Terrorists on Trial

TERRORISTS ON TRIAL

A Performative Perspective

Edited by Beatrice de Graaf and Alex P. Schmid

Leiden University Press

The publication of this book was made possible by a grant from the Netherlands Institute for Advanced Study in the Humanities and Social Sciences (NIAS) where the editors and several of the chapter authors conducted their research for this volume.

Cover design: Studio Jan de Boer
Cover illustration: ITALY—APRIL 01: Trial of 63 Red Brigade Suspects on April 1982 (Photo by Keystone-France/Gamma-Keystone via Getty Images)
Lay-out: TAT Zetwerk, Utrecht

ISBN 978 90 8728 240 0
e-ISBN 978 94 0060 235 9 (e-pdf)
e-ISBN 978 94 0060 236 6 (e-pub)
NUR 824

This book is distributed in North America by the University of Chicago Press (www.press.uchicago.edu).

Contents

Tables and Figures · 7

1. Introduction: A Performative Perspective on Terrorism Trials · 9
Beatrice de Graaf, in cooperation with Liesbeth van der Heide

2. Terrorism, Political Crime and Political Justice · 23
Alex P. Schmid

3. The Trial of Vera Zasulich in 1878 · 51
Alex P. Schmid

4. Stalin's 1936 Show Trial against the 'Trotzkyite-Zinovievite Terrorist Centre' · 93
Alex P. Schmid

5. 'Is There any Justice Left in this Country?' The IRA on Trial in the 1970s · 173
Joost Augusteijn

6. Germany Confronts the Baader-Meinhof Group. The Stammheim Trial (1975–1977) and Its Legacies · 231
Jacco Pekelder and Klaus Weinhauer

7. National Security on Trial: The Case of Zacarias Moussaoui, 2001–2006 · 311
Geert-Jan Knoops

8. Guantánamo as Theatre: Military Commissions as a Performance in the Court of Public Opinion, 2003–2004 · 345
Fred L. Borch

9. The Hofstad Group on Trial: Sentencing the Terrorist Risk, 2005–2014 · 371
Beatrice de Graaf

10. Supporting Prisoners or Supporting Terrorists: The 2008 Trial of Gestoras Pro Amnistía in Spain · 419
Carolijn Terwindt

11. Performing Justice, Coping with Trauma: The Trial of Anders Breivik, 2012 · 457
Tore Bjørgo, Beatrice de Graaf, Liesbeth van der Heide, Cato Hemmingby and Daan Weggemans

12. Conclusion · 503
Beatrice de Graaf

13. Literature on Terrorism Trials—A Selective Bibliography · 529

14. Notes on Contributors · 577

15. Index · 583

Tables and Figures

Tables

2.1. Typology of crime (adapted from Lee Ellis and Anthony Walsh) · 25
2.2. Severity of sentences for terrorism and other charges (USA) 2001–2009 · 42
6.1. Actors at the Stammheim trial · 288
11.1. Opinion on Breivik's sanity/accountability · 482
11.2. Opinion on the media attention to Breivik's perspective · 484
11.3. Judicial goals: important and attained · 486

Figures

8.1. Diagram showing prosecution theory of terrorist conspiracy · 356
12.1. A communicatively oriented typology of terrorism trials · 513

1. Introduction: A Performative Perspective on Terrorism Trials

Beatrice de Graaf, in cooperation with Liesbeth van der Heide[1]

1.1. Introduction[2]

On 6 May 2011, *Washington Post* journalist Jeff Greenfield painted a vivid picture of what would have happened had operation *Geronimo* (which resulted in the killing of Osama Bin Laden) resulted in capturing the leader of Al Qaeda alive. After the initial congratulations, the consequences might soon have created problems. Putting Bin Laden on trial for mass murder in a New York federal court—aside from the fact that it is very unlikely that Congress would allow this in the first place—would have caused major headaches:

> ... what if information about his location had been obtained through 'enhanced interrogation techniques' and was ruled inadmissible? What if Bin Laden acted as his own lawyer, turning the trial into a months-long denunciation of America? What if one holdout resulted in a hung jury? [...] A military commission at Guantánamo Bay, then? The process was agonizingly slow (only five cases concluded in nine years), and a death sentence for Bin Laden would mean years of appeals.[3]

Moreover, legal questions would, according to Greenfield, have been 'nothing next to the security consequences of taking Bin Laden alive'. What if any terrorist organisation worldwide seized an elementary school, threatening to kill all of the children unless Bin Laden were released?

Utilising criminal law and ultimately making use of civilian courts to try, sentence and imprison terrorists has often been criticised as a viable option in countering terrorism. Former Vice President Dick Cheney vehemently opposed organising terrorism trials in civilian courts in the United States (US). In a reaction to Attorney General Eric Holder's decision to prosecute Khalid Sheikh Mohammed (KSM) before a civilian court in 2009, he lamented: 'I can't for the life of me figure out what Holder's intent here is in having Khalid Sheikh Mohammed tried in civilian court other than to have some kind of show trial.'[4] Cheney objected to this decision, arguing that giving

KSM and other suspected terrorists a civilian trial in New York would be strategic disaster: 'they'll simply use it as a platform to argue their cases—they don't have a defence to speak of—it'll be a place for them to stand up and spread the terrible ideology that they adhere to'.[5]

Indeed, even when the rule of law is strictly observed, terrorism trials can easily turn into a show, a spectacle, run by the terrorist suspects in order to further their cause by communicative means. Or trials may lead to a (partial) acquittal, legally flawless but from a security perspective potentially disasterous. This concern, as voiced by many executive professionals, has been corroborated by the outcome of the first trial against a Guantánamo 'ghost prisoner', Ahmed Khalfan Ghailani, which sparked off a heated political debate. The defendant was convicted in a federal court in Manhattan for his role in the 1998 embassy bombings in Kenya and Tanzania, which earned him a 20-year sentence. Republican critics objected to the fact that the jury acquitted Ghailani of all other charges, more than 280 in total, including every single count of murder. This outcome was used as proof that terrorism detainees should be prosecuted solely by a military commission.[6] It was not so much the final verdict that was contested but the use of civilian courts—with all the unpredictability and risks involved for combating terrorism.

Notwithstanding such criticism, terrorism trials can be an exceptional opportunity better to understand and, hence, counter terrorism, since they are the only place where most, if not all, of the actors in a terrorist incident meet again: terrorists, state representatives, the judiciary, the audience, surviving victims, terrorist sympathisers, etc. The media will report and broadcast their respective performances. Forming a nexus between terrorist violence, law enforcement and public opinion, terrorism trials thus offer the prospect of showcasing justice in progress, and in so doing of demonstrating to the world how terrorist suspects are dealt with under the laws of the land. Ideally, criminal investigation and prosecution result in bringing terrorist suspects to court, where by solely legal and constitutional means, their purported crimes are adjudicated and justice is restored. However, governments and security officials are more often than not reluctant to put terrorist suspects in front of civilian courts. This reluctance can be explained if we view terrorism trials as a form of theatre, where the 'show' can develop its own, often unexpected, dynamics, which at times might inconvenience the government, most notably when terrorist suspects appropriate the trial to continue their struggle by communicative means. Terrorism trials almost inevitably give rise to political controversies. The crime of terrorism (not its direct effects—e.g. murder and hostage-taking) is a political construct and an essentially contested one as well.[7] Terrorism trials deal with suspects who are being charged with challenging the existing political system—or, at the very least, are seen as posing a political threat. The government's unease is owing to the fact that it has to hand over control to the judiciary, which has its own criteria for dealing with criminal offences (rather than viewing an act of terrorism primarily as a security threat). Governments also face the reaction of national and international public opinion, which might, in the worst case, even create new security threats.

In this volume, we are introducing a *performative perspective* on terrorism trials: these are viewed as a site of ongoing communicative struggle. The court room is a stage, not of warfare, but *lawfare* where legal instruments are used (and abused) by prosecution and defence and all kinds of performative acts are executed and (communicative) strategies are adopted to convince the court and audiences outside the courtroom of the validity of their respective narratives of (in)justice. In and outside the courtroom democratic states have much to lose when combating terrorism; respect for the rule of law, legitimacy and justice can become casualties. Therefore closer attention needs to be paid to the communicative aspects, judicial and socio-political mechanisms and effects of terrorism trials, especially with regard to their performative power which, in turn, may create and bolster new narratives of justice and/or injustice.[8]

In this introductory chapter, by combining the notion of *lawfare* with that of *performance*, we will present a new framework for analysing terrorism trials as sites of communicative contestation of political, ideological, religious ánd legal aims, pivoting around the concepts of (in)justice and legitimacy. At the end, we will briefly explain the place of individual chapters in this volume.

1.2. Terrorism Trials as a Places of Lawfare

Research on *political trials* in contemporary history has matured over recent decades. For instance, Awol Kassim Allo has analysed the show element in several political trials.[9] However, a specific focus on *terrorism trials* is still rare. As mentioned above, in the present volume we use the concepts of lawfare and performance as general frameworks for analysis.

The Prussian military strategist Carl von Clausewitz described war as 'merely a continuation of politics by other means'.[10] In the same way, terrorism trials can be viewed as the continuation of political violence by other—legal and non-legal, communicative means—in the courtroom.[11] In such trials, both terrorists and their defence lawyers on the one side and the government and its judiciary on the other hand operate within the framework of the law and legal procedures, engage with this communicatively, and either uphold and confirm or attempt to break and replace it with other sources of legitimacy to justify their actions. This process of waging war through law—or 'the art of managing law and war altogether' is what David Kennedy called *lawfare*.[12] 'Lawfare' has been used in more senses than one. The concept can be traced back to Charles Dunlap, a US Major General, who used the term as a 'bumper sticker' to describe how law had altered warfare.[13] In his view, lawfare denotes 'the use of the law as a weapon of war' that can be used both for the greater good as well as to do harm. Another aspect of lawfare has to do with the public support needed for armed conflict and the dependence of that support on upholding the rule of law. Legal scholar William Eckhardt, well-known for having prosecuted the My Lai cases during his service as Judge Advocate, observed that 'Knowing that our society so respects the rule of law that it demands compliance with it, our enemies carefully attack our military plans as illegal and immoral and our execution of those plans as contrary to the laws of war. Our vulnerability here is what philosopher of war Carl von Clausewitz would term our "center of gravity".'[14] From this perspective, lawfare can be seen as a means to claim legitimacy through the use (and abuse) of law and legal systems. Thus, lawfare is a tool where legality and legitimacy (two concepts that do not always overlap) can be used by either side, depending on political support, public opinion and the constellation of forces in a given social context.

In our view, terrorism trials can indeed also be analysed with the help of the concept of *lawfare*. Such trials constitute political arenas where the struggle for justification and legitimation continues by means of certain performative and communciative strategies. Here, in adaptation of Wouter Werner (who in turn refers to The Lawfare Project), we use the concept of *lawfare* as referring to the (ab)use of the law and legal systems for communicative and strategic ends.[15] It opens up a novel perspective on terrorism trials, viewing these as a continuation of a political struggle by other—both communicative and performative—means, namely competing narratives on the justice of a cause. Terrorist trials can remain firmly squared within the existing framework of law and legality, reinforce the authority of the state and communicate to the public at large that terrorist crimes are not acceptable, even if the grievances underlying them are real. Both the legal foundations and the communicative strategies adopted remain attached to status quo principles and paradigms. However, problems may arise when executive authorities try to divert from the aim of carrying out an open, transparent and legally grounded process of truth finding and adjudication, and instead put national security or protecting political order up front. The open, communicative space of the courtroom becomes restricted when governments put pressure on the judges, when populist politicians try to exert influence on court decisions and when judicial decisions run counter to government policies or when the general public does not accept the judicial verdict as just. While the ultimate verdict of the court might be considered as satisfactory by part of the public, another part may see it as another instance of injustice—contributing to further conflict escalation. The executive branch of the government may view an acquittal by a court as a reason to ask parliament to pass harsher laws. The terrorist's constituencies may consider a conviction as a reason to rally even more strongly behind those who have taken up arms against the government.[16]

As Alex P. Schmid will further elaborate in chapter two, terrorism trials might be turned into *political trials*, intended to evict (by legal, or illegal means) a political foe from the scene. Politicisation of trials may occur when court proceedings are deliberately manipulated for political reasons. The defendants can, however, also try to politicise the trial by directly challenging the authority of the court or the laws on the basis of which they are to be tried, to deny legitimacy to the court or disrepute the authorities.[17] In such cases, whether 'equality of arms' is involved or not, trials can divide audiences and conflict parties and intensify the conflict—hence the idea of 'lawfare'. Compared to the notion of political trials and political justice, where the power of the executive dominates the scene, 'lawfare' enables us to bring into focus the continuation of the struggle by communicative, legal and performative means of *all* parties involved, including the defendants.

Ideally, even with the possibility of protracted 'lawfare' involved, terrorism trials should be seen as the most fitting response of democratic states to terrorist attacks or threats thereof in a framework of rule of law.[18] Terrorist trials can be utilised to address core issues such as the need for retribution and the need to restore trust and stability and respect for the rule of law in society.[19] Trials are cornerstones of the criminal justice system in democratic societies that pride themselves on a tradition of 'fair' trials.[20] This vital demonstrative, and communicative function of terrorism trials is, however, often overlooked.

The existing body of research focusing on terrorism trials is limited and fragmented.[21] A great deal of research has been conducted into the goals of public trials,[22] and on changing attitudes with regard to accepting a system of global justice.[23] Less attention has been given to the role and place of terrorist trials in the framework of global justice,[24] or to the communicative, performative strategies and narratives used in court[25] and societal responses to terrorist trials.[26] De Graaf and De Goede have introduced a novel approach to terrorism trials, as sites where the precautionary turn (a tendency in criminal law to revert to risk justice, and to apply the law as precautionary measure rather than as a response to material evidence of terrorist attacks that have occurred) in criminal law manifests itself.[27] But more workneeds to be done. Research on radicalisation, the nature and effect of terrorism and ways and means to counter terrorism has generally overlooked the function of criminal trials in terrorism.[28] A well-conducted trial cannot only bring closure for surviving victims and their families, but can also bring some of those charged with terrorism to their senses and re-direct the life paths of some who previously identified with the terrorist cause.[29] When the performance in the courtroom is over, some lessons may have been learned by some audiences, if not the terrorists themselves. In a terrorism trial the main stakeholders accept or reject the legal system, but in either case they have to communicatively engage with the law in order to express their vision of what is just and unjust, legal or illegal, legitimate or not in the given political context.[30] Given these high stakes in the effect and impact of terrorism trials, this volume argues for adopting a new perspective on terrorism trials: The concept of *lawfare* allows us to bring into focus both the *strategies*, *performative acts* and the *rhetoric by means of which* the *main stakeholders* in a trial use the law and legal procedures to achieve an important objective: convincing their *target audiences* of their *political vision of justice/injustice*.

Terrorist trials are the sites where the process of lawfare reaches its climax. Witnessing audiences recognise, accept or reject the statements and the underlying strategies employed by key players. The stakeholders' visions of justice/injustice are more or less openly presented, debated and re-negotiated. The conduct or outcome of a trial can cause rupture (the rejection, obstruction or undermining of the legal system),[31] but it can also produce some forms of closure (solving a contentious issue one way or the other in the public debate[32]) in the eyes of some of the stakeholders and more distant audiences. Not infrequently, however, the outcome is an open-ended process of ongoing social feuds with unmet demands that foster resentment which, in turn, provides further ammunition for escalation. Given this situation, it is both relevant and timely to develop a better understanding of the communicative and performative aspects of terrorism trials.

Given our comments on the relevance of the performative element in terrorism trials, a definition of the concept of performativity needs to be presented here, a definition that refers to discursive efforts and actions to construct social realities,[33] as applied to terrorism trials:

> Performativity in terrorism trials refers to acts or strategies (stated or more incoherent) adopted by parties with a stake in the trial to try to persuade their target audience (s) in (and outside) the courtroom of the justice of their narrative(s) and the injustice of the one on the opposite side of the bar.[34]

The importance of studying communicative strategies and performative acts has been argued before.[35] Performative acts, according to Erika Fischer-Lichte, involve unpredictable and often (but not always) spontaneous interactions and exchanges between actors, spectators and others involved in the terrorism trial and do not leave them unchanged.[36] These transformative acts in the court room are based on explicit or implicit, stated or more incoherent strategies that have the potential to mobilise certain sectors of society, or certain groups outside it, by means of verbal statements or non-verbal behaviour in and outside the courtroom, e.g. in the form of hunger strikes. Their target audiences range from formal players within the legal system, such as judges and juries, to various publics outside the courtroom.[37]

Performance is an act, a process and a product at the same time; it provides consolidation of norms, re-enactment of identity and can also involve the transformation of these norms and identities. Performances are role plays, in which not only the individual but the community at large is involved. Interestingly, in courtrooms, performance takes place in a direct manner, in the art form of an Aristotelian drama: there is unity of time, place and action. Yet it also transcends the courtroom. The performances of the actors have a bearing on a broader audience, on the political context, on a society's culture and legal system as a whole, and this in three ways. First, there is *mimesis*: a (mostly verbal) re-enactment of the offence, performed in the hope of uncovering what actually happened. In addition to *mimesis*, there is *poiesis* as well, i.e. *making* not *faking*. Performances, like a driving test, a wedding, an examination or a defence in court, create identities, assert claims to selfhood and are part and parcel of confirming and producing social relations. The truth is not out there to uncover, but has to be (re)created in the courtroom. Moreover, apart from *faking* and *making*, performances also amount to *breaking* and *remaking*. Some narratives are upheld, others are disputed. In the end, often a new one emerges. This is called *kinesis*: movement, motion, fluidity. Performance can transgress existing boundaries, break structures and remake social and political rule. It intervenes and makes things anew.[38]

Through a trial, the members of the community participate in a possibly escalating and divisive debate: not only on the question of culpability and adjudication, but possibly also with respect to the communicative framework (the criminal law paradigm, rule of law, and justice) as such. Paraphrasing Bell's work on performative theories: during trials audiences will be induced to take sides; they will be inclined to be for or against the (alleged) rule breaker. Redress may be possible, when procedures to repair or remedy the breach are employed—a role the judicial machinery itself often plays. Trials not only involve re-establishment of the truth or stock-taking of the harm done; they also contain moments of liminality, a 'betwixt and between'[39] of suspended knowledge about the outcome of the social drama. Courtroom verdicts—guilty or not guilty—are exemplary of liminal moments in the redress phase of social drama. If the repair works the rule breaker is removed, and later reintegrated into the community. Every major social drama alters society to a certain extent. These alterations may not be permanent, but merely reflect a temporary mutual accommodation of interests. If this does not work, community splits or breaks apart into factions. This could be defined as a schism. In large scale complex communities continuous failure of repressive institutions may lead to a revolutionary situation in which at least one of the contending parties generates a programme of societal change, and the whole framework of the law is transformed.[40]

One critical note needs to be made, however. A performative act is not the same as a calculated strategy. And even if these two conflate, the exchange between actors and spectators remains unpredictable. The actual outcome of the trial and the question whose performance manages to mobilise or immobilise the public or more specific target audiences, is hard to assess conclusively. The outcome depends on a number of factors and may vary throughout the course of the trial. One major element of uncertainty in establishing the likely effect of a communicative strategy is the level of media coverage, and the degree of national public attention devoted to the trial.[41] This can be invoked by the agents directly involved in the trial, but media attention is—in some countries more than others—an autonomous factor in its own right. Distal and proximate context, historical experiences, media logistics at a specific time and place, other hypes on the political agenda, these all influence the way a trial is covered and reported. While mass media can have an independent agenda and independent interests, they are usually not just passive witnesses and conduits of factual information. In fact, sometimes the media have tried the suspects long before a case goes to court.

Like other political trials or media-saturated ordinary criminal trials (for example, the O.J. Simpson trial in California), terrorism trials can thus also be considered to be shows or, to use more accurate terminology, a dramaturgical play. This is not to say that terrorism trials are in all respects fundamentally different from other politicised trials, media-saturated trials or dramatic criminal trials. However, for terrorists and counter-terrorists, the presentation of, and contest over, credible narratives of justice and injustice are especially important. Compared to ordinary criminals who prefer a low profile in public, terrorist suspects often challenge the existing communicative frames and political rule or present contentious and violent views of justice and repression, and do so for all to see.

While combining these two concepts—lawfare and performativity—the guiding question for analysing terrorism trials should, in our view, be this: How do the main stakeholders in a terrorist trial (however coherently or incoherently) use the law and legal systems to achieve their goal of convincing their target audiences of their particular vision of justice/injustice? This question can be broken down into a number of sub-questions:

- Who are the main stakeholders in a trial and what are their visions of justice/injustice? Main stakeholders include the opposite parties within the legal system of criminal justice: the prosecutors and the defendant/legal counsel.
- Which performative acts and/or communicative strategies do they engage in in court? Do they follow strategies of rupture, i.e. strategies that intend to reject, obstruct or undermine the legal system? Strategies are defined as the total sum of performative actions, including the legal language (charges, legal paragraphs), narrative (either as a coherent plot line or explanation or as disparate statements), non-verbal expressions, behaviour, self-portrayal, etc., used to advance the stakeholder's vision of justice/injustice. These strategies might be visible as explicit attempts, or only to be perceived as post hoc rationalisations or implicit articulations.
- Which target audiences (judge and/or jury, real or potential terrorist constituencies, defendants, specific groups or society at large) are addressed, and how do these respond? Target audiences are understood here as the audiences implicitly or explicitly addressed by the stakeholder in the trial.
- To what extent do the stakeholders and/or their target audiences affirm closure? What are their ideas of (in)justice, defined as the implicitly or explicitly formulated goal and visions of moral rightness (or absence thereof)[42] of the stakeholder in the trial and his/her claim to legitimacy.

1.3. Outline of This Volume

In this volume a series of terrorism trials—some famous, others less so—are revisited. While the main focus is on trials held since the Second World War, we also look at two classical trials from Czarist Russia and the Soviet Union respectively. This is due in part to the special Russian background of one of the editors but it can also be justified in terms of their place in history; one taking place at the very beginning of modern terrorism and arguably (co-)inspiring the first anarchist wave of modern terrorism, the other, a classical Stalinist trial that was, in a way, the mother of all show trials. Somewhat closer to the present are the analysis of an ETA trial and the Stammheim trial of members from the German Red Army Faction. Altogether, the volume covers nine case studies, half of them taken from the post-9/11 period.

Following this introduction is a theoretical chapter by Alex P. Schmid, which focuses on the notions of political crime and political justice. Alex Schmid also authored the case study on the trial of Vera Zasulich in 1878 and offers a detailed account of the first of three Stalinist show trials in the mid-1930s, where alleged members of a 'Trotzkyite-Zinovievite Terrorist Centre' stood trial. The subsequent chapters deal with trials held in the 1970s. Joost Augusteijn analyses some of the more prominent IRA trials in the 1970s, while Jacco Pekelder and Klaus Weinhauer scrutinise the German Stammheim trial.

The next set of chapters deals with post-9/11 trials. First, Geert-Jan Knoops, international law scholar and practising lawyer, investigates the case of Zacarias Moussaoui, who—often referred to as the 20th hijacker of 9/11—was convicted of conspiring to kill US citizens. Knoops analyses the role of the theatre itself in setting the stage for the performative strategies of the parties involved. A federal trial, according to Knoops, is the best way to administer justice, and to conduct a fair trial. Next, Fred Borch considers the Guantánamo trials between 2003 and 2004. As a former US military prosecutor, he combines scholarly analysis with first-hand knowledge of some of the Guantánamo tribunals. Beatrice de Graaf then covers a number of trials against a group of jihadist terrorist suspects in the Netherlands. She notes that in the case of the Hofstad group in 2005–2006 it was not so much the thwarted attack, but the risk of such an attack, that was adjudicated upon—a new phenomenon in criminal justice. Carolijn Terwindt continues with an analysis of the support groups and sympathiser movement to the Gestoras pro Amnistía in Spain (who stood trial in 2008), a highly under-researched area.

The last trial discussed is the 2012 trial of Anders Behring Breivik, the perpetrator of a bomb plot and a massacre that cost the lives of 77 mostly young people in Oslo and Utøya. The authors of this last chapter, Tore Bjørgo, Beatrice de Graaf, Liesbeth van der Heide, Cato Hemmingby and Daan Weggemans take a broad look at the process timeline—from the time of Breivik's arrest to his sentencing—to assess the full impact of the trial on Norwegian society. They moreover carried out an investigation and inquiry during the Oslo trial and developed a methodology for assessing the quality of the trial in terms of closure or rupture for the different audiences involved and present in and around the courtroom.

In the conclusion, De Graaf will expand further on the insights drawn from these and other trials and propose a tentative typology of terrorism trials based on the two concepts of performativity and lawfare introduced briefly above, in order to prepare the ground for further research.

At the very end of the volume there is an extensive bibliography on terrorist trials and political justice which was prepared by Jaclyn Peterson, assisted by Susanne Keesman, Hannah Joosse, Jorrit Steehouder, Mike Spaans, Alex Schmid and Daan Weggemans.

Finally, the editors would like to thank the following persons: Susanne, Hannah and Jorrit for their crucial assistance and tireless dedication in the final stage of this project, and John Kok with his—as always—sound, swift and sensible editing. We would also like to express explicit words of gratitude to the Netherlands Institute for Advanced Study in the Humanities and Social Sciences (NIAS) and its two consecutive *rectores*, Wim Blockmans and Aafke Hulk, in Wassenaar for making this study possible. The editors and some of the contributors to this volume were invited to spend time at NIAS to conduct their research on terrorism trials in its wholesome halls. Leiden University Press/Chicago University Press, as represented by Anniek Meinders and Romy Uijen, similarly deserve our thanks for their interest in this project and their dedication in publishing such a voluminous manuscript.

Notes

1 Liesbeth van der Heide contributed to this introduction by writing the first page of the 1.2 section on 'lawfare'.

2 The author wishes to thank Fred Borch, Quirine Eijkman and Alex Schmid for their comments on an earlier draft of this introduction. The first author of this chapter took part in the 'Terrorists on Trial' Research Theme Group, hosted by the Netherlands Institute for Advanced Studies, Wassenaar/The Netherlands during the year 2010/2011. Parts of this introduction have been posted as an International Centre for Counter-Terrorism research paper: Beatrice de Graaf, 'Terrorists on Trial: A Performative Perspective', ICCT-*Research Paper* (June 2011), pp. 1–15, http://www.icct.nl/download/file/ICCT-de-Graaf-EM-Paper-Terrorism-Trials-as-Theatre.pdf.

3 Jeff Greenfield, 'What if we'd taken him alive?', *Washington Post* (8 May 2011), http://www.washingtonpost.com/opinions/what-if-bin-laden-had-been-captured-not-killed-an-alternate-history/2011/05/05/AFl7EO8F_story.html. Retrieved 11 May 2015.

4 Andrew Ramonas, 'Cheney Says Holder Wants "Show Trial" for KSM' (23 November

2009), http://www.mainjustice.com/2009/11/23/cheney-says-holder-wants-show-trial-for-ksm. Quoted in: Awol Kassim Allo, 'The "Show" in the Show Trials: Contextualizing the Politicization of the Courtroom', in: *Barry Law Review*, 15:1 (2010), pp. 41–72, here: p. 44.

5 Ramonas, 'Cheney Says Holder Wants "Show Trial" for KSM.'

6 Charlie Savage, 'Ghailani Verdict Reignites Debate Over the Proper Court for Terrorism Trials', *New York Times* (18 November 2010).

7 William E. Connolly, *The Terms of Political Discourse*. 3rd ed. (Princeton: Princeton University Press, 1993), p. 10. See also Alex P. Schmid, 'Terrorism: The definitional problem', in: *Case Western Reserve Journal of International Law*, 36:2 and 3 (2004), pp. 375–420.

8 For a theoretical and historical analysis of this concept see: Beatrice de Graaf, *Evaluating Counterterrorism Performance: A Comparative Study* (London/New York: Routledge, 2011).

9 Allo, 'The "Show" in the Show Trials', pp. 41–72. Parts of this introduction, and the conclusion, have also been used in a chapter in a German volume: Idem, 'Terroristen vor Gericht. Terrorismusprozesse als Fortsetzung des Kampfes um die Kommunikationshoheit. Eine Typologie', in: K. Weinhauer and J. Requate (ed.), *Terrorismus als Kommunikationsprozess. Eskalation und Deeskalation in historischer Perspektive* (Frankfurt/New York: Campus Verlag, 2012), pp. 281–298.

10 Actually, this is not what he said but that is how it is often quoted in English, a more correct translation of the German text is: 'the continuation of politics with a mixture of other means'. Carl von Clausewitz, *Vom Kriege: Hinterlassenes Werk des Generals Carl von Clausewitz* (Bonn: Dümmler Verlag, 1972), p. 12.

11 Martha Crenshaw, 'Current Research on Terrorism: The academic perspective', *Studies in Conflict & Terrorism*, 15:1 (1992), pp. 1–11.

12 David Kennedy, *Of War and Law* (Princeton: Princeton University Press, 2006), p. 5.

13 Charles Dunlap, 'Lawfare Today: A Perspective', *Yale Journal of International Affairs*, 3:1 (2008), p. 146.

14 William George Eckhardt, 'Lawyering for Uncle Sam When He Draws His Sword', *Chicago Journal of International Law*, 4:2 (2003), pp. 431–445.

15 Wouter Werner, 'The Curious Career of Lawfare', *Case Western Reserve Journal of International Law*, 43:1 and 2 (2010), p. 62. Whereas Werner and The Lawfare Project refer to the abuse, and negative manipulation of laws and judicial systems as a weapon of war, we take a broader view and apply a general notion of strategy to the uses and abuses of the law, while our main interest is in its strategic function.

16 Beatrice de Graaf, 'Terrorists on Trial: A Performative Perspective', ICCT *Expert Paper* (ICCT: The Hague, 2011), p. 11.

17 Roger Cotterrell, *The Sociology of Law: An Introduction* (London: Butterworths, 1992), pp. 231–232.

18 Council of Europe, ETS No. 005, *Convention for the Protection of Human Rights and Fundamental Freedoms*, http://conventions.coe.int/treaty/en/treaties/html/005.htm. Retrieved 13 May 2015.

19 Allan C. Hutchinson and Patrick J. Monahan, 'Law, Politics and the Critical Legal Scholars: The unfolding drama of American legal thought', *Stanford Law Review*, 36:1 and 2 (1984), p. 199. See also Constantijn Kelk, *Studieboek materieel strafrecht* (Deventer: Kluwer, 2005).

20 Jack Knight, 'Social Norms and the Rule of Law: Fostering Trust in a Socially Diverse Society', in: Karen S. Cook (ed.), *Trust in Society* (New York: Russell Sage Foundation, 2001), p. 355. See also: Harry C. Bredemeier, quoted in: Roger Cotterrell (ed.), *The Sociology of Law: An Introduction* (London: Butterworths, 1992), pp. 89–92.

21 Brian J. Ostrom, Charles W. Ostrom Jr., Roger A. Hanson and Matthew Kleiman, *Trial Courts as Organizations* (Philadelphia: Temple University Press, 2007). See also: Jacob Eisenstein and H. Jacob, *Felony Justice: An organizational analysis of criminal courts* (Boston: Little, Brown and Co., 1977).

22 Julian V. Roberts and Loretta J. Stalans, *Public Opinion, Crime, and Criminal Justice* (Boulder: Westview, 1997).

23 Thomas Nagel, 'The Problem of Global Justice', *Philosophy and Public Affairs*, 33:2 (2005), pp. 113–147.

24 Michael Freeman, 'Order, Rights, and Threats: Terrorism and Global Justice', in: Richard A. Wilson (ed.), *Human Rights in the 'War on Terror'* (New York: Cambridge University Press, 2005).

25 Philip L. Reichel, *Comparative Criminal Justice Systems: A topical approach* (Upper Saddle River: Prentice Hall, 2002). See also Mark A. Drumbl, 'Terrorist Crime, Taliban Guilt, Western Victims, and International Law', *Denver Journal of International Law and Policy*, 31:1 (2002), p. 69.

26 Ronald J. Sievert, 'War on Terrorism or Global Law Enforcement Operation?', *Notre Dame Law Review*, 78:2 (2002), pp. 308–349; cf. Herbert L. Packer, 'Two Models of the Criminal Process', *University of Pennsylvania Law Review*, 113:1 (1964), pp. 1–68.

27 Marieke de Goede and Beatrice de Graaf, 'Sentencing Risk: Temporality and precaution in terrorism trials', *International Political Sociology*, 7:3 (2013), pp. 313–331.

28 Wouter G. Werner, 'The Changing Face of Enmity: Carl Schmitt's international theory and the evolution of the legal concept of war', *International Theory*, 2:3 (2010), pp. 351–380; cf. Sarah Nouwen and Wouter Werner, 'Doing Justice to the Political: The ICC in Uganda and Sudan', *European Journal of International Law*, 11:4 (2010), pp. 941–965; Tim Meijers and Marlies Glasius, 'Expression of Justice or Political Trial? Discursive battles in the Karadžić case', *Human Rights Quarterly*, 35:3 (2013), pp. 720–752.

29 Daan Weggemans and Beatrice de Graaf, *Na de vrijlating. Een exploratieve studie naar recidive en re-integratie van jihadistische ex-gedetineerden* (Amsterdam: Stapel & De Koning, 2015).

30 Gunther Teubner, '"Global Bukowina": Legal pluralism in the world society', in: Gunther Teubner (ed.), *Global Law Without a State* (Dartmouth: Aldershot, 1997), pp. 3–28.

31 Martti Koskenniemi, 'Between Show Trials and Impunity', *Max Planck Yearbook of United Nations Law* (2002), p. 26.

32 Alan Keenan, *Democracy in Question: Democratic openness in a time of political closure* (Stanford: Stanford University Press, 2003), p. 12.

33 J.L. Austin, *How To Do Things with Words* (Cambridge, MA: Harvard UP, 1962); Malcolm Coulthard, *An Introduction to Discourse Analysis*. 2nd edition (New York: Longman, 1985); Judith Butler, *Excitable Speech: A politics of the performative* (New York: Routledge, 1997). Cf. also De Graaf, *Evaluating Counterterrorism Performance*, pp. 11–13.

34 Historically, this definition should only be applied to the modern period of the late 19th century and onwards, when the modern state managed to claim for itself the monopoly of legitimate use of violence, when a criminal justice system based on a parliament-approved penal code came to maturity at the same time as modern mass media emerged.

35 De Graaf, 'Terrorists on Trial'.

36 Erika Fischer-Lichte, 'Notwendige Ergänzung des Tekst-Modells', *Frankfurter Rundschau* (23 November 1999), p. 20; Idem, *Theater als Modell für eine performative Kultur. Zum performative turn in der europäischen Kultur des 20. Jahrhunderts (Universitätsreden 46)* (Saarbrücken: Pressestelle der Universität des Saarlandes, 2000); Idem, 'Performance, Inszenierung, Ritual. Zur Klärung kulturwissenschaftlicher Schlüsselbegriffe', in: Jürgen Martschukat and Steffen Patzold (ed.), *Geschichtswissenschaft und 'performative turn'. Ritual, Inszenierung und Performance vom Mittelalter bis zur Neuzeit* (Cologne/Weimar/Vienna: Böhlau Verlag, 2003), pp. 34–54.

37 Judith Butler, *Excitable Speech: A politics of the performative* (New York: Routledge, 1997).

38 Elizabeth Bell, *Theories of Performance* (Los Angeles: SAGE, 2008), pp. 12–15.

39 Bell, *Theories of Performance*, p. 108.

40 Bell, *Theories of Performance*, pp. 108–109.

41 'Media' in this sense covers all communicative media, including the media of the 'terrorists' or their constituency (pamphlets, grey literature, internet etc.).

42 John Rawls, *A Theory of Justice*. Revised ed. (Oxford: Oxford University Press, 1999).

2. Terrorism, Political Crime and Political Justice

Alex P. Schmid

> Any trial is a contest of dueling frames of reference, of alternate explanations.
>
> J. Post.[1]

2.1. Introduction

In the wake of the killing of Osama Bin Laden in Abbottabad, Pakistan, on 2 May 2011, there has been much talk on the subject of 'bringing terrorists to justice'. Yet such talk generally does not refer to bringing the alleged terrorists to a trial in court.[2] Debate over the last decade has ranged between those who favour a criminal justice approach to terrorism—based mainly on the use of the police and the judiciary—and those who favour a military warfare approach. On the whole, and certainly in the United States, the proponents of a military approach have dominated the field, even following a change of government in the United States in 2008. Attempts to try terrorists in civilian courts have often met resistance from those who would prefer military 'justice' or trial by a military commission. Underlying this debate is an uncertainty about whether terrorists should be treated as (political) criminals or as (enemy) combatants. In this chapter, I will address some conceptual issues on the subject of terrorism and justice, focusing in particular on the issue of extradition when a perpetrator is to be brought to trial from beyond national borders, and politics enters legal considerations.

The post-Cold War process of globalisation has allowed terrorists to expand the scope of their operations internationally, but justice is still largely a national prerogative. The only existing international terrorist court, the Special Tribunal for Lebanon in The Hague, still has to adhere to Lebanese national law.[3] The Lockerbie trial (2000–2001), held in the Netherlands, was conducted under Scottish national law. This illustrates that justice basically remains linked to national political communities, and is subject to national sovereignty. Terrorists, on the other hand, have traditionally breached national sovereignty and crossed international borders.

Terrorist trials are often considered 'political'. There is a widespread implicit assumption that a 'political trial' also amounts to 'political justice', i.e. that such trials are partisan, like some trials held by victorious powers at the end of a war. In this chapter, I will examine the notions of 'terrorism' and 'crime', and what we actually mean when we call a crime or a trial 'political'. I will also explore the notion of 'justice' and its dark twin brother 'revenge'. On closer inspection, all of these terms are ambiguous.

2.2. Political Crime and the Political Offence Exception

Perhaps the least controversial of these concepts would seem to be the concept of 'crime'. Yet even the notion of what is considered a crime varies greatly across time and cultural space, as the laws that define an offence vary, and as what is and what is not considered moral and legitimate varies. Crimes are often interpreted in terms of a conflict between a 'bad' individual and a 'good' society—with the government standing between the parties as the representative of society, bringing to trial those who violate its norms.[4] The state has the prerogative to proscribe an act against persons or property it deems dangerous or merely undesirable, thereby making it a crime. Many prohibited acts are, however, 'victimless', like some traffic offences or violations of migration law; these are crimes merely because the state has declared them to be punishable offences. They are defined as 'wrong' mainly or exclusively because they are prohibited (*mala prohibita*). However, some criminal offences are so harmful and serious that they are considered wrong in all civilised societies. They are not just legally prohibited but also considered morally 'evil' (*mala in se*). In particular, this applies to 'murder'—the premeditated, unprovoked killing of a human being. In murder cases, legal systems therefore tend to consider not only the criminal act (*actus reus*), but also the guilty mindset (*mens rea*), the underlying intention of the perpetrator.[5]

National courts deal with all sorts of crimes, while international criminal courts most often deal with serious war crimes, genocide or crimes against humanity. These crime categories (and others like piracy and slavery) are acknowledged and defined in international and humanitarian law; there is widespread transnational consensus as to what these entail. But when offenders operate outside the context of inter-state war and claim to have acted for ideological or religious reasons, our ability to distinguish between political offences and criminal offences often becomes blurred.

How should we distinguish a 'common crime' from a 'political crime'? The latter can be considered either more or less serious than the former, depending partly on where the crime takes place, and who claims jurisdiction over it. Political offenders often claim that the political nature of their deeds somehow decriminalises even violent acts. However, state officials who are on the receiving end often consider political crimes to be more serious than common crimes, even in cases where there is equivalence in terms of the victimisation resulting from a crime. The grey area between criminal and political offences is to some degree expressed in the following typology developed by Lee Ellis and Anthony Walsh.

Non-political crime:	1. Murder forcible rape, assault, kidnapping, robbery 2. Theft, burglary, fraud, vandalism, arson, shoplifting 3. Negligent manslaughter, driving while intoxicated
Quasi-political crime:	1. Violent rioting and pillaging 2. Destroying public property 3. Tax evasion, counterfeiting 4. Desertion of the armed forces, incitement to riot
Political crime:	1. Assassination political hostage-taking 2. Sabotage, desecration of national symbols 3. Advocating the violent overthrow of the government, treason

Table 2.1. Typology of crime (adapted from Lee Ellis and Anthony Walsh)[6]

This typology of crime, however, leaves no room for crimes typically performed by governments, e.g. crimes ranging from illegal police operations and gross human rights violations to ethnic cleansing and genocide.[7] Nor does it explain the difference between a murder and an assassination. The laws that outlaw these three types of offences have, at least in representative democracies, been made or confirmed by parliaments. In other words, political forces have been at the cradle of the creation of most criminal statutes.[8] In this sense, most crimes are 'political'. Yet the term 'political' can mean so many things—e.g. non-private, public, of collective interest—that it is difficult to nail down. Otto Kirchheimer's perceptive reflections help to illustrate the ambiguity of the term:

> There are no universally valid criteria for what constitutes political action as distinct from other types of social action. Something is called political if it is thought to relate

> in a particularly intensive way to the interests of the community. According to its own estimate of its needs (which does not always coincide with its 'objective' needs), each dominant group, class, or individual will develop criteria by which reprehensible acts, when grave enough, will necessitate public action. Correspondingly, infinite numbers of 'political' things might in the course of time enter, leave and re-enter the sphere of formalized public reaction.[9]

At least when it comes to domestic crimes (i.e. crimes on the territory of one state), most governments are reluctant to allow that domestic offences could be 'political' crimes. Former British Prime Minister, Margret Thatcher, for instance, abolished privileges such as wearing personal clothing for Provisional Irish Republican Army (IRA) prisoners in the 1970s, thereby portraying these militant nationalists as common criminals. This motivated IRA prisoners to engage in hunger strikes and 'blanket' protests. Thatcher's move was in fact no break with British legal tradition. When it comes to domestic crime, Anglo-American law does not recognise such crime as 'political crime' and, while it is prepared to consider the 'intent' behind a crime, it does not recognise 'motive' as bearing on guilt.[10]

Acts of lethal violence against human beings can be viewed and judged differently, depending on the frameworks used. This is most obvious when the perspective switches from a crime model to a war model. In inter-state war, most (though not all) acts of killing are viewed not as 'murder' but as legitimate acts of warfare. Those who kill in war, and do so courageously and successfully when ordered to by the state, can be rewarded with medals and promotion. However in peacetime the situation is altogether different. A decorated war veteran who comes home and continues to do to fellow citizens what he is good at—killing people—becomes a 'murderer' again, and may even receive the death penalty. Such a killing by the state, in turn, is framed differently again; what would otherwise be murder becomes a legal 'judicial execution'.

One way of exploring the notion of 'political crime' is to look at it through the lens of extradition practices between states in cases where killings and assassinations are committed by individuals against citizens or political and religious leaders.[11] If the perpetrator of such a killing is a citizen from another state and staying on the territory of a host country, a situation arises where one state might ask the other to bring him (or her) to trial or to extradite the person suspected to be the offender. However, such extradition requests are often refused for a variety of reasons when it comes to political (and some other) offenders, because:

- The suspect has dual citizenship, i.e. he/she is also national of the state from which extradition is requested;
- The crime may be a crime in one country but not in the other;
- The person sought may be unlikely to get a fair trial in the requesting country;
- The person sought may be subjected to torture in the requesting country;
- The death penalty may exist in the requesting country but not in the country from which extradition is requested.

Hesitancy to grant extradition requests for some forms of crimes makes it clear that while states are very reluctant to accept the category of 'political crime' for offences committed on their own territory, they will more readily distinguish between 'common' and 'political' crimes when it comes to foreign offenders who flee to their territory. There is greater consensus about what is a crime when it comes to war crimes and crimes against humanity. Because such crimes tend to affect also the peace and security of other states, the perpetrators can, in principle, be tried by any state—irrespective of the perpetrators' nationality or the location of the crime scene. However transnational terrorism is not yet subject to such universal jurisdiction and it is also not yet part of customary international law.[12]

Extradition is defined as 'the surrender by one State, at the request of another, of a person who is accused or has been accused of a crime committed within the jurisdiction of the requesting State'.[13] Most extradition treaties contain a 'political offence exception' and attempts to limit or abolish such exceptions have been only partly successful (for instance until quite recently, IRA terrorists sought by Great Britain were generally not extradited to Britain by the United States).[14] The Council of Europe tried to 'depoliticise' certain crimes (such as hijacking, bombing and hostage-taking) in the European Convention on the Suppression of Terrorism in 1977. However, the Council did not abolish the political offence exception itself. Nor did it define what exactly a 'political offence' is. Member states therefore still have some discretion to decide what they wish to consider a 'political offence',[15] despite the introduction of the European Arrest Warrant (2004) which recognises no political offence exception.[16] Nevertheless, even after 2004, France, for instance, continued to refuse extradition of fugitive Italian Red Brigade members.

This erratic use of the political offence exception can be better understood in the light of the historical experiences of European states. In the 1830s and in the decades thereafter, this exception was introduced by liberal democracies mainly because they felt that individuals have a right to rebel against an unjust government ruling through an undemocratic, autocratic regime.[17] There was widespread agreement that people who had fought for a liberal democracy should not be extradited for justifiable acts of political rebellion—even when these acts could be considered criminal in other contexts. Some states wanted to maintain neutrality in political conflicts affecting neighbouring states where they considered a revolution was long overdue.[18] Rather than extradition, many political offenders were granted asylum by host countries. However the nagging question remained: where to draw the line between a 'pure'—that is largely victimless—political offence like sedition, treason or espionage, and offences which included elements of violent crime, but were perpetrated to promote a political cause. An offence like the killing of a government official during an unsuccessful insurrection, leading to the perpetrator escaping to a neighbouring country, has generally been judged differently from an offence in which the link to a political goal was less direct.[19] Offences involving the assassination of a head of state (and family members), whether the rulers were autocrats or democrats, have never been taken lightly by states considering extradition requests. The Belgian parliament in the 1850s introduced an 'attentat clause',[20] which excluded the political offence exception for such serious crimes. Attentat clauses became quite common in extradition treaties after the 1850s.[21]

In the course of the 19th and 20th centuries a number of principles were established to determine how to evaluate a crime as a 'political offence exception'.[22] The points of importance to be considered have been summarised in the Norgaard Principles,[23] (named after the former Danish president of the European Commission of Human Rights):

- The motive of the offender (whether it was personal or political);
- The circumstances in which the act is committed (whether it was committed during an uprising or not);
- The legal and factual nature of the act, including its gravity;
- The political objective of the act: at whom it was directed (against government agents, property, or ordinary citizens);
- Whether it was committed following an order from a group of which the actor was a member;
- The relationship between the offence and the political motive—specifically, the proximity of the relationship and its proportionality.[24]

Despite the guidance provided by these principles, many offenders have mixed motives. It is often difficult to draw a line between an offender who acts for private (selfish/

profit) motives and one who is a convictional criminal (who acts on the basis of altruistic motives or for ideological and political, collective ends).[25]

In recent years, there has been a clear trend towards reducing the definitional scope of political offence exceptions for violent acts in political struggles, especially when it comes to terrorist offences. However a number of regional anti-terrorism conventions still contain exception clauses for fighters engaged in armed struggles for self-determination or national liberation. Where armed struggles for national liberation are conducted in accordance with the principles of international law, and in particular international humanitarian law, this is, in theory, less problematic.[26] Nevertheless while certain types of political violence by non-state actors are sometimes permissible under the laws of war (and/or can be morally justifiable and considered by many as legitimate), certain other acts of violence carried out by members of national liberation movements are not considered legal in terms of international law.[27] An offence committed in the name of self-determination, or in the name of a religion like Islam, or for some other political cause, may constitute a (war) crime depending on context, targets, method and actors involved. References to 'freedom fighters' and 'liberation struggles' have complicated the process of international legal cooperation. For instance, attempts by the Organisation of Islamic Cooperation (OIC) to exempt Palestinians (fighting Israel) and Kashmiris (fighting India) from being subject to anti-terrorist conventions[28] have inhibited reaching a consensus on a universal Comprehensive Convention on International Terrorism in the United Nations General Assembly.

Before we turn to the issues of political trial and political justice, it is important to look at the concept of terrorism as discussed in the framework of the United Nations.

2.3. The Definition of 'Terrorism'

The Ad Hoc Committee on Terrorism, a sub-committee of the Sixth (Legal) Committee of the United Nations General Assembly, has been attempting to draft a Comprehensive Convention on International Terrorism for more than a decade. The draft Article 2 of that incomplete Convention focuses on the definition of terrorism, and characterises 'terrorism' in these terms:

> Any person commits an offence within the meaning of this [the present] Convention if that person, by any means, unlawfully and intentionally, causes:

(a) Death or serious injury to any person; or
(b) Serious damage to public or private property, including a place of public use, a State or government facility, a public transportation system, an infrastructure facility or to the environment; or
(c) Damage to property, places, facilities or systems referred to in paragraph 1 (b) of this [the present] article, resulting or likely to result in major economic loss; when the purpose of the conduct, by its nature or context, is to intimidate a population, or to compel a Government or an international organization to do or abstain from doing any act.[29]

This proposed draft definition of terrorism avoids the word 'political'. The drafters, representing a club of states, also make no reference to state terrorism (though this issue is indirectly discussed in draft Article 18 which, like Article 2, is also subject to continuing debate). Rather, the draft definition refers to 'any person' both as perpetrator and as potential victim (and includes some attacks on property as falling under terrorism). The 'any person' as victim could cover military personnel as well. And the 'any act' at the end of sub-paragraph (c) opens the door to even wider interpretations.

Recent developments, like the emergence of suicide bombings against civilians as a major new form of terrorism, are not reflected in this definition. The communicative and performative aspect of terrorism ('propaganda by the deed'—a concept that has been developing since it was first invented in the second half of the 19th century),[30] is not reflected in any way in this UN draft definition. This means the UN definition, if it ever passes the drafting stage, is likely to be obsolete and out of touch with reality before it ever comes into force. To understand that, we only have to compare the above draft definition to recent developments in terrorism:

- The intense and extensive use of new communication technologies;
- Weak and failed states operating as safe havens;
- The globalisation of terrorism aided by diaspora bridgeheads;
- Kamikaze-type suicide attacks;
- The expansion of targets considered licit (children, tourists, the Red Cross and other NGOs, the UN);
- Attempts to engage in catastrophic terrorism (including Weapons of Mass Destruction);
- Pronounced religious fanaticism.

None of these aspects of terrorism are in any way reflected in the UN draft definition. This definition, with its broad vagueness—'any person', 'any act'—lacks the precision, objectivity and certainty required to make laws unequivocal (if it remains unchanged in the final document presented to the General Assembly).[31]

I worked formerly for the United Nations, and before I joined the UN full-time, I acted as a consultant to the secretariat of the UN Crime Commission. Back in 1992, I was asked to look into the definition of terrorism issue. At that time I proposed cutting through the Gordian knot of the definition issue by taking an existing, generally accepted definition and extending its reach. I suggested that we take the definition of 'war crimes' and extend it to analogue crimes committed in times of peace and outside zones of conflict, so that 'acts of terrorism' could be simply defined as 'peacetime equivalents of war crimes'. When that proposal was unsuccessful with the members of the international community (only one country, India, accepted it), I turned to academia and attempted to create greater consensus at least in the world of universities. The latest result of this effort is the Revised Academic Consensus Definition of Terrorism (2011):

> Terrorism refers on the one hand to a *doctrine* about the presumed effectiveness of a special form or tactic of fear-generating, coercive political violence, and on the other hand, to a conspiratorial *practice* of calculated, demonstrative, direct violent action without legal or moral restraints, targeting mainly civilians and non-combatants, performed for its propagandistic and psychological effects on various audiences and conflict parties. Terrorism as a tactic is employed in three main contexts: (i) to enforce illegal state repression; (ii) as propagandistic agitation by non-state actors in times of peace or outside zones of conflict; (iii) as an illicit tactic of irregular warfare employed by state- and non-state actors.[32]

Unfortunately, this Academic Consensus Definition differs markedly from the draft definition produced by the Ad Hoc Committee on Terrorism. The 'academic consensus' is also aspirational rather than fully realised. A related problem is that social and political scientists still disagree on the delineation of 'terrorism' from other forms of 'political violence'. Some scholars limit political violence to violent events short of war, while others do not.[33] Some equate 'political violence' and 'political terrorism', creating more confusion. Ted Hondrich, for instance, makes no distinction between the two, including both in his definition of 'violence with a political and social intention':

> Whether or not intended to put people in general in fear, and raising a question of its moral justification—either illegal violence within a society or smaller-scale violence than war between states or societies and not according to international law.[34]

In reality, there are many other forms of political violence short of war that are quite different from terrorism as practised currently by armed civilians against defenceless civilians for the purpose of intimidating, coercing or otherwise influencing other conflict parties and audiences. To give a few examples of political violence (not all of them are also political crimes) other than terrorism:

- Hunger strike/self-burning (political suicide)
- Blockade/public property damage/sabotage
- Hate crimes/lynching
- Violent demonstrations/mob violence/rioting
- Brigandry/warlordism
- Raids, razzia, pillage /pogroms
- Torture/mutilation/mass rape
- Tyrannicide
- Extra-judicial execution/massacre
- Ethnic cleansing/mass eviction, purge
- Guerrilla warfare/partisan warfare
- Subversion, intervention
- Revolt, coup d'état rebellion, uprising, insurgency, revolution.[35]

Whether political violence is used offensively or defensively, as a means of provocation or as a weapon of last resort, whether it is used against armed opponents or against defenceless people—these are all important moral distinctions that bear on the morality, legality and criminality of the act and determine whether it is perceived as legitimate or unjustified. We should distinguish terrorism from other forms of illegitimate political violence—some, like genocide, worse than terrorism, and others, like tyrannicide, less grave—though still criminal. On the other hand, we must acknowledge that there are certain forms of violent resistance to political oppression that are legitimate; to some extent these are already acknowledged in international humanitarian law. Terrorism ought to be considered unacceptable behaviour when it takes the form of violence without legal and moral restraints—violence that does not recognise and respect the existence of protected persons like unarmed non-combatants and defenceless civilians. Such unacceptable behaviour should be criminalised whether it occurs in wartime or peacetime, in zones of armed conflict or outside them, whether performed by state- or non-state actors and whether performed within or outside national jurisdictions.

While motive (as opposed to intent) should play no role in a legal definition of terrorism, the Academic Consensus Definition of Terrorism cited earlier includes a causal element as a driving force—the terrorists' belief in the effectiveness of their *tactic*. If terrorism did not 'work' on one level or the other, terrorists would presumably not engage in terrorism. However, since terrorists are no more rational than anyone else, they may engage in it despite the fact that, in a *strategic* sense, terrorism is more often than not counter-productive.[36] The fact that acts of terrorism often have a large impact does not mean that they are 'effective' in achieving the stated political goals (national liberation, a caliphate, etc.). An act of terrorism may satisfy the terrorists' less-than-rational desire for 'revenge'—vengeance to which they usually give the much more acceptable label of 'justice'. Revenge, in my view, is an altogether under-estimated cause of terrorism and probably also of much of counter-terrorism. Let us have a closer look at it.

2.4. Revenge and Justice

When President Bush declared a Global War on Terror and pursued Al Qaeda and the Taliban in Afghanistan from late 2001, this intervention was originally named 'Operation Infinite Justice'.[37] Later, when the President was told that 'Infinite Justice' is also a description of God in a certain religion, he had the intervention rebranded as 'Operation Enduring Freedom—Afghanistan (OEF-A)'.

The 'justice' label is one which—like the 'freedom' label in 'freedom fighters'—has widespread intuitive appeal. Unsurprisingly, terrorists too are all for 'justice'. A close associate of Bin Laden, the Egyptian Saif al-Adel, carried the *nom de guerre* 'sword of justice'.[38] History books also tell us that during the terror phase of the French Revolution (1793–1794), the guillotine was labelled the 'sword of justice'. Robespierre, the father of modern state terrorism, directly equated 'terror' with 'justice', claiming that 'Terror is nothing else than justice, prompt, secure and inflexible; it is therefore an outflow of virtue.'[39] Other terrorists followed him in this understanding: Osama Bin Laden declared in October 2004 that 'We have been fighting you because we are free men who do not remain silent in the face of injustice.'[40] Shamil Basayev, the Chechen warlord, claimed in 2005 'I have always fought for justice and justice has been my only goal.'[41]

Injustice—real or imagined—is widely seen as one of the most important social causes of rebellion, whether it is a terrorist revolt by a self-appointed vanguard or a more broadly based popular insurrection.[42] To give an example: after the attacks of 9/11, Bin Laden declared that he did not care if his life ended because his 'work was done', namely, having 'awoken Muslims around the world to the injustices imposed upon them by the West and Israel'.[43]

The justice narrative resonates strongly with people who have been wronged and crave revenge, but who label it justice because that word is more acceptable than vengeance.[44] From her study of the writings and pronouncements of terrorists, Louise Richardson contends that the revenge motive figures very prominently in the thinking of terrorists: 'The most powerful theme in any conversation with terrorists past or present, leader or follower, religious or secular, left wing or right wing, male or female, young or old, is revenge.'[45]

'Revenge' can be interpreted as 'primitive justice', an archaic form of retribution where the victim or his family or clan takes the law in their own hands and inflicts punishment on those considered guilty of having wronged, injured or killed one of its members. This desire to make someone pay for a transgression often manifests as an obsessive urge to rectify a grievance at all costs. Passionate impulses that result in revenge can be socially destructive, as a prolonged vendetta culture can break down the fabric of society.

'Revenge' has figured as a major theme in world history and literature. Cervantes' Don Quixote, for example, claimed that his mission was none other than that of helping those who cannot help themselves, avenging those who have been wronged.[46] Some terrorist groups have defined themselves as vicarious defenders of a constituency that cannot defend itself, 'adopting' a constituency and fighting on its behalf without a clear mandate from those concerned. Bin Laden, for instance, repeatedly reiterated the issue of Palestinian rights—but both Hamas and Al Fattah have rejected Al Qaeda's right to speak and act on their behalf.

Revenge can be seen as 'wild justice'; an alternative system of self-help justice, based on the archaic revenge framework. Nachman Ben-Yehuda's analysis of Jewish terrorists in the 1940s concluded that

> ... underlying vengeance is a very strong moral character, guided by a simple principle of justice that stipulates that symmetry must be restored to what is perceived to be an unbalanced situation. [...] Political assassination, as a particular rhetorical device, is invoked as a claim to explain and justify acts that the assassins want to project as a case of 'justice' in situations where they felt that they could not get a fair justice because of the opportunities for such 'justice' were felt to be blocked ...[47]

Uncomfortable as this thought may be, at least some of the violence of contemporary terrorists may be understood as a form of 'rough justice'. There are even similarities between state courts and what some terrorists do in their kangaroo courts—courts improperly constituted and illegal by the prevailing law. While an official state court, especially one with a jury, is widely seen as acting on behalf of society, the kangaroo court of the terrorist also professes to act on behalf of its constituency, for example:

- Some terrorist groups have guidelines for conducting trials within their own ranks (the 'Green Book' of the IRA) comparable to procedural codes for trials in civil society;
- Terrorist deeds are often meant to punish, e.g. 'enemies of the people';
- Terrorists seek to 'justify' their violence by referring to their ideological or religious code, while civil courts refer to a documented legal code;
- Terrorist punishment is sometimes performed in public or delivered as 'revolutionary justice' and documented on video.

The most significant difference between a legally established court and a terrorist kangaroo court is that in the latter the roles of prosecutor, judge, jury and executioner are often combined. In addition, the verdict is generally executed immediately—giving the defence not a semblance of the 'equality of arms'—a balance that would give the defendant at least the 'fighting chance' of a meaningful possibility of defence.

Terrorists have a different perception of justice, one that also includes 'might is right'. Historically, there have been a number of different bases of conceptualisations of justice. Aristoteles (384–322 BC), for instance, considered justice to be a personal virtue like prudence or fortitude. Others use a sacred text as the basis for justice (as do contemporary adherents to Sharia law). Some others equate justice simply with conformity to the current existing law. As one legal scholar has put it: 'Legal justice is justice according to law. It is not about the justice of the law.'[48] Democratic societies, however, tend to link justice to the equity principle to make the law 'fair'.

While terrorists and non-terrorists can agree that 'justice' is something positive, unfortunately no agreement can be reached on which particular conceptualisation of justice is just. 'Justice has no universally valid definition', lawyer Suri Ratnapala has observed.[49] His pronouncement is echoed in the social sciences: 'There does not appear to be universal consensus on what is considered to be just or unjust', L. Montada concludes in the *International Encyclopedia of the Social and Behavioural Sciences*.[50] When determinations of justice are based on different foundations, a clash between different notions of justices is a stark possibility. This is especially true where groups who claim to adhere to 'divine law' oppose more secular groups adhering to man-made laws rather than the authority of religious scholars claiming to speak in the name of a supreme being.

Aristotle posed a crucial question when he asked whether it is 'more advantageous to be ruled by the best man or by the best laws'.[51] Over time, the latter option has evolved into the concept of the Rule of Law. Most interpret the changing concept of justice—from privately delivered revenge or subject to the arbitrary decisions of a power-holder, to justice carried out by representatives of the community under the Rule of Law—in terms of human progress. As the International Commission of Jurists explains it, 'The rule of law is more than the formal use of legal instruments, it is also the rule of justice and of protection for all members of society against excessive governmental power.'[52] The Rule of Law, rather than rule by the personal preference of an arbitrary ruler, or rule by brute force, generally includes these agreed principles:

- Supremacy of the law: all persons are subject to the law (including those holding state power, who are also bound by a common law or constitution);
- The principle of *habeas corpus*: arbitrary or preventive detention is prohibited;
- Separation of powers: parliament exercises legislative power; there are restrictions on the exercise of power by the executive;
- State protection for all: nobody should be above the law, nobody should be outside the protection of the law;
- The principle of proportionality: only minimum force should be used to stop law-breakers; punishment must be relative to the seriousness of the offence;
- Judicial independence: an independent and impartial judiciary, and no 'special courts'.[53]

It is the last of these core principles of the Rule of law that is often challenged in terrorist court cases. Political offenders have often been tried in 'special courts'—e.g. Diplock courts with no jury, or military tribunals. This raises another issue for discussion: whether terrorists should be tried by regular courts.

2.5. Terrorism and Fair Trial

Since in liberal democratic Western legal systems, all citizens (and in many regards also denizens) are equal before the law, people accused of terrorism should, in principle, have the same rights to a fair trial as others accused of a crime. Extensive fair trial guarantees are provided by human rights instruments such as those found in Article 14 of the International Covenant on Civil and Political Rights, and in other UN and regional instruments. These cover, *inter alia*, these elements:

- The right to trial by a competent, independent and impartial tribunal;
- The right to defend oneself in person or through counsel;
- The right to be brought promptly before a judge or other judicial officer;
- The right to challenge the lawfulness of detention;
- The right to be tried without undue delay;
- The right to humane conditions of detention and freedom from torture;
- Exclusion of evidence elicited as a result of torture or other compulsion;
- The right to a public hearing;
- The right not to be compelled to testify or confess guilt;
- The right to call and examine witnesses;
- The right to appeal.[54]

Most of these rights are non-derogable—that is, even in armed conflict and in the face of severe peacetime attacks from terrorists, they cannot be waived.[55]

While democratic societies based on the 'one person-one vote' principle continue to manifest great social and economic inequalities, they nevertheless maintain that all persons are entitled to fair and equal treatment before the law. As a consequence, fair trial rights are in principle extended even to members of terrorist organisations who do not themselves respect the human rights of their adversaries.

Many terrorists who do not recognise the legitimacy of Western judicial systems nevertheless try to use the procedural rules of such judicial systems not just to their own advantage, but also to bring harm to others. Conversations between a defendant and the defence lawyer, for example, are considered confidential to ensure that a proper defence can be conducted, yet the instruments and safeguards of the legal system can be turned against it. There have been cases of collusion where the defence lawyers for terrorists have become de facto accomplices, smuggling messages out of prison for them, or smuggling weapons into prison—with often lethal consequences.[56] Defence lawyers have also successfully appealed to the European Court of Human Rights to overturn British court rulings against Irish terrorists who chose *not* to respect human rights. A number of problems arise in this context.

2.6. Terrorist Confrontations with the Judicial System

Terrorism has been characterised as an asymmetric mode of conflict waging. Terrorists know the location of their adversaries, while their own location is generally not known. Terrorists do not observe the humanitarian rules of warfare; their adversaries generally do. Terrorists ignore human rights but expect adversaries to adhere to them. What are the consequences when the democratic state respects the Rule of Law and the terrorist does not? If the conflict parties belong to different moral communities and play by different rules we are faced with the serious problem that there is no common ground between a judge and the accused, and that the outcome of a trial will not settle the case. Human rights lawyer Geoffrey Robertson has asked: 'How do you give fair trial to a person who does not accept your right to try him?'[57] Paradoxically, while a sentence may not be considered 'fair' by the defendant, the outcome of a trial (for example, punishment by the death penalty) may be welcomed by him or her when operating under an entirely different value system, one in which he or she may desire nothing more than to become a martyr. On a certain reading of Islam, martyrdom may offer 'a direct passport to paradise'.[58]

There may be problems even before the terrorist is brought to trial. The basic legal principle *aut dedere aut judicare* (extradite them or bring them to trial where they are) may not work for certain terrorists. A community hiding a terrorist suspect to protect him or her is unlikely to extradite the terrorist. After the attacks of 11 September 2011, the United States demanded that the Taliban, as de facto ruler of much of Afghanistan, extradite Osama Bin Laden. But Taliban rulers insisted that Osama Bin Laden could be tried only by a group of Islamic clerics committed to Sharia law.[59]

Terrorists have sought various other ways to attack the official justice systems of their adversaries. In early 2011, Greek terrorists claimed responsibility for a powerful explosion that damaged a court building in central Athens. They also threatened to target the individual judges presiding at the court over the trial of 134 suspected members of the 'Conspiracy of the Cells of Fire' organisation.[60] Other terrorists have threatened prosecutors with retaliation.[61] In November 1985 insurgents from the M-19 group in Colombia seized the Palace of Justice in Bogota, taking hostages. Over 70 people were killed in the ensuing fire and gun battle.[62] In Pakistan, courts regularly face the situation that witnesses recant earlier inculpating statements, fearing retribution by associates of the accused.[63] In Northern Ireland in the 1970s, some perverse verdicts resulted from clearly partisan juries. In other cases jurors were intimidated by defendants and their associates outside the courtroom. As a consequence, the so-called Diplock courts were established, with the jury replaced by judges.[64]

2.7. Political Trials

The court trial system is under attack not only by terrorists or—as in the case of the Stammheim trial (see case study in this volume)—by some of their defence lawyers. Under pressure from public opinion, from another state, or from the executive branch of government, attempts to bend the course of justice through unfair or illegal practices have repeatedly been made.

These practices may include the accused being denied access to a defence lawyer in a timely manner, or state prosecutors presenting unreliable or false confessions produced under intense police pressure, or forensic evidence against the accused being fabricated. In some cases, evidence exculpating those accused of a terrorist crime has been withheld from the court. Sometimes the accused have been presented to the jury in a prejudicial manner likely to influence them unduly.[65] Errors of justice based on such techniques have led to the conviction of innocent people as terrorist criminals.[66] Clive Walker has created a typology of miscarriages of justice, He explains that these occur when defendants' or suspects' human rights are breached, 'because of

1. Deficient processes or,
2. The laws which are applied to them, or
3. Because there is no factual justification for the applied treatment or punishment;
4. Whenever suspects or defendant or convicts are treated adversely by the State to a disproportionate extent in comparison with the need to protect the rights of others;
5. Whenever the rights of others are not effectively or proportionately protected or vindicated by State action against wrongdoers, or
6. By State law itself'.[67]

Miscarriages of justice are not confined to political trials of course, but such trials are probably more prone to them. Yet it is possible for a political trial to take place without violations of the Rule of law. It is a profound misunderstanding that a political trial will, by definition, result in political justice.[68] This perception has arisen because many political trials that stand out in collective historical memory were associated with political, i.e. partisan justice. The perception is reflected in the classical definition of a political trial elaborated half a century ago by Otto Kirchheimer, in his seminal work *Political Justice: The Use of Legal Procedures for Political Ends*. Kirchheimer distinguished three main categories of political trials:

1. The trial involving a common crime committed for political purposes and conducted with a view to the political benefits which might ultimately accrue from successful prosecution;
2. The classical political trial: a regime's attempt to incriminate its foe's public behaviour with a view to evicting him from the political scene; and
3. The derivative political trial, where the weapon of defamation, perjury, and contempt are manipulated in an effort to bring disrepute upon a political foe.[69]

Kirchheimer recognised that courts are battlegrounds over legitimacy, where the loyalty of the citizens is the ultimate prize. The narrative that wins over the jury and gains public support outside the courtroom can indeed influence and sometimes even shift the political balance of power—at least in high-profile cases. However, where this battle is fought without 'equality of arms' and the defence side has no 'fighting chance', a political trial is likely to become the scene of political (partisan) justice. Typical circumstances where this is the case have been described by Kirchheimer:

> The aim of political justice is to enlarge the area of political action by enlisting the services of courts on behalf of political goals. It is characterized by the submission to court scrutiny of group and individual action. Those instrumental in such submission seek to strengthen their own position and weaken that of their political foes. [...] If the foes should try to destroy the existing regime, the authority may conclude that it has no choice but to eliminate them. This necessarily involves recourse to the courts. In such circumstances the court proceedings will play a number of roles. First, they will serve as a forum for publicizing the vileness of the challengers. Second, they will conform and legitimize the power holders' proposals for disposing of their opponents. And finally, they might keep the power holders from giving in to the temptation to utilize the occasion for a wholesale elimination of all their political foes, even those unconnected with the group constituting the direct threat.[70]

The main guarantee to prevent political trials resulting in partisan political justice is the constitutional protection of the judiciary against encroachments by the executive branch of government and, to a lesser extent, by the legislative branch of government. This can be done by special provisions guaranteeing the judiciary's impartiality and independence. The importance of this guarantee was recognized in the 18th century by Charles de Montesquieu, who argued for the separation of governmental powers between the judicial, legislative and executive arms to create a system of checks and balances to prevent abuses of power. As he put it:

> There is no liberty, if the judicial power be not separate from the legislative and executive. Were it joined with the legislative, the life and liberty of the subject would be exposed to arbitrary control, for the judge would be then the legislator. Were the judicial power in a state joined to the executive power, the judge might behave with violence and oppression.[71]

Terrorists and their defence lawyers are sometimes accused of 'politicising' trials, as are governments. If both sides try to extend the process of seeking 'justice' to the court of public opinion, the question arises: who profits more from 'politicising' a trial—the prosecution or the defence? An American study (surveying hundreds of terrorist trials over nearly a quarter of a century) came to some counter-intuitive findings:

- The more politicised the prosecution strategy, the more likely the case will go to trial and the more likely it will result in acquittal or dismissal;
- Treating terrorist defendants like traditional offenders results in the highest plea and conviction rates;
- The most explicitly politicised prosecution strategies double the likelihood of acquittal and dismissal;
- Highly politicised defence strategies are associated with an increase in the likelihood of conviction[72]

If we are to believe these findings, the 'politicisation' of a trial is counterproductive for both sides. However in the study cited above, 'politicised' is defined in terms of 'tying the defendant's ideological motivation to the elements of the case'.[73] In my view, this is too narrow a definition of the performative manoeuvres engaged in by one or both sides in the 'lawfare' taking place in court in certain terrorist trials.[74]

Another American study showed that it does not pay to be seen as a 'terrorist' when it comes to sentencing since sentences for similar crimes are consistently harsher in terrorist cases, as the following table makes clear:

Average sentence for persons charged with terrorism	19.7 years
Average sentence for persons convicted of terrorism	16 years
Average sentence for persons charged with national security violations but not terrorism	10.4 years
Average sentence for persons convicted of national security violations but not terrorism	7.5 years
Average sentence for persons not charged with terrorism or national security violations	1.2 years

Table 2.2. Severity of sentences for terrorism and other charges (USA) 2001–2009[75]

Does this suggest that because terrorists are treated more harshly than others they therefore are not getting a fair trial? Not necessarily. Judges and juries not only assess the quality of the criminal deed (*actus reus* 'guilty act') itself, but also take into account the underlying intent (*mens rea* 'guilty mind'). In the case of terrorism, the tactical intent of an act of terrorism is often especially reprehensible. It can involve threatening to kill unarmed civilians to raise ransom money, provoking the repression of a sector of society in order to gain new recruits to a terrorist movement from disgruntled rebellious members of that sector of society, or instilling extreme fear in a population to induce people to leave a conflict zone (ethnic cleansing). It is this distinctive immorality which sets terrorism apart from other violent political crimes, even those with greater numbers of victims. For this reason, harsher sentences are justified although their deterrent value may not be great. However, they may go some way in placating feelings of anger among victims and survivors and the general public—thereby preventing acts of revenge.

2.8. Conclusion

When it comes to the question of how societies and governments should deal with terrorists, a crucial question is whether the criminal justice approach is the right one. Some argue that since jihadi terrorists declared 'war' on Western societies, states responding to terrorism also have to operate within a framework of war. Those taking this position are often not inclined to allow terrorists their day in court, at least not in a civilian court, and tend to prefer that captured terrorists be locked up until the war on terrorism is over (as with prisoners of war). The United States took this approach under the Bush administration and largely continued it under the Obama administration. Yet following more than ten years of fighting a global war on terror, and spending in the process more than one trillion dollars,[76] the results of the war on terror are less than satisfactory. There are more terrorists around than before as Al Qaeda mutated from a terrorist group to a conglomerate of jihadist groups and an even broader ideological movement. Deterrence clearly has not worked and terrorism has not been eradicated. Depending on the level of the terrorist challenge, both approaches—the criminal justice approach and the military approach—may indeed be needed side by side. However, given the less than persuasive results of the military war on terrorism, a reconsideration of the merits of the criminal justice approach to terrorism is warranted. Despite some apparent weaknesses which we have highlighted above, the criminal justice approach has considerable benefits, as Ben Saul has summarised:

> Set against the vain hope of pounding terrorists into oblivion through war, the criminal law offers the promise of restraint: individual rather than collective responsibility; a presumption of innocence; no detention without charge; proof of guilt beyond reasonable doubt; due process; the right to prepare and present an adequate defence; independent adjudication; and rational and proportionate punishment.[77]

These are the qualities that set the Rule of law apart from the 'rule of the jungle', where 'might is right'. Liberal democratic states adhering to these principles will occupy a moral high ground in the fight against terrorism. Even when terrorists and their defence lawyers abuse the legal system for tactical victories they do not deserve, this is a price well worth paying in defence of freedom and justice.

Terrorist trials will almost always be 'political' because terrorism is inherently a form of political violence. That the trials of those accused of terrorism are political despite the independence and impartiality of the judiciary does not mean that they are necessarily unfair. To be sure, many terrorist trials have fallen short of the highest standards of justice—as illustrated in this volume. However, the idea that justice should apply even to terrorists who deny justice to their opponents is one that makes the criminal justice approach ultimately superior to other systems of dealing with 'political crime', including terrorism. Used with wisdom and moderation, the criminal justice approach has the potential to break the cycle of revenge actions that feed terrorism.

Notes

1 Jerrold M. Post, 'Terrorist on Trial: The Context of Political Crime', in: Harvey W. Kushner. *Essential Readings in Political Terrorism* (Lincoln: Gordon Knot Books, 2002), p. 57.

2 After the killing of Bin Laden, US President Obama said that 'justice has been done'. However critics argued that proper justice should be administered by judges in a tribunal, not by Special Forces (cf. Daniele Archibugi, 'Should bin Laden have been tried?', *Open Democracy Forum* (4 May 2011), https://www.opendemocracy.net/daniele-archibugi/should-bin-laden-have-been-tried. Retrieved 4 May 2011).

3 Robert Cryer, Hakan Friman, Darryl Robinson and Elizabeth Wilmshurst, *An Introduction to International Criminal Law and Procedure*. 2nd ed. (Cambridge: Cambridge University Press, 2010), p. 338. The authors note that '[t]errorist acts can be prosecuted in an international court at present only if they amount to war crimes or crimes against humanity'.

4 Herman Thomas Bianchi, *Politiek en Criminaliteit* (Kampen: J.H. Kok, 1992), p. 63.

5 Based on the lemma 'crime' in: A.P. Schmid (ed.), *The Routledge Handbook of Terrorism Research* (London & New York: Routledge, 2011), p. 620.

6 Lee Ellis and Anthony Walsh, *Criminology. A Global Perspective* (Boston: Allyn and Bacon, 2000), p. 10.

7 Frank E. Hagan, *Political Crime: Ideology and Criminality* (Boston: Allyn and Bacon, 1997), p. ix.

8 Ellis and Walsh, *Criminology. A Global Perspective*, p. 11.

9 Otto Kirchheimer, *Political Justice. The Use of Legal Procedures for Political Ends* (Princeton: Princeton University Press, 1961), p. 25.

10 Hagan, *Political Crime*, p. 4.

11 Cf. Colin Wilson, *The History of Murder* (Edison, N.J.: Castle Books, 2004).

12 Anthony Aust, *Handbook of International Law*. 2nd ed. (Cambridge: Cambridge University Press, 2011), pp. 264–265; Cf. Ben Saul. 'Legislating from a Radical The Hague: The UN Special Tribunal for Lebanon Invents an International Crime of Transnational Terrorism', *Leiden Journal of International Law*, 24:3 (2011), pp. 677–700. See also: Ben Saul, *Defining Terrorism in International Law* (Oxford: Oxford University Press, 2006), p. 319: where he writes, 'In national criminal legislation, almost half of States now define terrorism generically (either in simple or composite definitions) although half of States still treat terrorism as ordinary crime. The variation in national definitions precludes the identification of any international customary definition, although generic definition is increasingly common'.

13 Kimberly Prost, 'Extradition: The Practical Challenges', in: Rodrigo Yepes-Enriquez and

Lisa Tabassi (eds), *Treaty Enforcement and International Cooperation in Criminal Matters. With Special Reference to the Chemical Weapons Convention* (The Hague: T.M.C. Asser Press, 2003), p. 202.

14 Louis G. Fields, 'Bringing Terrorists to Justice—The Shifting Sands of the Political Offence Exception', in: Richard B. Lillich (ed.), *International Aspects of Criminal Law Enforcing United States Law in the World Community* (Charlotteville, VA.: Michie Co., 1981), p. 15 (Abstract); Since then, the US–UK extradition treaty has removed the political offence exception.—Helen Duffy, *The 'War on Terror' and the Framework of International Law* (Cambridge: Cambridge University Press, 2005), p. 136.

15 Fields, 'Bringing Terrorists to Justice', p. 15.

16 Since 2004, extradition for criminal offences has been effectively replaced by the European Arrest Warrant, allowing the surrender of suspected or convicted criminals from one country to another with minimum formalities.—United Nations Office on Drugs and Crime (UNODC), *Handbook on Criminal Justice Responses to Terrorism* (New York: United Nations, 2009), p. 76; Cryer (et al.), *An Introduction to International Criminal Law and Procedure*. 2nd ed., p. 96.

17 In this context, M. Cherif Bassiouni noted: 'Legitimate resistance to oppression and tyranny is an internationally recognized right as a "last resort" when political and judicial avenues of redress have been exhausted. This does not justify, however, indiscriminate, disproportionate and unlawful use of violence or terrorism .... Such matters must be adjudicated preferably by an international body taking into account all factors underlying such acts for purposes of mitigation and aggravation'. Cit. M. Cherif Bassiouni (ed.), *International Terrorism and Political Crimes* (Springfield, Ill.: Charles C. Thomas Publisher, 1975), p. xxi.

18 Matthew Lippman, 'Political Offender Exception in International Extradition Law: Terrorism Versus Human Rights', *International Journal of Comparative and Applied Criminal Justice*, 13: 2 (1989), pp. 45–59 at p. 45 (Abstract).

19 Prost, 'Extradition: The Practical Challenges', p. 209.

20 'Attentat', in German, means making an attempt on a politically important person's life; if successful resulting in 'Politischer Mord' (political murder).

21 Ethan A. Nadelman, *Cops Across Borders. The Internationalization of U.S. Criminal Law Enforcement* (University Park: The Pennsylvania State University Press, 1993), p. 420; The trigger for the 'attentat clause' was the attempt by two Frenchmen to blow up a train carrying Napoleon III in Belgium. France requested their extradition which was first refused by a Belgian court on the basis of the political offence exception. However subsequently the Belgian parliament introduced the 'attentat clause', which made possible the extradition of the two culprits. The clause held that '[t]here shall not be

considered as a political crime or as an act connected with such a crime an attack upon the person of the head of a foreign government or of a member of his family, when the attack takes the form of either murder, assassination or poisoning'; Cit. Abraham D. Sofaer, 'The Political Offence Exception and Terrorism', *Current Policy*, no. 762 (Washington, D.C.: U.S. Department of State, November 1985), p. 3.

22 Cf. James J. Kinneally, III, 'The Political Offence Exception: is the United States-United Kingdom Supplementary Extradition Treaty the Beginning of the End?', *American University Journal of International Law and Policy*, 2:1 (1987), pp. 209–211.

23 Cit. Fred Hendricks, 'Jettisoning Justice. The Case of Amnesty in South Africa', p. 102, http://www.isa-sociology.org/colmemb/national-associations/en/meetings/reports/Southern%20Africa/Chapter%207.pdf. Retrieved 11 August 2011.

24 Cf. Staff Reporter, The Norgaard Principles; cit. *Mail & Guardian* (31 March 1995) www.mg.co.za/article/1995-03-31-the-norgaard-principles. Retrieved 19 May 2015.

25 This is the division introduced by Stephen Schafer in his book *The Political Offender: The Problem of Morality and Crime* (New York: Fee Press, 1974), pp. 380–387.

26 UNODC, Unpublished Report on the Treatment of the Political Offence Exception in International Anti-Terrorism Legal Instruments [ca. 2003], pp. 17–18; For a discussion of the issue see E. Chadwick, *Self-Determination, Terrorism and the International Humanitarian Law of Armed Conflict* (The Hague: Nijhoff, 1966). She argues that acts of terrorism during armed conflict in struggles for self-determination can be prosecuted as 'grave breaches' or terrorist war crimes. Cit. Peter van Krieken, *Terrorism and the International Legal Order* (The Hague: T.M.C. Asser Press, 2002), p. 221n.

27 Other problems of definition occur such as: who is the 'self' in 'self-determination', what is a 'nation' in 'national liberation', and indeed, who should be considered a 'people'? Does the term 'people', for instance, also apply to indigenous peoples? Neither 'nation' nor 'people' is defined in international law. In practice, self-determination in the UN context has meant freedom from white colonial overseas rule but not liberation from land-based, adjacent foreign rule as in the case of Tibet (from China) or other local non-white rulers dominating indigenous peoples (e.g. Morocco and the Sahrawi Arab Democratic Republic—Polisario—in former Spanish Western Sahara, or Indonesia in Western New Guinea—formerly Netherlands New Guinea).

28 Van Krieken, *Terrorism and the International Legal Order*, p. 221.

29 Annex II. Informal text of articles 2 and 2bis of the draft Comprehensive Convention, prepared by the Coordinator. Article 2. Reproduced from document A/C./6/56/L.9, annex I.B (emphasis in *italics* and underlined added by A.P. Schmid). This text represent the stage of consideration reached at the 2011 session of the Working Group of the Sixth Committee.—Cit. United Nations, *Report of the Ad Hoc Committee established by General*

Assembly resolution 51/210 of 17 December 1996. Sixth session (28 January–1 February 2002). General Assembly. Official Records. Supplement No. 37 (A/57/37), p. 6.

30 Typical for 'Propaganda by the Deed' is a statement by Mikhail Bakunin: 'We must spread out principles, not with words but with deeds, for this is the most popular, and the most irresistible form of propaganda'—Mikhail Bakunin, *Letters to a Frenchman on the Present Crisis* (1870), http://marxists.org/reference/archive/bakunin/works/1870/letter-frenchman.htm. Retrieved 11 August 2011.

31 These three criteria are from Saul, *Defining Terrorism in International Law*, p. 4.

32 Schmid (ed.), *The Routledge Handbook of Terrorism Research*, p. 86.

33 An example of an overly broad definition can be found in David Bloxham and Robert Gerwarth (eds), *Political Violence in Twentieth Century Europe* (Cambridge: Cambridge University Press, 2011), pp. 1–2, where the editors define 'political violence' in this way: '... it encompasses atrocities committed by the state in the form of genocide, but also of torture and extra-legal warfare; and atrocities committed by non-state actors, be they "terrorists" or paramilitary forces vying for political influence or territorial control. It includes violence in revolutionary and counter-revolutionary situations, violence within and outside conventional warfare, and violence committed in the name of ideological causes, both religious and secular. In short, the term "political violence" ... connotes all forms of violence enacted pursuant to aims of decisive socio-political control or change.'

34 Ted Honderich, *After the Terror* (Edinburgh: Edinburgh University Press, 2002), pp. 98–99. Cit. Tamara Meisels, *The Trouble with Terror. Liberty, Security, and the Response to Terrorism* (Cambridge: Cambridge University Press, 2008), p. 33.

35 Adapted from Schmid (ed.), *The Routledge Handbook of Terrorism Research*, pp. 5–6; It should be noted that some forms of political violence listed here can (also) be terroristic; there is a grey area with overlaps depending on context.

36 Max Abrahms, 'Why Terrorism Does Not Work', *International Security*, 31:2 (2006), pp. 42–78.

37 Geoffrey Robertson, 'Fair Trials for Terrorists?', in: Richard Ashby Wilson (ed.), *Human Rights in the 'War on Terror'* (Cambridge: Cambridge University Press, 2005), p. 169.

38 Daniel Fischer, 'Profile: al-Qaeda's Seif al-Adel', *The Telegraph* UK (12 February 2012), http://www.telegraph.co.uk/news/worldnews/al-qaeda/9113446/Profile-al-Qaedas-Seif-al-Adel.html. Retrieved 19 May 2012.

39 Maximilien Robespierre: 'La terreur n'est autre chose que la justice prompte, severe, inflexible: elle est donc une emanation de la vertu'. Cit. Andreas Musloff, *Krieg gegen die Oeffentlichkeit. Terrorismus und politischer Sprachgebrauch* (Opladen, Westdeutscher Verlag, 1996), p. 56.

40 Osama bin Laden, speech released on 29 October 2004, *Jihad and Terrorism Studies Project. http://www.memri.org/%20bin/%20articles.cgi?Page=subjects&Area=jihad&ID=SP81104.*

Retrieved October 2010; Cit. Steve Heitkamp, *Terrorism as Ethnic Antagonism and Violence: A View from Sociology*. Quoted from MS, p. 6.

41 Cit. ABC *News Nightline* (28 July 2005); Cit. Louise Richardson, *What Terrorists Want. Understanding the Enemy, Containing the Threat* (New York, Random House, 2006), p. 87.

42 Cf. Barrington Moore, *The Social Bases of Obedience and Revolt* (London: Macmillan, 1978); Manus I. Midlarsky, *Origins of Political Extremism. Mass Violence in the Twentieth Century and Beyond* (Cambridge: Cambridge University Press, 2011), pp. 39–45.

43 Cit. Frank Gardner, 'Obituary: Osama Bin Laden', BBC *News Middle East* (2 May 2011).

44 Cf. also Jeffry R. Halverson, H.L. Goodall, Jr., and Steven R. Corman, *Master Narratives of Islamist Extremism* (New York: Palgrave Macmillan, 2011).

45 Richardson, *What Terrorists Want*, p. 88.

46 Miguel de Cervantes, *Don Quijote de la Mancha* (1605), http://www.online-literature.com/cervantes/don_quixote/23/. Retrieved 19 May 2015.

47 Nachman Ben-Yehuda, 'Political Assassination Events as a cross-cultural form of alternative justice', *International Journal of Comparative Sociology*, 38:1 (1997), pp. 4–5.

48 Suri Ratnapala, *Jurisprudence* (Cambridge: Cambridge University Press, 2009), pp. 329, 357.

49 Ratnapala, *Jurisprudence*, p. 318.

50 L. Montada, 'Justice and its Many Faces: Cultural Concerns', in: Neil J. Smelser and Paul B. Baltes (eds), *International Encyclopedia of the Social & Behavioral Sciences*, 12 (Amsterdam: Elsevier, 2001), p. 8037.

51 Cit. Ratnapala, *Jurisprudence*, pp. 322–323.

52 Cit. Human Security Network, *Understanding Human Rights. Manual on Human Rights Education* (Graz: Human Security Network, 2003), p. 139.

53 Adapted from: Alex P. Schmid, 'The Concept of Rule of Law', In: Alex P. Schmid and Etihne Boland (eds), *The Rule of Law in the Global Village: Issues of Sovereignty and Universality* (Milan: ISPAC, 2001), p. xi.

54 Amnesty International, *Fair Trials Manual* (London: Amnesty International Publications, 1998), pp. i–v.

55 Evelyne Schmid, 'The Right to a Fair Trial in Times of Terrorism: A Method to Identify the Non-Derogable Aspects of Article 14 of the International Covenant on Civil and Political Rights', *Goettingen Journal of International Law*, 1:1 (2009), p. 30; see also: United Nations, *Digest of jurisprudence of the United Nations and regional organizations on the protection of human rights while countering terrorism* (New York: United Nations, 2003), p. 55, where it is noted: 'Although article 14 of the Covenant is not listed as non-derogable under article 4, the Human Rights Committee (in General Comment No. 29) has concluded that certain aspects of article 14 are obligatory, even in states of emergency: [T]he category of peremptory norms extends beyond the list of non-derogable provisions as given in

article 4, paragraph 2. States parties may in no circumstances invoke article 4 of the covenant as justification for acting in violation of humanitarian law or peremptory norms of international law, for instance by ... deviating from fundamental principles of fair trial, including the presumption of innocence'.

56 C. Revon, *Terrorism and Political Defence. Deviance et Societé* (Geneva, Faculte de Droit, 1978), NCJRS Abstract.

57 Robertson, 'Fair Trials for Terrorists?', p. 178.

58 Robertson, 'Fair Trials for Terrorists?', p. 174.

59 Amartya Sen, *The Idea of Justice* (London: Penguin Books, 2009), pp. 149–150.

60 Press report, reproduced in PTSS *summary of the German George Marshall Centre* (Garmisch-Partenkirchen, 10 January 2011).

61 UNODC, *Handbook on Criminal Justice Responses to Terrorism*, p. 93.

62 National Security Archive, *State Department Cable says Colombian Army Responsible for Palace of Justice Deaths, Disappearances* (Washington, DC: NSA, 8 October 2009), p. 1.

63 Alex Rodriguez, 'Pakistani criminal justice system proves no match for terrorism cases', *Los Angeles Times* (28 October 2010).

64 Philip B. Heyman, *Terrorism and America. A Commonsense Strategy for a Democratic Society* (Cambridge, Mass.: MIT Press, 1998), p. 122.

65 Cf. Clive Walker and Keir Starmer (eds), *Justice in Error* (London: Blackstone Press, 1993).

66 Kent Roach and Gary Trotter, 'Miscarriages of Justice in the War Against Terrorism', *Penn State Law Review*, 109:4 (2005), NCJRS Abstract.

67 Clive Walker, 'Miscarriages of Justice in Principle and Practice', in: C. Walker and K. Starmer. *Miscarriages of Justice: A Review of Justice in Error* (London: Blackstone Press, 1999), p. 33; Cit. Roach and Trotter, 'Miscarriages of Justice in the War Against Terror', p. 1035.

68 Ron Christenson, *Political Trials. Gordian Knots in the Law* (New Brunswick: Transaction Publishers, 1989), p. 10.

69 Kirchheimer, *Political Justice*, p. 46.

70 Kirchheimer, *Political Justice*, pp. 47, 419–420.

71 Charles Montesquieu, *The Spirit of the Laws* (Hafner Classics, 1949); cit. Paavo Kotiaho, *Challenges to Fair Trial in the 'Fight against Terrorism'* (Unpublished paper, n.d.), p. 13.

72 Christopher A. Shields, Kelly R. Damphousse and Brent L. Smith, 'Their Day in Court: Assessing Guilty Plea Rates Among Terrorists', *Journal of Contemporary Criminal Justice*, 22:3 (2006), p. v.

73 Chris Shields, Kelly R. Damphousse and Brent L. Smith, *Assessment of Defence and Prosecutorial Strategies in Terrorism Trials: Implications for State and Federal Prosecutors* (Rockville, MD: NCJRS, 2008), Abstract.

74 Lawfare has been defined as 'the cynical manipulation of legal and judicial systems and human rights law, for purposes other than those for which they were originally enacted, to achieve political ends—a kind of legal equivalent to asymmetric "warfare"'. See also: Zev Krengel, '"Lawfare" is the latest weapon used against Israel', *Mail & Guardian online* (4 February 2011), http://mg.co.za/article/2011-02-04-lawfare-is-latest-weapon-used-against-israel. Retrieved 19 May 2015. The meaning of the term in this chapter and in the Israeli context is not quite the same, although there is some overlap. According to the *Lawfare Project*, an American organisation dedicated to examine this phenomenon, '"lawfare" has three goals: To silence and punish free speech about issues of national and public concern; to delegitimize the sovereignty of democratic states; and to frustrate and hinder the ability of democracies to fight against and defeat terrorism.'

75 Centre on Law and Security, *Highlights from the Terrorist Trial Report Card, 2001–2009: Lessons Learned* (New York: CLS, 2009), p. 14. Based on 828 terrorism prosecutions (235 still pending; 593 resolved indictments). Out of these 593 defendants, 523 were convicted on some charge either at trial or by plea. Conviction Rate: 88.2%. (p. 2).

76 According to figures released on 30 April 2011, the Pentagon had spent at least US$1 trillion prosecuting the wars in Iraq and Afghanistan and defending the US homeland. Cf. Tony Capaccio, 'Pentagon Crosses $1 Trillion Threshold In War On Terror Spending', *Bloomberg News* (21 June 2011).

77 Saul, *Defining Terrorism in International Law*, p. 318.

3. The Trial of Vera Zasulich in 1878[1]

Alex P. Schmid

> Vera Zasulich's deed opened a new era of revolutionary terror ... it is difficult to imagine the now decisive turn of populism to terror without the Zasulich case. Society seemed to say through the court: yes, it is legitimate and necessary to resort to violence to shake up the autocracy. And the autocracy in turn gave up its last attempts to appease the intelligentsia and observe its own laws in dealing with sedition.
>
> A.B. Ulam (1977)[2]

3.1. Introduction

Trials sometimes become mirrors of their times, providing a glimpse into the state of a society.[3] In the 1870s, Russian society was divided into an educated westernised class (then called 'the intelligentsia'—perhaps 20 per cent of the population) and an illiterate, largely rural majority of 100 million common people, mostly peasants. While 23 million of them had been released from serfdom in 1861, they were still burdened by debts to their former owners; less than one third of Russia's land was in their hands; for many there was not enough land to make a decent living.[4] Russian government was divided into an autocratic executive (which also controlled the hand-picked Senate) and a judiciary that was, thanks to the reforms of 1864, based on democratic procedures.[5] By the mid-1870s, Russia also saw the rise of a mass-circulation press that was becoming commercially independent, less constrained by censorship, reflecting and shaping public opinion in the capital of St. Petersburg.[6] In 1877 and early 1878 Russia was at war with Turkey, initially against the wishes of the Tsar, though the press had pushed him into defending orthodox Christians in the Balkans who suffered from atrocities by the Ottoman empire. The war was costly, both in terms of finances and in terms of casualties, but Russia gained the upper hand and Turkey had to sue for peace in early 1878. Yet the spoils of victory were largely lost by mid-1878 when the Western powers at the Congress of Berlin forced Russia to make what many Russians considered humiliating concessions.[7]

It was against this general background that the assassination attempt by Vera Zasulich on 24 January 1878 and her trial on 31 March 1878 took place. The Zasulich trial has been called 'the most momentous trial in the history of imperial Russia'.[8] Zasulich's assassination attempt on the Governor of St. Petersburg and her acquittal by an independent jury set an example that stimulated the emergence of assassination as a form of 'vigilante justice' serving both as punishment and as 'propaganda by the deed'. At the end of a series of assassinations of government officials, on 1 March 1881, the reformist Tsar Alexander II was assassinated by the *People's Will* (*Narodnaya Volya*), a terrorist group led by another woman, Vera Figner. It was a moment when Russian and European history took a decisive turn in one direction at the end of which stood the assassination of Franz Ferdinand, the Austrian heir to the throne. This, in 1914, triggered the First World War which, three years later, would lead to the Russian Revolution. Indeed, to the extent that the emergence of 'propaganda by the deed' type terrorism can be linked to a single person and date, the assassination attempt by Vera Zasulich on 24 January 1878 would be a good candidate. While her assault on Governor Fyodor Trepov itself was unsuccessful—the governor survived—her trial made her, thanks to the attention given to this assassination attempt by the mass media, a celebrity and, in the eyes of those inspired by her, a heroine.

In the District Court of St. Petersburg she and, even more so, her defence lawyer 'out-performed' the prosecution. On 31 March 1878 the female assassin managed to gain the sympathy of the 18 jurors in the courtroom, captured the imagination of the crowd outside and, thanks to the press, touched a chord with much of the intelligentsia in Russia and beyond. How all this could happen to a shy woman with no personal charisma, a person who was not very confident of herself, is due to a confluence of circumstances in the peculiar historical context of the time. Before we turn to the trial and its judicial, social and political consequences, some historical background is in order for a better understanding.

3.1.1. *What Happened before the Trial*

Tsar Alexander II not only abolished serfdom in Russia in the March 1861, he also introduced a number of other reforms. Among these were judicial reforms that aimed to bring the country's judicial system more in line with West European standards.[9] Between 1864 and 1866 a unified court system was created for much of Russia. The judicial reforms also changed the way criminal trials were held. An adversarial criminal justice procedure was introduced, assigning to judges the role of acting as umpires between the defence and the prosecution. The courtroom became the stage where a defence attorney and the state's prosecutor would confront each other to establish truth and guilt.[10] Judges could, under the new reform scheme, no longer be removed by the government and verdicts by the courts could not be overturned by the executive. Professional advocates made their appearance, court hearings were held in public and juries represented in the first instance civil society and not the government.[11] This judicial reform was, however, not complete; a system of administrative justice co-existed with the new system; it allowed police and gendarmes to re-arrest defendants set free by the courts and exile them to the provinces—often Siberia. In addition, certain crimes against the state were excluded from the competence of juries by the new legislation.[12] Nevertheless, some quasi-political crimes, including Vera Zasulich's, were at times dealt with like common crimes.[13] The great reforms of 1864 had created a wave of expectation about further moves towards democratisation of the autocratic regime. However, after he had survived an assassination attempt in 1866, the reformist zeal of the Tsar declined sharply. The growing unrest among the educated part of the youth was met by the regime with increased repression and would even lead to the abrogation of some of the reforms of 1864.[14]

3.1.2. *The Bogoliubov Affair as Cause*

An example of this regression could be seen in the repression of a demonstration held in December 1876 by radical students on the Nevsky Prospect in St. Petersburg. The demonstration was led by Georgi Plechanov (who was later to become the founder of the Russian Social-Democratic Party). While it was meant as a workers' demonstration, most of the 200 to 250 participants were in fact students.[15] The police attacked them within five minutes after the demonstration had begun. A fight developed in which some constables were roughed up by some of the students. General Fydor Trepov, Governor and police chief of St. Petersburg, arrived on the scene with his mounted police to organise the arrests. Among those arrested was a 24-year-old man who had not even been on the scene; he was picked up in the neighbourhood because one of the policemen thought he recognised him as one of the students who had just fought with the police outside the Kazan Cathedral on the Nevsky Prospect. He gave his name as Arkhip Petrovich Bogoliubov (his real name was Aleksei Stepaniovich Emelianov) and he had a gun in his pocket.

Bogoliubov was one of the thousands of idealistic *narodniki* (populist) youth who, since 1874, had gone 'to the people', trying to incite the peasants to revolt against the owners of the large estates and take their land.[16] Many of these *narodniki* had already been apprehended by the police in 1874 and 1875, not infrequently after being denounced by the very people they wanted to liberate. Many of these populists were detained for years before they obtained their day in court, where they were charged with revolutionary propaganda. That was also to be the fate of Bogoliubov; but the charges brought against him were different. Based on the false testimony of six police witnesses, he was, in January 1877, sentenced to 20 years' hard labour.[17] He had been charged with resisting the police in the demonstration before the Kazan Cathedral and for having made threats to the life of a police aide. It was a tragic case of mistaken identity. Awaiting transportation to another prison, Bogoliubov was placed in the House of Preliminary Detention, the country's newest and most modern prison in St. Petersburg.[18]

Bogoliubov was still there in mid-1877 when General Trepov decided to inspect the House of Detention, after having heard that discipline there had become a problem. Trepov was a hardliner, widely known for taking bribes, often brutal but at times also sentimental.[19] Already in 1861, as police chief of Warsaw, he had ordered his policemen to fire on peaceful Polish demonstrators. After 1866, when the first of some ten attempts on the life of the Tsar failed, Alexander II had become almost paranoid about his personal security. Trepov was made Commandant of the St. Petersburg police where he arranged for a special police section dedicated to the protection of the Tsar.[20] Every morning Trepov would report directly to the Tsar about the security situation. He was also in charge of a police section that was investigating political crimes.[21]

Among these political crimes were also the revolutionary activities of the *narodniki*. 770 of these populists had been arrested in the mid-1870s. Some 70 had already died while in detention awaiting trial due to the unhealthy prison conditions. By October 1877, 193 of those arrested were brought to a trial in which Vladislav Zhelekhovskii acted as prosecutor. That *Trial of the 193* came to an end on 23 January 1878. The defendants' impassioned speeches, printed and distributed by the underground press, stirred emotions among revolutionary students and were sympathetically received by much of the reading public. These, mostly idealistic if somewhat naïve youths (overwhelmingly the sons and daughters of the nobility, the clergy, burghers and officials, including even the military) had agitated against the status quo, but most of them had not engaged in violence themselves. That was ultimately also recognised in court: the Senate's court in the end acquitted 153 of the 193 accused and most of the rest appeared at first to get off with light sentences.[22]

As mentioned above, on 13 July 1877 the House of Preliminary Detention was visited by the Governor of St. Petersburg, General Trepov.[23] In the courtyard of the prison Arkhip Bogoliubov apparently tried to speak to the Governor but was rebuked.

Later when Trepov passed him again, Bogoliubov failed to tip his cap (something he had done in the first encounter). Trepov was annoyed by this apparent lack of respect and hit him so that the cap flew off his head. This was seen as a humiliating blow by other prisoners who were watching the scene from their cell windows; they began to shout in protest. Angered by this and Bogoliubov's apparent insolence, Trepov ordered that he be flogged with birch rods.

Flogging a political prisoner was, in the view of Russia's intelligentia, unacceptable. It was also widely considered unlawful—a shameful practice from Russia's bad past. As a form of punishment, it had been abolished by the reforms of 1863. Yet, there were certain exceptions e.g. for soldiers and sailor and people who had lost their civil rights—which included some categories of prisoners. Trepov had, according to his own account, got permission for this particular act of corporal punishment from Konstantin I. Pahlen, the Minister of Justice. To make a stronger case for the punishment he also (falsely) claimed that Bogoliubov had given the other prisoners a sign to riot.[24]

In the afternoon of 13 July 1877, the acting prison administrator announced that Bogoliubov would be subjected to 'birching' for insubordination, which led to a major disturbance among the prisoners. It lasted 24 hours and 100 extra policemen had to be brought in to quell the riot.[25] The Minister of Justice had already approved the flogging when he heard about the initial rioting. The punishment was, in this particular case, apparently covered by law since Bogoliubov had lost his civil rights when the sentence against him (20 years' hard labour—itself unjust because based on mistaken identity) had become legally binding on 24 June 1878.[26] Bogoliubov was stripped to his waist and flogged. Rumour had it that he was beaten unconscious but he actually received only 13 of the 25 approved lashes; these he took bravely. Afterwards he was moved to the Lithuanian castle, one of the capital's worst prisons, where prisoners waiting for deportation to distant labour camps were assembled.[27] Trepov, possibly feeling sorry about the whole affair, later claimed that he had sent tea and sugar to Bogoliubov's cell. Due to the selective censorship of the press, what the public learned about the whole affair was limited; as a consequence rumours exaggerated both the circumstances and the severity of the flogging. Vera Zasulich had read about Bogoliubov's punishment in *Golos* (*The Voice*) in late July 1877.[28] As a former political prisoner, she became obsessed by this case and decided that this insult to a political prisoner was unacceptable. Without knowing either Trepov or Bogoliubov, she decided to take revenge.[29]

Here then we find, in an early manifestation, a familiar chain of events leading to terrorism: an outsider identifies him- or herself with a victim (or a victimised group) incapable of obtaining justice for an alleged or real wrong. He (or she) then decides to take vicarious revenge on the victim's behalf—without being appointed by the victim (group) and without a direct personal grudge against the original wrongdoer. Vera Zasulich decided to act for Bogoliubov against Trepov in order to appeal with her deed to a wider public. She had never personally met either of them.

3.2. The Unsuccessful Assassin

Before we proceed further to the terrorist act and the trial, we have to pause here and look at the personality and the motives of Russia's first female terrorist.

Like Bogoliubov, Vera Zasulich had been an unjustly condemned political prisoner herself and that bond contributed to trigger her fateful deed of 24 January 1878. It was her intent to use the court trial as a platform to bring an act of injustice to the attention of the public.[30] However, beyond that, there were other factors that set her on the path to assassination.

She was the daughter of Captain Ivan Zasulich, a despotic person who had been demoted for drunkenness in the army. Vera did not know her father; he died when she was three years old. Her mother, Feoktista, an impoverished woman from the lower nobility, could not afford to bring up all five of her children. Therefore Vera was sent away from home to be raised by wealthier relatives—a fact she deeply resented. Her education was strict, even when she was sent to a private boarding school in Moscow: running and laughing were forbidden and so was the use of Russian. Only German and French could be spoken. The only employment prospect open to a poor girl like her from the gentry was becoming a governess, a house teacher, for children of richer families than her own. It was not something she wanted. Joining the revolutionary movement was a way out—a choice also made by two of her sisters (the third had died). Vera was quite untypical of a revolutionary: shy and introverted, often depressive and at times even suicidal.[31] Originally very Christian, Vera later lost faith (Vera, in Russian, means 'faith') and became, for a while, a nihilist, which, for her, had more to do with liberation than with destruction—something that Sergei Nechaev had in mind.[32] Later she would write in her memoirs:

> But the older I grew, the more I became convinced that I was indeed an alien: I didn't belong. No one ever held me, kissed me, or sat me on his knees; no one called me pet names. The servants abused me [...] And then, the distant specter of revolution

> appeared, making me equal to a boy; I, too, could dream of 'action', of 'exploits', and of the 'great struggle' [...] I too could join those who perished for the great cause of love [...] I could imagine no greater pleasure than serving the revolution. I had dared only to dream of it, and yet now he [Sergei Nechaev,] was saying that he wanted to recruit me.[33]

Nechaev was the author of the *Catechism of a Revolutionary*, a nihilist pamphlet advocating ruthless assassination and shocking terrorism, a break with all conventions and morals that stood in the way of revolution—the end that justified all means. He had written in the *Catechism:*

> The Revolutionist is a doomed man. He has no private interests, no affairs, sentiments, ties, property nor even a name of his own. His entire being is devoured by one purpose, one thought, one passion—the revolution. Heart and soul, not merely by word but by deed, he has severed every link with the social order and with the entire civilized world: with the laws, good manners, conventions, and morality of that world. He is the merciless enemy and continues to inhabit it with only one purpose—to destroy it.[34]

While the majority of the Russian revolutionaries of the 1860s and 1870s were of upper middle class or noble origin,[35] Nechaev was the son of a house painter.[36] Through his charisma, he managed to gain a following among students when he came to St. Petersburg in 1868. There he set up the secret revolutionary society *People's Revenge* (*Narodnaya Rasprava*).[37] Vera Zasulich was two years younger than Nechaev. In 1867 she had found her first employment in Serpukhov, just outside Moscow, as a secretary. Here the future terrorist became an assistant to a Justice of the Peace, an institution introduced by the Judicial Reforms of 1864. The main goal of a Justice of the Peace was, according to the State Council, 'to satisfy this elemental need of administration of justice according to conscience'.[38] That stress on 'conscience' rather than merely 'the law' was, as it turned out, to become a crucial element in Zasulich's own trial in 1878.

Zasulich had met Nechaev in January 1869 and, like her two sisters, fell under his hypnotic spell. He declared his love for her (as he probably had done with other women he wanted to recruit). While Vera did not fall for this ruse of his Machiavellian character, she somehow admired his strong personality and agreed to act as a conduit for letters he planned to send from Switzerland to Vladimir Orlov, a fellow revolutionary who could not receive them directly as he was under police surveillance.[39] That cost her dearly. On 30 April 1869, while leaving for a holiday with her mother, she was arrested. Without even being interrogated or charged with a crime, she was first put into a cell in the Lithuanian Castle (a prison outside St. Petersburg) and then in the Peter and Paul Fortress in St. Petersburg. There had been no court hearing of her case; it was a routine administrative detention of a suspect. When Nechaev was extradited from Switzerland and charged with murder, she was brought to the trial to serve as witness. There she admitted to having passed on one of Nechaev's letters, claiming not to know what was in it.

After she had spent almost two years in prison, in March 1871, Minister of Justice K. Pahlen, decided to release her—there was not enough evidence to detain her further. However, the police had, in such cases, the administrative power to send suspects against whom there was not enough evidence into exile without a hearing or trial.[40] That was what happened to Vera Zasulich. She was exiled to the town of Krestsy. Later she was allowed to move to Kharkov to take a midwife's course which she finished in 1875. However, due to the stigma of police supervision, she could not find employment, although police surveillance had finally been lifted later that year.[41] Two years of prison and four years of exile, and the humiliations and the experience of injustice that accompanied them had scarred Vera; but had not broken her rebellious character. On the contrary, they turned her into a professional revolutionary.[42] Once free, equipped with false papers, in September 1875 she moved to Kiev. There she joined the 'Southern Rebels', a Bakuninist[43] group of some 20 revolutionaries linked to the populist *narodniki*. In Kiev she also met Masha (Maria) Kolenkina with whom she would, three years later, plot a double assassination in St. Petersburg.[44]

During those six years of prison and exile, she had become convinced that social justice in Russia could only be achieved by the violent transformation of the state.[45] She had also developed a keen sense of injustices suffered by others.[46] Looking back at this period, in 1883, five years after the infamous deed that brought her fame, she reflected on what had motivated her:

> I was a revolutionary, a Populist and, at the same time, always a great skeptic. The substantial points of my views of that time in regard to revolution: the ownership of the products of alien labor, and the authority of man over man are *unjust*, and hence it is right to destroy them, [yet] they will reemerge again and there will appear new destroyers: in no event will it be worse. That the revolutionary intelligentsia perish protesting injustice seemed to me, at the time, the best outcome and an obligatory one. [...].[47]

3.3. The Assassination Attempt on Governor Trepov

By the summer of 1877 Vera Zasulich had joined her mother in St. Petersburg, where she worked in a printing shop and again became involved in revolutionary activities. It was here that she learned about the beating of Bogoliubov. The accounts she heard were exaggerated (e.g. Bogoliubov was not beaten until he lost consciousness, as she believed). Vera apparently hoped that Governor Trepov would be punished, either by the government (since the flogging was in the eyes of many illegal) or by the revolutionaries. While her indignation at Boboliubov's humiliation was shared by many, nobody appeared prepared to do something about it. However, in reality she was not the only one. Alexander Mikhailov, the leader of *Land and Freedom* (*Zemlia I Volia*), a society of revolutionaries linked to the populists, had also decided that the Governor should be 'punished'.[48] Zasulich was in touch with Mikhailov and must have heard him discuss some plans. Yet apparently she had misunderstood him or, more likely, he had, in the interest of secrecy, not been open with her about his plan to make Trepov 'pay'.[49] In fact, among the revolutionaries of *Land and Freedom* in Kiev a committee had already been formed; Valerian Osinskii and four comrades were instructed to go to St. Petersburg and take revenge on Governor Trepov.[50] As it later turned out, there were two more groups planning to 'punish' Fydor Trepov.[51]

As weeks and months had passed since Boboliubov's flogging, Vera Zasulich apparently thought the conspirators she knew had lost their nerve; she and a girlfriend of hers decided to act on their own.[52] However, both the conspirators from Kiev and Vera Zasulich and her friend Masha Kolenkina first wanted to await the outcome of the so-called *Trial of the 193*[53] which had begun in October 1877 and would end on 23 January 1878, one day before Vera Zasulich and her friend planned to act. The two women had decided not only to shoot Trepov but also Vladislav Zhelikovskii, the prosecutor of the *Trial of the 193* as soon as that trial was over. It was thought that a revolver with a short barrel of the English bulldog type would be best for the task; a male friend of Vera acquired one for 21 roubles.[54]

Zasulich knew how to handle a gun. When with the 'Southern Rebels' between 1875 and 1877 and carrying out illegal propaganda among peasants, she had a pistol and practised how to use it in shooting exercises. However, among those 'Southern Rebels' she had been a marginal figure and, like most other women, was not invited to participate in some of the more daring actions. Now, in St. Petersburg, Vera and her comrade Masha decided on a very daring action indeed: two assassinations by two women on one and the same day. They drew lots for who should kill whom. Vera was to target Trepov.[55] As luck would have it, of the two would-be assassins only one succeeded in carrying out their plan. On that fateful day in January 1878, prosecutor Zhelekhovskii was not at home and Masha could not achieve her part in their plan to get public attention by a double murder.[56] Vera was luckier. She made it in time to Governor Trepov's residence where she found herself first in line among a dozen or so petitioners. Under the assumed name of Elizaveta Kozlova she submitted a petition to the Governor for a certificate of good conduct which she allegedly needed in order to obtain a diploma enabling her to work as a governess.

While Trepov wrote something in the margin of her petition, she took the revolver hidden under her cape and managed to fire one shot at the governor. The bullet hit the Governor on the left side of his buttock where it got stuck in the pelvic bone. Rather than firing another shot, Zasulich dropped her weapon on the floor, making no attempt to escape. Asked later for the reason she did not try to flee, she said: 'I am a terrorist, not a murderer!' Trepov whispered: 'I'm wounded.' Yet he did not lose consciousness and would eventually survive this attempt on his life. When arrested on the spot, Vera Zasulich was calm and polite, even helping the police inspector, Alexander Kabat, to tie her on a chair in a room next door.[57] But she refused to provide any information beyond giving them her (false) name Elizaveta Koslova. However, when asked why she had shot the Governor, she simply said 'for Bogoliubov'.[58]

In the meantime, Trepov was given first aid. With the physicians came well-wishers, including D.A. Miliutin, the Minister of War, and even the Tsar himself.[59] However, Alexander II was not amused when Trepov told him: 'This bullet might have been meant for you and I was happy to take it for you.'[60] In a memorandum Trepov dictated while recovering from the shooting, he claimed, however, that he did not know why he had been shot.[61] After her assassination attempt, Elizaveta Koslova's true identity soon became known. The chairman of the District Court in St. Petersburg learned the next day that her real name was 'Usulich' while the Chief of Gendarmes reported that she belonged to the so-called 'nihilists' and that, in the past, she had been detained as a defendant in the trial of Sergei Nechaev.[62]

The attempted murder was the talk of the town and the news spread with the speed of the telegraph to the capitals of Europe and beyond. Governor Trepov was widely loathed; there was considerable understanding and even sympathy for Vera's attack on him. Some sympathy for Vera Zasulich even reached the highest circles; one Russian general even declared her to be nothing less than a 'model of feminine bravery and self-sacrifice'.[63] The underground paper *Free Russian Press* went much further; it declared that Vera Zasulich had fired the shots in the struggle for 'human rights and the establishment of peace and humanity on earth', as well as to show that 'tyrants are not almighty'. The paper praised her further as 'the fearless girl who did not shrink from the awful bloody deed and her own ruin when no other means remained for the defence of the rights of man'.[64] By that time the revolutionaries had managed to make the flogging of prisoner Boboliubov a *cause célèbre*. Russian's first female assassin was taken to the same House of Preliminary Detention where, until recently, Bogoliubov had also been imprisoned. There she would have to wait for two months for her trial. She fully expected to pay for her deed with her life.[65]

3.4. Preparation of the Trial

The Minister of Justice, Count Konstantin Pahlen, wanted a fast conviction and was confident of the outcome:

> The jurors would deliver a guilty verdict and thereby teach a sobering lesson to the insane, small coterie of revolutionaries; they would show all the Russian and foreign admirers of Vera Zasulich's 'heroic exploit' that the Russian people bow before the Tsar, revere him, and are always ready to defend his faithful servants.[66]

When preparing for the trial of Vera Zasulich, the government had two basic options. If the crime was judged to be 'political', the case would go to a Special Committee of the Senate. The *Trial of the 193* had been dealt with there. The alternative was trial by jury, as was the rule for common crimes. Retrospectively, of course, it is clear that a political crime had been committed and that was also clear to most contemporaries. The fact that Zasulich knew neither Trepov nor Bogoliubov personally was indicative of a political crime. However, there were still some speculations floating around that Zasulich was Bogoliubov's lover and that the shooting of Trepov was the revenge of a mistress whose lover had been wronged.[67] Such an interpretation would have made it look like a personal rather than political affair. Treating the matter as a crime of moral indignation, an act of personal revenge had, from the Minister of Justice's point of view, certain advantages. The fact is that by March 1878 the Minister of Justice had decided to have Zasulich tried in a criminal court. Maybe he argued that in the event of a popular backlash against a harsh sentence, anger would not turn against the government but against the jury—a body consisting of representatives of society. Since the case appeared straightforward—there were plenty of witnesses to the attempted murder—there could be little doubt that any jury had to convict the would-be assassin.

One other reason the Minister of Justice might have decided on a trial by jury was that the alternative, trial by the Senate Committee, had not worked as well as he had expected in the recent *Trial of the 193*. That trial had lasted more than three months and only a minority of some 20 per cent of the accused could, for lack of evidence, be sentenced.[68] A number of the accused had died in prison through disease or had gone mad and committed suicide while waiting for months and years for their trial. The government wanted to avoid a long trial in the case of Vera Zasulich at all costs. What could go wrong? Minister Pahlen had discussed the case with Alexander Lopukhin, until recently chairman of the St. Petersburg District Court. Anatoli Koni, the newly installed chairman of the court, joined their conversation:

> 'Yes, Anatoli Fedorovich [Koni] will handle it for us beautifully.' 'Why, is it already so clear?' [Koni asked]. 'Oh yes', Lopukhin answered for Pahlen. 'Fully. This is a case of personal vengeance, and the jurors will convict her, this is clear as daylight.' To [Koni's] surprise, Pahlen, too, made some inherent predictions that the jurors will prove themselves, that they must show severity, etc.[69]

Since Lopukhin had already been informed on 25 January in a telegram from Odessa that there was a police dossier on Zasulich,[70] he should have known that the case was politically inspired. Nevertheless it was announced on 3 March 1878 that Zasulich would be tried by jury.

Also in March, the Minister of Justice had asked A.F. Koni directly, 'Can you, Anatoli Fedorovich, guarantee that Zasulich will be convicted?'[71] To his amazement Koni said, 'No, I cannot! [...] How can I guarantee their [the jury's] verdict? [...] However, I presume that common sense of the jury will suggest to them a decision that is just and dispassionate. The fact is obvious and it is unlikely the jury will venture to deny it. But I cannot guarantee a conviction!' 'You cannot? You cannot?' Pahlen [replied] agitatedly. 'In that case, I will report to His Majesty that the chairman cannot guarantee a conviction. I must report this to His Majesty!' he repeated, with a vague and pointless threat.'[72]

The Tsar himself also tried to exert pressure by expressing his hope to Koni that he would 'continue to serve successfully'.[73] Yet Koni was a man of principle. He had already told the Minister of Justice that 'the function of a court is not to render service but to pronounce judgment', reminding Count Pahlen that as President of the Court he, Koni, had to see to it that impartiality was maintained. The Minister called this all 'theory'. He suggested that Koni phrase the instructions for the jury in such a way that the conviction of the accused was inevitable. He even advised him to commit some technical violations of the procedural rules of the court so that, in the event that the jury acquitted her, the verdict could be overturned in an appeal court.[74]

How did things look on the side of the accused? Vera Zasulich first wanted to defend herself, yet she was told by her friends that it was important to get her acquitted, not just for herself but for 'the cause'. Her friends had collected money to pay for a good attorney. Peter A. Alexandrov, a defence lawyer who had distinguished himself in the *Trial of the 193*, was chosen. Alexandrov, visiting Vera Zasulich in the House of Preliminary Detention, tried to persuade her to tell the court that she had not wanted to kill Trepov but only intended to fire into the air to alert public opinion to Trepov's treatment of Bogoliubov. She refused. She also did not want to appear in court in the elegant coat Alexandrov had brought to her prison cell so that she would look more like a noble woman when entering the courtroom. However, she did promise not to bite her nails during the trial, something which at that time in Russia was considered a sign of 'evil'.[75] Defence Attorney Alexandrov was confident that he could obtain an acquittal for Vera Zasulich, and he said as much to his friends before the trial.[76] Others, on the contrary, thought that a conviction was a foregone conclusion, given the indisputable fact that an attempt at premeditated murder had taken place in front of many witnesses.

Alexandrov's opponent in the trial was Konstantin Kessel, the Deputy Prosecutor of the St. Petersburg District Court. He was not Minister Pahlen's first choice. Before him two more prominent prosecutors had been asked by the Ministry of Justice to serve in this matter but had refused to take on the case. Maybe they thought that there was not much to be gained in defending the widely disliked Governor Trepov; maybe they thought that the case against Zasulich was 'in the bag' since the evidence of the crime was there for all to see. Maybe they were afraid: several prosecutors in the *Trial of the 193* had learned about assassination plans being concocted against them.[77] Kessel was young and inexperienced. He did not make use of his right to reject members of the jury whom he might consider prejudiced. There was a pool of some thirty jurors available for the case; up to twelve of them could be rejected by the two sides combined. Since Kessel did not make use of his right to do so, Alexandrov made full use of it, rejecting eleven potential jurors. He selected mainly civil servants, plus one artist and one student, in the hope that they would be more impressionable than some merchants on the list of potential jurors he was given. He feared that some of those on the original list of jurors were more likely to cave in under government pressure than others and selected those he thought would be most sympathetic to his arguments.[78]

That such pressure by the government existed was also evident from another remark of the Minister of Justice to Anatoli Koni when the latter, just before the trial, lectured about the impartiality of the judiciary, 'Yes, justice, impartiality', the Minister said, 'but in this damned case the government has the right to expect special services from the court'.[79] The date of the trial was set for the last day of March 1878.

3.5. What Happened in Court during the Trial

The trial in the St. Petersburg Circuit Court began on 31 March 1878 at 11a.m. It would last eight hours. An hour before the trial the courtroom began to fill. Anatoli F. Koni was the President of the Court. The prosecutor was Konstantin I. Kessel while counsel for the defence was attorney Peter A. Alexandrov. The latter had, in the past, earned his reputation on the other side of the bar as an able prosecutor; indeed he had been one of the prosecutors in the trial of Sergei Nechaev when he was tried and convicted of murder in 1871. However, after a trial in 1875 where Alexandrov had argued for the freedom of the press while he was asked by Minister Pahlen to argue for the opposite, he had changed sides and joined the bar to become a defence attorney.[80] Alexandrov had just played an outstanding role as defence council in the *Trial of the 193*. One of his colleagues described him as 'sharp like a razor blade, cold as ice and shining like a hero'.[81] In the impending trial he was to give the performance of his life. The jury consisted, as mentioned before, mostly of low and middle level civil servants.[82] Since Alexandrov had carefully selected most of them, liberal-minded men were in the majority among the 18 jurors.[83]

The courtroom was crammed full. The President of the Court had distributed at his discretion 136 of a total of 300 tickets for the seats in the courtroom. They were sold out weeks before the trial began.[84] Many members of the aristocratic elite of Russia were curious to take a glimpse of someone from Russia's revolutionary underground. Present were, among other dignitaries, the Imperial State Chancellor, Prince Gorchakov, the War Minister Miliutin, Count Stroganoff, Secretary of State Solsky as well as members of the State Council and senators. They took their seats right behind the judges' bench. There were many more dignitaries in glittering gold-braided uniforms and high-society ladies loaded with jewels in the gallery. There also were about one hundred members of the legal profession in the room as well as foreign observers. When the trial began, some six hundred people were packed into the courtroom.[85] Ten members of the press, including F. Dostoyevsky, the writer, had also been admitted. The Minister of the Interior had originally suggested to the Minister of Justice that press access to the trial be minimised. Yet Count Pahlen thought this inadvisable, arguing that this would lead public opinion to suspect that Vera Zasulich had been unjustly convicted. He hoped that press reports would 'elicit general indignation'.[86]

All the display of rank and name in the seats behind the judges stood in sharp contrast to the defendant, Vera Zasulich. She was simply dressed, had an unassuming appearance and was modest in her manners. One observer saw in her 'pale, emaciated features' traces of 'spiritual suffering and physical deprivations'. Another observer thought that 'She looked almost saintly.'[87] Vera, then 29 years old, looked much younger. She spoke in a barely audible voice; it was hard to believe that this shy creature could be a threat to society.[88]

Not present at the trial was General Trepov himself. Although almost recovered from the attack by Vera Zasulich, he claimed to be ill that day. It is not clear why Alexandrov, the defence attorney, rather than the prosecutor had originally invited him to appear as witness. Nor is it clear why Trepov had refused to turn up. Probably he was afraid that he would, at least indirectly, also be judged. The fact is that he had already made public appearances, albeit in a wheelchair, telling everybody who wanted to hear it that he had asked for Bogoliubov to be flogged on the orders of Minister Pahlen. Stranger still, he was even reported to have expressed his hope that Zasulich would be acquitted![89]

The trial began exactly on time, at eleven o'clock. First the indictment was read, recounting the events of 24 January 1878 in the residence of the Governor of St. Petersburg. The charges brought against Vera Zasulich included planning of the assassination in advance and the point blank shooting of General Fyodor F. Trepov with a large-calibre revolver with the intent to deprive him of his life.[90] The defendant did not deny the crime and responded in a barely audible voice: 'I admit that I shot General Trepov but whether this would result in wounding or killing him was for me a matter of indifference.'[91]

The first of four witnesses called by the Prosecutor was Major Fedor Kurneev, Trepov's assistant. He had been present when the shooting took place. He was, at that time, also acting administrator of the House of Preliminary Detention. When Major Kurneev was interrogated by the Prosecutor, it surfaced that he was being investigated (and might be liable for prosecution) over his responsibility for disturbances in the prison which had accompanied the flogging of Bogoliubov. For a moment it looked as if the state admitted that a crime had occurred in the House of Preliminary Detention and that the state itself had been trying to seek and restore justice.[92] However Alexandrov, the Defence Attorney, quickly followed up on the Prosecutor's questioning of Kurneev and asked whether he was also responsible for the whipping of Bogoliubov which had occurred under his watch. 'Oh no', Kurneev answered (he had only announced the flogging to the prison population, not ordered it himself). That put the blame for the flogging back on Trepov.[93] The audience in the courtroom, which by that time had largely taken Vera's side, was audibly relieved. Another witness presented by the prosecutor was the owner of the shop where the bulldog gun had been bought. Kessel's pedantic interrogation of this and other witnesses produced nothing that grabbed the audience's imagination and did little to strengthen the prosecutor's case.[94]

Prosecutor Kessel's speech, while lacking passion, was logically compelling, but the public wanted drama, not reason. Kessel spoke for 45 minutes in a monotonous voice. He was handicapped in that he could or would not disclose the political motivation for the deed, the revolutionary background of Zasulich and her links to the nihilist Nechaev. This would have politicised the trial, something which the Minister of Justice had been trying to avoid, portraying her deed as an act of personal revenge.[95] Strangely, Kessel did not mention Bogoliubov at all.[96] He reminded the jury that it was not the duty of the court to judge Vera's motives or to judge whether Trepov, the victim, was guilty or innocent of anything. Nor was the court to adjudicate on the legitimacy of her emotions. She had to be judged solely on the basis of her action. Since she had bought one of the most powerful revolvers, it was clear that she did not expect Governor Trepov to remain alive. 'Every person', Kessel said, 'is free to love or hate whomever they choose, but no one is free to violate another's rights'.[97] Kessel depicted Zasulich's deed as a perverted form of trial, a kind of vigilante justice, arguing that:

> Having created her own court, Zasulich joined in her own person the roles of prosecutor, defendant, and judge: she, a young woman, thought it was possible to decree a death sentence, which fortunately she did not succeed in carrying out. I do not think for one minute that you will disagree that every public figure, whoever he may be, has the right to a legal trial and not a trial by Zasulich.[98]

The public was paying little attention to Kessel's dry reasoning; in fact his voice could barely be heard in the galleries as the people made a considerable noise.

Yet when it was Vera's turn to explain her case, the courtroom fell dead silent; nobody wanted to miss a word as she spoke with such a thin voice. Her manners were more those of a nun than a terrorist. She did not make any propagandistic speeches like many of those had done who stood accused in the *Trial of the 193*. She did not accuse the autocracy in her speech. Instead, she emphasised how humanitarian compassion for Bogoliubov had driven her to this deed.[99] Vera also recalled how, without ever having been judged by a court, she herself had, by administrative order, been condemned to spend years in prison and exile. Then she turned to the event that had triggered her deed.[100] It was, as she explained, an act of protest, a cry for justice:

> I waited for some response, [to the flogging incident] but everyone remained silent. [...] There was nothing to stop Trepov, or someone just as powerful as he, from repeating the same violence over and over. I resolved at that point, even if it cost my life, to prove that no one who abused a human being that way could be sure of getting away with it. I couldn't find another way of drawing attention to what had happened. I saw no other way [...] It's terrible to have to lift a hand against another person, but I felt that it had to be done.[101]

The public took a liking to her as she sobbed quietly while she spoke. As it was clear to everybody in the courtroom that her regret was real, compassion for her grew by the hour.[102] When it was the Defence Attorney's turn, Alexandrov began by saying that he was 'completely in agreement with much of what he [Kessel] said. We differ only in a few, small things.' This understatement was just one of his many rhetorical devices.

The Defence Attorney had, at his own expense, brought four former political prisoners as witnesses. They had been on the scene on 13 July 1878 when Governor Trepov clashed with prisoner Bogoliubov in the court of the House of Preliminary Detention.[103] (Later the President of the Court was to be blamed for having allowed Alexandrov to present such witnesses whose testimonies had no directly bearing on the crime that had taken place in the Governor's residence.) The sight of these witnesses—pale, thin young students, just acquitted after years in prison for no good reason—created a wave of compassion among the public. These *narodniki* idealists made the prison regime and, by implication, the political system that supported it look arbitrary and cruel.

Alexandrov used their testimonies to evaluate Trepov's behaviour and managed to place Trepov (and Kurneev) in the role of villains. He also lambasted a political system that had for so long allowed the regime and the landlords to flog people. He insinuated that there were still people in high places who felt that it was dangerous to leave Russia without the knout—that instrument of sanction that, in his words, had cemented the social foundations for so long. After giving a brief history of flogging in Russia until 17 April 1863 when 'the rod passed into the realm of history',[104] Alexandrov proceeded to say:

> Fifteen year after the abolition of corporal punishment a political prisoner was subjected to the ignominious punishment of whipping [...] The short newspaper accounts of the punishment inflicted on Bogoliubov could not but have an overwhelming impression on Zasulich [...] 'What terrible torture', thought Zasulich, 'what scornful profanation of everything which constitutes the most essential values of an intellectual ... of everyone to whom the sense of honour and human dignity are not foreign ...' [...] Bogoliubov was for Zasulich a political prisoner, and this word meant everything [...] A political prisoner was for Zasulich the bitter recollection of her own sufferings, of her terrible nervous excitement [...] everlasting though: '[...] When will an end be brought to all this?'[105]

Alexandrov then gave a dramatic description of the flogging as it must have appeared in Zasulich's mind. The audience began to applaud and shout 'bravo' at various points in his exposition.[106] He continued:

> The fateful question confronted her: 'Who will stand up for the insulted honour of a defenceless political convict? [...] Who will stand up for the fate of other wretches?' [...] She expected, finally, a word of justice [...] but justice remained silent. [...] And suddenly, an unexpected thought brightened her mind: 'Oh, I myself! [...] All is silent around Bogoliubov! A shout is needed' [...] Instant determination responded to this thought [...] 'If I commit a crime', Zasulich thought, 'the silent question about Bogoliubov's punishment will arise; my crime will provoke a public trial, and Russia, in the person of her people's representatives, the jury, will be compelled to pronounce a verdict not on me alone [...] and in the sight of Europe, this Europe which likes to call us a barbarian state, in which the attribute of the government is the knout [...]'

Turning to the jurors, Alexandrov continued:

> 'Gentlemen of the jury! It is not for the first time that a woman appears before the court of the people's conscience in this dock of crime and oppressive moral suffering. [...] Women who have steeped their hands in the blood of their lovers or of their more fortunate rivals, have been here. These women left this place acquitted. These sentences were just, an echo of divine justice, which takes into consideration not only the external side of an action, but also its inner meaning—the real guilt of the accused. These women did bloody, summary justice, they fought for and avenged themselves. But for the first time there appears here a woman who had no personal interest in her crime, who linked her crime with the fight for an idea, for the sake of a man who

> was for her no more than a companion in distress. If these reasons for crime prove lighter on a scale of public justice, if she must be punished for the sake of the general welfare, the triumph of justice and public safety—then let your chastising justice take place! Indeed, she may leave this court condemned, but not disgraced, and one may only wish that circumstances which provoke such actions and generate such culprits should not be repeated. [...] However somberly one looks at this deed, in the motives themselves it is impossible not to see an honest and noble impulse.'[107]

At one point Alexandrov compared the characters of the victim—Trepov—and Zasulich, the perpetrator. At another point, Alexandrov suggested that an acquittal of Zasulich might counteract Russia's reputation abroad as being a nation of barbarians.[108] Alexandrov's speech was a rhetorical masterpiece and, as we shall see, the jury fell into the trap he had laid: judging her on her apparently noble character and unselfish motives—not on the crime she had committed. In his account of what drove Vera Zasulich to her deed, Alexandrov had not stuck fully to the facts.[109] He completely omitted Vera Zasulich's revolutionary past and socialist convictions.[110] However, Alexandrov's rhetoric swayed the jury and the public much more than the monotonous speech of the Prosecutor had done. Zasulich herself was so impressed by her defence lawyer's account of her life story that she seemed to re-experience, while he spoke, some of her past agonies in front of jury and public. One eyewitness noted:

> [Her] head dropped on her hands, folded on the desk, and, concealing it in a crumpled kerchief, the girl tried to muffle and hide her sobs, but her thin, shuddering shoulders betrayed her. One could hear her sobs here and in the hall. I also wiped the tears that welled in my eyes. I looked behind me at the row of the public and saw the same tears in many an eye.[111]

Alexandrov pleaded with the jurors to judge Zasulich not for the intentions attributed to her by the prosecutor but for what she had actually done, the implication being that she had, after all, *not* killed the Governor.

The public was visibly moved. Here was a woman, herself an innocent victim of the unjust prison system, who identified with another political prisoner so much that she wanted, with her deed, to confront the public with Trepov's misdeed so that in the future such humiliating treatment would no longer be accepted. Dostoyevsky, the writer, whispered to his neighbour in the gallery: 'She should not be convicted, and punishment is inappropriate, superfluous; but one wishes one could say to her "go, and do not do that again".'[112]

A.F. Koni, the President of the Court, then asked Zasuliuch if she wished to have the last word. She declined. A wise decision: it could only have detracted from the profound impression left on public and jurors by the brilliant, two-hour-long speech of her defence lawyer.

The President of the Court then summarised the proceedings of the day, recapitulating the arguments of both Prosecutor and Defence Attorney. He also told the jurors that they should consider themselves 'the conscience of society',[113] asking them to answer three questions:

1. Was Zasulich guilty that, wanting to wreak vengeance on Commandant Trepov for his punishment of Bogoliubov and having acquired for this purpose a revolver, on January 24 with deliberate intent, inflicted on the General-Adjutant a wound in the region of the pelvis with a bullet of large calibre?
2. If Zasulich carried out this act, did she intend to deprive Commander Trepov of life? and
3. If Zasulich did intend to deprive Commander Fydor Trepov of life, did she do everything in her power to attain this objective, given that death did not ensue for reasons that did not depend on her?[114]

The balanced summing up by the Court's president which preceded these questions left much of the public—waiting in the corridors for the jury to return—in a gloomy mood. It seemed inevitable that Vera would be convicted.[115]

The jurors had withdrawn for deliberation for less than half an hour.[116] Then they came back. In the words of Koni:

> With pale faces, the jurors crowded around the corner of the judges' table. There was total silence in the court, everyone had bated breath. The foreman of the jurors, an official in the Ministry of Finances, hurried rattled off the question: 'Is Zasulich guilty of wounding' ... and then loudly, so that the whole room could hear: 'No! Not guilty!'[117]

Then, pandemonium broke out. The President of the Court later recalled:

> It is impossible for one who was not present to imagine the outburst of sounds that drowned out the [jury] foreman's voice and the movement that like an electric shock sped through the entire room. The cries of unrestrained joy, hysterical sobbing, desperate applause, the tread of feet, cries of 'Bravo! Hurrah! Good girl! Vera! Verochka!

> Verochka!' merged in one roar both moan and howl. Many crossed themselves; in the upper, more democratic sections for the public, people embraced; even in the places reserved for the judges there was enthusiastic applause.[118]

Another eyewitness from the audience, Elizabeth Naryshkin-Kurakin, confirmed that 'The judges, jury, dignitaries and officials grown grey in service, the whole public—everyone was carried away by the mood of the moment. One could not analyse it, but it swept over everyone, without exception, even the soberest of them, in that dramatic moment.'[119] Even Chancellor Gorchakov was clapping approvingly in the light of the verdict as did other dignitaries sitting behind the judges.[120] The President of the Court, turning to Zasulich, made no attempt to calm the courtroom down and simply said 'You are acquitted.' Then he told her to go to the House of Temporary Detention and collect her belongings before announcing 'The session is closed!'[121]

The verdict took Zasulich by complete surprise.[122] Upon hearing that she was acquitted, it was not joy she experienced, but 'extreme astonishment, immediately followed by a feeling of sadness', as she later told another, more successful, terrorist.[123] She had expected to be hanged and now she was to be free. When asked two hours later whether she was happy she said: 'Not very.'[124] That feeling persisted for the rest of her life. She would refer to her attempt to assassinate Governor Trepov as 'my crime' and experience much anguish when others tried to imitate her and succeed where she had failed.[125]

3.6. A Miscarriage of Justice?

How could the jurors reach such a decision when the incriminating facts were undisputed, plenty of witnesses to the crime were present and the defendant herself had admitted her crime? There is no simple answer; several elements came together on that day in court. The first element was that Governor Trepov was very unpopular among St. Petersburg society, including amongst the jurors. Another element was this: if a guilty verdict were to have been given by the jury, the consequences for the defendant would have been very serious. Article 9 of the Russian Penal Code, applicable in her case, would have meant a conviction to hard labour for 15 to 20 years. It was unlikely that she would have survived that. It was general knowledge that prisons in Russia were unhealthy; even someone who did not contract tuberculosis or some other deadly disease would, after years of confinement, often go mad or commit suicide.

Aware of this, juries like Zasulich's were typically mild in their verdicts, especially when it came to women.[126]

A third element was perhaps even more crucial: in the Russian legal system, guilt alone was not the only criterion for a sentence. A jury was expected to judge the defendant also according to 'conscience'. Indeed, evidence alone could not prevent acquittal.[127] The Russian system of justice, established in 1864, allowed the jury to acquit defendants considered guilty and even defendants who had confessed to the crime when the jurors decided that their decision to acquit was based on 'conscience'. An English observer of this trial, Sir Donald Mackenzie Wallace, offered this explanation for the seemingly paradoxical behaviour of Russian juries:

> [T]he juries often gave a verdict of 'not guilty' when the accused made a full and formal confession to the court [...] The Russian criminal law fixes minutely the punishment for each category of crimes, and leaves almost no latitude to the judge. The jury knows that if they give a verdict of guilty, the prisoner will inevitably be punished according to the Code. Now the Code [...] is found on conceptions very different from those of the Russian people, and in many cases it attaches heavy penalties to acts which the ordinary Russian is wont to regard as mere peccadillos, or positively justifiable. Even in those cases in which the Code is in harmony with the popular morality, there are many exceptional cases in which *summum jus* is really *summa injuria*. In such cases what is the jury to do? [...] There remains but one issue out of the difficulty—a verdict of acquittal; and Russian juries—to their honour be it said—generally adopt this alternative.[128]

As mentioned before, it did not take the jurors long to reach their verdict. We do not know whether the jury's verdict was unanimous or split. However, if the jury was split evenly in its opinion, a defendant was also acquitted.[129] The jury had two, perhaps three choices: (i) guilty, (ii) not guilty, and (iii) guilty but deserving leniency. Most of the audience, as well as A.F. Koni, the President of the Court, had hoped for the third outcome as the most likely. The law prescribed the severity of sentences; the jury had no influence on that. Even a lenient sentence would have been severe and might, given the conditions in Russia's prison system, cost Zasulich her life.

Yet the members of the jury were apparently concerned not only about Vera Zasulich's life but also about their own careers and even lives. Since all but two of the jurors were officials working for the government, acquitting the defendant was not without risk of retaliation from their employer. However, if they feared pressure from that side they did not say so. On the contrary, one of the jurors later claimed that he and his fellow jurors had acquitted Zasulich for fear of assassination by revolutionaries.[130] This is what he wrote in an anonymous letter to the Tsar, four days after the verdict:

> We, the jurors, *for all our indignation over [Zasulich's] crime*, were compelled to acquit her: 1. From the sense of self-preservation, and 2. To spare the government a scandal incomparably greater than that which, given the weakness of the police, inevitably would have followed a conviction [...] Had we convicted Zasulich then it is not only highly probable that some of us *would have been killed at the very entrance of the courtroom*, but for sure there would have been killed the prosecutor, the chairman and also, it may be, some prominent guests.[131]

Were the jurors intimidated? Were they following their conscience? Were they swayed by the defence lawyer? Were they caught by the mood of the audience in the courtroom? All these elements must have played a role. Today, with a distance in time of more than 135 years, it is impossible to discern what moved them most to reach their astonishing verdict. It had been a day of high drama. One journalist noted two days later:

> Only a few hours have passed, but it seems as if years have unfolded before you, as if a long repressed and gathering moral storm broke upon our heads, demanding that we evaluate everything that is good and bad within us, throwing open the doors of your soul and bringing it to an impartial, merciless court. Not one theater can provide you with this kind of drama.[132]

In a time span of eight hours, Vera Zasulich, the would-be assassin, had become a heroine. Her defender, Alexandrov, had become a star whose brilliant performance was even acknowledged by his adversaries.[133] Trepov, the victim of the crime, looked like the real culprit. Kessel, the prosecutor had been out-performed by Alexandrov. The President of the Court, Anatoli Koni, later gave his own private judgment on the outcome of this trial:

> The jury's verdict was, perhaps, not correct from the juridical point of view but it was true to moral feeling: it dissented from the dead letter of the law but it resounded the voice of living law; society cannot refuse it sympathy.[134]

However, the consequences of the jury's decision were far-reaching and fatal. More than a century later, with plenty of hindsight, Russian historian Edvard Radzinsky concluded in 2005:

> The trial by justice (by liberal rights) won a crushing victory over trial by law. It created a legal precedent for the right to shoot out of your convictions. From this moment of the great humiliation of the law, the clock of the revolution started ticking.[135]

3.7. How the Trial and Its Outcome were Received Outside the Court

Outside the St. Petersburg Courthouse a crowd of thousand or more people (the majority of them women) had been waiting for the outcome of the trial.[136] Already in the afternoon, the President of the Court had been informed by Alexander Lopukhin, the chief prosecutor of the St. Petersburg Court of Appeals, that the crowd was restless and that disorder could be expected.[137] There was fear that the jurors might be assaulted by the mob in the event of a conviction.[138]

When the acquittal became known, the crown welcomed it with shouts of joy and applause. The victorious Defence Attorney, Alexandrov, was carried through the streets all the way home on the shoulders of a jubilant crowd.[139] Emerging from the Courthouse, he told the waiting crowd that Vera Zasulich would soon be released from the nearby remand prison on Shpalernaia Street. However, when the crowd had moved there and Vera Zasulich was not seen for a long time, people got restless and aggressive. Vera had first been taken to her cell where she collected her belongings and had a cup of tea. When leaving, she took with her a candle and a pencil which she thought she might need in a prison cell in case she was re-arrested. That was, after all, what had happened to many of those who had been acquitted in the *Trial of the 193*. This almost happened to her that evening as well. Alexander Lopukhin asked the commander of the remand prison, Fedorov, not to release Zasulich until further written orders arrived. Indeed, one hour before midnight an order from the Tsar was delivered to Fedorov, saying that he commanded that spinster Vera Ivanova Zasulich be taken back to the House of Preliminary Detention until a special instruction was given. Fedorov, however, had by that time, on the authority of Koni, already let Zasulich go, despite Lopukhin's oral request to the contrary. This would soon cost him his post and earn him a week of arrest.[140]

One reason Fedorov acted without waiting any longer was that when Vera did not appear for almost an hour, the crowd actually tried to force the gates to liberate her. At that point Fedorov decided to push her through the gate.[141] The crowd greeted her enthusiastically and one man lifted her, despite her protests, on his shoulders to shouts of 'Long live Zasulich.'[142] She was marched around in the dense crowd until a carriage was found by one of the witnesses Alexandrov had summoned to the trial. Vera was then pushed into the carriage and the coachman began heading down Voskresenskii Prospekt. Then a medical student, Grigorii Sidoratskii, jumped on her carriage as a second carriage had come up next to hers. Vera Zasulich already feared that it had been sent to take her back to prison. Apparently Sidoratskii thought the same and began shooting—perhaps to distract attention from Vera so that she could escape, perhaps because he sought martyrdom for himself.[143] One shot hit a young woman in the arm, and when the student saw blood and heard shouts that he had also wounded Vera Zasulich he apparently lost his mind and shot himself through the temple (which was later erroneously blamed on the police). In the tumult and confusion, Zasulich's carriage sped away. She disappeared from the scene and made it to the apartment of a sympathiser who hid her from the police. It later turned out that the original address she was to be taken to had already been visited by the police with an order to arrest her again.[144]

In the meantime, Vera Zasulich had become a European celebrity. At least one newspaper in St. Petersburg came out with an extra edition on the sensational outcome of the trial. Not only St. Petersburg but, thanks to the telegraph, much of Europe was served with the extraordinary news of her acquittal. In the words of Gustave Valbert, a contemporary writing in the *Revue des deux mondes*:

> For forty-eight hours Europe forgot everything about peace, war, Bismarck, Lord Beaconsfield, Prince Gorchakov—so as to occupy itself with nothing except Vera Zasulich and the strange judicial adventure of which this unknown woman was the heroine.[145]

Many newspapers in the capital, St. Petersburg, gave ample coverage to the outcome of the trial. One of them, the *Telegraph*, even decided to serialise the entire trial proceedings in four instalments.[146] Most newspapers were supportive of the acquittal; some suggested that it might serve as a lesson to the autocratic regime. The *St. Petersburg Register* declared that the verdict was 'the voice of the people'.[147] *The New Times* (*Novoe vremia*) called the jurors' decision 'a verdict of social conscience not against state and law, but in defence of lawfulness and consequently for state and law'.[148] Not just the revolutionaries, but also liberals and even members of the aristocracy celebrated her. Some compared her to William Tell, others to Charlotte Corday or even Jeanne d'Arc.[149]

Few voices at that time were critical. Prince V.P. Meshchersky recalled in his memoirs:

> The solemn acquittal of Vera Zasulich happened as in a nightmare [...] Nobody could understand how such a frightful mockery of the highest servant under the Tsar and such an impudent triumph of faction could take place in the courtroom of an autocratic empire. The sad and fateful acquittal of Vera Zasulich showed, alas, too eloquently the disposition and mood of the contemporary society. [...] I remember how persons who later, under Alexander III, spoke about this acquittal with loud indignation, had quite forgotten that in 1878 they had joined those dignitaries who had dared to shout 'bravo' when they heard about the acquittal of Vera Zasulich, and lifted their glasses to the victory of justice at home and in their clubs.[150]

Much of public opinion in Russia and abroad was overwhelmingly pleased with the verdict, except in some conservative circles. Dimitri Miliutin, the Minister of War who had been watching the trial with his own eyes, later wrote:

> The entire public split into two camps [...] Any such case creates rumors and stirs up protest in society, on the one hand against our new legal procedures and especially against the institution of juries, and on the other hand against the arbitrariness and despotism of the administrative authorities.[151]

Vera Zasulich, hearing about the police's attempts to locate and arrest her, wrote in a letter published four days after her acquittal in the newspaper *Severnyi Vestnik*: 'I am prepared unquestioningly to submit to the judgment of the court, but I am not prepared again to expose myself to endless and indeterminate administrative prosecutions and I am compelled to hide until convinced that I have been mistaken and that I am not threatened by the danger of arrest.'[152]

Zasulich spent the next weeks in hiding, moving from location to location—there was no shortage of people prepared to hide her—until, in late May 1878, she finally decided, disguised as a peasant woman, to leave Russia secretly by train for Switzerland. Vera Zasulich would spend much of her political life in exile, first Switzerland, then France, then Great Britain and then Switzerland again. Her exile was interrupted by at least one brief secret trip to Russia in 1880. Then, in 1905, a general amnesty was proclaimed which allowed her to return legally and permanently to her country.[153]

To go into exile was, for her and for many other revolutionaries, a sign of defeat and not an easy decision to take. Yet the Tsarist regime, rather than accepting the jury's decision and trying to make the best out of it, reacted fiercely—with predictable results. In the words of J. Bergman:

Whatever moral capital the government might have gained from the trial was irrevocably lost in its denouement. If Zasulich had been left alone by the authorities, and Koni applauded by his superiors for his impartiality, the acquittal might have been received as a vindication of the Russian legal system and proof that Russia was evolving at last in the direction of a *Rechtsstaat*. But because the government reacted to the acquittal in ways that made its pretensions to judicial procedure seem hypocritical, it made Zasulich the martyr she would have been if the jury had convicted her, and imprinted her trial in people's consciousness as evidence of its own brutality and hypocrisy.[154]

3.8. Conclusion: Long-term Judicial, Social and Political Consequences

3.8.1. *Judicial Consequences*

Tsar Alexander II was shocked and furious by the trial's outcome.[155] He immediately issued, as mentioned above, a secret order to re-arrest Vera Zasulich.[156] When, after a massive search in the capital, Zasulich could not be found, the government was looking for scapegoats in its own ranks. In the following weeks several heads would roll. On 13 May 1878 Count Pahlen was forced to resign for the 'negligent handling of the Zasulich case', as the Tsar put it.[157] Earlier Pahlen had tried, but failed, to fire Koni.[158] The safeguards of the reform measures of 1864 made Koni's dismissal impossible. Koni had sent a personal apology to the Tsar but had refused to resign.[159] He was transferred to the Civil Chamber and remained disgraced for seven years.[160] Alexandrov, the defence lawyer, was forced to leave St. Petersburg. Kessel, the Prosecutor was also sent to the provinces. Andreevskii and Zhukovskii, the two prosecutors who had earlier refused to take on the assignment to prosecute Zasulich (a task that then went to the less experienced Kessel) were equally punished and resigned.[161] For a brief moment the government even considered punishing the jurors for their acquittal of Zasulich; but the idea was soon dropped.[162]

What about Governor Trepov, who had decided to stay at home during this trial? He felt that he had been maligned in the courtroom and by the press, accused of a crime which he felt he had not committed. In a memorandum submitted on 11 April to the Ministry of the Interior, he offered proof that the flogging of a convicted criminal had, in this case, after all been legal according to existing law, citing article and paragraph. Zasulich's assault on him, he said, had nothing to do with the Bogoliubov affair, adding, 'At issue, therefore, is not the security of a single person, but the security of entire society, the entire state and state authority.' Trepov also accused Koni of sympathising with the defendant.[163] The Ministerial Council and the Tsar did not want to act publicly on his memorandum, but Trepov would not take 'No' for an answer. Three weeks later he sent another, lengthier memorandum to the Tsar, with copies to other dignitaries, complaining, inter alia, about the democratic tendencies in the courts.[164] But this was to no avail: when he was not publicly rehabilitated he offered his resignation to the Tsar. He was unpleasantly surprised that it was accepted.

Three days after the trial had ended, on 2 April 1878, Count Pahlen submitted a proposal to the State Council to enact a law that would place all assassinations and acts of terrorism under the jurisdiction of military tribunals. On 9 May the new law came into force.[165] From then on, all cases of 'resistance to the authorities, rebellion, assassination or attempts on the lives of officials' would be dealt with by military courts.[166] In addition, the Ministry of Justice submitted, on 21 April, new legislation to the State Council which would allow it to supervise the activities of lawyers and give it the authority to prohibit individual lawyers from practising law if their behaviourwas judged to be incompatible with their duties.[167]

The Prosecutor, Kessel, on 24 April submitted an appeal to the Senate's Cassation Court, citing seven reasons why the verdict should be dismissed. He suggested that another court outside St. Petersburg should start a new trial of Zasulich. One of the reasons he gave for a re-trial was that in his view the jurors had been influenced by applause from the public and thereby had lost their objectivity. He also complained that the prosecution and defence were not given equal treatment by the President of the Court. On 20 May the Senate decided in Kessel's favour.[168] It declared the trial of Vera Zasulich on 31 March 1878 invalid and ordered a retrial of the case far away from the capital in the Novgorod Circuit Court.[169] Yet that new trial never took place. When it became known that Zasulich had escaped to Switzerland the Tsar first wanted her extradited (as had happened in the case of Nechaev who also had fled to Switzerland and was extradited in 1872). Yet in the end the Russian government only placed advertisements in foreign newspapers, ordering Vera Zasulich to present herself to the district court in Novgorod.[170] It was a vain gesture; in October 1878 the regime decided to give up the pursuit of Vera Zasulich in court.[171] Others than her had to pay a price. Those *narodniki* who had been tried and found guilty in the *Trial of the 193* but had hoped for leniency in an appeal could no longer hope for mercy. Indeed many of those who had been acquitted in that trial were arrested again and sent to the provinces in the usual procedure of administrative detention.[172]

As a consequence of the miscarriage of justice in the case of Vera Zasulich, Russia's legal system, especially the jury part of it, was weakened and some of the reforms of 1864 were in fact undone. The Zasulich case was to remain the only major case where jurors had been given an opportunity to decide on a political crime.[173]

3.8.2. *Social and Political Consequences*

It is, in this case, difficult to separate social from political consequences. We will therefore look at them together. Everybody agreed that the acquittal of Vera Zasulich was a 'slap in the face' for the autocratic regime.[174] As A. Koni, the President of the Court put it: 'The trial of Zasulich [...] showed the profound dissatisfaction of society with the government and its indifference to the government's fate.'[175] While that might have been true for the capital and major towns like Kiev and Odessa, it was far less true for the countryside where support for the Tsar had not eroded to the same extent as in the cities.

The trial of Vera Zasulich in late March 1878 had coincided with the return of the Tsar from the front. His armies, after a difficult campaign, had been victorious against the Ottoman Empire. The anti-government mood in the capital's press was not what he expected. He was not willing to compromise but wanted to show a firm hand. His reaction to the outcome of the trial of Vera Zasulich therefore meant renewed repression and enlarged police control.[176] A number of measures were taken to prevent a repetition of the events. One of them was that civilians were forbidden to carry weapons.[177] In the light of the backlash, the dreams of liberals for further reforms and a constitution for Russia vanished. Many of them gave up their hope for reforms from this Tsar and many liberals began to move closer to the revolutionaries in the aftermath of 1878.[178]

The government also cracked down on universities as many of the revolutionaries were students. 600 students were banned from St. Petersburg, 140 from Kiev, while in Charkov Cossaks were brought in to beat up demonstrating students.[179] Another casualty of the reaction to the Zasulich acquittal was press freedom. Under Tsar Alexander II the universities and the press had both enjoyed considerable freedom by the mid-1870s.[180] The press in St. Petersburg had given maximum coverage to Zasulich's attempt on Trepov's life and, even more so, to the subsequent trial of the would-be female assassin. Several newspapers reprinted in full Defence Attorney Alexandrov's eloquent speech in her defence. Two newspapers were punished for spreading 'false news'; one of them, *Severnyi Vestnik* (*Northern Herald*) had to close down. In its last issue of 4 April 1978 *Severnyi Vestnik* had printed Alexandrov's speech in court and a letter written by Vera Zasulich from her hideout.[181] Since the press had been largely sympathetic to Zasulich and critical of the government, censorship, which had become relaxed in recent years, was strengthened again, although in a haphazard way. A limitation of the freedom of expression was one social consequence of the Zasulich trial, or, perhaps, the press' extensive coverage of it.[182]

The press, reflecting urban public opinion, showed that there was much support for Vera Zasulich in the capital. However, in the provinces, common folk were more conservative. They could not understand how someone who would try to kill a Governor could get away with attempted murder. The people in the countryside, admonished by the Orthodox Church, were by and large still loyal to the Tsar and, by extension, to his servants.

Many political commentators interpreted the outcome of the trial as confirmation of what they wanted to believe. G.V. Plechanov, the father of Russian Marxism, as he would later be called, for instance, wrote with considerable exaggeration and wishful thinking, 'On the 31 of March 1878 the prologue of a great historical drama began for Russia, one can call it the judgment of the people over the government. On this day the split of Russian society from the government was de facto executed.'[183]

The shift from rural propaganda to urban terrorism was inspired, or at least speeded up, by the assassination attempt by Vera Zasulich. Her deed and, even more than that, her trial received extensive coverage in Russia and abroad. It had, in a matter of weeks, a greater propagandistic effect that the work of more than 20,000 *narodniki* in the years from 1874 to 1877. As a consequence, the Russian Socialists themselves split. Some young revolutionaries from the *Land and Freedom* party wanted to continue the approach of the populists who had gone to the people; others wanted to build on the momentum created by Vera Zasulich and go down the terrorist path.[184] The second, violence-oriented group later organised itself into *Narodnaya Volya* (and later evolved into the Socialist-Revolutionary Party). The first, more peaceful, group became known as the *Black Partition* group (and later evolved into the Marxist Social-Democratic Party). This split of the original *Land and Freedom* party was arguably an outflow of the polarisation brought about by Vera Zasulich's assassination attempt and her trial.[185]

Zasulich soon found imitators, especially among the revolutionaries who in early 1879 formed *Narodnaya Volya* (*People's Will*).[186] Acting in urban rather than rural surroundings, a series of terrorist assassins from the *People's Will* managed to capture the attention of the press and thereby achieved, at least among the urban educated classes, much bigger propaganda successes than the populists in their rural face-to-face campaigns could ever hope to enjoy. The terrorists were not concentrating on organising the peasants against the landlords. They were concentrating more on 'disorganisation', the assassination of what were in their eyes the most dangerous or harmful individuals in the government.[187]

Vera Zasulich's pivotal role in triggering with her deed and her trial a wave of terrorist assassinations in Russia is widely acknowledged by contemporaries and confirmed by historians.[188] Lev Deich, a fellow revolutionary, claimed, 'Quite rightly Vera Zasulich is celebrated as the founder of the terrorist struggle in Russia.'[189] Sergei Kravchinskii, in 1882, made this judgment of her:

> Vera Zasulich was not a terrorist. She was an angel of vengeance, and not of terror. She was a victim who voluntarily threw herself into the jaws of the monster in order to cleanse the honour of the party from a moral outrage. Yet this occurrence gave to the Terrorism a most powerful impulse. It illuminated it with its divine aureola, and gave to it the sanction of sacrifice and of public opinion.[190]

Kravchinskii held that Zasulich's assassination attempt on Trepov 'gave such a strong impetus to the [revolutionary] movement, that this step, which otherwise would perhaps have required several years, was taken at a single bound'.[191]

The new type of revolutionary, modelled after Vera Zasulich as much as after what revolutionaries preferred to see in her, was 'the terrorist'. Kravchinskii described him in these exalted words:

> He is noble, terrible, irresistibly fascinating, for he combines in himself the two sublimes of human grandeur: the martyr and the hero. [...] Alone, obscure, poor, he undertook to be the defender of outraged humanity, of right trampled under foot, and he challenged to the death the most powerful Empire in the world, and for years and years confronted all its immense forces. Proud as Satan rebelling against God, he opposed his own will to that of the man who alone, amid a nation of slaves, claimed the right of having a will. [...] And if the people, ill-counseled, say to him 'Be a slave', he will exclaim 'No'; and he will march onward, defying their imprecations and their fury, certain that justice will be rendered to him in his tomb. Such is the Terrorist.[192]

Kravchinskii ('Stepniak') was himself inspired by Vera Zasulich. In the summer of 1878 he assassinated with a dagger General Mezentsev, the chief of the political police (Third Section) in St. Petersburg. He was not the only one who drew inspiration from Zasulich's deed and trial. N.I. Kibalchich, the explosives expert and bomb-maker of

Narodny Volya, whose bomb would kill the Tsar three years later, was also directly inspired by Zasulich's attempt on Trepov and because of her joined the underground group of urban terrorists.[193]

A whole series of other copycat crimes were triggered by Zasulich's example and the outcome of her trial: on 23 February 1878 an unsuccessful attempt on the life of an assistant prosecutor Kotljarevskii was made in Kiev by Verian Osinsky; on 25 May 1978 Baron F.E. Geiking, chief gendarme, was assassinated in Kiev; in February 1879 there was the assassination of Governor Dimitri Kropotkin in Khrakov; in March 1879 an unsuccessful attempt on the life of Alexander Drenteln, Mezentsev's successor, was made; on 19 November 1879 a bomb exploded prematurely close to the Tsar's railway carriage as he travelled near Moscow; on 2 April 1879 an assassination attempt by A.K. Soloviev on Alexander II failed; on February 1880 an unsuccessful attempt on the life of Minister of Interior, General Count Loris-Melikov, took place; on 5 February 1880 one hundred pounds of dynamite placed by the carpenter Stephan Khalturin exploded in the Winter Palace under the Tsar's dining room but Alexander II survived; on 1 March 1881 Narodnaya Volya finally managed after six failed attempts to assassinate Tsar Alexander II, with the help of a nitroglycerine grenade.[194]

The 'Russian method', as it became known, was soon making its way abroad. It even inspired a number of attempted regicides. Soon after Zasulich's trial, there were two attempts on the life of William I, the German emperor, one attempt on the Italian King Umberto I in November 1878 and, the month before, in October one on King Alfonso XII of Spain.[195] Without Zasulich's example and the broad publicity given to her in the press, some of these and other assassination attempts would probably not have occurred. Vera Zasulich herself felt guilty about this chain of assassinations and, in late 1880, she secretly returned to Russia and tried to persuade the revolutionaries to stop terrorism and refocus on the struggle in the countryside. She came too late and did not succeed; terrorism had become the new mode of political struggle.[196] When, after several failed attempts, the Tsar was killed on 1 March 1881, she was dismayed.[197]

She would spend more than 25 years abroad and spoke out repeatedly against the systematic terror of revolutionary organisations from the underground by self-appointed 'heroes'. Her own 'terror', in the case of Trepov, was later described by her as an instinctive reaction to evil acts by government officials: 'When it is impossible to avert villainy perpetrated before one's eyes, then the feeling of revenge becomes the most legitimate social emotion.'[198] After her final return to Russia in 1905 she gave up politics and worked mainly as a translator. Between 1909 and 1919 she lived in the Writer's House in St. Petersburg from where she was evicted by Bolshevik soldiers. She did not survive this eviction and died on 8 May 1919 from pneumonia.[199] The

Russian Revolution—in reality more of a coup d'etat consolidated by Red Terror—had not brought the revolution she had fought for in her youth. She died disillusioned, writing in her last year, 'The Russia I knew and loved is gone.'[200]

Let us, after this glimpse into the future, return to the late 1870s and the 1880s. The unfortunate result of the Zasulich trial's outcome was, as indicated above, the impression prevailing in revolutionary circles that one could get away with murder and be applauded for it by the people. Her trial seemed to give political terrorism a semblance of legitimacy.[201] Many would-be terrorists thought they had a licence to kill, hoping to get a similar degree of understanding from society as Vera Zasulich had received from her jurors and the press. While Zasulich's own attempt on Governor Trepov was born out of a personal feeling of moral indignation and a desire to take revenge, those who followed in her footsteps tried to elevate assassination to an impersonal political doctrine. As a Russian counter-terrorist official from the Ministry of the Interior wrote perceptively in the late 1880s:

> Encouraged by the success of the first terrorist outbreaks, the devotees of anarchism from then on considered the principle of 'terror' as the most propitious mode of action and the most rational slogan for their plots and their agitations. They busied themselves with creating 'theories' and 'systems', seeking to convince the government and the public of the legitimacy of their crimes. The origin of the terrorist principles is thus explained more logically by consideration of an opportunistic character.[202]

The emergence of terrorism as a doctrine—the 'philosophy of the bomb'—was advanced by the writings of *Narodnaya Volya*. It was born out of the apparent failure of the populists to mobilise the peasants and from the absence of a sizeable urban working class ready to rise against the state. The populist revolutionaries' inability to mobilise the masses led some of them to have recourse to murderous attacks on government officials.[203] Amplified by the press, the impression was created by spectacular acts of terrorism that there was a sizeable and growing revolutionary movement, willing and able successfully to challenge the state. However, in reality the Russian terrorists were weak—estimates vary from a few dozen to a few hundred at best, with a few hundred (some say thousands) more sympathisers actively supporting their efforts. In a country of hundred million people they were no more than a drop in the ocean. The Tsarist police managed to round up most of them—so much so that the first wave of Russian terrorism, triggered by Vera Zasulich, practically came to an end with the massive crackdown following the assassination of Alexander II on 1 March 1881.[204]

Deborah Hardy, who studied the origins of Russian Terrorism in the years 1876–1879 concluded:

> Terrorism was too often a state of mind. It grew from feeding on its own danger, daring, and heroics. [...] Too many [...] were dominated by their emotional reactions to the magnetism of violence: by their need to act, their drives to become heroes, a strange attraction to martyrdom, their feeling for each other, their fervor about something that was 'contagious' or 'in the air' or 'inevitable'. Few of them, according to their memoirs, did much careful analyzing at all, beyond the intricate planning of the next, ever more spectacular and gruesome, terrorist deed. Their ultimate failure to attain their goal [...] became a personal tragedy for many of them.[205]

That was certainly true for Vera Zasulich. Her search for 'justice' for Bogoliubov brought her before a Court of Justice which, despite her crime, showed mercy towards her. Yet by side-stepping the provisions of the law for her crime, the court involuntarily legitimised, at least in the eyes of fellow revolutionaries, others to go and take the pursuit of 'justice', as they understood it, into their own hands. The consequences of that decision of 31 March 1878 were far-reaching. Her deed inspired, as mentioned above, the bomb-maker whose bomb killed the Tsar to join 'The People's Will'. The killing of the Tsar in 1881 in turn led to pogroms against Jews who were (wrongly) blamed for the conspiracy that led to the assassination. Such pogroms involving murder, rape and plunder would continue until 1884. In 1891, the systematic expulsion of most Jews from Moscow set in. These developments forced many Jews to move to Central and Western Europe. However, anti-Semitism followed them and met them in full force in post-World War I Germany.

There can be no doubt that Zazulich's crime had consequences that were far-reaching. Some of the consequences are still with us today. Where one wants to draw the line of her ebbing influence is a fascinating question. Yet there can be no doubt that her example set in motion a new model of political violence.

Notes

1 I am indebted to Ana Siljak, *Angel of Vengeance. The Girl Who Shot the Governor of St. Petersburg and Sparked the Age of Assassination* (New York: St. Martin's Griffin, 2008). Another work which was equally helpful is Richard Pipes, 'The Trial of Vera Z', *Russian History*, 37:1 (2010),

pp. 1–68. To a lesser degree, I am also indebted to Jay Bergman, *Vera Zasulich: A Biography* (Stanford: Stanford University Press, 1983) and, indirectly, to Wolfgang Geierhos, *Vera Zasulic und die russische revolutionäre Bewegung* (Munich: Oldenburg, 1977).

2 Adam B. Ulam, *In the Name of the People. Prophets and Conspirators in Prerevolutionary Russia* (New York: The Viking Press 1977), pp. 11 and 274.

3 In the words of Ron Christenson: 'Trials can become interpretative moments for a society.' Cit. Ron Christenson, *Political Trials in History. From Antiquity to the Present* (New Brunswick: Transaction Publishers, 1991), p. xv.

4 Tim Chapman, *Imperial Russia, 1801–1905* (London: Routledge, 2001), p. 95.

5 Samuel Kucherov, *Courts, Lawyers, and Trials under the Last Three Tsars* (New York: Praeger, 1953), pp. 304–305.

6 Louise McReynolds, *The News under Russia's Old Regime. The Development of a Mass-Circulation Press* (Princeton: University Press, 1991), p. 73.

7 Anatole G. Mazour, *Russia. Tsarist and Communist* (New York: Van Nostrand, 1962), pp. 302–303.

8 Ulam, *In the Name of the People*, p. 273; Pipes, 'The Trial of Vera Z.', pp. 5–6.

9 Cf. Kucherov, *Courts, Lawyers and Trial under the Last Three Tsars.*

10 For an overview of the judicial reforms in Russia see: Peter H. Solomon, Jr. (ed.), *Reforming Justice in Russia, 1864–1996* (Armonk, N.Y.: M.E. Sharpe, 1997).

11 Kucherov, *Courts, Lawyers and Trial under the Last Three Tsars*, pp. 304–305.

12 Ibid., p. 222.

13 Ronald Seth, *The Russian Terrorists: The Story of the Narodniki* (London: Barrie & Rockliff, 1967), p. 55.

14 Pipes, 'The Trial of Vera Z.', p. 6.

15 W.E. Mosse, *Alexander II and the Modernization of Russia* (London: English Universities Press, 1958), p. 159.

16 Siljak, *Angel of Vengeance*, p. 167.

17 Some sources cite 15 years.

18 Pipes, 'The Trial of Vera Z.', pp. 7–10.

19 Siljak, *Angel of Vengeance*, p. 219.

20 Pipes, 'The Trial of Vera Z.', p. 12.

21 Siljak, *Angel of Vengeance*, pp. 110–111.

22 Chapman, *Imperial Russia*, p. 117; McReynolds, *The News under Russia's Old Regime*, p. 92. Later the Tsar would increase some of the sentences.

23 Bergman, *Vera Zasulich*, pp. 33–34.

24 Pipes, 'The Trial of Vera Z.', pp. 15–16.

25 Siljak, *Angel of Vengeance*, p. 181.

26 Geierhos, *Vera Zasulich und die russische revolutionäre Bewegung*, p. 47. However, some participants, including A. Koni, considered the flogging illegal. Cf. Geierhos, p. 49.

27 Bogoliubov could not serve out his long sentence: after almost a decade of imprisonment and hard labour he began to showed signs of insanity and was sent to a psychiatric ward in Kazan. He died in 1887, back home with his family. Cf. Pipes, 'The Trial of Vera Z.', p. 17.

28 Bergman, *Vera Zasulich*, p. 29.

29 Siljak, *Angel of Vengeance*, p. 188.

30 Bergman, *Vera Zasulich*, p. 43.

31 Pipes, 'The Trial of Vera Z.', pp. 18–21 and 78.

32 'Our work is destruction, terrible, complete, pervasive, ruthless', was Nechaev's doctrine.—Cit. E. Radzinsky, *Alexander II. The Last Great Tsar* (London: The Free Press, 2005), p. 222.

33 Excerpts from Zasulich's memoirs cited in: Barbara A. Engel and Clifford N. Rosenthal, *Five Sisters: Women Against the Tsar. Edited and translated from Russian* (London: Weidenfeld and Nicolson, 1975), p. 73.

34 Lemma S.G. Nechaev, *Spartacus International* (no date), http://spartacus-educational.com/RUSnechayev.htm. Retrieved 18 May 2015.

35 Siljak, *Angel of Vengeance*, p. 39.

36 Matthew Carr. *The Infernal Machine. A History of Terrorism from the Assassination of Tsar Alexander II to Al-Qaeda* (New York: The New Press, 2006), p. 17.

37 Matthew Carr. *The Infernal Machine*, p. 18.

38 Bergman, *Vera Zasulich*, p. 8n.

39 Pipes, 'The Trial of Vera Z.', p. 25.

40 Siljak, *Angel of Vengeance*, p. 128.

41 Kucherov, *Courts, Lawyers, and Trials under the Last Three Tsars*, p. 217.

42 Siljak, *Angel of Vengeance*, p. 150.

43 Mikhail Bakunin was a figurehead of European anarchism. He had briefly been associated with Nechaev and had helped him to write the *Catechism of a Revolutionary*. He was an advocate of terrorist 'propaganda by the deed'.

44 Pipes, 'The Trial of Vera Z.', pp. 26–27.

45 Bergman, *Vera Zasulich*, p. 17.

46 Bergman, *Vera Zasulich*, p. 21.

47 Vera Zasulich, *Knigi Arkhivy. Avtografy* (Moscow: 1973), pp. 152–143, as cited in Pipes, 'The Trial of Vera Z.', pp. 28–29.

48 *Land and Freedom* had been founded in 1876 and pleaded that land be given to the peasants and their redemption payments (from their release from serfdom) should be abolished so that they would be really free. It also hoped to dismantle the autocratic system of

government. Contrary to many other populists, the members of *Land and Freedom* were tightly organised, with a central committee giving orders to its members. Cf. Chapman, *Imperial Russia*, pp. 117–118.

49 Seth, *The Russian Terrorists*, p. 54.

50 Pipes, 'The Trial of Vera Z.', p. 34.

51 Radzinsky, *Alexander II*, p. 276.

52 Reports on this aspect are contradictory. An alternative explanation is that Zasulich wanted to free some other conspirators preparing the attack on Trepov, so that they could return to Kiev and liberate a group of prisoners, including a close friend and later lover of Zasulic, Lev Deich. Cf. Geierhos, *Vera Zasulich und die russische revolutionäre Bewegung*, pp. 40–41.

53 The *Trial of the 193* involved students and other intellectuals who had 'gone to the people' in 1874 and 1875 to agitate among the peasantry for the overthrow of the government. The authorities arrested altogether some 4,000 of them. Others present at this trial were arrested during demonstrations in 1876. The *Trial of the 193* was the largest political trial in 19th century Russia. It ended in a mass acquittal, with only 40 of the 193 brought to court being sentenced to prison for hard labour. Two of those acquitted would later be involved in the successful assassination of Alexander II.

54 Pipes, 'The Trial of Vera Z.', p. 35.

55 Clark McCauley and Sophia Maskalenko, *Friction. How Radicalization Happens to Them and Us* (Oxford: University Press, 2011), p. 22.

56 Siljak, *Angel of Vengeance*, p. 2.

57 Anatoly F. Koni, *Sobranie sochinenii: vospominaniia o dele Very Zasulich* (Moscow: Juridičeskaja literatura, 1966), p. 65; cit. Pipes, 'The Trial of Vera Z.', p. 39.

58 Siljak, *Angel of Vengeance*, p. 8.

59 Pipes, 'The Trial of Vera Z.', p. 39.

60 Siljak, *Angel of Vengeance*, p. 9.

61 Pipes, 'The Trial of Vera Z.', p. 40. Since Trepov's memorandum contained a number of inaccuracies (he said that she had offered physical resistance, had refused to surrender the handgun and had tried to shoot him again), not too much credence can be given to this statement.

62 Ibid.

63 Siljak, *Angel of Vengeance*, p. 10.

64 Bergman, *Vera Zasulich*, p. 43; cit. Siljak, *Angel of Vengeance*, p. 11.

65 Pipes, 'The Trial of Vera Z.', p. 41; Bergman, *Vera Zasulich*, p. 39.

66 Koni, *Sobranie sochinenii*, pp. 72–74; as cited in: Bergman, *Vera Zasulich*, p. 40.

67 Bergman, *Vera Zasulich*, p. 43.
68 Mosse, *Alexander II and the Modernization of Russia*, p. 159.
69 Koni, *Sobranie sochinenii*, p. 66, as cited in Pipes, 'The Trial of Vera Z.', p. 41.
70 Pipes, 'The Trial of Vera Z.', p. 40.
71 Cit. Pipes, 'The Trial of Vera Z.', p. 47.
72 Koni, *Sobranie sochinenii*, pp. 69–72.
73 Koni, *Sobranie sochinenii*, p. 71; as cited in Bergman, *Vera Zasulich*, p. 41.
74 Bergman, *Vera Zasulich*, p. 41.
75 Pipes, 'The Trial of Vera Z.', p. 48.
76 Siljak, *Angel of Vengeance*, p. 230.
77 Geierhos, *Vera Zasulich und die russische revolutionäre Bewegung*, pp. 74–75.
78 Pipes, 'The Trial of Vera Z.', p. 49.
79 Samuel Kucherov, 'The Case of Vera Zasulich', *Russian Review*, 11:2 (1952), p. 87.
80 Siljak, *Angel of Vengeance*, pp. 227–228.
81 V.D. Spasovic, as cited in: Geierhos, *Vera Zasulich und die russische revolutionäre Bewegung*, p. 50.
82 Bergman, *Vera Zasulich*, p. 43.
83 Radzinsky, *Alexander II*, p. 277.
84 Geierhos, *Vera Zasulich und die russische revolutionäre Bewegung*, p. 53.
85 Siljak, *Angel of Vengeance*, p. 223.
86 Cit. Siljak, *Angel of Vengeance*, p. 221.
87 Cit. Siljak, *Angel of Vengeance*, p. 224.
88 Bergman, *Vera Zasulich*, p. 45; Pipes, 'The Trial of Vera Z.', p. 52.
89 Pipes, 'The Trial of Vera Z.', p. 54. Koni claimed later that Trepov told him after the trial that he "thanked God" for the acquittal of Zasulich. Cf. Pipes, p. 71.
90 Bergman, *Vera Zasulich*, p. 45.
91 Cit. Pipes, 'The Trial of Vera Z.', p. 55.
92 The Trepov flogging and the conditions in the House of Preliminary Detention were the subject of some internal investigations but in the end no case was brought against Trepov or Kurneev. Cf. Geierhos, *Vera Zasulich und die russische revolutionäre Bewegung*, pp. 36–37.
93 Siljak, *Angel of Vengeance*, p. 231.
94 Siljak, *Angel of Vengeance*, pp. 225–226.
95 Pipes, 'The Trial of Vera Z.', p. 67.
96 Geierhos, *Vera Zasulich und die russische revolutionäre Bewegung*, p. 54.
97 Cit. Siljak, *Angel of Vengeance*, p. 236.
98 Koni, *Sobranie sochinenii*; as cited in Bergman, *Vera Zasulich*, p. 47.

99 Geierhos, *Vera Zasulich und die russische revolutionäre Bewegung*, p. 54.

100 Kucherov, *Courts, Lawyers, and Trials under the Last Three Tsars*, p. 214; Siljak, *Angel of Vengeance*, p. 234.

101 Ezhov Tsederbaum, S. *Zhenshchina v russkom revoliutsionnom dvizhenni* (Leningrad: 1927), p. 69 as quoted in Engel and Rosenthal, *Five Sisters*, p. 78.

102 Siljak, *Angel of Vengeance*, p. 235.

103 Siljak, *Angel of Vengeance*, p. 230.

104 As quoted in Siljak, *Angel of Vengeance*, p. 239.

105 Quoted in: Kucherov, 'The Case of Vera Zasulich', p. 90.

106 Kucherov, *Courts, Lawyers, and Trials under the Last Three Tsars*, p. 218.

107 Cited in S. Kucherov, 'The Case of Vera Zasulich', p. 92; and in Bergman, *Vera Zasulich*, p. 49.

108 Bergman, *Vera Zasulich*, p. 44.

109 Bergman, *Vera Zasulich*, p. 42.

110 Siljak, *Angel of Vengeance*, p. 229.

111 As cited in Pipes, 'The Trial of Vera Z.', p. 58.

112 As cited in Siljak, *Angel of Vengeance*, p. 245.

113 McReynolds, *The News Under Russia's Old Regime*, p. 93.

114 Koni, *Sobranie sochinenii*, p. 157, as cited in Pipes, 'The Trial of Vera Z.', p. 60.

115 Siljak, *Angel of Vengeance*, p. 245.

116 Sources differ about the time it took the jury to reach its verdict. Michael Burleigh claims that the jury returned already after seven minutes; another source mentions ten, a third, 30 minutes. Cf. Michael Burleigh, *Blood & Rage. A Cultural History of Terrorism* (London: Harper Press, 2008), p. 44.

117 Cit. Radzinsky, *Alexander II*, p. 278.

118 Koni, *Sobranie sochinenii*, pp. 171–172, as cited in Kucherov, *Courts, Lawyers, and Trials under the Last Three Tsars*, p. 221.

119 Cit. Kucherov, *Courts, Lawyers, and Trials under the Last Three Tsars*, pp. 221–222.

120 Kucherov, 'The Case of Vera Zasulich', p. 92.

121 Siljak, *Angel of Vengeance*, p. 247.

122 Stepniak [pseud. for S. Kravchinskii], *Underground Russia: Revolutionary Profiles and Sketches from Life* (London: Smith, Elder & Co, 1883), p. 121.

123 Stepniak, *Underground Russia*.

124 Pipes, 'The Trial of Vera Z.', p. 61.

125 Pipes, 'The Trial of Vera Z.', p. 78.

126 Pipes, 'The Trial of Vera Z.', p. 47.

127 Ibid., p. 45.

128 Donald Mackenzie Wallace, *Russia. Vol. II* (London: Cassell, Petter & Galpin, 1912), p. 597, as cited in Pipes, 'The Trial of Vera Z.', p. 46.

129 Pipes, 'The Trial of Vera Z.', pp. 45–47.

130 Bergman, *Vera Zasulich*, p. 44n.

131 Cit. Pipes, 'The Trial of Vera Z.', p. 62.

132 G. Gradovskii, *Golo* [*The Voice*] (2 April 1878), as cited in Siljak, *Angel of Vengeance*, p. 222.

133 Geierhos, *Vera Zasulich und die russische revolutionäre Bewegung*, p. 55. Alexandrov's defence of Zasulich was translated into several languages.

134 Koni, *Sobranie sochinenii*, p. 180, as cited in Pipes, 'The Trial of Vera Z.', p. 61.

135 Radzinsky, *Alexander II.*, p..

136 Pipes, 'The Trial of Vera Z.', p. 53.

137 Siljak, *Angel of Vengeance*, p. 215.

138 Pipes, 'The Trial of Vera Z.', p. 60.

139 Kucherov, *Courts, Lawyers, and Trials under the Last Three Tsars*, p. 222.

140 Pipes, 'The Trial of Vera Z.', p. 63.

141 Siljak, *Angel of Vengeance*, p. 251.

142 Bergman, *Vera Zasulich*, p. 57.

143 Deborah Hardy, *Land and Freedom. The Origins of Russian Terrorism, 1876–1879* (Westport, Conn.: Greenwood Press, 1987), p. 61.

144 Pipes, 'The Trial of Vera Z.', pp. 65–66; Bergman, *Vera Zasulich*, pp. 51–52.

145 *Revue des Deux Mondes* (1 May, 1878) as quoted in Bergman, *Vera Zasulich*, p. 54.

146 Siljak, *Angel of Vengeance*, p. 254.

147 Ibid., p. 255.

148 McReynolds, *The News under Russia's Old Regime*, p. 93.

149 Ulam, *In the Name of the People*, p. 270.

150 Cit. Kucherov, *Courts, Lawyers, and Trials under the Last Three Tsars*, p. 223.

151 Cit. Bergman, *Vera Zasulich*, p. 53.

152 Cit. Pipes, 'The Trial of Vera Z.', p. 65.

153 Pipes, 'The Trial of Vera Z.', p. 68.

154 Cit. Bergman, *Vera Zasulich*, p. 54.

155 Radzinsky, *Alexander II*, p. 280.

156 Geierhos, *Vera Zasulich und die russische revolutionäre Bewegung*, p. 64.

157 Cit. Kucherov, 'The Case of Vera Zasulich', p. 96.

158 Geierhos, *Vera Zasulich und die russische revolutionäre Bewegung*, p. 67.

159 Siljak, *Angel of Vengeance*, p. 258.

160 Vera Zasulich entry in: http://yqyq.net/27244-Vera-Zasulich.html. Retrieved 5 January 2011.

161 Kucherov, 'The Case of Vera Zasulich', p. 96; Pipes, 'The Trial of Vera Z.', pp. 71–72.
162 Pipes, 'The Trial of Vera Z.', p. 72.
163 Pipes, 'The Trial of Vera Z.', p. 70.
164 Geierhos, *Vera Zasulich und die russische revolutionäre Bewegung*, p. 71.
165 Siljak, *Angel of Vengeance*, 258; Kucherov, 'The Case of Vera Zasulich', p. 93.
166 Mosse, *Alexander II and the Modernization of Russia*, p. 160.
167 Kucherov, *Courts, Lawyers, and Trials under the Last Three Tsars*, p. 269.
168 Geierhos, *Vera Zasulich und die russische revolutionäre Bewegung*, pp. 64–65.
169 Bergman, *Vera Zasulich*, p. 57.
170 Pipes, 'The Trial of Vera Z.', p. 67.
171 Siljak, *Angel of Vengeance*, p. 256.
172 Geierhos, *Vera Zasulich und die russische revolutionäre Bewegung*, pp. 43–44.
173 Ibid., p. 70.
174 Mosse, *Alexander II and the Modernization of Russia*, p. 161.
175 Koni, *Sobranie sochinenii*, p. 247, as cited in Pipes, 'The Trial of Vera Z.', p. 69.
176 The level of repression was, compared with what was to come after the end of the Romanovs, minor. *Narodnaya Volya* listed, for the last four years of Alexander II, 22 executions for 'political' crimes and some 160 sentences of forced labour to be served in Siberian camps. F.L. Ford, *Political Murder. From Tyrannicide to Terrorism* (Cambridge: Harvard University Press, 1985), p. 227.
177 Pipes, 'The Trial of Vera Z.', p. 70.
178 Stepniak, *Underground Russia*, p. 40.
179 Geierhos, *Vera Zasulich und die russische revolutionäre Bewegung*, p. 86.
180 Chapman, *Imperial Russia*, p. 121.
181 Pipes, 'The Trial of Vera Z.', pp. 72–73.
182 McReynolds, *The News under Russia's Old Regime*, pp. 93–96.
183 Cit. Geierhos, *Vera Zasulich und die russische revolutionäre Bewegung*, p. 79.
184 Peter Lavroff, in "Preface", Stepniak, *Underground Russia*, p. ix.
185 Chapman, *Imperial Russia*, p. 118; Pipes, 'The Trial of Vera Z.', p. 74.
186 Chapman, *Imperial Russia*, p. 118.
187 Ibid., p. 48.
188 Ulam, *In the Name of the People*, p. 11.
189 Lev Deich, 'Valerian Osiunsky', in: *Hard Labor and Exile*, LIV (Moscow: 1929), p. 27, as cited in Ulam, *In the Name of the People*, p. 275.
190 Stepniak, *Underground Russia*, p. 38.
191 Ibid., p. 42.
192 Stepniak, *Underground Russia*, pp. 42 and 44–45.

193 Hardy, *Land and Freedom*, pp. 61–62.

194 Engel and Rosenthal, *Five Sisters*, p. xxix; Siljak, *Angel of Vengeance*, pp. 275–276; Ford, *Political Murder*, p. 227.

195 Radzinsky, *Alexander II*, pp. 280–281.

196 Siljak, *Angel of Vengeance*, pp. 302–303.

197 Hardy, *Land and Freedom*, pp. 61–62.

198 Vera Zasulich. *Iskra* [*The Spark*] (3 April 1901) as cited in Pipes, 'The Trial of Vera Z.', p. 76.

199 In a note to Zinoviev, the chief of Communist Petrograd, Lenin called the eviction a 'disgrace'; but neither he nor Zinoviev took action to reverse it.—Pipes, 'The Trial of Vera Z.', pp. 81–82.

200 Cit. Pipes, 'The Trial of Vera Z.', p. 311.

201 Bergman, *Vera Zasulich*, p. 57.

202 Cf. *Chronique du movement socialiste en Russia, 1878–1887* (St. Petersburg: Imp. Officielle du Ministre de l'Interieur, 1890), p. 29, as cited in Hardy, *Land and Freedom*, p. 156.

203 Walter Laqueur, *Terrorism* (London: Sphere Books, 1978), p. 46.

204 Laqueur, *Terrorism*, p. 54.

205 Hardy, *Land and Freedom*, pp. 163–164.

4. Stalin's 1936 Show Trial against the 'Trotzkyite-Zinovievite Terrorist Centre'

Alex P. Schmid

> The show trial is a propaganda arm of political terror. It aims to personalize an abstract political enemy, to place it in the dock in flesh and blood and, with the aid of a perverted system of justice, to transform abstract political-ideological differences into easily intelligible common crimes. It both incites the masses against the evil embodied by the defendants and frightens them away from supporting any potential opposition.
>
> George H. Hodos (1987)[1]

4.1. Introduction

This chapter on the first of the three show trials staged in the Soviet Union in the years 1936–1938 offers a comprehensive reconstruction of an enormous travesty of justice. Recounting a complex 'Orwellian' conspiracy, in which perceptions and realities stood far apart, it is longer than the other chapters in this volume. In part this is also due to the fact that it goes beyond a mere description of the trial itself, a trial that was the catalyst to a tragedy leading to the death of hundreds of thousands of innocent people. A broad contextualisation of events that preceded, accompanied and followed the trial that took place more than three quarters of a century ago in a closed society is necessary for its full understanding. Given the fact that this trial was one of the most brazen miscarriages of justice in the 20th century and its consequences have nevertheless been largely forgotten, this chapter also serves as a reminder of what totalitarianism can do to individuals and whole societies, using the justice system to enable and 'legitimise' injustices on a large scale.

In our previous case study on the trial of Vera Zasulich, it was demonstrated that the defence had the greater 'performative power'. In this chapter the balance of power is altogether on the side of the prosecutor. The real target of the trial, Lev Trotzky, called it 'the greatest frame-up in the political history of the world'.[2] He was not far off the mark.

In the Zasulich case, the perpetrator was declared innocent of the alleged crime, although her crime had been objectively established and, as such, was not contested.

In the present case study, those accused were de facto innocent, at least of the crimes they were charged with. The real perpetrators were Joseph Stalin, General Secretary of the Central Committee of the Communist Party of the Soviet Union, and some members of his innermost circle—Nikolai I. Yezhov, Andrei Y. Vyshinsky and Genrikh G. Yagoda. The trial was set up as part of a campaign to eliminate the 'Old Bolsheviks'. The outcome was that Stalin won the trial, justice was denied, truth was trampled upon and much of the world fooled. Many local and foreign observers, especially those who stood on the left side of the political spectrum, professed that this trial against Kamenev and Zinoviev—Lenin's closest comrades, according to Lenin's wife[3]—and their co-defendants was fair and that the confessions made by those accused were genuine. The show was so well orchestrated that the term 'show trial' was later invented to describe this and subsequent trials that were perversions of justice.

Jeremy Peterson wrote that a 'show trial' requires two essential elements: a heightened probability of the defendant's conviction, and a focus on the audience observing the trial rather than on the defendant.[4] Peterson's characterisation applies here but does not go far enough. Instead of 'a hightened probablility' of conviction the verdicts in the Moscow show trials were a foregone conclusion.[5] Show trials are often characterised by apparently unforced and completely unexpected confessions by defendants to improbable crimes.[6]

Between 1936 and 1938, three major show trials were held in Moscow. The key crime in the first trial was 'terrorism', in the second trial it was 'wrecking' and 'high treason', and in the third it was 'espionage'.[7] Those accused in the first Moscow trial in August 1936 were Grigory Zinoviev, Lev Kamenev and 14 others; in the second, held in late January 1937, Levid Pyatakov, Karl Radek and 15 others stood in front of the bench. The third trial saw Nikolai Bukharin, Alexei I. Rykov and 19 others accused in March 1938.[8] Of the 54 people accused in these three trials, 47 were sentenced to death; the others received long prison sentences.[9]

Here the focus is on the first of these three show trials. Between 19 and 24 August 1936, the trial against the so-called 'Trotzkyite-Zinovievite Terrorist Centre' was conducted at a Military Collegium of the Supreme Court of the USSR in Moscow and given great publicity.[10] Those accused were charged, inter alia, with forming a terrorist organisation with the purpose of killing Joseph Stalin and other members of the Soviet government. Before their trial, there had been a secret trial of a disturbed young Communist, Leonid Nikolayev, who had been charged with killing Sergei Kirov on 1 December 1934. In some respects, his case was comparable to that of Dutch Communist Marinus van der Lubbe, who allegedly set fire to the German Reichstag building on 27 February 1933. The Nazis implicated Van der Lubbe in a Comintern (Communist International) plot and staged a trial in Leipzig. In both cases—Stalin's and Hitler's—there are indications of a false flag operation where those accused were pawns in a larger game. Their crimes and the trials were designed to consolidate power for each leader. The trial against Van der Lubbe and other alleged conspirators was public and did not quite play out the way Hitler had intended—only Van der Lubbe was sentenced to death, not his alleged Comintern comrades. The Zinoviev-Kamenev trial was staged more successfully, despite the fact that the prosecutor, Andrei Vyshinsky, had practically no evidence to prove his case—only the coerced confessions of the accused and those of equally coerced witnesses.[11] Nevertheless the Soviet prosecutor managed to persuade (or fool) most of the public and, incredibly, to some extent, even some of the defendants themselves. They played their roles completely against their own best interests, for reasons to be explored later.

The Kirov murder, the three Moscow show trials and the Great Purges that accompanied them still baffle historians—though not as much as those who lived through them. The chain of events is complex, and many documents relating to them have been hidden, destroyed or falsified.[12] Those writing about these events have often had political, ideological and personal motives to stress one interpretation over the other—for example, to whitewash Communist policies or to place most of the blame exclusively on Stalin. Not all archives are accessible and what they have yielded so far is complex and often confusing. As one recent Stalin biographer put it 'The events of 1935–1938, which led to the total destruction of the Leninist Party, remain the greatest riddle of Stalin's reign. Why did he destroy the Party, now completely subservient to him, with such inordinate cruelty?'[13] The interpretation presented here is based on a broad reading of secondary sources; it is also based on the official 'Report of the Court Proceedings' of the first show trial. These texts from the trial sometimes only offer summaries of what was said, while at other times reproducing the courtroom dialogues verbatim. The Report is the only officially approved version of the recordings as they were published in 1936; it is neither complete nor fully accurate. The original protocols were apparently destroyed in a fire.[14]

The first Moscow show trial was a political trial, that is, legal procedures were used for political ends by a regime that did not recognise the separation of powers between legislative, executive and judicative branches of government as it evolved in Europe since the 18th century. The classical political trial involves, in the words of Otto Kirchheimer, 'a regime's attempt to incriminate its foe's public behaviour with a view to evicting him from the political scene'. A variant on this, the 'derivative political trial', Kirchheimer identifies as one 'where the weapon of defamation, perjury, and contempt are manipulated in an effort to bring disrepute upon a political foe'.[15] Both definitions are fully applicable in this case.

The trial under consideration was also 'political' in a peculiarly Marxist sense, explained by George Katkov:

> Law, being like the state, only a superstructure in the organization of human society, was interpreted as one of the instruments of the class struggle, an instrument which in the hands of the property-owning classes served to maintain their privileges but which in the hands of a proletarian dictatorship (in the period of transition to socialism and Communism) was to be a revolutionary weapon to bring about the desired historical changes. Not merely legislation itself, but its practical application in court was to serve the militant purpose of the Party. It would be self-contradictory, un-Marxist and counter-revolutionary for a Marxist to object to the use of legal procedures for political ends.[16]

While in the beginning of Soviet rule the judiciary was politically instrumentalised mainly against class enemies, under Stalin it was also used against rivals, enemies and deviationists in the ruling Bolshevik Party as we shall see in the unfolding of events between 1934 and 1936.

4.2. What Happened before the Trial

4.2.1. *The Stalin–Trotzky Rivalry*

It has been said that all history is biography. To the extent that this is true, the present case reflects also a clash of two biographies, those of Joseph Stalin and Lev Trotzky. The Bolshevik Revolution of 1917 was, initially, little more than a coup d'état the main architect of which was Lev Trotzky. Joseph Stalin, writing about the seizure of power in St. Petersburg on the first anniversary of the revolution in the *Pravda* (the Party newspaper), acknowledged this:

> All practical work in connection with the organization of the uprising was done under the immediate direction of Comrade Trotzky, the president of the Petrograd Soviet. It can be stated with certainty that the Party is indebted primarily and principally to Comrade Trotzky for the rapid defection of the garrison to the Soviet side and for efficiently organizing the work of the Military-Revolutionary Committee.[17]

The origins of the conflict between Josef Stalin and Lev Trotzky go back to the civil war (1918–1920). Trotzky was the founder of the Red Army and the leading force in the civil war victory against the 'White Guards'.[18] Stalin played a very minor role in these events but later rewrote history to enhance his place in it. By the early 1920s that civil war, and a war with Poland, had come to an end and an internal power struggle within the Bolshevik cadres took shape. The struggle for control of the Bolshevik Party intensified from 1922 onwards, when Lenin had his first incapacitating stroke. In that year Stalin became Secretary of the Party, a position for which Ivan N. Smirnov had also been proposed. By 1923 the Politburo consisted of V. Lenin, L. Kamenev, A. Rykov, M. Tomsky, G. Zinoviev, L. Trotzky and J. Stalin.[19] The struggle for leadership which followed Lenin's death in January 1924 lasted more than three years. At the end Trotzky (and others) were defeated and Stalin had consolidated his power by 1927. In the beginning, this power struggle had not been overtly violent. After Lenin's death, as one of the six remaining Politburo members, Stalin proclaimed in 1924:

> It is the task of the Party to bury Trotzkyism as an ideological trend. There is talk about measures of repression against the opposition and of the possibility of a split. This is all nonsense, comrades. Our Party ... will not allow any splits. As for repressions, I am decidedly opposed to them. What we want now is not repressions, but a[n] ... ideological struggle against ... Trotzkyism.[20]

That was his declaratory policy, but Stalin's vindictiveness already surfaced in a conversation he had in the summer of 1923 with Felix Dzerzhinski, the chief of the Cheka, the political police (later renamed NKVD)[21]—a conversation Lev Kamenev also witnessed. Stalin: 'To choose one's enemy, to prepare every detail of the blow, to slake an implacable vengeance, and then go to bed. [...] There is nothing sweeter in the world!'[22] Stalin developed a simple conflict resolution model early in his career: 'Death solves all problems. Where there are no people, there are no problems.'[23]

Stalin was a master 'technician of power', his love of political intrigue driven by a thirst for revenge, and haunted by constant suspicion, bordering on paranoia in later life.[24] He could not forgive past insults and humiliations. In 1926 Trotzky had called Stalin the 'gravedigger' of the Party and the revolution. Pyatakov (who was to be tried ten years later in the second show trial), told Trotzky '[Stalin] will never forgive you for this, neither you nor your children, nor your grandchildren'.[25] During the 14th Party Congress in 1926, Kamenev and Zinoviev had also broken with Stalin, who formed a new coalition with the 'Party's favourite' (as Lenin called him) Nikolai Bukharin.[26] The following year, in August 1927, Stalin had Trotzky and Zinoviev expelled from the Central Committee. Numerically, the Trotzkyists were only a very small faction in the Party: out of 854,000 Party members only 4,000 voted for the Trotzkyists and only about 12,000 Party members at that time openly sympathised with Trotzky.[27] Trotzky tried to regain lost ground by revealing the existence (but not the content) of Lenin's testament in public in October 1927.[28] In this document Lenin had discussed five possible successors: Trotzky, Zinoviev, Kamenev, Bukharin and Pyatakov; at the same time he had suggested the removal of Stalin who was judged to be too brutal.[29] However, that did not help Trotzky; he was exiled to Alma Ati in 1927. Later he fled to Norway where he stayed during the first show trial. When Stalin put pressure on Norway, he sailed to Mexico.

After Lenin's death, there were shifting coalitions among the main actors in the Communist Party's power struggles. The events of 1936–1938 were in part a replay of these alliances and splits.[30] Yet at the same time, by the mid-1930s, the power struggles of the 1920s were largely history; Stalin was the acknowledged supreme leader of the Party and the Soviet state.[31] He had implemented his first Five-Year Plan (1928–1933) with an emphasis on heavy industrialisation and arms production on the one hand and a collectivisation of agriculture on the other. The human costs, especially in the countryside, were enormous: six million died in 1932–1933 alone, as collectivisation led to repression through forced deportations, and to famine.[32] As a consequence, in the late 1920s and early 1930s criticism of Party politics was widespread, but subdued and unorganised.[33] Throughout the 1920s, the Bolshevik Party had not been held in high esteem by most of the workers, let alone the peasants. They experienced a continuation of repressive tactics used during the Red Terror and the civil war. These tactics had kept the Bolsheviks in power.[34]

By the early 1930s, those Party members (and common people) who took issue with the brutality of collectivisation created more problems for Stalin than the Trotzkyists.[35] To escape deportation and starvation, some 12 million peasants had fled to the cities.[36] Reflections of widespread social unrest surfaced at the Party Congress in 1933. The gross mismanagement of the economy motivated some Congress delegates to discuss among themselves the possibility of replacing Stalin with the Party's chief in Leningrad, who was Zinoviev's successor. Kirov was more popular among the workers than most other Party bosses. He actually ventured into the factories, spoke to and listened to workers—something most Party bosses did not dare or care to do any more, except in tightly controlled settings. Kirov was asked privately whether he would accept Stalin's position if it was offered to him. Yet Kirov informed Stalin about this exploratory move to replace him, and said he had no interest in becoming leader of the Party.[37] Stalin was nevertheless anxious about this challenge. Kirov in turn became worried too as now he felt threatened.[38]

In order to address the latent revolt by those who had wanted to see Kirov replace him, Stalin came up with the idea of bringing Kirov from Leningrad to Moscow to be appointed as one of the four Party secretaries. On the surface, this would appear to be a concession to the wishes of many in the CommunistParty. In reality, it would bring Kirov under the direct control of Stalin, his bodyguards and his secret police. Kirov tried to avoid and then postpone the promotion. A compromise was reached: Kirov became third secretary of the Party but would stay for the time being in Leningrad. Stalin and Kirov had once been friends, but now Stalin saw Kirov as his rival. The events that follow are difficult to understand without acknowledging the duality of this love/hate relationship. Sergei Kirov had a number of qualities Stalin admired—popularity, eloquence, charisma—and Stalin was also jealous of Kirov. Ominously, when Kirov postponed his move to Moscow, Stalin tried to replace some of Kirov's personal security personnel in Leningrad.

Events taking place in Germany around this time may have influenced Stalin. On 30 June 1934, Adolf Hitler arranged what has become known as the 'Night of the Long Knives'. With his close allies Hermann Goering, (Prime Minister of Prussia), Joseph Goebbels (Propaganda) and SS chief Heinrich Himmler and his Deputy Reinhard Heydrich, Hitler had manufactured false evidence, implicating the chief of the Sturm Abteilung SA—a paramilitary unit of Hitler's party, Ernst Röhm, in a conspiracy to organise a Putsch and execute the Fuehrer and his closest allies. On 30 June, when all the SA leaders were meeting in Bad Wiessee, Hitler ordered a commando action to have them arrested, purged and, as in Röhm's case, killed (after he refused to commit suicide). Altogether some 130 SA members as well as some others were executed. Hitler's bold move to get rid of his rivals impressed Stalin, who commented to Politburo member Anastas Mikoyan, 'Did you hear what happened in Germany? Some fellow that Hitler! Splendid. That's a deed of some skill!'[39]

What Stalin did to his own Old Bolsheviks in the coming years was many times 'bolder' (and deadlier) than Hitler's purge of the rival SA leaders. It was a nightmare that engulfed the Party, then the country and even the Comintern (the Communist International Organisation), for more than four years. We know that he conceived the idea to purge the Party of oppositionists and rivals in the summer of 1934,[40] at the same time as the SA purge took place in Germany. There is an ongoing controversy among historians as to the planning for each consecutive step in Stalin's ascent to total power in the USSR. Some argue that he followed a diabolical strategy; others see him stumbling from one deadly game of chess to another, sometime retreating, then attacking again.[41] Newly released sources tend to support the first view.

What triggered the Great Purge and the first Stalinist show trial was the murder of the Leningrad Party chief Sergei Kirov, on 1 December 1934. The apparent murderer was Leonid Nikolayev, but there is an ongoing controversy as to whether or not Stalin personally ordered Kirov's assassination. Some questions remain unanswered, such as who tipped off Nikolayev that Kirov was making an unplanned visit to his office at the Smolny Institute? Khrushchev later thought that Stalin had a hand in this, and Mikoyan also believed that Stalin 'was somehow involved in the death'.[42] The murderer and key witnesses conveniently disappeared under dubious circumstances,[43] evidence was lost or altered,[44] and different interest groups, then and later, pushed or prevented interpretations as to who was behind Kirov's murder. Kirov's bodyguard (M.D. Borisov) was killed the next day in a contrived car accident. On the afternoon of the murder, as Borisov had accompanied Kirov to his office on the third floor of the Smolny Institute, he lagged behind him on the staircase—either because he could not keep pace with the more agile Kirov or because he was apparently held back for a few moments by some Chekists from Moscow. This gave Nikolayev, who was waiting for Kirov in the corridor on the third floor, the opportunity to approach him from behind and shoot him in the neck. A second shot was fired in the corridor shortly afterwards and hit the ceiling. It is unclear whether this shot was a bungled attempt at suicide by the assassin, perhaps prevented by the interference of an electrician who happened to step into the corridor. When Borisov arrived moments later with his pistol drawn, Kirov was already mortally wounded.[45]

The assassin was a disgruntled young Communist who felt mistreated by the Party bosses. In this he was not alone; feelings of resentment were widespread among the population, as revealed by secret reports the NKVD produced on reactions to Kirov's murder.[46] In the month before the murder, Nikolayev had lost his job, and was first excluded but then reinstated in the Party. He had written to both Stalin and Kirov in desperation, saying, 'I am ready to do anything if no one responds.' Perhaps this gave Stalin the idea of using him as his instrument to get rid of Kirov.[47] However, no 'smoking gun' points directly to Stalin. Some pieces of the evidence puzzle are difficult to reconcile, perhaps also because evidence was altered in the aftermath of the murder, but the case against Stalin is a strong one.[48] Philip Medved, Leningrad NKVD chief, later held that Stalin had suggested the assassination of Kirov to Yagoda. He did not survive the purges, probably because he knew too much.[49]

The murder of Kirov marks the beginning of a chain of events that cost the lives of hundreds of thousands of people, and affected countless others who were exiled to Siberia or placed in camps.[50] The Great Terror of 1936–1938 was mainly a purge of the Bolshevik Party. The Party had grown considerably during the First Five-Year plan, more than doubling between 1929 and 1933 to 3.5 million members. Communist Party insiders enjoyed privileges and protection from persecution, so membership was sought not only by true believers, but by opportunists and careerists of all hues. Attempts were made to control the influx into the Party, for example by withdrawing old Party cards and issuing new ones, and in 1933 alone more than 18 per cent of Party members lost their membership. This process of purging Party membership continued throughout the 1930s.[51] Until 1936, exclusion from the Party meant at worst exile, prison or labour camp. In the 1920s, a show of regret had often been sufficient for re-admission to the Party, certainly for Old Bolsheviks (who had been Party members before 1917, or had distinguished themselves in the civil war against the 'White Guard' counter-revolutionaries). Zinoviev and Kamenev, who had been expelled twice from the Party, were readmitted in the late 1920s after showing repentance.[52]

By the mid-1930s the Communist Party was the new elite, far removed from the proletariat it was supposed to represent. In reality, the 'dictatorship of the proletariat' meant rule by cliques of local bosses with their patronage networks. Party discipline had brought the Bolsheviks to power in 1917. Stalin and others considered the Party as the instrument to bring about a new society. But first the Party had to be cleansed of parasites, opportunists and 'double-dealers' (those who professed Bolshevik principles but secretly advanced their own careers). Vigilance was called for to keep the Party 'pure'. Those who deviated from the Party line had to be purged. Although Kirov had not openly deviated from the Party line, he wanted reconciliation within the Party, as well as between the Party and the 165 million citizens of the Soviet Union.[53] He was also, as we have seen, Stalin's potential rival. His murder marked the beginning of a catastrophic series of events. To understand the show trial that began on 19 August 1936 some additional background information—provided here in the following paragraphs in chronological fashion—is necessary.

On 1 December 1934, within hours of learning of the Kirov murder, Stalin drafted a new law, published in *Pravda* on 5 December; it stipulated rapid procedures for processing cases involving terrorism. Investigations of terrorist cases were to be completed within ten days; the accused would be informed of the charges only 24 hours before the trial, and the trial would take place without the presence of the defendant or counsel. Appeals for clemency would not be permitted and death sentences would be carried out immediately. This decree was soon to be included under Article 58 of the Penal Code (1927) and gave the NKVD a licence to kill suspects without due process. This fateful decree was to provide the legal basis for the arrest, trial and execution or deportation to labour camps of up to two million people over the next four years.[54] On the same day he drafted the draconian new law, Stalin travelled to Leningrad in order to supervise the investigation into Kirov's murder. He personally spoke with the assassin Nikolayev, seeking to link him to a group of Zinovievites, an allegation Nikolayev denied.[55]Following Kirov's state funeral on 3 December 1934, Stalin created a personality cult around the fallen comrade; within a week, several books in praise of Kirov were published.[56] By mid-December, Kamenev and Zinoviev, already confined in a 'political isolator' (a procedure similar to house arrest) since 1932, were arrested in Moscow;[57] In Leningrad, 843 others were arrested in the two and a half months after the murder. Until 1938, more than 90,000 others were to follow them in the Leningrad district alone.[58] By 22 December 1934, the NKVD announced that investigations had shown that Nikolayev was a member of an underground terrorist organisation established by Zinoviev oppositionists in Leningrad.[59] Stalin instructed that all involved should be condemned to death.[60] A week later Soviet newspapers reported that Nikolayev and 13 'young Zinovievites' associated with a Leningrad terrorist Centre had been sentenced in a closed trial and executed.[61] Neither the indictment nor the verdict mentioned Zinoviev and Kamenev.[62] During December, 6,501 people were shot, many of them from Kirov's entourage.[63]

At the beginning of 1935, Stalin instructed the NKVD to find and bring to trial any members of the Zinovievite 'Moscow Centre'. In a secret trial, 19 accused persons were found guilty of 'objectively contributing to inflaming terrorist moods' among adherents in Leningrad. They were tried on 15–16 January; Kamenev received a five-year prison sentence and Zinoviev ten years.[64] Yezhov, speaking on behalf of Stalin, had assured Zinoviev that the secret trial would be the last sacrifice he would have to make 'for the sake of the Party'.[65] No death sentences were issued. In a secret letter Stalin ordered that all opposition had to be treated like White Guards, i.e. were to be arrested and taken to camps.[66] On 16 January it was announced that further investigations had produced 'new material relating to the underground counter-revolutionary activities of G.Y. Zinoviev, G.E. Evdokimov, L.B. Kamenev and G.F. Fedorov'.[67] Two days later Stalin drafted a letter on the lessons of the events connected to the Kirov murder, calling the Zinoviev oppositional group 'the most treacherous and despicable of all fractional groups in the history of our country', adding that 'with such double-dealers we cannot restrict ourselves to their exclusion from the Party'.[68] Stalin also demanded a check of all Party membership cards by the Party. It was alleged that Kirov's murderer had entered the Smolny Institute with a falsified Party card. Some 250,000 members were subsequently deprived of Party membership.[69]

On 23 February 1935, after a series of arrests, during which part of Trotzky's archive from the 1927 period was recovered (from I.I. Trusov), Stalin asked Yezhov to build a case against a 'Trotzky–Zinoviev Centre'.[70] By late April or early May, Yagoda, Commissar-General of State Security, in a text edited by Stalin and entitled 'From Factionalism to Open Counter-revolution', 'proof' was offered that in its struggle against the Party the former opposition around Zinoviev had resorted to methods of terror.[71] On 13 May, a secret Central Committee decree led to the creation of a Special Security Commission of Politburo members charged with directing the liquidation of 'enemies of the people'. Its members included Stalin, Yezhov, Vyshinsky, Zhdanov, Malenkov and Shkiryatov.[72] In mid-1935, Yezhov announced the existence of a Centre of Trotzkyists. Yezhov said that he was sanctioned to carry out operations against Trotzkyists in Moscow.[73] Towards the end of the year Yezhov, by now the deputy chief of the NKVD, reported to the Central Committee that 33 per cent of all those purged from the Party since July 1935 had been spies, White Guards and Trotzkyists.[74] Yezhov initiated an investigation into the case of a 'United Trotzky–Zinoviev center'.[75] In early 1936, Valentine Olberg, a former Trotzky associate, was arrested in Gorky. Under interrogation, Olberg 'confessed' to being a Trotzky emissary.[76] On the last day of March 1936, Stalin ordered Yagoda and Vyshinsky to submit a concrete proposal for the trial of 82 Trotzkyists. Among those interrogated during April in preparation of such a trial were Smirnov, Mrachkovsky and Ter-Vaganyan.[77] When Yagoda, Commissar-General of State Security, looked at the evidence, he came to the conclusion that the charge that Trotzky had ordered terrorism in the USSR was 'nonsense'.[78] Stalin threatened to 'punch him in the nose' if he continued to drag his feet with the investigations.[79]

In mid-May, Molchanov, an NKVD investigator, presented to Stalin, Yezhov, Yagoda and others a diagram depicting Trotzky as part of a 'terrorist conspiracy' in the USSR.[80] By 20 May the Politburo decided that Trotzkyists already in prison were to be handed over to the NKVD so that death sentences could be passed on them.[81] By 19 June 1936 Yagoda and Vyshinsky, the State Prosecutor, presented to Stalin the requested list of 82 Trotzkyists who could be brought to trial for participating in terrorist activity. Stalin suggested that a combined case against Trotzkyists and Zinovievites should be prepared for an open trial.[82] In preparation of a public trial, by mid-July 'confessions' were obtained from Kamenev, Zinoviev, Bakayev, Dreitzer and Mrachkovsky.[83] On 29 July 1936, just before going on holiday to Sochi, Stalin sent a secret letter, which had been drafted by Yezhov, to the Politburo, the Central Committee and the Party organisations. This letter, 'On the Terrorist Activity of the Trotzky–Zinoviev Counter-revolutionary Bloc', came as a total surprise to most of the recipients.[84] It claimed that plans to assassinate Stalin, Voroshilov, Kaganovich, Ordzhonikidze, Zhdanov, Kosior and Postyshev were the 'main and principal task of the [Trotzky–Zinoviev] Centre'.[85] A week later, on 7 August 1936, Vyshinsky sent Stalin a draft indictment for the forthcoming trial of Zinoviev, Kamenev et al.; Stalin edited it twice and accepted the third version.[86] In preparation of the trial a further decree was issued with regard to terrorist trials, apparently to create the illusion for those accused that all would be window dressing and that in the end they would be spared the full weight of the verdict. To achieve this, on 11 August 1936, partly undoing the decree of 1 December 1934, a further decree was issued re-establishing public hearings for terrorist trials. Contrary to the decree of 1 December (which had entered the Penal Code under article 58), appeals from the accused were allowed for three days after a sentence had been passed, and the use of defence lawyers was again permitted.[87] This opened the possibility of a public show trial. Four days later, on 15 August 1936, *Pravda* announced that the NKVD had uncovered a Trotzkyist–Zinoviev plot to murder Stalin and other leaders, and that these 'enemies of the people' were the same who had also killed Kirov.[88]

Three days later, on 19 August 1936—which, by coincidence, was also the day the official theatre season in Moscow began[89]—the show trial could begin. The person who had done the *mise en scène*, Stalin, had, in the meantime, left the scene; on 13 August he arrived at the Black Sea where he would spent the coming six weeks on holiday in Sochi. However, how well he prepared the show can be gathered from his involvement in the preparations, including the production of 'confessions'.

4.2.2. *How 'Confessions' were Secured*

In 1939 chief prosecutor Andrei Vyshinsky published a book with the title *The Theory of Legal Evidence in Soviet Law*. In this work he postulated that 'confession is a queen over all sorts of evidence'.[90] Confession also happens to be the essence of show trials. Before we turn to the trial itself, it is important to examine the way the evidence for the trial was collected. It consisted almost exclusively of self-incriminating 'confessions'. How were these astounding confessions obtained? At the time, some suggested the defendants had been given chemical substances, or were hypnotised. Another theory was that actors (who resembled the more well-known defendants) sat in the courtroom, rather than the Old Bolshevik heroes themselves. Others thought that torture had elicited the confessions.[91] There is some substance to this last charge, but the issue depends on how torture is defined. According to Khrushchev, extreme torture only became, on Stalin's initiative, standard practice by 1937.[92] However the defendants of the 1936 show trial were certainly under great pressure. The key defendants, Zinoviev and Kamenev, were broken men after years of imprisonment. They had been twice excluded from the Party and then readmitted after submitting to the Party line. They may have hoped that the trial was the final humiliation to undergo before they were welcomed back into the arms of the Party. Or they may have hoped that if the death sentence was pronounced, it would be commuted immediately to a lesser penalty. There is some dispute as to whether or not they were tortured to extract confessions. Yet this does not seem to have been the case, at least for these two defendants. Yet those arrested and prepared for trial were certainly placed under enormous psychological pressure. Originally, some 300 'Trotzkyists' had been rounded up from prisons and the Gulag and brought to Moscow where they had been prepared for possible use in the trial.[93] Within such a large group, some prisoners would inevitably be prepared to confess anything and denounce anybody if it would help to save themselves, or at least the lives of their family members. Some of those brought to trial were actually, as we shall see, provocateurs—pseudo-defendants working for the NKVD who were instructed to denounce some of the real defendants.

When the usual interrogative methods (sleep deprivation, sub-standard food and general bullying) used on Kamenev did not produce the desired result, Stalin was annoyed. He reprimanded one of the interrogators, Mironov: 'Now, then, don't tell me anymore that Kamenev, or this or that prisoner, is able to withstand that pressure. Don't come to report to me until you have Kamenev's confession in this briefcase!'[94] Further 'pressure' was brought on Kamenev, including Yezhov's threat to shoot Kamenev's son if he did not submit. During a critical phase of the interrogations, Stalin's secretary would phone every two hours to find out whether Kamenev and Mrachkovsky had been 'broken' (had confessed).[95] Stalin's instructions on how to obtain a confession on another occasion had been: 'Mount your prisoners and don't dismount till they have given you the testimony!'[96] At one point in the summer of 1936, Kamenev and Zinoviev were allowed to consult with each other. As a consequence, they 'agreed to go on trial on condition that Stalin would confirm his promise to them of executing neither themselves nor their followers, in the presence of the whole Politburo'.[97] According to Orlov, an NKVD chief, they were then brought to the Kremlin, but instead of the full Politburo only Stalin, Voroshilov and Yezhov were present. Stalin explained that they formed the special 'commission' of the Politburo authorised to hear the case. The two defendants asked for a guarantee that their lives would be spared in exchange for confessions. Stalin made it clear that they were in no position to make demands, but also gave them false hope, telling them:

> First: that the trial is directed not against them, but against Trotzky, the principal enemy of the Party; Second: if we did not shoot them [Zinoviev and Kamenev] when they fought actively against the Central Committee, then why should we shoot them after they have helped the Central Committee in the struggle against Trotzky? Third, the comrades forget also ... that we are Bolsheviks, disciples and followers of Lenin, and that we don't want to shed the blood of Old Bolsheviks, no matter how grave their past sins against the Party.

Zinoviev and Kamenev consented to go on trial 'if it were promised that none of the Old Bolsheviks would be executed, that their families would not be persecuted and that in the future the death sentence would not be applied to any of the former members of the opposition'. Stalin's reply was, according to Orlov, 'That goes without saying.'[98] As soon as Zinoviev and Kamenev had made what they thought was a deal with Stalin, their surrender was rewarded: by mid-July 1936, they were held in much better conditions of detention—more like a sanatorium than a prison.[99] They were no longer subject to the 'conveyor belt' (non-stop interrogations by a series of NKVD interrogators) that had deprived them of sleep.[100] The other main defendants—Bakayev, Dreitzer, Mrachkovsky—confessed between 13 and 21 July. Mrachkovsky had endured the 'conveyor belt' for hours in a row.[101] In the end, all but Smirnov confessed, and even he seemed to be close to a confession by the 5th of August.[102] Two days later, the prosecutor, Andrei Vyshinsky, felt confident that he had a sufficiently large pool of 'confessing' oppositionists to present a list of twelve to be indicted. Stalin changed parts of Vyshinsky's draft indictment and added two more names (Moissei Lurye and Nathan Lurye). A revised indictment draft reached Stalin on 10 August, and Stalin again added two more names—Ter-Vaganyan and Evdokimov.[103]

These men were all Old Bolsheviks for whom the Party was sacred. For the sake of the Party, they were expected to make great personal sacrifices. Zinoviev was asked by Molotov:

> How many times have you lied to the Party? How many times have your lies damaged the Party? You are now asked to calumniate yourself for the good of the Party. At a time when Trotzky is trying to split the workers' movement, and the Germans are preparing to attack us, your lies will undoubtedly be of help to the Party. That is undeniable. So what is there to discuss? If the interests of the Party demand it, it is our duty to sacrifice not only our miserable reputations but our very lives. Although, objectively, you are not being asked to lie. Objectively, everything you did was [a] betrayal of the Party's interest.[104]

Molotov assumed that if Zinoviev and Kamenev played the game in the show trial well, they would be pardoned and he told Stalin so.[105] That belief would put Molotov himself for a while in the danger zone.[106]

The scriptwriter for the trial was Stalin, who followed the interrogations in every detail.[107] Russian historian Roman Brackman, author of a recent biography of Stalin, writes:

> The interrogators had to force the defendants to confess their roles in the plot, the details of which had been provided by Stalin who probably convinced himself that the plot indeed existed. But to buttress his conviction, he felt the need to force the defendants to confess their involvement in it. When some of his subordinates dared to suggest that many people at home or abroad would not believe these accusations against Old Bolsheviks, Stalin's contemptuous reply was: 'Never mind, they'll swallow it.'[108]

Not only was the audience to be fooled; the accused were also misled. Before the trial began, Yagoda and Yezhov met with the chief defendants—Zinoviev, Kamenev, Evdikomov, Mrachkovsky, Bakayev and Ter-Vaganyan. They were reminded of Stalin's promise that their lives would be spared if they all played their roles as expected. Yezhov also warned them that the whole group would suffer if there was a single attempt at 'treachery'.[109]

During the trial, Yagoda would monitor the performance of the accused through a loudspeaker from an adjacent room.[110] In the Kremlin, Lazar Kaganovich ('Iron Lazar', the Politburo member who had been one of the chief people responsible for the genocidal famine in the Ukraine) was entrusted with controlling the course of the trial.[111] Each day, protocols of the court proceedings were brought or transmitted to Stalin. His hand had been in almost every detail of the trial, including selecting the cast of defendants, rewording the indictment prepared by Vyshinsky, and pre-determining the sentences to be meted out by the court.[112] His invented plot for this play was guided by his paranoia and a desire for revenge against Trotsky and others who had crossed his path, rather than on credible evidence.

One would have expected that Stalin would want to be close to the trial and watch the show. Indeed, there was a story circulating that Stalin watched the show trials from behind a curtained window overlooking the October Hall where the trials took place. Stalin could also listen to the trial, transmitted from microphones placed in the October Hall through a loudspeaker in his office in the Kremlin.[113] This was probably true for the show trials of 1937 and 1938, but in August 1936[114] Stalin was far away from Moscow. This may have been a deliberate tactic to obscure his role in the trial. Neither the Central Committee nor most members of the Politburo were really aware of what was going on. Many were also away on summer holidays. Stalin had, in the preparations, worked closely with an eager Yezhov, a reluctant Yagoda and a servile Vyshinsky. But Stalin himself was the stage manager, he 'personally conceived, initiated, and directed the entire process, including the planning, preparation, and actual conduct of the purge trials', as Tucker and Cohen concluded in their study.[115] Recent research has made this even clearer. Simon S. Montefiore, for instance, found that 'Stalin set to work on the script for the Zinoviev trial, reveling in his hyperbolic talents as a hack playwright. The new archives reveal how he even dictated the words of the new Procurator-General, Andrei Vyshinsky, who kept notes of his leader's perorations.'[116]

The trial was to be a travesty of justice. As one historian put it, 'The spectacle about to be performed would not be a trial with elements of a show, but a show with elements of a trial.'[117] As in real theatre performances, there were rehearsals. An NKVD chief (who later defected) wrote, 'The last week before the opening of the trial was spent in giving detailed instructions to the defendants, who were made to rehearse their parts under the direction of ProsecutorVyshinsky and the NKVD interrogators.'[118] We do not know in detail what they were told, but we know that in the third show trial the defendants were instructed that if they did not give the necessary testimony, torture would continue even after the trial.[119] Similar pressure may have also played a role in the first show trial.

Press coverage had been fixed by Yezhov and Kaganovich: every day both *Pravda* and *Izvestiya* would publish a full-page account of the trial. Stalin had instructed that the trial should begin on 19 August 1936. He could rely on Vyshinsky—they had once shared a prison cell together in their underground days before the revolution. Vyshinsky had already conducted a successful show trial for Stalin in 1928.[120] Now, in August 1936, Yezhov and Kaganovich reported the trial's progress to Stalin every day—altogether 87 packages of trial-related materials were sent to Sochi.[121] Stalin had been involved in every phase of the trial's preparations. As Vishinsky's biographer, A. Vaksberg, noted: 'The final version of the Prosecutor-General's speech for the prosecution—a model of impassioned eloquence by a great orator—was edited and approved by the Leader and Teacher [Stalin] before he set off on holiday to the shores of the Black Sea.'[122]

The script was Stalin's, based on drafts from the prosecutor, Vyshinsky, and Lev Sheinin, chief investigator at the Procurator's office, who, ironically, was also the author of various real plays for theatre performances.[123] The sixteen players in the show trial belonged to two different groups and were not all known to each other. One group of eleven defendants belonged to a 'united opposition bloc' of Old Bolsheviks who had opposed Stalin mainly in the 1926–1927 period. A younger group of five defendants were members of the German Communist Party who had emigrated to the Soviet Union, and worked in the Comintern department where they had been writing anti-Trotzkyist articles. Yet in the trial it was implied that they constituted the link between the Zinoviev group and Trotzky in exile, with the German Gestapo acting as go-between and facilitator.[124]

4.3. What Happened in Court during the Trial

For the trial itself, our main source is a much condensed printed version of the court proceedings, edited to fit the propaganda needs of Stalin and his entourage.[125] For example in this official document all sixteen defendants are identified simply as 'employees'. In fact, many had held outstanding positions and it is worth recalling some biographical data here:

1. **Grigory Y. Zinoviev**, chairman of the Comintern (1919), editor of *Pravda* (1917), full member of the Politburo since 1921, member of the ruling triumvirate with Stalin and Kamenev, 1923–1924, head of the Leningrad Soviet before Kirov. Close friend of Lenin.
2. **Lev B. Kamenev**, head of the Moscow Soviet section (1919–1925), founding member and later chairman of the Politburo, member of the ruling triumvirate with Stalin and Zinoviev, 1923–1924. Close friend of Lenin.
3. **Sergei V. Mrachkovsky**: hero of the Russian Civil War in Siberia and the Far East; Deputy People's Commissar for Agriculture.
4. **Vagarshak A. Ter-Vaganyan**: former leader of the Military Department of the Moscow Committee of the Party, leader of the Armenian Communist Party; founding editor of the Party's scientific monthly *Under the Banner of Marxism*.
5. **Ivan N. Smirnov**: founder of the Bolshevik Party; leader of the 5th Army that defeated Kolchak's White Guards in the civil war; member of the Executive Committee of the Russian Communist Party (1920–1923), People's Commissar for Communications (1923–1927); expelled from Party in 1927.
6. **Ivan F. Bakayev**: former chairman of the Petrograd (Leningrad) Cheka, a major figure in the civil war who was also a member of the Central Committee.

These 'employees'—like some of those who would be facing similar show trials in 1937 and 1938—were the cream of the Old Bolsheviks. Zinoview, Kamenev and the absent Trotzky had been named in Lenin's will as his potential successors[126] The remaining ten defendants were a mixed group, including Old Bolsheviks and the five young members of the German Communist Party.[127] Three, perhaps four, among the sixteen accused were pseudo-defendants—accomplices of the NKVD mobilised as provocateurs and false witnesses for the judicial frame-up: Valentine Olberg, Fritz David and Berman-Yurin and, to a lesser extent, Isak Reingold, a former acquaintance of Kamenev, and Richard V. Pickel, the former head of the secretariat of Zinoviev in Leningrad (before Kirov succeeded Zinoviev).[128] At least three of them saw themselves more as actors executing secret NKVD directives rather than as genuine defendants in this trial.[129] The real defendants had been carefully selected. As an NKVD insider explained later:

> At the beginning Stalin planned to stage the first Moscow trial with at least fifty defendants; then, as the investigation progressed, that figure had been decreased several times and finally reduced by Stalin to sixteen men. For the trial only those of the accused were selected who promised to repeat in court the false testimony which they had signed at the NKVD. Even some of those who agreed to play the part of conspirators and terrorists were not admitted to the trial, because the NKVD chiefs were not completely sure that they would scrupulously carry out their promises.[130]

The chief target of this trial was not in court: Lev Trotzky was in exile in Norway.[131] Some of those in the dock who had been associated in the past with Trotzky had to serve as scapegoats for the absent Trotzky.

The show trial opened on 19 August 1936. The scene of the trial was the House of Trade Unions, where in early December 1934 the slain Sergei Kirov had laid in state. While there were larger halls in the building, the sixteen defendants were tried in the October Room, a small hall able to accommodate only three hundred people. The room was re-decorated in various shades of red for the purpose of the trial. The judge's desk was covered with bright red cloth and the chairs were embossed with the Soviet Union's coat of arms. The three judges and the court's president, Military Jurist Vasiliy Ulrich, sat in the centre on throne-like, decorated chairs.[132] Zinoviev, Kamenev and the other 14 defendants sat in four rows, within a fenced wooden dock on the right side. Opposite them, near the left wall, Prosecutor Vyshinsky sat at a small table.[133] At the back stood uniformed guards, their rifles fixed with bayonets. There was no jury,[134] and no defence lawyer was present. Before the trial, the defendants had been made to promise that they would defend themselves.[135] President of the Court, Ulrich, consequently announced that 'all the accused [had] declined the services of counsel for defence'. They would, he said, defend themselves personally.[136] No relatives of the defendants were allowed among the public in the hall.[137]

In fact, the public consisted predominantly of NKVD personnel in civilian clothes.[138] On Stalin's orders, no member of the Central Committee of the Party or the government was admitted.[139] There were a few carefully selected guests of honour—some 30 foreign journalists and diplomats.[140] The International Association of Lawyers had been invited by the authorities to attend and it had sent Joseph Edelman (an American) and Denis Noel Pritt, Dudley Collard and Robert Lazarus (all British) to the trial.[141] Many of the foreigners may not have understood Russian. One wonders whether they could, as they entered the courtroom, read the writing on the wall: a banner, allegedly from the 'Workers of Moscow', which read 'To the mad dogs—a dog's death.'[142]

This slogan would at the end of the trial be alluded to by Andrei Vyshinsky, Stalin's Prosecutor. He had already helped shape the pre-trial interrogations. Years later, after de-Stalinisation, a historical commission of the Politburo would conclude that this son of Polish nobility from Odessa, who was a former Menshevik, now played a 'provocative role in the judicial inquiries'. Like Nikolai Yezhov from the NKVD, the chief prosecutor had pressured the investigators to obtain direct evidence from the accused. As a report to the Politburo in the 1950s found, 'When the evidence was analysed, he demanded sharper political conclusions and generalizations and, essentially, the falsification of cases.'[143] Vyshinsky's biographer wrote on this trial:

> ... Vyshinsky was himself the principal falsifier. In the most important cases the indictments were compiled by him personally before the investigation was even over, and the drafts were then presented to Stalin so that he could edit them, ascribing to the accused other 'crimes' as he saw fit. [...] Vyshinsky fulfilled his wish by making an appropriate entry in the indictment, after which the investigators had no difficulty in obtaining the necessary confession from the 'assassin'.[144]

The trial began shortly after noon with the reading of the indictment by the secretary of the court. The indictment was partly based on the charges issued at a previous secret trial held in January 1935 against Zinoviev and Kamenev. At that closed January trial there had been 19 defendants. Of these, only four were at this new trial; the rest were not even there as witnesses,[145] probably because they had already been executed. The indictment was based on Article 58 of the Criminal Code of the Russian Soviet Federative Socialist Republic (RSFSR), drawn from the 1 December 1934 decree Stalin had drafted immediately upon hearing of the assassination of Sergei Kirov.

The relevant paragraph in the article (58.8) referred to 'The perpetration of terrorist acts, directed against representatives of Soviet authority or activists of revolutionary workers' and peasants' organizations, and participation in the performance of such acts, even by persons not belonging to a counter-revolutionary organization ...'[146]

The underlying charge was 'terrorism', a code word for anti-Stalinism. As one of Stalin's biographers explained: '"terrorism" simply signified "any doubt about the policies or character of Stalin". All his political opponents were *per se* assassins. More than two "terrorists" was a "conspiracy" and, putting together such killers from different factions created a "Unified Centre" of astonishing global ... reach.'[147]

The indictment claimed that the preliminary and court investigations of that secret trial held in January 1935 had 'established that for a number of years this so-called "Moscow Centre" guided the counter-revolutionary activities of diverse underground groups of Zinovievites, including the counter-revolutionary activities of the Leningrad group of *Nikolayev-Kotolynov* which on Dec. 1, 1934, foully murdered Comrade S.M. *Kirov*'. At that secret trial Zinoviev and Kamenev had denied that they had any part in the murder, but in the end accepted that they bore moral and political responsibility for the assassination.

The long indictment read out on the afternoon of 19 August 1936 claimed that since January 1935 new facts had surfaced which showed that the accused not only 'knew their adherents in Leningrad were inclined towards terrorism', but 'were the direct organizers of the assassination of Comrade S.M. *Kirov*'. According to the indictment, the investigation also revealed that Zinoviev, Kamenev and others accused in this court were the 'initiators and organizers of attempts on the lives of other leaders of the Communist Party of the Soviet Union and of the Soviet Government'. In particular, it named Stalin, Voroshilov, Kaganovich, Orzhonikidze, Zhdanov, Kosior and Postyshev as their targets. Furthermore the indictment claimed that the Zinovievites had acted in conjunction with Trotzkyites and with L. Trotzky himself since 1932. The alleged goal of the Trotzkyite–Zinovievite bloc, according to the indictment, was 'to seize power at all costs', by terrorist means—'the most detestable method of fighting'. The conspirators chose the strategy of political assassination due to lack of support from the working class, it claimed, and due to their own ideological bankruptcy. The indictment quoted from a 'confession' which Zinoviev, 'compelled by the weight of evidence', had allegedly made, namely that 'The main object which the Trotzkyite–Zinovievite Centre pursued was the assassination of the leaders of the CPSU [Communist Party of the Soviet Union], and in the first place the assassination of *Stalin* and *Kirov*.'[148] 'Confessions' along the same lines made by others during the investigation phase were also quoted, including a statement, attributed to Kamenev, stressing the necessity of killing Stalin, the head of the Party and state. Kamenev was quoted as saying that 'heads are peculiar in that they do not grow back again'. The indictment concluded that 'there is no doubt left that the Trotzkyite–Zinovievite *bloc* had turned into a group of unprincipled, political adventurers and assassins striving at only one thing, namely, to make their way to power even through terrorism'. The chief instigator behind this was, according to the indictment, Lev Trotzky. His son, Lev Sedov, was said to have acted as go-between and liaison to the conspirators in the Soviet Union, including the 'Trotzkyite agent' Olberg, who allegedly was arrested travelling with a Honduran passport, which he had obtained 'with the aid of the German Secret Police (Gestapo)'. This passport was presented as an 'exhibit' during the trial—the only material evidence in the case against the sixteen.

The case rested almost exclusively on the confessions of the accused about their own misdeeds, and those of their alleged fellow conspirators. Some witnesses, under threat of being accused themselves, also testified against those in the dock. This group included Ms. Safonova, who testified against her former husband I. Smirnov. After Khrushchev had informed the 20th Party Congress about the true nature of Stalinism (on 25 February 1956), she would explain that her testimony, like that of others who had testified at the trial and the pre-trial investigation, 'did not correspond to reality 90 percent of the time'.[149]

The link with fascist Germany and its Gestapo (roughly the equivalent of the NKVD) was a side theme in the indictment. Two of the accused, M. Lurye and N. Lurye in particular, were included in the cast of defendants by Stalin himself to suggest a plausible link to the German Secret State Police. Yet the main tie, the indictment stressed, was the one between Trotzky and the 'Moscow Centre' of Zinoviev et al. Both were now linked to the assassination of Kirov. Kirov's murder was portrayed as a first blow in a planned series of assassinations to eliminate the leadership of the USSR.[150] Zinoviev was quoted from pre-trial testimony as saying, 'while speaking of the necessity of assassinating Comrade Kirov as Comrade Stalin's closest assistant ... It is not enough to fell the oak; all the young oaks growing around it must be felled too.' These words were dictated by Stalin himself.[151] Later in the trial another of Stalin's own additions was again spoken by Kamenev: 'Stalin's leadership has become as solid as granite, and it would be foolish to hope that this granite will begin to crack.'[152]

The indictment charged the 16 accused of organising 'in the period 1932–1936 a united Trotzkyite–Zinovievite Centre ... in the city of Moscow with the object of committing a number of terroristic acts against the leaders of the CPSU and the Soviet Government for the purpose of seizing power' and of having 'carried out the foul murder of Comrade S.M. *Kirov* on December 1, 1934'. It ended by stating that all but one of the accused 'have fully admitted their guilt of the charges preferred against them'. The exception was Ivan N. Smirnov who 'categorically denies that he took part in the terroristic activities of the united Trotzkyite–Zinovievite Centre'. However, the indictment listed statements made by his ex-wife A.N. Safonova, and by his alleged fellow conspirators, that served to incriminate him as well. The indictment, signed by Vyshinsky, also instructed that Trotzky and his son, 'in the event of their being discovered on the territory of the U.S.S.R., are subject to immediate arrest and trial'. While Trotzky and son were not in the courtroom, E.A. Dreitzer, the former chief of Trotzky's bodyguard, was in the dock to suggest proximity and guilt by association.

The opening session concluded with the President asking the accused whether they pleaded guilty as charged. All but Smirnov and Holtzman accepted the charges, although they denied 'personal participation in the preparation of terroristic acts'. When such apparent dissent arose, some defendants would pitch in to denounce others. Dreitzer, according to the Report of Court Proceedings, objected to Smirnov's denial: 'I am surprised at the assertions of Smirnov, who, according to his words, both knew and did not know, spoke and did not speak, acted and did not act. This is not true!'[153] Some defendants also tried to shift blame to other defendants. Zinoviev, for instance, said at one point, 'Smirnov, in my opinion, displayed more activity than anyone else, and we regarded him as the undisputed lead[er] of the Trotzkyite part of the *bloc*, as the man best informed about Trotzky's views, and fully sharing these views.'[154]

After a 15 minute break—it was already late afternoon—the examination of the accused followed. Mrachkovsky, the first to be interrogated in public, was accused of conducting 'Trotzkyite anti-Soviet work' since 1923.[155] However, according to his testimony, 'The terrorist *bloc* of the Trotzkyites and the Zinovievites was only formed at the end of 1932.' There was reference to a 'letter of Trotzky's, written in invisible ink'—but no such letter was produced as evidence in court. It was said that Mrachkovsky, 'after reading it, burnt it for reasons of secrecy'.[156] Part of the proceedings took the form of a defendant being asked to read passages from his own 'confession' as laid down in the signed interrogation protocols (which in some cases had been prepared for signature before the interrogations had even begun!). The prosecutor would also quote from pre-trial examinations and the defendants, except for minor details, confirmed now in public—to the extent that the predominantly NKVD audience could be considered 'the public'—what was 'agreed upon' behind closed doors. Sometimes the accused gave only very brief, self-incriminating answers. We do not know whether the explanations offered in court are summaries or directly transcribed. A typical excerpt reads:

Vyshinsky: Did you receive from Trotzky instructions on terrorism as a means of struggle?

Smirnov: Yes[157]

Mrachkovsky then goes on to tell the Court about the activities of the Trotzkyite–Zinovievite terrorist Centre.

Vyshinsky: In that centre there were you, Kamenev, Smirnov, Mrachkovsky and Ter-Vaganyan?

Zinoviev: Yes.

Vyshinsky: So you all organized the assassination of Kirov?

Zinoviev: Yes.

Vyshinsky: So you all assassinated Comrade Kirov.

Zinoviev: Yes.

Vyshinsky: Sit down.[158]

What the Report of Proceedings tells us and what actually happened in court may not be quite the same.[159] That even Smirnov confessed with a monosyllabic 'Yes' is doubtful, as reports on his behaviour in court showed that he used irony and other devices to distance himself from the mechanical routines prescribed by the prepared script. Precautions had been taken in case one of the accused should attempt to deviate from the script. The following strategy was agreed upon, as one NKVD chief later revealed:

> In the courtroom, among the 'public' were seated several groups of specially trained officers of the NKVD. At the first attempt of a defendant to expose the judicial frame-up, these groups were ready, at a signal from the prosecutor, to spring up from their chairs and with loud outcries drown the words of the rebellious defendant. The commotion was then to be used by the President of the Court as a pretext for declaring a recess.[160]

The culprit who had deviated from the script could then be given the necessary 'treatment' in an adjacent room. Failing that to achieve the desired result, he would not be brought back into the court. Judging from the available transcripts we have, this measure was not necessary. The interrogators had done their work well. Almost everybody 'played' their role as Stalin had script it.

One of the accused, Bakayev, admitted to having met Nikolayev, Kirov's murderer, in Leningrad, and to having discussed details of the crime with him. Kamenev also admitted to having been involved in the plot, saying 'The blow [against Kirov] was planned and prepared on the order of the centre of which I was a member, and I regarded it as the fulfilment of the task we had set ourselves.'[161]

The choice of assassination as a tactic was portrayed in the examination as weapon of last resort. Reingold 'recalled' that back in 1932 Zinoviev had argued that 'although terror is incompatible with Marxism, at the present moment these considerations must be abandoned. There are no other methods available of fighting the leaders of the Party and the Government ... Stalin combines in himself all the strength and firmness of the present Party leadership. Therefore Stalin must be put out of the way in the first place.' Kamenev enlarged on this 'theory', adding that the former oppositional methods, namely, attempts to win the masses, combining with the Rightists, and banking on economic problems, had failed. That left only terroristic acts against 'Stalin and his closest comrades-in-arms, Kirov, Voroshilov, Kaganovich, Orjonikidze, Postyshev, Kosior and the others' as a means of struggle.[162]

According to Reingold's testimony, summarised in the available proceedings, Zinoviev and Kamenev insisted that 'every advantage be ... taken of legal possibilities for the purpose of "crawling on the belly into the Party"—this he said was Zinoviev's favourite expression—and of winning the confidence of the Party, particularly Stalin's. After this confidence had been restored, strictly secret terroristic work was to be carried out in parallel with open work.'[163] (Reingold was probably a pseudo-defendant, planted among the 16 defendants due to his former close ties with Kamenev). Both Kamenev and Zinoviev admitted to this 'monstrous plan' (Vyshinsky's words), portrayed as a coup d' état. According to Reingold's summarised testimony, this would lead to a seizure of power after which Trotzky would be recalled from exile abroad, and with his support 'all those who were most devoted to Stalin were to be removed from Party and Soviet posts'.[164]

Each of the cross-examinations revealed more details of an alleged plot or sub-plots. Bakayev, for instance, testified that in October 1934 Kamenev had already organised an attempt on Stalin's life in Moscow—a 'failure', like another attempt (equally fictional), the year before, 'confessed' by another probable pseudo-defendant, Richard Pickel.[165] Pickel, a member of the Soviet Writers' Union, had visited Spitzbergen 'for creative work' in 1934—hardly the place to conspire against the Kremlin. However, at the trial even such an innocent 'fact' was turned by the prosecutor against the accused. In this case, Pickel's sojourn close to the North Pole was said to serve 'to wipe out all traces and save their terrorist organization'.[166]

The morning session of the second day began with the examination of Lev Borisovich Kamenev, the former head of the Moscow Soviet and, briefly in late 1917, nominally the first President of the Soviet Union. When he gave his 'evidence', he still displayed a certain dignity but soon lost it in the cross-examination.[167] His opening sentence must have come straight out of the 'script': 'The terrorist conspiracy was organized and guided by myself, Zinoviev and Trotzky.'[168] Vyshinsky then set out to expose Kamenev's apparent 'double-dealing' in his attempt to regain a central place in the Communist Party. Here is a typical extract from the pre-arranged exchange of words:

> *Vyshinsky*: What appraisal should be given of the articles and statements you wrote in 1933, in which you expressed loyalty to the Party? Deception?
> *Kamenev*: No, worse than deception.
> *Vyshinsky*: Perfidy?
> *Kamenev*: Worse.
> *Vyshinsky*: Worse than deception, worse than perfidy—find the word. Treason.
> *Kamenev*: You have found it.
> *Vyshinsky*: Accused Zinoviev, do you confirm this?
> *Zinoviev*: Yes.[169]

In this courtroom spectacle, past Bolshevik heroes had become present anti-Soviet villains. The main defendant in the dock was Grigory Zinoviev. Previously a great orator, he now appeared cowed after years of imprisonment, gasping for air due to his asthma.[170] He 'confessed' that at the secret trial in January 1935 he had not told the court the 'whole truth', adding that he was prepared to do so now. In self-accusations he 'revealed' that 'After the murder of Sergei Mironovich Kirov our perfidy went to such lengths that I sent an obituary about Kirov to *Pravda*' (a text that had not been published).[171] Zinoviev's cross-examination added little to the accusations in the indictment, except for references to alleged links with the German Gestapo and its chief Heinrich Himmler. More ominous was Zinoviev's name-dropping of Old Bolsheviks, listing them as potential allies he had hoped to win against Stalin. Many of them would soon also appear in show trials. Zinoviev's public examination by the prosecutor was relatively short, if we can believe the transcripts in the Report of Court Proceedings.

Zinoviev was followed by a witness, Smirnov's former wife, A. Safonova. Smirnov's denials about the extent of his involvement with the 'Trotzkyite centre' required the testimony of his former wife to fill the gaps and implicate him in the plot, which she did.[172] Smirnov's own turn came in the evening session of 20 August. He, a former leader of the Red Army who had defeated Admiral Kolchak and the 'White Guards' on the eastern front in the civil war, and who later had become a member of the praesidium of the eleventh Bolshevik Conference, was now portrayed as 'the closest friend of Trotzky and the actual organiser and leader of the underground Trotzkyite counter-revolutionary activities in the U.S.S.R.'.[173] Smirnov apparently put up some verbal resistance during the public trial. As a consequence, much of his testimony was abridged and only summarised in the published proceedings.[174] Nevertheless, traces of his resistance remain in his testimony—for example when he was interrogated about the 'Trotzkyite centre'. His sarcasm must have kept Vyshinsky on guard.[175] An example:

> *Vyshinky*: So when did you leave the centre?
> *Smirnov*: I did not intend to resign; there was nothing to resign from.
> *Vyshinsky*: Did the centre exist?
> *Smirnov*: What sort of a centre ...
> *Vyshinsky*: Mrachkovsky, did the centre exist?
> *Mrachkovsky*: Yes.
> *Vyshinsky*: Zinoviev, did the centre exist?
> *Zinoviev*: Yes.
> *Vyshinsky*: Evdokimov, did the centre exist?
> *Edokimov*: Yes.
> *Vyshinsky*: Bakayev, did the centre exist?
> *Bakayev*: Yes.
> *Vyshinsky*: How, then, Smirnov, can you take the liberty to maintain that no centre existed?[176]

The trial record noted that 'Under the weight of all these irrefutable facts, Smirnov at last admits that it was he and no one else who was the head of the Trotzkyite organization.'[177] As Smirnov had been in prison since January 1933, it was not very credible to suggest he was a leader of a terrorist centre supposedly operating for the past four years. At one point, when a fellow defendant incriminated him as the leader of the conspiracy, Smirnov turned on him sardonically: 'You want a leader! Well, take me!' Vyshinsky interjected by explaining that this was said 'in rather a jocular way'.[178] Of all the defendants, Smirnov managed, within the little room for manoeuvre that was granted to them, to sow confusion; his public confession was only partial.[179]

Next in line was pseudo-defendant Valentine Olberg. He 'confessed' his personal connection with the Gestapo, saying that 'in 1933 there began organized systematic connection between the German Trotzkyites and the German fascist police'.[180] He admitted to travelling on a Honduran passport into the USSR. Oddly, the passport was allegedly *given* to him by the Gestapo, but according to the proceedings he also had to *pay* a large sum of money for it. Olberg admitted to being directly involved in a plan for the assassination of Stalin in Moscow on 1 May 1936.[181]

The second day closed with the cross-examination of yet another pseudo-defendant, Berman-Yurin. He admitted to yet another failed (because fictional) attempt on Comrade Stalin's life and also claimed to have been inspired by Trotzky: 'He [Trotzky] said that the terroristic act should, if possible, be timed to take place at a plenum or at the congress of the Comintern, so that the shot at Stalin would ring out in a large assembly. This would have a tremendous repercussion far beyond the borders of the Soviet Union and would give rise to a mass movement all over the world. This would be an historical political event of world significance.'[182]

The third day began with the ritualistic examination of E.S. Holtzman, a genuine ex-Trotzkyite and former friend of Smirnov. He recalled meetings in Berlin with Trotzky's son Sedov who was said to have invited him to accompany him to Copenhagen to see his father (there in exile before moving to Norway). Holtzman: 'I agreed, but told him that we could not go together for reasons of secrecy. I arranged with Sedov to be in Copenhagen within two or three days, to put up at the Hotel Bristol and meet him there. I went to the hotel straight from the station and in the lounge met Sedov. About 10 a.m. we went to Trotzky.'[183] Vyshinsky prodded him: 'So Trotzky plainly told you that the fundamental task now (that is in the autumn of 1932) was to assassinate Comrade Stalin? You remember for sure?' Holtzman: Yes.[184]

Probably neither the audience nor the rest of those present in the courtroom (except Holtzman who knew it was a lie) were aware that the Hotel Bristol in Copenhagen—the alleged venue of the 1932 conspiratorial meeting—had been demolished in 1917, a fact which also demolished this story (but only after the trial was long over).[185] In addition, it later turned out that he could not possibly have met Sedov in Copenhagen, as Sedov was taking examinations at that same time in a technical institute in Berlin.[186] When a Danish Social-Democratic newspaper revealed that the Bristol Hotel had ceased to exist 19 years before the trial, the defendants had already been executed.[187] Apart from Smirnov's, Holtzman's was the only confession that was incomplete. Perhaps he was inspired by Smirnov's subliminal resistance. Despite his claim not to share Trotzky's view about the necessity of terror, Vyshinsky managed to get him to confess that he nevertheless remained a member of the Trotzkyite organisation.[188]

In the evening session of 21 August the examination of the pseudo-defendant Fritz David (aka I.I. Kruglansky) followed. He declared, inter alia, that in alleged meetings with Trotzky he learned from him that 'the advent of the Trotzkyites to power in the

U.S.S.R. was possible only if Stalin was physically destroyed'.[189] He confessed that he had been unable to commit the terroristic act 'because it was impossible to get near Comrade Stalin'.[190]

Some ominous name-dropping occurred during the trial. Zinoviev had been the first to implicate others in his testimony, and later Reingold 'confessed' that not only had the Trotzkyites and the Zinovievites joined forces, but negotiations were carried on about joint activity with 'Leftists' like Shatskin, Lominadze and Sten, as well as with representatives of the Right like Rykov, Bukharin and Tomsky.[191] In total, 123 individuals were incriminated in this trial, not counting those already in the court who often incriminated each other.[192]

At the end of the 21 August session, Vyshinsky cultivated these cues when he announced:

> At preceding sessions some of the accused (Kamenev, Zinoviev and Reingold) in their testimony referred to Tomsky, Bukharin, Rykov, Uglanov, Radek, Pyatakov, Serebryakov and Sokolnikov as being to a greater or lesser degree involved in the criminal counter-revolutionary activities for which the accused in the present case are being tried. I consider it necessary to inform the Court that yesterday I have orders to institute an investigation of these statements of the accused in regard to Tomsky, Rykov, Bukharin, Uglanov, Radek and Pyatakov, and that in accordance with the results of this investigation the office of the State Attorney will institute legal proceedings in this matter.[193]

Vyshinsky's statement at the end of the day's session was printed in the newspapers the next morning, together with a demand from a workers' meeting at the Dynamo Factory that this should be 'pitilessly investigated'.[194] Vyshinsky's words ('I have orders ...') did not make explicit from whom the State Attorney of the USSR took his orders. But it could be only from Stalin.

This list of names was a time bomb, pointing to events to come in the next two years—presaging the purge of almost the entire Old Bolshevik elite. Mikhail Tomsky, the head of the Combined State Publishing House and a former civil war hero, saw the writing on the wall and shot himself the same day, leaving behind a letter in which he tried to prove his innocence.[195] Stalin learned of this suicide the next morning. Kaganovich, Yezhov and Ordzhonikidze wrote to him, with a cynicism typical for Stalin and his entourage, 'We have no doubt that Tomsky ... knowing that now it is no longer possible to hide his place in the Zinoviev–Trotzkyite band had decided to dissimulate ... by suicide ...' Alexei Rykov (the former Premier who had ruled the

Soviet Union from 1925 to 1928 together with Bukharin and Stalin) having read this list in *Pravda* and heard about Tomsky's fate, was also on the point of committing suicide but his family held him back.[196] Not all of those mentioned by Vyshinsky were arrested immediately. Stalin decided that Karl Radek, a German revolutionary who had become secretary of the Comintern, could be a 'useful idiot' (to use one of Lenin's terms) and ordered on 19 August '... to delay for the moment the question of Radek's arrest and to let him publish in *Izvestiya* a signed article ...'[197] Radek duly complied, writing in support of the liquidation of the 16 defendants in the dock.[198]

The climax of the trial was Vyshinsky's long rhetorical summary of the 'crimes'. As one of Stalin's biographers puts it:

> Procurator-General Vyshinsky brilliantly combined the indignant humbug of a Victorian preacher and the diabolic curses of a witch doctor. Small, with 'bright black eyes' behind horn-rimmed spectacles, thinning reddish hair, pointed nose, and dapper in 'white collar, checked tie, well-cut suit, trimmed grey moustache', a Western witness thought he resembled 'a prosperous stockbroker accustomed to lunching at Simpson's and playing golf at Sunningdale'.[199]

On 22 August in the morning session, the prosecutor summarised what had emerged so far: 'Horrible and monstrous is the chain of these crimes against our socialist fatherland; and each one of these crimes deserves the severest condemnation and severest punishment.' He then referred to the murder of Kirov, eulogising Kirov as 'one of the best sons of the working class, one of the most devoted to the cause of socialism, one of the most loved disciples of the great Stalin, the fiery tribune of the proletarian revolution, the unforgettable Sergei Minronovich Kirov'.[200] Vyshinsky then referred to Comrade Stalin, quoting him as saying that 'We must bear in mind that the growth of the power of the Soviet state will increase the resistance of the last remnants of the dying class.' He also complimented Comrade Stalin for his foresight: 'Three years ago Comrade Stalin not only foretold the inevitable resistance of elements hostile to the cause of socialism, but also foretold the possibility of the revival of Trotzkyite counter-revolutionary groups. This trial has fully and distinctly proved the great wisdom of this forecast.'[201] The prosecutor's rhetoric, including phrases directly dictated by Stalin himself, was becoming more exaggerated:

> This contemptible, insignificant group of adventurers tried with their mud-stained feet to trample upon the most fragrant flowers in our socialist garden. These mad dogs of capitalism tried to tear limb from limb the best of the best of our Soviet land.

> [...] They killed our Kirov; they wounded us close to our very heart. To the murderers' treacherous shot of December 1, 1934, the whole country replied with unanimous execration. The whole country, millions and tens of millions of people, were aroused and once again proved their solidarity, their unity, their loyalty to the great banner of the Party of Lenin–Stalin. The land of Soviets rose up like an unshakable, iron wall in defence of its leaders, its guides, for every hair of whose heads these criminal madmen will answer with their lives.[202]

The prosecutor then went into overdrive in his praise of Stalin: 'With great and unsurpassed love, the toilers of the whole world utter the name of the great teacher and leader of the peoples of the U.S.S.R.—Joseph Vissarionovich Stalin!'[203] Vyshinsky lauded the victories of the 'great Stalin': 'These victories have brought our whole country, every factory worker and collective farmer, every office worker and intellectual, a happy and a well-to-do life. And these victories are the guarantee of the unity of all the Soviet people with our government, with our Party, and with its Central Committee.'[204]

Vyshinsky juxtaposed the genius Stalin with the 'gang of contemptible terrorists' who 'tried to pose as genuine political figures in the Court', calling them 'Liars and clowns, insignificant pygmies, little dogs snarling at an elephant.'[205] Vyshinsky continued:

> After this, can we speak with these people in any sort of political language? Have we not the right to say that we can speak with these people in one language only, the language of the Criminal Code, and regard them as common criminals, as incorrigible and hardened murderers. [...] They came to terrorism, because their position had become hopeless, because they realized that they were isolated from power, from the working class. They came to terrorism because of the complete absence of favourable prospects for them in the fight for power by other methods and by other means.

Turning to the judges, the prosecutor proceeded:

> Comrade judges, in drawing up your verdict in your council chamber, you will carefully—I have no doubt about that—once again go over not only the material of the court investigation but also the records of the preliminary investigation and you will become convinced of the animal fear with which the accused tried to avoid admitting that terrorism was precisely the basis of their criminal activities. That is why Smirnov wriggled so much here.[206]

At one point Vyshinsky even invoked Lenin's last will and testament:

> All their bestial rage and hatred were directed against the leaders of our Party, against the Political Bureau of the Central Committee, against Comrade Stalin, against his glorious comrades-in-arms. It was upon them, headed by Comrade Stalin, that the main burden of the struggle against the Zinovievite-Trotzkyite underground organization lay. It was under their leadership, under the leadership of Comrade Stalin, that great executor and keeper of Lenin's will and testament, that the counter-revolutionary Trotzkyite organization was routed.[207]

This was a somewhat risky manoeuvre since Lenin's will had been a sore point with Stalin. Apparently the trial also provided Stalin with an opportunity to rewrite Lenin's secret testament. Lenin's political testament, written in 1922 and 1923 after his incapacitating strokes, said something quite different, namely: 'Stalin, having become General Secretary has concentrated enormous power in his hands, and I am not sure that he always knows how to use that power with sufficient caution.' In a postscript Lenin had added, 'I propose to comrades to find a way to remove Stalin from that position and appoint to it another man' who would be 'more loyal, more courteous and more considerate to comrades, less capricious, etc.'[208] It was Kamenev who had made the testament known to the Central Committee and, at the time, a secretary of Stalin noted that 'Terrible embarrassment paralyzed all those present. Stalin, sitting on the steps of the praesidium's rostrum, felt small and miserable. I studied him closely: notwithstanding his self-possession and show of calm, it was clearly evident that his fate was at stake ...'[209]

Lenin's testament had never reached the public, but for Kamenev and Zinoviev, who knew of its contents, this reference must have been especially hurtful. However, there can be no doubt that this passage entered the prosecutor's speech with Stalin's approval. We know that the final version of the Prosecutor General's summing up speech had been edited by Stalin before he left Moscow for his holiday on the Black Sea.[210] Then, the prosecutor asked:

> I would like now to get a straight answer from Zinoviev to the following question: Does Zinoviev now accept only moral responsibility [as he had done in the January 1935 trial behind closed doors], or the whole criminal responsibility, full responsibility, for preparing, organizing and committing the murder of Sergei Mironovich Kirov?[211]

Not waiting for the defendant's response Vyshinksy provided the answer himself:

> Of course, Zinoviev will say 'yes'. He cannot say anything else. He said this on the very first day of this trial when caught in the grip of the iron chain of evidence and proof.[212]

In fact there was no proof, beyond false witness testimonies and coerced confessions—except for that odd Honduran passport which was shown during the trial.[213] The passport in itself, of course, did not prove the existence of a 'terrorist centre' or the responsibility of anyone for the Kirov murder. Yet Vyshinsky repeated in many variations in his long statement that 'This centre existed, and, what is most important, it was formed on the direct instructions of Trotzky, Zinoviev and Kamenev', adding: 'I take it as absolutely proven by the personal evidence of literally all the accused, including Smirnov on this point, that this centre was organized on a terroristic basis ....'[214]

How this centre could have existed was hard to understand. Even the prosecutor admitted at one point during the trial that 'In 1932–1933 Kamenev and Zinoviev were in exile ... It is known that in 1934 Smirnov, too, was not at liberty; he was arrested in January 1933 ...' His conclusion was a kind of *conclusio ad absurdum*. Despite the absence of the central players—Kamenev, Zinoviev and Smirnov—the centre was there: 'I draw the conclusion that if the centre functioned it was because of the well-organized technique of communication which enabled even those who were not at liberty, Smirnov, for example, to take part in guiding the work of this centre'.[215]

Turning to Kamenev, the Prosecutor reminded the court that in 1934 Kamenev was head of the 'Academia' Publishing House, which had printed a translation of *The Prince* by Niccolo Machiavelli. Kamenev had written a preface to the Russian edition, calling the Italian political thinker 'A master of political aphorism and a brilliant dialectician.' Vyshinsky, turning to the accused, claimed, 'You, Kamenev, adopted the rules of Machiavelli, you developed them to the utmost point of unscrupulousness and immorality, you modernized them and perfected them.'[216] In his preface to the Russian edition, Kamenev had apparently called Machiavelli's book 'a shell of enormous explosive force'. Twisting these words, Vyshinsky concluded that 'Evidently Kamenev and Zinoviev wanted to use this shell to blow up our socialist fatherland. [...] They miscalculated!' he announced triumphantly, 'Their program of home policy was confined to murder; their program of foreign policy was confined to defeat of the U.S.S.R. in war; their method was perfidy, cunning and treason.'[217] Generously, he added that he did not ask the comrade judges to regard this book as material evidence in this case. With hindsight, we might add that if anyone was a pupil of Machiavelli in the Moscow of 1936, it was Stalin. In fact, Machiavelli could have learned a lesson or two from Stalin rather than the other way round.

Vyshinsky emphasised the highlights of previous days and the 'confessions' of the accused and their mutual 'denunciations' (either in the pre-trial phase or in court) to build a case: that they deserved the penalty provided for by Article 58 of the Penal Code. In the case of Moissei and Nathan Lurye, for example, he used the formula of guilt by association, elaborating on their alleged link to a certain Franz Weiss, 'the fascist agent and a trusted man of Himmler, chief of the fascist black secret service, chief of the German S.S. detachments and subsequently, chief of the German Gestapo'.[218]

Coming to the end of his final speech, the Prosecutor turned to Russia's terrorist heyday in the 1880s and noted that some of the accused tried to draw a parallel with the historical past, with the period of the *Narodnaya Volya* (the People's Will). He said that they tried to compare some people with the heroic terrorists who in the last century entered into combat with the 'terrible, cunning and ruthlessly cruel enemy, the tsarist government'. But the prosecutor concluded that 'This argument does not hold water', explaining:

> That was a struggle by a handful of self-sacrificing enthusiasts against the gendarme giant: it was a fight in the interests of the people. We Bolsheviks have always opposed terrorism, but we must pay our tribute to the sincerity and heroism of the members of the Narodnaya Volya [...]. You, however, a handful of downright counter-revolutionaries ... you took up arms against the vanguard of the world proletarian revolution! You took up arms against the liberty and happiness of the peoples. The comparison with the period of Narodnaya Volya terrorism is shameless.[219] [...] I empathetically reject this sacrilegious parallel. I repeat this parallel is out of place here. Before us are criminal, dangerous, hardened, cruel and ruthless towards our people, towards our ideals, towards the leaders of our struggle, the leaders of the land of Soviets, the leaders of the toilers of the whole world![220]

What the prosecutor did not and could not mention was that both he and Stalin had, at one time, actually been working, before the revolution, as agents or informers for the same Tsarist secret police that was fighting Narodnaya Volya.[221] Incidentally, the defendants themselves, at least in the Report of the Proceedings, did not mention *Narodnaya Volya*—one of the many inconsistencies of the official report.

In conclusion, the prosecutor reminded the comrade judges of those demands the law makes in cases of the gravest crimes against the state. He reminded the court to apply to the accused in full measure the articles of the law, ending with a reference to the slogan written on a large banner on the wall hanging in the court room: 'I demand that dogs gone mad should be shot—every one of them!'[222]

The next day, 22 August, there was no morning session. In the evening session the court began hearing the last pleas of the accused. The texts of these pleas had been revised by Yezhov,[223] and the protocol we have here is very thin, probably because the accused tried to elaborate on their past services to the Party—something they had been instructed to avoid. We glimpse this where the protocol notes that 'The accused Mrachkovsky starts his last plea by relating his autobiography.' Mrachkovsky went on to say, 'In 1923 I became a Trotzkyite. I took a despicable path, the path of deception of the Party [...] I am a counter-revolutionary ... I do not ask for mitigation of my punishment. [...] I want to depart from life without carrying any filth with me. [...] I depart as a traitor to my Party, as a traitor who should be shot'. While the official minutes in the Report of Court Proceedings of the session provide us with few details of the 'last pleas', Alexander Orlov (then an NKVD official) later gave us these details:

> He [Mrachkovsky] recounted that his grandfather had been an organizer of the famous Southern Russian Workers Union, that his father and mother, both factory workers, had served prison sentences for revolutionary activities, and that he himself, at the age of thirteen, had been arrested for disseminating revolutionary leaflets. 'And here I stand before you as a counter-revolutionary!' exclaimed he with bitter resentment and irony in his voice.[224]

Next came Evdokimov. Rather than trying to defend himself, he too was self-incriminating: 'Who will believe us, who played so detestable a comedy at the fresh grave of Kirov whom we had killed; who will believe us, who only by accident, not through any fault of our own, did not become the assassins of Stalin and other leaders of the people?' [...] He finished by saying that 'Our crimes against the proletarian state and against the international revolutionary movement are too great to make it possible for us to expect clemency.'[225] For those who could read between the lines at the trial, Evdokimov's exclamation, 'Who will believe us ...?' hinted at the show being put on.[226]

Isak Reingold, one of the pseudo-defendants, came next, saying, 'Whatever our fate may be, we have been already shot politically', and then went to quote the representative of the state Prosecution who, 'speaking with the voice of 170,000,000 Soviet people, demanded that we be shot like mad dogs'. He ended by saying, 'I fully admitted my guilty. It is not for me to plead for mercy.'[227] Reingold was the best actor among the pseudo-defendants, Orlov recalled:

> Assisting Vyshinsky during the whole trial, he displayed a remarkable ability as a prosecutor and a brilliant memory. Every time when he noticed in the testimony of some other defendant a slight deviation from the approved scenario, he would jump up from his seat and angrily correct him, as if that defendant wanted to conceal something. If Reingold noticed that the prosecutor made an error, he would get up and respectfully ask permission to add something to what the prosecutor had just said, using that pretext for the purpose of correcting him. Vyshinsky would rein up quickly and accept Reingold's prompting with a smile of gratitude.[228]

After Reingold came I.F. Bakayev, the former Cheka chief of Leningrad. He began by saying, 'I am guilty of the assassination of Kirov', and ended by declaring that he awaited 'the deserved and just verdict of the proletarian court'.[229] Richard Pickel was next to plead. The former head of Zinoviev's secretariat when the latter was Party boss in Leningrad, Pickel was the other probable pseudo-defendant. He too concluded by saying 'I must bear my deserved punishment'.[230]

It had been a perverse performance of those who said they would need no defence counsel: rather than *defending* themselves, they used the opportunity of the last plea to *accuse* themselves, no doubt hoping that such a performance would be rewarded rather than used against them when it came to the court's sentence.

The morning session of 23 August continued with Kamenev's plea. His too, was a full confession. He ended by saying, 'Thus we served fascism, thus we organized counter-revolution against socialism, prepared, paved the way for the interventionists. Such was the path we took, and such was the pit of contemptible treachery and all that is loathsome into which we have fallen.'

Having spoken what must have been his prescribed lines, Kamenev rose again from his chair and made a desperate attempt to save at least the lives of his children:

> I should like to say a few words to my children ... I have no other way of addressing them. I have two children: one is a military pilot, the other a Pioneer. Standing, maybe, with one foot in the grave, I want to tell them: no matter what my sentence will be, I in advance consider it just. Don't look back. Go forward. Together with the Soviet people follow Stalin.[231]

Orlov continued, explaining that:

> Having spoken these simple words, Kamenev sat down and shielded his eyes with his hand. Those who were present in the courtroom were shaken by this tragic moment. Even the faces of the judges lost the studied expression of stony indifference.[232]

Kamenev's plea for his children—the elder a pilot (already in prison), the younger, Yuri, only 16—was in vain; both would be shot, like their father.[233]

Then it was Grigory Zinoviev's turn. Again, we have only Orlov's account beyond the censored words of the official minutes of proceedings:

> When he began to speak, it was impossible to recognize the brilliant orator, who in the old times charmed huge audiences at Party conferences and congresses of the Comintern. Breathing with difficulty, he began to speak incoherently and without emotion. Zinoviev didn't look at the audience and did not seek contact with it, as he used to do in his famous appearances of the past. But within a few minutes he regained his self-possession and skill, and his speech began to flow easily. Standing in the dock and speaking the words which were written for him by Stalin's inquisitors, he was like a superb actor, using the oratorical technique of the great Zinoviev in order to give a new interpretation of the personality of the Old Bolshevik Zinoviev and to demonstrate that Zinoviev's revolutionary past was a myth and that in reality he had always been an enemy of socialism and a traitor. Zinoviev's speech was patterned along the same lines as Kamenev's. He also defended not himself but the Party and Stalin. Zinoviev concluded his speech with an involved syllogism, the literary form of which resembled very much the clumsy style of Stalin, but by no means the refined style of Zinoviev. 'My defective Bolshevism became transformed into anti-Bolshevism, and through Trotzkyism I arrived at fascism. Trotzkyism is a variety of fascism and Zinovievism is a variety of Trotzkyism.'[234]

Zinoviev, also pleaded 'fully and completely guilty ... of having been an organizer of the Trotzkyite–Zinovievite *bloc* second only to Trotzky, the *bloc* which set itself the aim of assassinating Stalin, Voroshilov and a number of other leaders of the Party and the government. I plead guilty to having been the principal organizer of the assassination of Kirov.'[235]

Ivan Smirnov, in turn, was dealing 'in detail with the history of his struggle against the Party leadership after he was forgiven by the Party and reinstated into its ranks in 1929', as the protocol summarises. However, Smirnov apparently did not make a full guilty plea. The protocol notes that 'Smirnov continues, just as during the preliminary investigation and the trial, to deny responsibility for the crimes committed by the Trotskite–Zinovievite terrorist centre after his arrest.' Smirnov did turn against Trotzky, appealing 'to all his adherents resolutely to break with the past, to fight Trotzkyism and Trotzky'.[236] But his testimony during nearly three hours of interrogation by Vyshinsky, is reduced to only a very brief record in the transcript.[237]

The pseudo-defendants' pleas contained no drama. As an NKVD witness recalled later, 'As fictitious defendants, they were sure their lives were not in danger.'[238] The last two pleas were made in the evening session of 23 August 1936. The testimonies of Fritz David, a pseudo-defendant, and Ter-Vaganyan, a real defendant, take only twelve lines in the protocol. Ter-Vaganyan claimed to be 'crushed by the speech of the State Prosecutor' and assured the Court that whatever its decision may be, 'I accept it as deserved'. Due to the short preparation time before the trial (he had not been on the original list of those accused), there was no evidence against Ter-Vaganyan, not even falsified evidence. However, Vyshinsky, following Stalin's instructions, also 'substantiated' his guilt: '... all the investigators could do was to obtain the necessary "confession" from the accused at lightning speed', Vyshinsky's biographer found.[239]

Even in their last pleas, the defendants were prohibited from saying what they wanted to say. Their final words were edited by Yagoda or Stalin. References to their closeness to Lenin, their past positions in the Soviet government and the Party, and their revolutionary credentials were replaced in the final script prepared for the session with words like 'traitors and murderers'.[240]

Why would the defendants engage in such masochistic self-accusations even to the end? We have no better answer than Orlov's: 'The defendants were struggling for their lives with desperation, but they did it not by trying to prove their innocence, as is done in genuine and impartial courts of law, but by striving to carry out with the utmost precision the conditions which Stalin had laid down for them: to slander themselves and glorify him.'[241] The pseudo-defendants, on the other hand, testified as they did because they thought they were 'on a secret assignment of the Party'.[242] In a similar way, the main defendants, Zinoviev and Kamenev, also thought they had struck a bargain with Stalin, namely, that in return for playing their role in court their lives would be saved. They now stuck to their side of the bargain. But Stalin would not.

The verdict had already been written before the trial was completed, but a decent interval was created before it was announced.[243] On the afternoon of the following day, 24 August 1936, Ulrich, the president of the Court, read the verdict. Ulrich again summarised what would pass as 'evidence' against the accused. His focus, however, was more on the distant target of the trial, Lev Trotzky, and his influence on the international workers' movement. According to Ulrich, Trotzky had been '... systematically sending a number of terrorists into the U.S.S.R. from abroad', to target 'the leaders of the Soviet Government and the C.P.S.U.'. Among these emissary terrorists were, according to the verdict, Berman-Yurin, Fritz David, Dr. Nathan Lurye and Moissei Lurye, as well as Valentine Olberg. Seven of the accused, including Zinoviev, Kamenev and Smirnov, were found guilty of having organised the 'united Trotzkyite-Zinovievite terrorist centre', having prepared and perpetrated the murder of Kirov, and having organised a number of terrorist groups who made preparations to assassinate seven Communist leaders, including Stalin, Voroshilov, Zhdanov and Kaganovich—crimes covered by one or several of the 14 paragraphs of Article 58 of the Criminal Code of the RSFSR.[244] The remaining nine, including David, Olberg and Berman-Yurin, were found guilty of having been 'active participants in the preparations for the assassination of the leaders of the Party and the Government, Comrades Stalin, Voroshilov, Zhdanov, Kaganovich, Ordzhonikidze, Kosior and Postyshev'. In addition, the president of the Court also ordered that Trotzky and his son Sedov, who were in exile, were 'convicted by the evidence of the accused'.[245]

When Ulrich finally announced that all were sentenced to 'the supreme penalty—to be shot—there was silence and consternation, even among the NKVD employees who formed most of the audience. They had expected the President to add: '.... but taking into consideration the past revolutionary services of the defendants, the court has decided to commute the death penalty'. When these expected words did not come, one of those just condemned to death, broke the silence—it was either M. or N. Lurye—and rose to shout hysterically, 'Long live the cause of Marx, Engels, Lenin and Stalin!''[246]

The trial had come to an end after six days. Those sentenced were taken back to prison, where they began to work on their appeals for mercy.[247] It was the customary rule at the time that when an appeal for mercy was made, any death sentence would be suspended for 72 hours, even when no pardon was granted.[248] Those just condemned to death still had one last hope. After all, Stalin had promised them *in camera* that, as Old Bolsheviks, their lives would be spared.

Stalin did not keep his word.[249] Still on holiday, he was informed shortly before nine on the evening of 24 August 1936 in a telegram sent by Kaganovich, Yezhov and two others. They wrote, 'The Politburo proposed to reject the demands and execute the verdict tonight.'[250] Stalin waited until almost midnight before he gave his one word reply: 'okay'. The execution of the three main 'terrorists', Zinoviev, Kamenev and Smirnov, took place in the Lubianka prison. Yezhov and Yagoda were present. Stalin had also sent Voroshilov to the headquarters of the NKVD's slaughter chamber to supervise the execution. A dignified Smirnov apparently said, 'We deserve this because of our unworthy attitude at the trial.'[251] Kamenev was said to be calm, walking as if in a dream when he was shot from behind. Zinoviev, however, was hysterical and, according to one account, shouted, 'This is a fascist coup!'[252] To silence his screams an NKVD officer reportedly took him to a separate cell and shot him in the back of the head. Later, that officer received a citation for 'acting expeditiously under difficult conditions'.[253] Yagoda apparently kept the bullets that killed Zinoviev and Kamenev as trophies.[254] The other defendants—except three planted NKVD agents—David, Olberg and Berman-Yurin—were also shot that night.[255] Their families would soon suffered similar fates; they were either shot or sent to labour camps.[256]

This tragedy was turned into a macabre comedy show four months later. At the end of 1936, on 20 December, on the occasion of the anniversary of the founding of the secret police, Stalin gave a small banquet for the heads of the NKVD. After much drinking by the party, the head of Stalin's personal security, Karl Pauker, who had personally witnessed the execution of Zinoviev and Kamenev, put on a show for Stalin. Assisted by two officers who played the parts of warders dragging Zinoviev to the site of execution, Pauker is said to have dramatised Zinoviev's last desperate moments, falling on his knees and clinging to the boots of one of the warders: 'Please, for God's sake, Comrade, call Yosif Vissarionovich!' Yosif Vissarionovich Stalin liked the parody so much that Pauker had to re-enact the scene once more. This time he added new elements to the role, raising his hands and crying, 'Hear, Israel, our God is the only God!' Choking with laughter, Stalin had to wave Pauker to stop.[257]

4.4. What Happened outside the Courtroom

In parallel with the show trial, a press campaign had been set up by the authorities in the Kremlin. A secret letter sent from Stalin to all Party organs, dispatched on 29 July 1936, called for extra vigilance: 'The indelible mark of every Bolshevik in the current situation ought to be the ability to recognize and identify the enemies of the Party, no matter how well they may have camouflaged their identity.'[258] Two weeks later, *Pravda* carried the announcement from Procurator Andrei Vyshinsky, stating that a case on 'the United Trotzky–Zinoviev Centre' had been transferred to the Military Collegium of the Supreme Court of the USSR. The trials were given saturation coverage in the Soviet media. The press contained what purported to be verbatim reports of the daily proceedings, parts of which were broadcast by radio and filmed for cinema audiences.[259] The newspapers reproduced multiple resolutions from 'workers' meetings' demanding, to quote from one, 'No mercy, no leniency for enemies of the people who have tried to deprive the people of its leaders.' One telegram from the Dagestani Party organisation in Makhachkala, insisted '... that the Supreme Court execute the three-time contemptible degenerates, who have slid into the mire of fascism and aimed their guns at the heart of our Party, the great Stalin'.[260] Directives from the Kremlin had mobilised such propaganda support, which resulted in local Party resolutions as well as letters purporting to come from ordinary citizens.[261]

Well-known public figures were also pressed to publish press statements of support for the prosecutor.[262] The poet Demian Bedny was forced by Kaganovich and Khrushchev to write some verses for *Pravda* which played on the theme of 'no mercy'.[263] Editorials with titles like 'Trotzky-Zinoviev-Kamenev-Gestapo' and 'The People's Wrath is Mighty and Terrible' appeared.[264] Karl Radek, the former secretary of the Comintern, wrote (prodded by Stalin) a piece in the *Izvestia* of 21 August 1936, demanding that 'The people who raised their weapons against the lives of the favourite leaders of the proletariat must pay with their heads for their boundless guilt.'[265] (Maybe he did so hoping to avoid arrest, but 28 days later he too was apprehended). Another prominent Party figure who raised his voice against Zinoviev and his co-defendants was Pyatakov, the former first President of the Government of the Soviet Ukraine. Like Radek, he too would soon be subject to a show trial. In many cases we do not know where pressure was applied, where pre-emptive opportunism was at work, or whether they really believed what they wrote.

However, we know that Pyatakov was motivated by fear. When his former wife was arrested by the NKVD, some old correspondence found in the apartment linked him to the opposition of the 1920s. In an attempt to save himself, he wrote an article in *Pravda* demanding the accused 'be destroyed like carrion'.[266] He even asked Yezhov that he, Pyatakov, be allowed to shoot all those sentenced to death in the trial, as well as his former wife [sic!].[267] A month later he was arrested and prepared for the second show trial to be held the following year, in January 1937. Alexei Rykov, former Premier and Lenin's successor as Chairman of the Council of People's Commissars, and K. Rakovsky, former head of the Ukrainian Government and a well-known figure in the international workers' movement, also turned against their former colleagues, demanding in the press that no pity be shown towards Kamenev and Zinoviev.[268] Even Lenin's widow, Nadezhda Krupskaya, was mobilised. She lent her name to an article entitled 'Why the Second International Defends Trotzky', asserting that 'It is also no accident that the Second International rants and raves, raises the Trotzky–Zinoviev gang of killers on its shield, and tries to break up the [anti-fascist] Popular Front.'[269]

These orchestrated endorsements of the trial and calls for the death penalty were meant to give a semblance of legitimacy to the trial. The charges which surfaced in the trial were given more credence with the endorsement of respected commentators like Lenin's widow. Their voices, and the resolutions from local Party organisations that were flooding the newspapers, created a momentum and rationale for the nightly arrests by the NKVD. As Tucker and Cohen's study of the third Moscow trial points out:

> ... the purge trials had, in the first place, a political symbolic function, which was to provide a rationale for the purge, to make publicly meaningful the campaign of arrests that was going on night after night. The underlying assumption of the Great Purge was that treason was abroad in the land, especially among Party members, and that it had to be cleaned out and exterminated on the massive scale that this treason itself had assumed. The three great Moscow show trials and a number of lesser local trials held at this time were designed to dramatize this idea, to show the existence, enormity, and scope of the purported treasonable activity, which had—it was thus made to appear—been organized and directed by men at the pinnacle of the Party and state as well as their counterparts at the provincial level.[270]

There was no civil society in Russia at the time. All public opinion was controlled by Party and state. While many people must have been shocked to see that the former Bolshevik heroes were exposed as traitors and murderers, they could not articulate this in public. The NKVD, however, did report anonymous protests to Stalin: messages like 'Down with the murderers of the leaders of October' and 'Too bad they didn't finish off the Georgian snake', appeared on the walls of several factories in Moscow.[271] Yet such voices did not reach a wider public. The voice of 'the people' was expressed by *Pravda*, Stalin's official mouthpiece. *Pravda* stated on 25 August 1936, for example, reporting on the execution of sixteen 'terrorists', that millions of working people were starting their day with the joyful feeling that a loathsome creature had been crushed.[272] By the time of the second show trial, in January 1937, against Pyatakov, Radek and twelve others, the mobilisation of the public to support the court's decision ('The court's verdict is the people's verdict') was even more frenetic. On 29 January 1937, a crowd of 200,000 people gathered in Red Square despite sub-zero temperatures, denouncing 'Judas-Trotzky'. They were addressed by a member of the Politburo in these words, 'By raising their hand against Comrade Stalin, they raised their hand against all the best that humanity has, because Stalin is hope ... Stalin is our banner. Stalin is our will, Stalin is our victory.'[273] The public speaker was none other than Nikita Khrushchev, who in 1956 would denounce Stalin in a 'secret speech' to the Twentieth Party Congress.

Why did the masses acquiesce to Stalin and his colleagues in the Politburo? The First Five-Year Plan and its aftermath had created great confusion in the country. The massive forced social and economic changes—and the traumatic disruptions these triggered in people's lives—called for an explanation. To blame the regime was risky. In this situation the regime offered scapegoats to blame: economic saboteurs termed 'wreckers' and political saboteurs called by various other names—White Guards, Trotzkyists, or simply 'enemies of the people'. As historians Getty and Naumov put it:

> From peasant to Politburo member, the language about evil conspirators served a purpose. For the plebeians, it provided a possible explanation for the daily chaos and misery of life. For the many committed enthusiasts it explained why their Herculean efforts to build socialism often produced bad results. For the nomenklatura member, it was an excuse to destroy their only challengers. For local Party chiefs, it was a rationale for again expelling inconvenient people from the local machines. For the Politburo member, it provided a means to avoid self-questioning about Party police and a vehicle for closing ranks. The image of evil, conspiring Trotzkyists was convenient for everybody ...[274]

However, many foreign observers in Moscow and abroad were also accepting the trials as real, rather than as a parody of justice. Great care had been taken to prepare the defendants and witnesses for the trial. As a consequence, the fake character of the first Moscow trial was missed by many, if not most, especially if they had no command of the Russian language. The American ambassador to Moscow, Joseph Davis, for instance, held that the treason charges—in particular the collaboration of the accused with the Gestapo—were factually true.[275]

We do not know whether he was among the few foreign observers who were invited to attend the first Moscow trial. However, the delegation from the International Association of Lawyers, who had attended the trial, issued this statement:

> We consider the claim that the proceedings were summary and unlawful to be totally unfounded. The accused were given the opportunity of taking counsel; every counsel in the Soviet Union is independent of the Government. The accused, however, preferred to be defended individually. Hardly a state exists in which people involved in terrorist acts are not given the death penalty. [...] We hereby categorically declare that the accused were sentenced quite lawfully. It was fully proven that there were links between them and the Gestapo. They quite rightly deserved the death penalty.[276]

One of the delegation's members, British Labour Party Member of Parliament Denis Pritt, added in a newspaper article, 'What first struck me as a British lawyer was the defendants' completely free and unconstrained conduct. They all looked well; they all stood up and spoke when they wanted to ... I consider the entire trial and the manner of addressing the defendants to be an example for the whole world in a case where the defendants are charged with the conspiracy to assassinate leading statesmen and to overthrow the government, which the defendants confessed to'.[277] Pritt's article for the British *News Chronicle* was entitled 'The Moscow Trial was a Fair Trial'. *Pravda* did not miss the opportunity to reprint such an endorsement in block letters.[278]

The International Human Rights League also took the confessions at face value, calling the trial lawful. Left-wing intellectuals in Europe were fooled, among them Bernard Shaw, André Malraux and Romain Rolland. In public they all took Stalin's side—although at least one of them (Rolland) privately held grave concerns about the conduct of the trial.[279]

However not everybody was fooled. In the United States a Commission of Inquiry was set up in May 1937, chaired by 78-year-old philosopher John Dewey, to investigate the Moscow show trial. The Inquiry was responding to appeals from an American Committee for the Defence of Lev Trotzky, and from French intellectuals, trade unionists and some parliamentarians. Trotzky and his son Sedov provided the Dewey Commission (of eighteen men) with documents and evidence. At the same time, Soviet diplomats abroad worked hard to discredit this fact-finding exercise.[280] Journalists from a number of countries had covered hearings in Cocoyan, Mexico, where Trotzky had been given asylum by the Mexican president after pressure was put on Norway to have him extradited to the Soviet Union. Since most charges of the Moscow trial were linked to a conspiracy allegedly masterminded by Trotzky, his explanations and refutations were crucial in determining the truthfulness of such accusations. Trotzky defended himself forcefully on this and other occasions. Here he replies to accusations from the Moscow trials in his own words:

> According to the statements in both trials [the first and the second], the content of my criminal work was as follows: Three meetings in Copenhagen, two letters of Mrachkovsky and others, three letters to Radek, a letter to Pyatakov, another to Muralov, a meeting with Romm lasting twenty to twenty-five minutes, a meeting with Pyatakov lasting two hours ... Altogether, the conversations and correspondence of the conspirators, according to their own testimony, did not take more than twelve or thirteen hours of my time. I do not know how much time was taken up by my

> conversations with Hess and the Japanese diplomats. Let us add twelve more hours. Altogether, this totals a maximum of three working days ... the eight years of my most recent exile comprise two thousand nine hundred and twenty possible working days ... During two thousand nine hundred and seventeen working days I wrote books, articles and letter and held conversations devoted to the defence of Socialism ... On the other hand, I devoted three days ... to a conspiracy in the interests of fascism.[281]

The report of the Cocoyan hearings was six hundred pages long and managed to question many of the assertions made during the Moscow trial.[282] The Dewey Commission's final report was 422 pages long and published in 1937 under the title *Not Guilty*, with the conclusion, 'We therefore find the Moscow Trials to be frame-ups.'[283] That conclusion did not reach many in the Soviet Union, nor did it manage to convince many on the political Left, outside the inquiry. Although part of the less doctrinaire democratic intelligentsia did have second thoughts about the character of the Soviet regime following the publication of the Dewey report, those on the political Right tended to accept the veracity of the charges brought against Trotzky and his followers.[284]

The sad truth about the reaction to the trial was that many people in the Soviet Union believed what they were told to believe, while others outside Russia believed what they wished to believe. Evidence and counter-evidence were accepted or ignored based on ideology, convenience or short-term self-interest. That said, however, most people were simply confused about what was going on. As Robert Tucker put it, '... even politically literate people were [far] from understanding what was happening in the country, who was behind it, and "why"'.[285] In many ways, what happened was simply beyond comprehension.

4.5. Judicial, Social and Political Consequences

4.5.1. *Judicial Consequences*

On 5 December 1936, the Soviet Union received a new Constitution from the Communist Party, the product of a commission set up in February 1935. This Constitution had been drafted mainly by Nikolai Bucharin, with the help of Karl Radek. They would be among the main defendants in the second (January 1937) and third (March 1938) Moscow trials. The new Constitution 'guaranteed' freedom of speech, freedom of assembly, freedom of the press and freedom of religious worship as well as the inviolability of individuals, their homes and their correspondence. More to the point, it also 'guaranteed' Soviet citizens freedom from arbitrary arrest and the right to defence in a public trial before an independent judge[286] The Constitution was supposed to identify the superior democratic and humanistic features separating Communism from Fascism.[287] Yet the contrast between the 'theory' of the Constitution and the practice, manifested in the show trials and the purges, could not have been greater.[288]

On 1 September 1935, one week after the execution of Zinoviev, Kamenev, and the other defendants, Stalin issued an order to Yagoda and Yezhov. Five thousand members of the former opposition, who were already held in concentration camps, were to be secretly executed. Former NKVD chief Orlov remembered this as an order 'which shocked even the most callous of the NKVD chiefs'. That order was soon followed by another, asking the NKVD to prepare a further list of five thousand opponents destined to be executed.[289] Compiling such lists of names would become a frequent occurrence. On some evenings, Stalin would sign off on more than thousand names.

This was the beginning of a purge that would, according to a conservative estimate, cost some 700,000 lives over the next two years.[290] What were the 'crimes' of those who were executed? Perhaps they had, somewhere in the past, abstained from voting in a resolution against Trotzky, or made a careless remark that was recorded by NKVD informers. Others may have shown a perceived lack of faith in the Party line. 'Trotzkyism' was not specifically named as a crime in the Penal Code. The definition of Trotzkyism was very fluid and included not only opponents left and right of Stalin's line in the past, but also 'wreckers' and 'fascist spies'.[291] In November 1937, during a toast for the twentieth anniversary of the Bolshevik Revolution, Stalin told the Politburo members and a few select others, 'We will destroy every enemy, even if he is an Old Bolshevik, we will destroy his kin, his family. Anyone who by his actions or thoughts encroaches on the unity of the socialist state, we shall destroy relentlessly.'[292] It was Stalin and the NKVD who decided what was a crime, not the Constitution, the Penal Code or the Ministry of Justice.

Show trials like those held in Moscow were also conducted in the republics, regions and districts of the Soviet Union in the following two years. They served to provide the rationale for local purges.[293] The following two major show trials held in Moscow in 1937 and 1938 clearly indicated that Stalin must have considered the first show trial a success. While that trial had been targeting the Trotskyist Left, and the second targeted Trotzkyist 'wreckers', the third trial focused mainly on the 'Bloc of Rightists and Trotzkyists', with Bukharin as the most prominent representative.[294]

Legal safeguards, which existed at least on paper, had gravely deteriorated since Kirov's murder and the first Moscow trial. Until December 1934, for example, executions of political opponents had to be confirmed by a commission of the Politburo. However, by September 1934 in some regions of the Soviet Union, the death penalty no longer had to be confirmed by Moscow if the matter was judged to be only of local concern.[295] Until early 1936, Vyshinsky had advocated reducing the NKVD's powers to impose sentences directly. We must assume that he did this mainly to preserve this power for the judiciary rather than the NKVD.[296] Vyshinsky was not averse to drastic measures—in 1937 he said that 'One has to remember Comrade Stalin's instruction that there are sometimes periods, moments in the life of a society and in our life in particular, when the laws prove obsolete and have to be set aside.'[297] In April 1938 he instructed his procurators not to obstruct the 'mass operations' of the NKVD.[298] 'Troikas' (consisting of the local Party boss, the local NKVD chief and the local procurator) were at that time arranging and supervising mass arrests and executions in the provinces.[299] Often, the representative from Vyshinky's office was not even consulted. In late 1938, Vyshinsky managed to regain some lost ground in that regard. The activities of the 'troikas' were in practice brought to an end by mid-November 1938 by a Politburo decree.[300] Some dubious cases of NKVD arrests were even reopened and some of those unjustly sent to labour camps were freed. But this affected only a minority of the nearly two million people who had been sent to the camps by that time.[301]

The purges that followed did not stop when it came to the Soviet criminal justice system itself. The search for political enemies meant that ordinary criminal justice cases became political cases, and the standards for issuing convictions were lowered. The judiciary was also purged. Those within its ranks who did not sufficiently facilitate the work of the NKVD became objects of persecution themselves. Almost half of all judges and prosecutors lost their jobs in 1937 and 1938; many of them were arrested. Some two thousand new investigators and prosecutors hired in early 1938 could not fill all the vacancies created by the purges.[302]

The Military Collegium of the Supreme Court which had sentenced Zinoviev, Kamenev and the others would, in the next two years, rubber-stamp the death sentences and other sentences not only for tens of thousands of old Party members, but also bring death to young Komsomol (Communist Youth Organisation) members, economic and military functionaries, writers, artists and others. The Committee of Justice of the Politburo, which included Nikolai Yezhov, would draw up hundreds of lists of names. Stalin and a few colleagues from his inner circle in the Politburo would sign them, often dealing with thousands in a single day; de facto pronouncing the sentence—death or camp. Stalin signed 362 such lists, Molotov 373, Voroshilov 195, Kaganovich 191, Zhdanov 177 and Mikojan 63. In this way, lists containing 44,000 names passed through their hands and were forwarded to the Military Collegium. 39,000 thousand of the 44,000 were then sentenced to death by the Collegium.[303]

This procedure did not apply to the 'national operations' which paralleled the Party purges. The Soviet Union was home to people of more than hundred different nationalities. From this large pool of non-ethnic Russians, large numbers of people were sent to the camps or sentenced to death. According to one NKVD document dated December 1938, between 1 October 1936 and 1 November 1938, 1,565,041 people had been arrested in national and other operations.[304] Of these, 1,336,863 were sentenced. The first category of punishment was death, the second was being sent to camps. Of those arrested, more than 90,000 people died in camps in 1938,[305] and 668,305 of them were given the death sentence.[306] These figures are incomplete; there were also other operations. Operational order No. 00486, dated 15 August 1937, for instance, ordered the 'Liquidation of the families of arrested enemies of the people.'[307] When Yezhov sent Stalin a list with the names of wives of 'enemies of the people', he signed that list as well.[308] The slaughter was on an almost industrial scale. In one instance, between August 1937 and October 1938, twelve NKVD men in a special facility for killing people by neck-shots in Butovo, outside Moscow, killed 20,000 people. As the volume of liquidations increased, gassing in carriages was also said to have occurred.[309] The purges gradually shifted focus, from Old Bolsheviks to members of non-Russian nationalities. This continued until at least late 1938. In addition, the NKVD also operated abroad. Its most prominent target was Trotsky himself, who was assassinated in Mexico in 1940 at Stalin's order.

It took the Soviet Union a long time to admit to the miscarriage of justice in this trial. In 1956 Khrushchev admitted to 'glaring abuses of Socialist legality which resulted in the death of innocent people' in his secret speech to the twentieth Party Congress. However, it would take 32 more years before at least some symbolic measures were taken to address some of the damage. In 1988, the USSR Supreme Court reviewed the evidence against Zinoviev and Kamenev and others tried in August 1936, and rehabilitated them, declaring that all the defendants in the first Moscow trial had been innocent of the charges.[310]

4.5.2. *Social and Political Consequences*

With hindsight, it seems astounding that nobody realised what would stem from the Kirov murder—nobody except Trotzky. Yet even he did not attribute Kirov's murder in December 1936 to Stalin. Yet he had suggested in the same month that Stalin's goal was 'to terrorize completely all his critics and oppositionists, and this not by expulsion from the Party nor by depriving them of their daily bread, not even by imprisonment or exile, but by the firing squad. To the terrorist act of Nikolayev, Stalin replies by redoubling the terror against the Party.'[311]

Despite the breadth and the horror of the purges, they were smaller in terms of casualties than the deaths accompanying the forced collectivisation of the peasantry in the late 1920s and early 1930s. According to the highest estimates, two million people were killed or sent to the camps during the Great Purge. At least three times as many people had perished through hunger or shootings during the forced collectivisations. The common people were affected by the purges less than Party members and the middle levels of society. In fact, Stalin tried to tap into the discontent of the common man, including those at the bottom of the Party pyramid, using their dissatisfactions and denunciations as the rationale and engine for his purges against the Old Bolsheviks.[312]

When the death sentences against Zinoviev and Kamenev were carried out in the early hours of 25 August 1936, and *Pravda* had announced this, many in the Communist Party were shocked. An unwritten contract had been broken: Party members do not kill Party members and, above all, Old Bolsheviks do not kill Old Bolsheviks.[313] While Stalin was still in Sochi (where he stayed until the end of September), the Politburo discussed the trial on 27 August 1936. While nothing could now be done about Zinoviev's, Kamenev's, Smirnov's and Tomsky's deaths (Tomsky had committed suicide), many worried as their names had also been mentioned by defendants or by the prosecutor during the trial. Rykov and Bukharin were the most prominent members named—and two days after the executions, most Politburo members were not ready to let them share the same fate. Confronted with a false witness Yezhov had presented to denounce Bukharin (editor of *Izvestia*), Lazar Kaganovich reportedly told Bukharin, 'He's lying, the whore, from beginning to end! Go back to the newspaper, Nikolai Ivanovich and work in peace.'[314] The wide-ranging purge Stalin had in mind for even the top ranks of the Party was still alien to many Politburo and Central Committee members. Their instincts told them, 'Repression was something *we* did to *them* [the enemies of the Party] ... and it was inconceivable that *we* would repress *us*.'[315] Due to this resistance, Stalin, still away from Moscow, had to take a step back. On 10 September 1936 Vyshinsky announced in *Pravda* the closure of investigations against the two 'Rightists' (Bukharin and Rykov—both non-voting members of the Central Committee) for lack of evidence.[316]

Stalin blamed Yagoda for this setback in going after the 'enemies of the people', a term soon applied, as Khrushchev later explained, to all 'those who in any way disagreed with Stalin' as well as to 'those who were only suspected of hostile intent'. Khrushchev called Stalin 'a very distrustful man, sickly suspicious'.[317] In Stalin's dictionary 'anti-Stalin' meant 'counter-revolutionary', 'oppositional activity' meant 'treason', and 'anti-Stalin grouping' meant 'conspiratorial terrorist centre'. In short, anyone who engaged in criticising or opposing Stalin's policies could be charged with 'counter-revolutionary terrorism'.[318] Few claims that surfaced in the first show trial had been true, although there *was* an undercurrent of opposition in the Bolshevik Party, and this opposition had been linked with Trotzky and one of his sons abroad in the past. All the evidence we have indicates that they planned no terrorist assassinations.[319] Yagoda, the NKVD chief who studied the pre-trial 'confessions' and 'evidence' of Pickel, Dreitzer and others in the first show trial, annotated one report supposedly documenting Trotzky's terrorist orders with words like: 'untrue', 'nonsense', 'rubbish' and 'this cannot be'.[320] Yagoda's unwillingness to purge Old Bolsheviks on the basis of blatant lies would soon cost him his job and, in the third show trial, his own life. Perhaps Stalin was 'inventing new enemies to intimidate his real opponents' and to 'destroy not only his opponents but the less radical among his allies', as Montefiore has suggested.[321]

Given Yagoda's reluctance to act on false evidence, Stalin was determined to replace him with the more aggressive Nikolai Yezhov. In a telegram of 25 September 1936, co-signed by Andrei Zhdanov, Secretary of the Central Committee, Stalin demanded that Yezhov be made People's Commissar for Internal Affairs, blaming Yagoda for handling the trial poorly.[322] Yagoda, like Molotov, had probably expected that Zinoviev and Kamenev would be pardoned. An Old Bolshevik himself (he had joined the Party in 1907), he was sceptical about the widening of the purges, knowing that the charges were fabricated and supported only by false confessions.[323] Nikolai Yezhov became Yagoda's successor by the end of September 1936.

When Yezhov became chief of the secret police, he quadrupled NKVD salaries, making them higher than those of others who worked in comparable positions in government or the Party.[324] Yezhov took with him from the staff of the Central Committee three hundred men loyal to him. These men were the inner core to administer the purges to come—purges that would include the old Chekist Bolsheviks in the NKVD as well.[325] With their help Yezhov would soon purge another 14,000 people. Why did they have to go? Perhaps because Stalin thought they knew too much about the crimes he had ordered them to commit in the past. The purge of the Old Chekists in 1937 occurred without trials.[326] Yezhov, the 'poison dwarf' (he was just 151 cm tall, about 10 cm shorter than Stalin) was notorious for his ruthlessness. On one occasion, he claimed it was 'better that ten innocent people should suffer than one spy get away', and on another he declared, 'If during this operation an extra thousand people will be shot, that is not such a big deal.'[327] He participated personally in shootings, and also engaged in torture, sometimes cutting off the ears and noses of his victims.[328] In 1937, Stalin promoted Yezhov, the 'Iron Commissar', to the position of candidate member of the Politburo.[329] Except for Molotov, who was a full member of the Politburo, Yezhov was Stalin's most frequent visitor at that time; Stalin's appointment book records 278 of his visits, averaging three hours in length each, during 1937–1938.[330] Stalin told Yezhov on the occasion of his appointment as head of the NKVD that there was a four-year backlog of 'work' to be done (presumably a hint at the insufficient punishment meted out to the 1932 supporters of the Ryutin platform).[331] Stalin authorised Yezhov to impose death sentences when it came to 'national operations'. But he kept the 'political' Party purges under his own tight control.[332]

The show trials provided sensational confessions which, when publicised, created an atmosphere of crisis, tension and suspicion—enemies could be everywhere, even in the Party, and the utmost vigilance was called for. In this sense, the trials served to 'legitimise' the purges, suggesting an enormous conspiracy that justified drastic measures.[333]

The second Moscow trial (also known as the Pyatakov–Radek trial) in January 1937 was ostensibly 'necessitated' by the fact that, in addition to the 'Leningrad Centre' (consisting of Nikolayev and others) and the 'Moscow Centre' (Zinovievites and Trotzkyites), a third, 'Parallel Centre' (or 'Reserve Centre') had been 'discovered' by the NKVD investigators. Among those arrested and brought to trial were, in addition to the Party's renowned theorist Bukharin, Karl Radek, former secretary of the Comintern, Leonid Serebriakov, former secretary of the Central Committee, and Mikhail Sokolnikov, former candidate member of the Politburo. This 'Parallel Centre' was said to have organised since 1933 sabotage and terrorist groups engaged in 'wrecking' at industrial plants, especially those of the defence industry. It was claimed they had been preparing terrorist attacks against Soviet leaders and engaged in spying for foreign states, ultimately aiming to overthrow the Soviet regime and restore capitalism.[334] The outcome of the second Moscow trial was that 13 out of 17 defendants were sentenced to death; the remainder received lesser sentences. Pyatakov (whom Lenin had described in his testament as 'undoubtedly a person of outstanding strength of purpose and abilities'[335]) was executed, while Radek was given ten years in the camps. He did not survive; Lavrentiy Beria who became chief of the NKVD following Yezhov ordered his murder despite the fact that Radek was already in a prison camp.[336]

In March 1938 the largest of the show trials was held, against Nikolai Bukharin, the former head of the Communist International and member of the Politburo (according to Lenin 'the darling of the Party'),[337] Alexei Rykov (Lenin's deputy and later head of the Soviet government), and more than a dozen others.[338] Among those others was Arel Yenukidze, the Secretary of the Central Executive Committee, who had helped Stalin in drafting the 1 December 1934 decree and Yagoda, who had prepared the first show trial together with Yezhov. Yagoda was accused of belonging to a 'Bloc of Rightists and Trotzkyists' who had allegedly conspired with foreign powers; he was also accused of complicity in the murder of Kirov. He had allegedly instructed his deputy in Leningrad 'not to place any obstacles in the way of the terrorist act against Kirov'.[339] This may have been the only true charge made at this trial. However, if it was true, Yagoda could not have done it without the approval of Joseph Stalin.[340]As Stalin's biographer, Montefiore, found: 'Stalin sometimes accused others of his own crimes'.[341]

It goes beyond the scope of this chapter to give a detailed account of the Great Terror that followed the show trials. It engulfed ever widening circles. Quotas were set on how many 'former kulaks and criminals' had to be arrested in 'mass operations' and the specific selection of the victims was often left to lower level officials who were even encouraged to exceed their quotas.[342]

To create the right public atmosphere for the country-wide purges, local show trials were organised across the Soviet Union. The audience was no longer NKVD people only, as in the first Moscow trial. Workers and farmers were brought in to attend the trials and local newspapers published full accounts. There was also a spin-off into real theatre, as Sheila Fitzpatrick writes:

> The show trials, which were themselves political theater, spawned imitations in the regular theater, both professional and amateur. Lev Sheinin, whose cross-over activities between criminal investigation and journalism we have already encountered, was coauthor of one of the most popular theatrical works on the themes of the Great Purges, a play called *The Confrontation*, which played in a number of theaters throughout the Soviet Union in 1937. Since Sheinin was reputed to be the author also of the scenarios of the big Moscow show trials, this switch to 'legitimate' theater, using the same themes of spies and their unmasking and interrogation, is intriguing.[343]

The purges also affected the NKVD and the Red Army, the two wings of government with the largest capacity for organised violence. Here Stalin did not dare to use a show trial as the instrument of bringing the Army under his full control The Red Army, created and led by Trotzky in the years of the Civil War, still contained many who had served under his command and who now risked being labelled as

'Trotskyists'. On 1 May 1937, after the annual May Day parade, Stalin told his inner circle that it was time 'to finish with our enemies because they are in the army, in the staff, even in the Kremlin'.[344] And indeed, in 1937 an 'Anti-Soviet Trotzkyist Military Organization in the Red Army', allegedly led by Marshal Mikhail Tukhachevsky, was 'discovered'.[345]Tukhachevsky, the Deputy Commissar, was arrested on 22 May 1937, and admitted under torture to both having been a German agent and having tried to seize power together with Bukharin. The charismatic commander of the Red Army was secretly tried by the Military Collegium of the Supreme Court and shot on 12 June 1937.[346] The people of the USSR learned of his death in a brief newspaper notification.[347] About 10,000 officers of the Red Army were purged, including three (out of five) marshals, fifteen army commanders, fifteen army commissars, 63 commanders of corps and an equal number of their commissars, 151 division commanders and 86 division commissars, 243 commanders of brigades and 143 respective commissars, 318 commanders of regiments and 163 of their commissars.

The purges in the Party were equally drastic. In the spring of 1937 Stalin had told NKVD leaders that the entire pre-revolution and civil war generations of the Old Bolsheviks were a millstone around the neck of the revolution.[348] While he did not destroy them all, his purge was extensive: the Central Committee, formally the supreme authority in the Party, saw 70 per cent of its members and candidate members—98 men in total—arrested and shot in 1937–1938.[349] The purges did not stop at the Politburo either: five of its members—Rudzutak, Eiche, Cubar, Kosior and Postyshev—were arrested and shot.[350] When the eighteenth Party Congress began on 10 March 1939, 90 per cent of the 1,900 attending were under 40 years of age. The Old Bolsheviks—apart from Stalin, Molotov, Voroshilov, Kaganovich, Zhdanov and a few others—had all gone. They were replaced by rising stars like Andrei Gromyko, Yuri Andropov and Leonid Brezhnev. Nearly 60 per cent of those who had belonged to the Party in 1933 were no longer part of it.[351] Of the regional Party leaders, 293 out of 333 had been replaced. Altogether half a million new appointments had been made in the Party and the state, as the Party Congress learned from 'the wisest man of the epoch', the 'genius' Stalin.[352] Speaking at the opening of the Congress, Stalin, with characteristic duplicity, also referred to the Old Bolsheviks, saying '... there are never enough Old cadres, there are far less than required, and they are already partly going out of commission owing to the operation of the laws of nature'.[353]

By early 1939 the purges had practically come to an end. From January 1938 onwards, the Central Committee had begun to criticise 'false' or 'excessive' vigilance.[354] But this referred more to unrestrained repression from below, especially in the provinces, which was often fuelled by denunciations and personal vendettas by Party bosses.[355] On 17 November 1938 the Politburo had abolished the 'Troikas' that had been so active identifying and trying 'enemies of the people' in the country, often exceeding quotas set by the Kremlin.[356] Yezhov was first side-lined and later arrested. He was replaced in December 1939 by Lavrentiy Beria, the Stalin confidant from Georgia. What had Yezhov done wrong? His biographers, Marc Jansen and Nikita Petrov, hold that 'there are no indications that Yezhov ever exceeded the role of Stalin's instrument'.[357] However, Stalin was now eager to shift the blame onto him: 'Yezhov was a scoundrel. He ruined our best cadres. He had morally degenerated.'[358] The manoeuvre of blaming Yezhov for 'excesses' was successful. The Great Terror of 1937–1938 is still referred to in Russian history as 'Yezhovshchina', the 'time of Yezhov',[359] as if it was principally Yehzhov's crime and not Stalin's. The General Secretary claimed in March 1939 at the Party Congress that 'serious mistakes' had been made by the NKVD.[360] On 10 April 1939, Yezhov was arrested by Beria at a meeting Stalin had ordered Yezhov to attend.[361] Yezhov was to be accused of planning a coup d'état on the 21st anniversary of the Bolshevik revolution. He was accused of treasonable espionage for Poland, Germany, England and Japan. Under torture Yezhov admitted it all, and much more readily than many of his own victims. He was shot on 4 February 1940, probably at the same special execution site near the Lubianka NKVD headquarters he had built for some of his victims: a declining concrete floor with wooden logs at one end to absorb the bullets and a hose to flush away the blood. Yezhov's last request reportedly was 'Tell Stalin I shall die with his name on my lips.'[362] However after his death, when his personal safe was opened, materials about Stalin's pre-1917 past were allegedly found, including police records which contained incriminating evidence of Stalin's relationship with the Tsarist secret police, the Okhrana.[363] Yezhov's relatives and close collaborators as well as their wives and children—altogether 346 people—were also shot.[364] His divorced wife had already committed suicide before she could be arrested (she was accused of being an English spy) and made to testify against Yezhov, as Stalin and Beria reportedly had planned.[365]

Yezhov's successor, L. Beria, managed to survive Stalin (and may even have had a hand in his death by poisoning him in 1953).[366] He also succeeded in killing Stalin's distant rival, Trotzky, the author of the volume *The Revolution Betrayed*. Stalin's order to Beria in 1939 was that 'Trotzky should be eliminated within a year.'[367] Beria set up a special team, giving them three floors at NKVD headquarters. It required several attempts before Beria succeeded. Trotzky had fled Norway for Mexico in 1937. In 1938,

Trotzky's son Sergei was arrested and his older son Sedov was killed.[368] Beria managed to infiltrate Ramon Mercader into Trotzky's inner circle. Mercader was an NKVD recruit from the Spanish civil war. He killed Trotzky in Mexico City at his desk with an ice axe on 20 August 1940.[369] The previous day Stalin had Molotov, his Minister of Foreign Affairs, sign a non-aggression pact with Hitler—the fascist leader Stalin had accused Trotzky of conspiring with.[370]

4.6. Conclusion

Following the Kirov murder, there were two secret trials (in December 1934 and January 1935) and three show trials (in 1936, 1937 and 1938). We have focused here in some detail on the first of the public Moscow trials and its consequences. Today we know much more about what happened behind the scenes than most contemporaries did in August 1936. During the Great Purge, even otherwise well-informed people like the writers Ilya Ehrenburg and Boris Pasternak thought that Stalin had nothing to do with the mass violence. 'If only someone would tell Stalin about it', Pasternak said at the time—and he was not alone.[371] Those who were at the receiving end of the terror wanted to know the reason for it all. 'Koba, [Koba was Stalin's name from the days in the underground before the revolution] why do you need me to die?', wrote Nikolai Bukharin on 13 March 1938, after he (who had saved Stalin in the 1920s from being politically side-lined) was also condemned to death.[372] Could someone with paranoia have acted the way Stalin did? While there is considerable evidence of paranoia in Stalin's last phase of life after the Second World War, pathological paranoia does not conform well with the precision of his manoeuvres during the years of the Great Purge, as Vadim Rogovin, and, before him, Boris Nicolaevsky have pointed out.[373] Rogovin rightly observes that:

> Stalin was not mad, and he conducted a precisely determined line. He arrived at the conclusion about the need to destroy the layer of Old Bolsheviks not later than the summer of 1934, and then he began to prepare this operation. [...] in 1937 Stalin held the entire grandiose mechanism of state terror under his unwavering and effective control. Without weakening or losing this control for even a minute, he displayed in his actions not the nervousness and alarm of a paranoiac, but on the contrary, a surprising, almost superhuman self-control and the most refined calculation. During the 1930s, he conducted the 'Yezhov' operation very precisely (from his point of view),

> since he prepared everything and seized his enemies unawares; they didn't understand him ... Even many of his supporters didn't understand him.[374]

It is clear that Stalin wanted to maintain a 'monolithic structure of the Party'[375] with himself undisputedly at the top. The Old Bolsheviks were the only ones who could combine and challenge him, and in that sense they posed a potential danger. However, they were divided and had in fact already lost their battle by the late 1920s. In the end one has to search for explanations within Stalin himself. Bukharin found one possible answer:

> He [Stalin] is ever unhappy because he cannot convince everyone, even himself, that he is greater than everybody else, and this is his misfortune, perhaps his only human trait .... But what is no longer human, but something diabolical is that for his 'misfortune' he cannot help but get revenge over people, all people, and particularly those who are higher in some way, or better than him.[376]

How did Stalin manage to lead his closest allies and countless others he did not even know, to the Gulag camps and the execution sites? Perhaps the main reason he succeeded was that he was a good actor. As Robert Tucker observed, '... noteworthy is the extraordinary cunning and duplicity that Stalin showed in his dealings with various individuals who were condemned in his own mind to destruction. He would convincingly reassure them that they had nothing to worry about.'[377] In March 1937, when the purges he had ordered were already in full swing, he could sanctimoniously caution other members of the Central Committee against 'a heartless attitude toward people' and blame those who 'think it is a mere bagatelle to expel thousands and ten thousands of people from the Party'.[378] His ability to manipulate his colleagues and subordinates was extraordinary.[379] While it is true that he needed helpers and willing executioners, one year after the first Moscow show trial, by mid-1937, as Robert Tucker put it, '... he effectively *was* the regime'.[380]

New evidence which has surfaced since the Soviet Union came to an end basically corroborates (for the first show trial) what Tucker and Cohen concluded in 1965 when they wrote about the third Moscow trial:

> As we re-examine the problem of the Moscow show trials, then, it is essential to bear in mind that these were basically one-man shows of which Stalin himself was organizer, chief producer, and stage manager as well as an appreciative spectator from a darkened room at the rear of the Hall of Columns, where the trial was held. Vyshinsky spoke

> for the prosecution, but we must understand that he spoke with the voice of Stalin. Although he did not claim personal authorship, Stalin was the chief playwright of the case of the 'Anti-Soviet Bloc of Rights and Trotzkyites' and the other cases enacted in the show trials.[381]

With his show trials, Stalin managed to frighten his enemies, punish his former opponents in the Party, mobilise the public to be 'vigilant' and expose and denounce 'enemies of the people', while at the same time shifting the blame for the crimes he committed to others. Perhaps that was also the deeper purpose of the 'confessions'—if he was at all capable of feelings of guilt, the confessions of others to *his* crimes could serve to take away that guilt. This is the interpretation proposed by Robert Tucker:

> For Stalin, the execution of Zinoviev and Kamenev, in violation of his promise to spare their lives, represented the final measure of vindictive triumph over loathsome enemies. He not only humiliated, exploited, and destroyed them, but he caused them to die knowing they had publicly abased and besmirched themselves and very many others, taken on the guilt for *his* murder of Kirov, *his* duplicity, and *his* terrorist conspiracy against the Party state. They had confessed to representing a variety of fascism when he was introducing just that in Russia by, among other things, this very pseudo-trial; and they wound up groveling at their murderer's feet and glorifying him—*all for nothing but to serve his purposes*.[382]

The 'show' trial was, if we follow this line of interpretation, perhaps first of all a show for himself, and then only one for the 165 million people in the Soviet Union and the workers' movement beyond the USSR. Of his opponents, only Trotzky stood up to challenge him from abroad, for which he paid the same price as those who had 'crawled on their bellies' during the trial in an attempt to save their lives.[383] Not only are the ruthlessness and vindictiveness of Stalin reflected in the crimes he attributed to his enemies in the show trial. The trials also became the model for the kind of society the Soviet Union became under Stalin after he seized on the Kirov murder to shape Russia in his own image. Amy Knight has correctly observed that:

> The Kirov case—not just the murder, but the investigation, trials, and propaganda that followed—served as a prototype for all future cases that the secret police would investigate. Marking the beginning of a collusion between Party leadership and the secret police in a travesty of justice for the Soviet people, it incorporated all the elements of the Soviet system of repression that would be refined in the decades to come—

> falsified testimonies, scapegoats, arbitrary punishments, physical and psychological torture, intimidation and threats, and meaningless judicial jargon.[384]

Before the advent of electricity (and even thereafter), theatres in Russia and elsewhere had to have an 'iron curtain', a barrier that could separate the stage, with its petrol lamp illumination, from the audience. In case of fire the curtain could be lowered to the edge of the stage, allowing the audience to escape unharmed. After the Second World War, Stalin put up an Iron Curtain around the Soviet Union and its satellites. It served the opposite purpose, namely to *prevent* the audience from escaping. Those in the Soviet Union who did not like his 'show' were put away and, in many cases, were worked to death in labour colonies and camps. By 1939 the camp population numbered 1.7 million people (not all of them political prisoners). By 1941 some seven million people had passed through the Gulag and labour colony system since 1934. By the time Stalin died, in 1953, there were 12 million in the Gulag system.[385] In the years 1937–1938 alone, 680,000 people had died following the monstrous trials and special tribunals at the hands of the NKVD. To this day, even these figures are incomplete and provisional.[386]

The chain of events that had led to this national tragedy began on 1 December 1934 with the assassination of Sergei Kirov and the decree that Stalin drafted in response, which became the heart of Article 58 of the Soviet Penal Code. The Great Purge ended four years later on 17 November 1938 with a decree of the Central Committee that put a stop to the extensive arrest and deportation operations. As Nikolaus Werth has observed, 'The Great Terror ended as it had begun, with an order of Stalin.'[387] He had never lost control of the 'show'. Stalin's compelling performative power has been unmatched to this day—as has his moral depravity.

Notes

1 George W. Hodos, *Show Trials. Stalinist Purges in Eastern Europe, 1948–1954* (New York: Praeger, 1987), p. xiii.

2 Cit.Vadim Z. Rogovin, *1937. Stalin's Year of Terror* (Oak Park, Michigan: Mehring Books, Inc., 1998), p. 46.

3 Arkady Vaksberg, *The Prosecutor and the Prey. Vyshinsky and the 1930s Moscow Show Trials* (London: Weidenfeld and Nicolson, 1990), p. 73.

4 Jeremy Peterson, 'Unpacking Show Trials: Situating the Trial of Saddam Hussein', *Harvard International Law Journal*, 48:1 (2007), p. 257.

5 Ernest Clark, 'Revolutionary Ritual: A Comparative Analysis of Thought Reform and the Show Trial', *Studies in Comparative Communism*, 9:3 (1976), pp. 226–227, 232–233 and 243.

6 Robert C. Tucker and Stephen F. Cohen (eds), *The Great Purge Trial* (New York: Grosset & Dunlap, 1965), pp. ix–x.

7 Nathan Leites and Elsa Bernaut, *Ritual Liquidation. The Case of the Moscow Trials* (Glencoe, Ill.: The Free Press, 1954), p. 449.

8 Ron Christenson (ed.), *Political Trials in History. From Antiquity to the Present* (New Brunswick: Transaction Books, 1991), p. 304.

9 Gudrun Persson, 'And they all confessed ...', http://art-bin.comart/amosc_preeng.html. Retrieved 9 June 2011.

10 Documents relating to the trial were destroyed in a fire in Moscow's *Pravda* building in February 2006. Adrian Blomfield, 'Stalin show trial files go up in smoke', *The Telegraph* UK (15 February 2006). The official transcript is partly paraphrased, shortened and incomplete; it has certainly been edited. It can be found in: People's Commissariat of Justice of the USSR. Report of Court Proceedings. The Case of theTrotzkyite-Zinovievite Terrorist Centre. Heard before the Military Collegium of the Supreme Court of the USSR, Moscow (19–24 August 1936). In re G.E. Zinoviev, L.B. Kamenev, G.E. Evdokimov, I.N. Smirnov, I.P. Bakayev, V.A. Ter-Vaganyan, S.V. Mrachkovsky, E.A. Dreitzer, F.S. Holtzman, I.I. Reingold, R.V. Pickel, V.P. Olberg, K.B. Berman-Yurin, Fritz David (I.I. Kruglyansky), M. Lurye and N. Lurye. Charges under Articles 19, 58.8 and 58.11 of the Criminal Code of the R.S.F.S.R. Published by the People's Commissariat of Justice of the USSR Moscow (1936).

11 Alexander Orlov, *The Secret History of Stalin's Crimes* (New York: Random House, 1953), p. 43. Orlov (pseudonym. for Lev Feldbin), himself a high-level former NKVD agent, noted: '... at the three Moscow trials the state prosecutor was unable to produce a single material proof of the defendants' guilt: not a conspiratorial letter, not a document relating to espionage, and not even a single political proclamation or leaflet'.

12 One of our chief sources is Alexander Orlov whose account was published in 1953. While its authenticity has been doubted in the past, recent archive findings corroborate what he wrote. In the words of Rogovin: 'The Secret History of Stalin's Crimes is the most complete and reliable account of the mechanism of Kirov's murder and the organization of the Moscow Trials, especially the first, which occurred when Orlov was in the USSR'. See Rogovin, *1937*, p. 469.

13 Edvard Radzinsky, *Stalin. The First In-Depth Biography Based on Explosive New Documents from Russia's Secret Archives* (London: Hodder & Stoughton, 1996), p. 310.

14 A fire in the Pressa Printing complex in Moscow on 14 February 2006 destroyed files of

the Stalin show trials. See Adrian Blomfield, 'Stalin show trial files go up in smoke', *The Telegraph* UK (15 February 2006); cit. *The Telegraph* (23 January 2011).

15 Otto Kirchheimer, *Political Justice. The Use of Legal Procedures for Political Ends* (Princeton: Princeton University Press, 1961), p. 46.

16 George Katkov, *The Trial of Bukharin* (London: B.T. Batsford, 1969), pp. 9–10.

17 *Pravda* (6 November 1918); cit. Leites and Bernaut, *Ritual Liquidation*, p. 444.

18 Alex P. Schmid, *Churchill's privater Krieg. Intervention und Konterrevolution im Russischen Bürgerkrieg, 1918–1920* (Zürich: Atlantis Verlag, 1974), p. 26.

19 Robert Conquest, *Stalin and the Kirov Murder* (London: Hutchinson, 1989), p. 122. The first Politburo consisted of five members; later it was expanded to fourteen full members and eight candidate (non-voting) members, but its actual size varied over time.

20 Stalin, in a speech at a trade union conference (19 November 1924); cit. Leites and Bernaut, *Ritual Liquidation*, p. 192.

21 NKVD stands for NarodnyiKommissariat Vnutrennych Diel (People's Commissariat for Internal Affairs). The secret police changed its name many times: from 1917 to 1922 it was known as Cheka (All-Russian Extraordinary Commission for Fighting Counter-Revolution and Sabotage), and as GPU or OGPU (State Political Administration/Combined State Political Administration), 1923–1934; NKVD, 1934–1946; Ministry of State Security (MGB), 1946–1953, and KGB (Committee for State Security) from 1953 to the early 1990s—Roj Medvedev, *All Stalin's Men* (Oxford: Blackwell, 1983), p. 169.

22 Boris Souvarine, *Stalin: A Critical Survey of Bolshevism* (New York: Alliance Book Corporation, 1939), pp. 482–485; cit. Orlov, *The Secret History of Stalin's Crimes*, p. 25; Tucker and Cohen (eds), *The Great Purge Trial*, p. xviii.

23 Simon Sebag Montefiore, *Stalin. The Court of the Red Tsar* (London: Phoenix, 2004), p. 34.

24 Amy Knight, *Who Killed Kirov? The Kremlin's Greatest Mystery* (New York: Hill and Wang, 1999), p. 248. Cf. Stalin's fear of assassination was real. While he could have an eye on his main political opponents, a lone-wolf-type of attack like Nikolayev's murder of Kirov was always a possibility although his personal security measures were extremely thorough. Cf. Robert Conquest, *The Great Terror: Stalin's Purge of the Thirties* (Harmondsworth: Penguin, 1968), p. 172; cf. Concern about terroristic assassinations also prompted Stalin to launch a campaign for the creation of an international court against terrorism after the assassination of the king of Yugoslavia and the French foreign minister in 1934. The Geneva-based Commission of Lawyers worked on the status of the future tribunal. However, when on 22 October 1936 Trotzky demanded that his case be brought to the tribunal once it was established, Stalin's efforts to bring about such an international court came to a halt. Cf. Rogovin, *1937*, p. 85.

25 Cit. Rogovin, *1937*, pp. 146–147.

26 Stuart Kahan, *The Wolf of the Kremlin. The First Biography of L.M. Kaganovich, the Soviet Union's Architect of Fear* (New York: William Morrow & Co., 1987), pp. 137–138.

27 Robert C. Tucker, *Stalin in Power. The Revolution from Above, 1928–1941* (New York: ww. Norton, 1990), p. 431.

28 Kahan, *The Wolf of the Kremlin*, p. 138.

29 Alexander Dallin and George W. Breslauer, *Political Terror in Communist Systems* (Stanford: Stanford University Press, 1970), p. 28.

30 Leites and Bernaut, *Ritual Liquidation*, pp. 9–10.

31 Tucker and Cohen (eds), *The Great Purge Trial*, p. xxviii.

32 Nicolas Werth, *Ein Staat gegen sein Volk. Das Schwarzbuch des Kommunismus—Sowjetunion.* (München: Piper Verlag 2002), pp. 186–187; Tucker and Cohen (eds), *The Great Purge Trial*, p. xviii; Montefiore, *Stalin*, p. 87n.

33 John Arch Getty & Oleg V. Naumov, *The Road to Terror. Stalin and the Self-Destruction of the Bolsheviks, 1932–1939* (New Haven: Yale University Press, 1999), p. 473.

34 F. Beck and W. Godin, *Russian Purge and the Extraction of Confession* (London: Hurst &Blackett, 1951), p. 27.

35 Tucker, *Stalin in Power*, p. 372.

36 Werth, *Ein Staat gegen sein Volk*, p. 151.

37 Cit. Montefiore, *Stalin*, pp. 131–132.

38 Rogovin, *1937*, p. xiii.

39 Cit. Montefiore, *Stalin*, p. 133; Michael Heller and Alexander Nekrich, *Geschichte der Sowjetunion. Vol. 1: 1914–1939* (Königstein: Athenäum, 1981), p. 266.

40 Rogovin, *1937*, p. xv.

41 John Getty, for instance, adheres to one theory, writing 'he [Stalin] was not a master planner, and studies of all of his policies before and after the 1930s have shown that he stumbled into everything from collectivization to foreign policy. Stalin's colossal felonies, like most violent crimes everywhere, were of the unplanned, erratic kind'. Cit. John Arch Getty & Oleg V. Naumov, *The Road to Terror. Stalin and the Self-Destruction of the Bolsheviks, 1932–1939* (New Haven: Yale University Press, 1999), p. 62; Rogovin takes the opposite position: '... the idea that the entire 'Yezhov period' was a diabolically calculated game, a crime, but not madness is profoundly justified. Cit. Rogovin, *1937*, p. xv. R. Tucker and S. Cohen also support this position: 'A crucially important point that emerges from the post-Stalin Soviet revelations about the Great Purge is that Stalin personally conceived, initiated, and directed the entire process, including the planning, preparation, and actual conduct of the purge trials'. Cit. Tucker and Cohen (eds), *The Great Purge Trial*, p. xii. This position has been strengthened by analyses based on archive materials released after the demise of the USSR.

42 Montefiore, *Stalin*, p. 154.

43 A German historian, Jörg Baberowski, noted that 'Following the trial [of Nikolayev and others, AS] NKVD people from Leningrad mysteriously lost their lives, others were arrested, shot or placed elsewhere as punishment'. Cit. J. Baberowski, *Der Rote Terror. Die Geschichte des Stalinismus* (Frankfurt a. M.: Fischer, 2007), p. 14.

44 Baberowski, *Der Rote Terror*, p. 144.

45 Montefiore, *Stalin*, pp. 146–147.

46 Knight, *Who Killed Kirov?*, p. 267.

47 Cit. Knight, *Who Killed Kirov?*, pp. 203–204; Montefiore, *Stalin*, p. 155.

48 Knight, *Who Killed Kirov?*, p. 229.

49 Knight, *Who Killed Kirov?*, pp. 224–225.

50 The numbers of those who were then in the camps was, according to one estimate, around 3.5 million but not all of them were 'political' criminals; J. Getty and O. Naumov cite a statistical report of the NKVD from 1953 who showed that 1,575,259 people were arrested by the security police in 1937–1938 (87 per cent of them on political grounds) of whom 1,344,923 were convicted and taken to the camps. However, this report covered only one part of those who during those two years were arrested, imprisoned and taken to labour colonies and camps. Cf. Getty and Naumov, *The Road to Terror*, pp. 589–590. Many of those who managed to survive in the camps were only released after Khrushchev's secret speech to the twentieth Party Congress in 1956. Cf. Sheila Fitzpatrick, *Everyday Stalinism. Ordinary Life in Extraordinary Times: Soviet Russia in the 1930s* (Oxford: Oxford University Press, 1999), p. 217. When the Presidium of the Supreme Soviet on 25 August 1938 discussed the possibility of an early release of prisoners who had distinguished themselves in the camps, Stalin was opposed to this, arguing, 'From the point of view of the economy it is a bad idea'. He made sure that those convicted would serve their full sentence because his 'dictatorship of the proletariat' needed slave workers. Cit. Radzinsky, *Stalin*, p. 402.

51 Baberowski, *Der Rote Terror*, pp. 157–160.

52 Conquest, *Stalin and the Kirov Murder*, p. 59.

53 Conquest, *Stalin and the Kirov Murder*, p. 35.

54 Knight, *Who Killed Kirov?*, p. 200; The Politburo approved the decree only *after* it had been published by *Pravda* on 5 December. Cf. Conquest, *Stalin and the Kirov Murder*, p. 38. This decree, which became Article 58 of the Russian Penal Code, penalised high treason, armed revolt, espionage, sabotage, terror, counter-revolutionary propaganda and association with a counter-revolutionary organisation. Cf. Beck and Godin, *Russian Purge and the Extraction of Confession*, p. 43. For an English translation of Art. 58, see: http://www.cyberussr.com/rus/uk58-e.html#58-1a.

55 Knight, *Who Killed Kirov?*, p. 220. According to one source, 'The murderer told the prison guard who brought him back to his cell that Stalin 'promised me my life if I named my accomplices, but I had no accomplices''. (p. 207).

56 Knight, *Who Killed Kirov?*, p. 6 and 205; The personality cult of the dead Kirov in subsequent years, encouraged by Stalin, placed him almost on the same saintly pedestal as Lenin. Cf. Ibid., pp. 235–236.

57 Wladislaw Hedeler, 'Ezhov's Scenario for The Great Terror and the Falsified Record of the Third Moscow Show Trial', in: Barry McLoughlin and Kevin McDermott (eds), *Stalin's Terror. High Politics and Mass Repression in the Soviet Union* (New York: Palgrave Macmillan, 2003), p. 37; Radzinsky, *Stalin*, pp. 317–321.

58 Knight, *Who Killed Kirov?*, p. 243.

59 Ibid., p. 14; Stalin had earlier instructed the interrogators: 'Nourish Nikolaev well, buy him chicken and other things, nourish so that he will be strong and then he will tell us who was leading him. And if he doesn't talk we will give him ... and he will tell and show everything'. Cit. Ibid., p. 214.

60 Ibid., p. 220.

61 Orlov, *The Secret History of Stalin's Crimes*, pp. 4–5; Their families were executed soon thereafter. Cf. Montefiore, *Stalin*, p. 167.

62 Cf. Montefiore, *Stalin*, p. 167.

63 Ibid.

64 Knight, *Who Killed Kirov?*, p. 222; Rogovin, *1937*, p. 1.

65 Rogovin, *1937*, p. 8.

66 Montefiore, *Stalin*, p. 167.

67 Conquest, *Stalin and the Kirov Murder*, p. 59.

68 Cit. Knight, *Who Killed Kirov?*, p. 222.

69 Baberowski, *Der Rote Terror*, p. 159; Werth, *Ein Staat gegen sein Volk*, pp. 158–159.

70 Rogovin, *1937*, p. 2.

71 Marc Jansen and Nikita Petrov, *Stalin's Loyal Executioner: People's Commissar Nikolai Ezhov, 1895–1940* (Stanford: Hoover Institution Press, 2002), p. 20.

72 Vaksberg, *The Prosecutor and the Prey*, p. 70.

73 Rogovin, *1937*, p. 1.

74 Baberowski, *Der Rote Terror*, p. 159.

75 Rogovin, *1937*, p. 4; In the February-March 1937 Plenum of the Central Committee, Yezhov, secretary of the Central Committee and boss of the NKVD, recalled that 'the person responsible for opening the case [of the Trotzky-Zinoviev Centre] was essentially Comrade Stalin'. Cit. Rogovin, *1937*, p. 2.

76 Getty and Naumov, *The Road to Terror*, p. 247.

77 Robert Conquest, *The Great Terror. A Reassessment* (Oxford: Oxford University Press, 1990), p. 83.

78 Montefiore, *Stalin*, pp. 189–190.

79 Getty and Naumov, *The Road to Terror*, p. 247.

80 Orlov, *The Secret History of Stalin's Crimes*, p. 107.

81 Hedeler, 'Ezhov's Scenario for The Great Terror', p. 38.

82 Rogovin, *1937*, p. 5.

83 Conquest, *The Great Terror*, pp. 87–88.

84 Jansen and Petrov, *Stalin's Loyal Executioner*, p. 204.

85 Rogovin, *1937*, p. 12.

86 Hedeler, 'Ezhov's Scenario for The Great Terror', p. 38.

87 Conquest, *The Great Terror*, pp. 90–91. Art. 58 of the Penal Code with Stalin's amendments of 1 December 1934 did not allow for appeal or clemency. However, since the expectation of a pardon was what made the defendants confess this revision was necessary to lull the defendants in a false sense of security.

88 Tucker, *Stalin in Power*, p. 367.

89 Radzinsky, *Stalin*, p. 332.

90 Cit. Hans Sherrer, 'Stalin's Prosecutor: the Life of Andrei Vyshinsky—Review by Hans Sherrer', *Justice Denied Magazine*, http://forejustice.org/wc/vyshinsky/stalin%27s_prosecutor.html. Retrieved 19 May 2015.

91 Rogovin, *1937*, p. 164.

92 Tucker, *Stalin in Power*, p. 378; Rogovin, *1937*, p. 93 also underlines that '.... according to the documents and eyewitness accounts we have, in 1936 the people under investigation were still not subjected to inhuman physical torture. The investigators limited themselves to such devices as sleep deprivation, conveyor belt interrogations lasting many hours, and threats to shoot or arrest relatives.'; In 1937, Stalin had hand-written the secret document allowing torture of arrested persons and had the other members of the Politburo to sign it. Cf. Rogovin, *1937*, p. 499. Sometimes, when Stalin went through the arrest lists prepared for him by Yezhov, he would add behind a name as specific instruction 'beat, beat!'. Cf. Jansen and Petrov, *Stalin's Loyal Executioner*, p. 111. A rationale given for torture, in a telegram signed by Stalin to provincial Party committees, informing them that the application of physical pressure by the NKVD had been authorised by the Central Committee argued that 'It is well known that all bourgeois agencies use physical pressure on representatives of the proletariat. The question is why should socialist countries have to be more humane with sworn enemies of the working class?' Cit. Radzinsky, *Stalin*, p. 343.

93 Conquest, *The Great Terror*, p. 83.

94 Orlov, *The Secret History of Stalin's Crimes*, pp. 129–130.

95 Rogovin, *1937*, p. 10.

96 Cit. Orlov, *The Secret History of Stalin's Crimes*, p. 74; Montefiore, *Stalin*, pp. 189–190.

97 Conquest, *The Great Terror*, p. 87.

98 Orlov, *The Secret History of Stalin's Crimes*, pp. 126–127.

99 Before that, they had been put in overheated cells despite the fact that it was summer; as a consequence, Zinoviev who suffered from asthma, could hardly breathe. Cf. Orlov, *The Secret History of Stalin's Crimes*, p. 122; Montefiore, *Stalin*, pp. 189–190.

100 Montefiore, *Stalin*, p. 190.

101 Rogovin, *1937*, p. 10.

102 During the pre-trial interrogations Smirnov asked Abram Slutsky, one of the interrogators, 'I should like to see how you are going to prove in court that I organized the assassination of Kirov in 1934 and that I was preparing a terrorist act against Stalin, when everybody knows that since January 1933 I have been in prison'. Slutzky's reply was 'We don't have to prove that. The Politburo expects that you confirm that yourself. If you refuse, you won't be taken to the trial'. At this point Slutsky reminded '.... Smirnov of Stalin's word that the life of those who consented to testify at the trial would be spared, and that those who refused to carry out the demands of the Politburo would be shot without trial by order of the Special Council of the NKVD'. Cit. Orlov, *The Secret History of Stalin's Crimes*, pp. 99–100.

103 Conquest, *The Great Terror*, p. 87.

104 Cit. Radzinsky, *Stalin*, pp. 329–330; Yezhov used similar language when trying to persuade Zinoviev to confess, telling him that his testimony was a political necessity since '.... Soviet intelligence had seized documents of the German general staff which showed the intentions of Germany and Japan to attack the Soviet Union the following spring. Therefore, what was now needed more than ever was the support of the international proletariat for the 'fatherland of all labourers''. Trotzky was impeding this support with his 'anti-Soviet propaganda'. Zinoviev must 'help the Party strike a shattering blow against Trotzky and his band in order to drive the workers away from his counterrevolutionary organization' [summary of Rogovin]. Cit. Rogovin, *1937*, p. 7. The same type of reasoning was also given by one of the few surviving witnesses, Smirnov's former wife, A. Safonova, who testified in 1956 before a Party Control Commission: 'Yes, it was with this understanding—that the Party demands this and we were obliged to pay with our heads for Kirov's murder—that we arrived at giving false testimony, not only I, but all other accused ... That's what happened during the pretrial investigation, and at the trial this was aggravated by the presence of foreign correspondents; knowing that they could use our testimony to harm the Soviet state, none of us could tell the

truth'. Cit. Rogovin, *1937*, p. 18; Robert Conquest also noted that 'Their surrender was not a single and exceptional act in their careers, but rather the culmination of a whole series of submissions to the Party made in terms they knew to be 'objectively' false [...] The oppositionists—with the exception of Trotzky himself—had made a basic tactical error. Their constant avowals of political sin, their admissions that Stalin was after all right, were based on the idea that it was correct to 'crawl in the dust', suffer any humiliation, to remain in or return to the Party'. Cf. Conquest, *The Great Terror*, p. 179.

105 Conquest, *The Great Terror*, p. 216.

106 Radzinsky, *Stalin*, p. 330; One way this showed was that during the trial Molotov's name was not on the list of those the defendants had drawn up as their victims. Kaganovich had put his own name on that list while Molotov's name was missing. Cf. Orlov, *The Secret History of Stalin's Crimes*, pp. 151–156.

107 Montefiore, *Stalin*, p. 189.

108 Roman Brackman, *The Secret File of Joseph Stalin. A Hidden Life* (London: Frank Cass, 2001), p. 254; Stalin had dissolved the Society of Old Bolsheviks in May 1935. That society had its own publishing house. In the Party, the revolution and civil war history of these Old Bolsheviks, Stalin's minor role in the Bolshevik Party's history was almost never mentioned. This irritated Stalin and inspired him to re-write the history of Bolshevism in his own 'official' Party publications. Cf. Orlov, *The Secret History of Stalin's Crimes*, p. 32.

109 Conquest, *The Great Terror*, p. 154.

110 Montefiore, *Stalin*, p. 194.

111 Rogovin, *1937*, p. 13.

112 Getty and Naumov, *The Road to Terror*, p. 256; Montefiore, *Stalin*, p. 160.

113 Tucker, *Stalin in Power*, p. 500.

114 Radzinsky, *Stalin*, p. 369; Conquest, *The Great Terror*, p. 154.

115 Tucker and Cohen (eds), *The Great Purge Trial*, pp. xiii–xiv.

116 Montefiore, *Stalin*, p. 193.

117 Tucker, *Stalin in Power*, p. 367.

118 Orlov, *The Secret History of Stalin's Crimes*, p. 157.

119 Conquest, *Stalin and the Kirov Murder*, p. 131.

120 According to R. Brackman, 'Stalin first used Vyshinsky's animosity toward the Old Bolsheviks in 1928 when he appointed Vyshinsky to preside over the Shakhty show trial. Vyshinsky performed to Stalin's satisfaction ....' Cit. Brackman, *The Secret File of Joseph Stalin*, p. 252.

121 Montefiore, *Stalin*, pp. 194–196.

122 Vaksberg, *The Prosecutor and the Prey*, p. 80.

123 Vaksberg, *The Prosecutor and the Prey*, p. 74.

124 Rogovin, 1937, p. 14.

125 People's Commissariat of Justice of the USSR. Report of Court Proceedings. The Case of the Trotzkyite-Zinovievite Terrorist Centre. Heard before the Military Collegium of the Supreme Court of the USSR. Moscow, August 19–24, 1936 In re G.E. Zinoviev, L.B. Kamenev, G.E. Evdokimov, I.N. Smirnov, I.P. Bakayev, V.A. Ter-Vaganyan, S.V. Mrachkovsky, E.A. Dreitzer, F.S. Holtzman, I.I. Reingold, R.V. Pickjel, V.P. Olberg, K.B. Berman-Yurin, Fritz David (I.I. Kruglyansky), M. Lurye and N. Lurye. Charges under Articles 58.8, 19 and 58.8, 5811 of the Criminal Code of the R.S.F.S.R. Published by the People's Commissariat of Justice of the USSR Moscow, 1936.

126 Tucker, *Stalin in Power*, p. 374.

127 Rogovin, 1937, p. 14.

128 Orlov, *The Secret History of Stalin's Crimes*, p. 157.

129 Ibid., p. 157; Conquest, *The Great Terror*, p. 154; Olberg, for instance, had in 1930 been ordered by Stalin to infiltrate Trotzky's exile circle and kill him, but Trotzky mistrusted him and excluded him. During the pre-trial investigation, Molchanov had explained to Olberg that he would now be given a chance to expose Trotzky in the impending trial and he was told that he would be given an important position after the trial if he agreed to confess to a plot, involving several students, who were planning to assassinate Stalin during a parade on the Red Square. Olberg also agreed to state in his signed deposition that he had met Trotzky's son Lev Sedov who was to be depicted as a Gestapo agent. To strengthen Olberg's testimony, two other NKVD agents were to confess that they had met Trotzky himself in 1932 in Copenhagen where they were given the assignment to kill Stalin and other members of the Politburo. Cf. Brackman, *The Secret File of Joseph Stalin*, pp. 254–255.

130 Orlov, *The Secret History of Stalin's Crimes*, p. 157.

131 Montefiore, *Stalin*, p. 193.

132 Ibidem, p. 194.

133 Orlov, *The Secret History of Stalin's Crimes*, p. 159.

134 A. Orlov explained the absence of defence lawyers in these words: '... before the defendants were brought into court they were made to promise that they would decline counsel. Besides that, they promised their inquisitors that they themselves would not raise a finger in their own defence. And indeed, when the time came for them to make speeches of defence, all the defendants, with one voice, declined to do so'. Cit. Orlov, *The Secret History of Stalin's Crimes*, p. 161.

135 Ibid.

136 Report of the Court Proceedings. The Case of the Trotzkyite-Zinovievite Terrorist Centre Centre. Heard Before the Military Collegium of the Supreme Court of the USSR

Accused: G.E. Zinoviev, L.B. Kamenev, G.E. Evdokimov, I.N. Smirnov, I.P. Bakayev, V.A. Ter-Vaganyan, S.V. Mrachkovsky, E.A. Dreitzer, E.S. Holtzman, I.I. Reingold, R.V. Pickel, V.P. Olberg, K.B. Berman-Yurin, Fritz David (I.I. Kruglansky), M. Lurye and N. Lurye. Charged under Articles 58.8 58.11 of the Criminal Code of the RSFSR. Moscow: People's Commissariat of Justice of the USSR 1936; August 19 [1936] (morning session).

137 Orlov, *The Secret History of Stalin's Crimes*, p. 158.

138 A. Orlov noted, 'Stalin ordered Yagoda to fill the hall only with NKVD officials and not to admit there any 'outsiders', even members of the Central Committee and of the government. [...] Yagoda carried out Stalin's order with unusual thoroughness and filled the hall with NKVD office employees—filing clerks, typists and code clerks. These employees received passes valid for half a day only and attended the trial in shifts. They had been instructed to come dressed in civilian clothes and to sit there the number of hours allotted them. Only the NKVD chiefs were allowed to attend the court proceedings in uniform'. Cf. Orlov, *The Secret History of Stalin's Crimes*, p. 158.

139 Ibid.

140 Conquest, *The Great Terror*, p. 152.

141 Vaksberg, *The Prosecutor and the Prey*, p. 123.

142 Vaksberg, *The Prosecutor and the Prey*, p. 81.

143 Report prepared for the Politburo; cit. Vaksberg, *The Prosecutor and the Prey*, pp. 78–79.

144 Vaksberg, *The Prosecutor and the Prey*, p. 79.

145 Rogovin, *1937*, pp. 15–16.

146 Article 58, Criminal Code of the RSFSR (1934), http://www.cyberussr.com/rus/uk58-e.html#58-1a. Retrieved 22 March 2011.

147 Montefiore, *Stalin*, p. 195.

148 RCP, pp. 3–4.

149 Cit. Rogovin, *1937*, p. 60.; Trotzky's son, L. Sedov would later write on the veracity of the trial, 'These two facts, i.e. that the meetings of Smirnov and Holtzman with Sedov actually took place, were the *only* grains of truth in the sea of lies at the Moscow Trial'. Cit. Rogovin, *1937*, p. 61; The chance meeting between Smirnov and Sedov in Berlin was, however, in 1931. In reality, there was a bit more substance to contacts between Trotzky and some members of the 16 defendants. However, there was no *terrorist* plot involved. Cf. Rogovin, *1937*, pp. 62–63.

150 RCP, p. 15 (19 August 1936; morning session).

151 RCP, p. 8. (19 August 1936; morning session). Quoting from Vol. XXVII, p. 70 of the interrogation files. According to A. Orlov, Stalin himself added this sentence to Reingold's testimony. Cf. Orlov, *The Secret History of Stalin's Crimes*, p. 69.

152 Orlov, *The Secret History of Stalin's Crimes*, pp. 69–70.

153 RCP, p. 1 (19 August 1936; evening session).

154 RCP, p. 3 (19 August 1936; evening session).

155 RCP, p. 22 (19 August 1936; morning session).

156 RCP, p. 1 (19 August 1936; evening session).

157 It is doubtful whether Ivan N. Smirnov simply said 'Yes' as the proceedings state. In prison, in a confrontation with Mrachkovsky who had tried to convince him to confess ('Ivan Nikitich, let us give them what they want. It has to be done'), Smirnov replied: 'I have nothing to confess to. I never fought against the Soviet power. I never fought against the Party. I was never a terrorist. And I never tried to murder anyone'. Cit. W.G. Krivitsky, *In Stalin's Secret Service. Memoirs of the First Soviet Master Spy to Defect* (New York: Enigma Books, 2000), p. 176. Like Trotzky, Krivitsky was assassinated abroad in 1940 on the orders of Stalin.

158 RCP, p. 25 (19 August 1936; evening session).

159 This also emerges from some references to the secret trial in mid-January. – Conquest, *Stalin and the Kirov Murder*, p. 65.

160 Orlov, *The Secret History of Stalin's Crimes*, p. 159; see also: Radzinsky, *Stalin*, pp. 332–333; Conquest, *Stalin and the Kirov Murder*, p. 80; Vaksberg, *The Prosecutor and the Prey*, p. 81.

161 RCP, p. 30 (19 August 1936; morning session).

162 RCP, p. 4 (19 August 1936; evening session).

163 Ibidem.

164 RCP, p. 6 (19 August 1936; evening session).

165 RCP, p. 7 (19 August 1936; evening session).

166 RCP, pp. 9–10 (19 August 1936; evening session); Pickel, who, at the time of his arrest was director or commissar of the Kamerny theatre in Moscow, had been promised a light sentence for his cooperation and testimony in the trial. In the words of Alexander Orlov: 'Pickel's friend told him frankly that they could not save him from the trial, because that had been decreed 'from above', but if he would agree to assist the NKVD against Zinoviev they promised him that he would serve his term, whatever the court sentence might be, not in prison, but at liberty, as one of the chiefs of a new big construction job on the Volga'. Cf. Orlov, *The Secret History of Stalin's Crimes*, p. 71.

167 Conquest, *The Great Terror*, p. 159.

168 RCP, p. 1 (20 August 1936; morning session).

169 RCP, p. 3 (20 August 1936; morning session).

170 Conquest, *The Great Terror*, p. 160.

171 RCP, p. 7 (20 August 1936; morning session).

172 RCP, p. 3 (20 August 1936; morning session); During the pre-trial interrogations, Smirnov was shown a deposition made by his former wife in which she 'confessed' that Smirnov

had received 'terrorist instructions' from Trotzky in 1932. When confronted with him in prison she had pleaded with her former husband to save both himself and her by agreeing to provide the required testimonials in court. He finally agreed, provided that Safonova would not be hurt. Cf. Brackman, *The Secret File of Joseph Stalin*, p. 256. Safonova managed to survive Stalin—probably more by good luck than thanks to a promise kept.

173 RCP, p. 1 (20 August 1936; evening session); A. Orlov had this to say about Smirnov's previous relationship with Stalin after Lenin's death: 'but Smirnov was one of the first who had demanded that Lenin's Testament, which recommended the removal of Stalin from the post of General Secretary, be carried out. Stalin knew how great was Smirnov's popularity within the Party and how the Old Bolsheviks heeded Smirnov's advice. Now, being firmly in the saddle, Stalin could not deny himself the long awaited pleasure of taking revenge on Smirnov by dragging him through the excruciating inquisition of the NKVD and the comedy of the trial to the cellar of the executioner'. Cit. Orlov, *The Secret History of Stalin's Crimes*, p. 96.

174 Rogovin, *1937*, p. 177.

175 A. Orlov commented: 'Of all the defendants only Smirnov gave his testimony in a manner so ironical as to leave no doubt that he considered that all the charges against him and the other Bolsheviks were trumped up. His sarcastic remarks and frequent hints that the whole story about the conspiracy was a pure myth kept Prosecutor Vyshinsky on tenterhooks. Before conceding some point of the accusation, Smirnov took care to discredit first the whole accusation and only then would say in a contemptuous tone, 'Well, let it be so''. Cit. A. Orlov, *The Secret History of Stalin's Crimes*, p. 162.

176 RCP, p. 3 (20 August 1936; evening session).

177 RCP, p. 4 (20 August 1936; evening session); Earlier, during the interrogation phase, Y.D. Agranov who had to interrogate him, had told Stalin: 'I am afraid that we won't be able to accuse Smirnov. He, after all, was in prison for a number of years'. Cit. Orlov, *The Secret History of Stalin's Crimes*, p. 96. (Smirnov had been in prison since at least the beginning of 1933; some of his 'crimes' therefore had to be situated in the year 1932).

178 Conquest, *The Great Terror*, p. 161.

179 Ibidem.

180 RCP, p. 9 (20 August 1936; evening session).

181 RCP, p. 12 (20 August 1936; evening session).

182 RCP, p. 14 (20 August 1936; evening session).

183 This meeting was also subject to investigation, in 1937, by the so-called Dewey Commission (more on it later) which wrote in its report: '… Trotzky, testifying before the preliminary Commission … stated that … Sedov had met Smirnov on the street in Berlin in 1931. Trotzky said that his son thereafter wrote him that Smirnov was unhappy and

without political orientation, and had given him information about Old friends .... Sedov testified before the *Commission Rogatoire* ... that he did meet Smirnov accidentally in Berlin in July 1931; that he did subsequently have an interview with him at Smirnov's apartment during which he gave him two addresses and a phone number, and suggested that Smirnov should take advantage of the trips of comrades to send him information on conditions in the Soviet Union; that Smirnov said jokingly that if anyone came to find Sedov he would present himself in the name of Galya ... the little girl who had accompanied Smirnov at their first meeting .... Sedov further affirmed that the defendant Holtzman did get in touch with him in Berlin around the end of September or the beginning of October 1932, that in presenting himself he stated that he brought ... a document for Trotzky from Smirnov which he had carried in a spectacle case ...' Sedov further testified that the document delivered to him by Holtzman was an unsigned report on economic conditions in the Soviet Union, which he, Sedov, published in the *Bulletin of the Opposition*, No. 31, of November 1932, p. 20. Sedov said that in publishing it he affixed as a signature the syllable 'Ko' [from Kolokol, a bell] which was an allusion to Trotzky's having compared Smirnov, in polemicizing with him, to a bell-ringer'. Cit. Leites and Bernaut, *Ritual Liquidation*, pp. 323–324.

184 RCP, p. 3 (21 August 1936; morning session).

185 This point was later highlighted by Sedov in a book trying to expose the lies of this trial. The 'mistake' arose perhaps as the NKVD's script for this session had originally situated the meeting in Norway (where there was a Hotel Bristol). When this blunder was later brought to Stalin's notice, he shouted, according to one account: 'What the devil did you need the hotel for? You ought to have said 'railway station'. The station is always there'. Cit. Montefiore, *Stalin*, p. 196. However, according to R. Brackman, the Bristol Hotel in Copenhagen could, in fact, have been Stalin's own idea: in 1906—according to Brackman's account—Stalin, like Yagoda, a former part-time informer (code name 'Vasily') for the Okhrana, the Tsarist secret police, apparently met the chief of Okhrana's Foreign Agency, Arkady Garting, in the Bristol hotel which was destroyed in 1917. Cf. Brackman, *The Secret File of Joseph Stalin*, p. 255 and 233–234. See also: Tucker, *Stalin in Power*, pp. 501 and 377.

186 Conquest, *The Great Terror*, p. 164.

187 Rogovin, *1937*, p. 17.

188 Conquest, *The Great Terror*, p. 163.

189 RCP, pp. 1–2 (21 August 1936; evening session).

190 RCP, p. 2 (21 August 1936; evening session).

191 RCP, p. 3 (21 August 1936; evening session).

192 Tucker, *Stalin in Power*, p. 374.

193 RCP, p. 15 (19 August 1936; evening session).

194 Conquest, *The Great Terror*, p. 166; Karl Radek, a prominent journalist and former secretary of the Communist International and Yuri L. Pyatakov, Deputy Commissar of Heavy Industry, had been siding with Trotzky in the 1920 but had forsworn Trotzkyism in the early 1930s. Cf. Getty and Naumov, *The Road to Terror*, p. 262.

195 Tucker, *Stalin in Power*, p. 374.

196 Ibidem, p. 375.

197 Cit. Radzinsky, *Stalin*, p. 338.

198 Montefiore, *Stalin*, p. 197.

199 Cit. Montefiore, *Stalin*, p. 195.

200 RCP, p. 1 (22 August 1936; morning session).

201 Ibid., p. 2.

202 Ibid., p. 3.

203 Ibid.

204 Ibid., p. 4.

205 Ibid., pp. 4–5.

206 RCP, p. 6 (22 August 1936; morning session).

207 Ibid., p. 7; Vyshinsky, like Stalin, had been an agent/informer for the Tsarist secret police, the Okhrana, a fact with which Stalin was familiar and which allowed him to blackmail Vyshinsky if necessary. Roman Brackman writes: 'Stalin kept in Vyshinsky's dossier an order, signed by Vyshinsky in 1917, to arrest Lenin. [...] Stalin's blackmail worked: Vyshinsky was his obedient tool. The Old Bolsheviks despised Vyshinsky, whom they called 'a rat in human image', and he hated them for this. Stalin first used Vyshinsky's animosity toward the Old Bolsheviks in 1928 when he appointed him to preside over the Shakhty show trial. Vyshinsky performed to Stalin's satisfaction, and Stalin chose him to play the leading role of prosecutor in the show trial of Kamenev, Zinoviev and other defendants scheduled for the summer of 1936'. Cf. Brackman, *The Secret File of Joseph Stalin*, p. 252; E. Radzinsky also refers to Vyshinsky as a '... former enemy of the Bolsheviks, a man who had called for Lenin's arrest in 1917 as a traitor and a German spy ...' Cit. Radzinsky, *Stalin*, p. 382; see also: Rogovin, *1937*, p. 57.

208 Cit. Lev Trotzky, *Stalin. An Appraisal of the Man and His Influence* (New York: Harper & Bro., 1941), p. 375.

209 Cit. Brackman, *The Secret File of Joseph Stalin*, p. 183; When Lenin's Testament was read at a special closed session of the Central Committee on 22 May 1924, Zinoviev and Kamenev had come to Stalin's rescue. In the words of Brackman, 'It hardly seemed possible for the Central Committee members to ignore Lenin's wish, having loudly pledged to 'hold Lenin's word sacred'. But Zinoviev and Kamenev did the impossible. Stalin's fate was

in their hands; they could have used Lenin's words to remove Stalin from power, but instead rushed to his rescue, imploring the Central Committee not to deny him the post of general secretary. 'Lenin's word is sacred', Zinoviev exclaimed. 'But Lenin himself, if he could have witnessed, as you all have, Stalin's sincere efforts to mend his ways, would not have urged the Party to remove him'. Displaying a considerable flair for theatrical performance, Kamenev and Zinoviev persuaded delegates that Stalin was a reformed man. The majority voted in Stalin's favour. Trotzky watched the scene, remaining aloof and silent. Stalin pretended to offer his resignation, but Zinoviev and Kamenev 'persuaded' him to stay. The decision was not to read Lenin's Testament to the delegates of the congress and not to enter it into the congressional record. [...] Why Trotzky did not use Lenin's 'Testament' as a weapon to fight Stalin remains an unanswered question'. Cf. Brackman, *The Secret File of Joseph Stalin*, p. 183.

210 Vaksberg, *The Prosecutor and the Prey*, p. 80.

211 RCP, ibid., p. 20.

212 RCP, ibid.

213 There are multiple testimonies about the falsifications in this trial, both contemporary and from the post-Stalin period. For instance, G.S. Lushkov, the deputy chief of the Secret Political Department who had assisted Molchanov, the chief of the Secret Political Department of the NKVD, in organising the first Moscow trial and who had fled the USSR in 1938, declared: '... at the trial ... accusations that Trotzky via Olberg, was connected with the German Gestapo; accusations against Zinoviev and Kamenev for espionage; accusations that Zinoviev and Kamenev were linked to the so-called 'Right Centre' via Tomsky, Rykov and Bukharin—all these accusations were completely fabricated.' Cit. Rogovin, 1937, pp. 17–18; Orlov, *The Secret History of Stalin's Crimes*, p. 219.

214 RCP, ibid, p. 22.

215 RCP, ibid., p. 24. Elsewhere the prosecutor said, 'And they must bear full responsibility for this, irrespective of whether any one of them was at liberty at the time or not' (ibid).

216 RCP, p. 15 (22 August 1936; morning session).

217 Ibid., p. 16.

218 Ibid., p. 28.

219 Actually the published version of the proceedings make no mention that the defendants referred to *Narodnaya Volya* (the People's Will) themselves.

220 RCP, ibid., p. 30.

221 See: Brackman, *The Secret File of Joseph Stalin*; Vaksberg, *The Prosecutor and the Prey*.

222 RCP, ibid., p. 31.

223 Orlov, *The Secret History of Stalin's Crimes*, p. 163.

224 Orlov, *The Secret History of Stalin's Crimes*, pp. 164–166.

225 RCP, p. 2 (22 August 1936; evening session).

226 Conquest, *The Great Terror*, p. 168.

227 RCP, pp. 2–3 (22 August 1936; evening session); According to A. Orlov, Rinegold was included among the defendants, '... because his personal acquaintance with Kamenev and Sokolnikov afforded an opportunity to use him as witness against them, and also because his short-lived membership in the opposition could be used against ...' Reingold was arrested. Cf. Orlov, *The Secret History of Stalin's Crimes*, p. 65. Orlov added: 'The testimony of Reingold, carefully revised by Moronov, chief of the Economic Administration, and Agranov, Yagoda's assistant, was taken by Yagoda to Stalin. On the next day Stalin returned Reingold's [pre-trial, AS] testimony with corrections which created the incredible sensation among the chiefs of the NKVD. From the part of the written testimony where Reingold testified that Zinoviev insisted on the assassination of Stalin, Molotov, Kaganovich and Kirov, *Stalin with his own hand crossed out the name of Molotov*.' Cf. Orlov, *The Secret History of Stalin's Crimes*, pp. 68–69.

228 Orlov, *The Secret History of Stalin's Crimes*, p. 163.

229 RCP, p. 3 (22 August 1936; evening session).

230 Ibidem.

231 Orlov, *The Secret History of Stalin's Crimes*, p. 166.

232 Ibidem.

233 Brackman, *The Secret File of Joseph Stalin*, p. 259; Radzinsky, *Stalin*, p. 333; Rogovin, *1937*, p. 8; Earlier, in the pre-trial investigation, when Kamenev refused to confess, Stalin told his interrogator: 'Tell him [Kamenev] that if he refuses to go to the trial, we'll find a suitable substitute for him—his own son, who will testify at the trial that on instructions from his dad he was preparing terroristic acts against the leaders of the Party. Tell him that you have information that his son together with Reingold were trailing the automobiles of Voroshilov and Stalin on the Mozhaisk road. This will bring him to his senses at once ...' Cit. Orlov, *The Secret History of Stalin's Crimes*, p. 118.

234 Orlov, *The Secret History of Stalin's Crimes*, pp. 166–167.

235 RCP, p. 2 (23 August 1936; morning session).

236 Ibid., pp. 2–3.

237 Rogokin, *1937*, p. 22.

238 Orlov, *The Secret History of Stalin's Crimes*, p. 167.

239 Vaksberg, *The Prosecutor and the Prey*, p. 79.

240 Brackman, *The Secret File of Joseph Stalin*, p. 259; Orlov, *The Secret History of Stalin's Crimes*, p. 164.

241 Orlov, *The Secret History of Stalin's Crimes*, pp. 48–49.

242 Ibid., p. 72.

243 Conquest, *The Great Terror*, p. 169.
244 RCP, p. 5 (24 August 1936; afternoon session).
245 Ibid., pp. 6–7.
246 Cit. Orlov, *The Secret History of Stalin's Crimes*, p. 167.
247 Tucker, *Stalin in Power*, p. 371. One of them, Hotzmann, apparently did not appeal for clemency.
248 Orlov, *The Secret History of Stalin's Crimes*, p. 168.
249 Conquest, *The Great Terror*, p. 169.
250 Cit. Montefiore, *Stalin*, p. 198.
251 Conquest, *The Great Terror*, p. 170.
252 Tucker, *Stalin in Power*, p. 373.
253 Conquest, *The Great Terror*, p. 170.
254 Radzinsky, *Stalin*, pp. 334 and 337.
255 Brackman, *The Secret File of Joseph Stalin*, p. 260. However, the other two pseudo-defendants were apparently also shot.
256 Conquest, *The Great Terror*, pp. 170–171.
257 Cit. Montefiore, *Stalin*, p. 202; Pauker, a former hairdresser at the Budapest opera, was, according to Montefiore, 'an accomplished actor performing accents, especially Jewish ones, for Stalin'. Cf. Montefiore, *Stalin*, p. 69. Pauker too would soon fall from grace; he disappeared without a trace. Cf. Radzinsky, *Stalin*, p. 381.
258 The Central Committee of the VKP(b), Moscow (29 July 1936), repr. in Getty and Naumov, *The Road to Terror*, p. 255.
259 Fitzpatrick, *Everyday Stalinism*, pp. 202–203.
260 Repr. In Getty and Naumov, *The Road to Terror*, p. 257.
261 Getty and Naumov, *The Road to Terror*, p. 257.
262 Rogovin, *1937*, p. 14.
263 Montefiore, *Stalin*, p. 197.
264 Tucker, *Stalin in Power*, p. 320.
265 Cit. Rogovin, *1937*, p. 67.
266 Ibid., p. 70.
267 Ibid.
268 Rogovin, *1937*, p. 54; Conquest, *The Great Terror*, p. 162. All three would soon be arrested and tried.
269 Cit. Rogovin, *1937*, p. 40.
270 Tucker and Cohen (eds), *The Great Purge Trial*, pp. xxviii–xxix.
271 Cit. Rogovin, *1937*, p. 83.
272 Cit. Tucker, *Stalin in Power*, p. 371.

273 Cit.Montefiore, *Stalin*, p. 214.
274 Getty and Naumov, *The Road to Terror*, pp. 273–274.
275 Tucker and Cohen (eds), *The Great Purge Trial*, p. xxxiii.
276 Cit. Vaksberg, *The Prosecutor and the Prey*, p. 123.
277 Vaksberg, *The Prosecutor and the Prey*, p. 123. In 1954 Pritt would receive the Lenin Award from the USSR.
278 Tucker, *Stalin in Power*, pp. 372–373.
279 Vaksberg, *The Prosecutor and the Prey*, pp. 124–125.
280 Rogovin, *1937*, pp. 305–307.
281 Cit. Leites and Bernaut, *Ritual Liquidation*, p. 207.
282 Rogovin, *1937*, p. 309.
283 Not Guilty. The Dewey Commission Report (New York: Harper & Brothers, 1938), p. xv.
284 Rogovin, *1937*, pp. 41 and 43.
285 Tucker, *Stalin in Power*, p. 391.
286 Constitutional Rights Foundation, 'The Stalin Purges and "Show Trials"', *Bill of Rights in Action*, 7:4 (1991), http://www.crf-usa.org/bill-of-rights-in-action/bria-7-4-a-the-stalin-purges-and-show-trials. Retrieved 9 April 2014.
287 Conquest, *Stalin and the Kirov Murder*, p. 35; Tucker and Cohen (eds), *The Great Purge Trial*, p. xxxv.
288 However, maybe there was a link between the Constitution which promised to erase class borders and give back suffrage to former White Guards, Kulaks and priests: if these classes were eliminated by the purges, then they could be safely given the vote. See: Jansen and Petrov, *Stalin's Loyal Executioner*, pp. 107–108.
289 Orlov, *The Secret History of Stalin's Crimes*, p. 170.
290 Werth, *Ein Staat gegen sein Volk*, p. 181.
291 Getty and Naumov, *The Road to Terror*, pp. 272–274.
292 Cit. Georgii Dimitrov, Secretary of the Comintern; as quoted by Jansen and Petrov, *Stalin's Loyal Executioner*, p. 111. Later, when Dimitrov would plead with Stalin on behalf of arrested colleagues of his, Stalin lied to him: 'What can I do for them, Georgi? All my own relatives are in prison too'. Cit. Montefiore, *Stalin*, pp. 296–297.
293 Peter H. Solomon, *Soviet Criminal Justice under Stalin* (Cambridge: Cambridge University Press, 1966), pp. 238–239.
294 Hedeler, 'Ezhov's Scenario for The Great Terror', pp. 51–52.
295 Werth, *Ein Staat gegen sein Volk*, pp. 156–157.
296 Baberowski, *Der Rote Terror*, pp. 146–148.
297 Cit. Vaksberg, *The presecutor and the prey*, p. 105; His attitude and loyalty to Stalin got him far. In 1939, Vyshinsky was promoted to Deputy Chairman of the Soviet People's

Commissariat. Later Vyshinsky became Minister of Foreign Affairs (1949–1953) and then the Soviet Union's Permanent Representative to the United Nations (1953–1954).

298 Getty and Naumov, *The Road to Terror*, p. 546. On 7 August 1937 Vyshinsky instructed the regional procurators to attend the troika meetings, adding, 'The observance of legal procedure and the preliminary approval of arrests are not demanded'. Cit. Jansen and Petrov, *Stalin's Loyal Executioner*, p. 88.

299 Baberowski, *Der Rote Terror*, p. 191.

300 Getty and Naumov, *The Road to Terror*, p. 530.

301 Ibid., p. 547; After April 1939, 327,000 people, many of them from the armed forces, were freed, pardoned by Stalin after Yezhov's arrest. Cf. Radzinsky, *Stalin*, p. 415.

302 Solomon, *Soviet Criminal Justice under Stalin*, pp. 1 44–145, 252.

303 Werth, *Ein Staat gegen sein Volk*, p. 167.

304 All told, the 'national operations' affected more than 350,000 people of whom almost 250,000 were shot by NKVD commandos. Cf. Baberowski, *Der Rote Terror*, p. 200.

305 Werth, *Ein Staat gegen sein Volk*, pp. 170 and 184.

306 Jansen and Petrov, *Stalin's Loyal Executioner*, pp. 102–104.

307 Werth, *Ein Staat gegen sein Volk*, pp. 166–167.

308 Baberowski, *Der Rote Terror*, p. 182; The interpretation of Edvard Radzinsky is illuminating in this context: '... Stalin had been reared in the Caucasus, where the blood feud was a living tradition, and he was afraid that he might be rearing his own future assassins. As always, he found a revolutionary solution. At Yezhov's (and not, of course, the Boss' [Stalin's]) suggestion, the Politburo adopted a secret resolution on July 5, 1937. [...] The wives of convicted enemies of the people were sent to prison camps for a term of five to eight years. Children under the age of 15 were cared for by the state (that is, they were consigned to a dreadful state orphanage).' Cf. Radzinsky, *Stalin*, p. 407.

309 Baberowski, *Der Rote Terror*, p. 195.

310 Knight, *Who Killed Kirov?*, p. 15.

311 Ibid., p. 260.

312 Werth, *Ein Staat gegen sein Volk*, p. 171.

313 Tucker, *Stalin in Power*, p. 372.

314 Cit. Montefiore, *Stalin*, p. 203.

315 Getty and Naumov, *The Road to Terror*, p. 326.

316 Conquest, *The Great Terror*, p. 214.

317 Cit. Tucker and Cohen (eds), *The Great Purge Trial*, pp. xxx–xxxi.

318 Ibid., p. xxxi.

319 Rogovin, *1937*, p. 63. Most of the oppositional activities of Trotzky against Stalin dated back to 1926 and 1927 when he was heading a United Left Opposition inside the Bolshevik

Party, numbering some 8,000 adherents. In the description of Stuart Kahan, 'Clandestine meetings of the Left Opposition were held in workers' homes outside Moscow, almost like old times; almost, but not quite [...] But the new front, led by Trotsky, Kamenev, and Zinoviev, was determined not to attack the principle of Party unity but rather the Party bureaucracy, which they blamed for many defects ...' Cf. Stuart Kahan, p. 137; By 1927–1929 the Old Bolsheviks who had opposed Stalin's rise to supremacy had (with the exception of Trotzky who went into exile) capitulated and publicly renounced their opposition. Cf. Rogovin, *1937*, p. 374; Leites and Bernaut noted that, 'According to the *Letter of an Old Bolshevik*, the Leningrad Zinovievites had before the assassination of Kirov: ... no secret organization, but maintained mutual friendly relations, which, in some cases, had been of long standing. At their gatherings they exchanges information about Party affairs and ... comrades still in prison or in exile. They took up collections on their behalf, and ... abused opponents ... This was ... the limit of their political activity ...' Cit. Leites and Bernaut, *Ritual Liquidation*, p. 133.

320 Cit. Rogovin, *1937*, pp. 4–5.

321 Montefiore, *Stalin*, pp. 58, 156.

322 Conquest, *The Great Terror*, p. 218; In this telegram he said that 'Yagoda has definitely proved himself to be incapable of unmasking the Trotskyite–Zinovievite bloc. This is noted by all Party workers and by the majority of the representatives of the NKVD'. Cit. Robert Conquest, *Inside Stalin's Secret Police. NKVD Politics, 1936–1939* (London: Macmillan, 1986), p. 11. Yagoda could not find such a 'bloc' because it never existed as was admitted by the Soviet regime after Stalin's death. Cf. Tucker and Cohen (eds), *The Great Purge Trial*, p. xxiv.

323 Montefiore, *Stalin*, p. 203; Tucker, *Stalin in Power*, p. 376.

324 Radzinsky, *Stalin*, p. 336.

325 Tucker, *Stalin in Power*, p. 378.

326 Getty and Naumov, *The Road to Terror*, p. 80; Orlov, *The Secret History of Stalin's Crimes*, p. x.

327 Jansen and Petrov, *Stalin's Loyal Executioner*, p. 201.

328 Baberowski, *Der Rote Terror*, p. 206.

329 Tucker, *Stalin in Power*, p. 444.

330 Jansen and Petrov, *Stalin's Loyal Executioner*, pp. 206–207.

331 Hedeler, 'Ezhov's Scenario for The Great Terror', p. 39; Baberowski, *Der Rote Terror*, p. 164.

332 Jansen and Petrov, *Stalin's Loyal Executioner*, p. x.

333 Robert C. Tucker, 'Stalin, Bukharin, and History as Conspiracy', in: Tucker and Cohen (eds), *The Great Purge Trial*, p. xxix.

334 Tucker, *Stalin in Power*, p. 415.

335 Cit. Radzinsky, *Stalin*, p. 337.

336 Orlov, *The Secret History of Stalin's Crimes*, p. 187.

337 Montefiore, *Stalin*, p. xxxi.

338 See Tucker and Cohen (eds), *The Great Purge Trial* for a transcript. With notes by the editors.

339 Cit. Knight, *Who Killed Kirov?*, p. 205.

340 In court, Yagoda testified that 'In 1934, in the summer, Yenukidze informed me that the centre of the "bloc of Rights and Trotskyites" had adopted a decision to organize the assassination of Kirov. Rykov took a direct part in the adoption of this decision [...] Needless to say, my objections were not taken into consideration and had no effect. Yenukidze insisted that I was not to place any obstacles in the way; the terrorist act, he said, would be carried out by the Trotzkite–Zinovievite group. Owing to this, I was compelled to instruct Zaporozhetz, who occupied the post of Assistant Chief of the Regional Administration of the People's Commissariat of Internal Affairs, not to place any obstacles in the way of the terrorist act against Kirov. Some time later Zaporozhetz informed me that the organs of the People's Commissariat of Internal Affairs had detained Nikolayev, in whose possession a revolver and a chart of the route Kirov usually took had been found. Nikolayev was released. Soon after that Kirov was assassinated by this very Nikolayev.' Cf. Tucker and Cohen (eds), *The Great Purge Trial* [Transcript], pp. 493–494.

341 Montefiore, *Stalin*, p. 295.

342 Solomon, *Soviet Criminal Justice under Stalin*, pp. 235–236.

343 Fitzpatrick, *Everyday Stalinism*, p. 203; She called Lev Sheinin 'an intriguing figure who combined a day job as a high-ranking investigator ... [and] deputy to Andrei Vyshinsky, with an avocation as a writer and journalist'. Cf. Fitzpatrick, *Everyday Stalinism*, p. 78.

344 Cit. Montefiore, *Stalin*, p. 225.

345 Tucker, *Stalin in Power*, pp. 379–380.

346 Montefiore, *Stalin*, pp. 226–227.

347 Baberowski, *Der Rote Terror*, pp. 169–172.

348 Krivitsky, *In Stalin's Secret Service*, p. 151; cit. Leites and Bernaut, *Ritual Liquidation*, p. 409.

349 Tucker and Cohen (eds), *The Great Purge Trial*, p. xx.

350 Baberowski, *Der Rote Terror*, p. 179.

351 Tucker, *Stalin in Power*, pp. 526–529.

352 Radzinsky, *Stalin*, p. 413.

353 Cit. Leites and Bernaut, *Ritual Liquidation*, p. 403.

354 Getty and Naumov, *The Road to Terror*, p. 493.

355 Ibid., p. 523.

356 Ibid., p. 530; These 'troikas'—groups of three—consisted of the local Party secretary, the local NKVD chief and the local prosecutor. Together they decided about the categorisation of the victims (category 1: execution; category 2: deportation to camps). Often the Troikas existed only on paper and the local prosecutor did not participate in the decision-making. The fate of most of those placed on lists was decided in their absence and neither prosecutors nor judges were present. Cf. Baberowski, *Der Rote Terror*, pp. 191–193.

357 Jansen and Petrov, *Stalin's Loyal Executioner*, p. 208.

358 Cit. Ibid., p. x.

359 Tucker and Cohen (eds), *The Great Purge Trial*, p. xiii; According to Jansen and Petrov, the *Yezhovshchina* period saw some 1,5 million people arrested, of whom 700,000 were shot. Cf. Jansen and Petrov, *Stalin's Loyal Executioner*, p. 104.

360 Radzinsky, *Stalin*, p. 412.

361 Montefiore, *Stalin*, p. 304.

362 Cit. Radzinsky, *Stalin*, p. 417.

363 There was, according to the testimony of the son of one of the closest collaborators of Stalin, Malenko, a file on Stalin in Yezhov's safe, showing that Stalin had, in his previous career, also been an agent provocateur of the Tsarist secret police. Cf. Radzinsky, *Stalin*, pp. 334, 337; Leites and Bernaut noted that 'In the late period of tsarism there was a distinctive pattern of police agents occupying *top* positions in revolutionary organizations'. Cit. Leites and Bernaut, *Ritual Liquidation*, p. 450; see also: Montefiore, *Stalin*, p. 304.

364 Baberowski, *Der Rote Terror*, p. 203.

365 Jansen and Petrov, *Stalin's Loyal Executioner*, pp. 166–167.

366 'I did him in, I saved you all', Beria later reportedly told Molotov and Kaganovich. Cit. Montefiore, *Stalin*, p. 655.

367 Montefiore, *Stalin*, p. 302.

368 Radzinsky, *Stalin*, pp. 423–424.

369 Franklin L. Ford, *Political Murder. From Tyrannicide to Terrorism* (Cambridge: Harvard University Press, 1985), pp. 269–270; In order to deflect attention away from Stalin, a letter found in his pockets made it appear that he was a disillusioned Trotzkyist. Cf. Tucker, *Stalin in Power*, p. 613.

370 Werth, *Ein Staat gegen sein Volk*, p. 187. A week after the Ribbentrop–Molotov Pact was signed, the German Army attacked Poland and Stalin followed on 17 September to take his share of Poland.

371 Cit. Tucker and Cohen (eds), *The Great Purge Trial*, pp. xii–xiii.

372 Cit. Tucker, *Stalin in Power*, p. 500. 'Koba' was one of the names used for Joseph Stalin by his friends from the pre-1917 days of life in the underground.

373 Rogovin, 1937, pp. xvi–xvii; B. Nicolaevsky, a prominent Menshevik, published in late 1936/early 1937 an anonymous 'Letter of an Old Bolshevik' in the *Bulletin of the Opposition*, an exile journal. The Letter was largely based on conversations he had with Nikolai Bukharin whom he had met in the spring of 1936 in Paris. Cf. Knight, *Who Killed Kirov?*, p. 248.

374 Rogovin, 1937, p. xiii, xvi.

375 Leitens and Bernaut, *Ritual Liquidation*, p. 15.

376 Cit. Rogovin, 1937, p. 238.

377 Tucker, *Stalin in Power*, p. 446.

378 Cit. Tucker and Cohen (eds), *The Great Purge Trial*, p. xiv.

379 Knight, *Who Killed Kirov?*, p. 267.

380 Tucker, *Stalin in Power*, p. 475.

381 Tucker and Cohen (eds), *The Great Purge Trial*, pp. xi–xv.

382 Tucker, *Stalin in Power*, p. 373. Expanding on this line of thought, Robert Tucker also wrote, 'He [Stalin] was driven to 'see through and expose' in others the duplicity that he had to remain blind to himself. Then, with a sense of only meting out justice, he could and did visit on those unfortunates the rage and fury that he could not bear to direct at himself. No torture, he seems to have thought, was too cruel as punishment for *their* villainy. As a result, he virtually wrecked Soviet Russia in the great manhunt against 'wreckers', and by means of the Terror that purported to cleanse the land of enemies, he made many very loyal citizens into real covert enemies of his state'. Cf. Tucker, *Stalin in Power*, p. 478.

383 Stalin had instructed the NKVD chiefs regarding the interrogation of Zinoviev and Kamenev in the pre-trial phase: 'Tell them that no matter what they do, they won't be able to stop the march of history. The only thing that they still can do is—either die or save their hides. Give them the works until they come crawling to you on their bellies with confessions in their teeth!' Cit. Orlov, *The Secret History of Stalin's Crimes*, p. 117.

384 Knight, *Who Killed Kirov?*, pp. 268–269.

385 Werth, *Ein Staat gegen sein Volk*, pp. 185–186; H. Rappaport, *Joseph Stalin: A Biographical Companion* (St. Monica: ABC-CLIO, 1999).

386 Werth, *Ein Staat gegen sein Volk*, pp. 185–186.

387 Ibid., p. 168.

5. 'Is There any Justice Left in this Country?' The IRA on Trial in the 1970s

Joost Augusteijn

5.1. Introduction

In the course of their long-standing struggle for independence, Irish Republicans have become well aware of the performative power of trials. The rebellion of 1803, for instance, is best remembered not for its somewhat farcical military exploits, but for the speech given by its leader Robert Emmet after his conviction. Indeed, statements delivered by Irish defendants in the courts became a key mobilising tool for nationalists in the nineteenth century. This is attested to by the popularity of publications like *Speeches from the Dock*, first published in 1867, which contained arguments made in court by men like Wolfe Tone, the leader of the first Republican uprising in 1798, up to those who had been involved in the Fenian rebellion in the year of publication. The influence of these speeches on the formation of the Irish Republican Army (IRA) in 1913 was acknowledged by one of the first IRA leaders.[1]

Speeches by imprisoned leaders declined in significance in the twentieth century, but court cases and the imprisonment of IRA activists did not. The outcome of some IRA campaigns, beginning with the execution of the leaders of the 1916 rebellion, had a substantial impact on society. After southern Ireland gained independence following a guerrilla war in 1920–1921, the IRA was involved in further violence during the short-lived but vicious civil war of 1922–1923, and in low-key campaigns against Britain and Northern Ireland between 1939 and 1944 and from 1956 to 1962. After the IRA acknowledged in 1962 that the Border Campaign had failed it shifted to a peaceful strategy in conjunction with a quest for civil rights engaged in by large sections of the Catholic population in the North. However, this generated such extreme anxiety among Protestants that at the end of the 1960s communal violence erupted, threatening to lead to a civil war. In these circumstances, the IRA was called upon to help protect Catholic neighbourhoods against attacks from Protestant civilians. A section of the IRA that responded to this call set up the Provisional IRA in December 1969, leading to a long period of conflict lasting to the end of the century.

At the same time as the formation of the Provisionals, British troops were brought out onto the streets of Northern Ireland to prevent further escalation. They helped to bring relative safety to Catholic areas, but conflict now developed between the IRA and the British army. In 1971 the IRA convinced itself that it could force the British to leave Northern Ireland by military means, and turned to a confrontational strategy. Thanks to the militarisation of the conflict by both sides, 1972 became the most violent year of 'The Troubles', with hundreds of bombs exploding in Northern Ireland and thousands of shooting incidents. To put a stop to this, peace negotiations between the IRA and the Secretary of State for Northern Ireland were held in the summer of 1972, but these failed over IRA demands for British withdrawal. When the desired results did not materialise, the IRA extended its activities to Great Britain's mainland, where car and parcel bombs became frequent occurrences from 1973 onwards. This offensive continued until 1975, when a cease-fire (which lasted from February 1975 until January 1976) initiated the turn to the so-called Long War strategy. The willingness of the British government to remain in Northern Ireland, the IRA now thought, could be undermined by sustained low-intensity violence. This soon created a deadlock, with neither side making substantial progress. Eventually this gave rise to the peace process which culminated in the Good Friday Agreement of 1998. Throughout this period, the survival of the IRA was dependent on the support it received from nationalists in Northern Ireland as well as in the Republic of Ireland. In the Republic the dominant ideology favoured a united Ireland, but an overwhelming majority of citizens were against the methods used by the Provisionals. An important element in generating and maintaining public support for them was the plight of prisoners. Their willingness to suffer for the shared ideal of a united Ireland, which came particularly sharply in focus during court cases, was able to mobilise many.

The four court cases investigated in this chapter, held against the backdrop of the Troubles of the early 1970s, represent conditions in the three jurisdictions involved in the conflict: Northern Ireland, England and the Republic of Ireland.

(i) the trial of two leading Belfast Republicans, William McKee and Francis Card, which took place in Northern Ireland on 16 May 1971;
(ii) the case of the chief of staff of the IRA, Sean MacStiofáin, in Dublin on 24–25 November 1972;
(iii) the case against ten IRA operatives from Belfast responsible for the first London bombings in the Provisionals' campaign, which was held in Winchester from 10 September to 14 November 1973;

(iv) the case of Bobby Sands, who was tried in Belfast on 8 September 1977, following the introduction in Northern Ireland of the Diplock courts system, which replaced jury trials.

Apart from the last case, these trials generated substantial media attention, and on occasion controversy and debate. This applied in particular to the cases against MacStiofáin and the 'Belfast Ten'. The former signalled the start of a confrontational policy of the southern authorities vis-à-vis the Provisional IRA, after a period when they had been essentially left alone. The trial of the Belfast Ten struck a raw nerve as the first major trial against IRA members in England. Far less attention was paid to cases tried in Northern Ireland, where the scale of violence was so vast that the impact of any one trial was relatively minor. The case against McKee and Card was an exception, in that it witnessed a change in policy by the authorities, a deliberate attempt to use the legal system to lock up known leaders of the IRA. The impact of this trial was augmented when the defendants went on a hunger strike, as all the other condemned Republicans in the cases under scrutiny here eventually did. The trial of prominent hunger striker Bobby Sands was chosen to serve as an example of how the Diplock courts, introduced in 1973, reduced the public impact of IRA trials in the North.

The performative power of these trials will be assessed according to the framework provided in this volume's theoretical chapters in the introduction and the conclusion by Beatrice de Graaf (and Liesbeth van der Heide). Trials are here seen as a stage where the different actors adopt and act out strategies with the aim of convincing their target audience(s) in and outside the courtroom of their narrative of (in)justice. Particular attention is paid to the way in which the various parties framed their positions and those of the opposing parties, as well as to the relative success of these attempts in convincing the general public. The focus lies not only on the intentions of those involved but also on effects on the ground. It will therefore look into proceedings during the trials as well as at the reactions of politicians and the general public in Northern Ireland, the Republic of Ireland and Great Britain. The analysis is based primarily on newspaper reports and parliamentary debates during and after the arrests and trials. The underlying premise is that a performative strategy that fails to make it into the public arena lacks resonance in society and can therefore be largely discounted. An attendant circumstance is that there is very little other source material on the trials, as proceedings were generally not recorded verbatim. The newspapers used for this chapter were chosen from among those searchable on the Internet. Within the Irish Republic the choice fell on the middle-class and traditionally slightly

Unionist *Irish Times*; the nationalist *Irish Press*; the more populist *Irish Independent* and *Sunday Independent*; and a number of provincial newspapers.[2] Those in Britain included the middle-class, fairly non-partisan *Observer* and the left-leaning *Guardian*. To gain insight into the Republican perspective, the hardcopy files of the southern-based weekly *An Phoblacht* and the northern-based *Republican News* were also consulted.

5.2. The Trial of William McKee and Francis Card (1971)

The first case pertains to William McKee and Francis Card, who were arrested after a car chase in Belfast on 14 April 1971. Both were known leaders of the Belfast IRA and they seem to have been targeted for arrest. McKee was commanding officer of the Belfast Brigade and Card was in charge of propaganda in the city, having previously served 13 years in detention. According to the *Irish Times*, they had been challenged in recent months by the British army to state whether they were in fact members of the Provisionals. As this was not the first arrest of known Republicans in unclear circumstances, the newspaper reported that there was much talk in Republican areas that the security forces

> were carrying out a policy of virtual internment: they were arresting known suspects and holding them, thereby hoping to capture the ringleaders of the Provisional I.R.A. [...] Certainly the absence of any major outbreak of I.R.A. activity against the troops could suggest that this policy is working and the arrest of Card and McKee could be seen as further evidence of this policy in action.[3]

The openly pro-IRA *Republican News*, one of the few other papers that reported on the case, paid no attention to the reasons for the arrest itself but highlighted the subsequent raid on the home of Pronnsias McAirt, as Francis Card called himself in an attempt to show his commitment to a Gaelic Ireland. They painted a picture of police brutality by printing photographs of his house and saying that it had been 'violated' in a raid executed with 'force of military jack-boots and padded shoulders and of course rifle butts'. As the *Republican News* put it, the 'assault on privacy clearly shows that we, the Nationalist people of the North, can expect no regard to our lives, limbs or property, by these monsters. No house in any Nationalist area is exempt from this brutal and hideous treatment.'[4]

At the remand hearing, Card was presented as a 47-year-old unemployed clerk and McKee as a 49-year-old unemployed labourer. Together with Bernard Burns, a shop owner of 33 who had driven the car and had been arrested with them, they were charged with unlawful possession of an explosive substance and a loaded firearm.[5] The three men were remanded in custody repeatedly, each period lasting a week before a next hearing was held, until their trial two months later. During one of the remand hearings, Burns, who was only a minor figure in the IRA, was released due to lack of evidence.[6] In the run-up to the actual trial, the charges against McKee and Card were modified; they were now accused of possession of a .45 revolver and one round of ammunition with intent to endanger life; possessing them under suspicious circumstances and without a licence; and having a stolen car and driving it knowingly. Card faced additional charges because he was serving a suspended sentence, and for possessing documents found in his home relating to the republican party, Sinn Fein, and the IRA. During the trial it became clear that the arrest of the two men took place after they were seen visiting a house in Belfast that was under police observation. The car in which they travelled was halted after they left the house, upon which they reversed direction and eventually fled on foot. During the pursuit they called upon people on the street to block the road to stop the police following them. Some of them did, and the police car was held up temporarily. The escape car was later found a few streets away, empty, with the doors open. When the police tried to investigate it they were forced to withdraw by a threatening crowd. Upon their return with reinforcements they found a revolver under the back seat. There were no fingerprints of the defendants on the gun—or for that matter in the car. What *was* found, on the gun was a combination of fibres that matched McKee's jacket pocket. However, during the trial the forensic expert agreed with Card that another coat of similar material would have shown the same results.[7]

Apart from some instructions to the jury, there were no reports of specific interventions by the judge in the case, which was conducted in the regular format of the British criminal justice system. Proceedings were overseen by a judge who determined the appropriate measure of punishment. The public prosecutor argued the case against the defendants and lawyers would normally speak in their defence. All of this took place in front of a jury that determined guilt or innocence. In the media, the impression one gets of the prosecution is that it simply presented evidence in court and questioned witnesses. However, the prosecution also emphasised that the defendants had portrayed themselves as leading men in their neighbourhoods, apparently in an attempt to make their conviction more urgent. This was in line with the policy that the *Irish Times* attributed to the authorities. Card was stated to have said during his interrogation, 'No one will say they saw us in that Cortina. We are the leaders in our area.' When asked whether it was the IRA to which he was referring he did not answer. When McKee was interviewed later he was reported to have said, 'We were up there because we heard there was trouble, so we went to see about it. When there is trouble we organise things and help defend our people.'[8]

The defendants also attempted to influence the way the case was perceived by the outside world. In keeping with the long-standing tradition among Irish Republicans, they refused to recognise the court and consequently rejected any form of legal counsel, nor did they enter a plea after the charges were read. They did, however, defend themselves when they felt it was opportune.[9] During the remand hearings they tried to undermine the case of the prosecution, playing to a courtroom audience that was apparently generally packed with sympathisers. One simple ploy was to initiate a positive response by waving at the audience, but a more elaborate tactic would involve the ridiculing of witnesses for the prosecution. The court erupted in laughter when Detective Chief Inspector Robert Wilson of the London Metropolitan Police could not recall how many cars the defendants had been driving when caught because he had not been there. The judge threatened to clear the courtroom, instructing the officers to remove one woman who then shouted, 'This is no court!' She was sentenced on the spot to three days' imprisonment for contempt of court, but this punishment was waived after she apologised.[10]

In their defence the men tried to brush off the case as a 'frameup' and 'legalised internment'. In the history of the Irish struggle for independence the term 'internment' carried a strong negative ring, implying the exercise of injustice. Tarring the trialwith that brush undoubtedly resonated with a large part of the nationalist population in Northern Ireland and the Republic of Ireland. The defendants demanded to know where the gun, which did not have any fingerprints on it, was found. They argued that the fibres on the gun that matched McKee's coat were put on the gun later. McKee stated that it would have been very conspicuous had he carried a gun in his coat pocket: 'No fool would walk about the streets of Belfast with such a gun in an outside pocket', even climbing onto a seat to demonstrate the truth of this statement. Card finished up by dismissing all the evidence connecting him to any of the charges. He denied ever having stated they were leaders in the area and reminded the court that the onus was on the prosecution to prove their guilt, not on them to prove their innocence. McKee concurred, adding for good measure that a critical examination would reveal that there was no case whatsoever.[11] The defendants' arguments did not convince jury or judge. Card and McKee were both found guilty and sentenced to five years for the gun-related charges. The judge had instructed the jury to exonerate them of the charges linking them to the stolen car, for which there was no evidence.[12]

Outside the court the portrayal of the case as a set-up had somewhat more impact. In what seems to have been a staged reaction to the arrest, already during the second remand hearing, a dozen men carrying placards protested outside the court building against 'State repression'.[13] The IRA made its presence known immediately after the first hearing by bombing the house of the presiding judge, damaging the windows, car and garage door. This was the only aspect of developments prior to the court case itself reported in any of the papers besides the *Irish Times*.[14] Although the *Irish Press* only referred to the case during the trial, it claimed that the impact of the arrests had been widespread: 'The recent bombing campaign began in earnest after the arrest of these men—the Provisional IRA wanted to make the point that the imprisonment of two of their leaders did not in any way incapacitate the organisation or diminish its effectiveness.' The *Irish Press* was the only mainstream paper that considered the sentence 'unexpectedly heavy' and that detected a mood of dismay and despondency in Republican circles, from whom they expected agitated reactions.[15]

Republican newspapers indeed picked up on the suggestion that the two were framed and that there was no justice for nationalists in Northern Ireland. The main headline in *An Phoblacht*—'Belfast Men Framed'—referred to the claim that the pistol found in the car was planted: 'What Scotland Yard liars did not say was that the car had been searched previously by a British Army Patrol and that the back seat had been removed by the British Troops who found nothing.' The absence of real evidence should in their minds have led to an acquittal, and the fact that this did not happen supported their narrative of injustice. 'In any impartial court the case would have been stopped by the judge. But in the corrupt Judicial system in Orangist Ireland there is no justice for anyone who cherishes Republican or Nationalist aspirations.' They contrasted the heavy sentence with what they considered the light sentences handed down to Loyalist paramilitary men found in possession of arms or ammunition, ending their argument with a call to each and every one to do more to support the cause.[16] The *Irish Press* reported that at meetings organised by Sinn Fein in Belfast speakers and placards referred to the case as based on 'thrumped [sic] up charges'. In the end it was not just the immediate friends and supporters of the defendants and the IRA who were convinced by these claims. Frank Gogarty, the vice-chairman of the non-violent Northern Ireland Civil Rights Association, also credited the accusation that Card and McKee had been framed by Scotland Yard detectives.[17]

From the reports in the newspapers it appears that at this stage the IRA was more aware than the other participants of the publicity value of a court case. Because the court system tried to maintain the rule of law and legal standards in a traditional way, the prosecution assumed that everybody would be against what they saw as crime.

That being the case, there was little need to do more than to identify the defendants as leading IRA members. This may have had little impact on the Republican constituency, but in Unionist circles it was enough to justify a harsh sentence. What seems to have happened is that the authorities, in an attempt to stem the sudden rise of anti-state violence, resorted to the tactic of putting the accused away for as long as possible. Heavy sentences were handed down even in cases where the charges were minor and the evidence not particularly strong. In a period in which violence was flaring up with hitherto unknown intensity, this seemed an understandable reaction. The IRA and the defendants involved had a great deal of experience with the impact of violence and court cases. This applied particularly to McKee, who had been involved in campaigns in the 1940s and 1950s and, like Card, had spent long periods in prison. The Republicans were out to frame the case for its public impact, while the authorities seemed to treat it as a simple security issue. The *Irish Times* was the only paper to pay extensive attention to the legal process from arrest to trial. The only other mainstream paper that reported on the trial itself, the *Irish Press*, seemed to address the Republican constituency in Ireland. The *Irish Independent*, the local papers in the Republic in the south and the English papers did not pay any attention to it, indicating that the performative quality of the trial of McKee and Card was limited and largely confined to Republicans and the southern elite.

5.3. The Trial of Sean MacStiofáin (1972)

The arrest in Dublin of Sean MacStiofáin on 19 November 1972 and his subsequent trial had a great deal more performative power than the conviction of Card and McKee the year before. In 1972 the violence in Northern Ireland escalated to new heights. MacStiofáin had become widely known as the chief of staff of the Provisional IRA and essentially acknowledged this in his conversations with the press. His speech to the Sinn Fein Ard Fheis, the annual conference, of October 1972, where he had been openly described as such, had badly irked both Irish and English politicians. On 1 November, opposition politicians in the Dáil, the Irish parliament, asked why MacStiofáin was not arrested following this appearance.[18] Similar questions were raised in Great Britain. The *Guardian* wondered how it was possible that until recently people had been allowed to describe themselves openly on television and radio as IRA leaders without consequences. The *Observer* called upon the Irish government 'to make a conciliatory gesture' following the British government's recent Green Paper, which acknowledged the need for a role of the South in the future of Northern Ireland.

It was time for the Irish to act, they argued: 'The Irish police so often seem to blow hot and cold, one day closing Sinn Fein's Dublin headquarters and the next permitting a Sinn Fein meeting, at which Mr Mac Stiofáin made a well-publicised and markedly unhelpful address.' It was clear that pressure was building on the Irish Government to act against the IRA and MacStiofáin in particular.[19]

However, due to the fraught historic relationship with Britain and its precarious majority in parliament, the Irish government felt unable to take on MacStiofáin directly; put bluntly, the government was afraid to be seen to act on the bidding of the British. The very suspicion would lead to repercussions in their own Fianna Fáil party, which had strong historic connections with the IRA. The Minister of Justice, Desmond O'Malley, went only so far as to say in a radio interview that he would like to arrest MacStiofáin but that he had nothing to charge him with. He added that he would introduce fresh legislation to deal with violence.[20] The *Guardian* reacted positively: 'The problem of locking up Fenians,[21] which seems to concern almost every politician in Ireland, might be solved later this month.'[22] The opposition TD (member of the Dáil) Gerald L'Estrange was less optimistic. The next day he countered, 'Surely we are entitled to know how a man could have a bodyguard around him, a man who is a wanted member of the council of the IRA. These people were not apprehended. We are entitled to ask what is happening in this country at present. Is there any justice left in the country?'[23]

Increased pressure nonetheless had its effect. Two weeks later, before there was time to enact new legislation, the government detained MacStiofáin. The arrest followed a pre-arranged interview with the well-known RTE journalist and broadcaster Kevin O'Kelly in the very early hours of Sunday, 19 November 1972. They spoke to each other in O'Kelly's house, which was apparently watched by Irish policemen waiting for an opportunity to pounce. When O'Kelly went to the studio to report on the interview MacStiofáin got into his car to drive home. At 3:15 a.m. he was captured, apparently at gunpoint, on the charge of membership of an unlawful organisation. The arrest was headline news in all the Irish newspapers. In their initial response even the *Irish Press*, which had strong ties to the government party, questioned the legality of the arrest. Asking rhetorically whether the legal system had been changed or whether MacStiofáin had broken any laws since the recent statement by Minister O'Malley, the *Irish Press* hinted at other reasons when it asked, 'or was his arrest the direct result of pressure from Britain'?[24]

MacStiofáin was tried by the Special Criminal Court established earlier that year to deal with cases where 'the ordinary courts were deemed inadequate to secure the effective administration of justice'. Juries in these courts were replaced with a panel of three judges; verdicts were delivered by majority vote. At the start of the trial, on Friday, 24 November 1972, MacStiofáin was described as a 44-year-old man born in London. He was arraigned on two charges: membership of an unlawful organisation that raised or maintained an armed force, and membership of an unlawful organisation, namely the IRA. In line with official IRA policy, MacStiofáin refused to recognise the court and chose to represent himself, just like McKee and Card had done the previous year. One of his first allegations, which was reported in the more nationalist-minded newspapers, was that the whole proceedings were only initiated because the government was under pressure from the British—in particular the British press—and the northern Unionists to arrest him. The *Guardian* later acknowledged that the intensive discussions between the British and Irish governments following the abolition of the separate Northern Irish government seemed to justify this claim: 'Each move by the Irish Government has been followed by discussions with the British leaders, which has created in the minds of Irish Republicans the suspicion that, to say the least, actions and talks have somehow been connected.'[25] This idea was pressed particularly vigorously in the Republican press. *Republican News* opened its front page with the headline 'Lynch acts at Heath's Orders', arguing that the Irish Taoiseach (prime minister), Jack Lynch, had been instructed to arrest MacStiofáin by the British Prime Minister, Edward Heath. 'Herod Heath has called for a head on a plate. Saoirse Lynch will tell him the victim is already imprisoned.'[26] The newspaper further inferred that the government was only holding Ireland for the British Conservative Party by calling the governenment members 'quislings'. The Irish-based *Sunday Independent* followed this line of argument to some extent by claiming that in a jury trial the case would have been stopped dead in its tracks.[27]

Like Card and McKee, MacStiofáin challenged the legality of the proceedings and claimed that the court could not deliver proper justice. The main grounds for these protests were that the evidence lacked viability and that the court was prejudiced against him due to all the reporting in the media. 'It seems to him that the wells of justice had been staunched before beginning to flow.'[28] One weakness of the case was that the charges against MacStiofáin were laid after the mandatory deadline of 48 hours following arrest. The impression had been given by Minister O'Malley that the prosecution had no evidence against MacStiofáin. The *Republican News* put it succinctly, 'The man is held unjustly, no evidence being preferred against him, and no grounds for his detention.'[29] The English papers, the *Observer* and the *Guardian*, paid no attention to MacStiofáin's claims of injustice. They honed in on the peculiar position of the journalist Kevin O'Kelly, who stated in court that recordings played at the hearing represented an accurate and authentic representation of

MacStiofáin's position but refused to testify that it was MacStiofáin himself who could be heard on the tape. This got O'Kelly a sentence of three months' imprisonment for contempt of court. Kelly's assertion nevertheless formed the sole basis for MacStiofáin's conviction as it was the sole piece of concrete evidence. MacStiofáin's narrative of injustice also led him to state that although he did not doubt the integrity of those involved, as a Republican he had 'very very little chance of getting justice in a Free State Court' that had 'been set up by the most obnoxious piece of legislation' and that was being abused to serve the ends of the British government.[30] This charge was only reported in the Irish papers. The *Guardian* made reference to the lack of evidence and MacStiofáin's 'outrage' over the court system being abused by some members of the government, but did not refer to the accusation that he could get no justice in an Irish court. This may be because the journalist involved did not understand the implication of the use of the term Free State, which referred to the dominion status Britain had granted in 1921 and which had led to the Irish civil war of 1922–1923. The government party had fought against the Free State in this war and referring to it implicitly charged the government party with betrayal of their Republican principles.[31] Later in the trial MacStiofáin tried to undermine the perceived objectivity of the court further: 'It's a waste of time making objections. I am taking no further interest in these proceedings.' He nevertheless continued to debate with the judges on the value of the evidence presented and the competence of the witnesses.[32]

Public attention to the case, which was already considerable given MacStiofáin's high public profile, was further augmented by the hunger and thirst strike he started after his arrest. As this put him in danger of death within two weeks or less, the stakes for all parties became extremely high. MacStiofáin played upon this to get the court to speed up proceedings and to heighten public awareness of his situation. When he appeared before the court for the first time, on a Tuesday, the prosecution argued that it needed two weeks to prepare its case and that it needed the tapes O'Kelly had made of the interview. MacStiofáin argued that he had less than twelve days to live, so it was agreed to have the tapes heard three days later on the Friday and have the obligatory transcripts made afterwards. Whether taped interviews were admissible as evidence would yet have to be established, as this had never before been accepted in an Irish court.[33] During the Saturday it was decided, upon MacStiofáin's insistence, to continue late into the night to make sure the case was completed as quickly as possible. When a five-hour break was inserted to allow for the transcripts to be made, he publicly asked for a warm room, from which when proceedings were resumed he was carried back on a chair. Even before the case started, reports on his physical condition were brought out through his friend Myles Shevlin, a solicitor who seems to have been advising him. On Thursday, for instance, Shevlin stated that MacStiofáin had lost fifteen pounds in weight and was suffering from kidney pains. The *Irish Press* opened its Friday edition with this story on its front page and continued to pay a lot of attention to MacStiofáin's physical condition.[34] Despite the administration of medical treatment, the complaints worsened during the trial. After his sentence was read out on Sunday morning MacStiofáin was described as being 'determined and defiant, and, in spite of his weakness, he struck the bench in front of him with his fist and shouted to the three judges: "I will be dead in six days. Live with that."'[35] The less sympathetic *Irish Times* also dealt with the effects on the body of a hunger and thirst strike, reporting that a thirst strike carried a maximum survival period of eighteen days.[36]

While the judges were willing to take the physical effects of MacStiofáin's hunger and thirst strike into account and never put restrictions on reporting the case, they were less lenient concerning his attempts to put across his narrative of injustice. On the one hand the president of the court, Justice Frank Griffin, assured MacStiofáin that nothing written or said outside the court would have a bearing on the case, he also refused to allow any evidence regarding MacStiofáin's membership of the IRA beyond the date mentioned in the charge. On the other hand, he cut MacStiofáin off when he characterised the act establishing the Special Criminal Courts as obnoxious. In a move with major implications, apparently inspired by partisan considerations, Griffin pointed out to the prosecution that it could recall O'Kelly to take the stand again even after his conviction for contempt of court. Griffin added that if O'Kelly would then name MacStiofáin he would be allowed to negotiate the extent of his sentence with the authorities. In effect, in a move described by the *Guardian* as 'extraordinary', he invited the prosecution to make a deal with O'Kelly in order to get the main piece of evidence approved in court. O'Kelly was indeed recalled, the tape was admitted as evidence, and a conviction was handed down, based on the court's acceptance that the tape was a recording of the voice of MacStiofáin on the date alleged.[37] Not much attention was paid to the role of the prosecution, but even the *Guardian* felt it had put in a poor performance. The dismissal of all the evidence it presented except for a set of tapes the content of which was unknown to it until five hours before the trial opened was seen as particularly weak. This led the *Irish Press* to conclude that the prosecution had set out to frame MacStiofáin as a man of violence.[38]

Although the sudden arrest of its leader took the IRA by surprise, it was quick to respond. Since the introduction of the Special Criminal Court a few months earlier, about hundred Republicans had been convicted in the South for various, often minor, offences. The onset of this high profile case gave the movement the hope of using it to generate opposition to the court system. A public statement deploring the arrest of MacStiofáin was reported in the *Irish Times*:

> His arrest 'at this critical and most hopeful' stage of the struggle for over 50 years was calculated to give aid and comfort to the forces of British imperialism which he had relentlessly opposed. Equally his arrest is intended to strike at the morale of the beleaguered people of the North whose cause he so unselfishly espoused and who are now engaged in a fight for their very existence. 'The Leinster House politicians [Southern Irish politicians, JA] have nothing to offer the people of the Six Counties, neither Unionists nor Nationalists. Instead of bread they give them stones.'[39]

Provisional Sinn Fein, in a statement that emphasised the theme of injustice, called the arrest 'a blatant act of collaboration with the British army'. This reaction was the first item in the *Irish Press*'s coverage of the story. Both the IRA and the Provisional Sinn Fein called for a wave of protest against this 'latest act of appeasement of the enemies of Ireland'.[40] The movement expressed its conviction that the arrest would show up the corruptness of the Irish government and its lack of willingness to aid the nationalist community in the North in its fight against oppression. As painful as it was to them to accuse fellow countrymen of collaboration, they portrayed '[Prime Minister Jack] Lynch and [Minister Desmond] O'Malley as arch-collaborators; arch-quislings; and arch-traitors of the Irish people'. Lynch was 'a puppet on a string'.[41] The MacStiofáin case, they believed, would ultimately lead to the end of his rule. 'The sentence sums up the corruptness of the Free State regime, a regime soon to be given its marching orders by a risen Irish people.' 'Will the proud people of Ireland stand for this? Half a million northerners will shortly give Lynch his answer for he can no more stop the revolution which will now gain momentum, then he could stop the flowing tide.' The Irish government would soon go the way of the Unionist government in the North, which had just been abolished by Britain following the escalation of violence in 1972, 'ground down by the mills of justice. The mills of justice which grind exceedingly slow but exceedingly small.'[42]

The English newspapers were less sanguine than the *Irish Times* in their coverage of the IRA response. In a front-page article, the *Guardian* drew attention to the storm of protest in England and Ireland promised by the IRA. This had already begun, in a picket on the Irish embassy in London and a series of meetings in Dublin, including a picket on the Bridewell police station, a large photo of which appeared in the *Irish Press*. The next day 2,000 people headed by masked men marched through the rain in Dublin carrying a coffin draped in the tricolour with the inscription 'Justice is dead.' A violent response took place in Londonderry, 'when a crowd incensed by the arrest' attacked the police, who responded with rubber bullets and CS tear gas. 'Republicans in the North see the arrest as the betrayal of their cause by the authorities in the South, and many nationalists are convinced that the Dublin Government and police are working to the instructions of the British.'[43] The weekly *Republican News* recounted how Sinn Fein called upon the legal profession to protest vigorously against the attempt to subvert the cause of justice. People should 'recoil in revulsion', the paper argued, if the state could pick up any person it liked while looking around for evidence to justify the arrest.[44] In the beginning of December MacStiofáin tried to reinvigorate the injustice narrative by writing to the Incorporated Law Society asking them to have the three judges who sentenced him struck off the roll for having let down the profession.[45]

Leading Republicans reiterated the accusation that the arrest was made either at the behest of the British government or to force the Dáil to enact further repressive legislation, statements tantamount to accusing the Irish government of collaboration and treachery. In a speech during a protest meeting on the day of his arrest, praise was lavished on MacStiofáin's long career in the Republican movement, for which he had been jailed in England from 1953 to 1959. Even the civil rights leader Aidan Corrigan proclaimed that MacStiofáin had done more for Irish freedom and unity than the governing party, Fianna Fáil, which claimed to be *the* Republican party, had done in 50 years. Corrigan called MacStiofáin the man most maligned in Ireland by press, radio and television, a man who deserved to stand proudly beside Jomo Kenyatta[46] and Desmond Greaves[47] as the leader of a great guerrilla movement. 'The fact of the matter is that Sean MacStiofáin has headed the movement which brought down Stormont [the Northern Irish Unionist Government].'[48]

Similar plaudits for MacStiofáin could be found in *Republican News*. 'To Sean McStiofain, as to all previous men of his calibre, we pledge our support in your stand. We will tread your way side by side and we will never desert you. Long live the cause of Freedom enshrined in your sacrifice.'[49] *An Phoblacht* tried to counteract the deliberate campaign of character assassination which it argued had found its way into the Irish and British press: 'never were such depraved, cowardly and untruthful methods used in the attempts to assassinate the character of an Irish leader. The real Sean Mac Stíofáin already belongs to the pages of history; nothing indeed the yellow Fleet Street or Seoinin Abbey Street press can spew forth will ever tarnish that Pearse-like image.'[50] Needless to say, the framing of MacStiofáin as a better Irishman than the government could only work in an Irish context where every politician had to show his or her nationalist credentials. To allay fears among its supporters of the repercussions of

MacStiofáin's arrest for the IRA, a movement spokesman found it necessary to add, 'Of course, we are concerned that MacStiofáin has been arrested but we are just as concerned when a young volunteer gets picked up in Derry or wounded in Belfast. There are leaders of the Republican movement and MacStiofáin happens to be one of them, but the movement doesn't stop when he gets lifted.' The *Guardian* claimed that the timing of the arrest was a surprise to the IRA, which had expected the announced new legislation to be introduced first. The newspaper added however that they had naturally prepared for it and it was 'unlikely therefore to pose any great organisational problems for the IRA'.[51]

The Irish government, manoeuvred into a difficult position, took resolute measures to counter the way it was being framed by Republicans. Following the broadcast of the interview with MacStiofáin, the government, possibly in an attempt to distract attention, dismissed the RTE Authority, which overlooked the running of the public television service, for giving airtime to a terrorist, and it introduced a bill that included stringent security measures. RTE authorities, it argued, had contravened section 31 of the Broadcasting Act, enacted the previous year, that forbade the airing of live interviews with Sinn Féin members. To counter the sympathy generated by the reporting on MacStiofáin's physical suffering, stories were put out that he was breaking his thirst strike by drinking water. Apparently he had at one stage tried to take an aspirin with water and he might have drunk some while taking a shower. MacStiofáin's spokesmen responded by declaring that he had vomited immediately upon taking the aspirin.[52]

British politicians publicly expressed their contentment with the Irish government's response. Even the Labour leader, Harold Wilson, who backed the Conservative British government in its Irish policies, said on television that the Irish had been acting on inadequate laws in its dealings with the IRA, but that it was now taking them on properly.[53] Opposition politicians in Ireland were less enthusiastic. Although most supported the arrest of MacStiofáin, there was much criticism of the sacking of the RTE Authority, which was seen as an attack on the independence of the public media. They argued that the RTE interviewer had done everything he could to show up the IRA. The hunger and thirst strike also generated concern in the Dáil, where questions were asked on the floor about MacStiofáin's health.[54]

The English press was not always convinced by the actions and intentions of the Irish government. The leftish *Guardian* shared concern for the threat to freedom of speech in the Republic after the sacking of the RTE Authority. It felt that the interview had been used to get not only at MacStiofáin but also at the RTE Authority, which the government felt had been acting against its interests.[55] In relation to the IRA, it referred in particular to the charge of 'collaboration with enemies of the Irish people', a frequent accusation in public protests in Ireland. In response to this charge the Association of Legal Justice had recently urged the government to revoke the 1965 extradition agreement with Britain, in order to prevent the expulsion of three Republican prisoners to the North. Some commentators, the paper argued, believed the Irish government was sensitive to this issue. They considered the arrest and an attendant minor wave of extraditions to be nothing more than a PR exercise to show the British government and the Unionists of Belfast that they had done everything they could to 'rid the Republic of the IRA menace and cooperate with the British Army and the RUC [the Royal Ulster Constabulary, the Northern Irish police]'. The paper moreover surmised that the government secretly had hoped that the courts, by refusing the extradition orders and by finding that no evidence existed to convict MacStiofáin, would help them off a political hook. The great importance the *Guardian* attached to the arrest of MacStiofáin was clear from the start, when it reported on the original charge on the front page.[56] To explain the predicament of the Irish government, it speculated on the public impact that a hunger strike by MacStiofáin would have in Ireland. Many who would not normally sympathise with the IRA, the paper supposed, would be moved by a hunger strike. Emotional reactions of this kind could have consequences with which the authorities would find it hard to deal. The paper took a comparable line in explaining the attitude taken by MacStiofáin in court: 'Many probably expected Mr MacStiofáin to turn his back on the court and say nothing.' Although he did not recognise the court, did not submit a plea and refused to apply for bail, he did defend himself, which was allowed under IRA policy. At the same time the paper tried to play down MacStiofáin's opposition to the system by mentioning that he addressed Justice Griffin as 'Sir'.[57]

The public response to the plight of MacStiofáin was much stronger than in the case of Card and McKee. Even the *Irish Times* painted a picture of a heroic man who in the 1950s had been imprisoned for years for the cause, a man who had an eye damaged when a bomb exploded at his house the previous March and who was one of five Republicans flown by the British to England for negotiations during the recent IRA ceasefire.[58] MacStiofáin's physical condition was reported on with sympathy in most major newspapers in Ireland and England. The *Guardian* expressed doubt that he would survive, adding that in Ireland—contrary to the situation in Britain—forced feeding was not allowed before a prisoner was convicted. The most detailed description of MacStiofáin's condition was offered by the *Observer*, clearly ringing a sympathetic note:

> When he heard the sentence he dragged himself from the blanket in which he had been covered during the trial, and said 'I will be dead in six days' time' [...] his voice trailed off and he had to drag himself into a sitting position before he could go on: [...] before falling back to be cradled in the arms of a prison officer. [...] Earlier he had collapsed in court. He was given painkilling injections. His shoes were removed and his feet massaged. A hot-water bottle was called for and a doctor took his pulse.

His weak voice was remarked upon in the *Irish Times* and it was stated that he 'staggered slightly, spoke with difficulty, eyes glazed, scarcely audible and pale'. The intended effect of this writing is not unambiguous. It might have been designed to portray him as a weakling. This was also implied in the description of MacStiofáin's physical reaction to the verdict in the Irish papers: 'as he lay wrapped in a rug with a hot-water bottle clutched to his chest, he shouted with a sobbing voice at the three members of the court: "It might as well be six years. I'm going to die in six days." The presiding judge retorted by stating this was something over which they unfortunately had no control.' The *Irish Independent* gave most detail. According to the story in that paper, the incident described took place after the members of the court began to leave. Rather than being proudly defiant, he is described as prostrated and weeping, to be joined 'by sobbing wife who hugged and kissed him as he lay cradled in the arms of a male nurse. He embraced her for several minutes. It was a moving moment in an otherwise tense and dramatic day.' More simply, the *Observer* stated that his wife rushed crying into the arms of her husband. The seriousness of his condition was indicated by the fact that MacStiofáin was taken to intensive care in the Mater Hospital immediately following the sentencing.[59]

There was s strong public response to the framing of the case. On the night of MacStiofáin's arrest, there were riots in Derry which lasted for more than two hours, and a number of relatively small public protests in other places both in the North and the South, each attended by fifty to two hundred people—probably Sinn Fein supporters for the most part.[60] Three former IRA chiefs of staff, Tom Barry, Sean Cronin and Maurice Twomey, who all had become well-known public figures, issued a joint statement calling for MacStiofáin's release. They argued that his death would only please Britain and lead to further oppression in the North: 'No Irish person, irrespective of position, should assist Britain in maintaining her grip on this country.'[61] There was also support from less partisan quarters. The largest Irish trade union, the ITGWU, sent a telegram to the Irish president asking for clemency, and a few days after the arrest the most famous English university debating society, the Oxford Union, voted for a reunification of Ireland. During the debate, attended by the

Irish Taoiseach, Jack Lynch, John Hume, the new leader of the SDLP (the moderate nationalist Social Democratic and Labour Party of Northern Ireland), and Roy Bradford, a former Unionist minister, appeals were also voiced for the release of MacStiofáin.[62]

After being convicted and sentenced to (the minimum term of) six months' imprisonment, MacStiofáin continued his hunger and thirst strike. The prospect of his death generated growing public attention and support. After the verdict was read there were shouts of 'British traitor' from the public gallery, directed at the judge. One man, accused him of fighting a war for the English, and threw a handful of coins that according to the *Observer* 'smashed a chandelier and glass rained over the court room'; the *Irish Independent* less dramatically reported that the coins 'broke a light'. In his memoirs MacStiofáin stated that 'splinters fell around Mary and me as she came over to embrace me'.[63] There were scuffles outside the courtroom and outside the Mater Hospital in Dublin, to which MacStiofáin was taken in what *An Phoblacht* described as 'inclement weather', no fewer than seven thousand people were reported to have come out in protest. There was some bottle-throwing, injuring four policemen and two civilians, while the crowd chanted, 'We want Sean out.' They were addressed by opposition TDs (members of parliament), civil rights activists from Northern Ireland and prominent Republicans. Sinn Fein leader Daithi O Connaill called for a large protest meeting on Wednesday or Thursday, optimistically arguing, 'We are going to bring this government down and we will not finish until we do so.' In response to the violence on the street and a bomb attack on a nearby cinema, MacStiofáin had a message read out in which he called for peaceful protest in the South and to take the fight to the North. During the protest at the hospital an attempt was made to free MacStiofáin by eight armed men, two dressed as priests and six as hospital staff. The rescue failed, and after a shoot-out in the corridors of the hospital four of the men were arrested. The crowd remained outside until the early hours of Monday morning, when the last three hundred protesters moved to the General Post Office in O'Connell Street.[64]

In a personal response, another Sinn Fein leader, Ruari O Bradaigh, summarised the movement's attitude to the case, saying that the English had instigated the prosecution of MacStiofáin and thereby had effectively signed his death warrant. He further accused the Irish government of trying to provoke a confrontation with the Republican movement on the streets. The entire affair betrayed a pattern that he asked people to recognise. The connected pieces included the muzzling of the media to prevent people from hearing the news; the closure of Sinn Fein offices; the issuing of extradition orders 'to hand over gallant Republicans to the RUC and British army who are investigated by human rights court'; and the meetings between the two prime ministers prior to the action against MacStiofáin. 'All these pieces of the jigsaw indicated the coming to a head of an attempt to impose the latest British "settlement" to the "Irish problem" because southern politicians realised that they could not last in a 32-county context but needed a British created state to survive.' He hoped the newspapers would deliver this message to the country.[65]

Following MacStiofáin's conviction there were also protest meetings in other parts of Ireland. The Aer Lingus office in London was occupied by members of Sinn Fein. The Cork command of the Republican splinter group Saor Eire threatened retaliatory action against the people responsible if MacStiofáin died. There were protests from trade union officials, the Socialist Workers Movement, the National Graves Association, a branch of the Gaelic Athletic Association (GAA) and Republican Clubs in Northern Ireland. Resolutions were passed, a black coffin with 'Justice is Dead' was again carried around, some short strikes broke out in various companies, pickets were staged, petitions were signed and masses were said in church. Nevertheless, the scale of protect in Ireland was insufficient to bring the country to a standstill.[66] Although a small peaceful protest against MacStiofáin's conviction led to a gun battle in Belfast between the IRA and Loyalist gunmen, the *Guardian* claimed that:

> apart from diehard Republicans, there was surprising little sympathy for Mr MacStiofáin's physical plight among Belfast Catholics. Martyrs appear out of fashion in the city, and although there was a good deal of general sympathy for Mr MacStiofáin and his principles, his behaviour, to many, appeared a needless sacrifice.[67]

In contrast, the *Irish Press* observed many reactions in the North, with hundred people going on hunger strike in Andersonstown and others picketing RUC stations. Generally they reported on the appeal for MacStiofáin's release issued by several organisations, including trade unions and GAA clubs.[68]

The bungled rescue attempt in the hospital and the bomb attack on the Dublin cinema did not do MacStiofáin's case much good in the public eye. In a front-page article, the *Guardian* reported on the rescue attempt in quite neutral tones before remarking, 'The attempt showed by its suicidal nature the length to which some of the Provisionals are prepared to go to try and free Mr MacStiofáin.' The *Irish Press*, whose entire front page was dedicated to the MacStiofáin case, agreed that the rescue was bad publicity for the IRA. The IRA denied responsibility for the attack on the cinema, instead accusing 'agents provocateurs', and even openly suggesting it was done by the Irish security forces: 'In the North such action by the S.A.S is commonplace and the Special Branch in the South have always been quick to learn from their counterparts in the North.'[69] The *Guardian* and the *Sunday Independent* agreed that the attack aided the passing of new repressive legislation through the Dáil.[70] In a government investigation conducted after the peace process in the 1990s it was concluded that IRA members from Derry had been involved in the bombing and that there was probably no sanction for it from their central command. Possibly to divert attention, MacStiofáin's wife produced telegrams of sympathy and support allegedly from two sons of the late Robert Kennedy at a press conference. The only paper to report this was the *Guardian*, which added that Joseph Kennedy, one of the two sons, described the claim as 'absolute rubbish'.[71]

The *Guardian* recognised the performative power of the hunger strike in Ireland but made a point of warning people against it:

> The martyred Republican hero goes deep in the Irish—not least in the Fianna Fáil—tradition. Yet it must not be forgotten that Mr MacStiofáin is the unashamed advocate, organiser, and defender of a vicious campaign that has killed hundreds of his fellow Irishmen and Englishmen. The IRA is not on the side of democracy or humane behaviour either in the North or the South. The plight in which Mr MacStiofáin has voluntarily placed himself will arouse human pity. But it is not a cause for criticising Mr. Lynch's government, which cannot allow the methods of a Gandhi to be used for the objectives of a Franco.[72]

In an attempt to marginalise opposition, the Irish government expressed confidence that even if MacStiofáin died, trouble would only come from the IRA, not from the people.[73] Nevertheless, after the conviction the hospital was protected like a fortress, surrounded by 150 policemen, with another six hundred soldiers kept in readiness.[74] In a rare move, Brian Faulkner, the Unionist leader in the North, supported the Irish government's approach: 'If someone was breaking the law, a Government had to act, even at the risk of producing martyrs.'[75] To some extent, the reaction of Sinn Fein leaders—that they had no desire to seek confrontation with the Irish police, only with politicians—indicated that the government assessment of limited potential popular support for Republicanism in the South was on the mark. During the protest meeting at the hospital, the IRA called for discipline and restraint, telling the protesters that 'the government would love the media to be able to report that a crowd of hooligans and hoodlums came up from O'Connell Street and desecrated a hospital'.[76] Instead they continued to project a picture of MacStiofáin as a strong, heroic figure suffering for the cause. When, following the failed rescue attempt, MacStiofáin was moved by helicopter from the Mater to a military hospital inside military barracks, his wife had it be known that 'One of the hospital staff said he put up a tremendous struggle which "must have taxed his strength immensely." '[77]

In the following days numerous demonstrations and demands for MacStiofáin's release were reported in Ireland, Britain and the USA. Republicans attributed the strong reactions to the absence of justice in the trial, but many others involved in the protests argued they came out on humanitarian grounds. Representatives of the latter group concentrated less on Republicanism and more on the issue of press freedom, a predilection that was also reflected in newspaper reporting.[78] Resolutions were passed by local authorities with the support of Fianna Fáil councillors, branches of political parties, sports clubs and schools. The teaching staff of Presentation Secondary School in Cashel held a prayer meeting in church and put out a statement saying that 'they upheld the principle of truth, justice and freedom and could therefore not accept that any Irishmen in 1972 should be allowed to die on hunger strike for those principles by the consent of our government'. Spontaneous strikes broke out in various parts of the country. Dockers and Ford plant workers in Cork as well as hundreds of workers in Monaghan walked out in protest, and in Tralee most businesses, including banks, were closed. MacStiofáin was even visited in hospita by the sitting archbishop of Dublin, Dr. Dermot Ryan, and his predecessor, Dr. John Charles McQuaid.[79]

The idea that the English were somehow behind the events did strike a chord with some papers. The local *Kerryman* picked up on the Republican narrative and criticised the positive reaction in English newspapers to the arrest of MacStiofáin and the new legislation brought in against the IRA. This, said the *Kerryman*, was simply an attempt by the government to keep control over the South and aid the British to do the same in the North. It was rare, it argued, for the British press to be so positive about Ireland, particularly in support of legislation they would never accept in their own country. 'But then in ultra-British terms, we were always just wogs anyway.'[80] The Republican interpretation also got a measure of credence in the Dáil, in particular from Sean Sherwin, a deputy of the government party, Fianna Fáil, who repeatedly raised the issue of MacStiofáin's plight. On 29 November, he read out a petition signed by 13,867 people, presented to him by a group of Derry women. It protested against the setting up of military courts, the introduction of repressive legislation and the imprisonment of Irish men and women at the bidding of the British government. Sherwin concurred. As far as he was concerned it was a lie to argue, as was being done by the government and the opposition, that the IRA was a threat to the Irish state. It was only a threat to the security of what he called the Six County Area, which, he implied, was a good thing. Far from being a threat to the Irish, MacStiofáin was enemy no. 1 for the British; his arrest was on instruction of their government.[81] When asked in the Dáil whether it would not be right to release MacStiofáin in light of his physical condition, Taoiseach Jack Lynch made clear that to his party the maintenance of the Rule of law was at stake and they were therefore not going to give in:

> Mr. Mac Stiofáin has been given a fair trial before the courts and has been found guilty. It is open to him to serve his sentence or to appeal against it or his conviction. Nothing can be gained by continuing the hunger strike in an attempt to frustrate the course of justice. If a member of such an organisation, and especially a self-confessed leader, could secure his release from prison through resort to a hunger or thirst strike, the inevitable consequence would be that not only he but all his associates would be effectively above the law of the land and free to act as they choose and would be seen to be so. This is so for the obvious reason that other prisoners, now or in the future, need only adopt the same tactics to ensure that they, too, would be released. Accordingly, the issue in the present case is nothing less than whether Parliament, Government, the courts and the law are all to surrender to an unlawful organisation. The challenge to the institutions of the State is direct, deliberate and unmistakable. The Government have no choice but to meet it. The consequences that may ensue are regretted by the members of the Government as they no doubt are regretted by everybody with a normal human concern for human life. The consequences, however, are not of the Government's making.[82]

MacStiofáin continued his hunger strike for the next seven weeks, but abandoned his immediately life-threatening thirst strike a few days after the trial. Public support and attention to his plight in the newspapers clearly declined in this period, except during Christmas, when 150 IRA supporters marched on the Irish embassy in London stating, 'We will stand with MacStiofáin and the Provisional Republican Movement even if we have to die.'[83] The *Sunday Independent* attributed the declining attention to the smart tactics of the Irish prime minister, Jack Lynch. Lynch had been using the unpopularity of the growing violence in Northern Ireland to gain support for a move not only against the IRA but also against the independence of the public broadcasting company, RTE, which had been very critical of corruption in government. The response of the Republican movement had also played into the hands of the government. The rescue attempt and the bomb attack only showed their political naiveté. 'At no stage was there any fear that the MacStiofáin hunger and thirst strike would actually create chaos within the State.'[84] Ultimately the Republicans took this message to heart. Although the Sinn Fein leader Ruari O Bradaigh had initially said that it was up to MacStiofáin to decide whether or not to continue his hunger and thirst strike, he was eventually ordered by the IRA leadership on 16 January to abandon his fast. 'After 57 days of hunger strike no useful purpose will be served by Mr Mac Stiofáin continuing his protest against his unjust imprisonment.'[85] After serving his sentence he was released two months later on 16 March 1973.

In the meantime, attempts to undermine MacStiofáin's credibility continued, particularly in the English press and with the support of the Irish government. A few days after his conviction, the *Guardian* opened with a headline stating that MacStiofáin had ended his hunger and thirst strike. Although mentioning further down the article that MacStiofáin's wife denied it, they sided with those who argued that taking tea put a hunger strike to an end. 'But the fact that he has, as the Government information bureau put it, "taken tea" does not mean that he has definitely decided to end his strike. It could be that the tea was taken in a moment of weakness, although judging by his previous behaviour it seems more likely that it was a definite and fully understood decision by him.' The *Irish Independent* was the only newspaper to report that according to the doctor the tea was necessary to prevent MacStiofáin's veins from collapsing.[86] The inducement for giving up the thirst strike seems to have been a request by MacStiofáin's friend Father Sean MacManus. MacManus later said he had persuaded him to take some water by arguing that if he died there was 'going to be bloodshed in the South of Ireland'. The *Irish Independent* also claimed that he was given oxygen and was in a state of semi-collapse, doing nothing except repeating the phrase 'I love Ireland' and asking to see some of his friends. These included Cathal Goulding. The leader of the rival Marxist Official IRA, an old friend with whom he had fallen out in 1969 over Republican policy.[87] Although an undertone of admiration rings through in the piece, the overall message tended to undermine MacStiofáin's credibility.

The reports questioning MacStiofáin's commitment and sincerity in maintaining his hunger strike continued until his release. The *Guardian* followed the allegations up with an article entitled 'MacStiofáin thirst strike suspicions', reporting that 'more than one source claimed last night that he had been drinking during the early days of his thirst strike'. The article quoted the opinion of many doctors that he could not have survived that long otherwise; the reports on his poor condition and his continued strike came from visitors and not from the authorities. The hunger and thirst strike, wrote the *Guardian*, had been purely tactical. It was 'significant that the announcement that Mr MacStiofáin had drunk half a cup of tea came shortly after Mr Lynch had announced that he would not consider releasing him. The Provisionals had hoped that a wave of public sympathy would secure his release and the announcement that he had drunk tea came when this hope had finally disappeared.' The paper also discounted Father MacManus's claim that he had asked MacStiofáin to drink in order to forestall future bloodshed.[88] The next day the *Guardian* acknowledged that his death would 'cause a great wave of political emotion' and reported that the names of Republicans who had died on hunger strike in the past were being mentioned widely. The same concerns were shared in Ireland, where police and military were kept on standby in case of rioting.[89] In response, MacStiofáin issued an appeal calling for peaceful protest—'no rioting, stonethrowing or abuse'—and reiterating MacManus' claim that 'the fight is in the North and must be kept there. I don't want anybody hurt or any blood spilt on my behalf in the 26 counties. That is why I am taking liquids.'[90]

Against this background the *Observer* as well as the Irish *Sunday Independent* did feature stories on MacStiofáin. In the *Observer*, Paul Ferris contrasted the Irish view of the revolutionary with the English. He acknowledged that 'many "good Irish people" regarded MacStiofáin as a hero and were very annoyed when his Irishness was questioned'. The fact that MacStiofáin, whose original name was John Stephens, was born in England from an English father and a mother of uncertain Irish parentage had given rise to such claims. As for the English, although they acknowledged that Ireland 'has been wronged for centuries', MacStiofáin to them was 'Mac the Knife'. He was described as 'a man of limited imagination and fanatical views' with 'no public glow' around his name.[91] The *Sunday Independent* published two full-page articles on him in consecutive weeks. 'Few men have influenced modern Irish history as much as Sean MacStiofáin', it wrote, but the paper did not fundamentally disagree with the *Observer*. It reiterated that MacStiofáin had apparently no Irish ancestry whatsoever, and only had become involved in Irish politics through a group of London Sinn Feiners that included Cathal Goulding. They described him as a very conservative Catholic with 'fanatically generated energy' and pointed out that he demanded total obedience, annoying many Republicans with his abstemious ways and abrupt manner. Although the paper later published an apology to Cathal Goulding for misrepresenting him and printed a letter from MacStiofáin in which he claimed there were at least eighteen inaccuracies in its articles, the public picture of MacStiofáin was no doubt influenced by these portrayals.[92]

During the next two months occasional reports were put out that the prisoner had abandoned his hunger strike. The credibility of MacStiofáin's position was not aided when he went on and off the thirst strike in a vain attempt to prove his commitment.[93] When after abandoning his thirst strike he took tea, glucose and orange juice, some senior Republicans felt this meant he had broken his hunger strike too. Hearing this, he cut back again to water alone.[94] To make clear that the strike was indeed life-threatening, his wife issued reports that he was weak, had lost a lot of weight and had no intention to abandon his strike.[95] To generate understanding, a friendly priest stated that he had only started to drink again so that he could take communion.[96] Nevertheless, the allegations eventually stuck and the perception among many since 1972 has been that MacStiofáin was not truly dedicated to the cause. In December 1974 Lord Dunleath said in the British House of Lords that MacStiofáin 'remains almost a forgotten name now and a figure of ridicule'.[97] Essentially, he stated, this was due to the fact he had not gone through with his hunger strike to the end. Some took this a step further. A few days after the conviction, Sherwin stated in the Dáil that there had been a calculated campaign in the previous year to make out that MacStiofáin 'was a British spy, that Seán Mac Stiofáin was an Englishman and therefore how could he be on the Irish side?'[98] In 1985 some RUC constables claimed that MacStiofáin had been an informer for the Garda, the Irish police force, from about 1970 to the 1980s, which MacStiofáin felt he was obliged to deny vociferously.[99]

At the root of these rumblings may have been some infighting in the IRA itself. The tensions that had prevailed between northern and southern leaders ever since the formation of the Provisionals in 1969 may have been responsible for the false reports a few months before his arrest that MacStiofáin had resigned as chief of staff. In October 1972, just before his arrest, rumours were discussed in a series of articles in the *Observer*, stating that MacStiofáin was to be deposed at the Army Council meeting of that month.[100] These speculations appear to have emerged every year and were said to be related to the rigid discipline on which MacStiofáin insisted. After the meeting, the *Irish Independent* reported that there had been no challenge to the existing leadership and that no changes in the Army Executive or Army Council were expected in the impending convention. This caused one reader to send in a letter accusing the British papers of character assassination on MacStiofáin.[101] His former comrades in the Official IRA argued that the fact that he was born in Britain and did not have an Irish Catholic background made him suspicious in the eyes of some Republicans.[102]

The existence of tensions in the leadership was confirmed in the following months. In December 1972 the *Irish Times* and the English papers reported that before his arrest, unknown to the other leaders, MacStiofáin had put out peace feelers to the British about a truce. The *Observer* argued that the IRA was losing in the North and that MacStiofáin wanted to be remembered as the leader who brought peace, not as one who lost the war.[103] The previous month, however, the same paper had claimed that these suggestions had been brought into the world by his rivals in the Provisionals' executive and that MacStiofáin had put a stop to them by disclosing what went on at the meeting. Afterwards his main rival, Daithi O Connaill, was ousted from the Army Council. After his conviction, the Belfast IRA denied any involvement of Republicans in the peace overtures and claimed they had been made by 'well-intentioned local people'.[104] In December 1972, the *Irish Times* told its readers that peace moves were afoot as soon as a change in IRA leadership had taken place.[105] The *Observer* saw MacStiofáin as a purely military figure whose inability to play a political role 'has reduced the Provisionals to a sterile campaign of violence' that had lost him support in the movement. The paper expressed the hope that he would be replaced by a more flexible leader, but feared that he would inherit a martyr's crown. After his release, when MacStiofáin was asked by reporters about his position in the Republican movement, he dismissed this as 'rubbish' allegations that his fellow prisoners had ignored him and refused to talk to him. Nevertheless, although it was not apparent in the short run, he found it difficult to regain a position of influence after his release. Public support continued to pour in in the fight for his release, even after he was ordered off the hunger strike.[106] Indicating that he had been physically affected by the strike, the *Irish Times* reported upon his release a few months later that 'he looked pale and weak and was visibly shaking while talking to newsmen and being photographed'.[107]

The struggle over public impact was most acute in the Republic of Ireland, where politicians had more to gain from a commitment to Irish unity than in the North. MacStiofáin and the IRA as well as all Irish politicians and the government were acutely aware of this. The IRA side emphasised that MacStiofáin was willing to go to extremes of suffering for the nationalist cause, a degree of commitment that one sought in vain in the behaviour of the government. The imprisonment was portrayed as unjust and vindictive and as having been carried out on the behest of the British government. This view of things would have had greater impact had it not been undermined by signs of disagreement within their own camp. As for the government, it had little choice but to position itself as the guardian of law and order. A campaign to undermine MacStiofáin's credibility that emanated from unclear sources did not seem to have much immediate impact, but in the long run this reflected what most people came to believe. Irish opposition politicians had many targets to criticise. They attacked the government for its failure to maintain law and order, in particular before the arrest; for the harshness of its treatment of MacStiofáin; and, in particular, the threat to freedom of speech implicit in its actions against RTE and O'Kelly. Large swathes of the populace—not just active nationalists but also public bodies such as trade unions, sport clubs and the Catholic Church—were potentially receptive to criticism of the government on these points.

The different newspapers took slightly different positions in the framing of events. They all reported the proceedings fairly faithfully; the distinctions lay in emphasis and the inclusion or exclusion of particular issues or events. Most remarkable was the total absence of reporting on the case by all Irish local newspapers except the *Kerryman*, which limited its remarks to plain reports on who brought out statements or went on strike in support of MacStiofáin. The British newspapers, which had to explain in more detail than the Irish ones the peculiarities of the Irish political and court systems and IRA tactics, seemed keen to report on matters that undermined MacStiofáin's credibility. Despite this bias, they devoted more space to his physical discomfort than the *Irish Times*, which remained fairly neutral while hinting at behaviour that would tarnish his image. The *Irish Independent* was notable for the copious attention it paid to the physical consequences of the hunger and thirst strike. The manner in which the paper did this generated a certain amount of sympathy, as witnessed by local reactions demanding the release of MacStiofáin on humanitarian grounds. Demands of this kind were quite popular, providing Republicans and other nationalists a cause on which they could agree. Few of the papers moved on from humanitarianism to adopt (as opposed to merely mentioning) the injustice frame advanced by the Republicans. Nationalist newspapers were more likely to concentrate on the humanitarian aspects of the case and the threat to press freedom posed by government tactics.

5.4. The Trial of the Belfast Ten (1973)

One of the first major trials of IRA activists in England after the outbreak of violence in 1969 took place in the autumn of 1973. Ten people[108] stood trial in Winchester: court for planting four car bombs, two of which went off, in London on 8 March of that year. Although a warning had been issued, 243 people were injured and one died of a heart attack when bombs went off outside the Old Bailey and the Scotland Yard building, which also housed an Army Recruiting Centre. The police later admitted that the great extent of the harm had been partly due to a delay in their control room as a result of human error.[109] These first major IRA bombings in London since the outbreak of the Troubles in 1969 were part of a wider campaign against a planned referendum to determine whether the people of Northern Ireland wanted to remain in the union with Great Britain or to join the Republic of Ireland. The poll was organised by the British government with the intention of undermining the legitimacy of the Republican claim to a united Ireland, as they were sure that the majority in Northern Ireland would vote in favour of the Union. Nationalists boycotted it, arguing that such a poll could only be held if the population of the whole of the island of Ireland could vote. Shortly after the bombs were found, ten people were arrested at Heathrow airport on their way to Dublin. After an unusually lengthy detention of over four days without charge or access to lawyers, they were accused of conspiring to cause explosives likely to endanger lives or damage property.[110]

During the trial, which lasted ten weeks, it became clear that the four cars used had probably been hijacked in Belfast, then taken to Dublin where they had received a fresh coat of paint and new number plates, were loaded with explosives and driven to London. The evidence against the ten, who included two sisters, Marian and Dolours Price, and the future leading Republicans Hugh Feeney and Gerry Kelly, was mainly circumstantial, namely that they had travelled to London by car and were returning by plane only a few days later, right after the bombings. The few minor clues included a notebook belonging to one of the Price sisters that contained the initials of those participating and a sketch of what looked like an electric circuit. The only direct evidence connecting the ten to the car bombs was a fingerprint of Robert Walsh on the rear-view mirror of one of the cars used and another on a parking ticket found in one of the other cars. The only 'weapons' found on them were two screwdrivers which Dolours Price was carrying in her bag. At the start of the trial the 19-year-old defendant William McLarnon pleaded guilty to membership of the IRA but claimed he was unaware of the mission they had been on. He then left the dock until the end of the trial. It also became clear that another defendant, the 18-year-old Roisin McNearney, who made a statement similar to McLarnon's but pleaded not guilty, had cooperated with the police. Eventually she was acquitted, while McLarnon received a 15-year sentence. The other eight got two life sentences and 20 years' imprisonment, to run concurrently.[111]

The authorities clearly wanted to give the case a high public profile. For what were claimed to be security reasons, the trial was moved from London to Winchester Castle, where the court was situated only 300 yards from the local prison. The courtroom was specially adapted for the trial, with an enlarged dock and a sound system. According to the *Observer*, the courtroom was specially painted in 'battleship grey'. At the opening of the trial, all of the government representatives arrived wearing their full regalia to show how seriously the authorities took the case.[112] Throughout the trial, details concerning security measures were reported in all the newspapers—except for *An Phoblacht*, which claimed that its reporter was refused admittance by the Special Branch.[113] Most Irish and British newspapers simply detailed the arrangements, but the *Irish Times* was more descriptive. It discussed how, when driven to court, the defendants were accompanied by a motorcycle convoy, a dog car and a police van, where they were awaited by armed police and then brought in through the front door while their relatives and friends had to wait until they were all safely inside. The paper was nevertheless not impressed, remarking drily that 'although security was tight it was minimal by Belfast standards'.[114] The *Sunday Independent* claimed that scores of Scotland Yard Special Branch officers had been drafted to join a strong local police force. Marksmen were stationed on rooftops overlooking the route from prison to courthouse; the perimeter wall of the prison was floodlit during darkness; special passes were required; and people were searched. Under the heading 'One of the biggest trials in British legal history opens this morning', the *Irish Independent* added that the judge would have a marksman riding alongside him in his limousine, and that detectives in the courtroom would be armed. The *Guardian* specified all the measures taken, which they believed was the biggest security operation ever mounted in a British court, involving hundred soldiers on standby, a ban on parking in the city, and a doubling of the guard at the prison. The supposed justification was that the police received a tip-off from Northern Ireland that the trial would be violently disrupted. The measures taken included intensified precautions at government buildings and the postal services to prevent a new outbreak of parcel bombs. Hospitals were prepared for large numbers of casualties.[115] The precautions were not entirely unjustified. On the first day of the trial two bombs went off in London and about hundred hoaxes were reported, causing widespread chaos and confusion. The consternation in England was great, with some MPs demanding such draconic measures as requiring identity cards for all Irishmen; a ban on the IRA; deportation of known sympathisers; and the death penalty for terrorist killers.[116]

The press and public were nevertheless allowed into the courtroom, and photographs of the judge and prosecutors were published freely. In light of the expressed fear of IRA retaliation and the bomb attack on the judge in the *Card and McKee* case, this seems somewhat inconsistent. In the courtroom, the defendants were put side by side in a lengthened dock, with numbers in front of them for easy identification; special tables were put behind them to accommodate their seventeen lawyers. The numbering could be seen as an attempt to dehumanise the defendants and reduce public sympathy. Before the opening sitting, the defendants were made to wait in the dock for an hour and twenty minutes. After that it took almost thirty minutes more to swear in the jury members. Eleven of them were challenged and another two were released on account of pressing commitments during the eight weeks the trial was expected to last. Compared to the one- or two-day trials in the cases discussed above, this was extremely long.[117]

The importance the government attached to presenting its case was highlighted by the choice of Sir Peter Rawlinson, the attorney general, as chief prosecutor. His opening speech alone lasted five and a half hours. Starting off, he stated that although the coming referendum on the Irish borders was expected to incite attacks in London, and even if car bombs had been an everyday experience in Northern Ireland for some time, the crime for which the defendants was charged marked the first time since the war that London had been rocked by massive explosions. The calling up of this sense of threat was amplified by the *Guardian*, which specified the probable weight of the explosives used, concluding that each car had been transformed 'into a moveable lethal bomb'.[118] Rawlinson sketched the IRA as less than heroic by understatedly arguing that the deed under judgment 'might be thought a cowardly form of attack' which 'left passers-by to suffer the consequences of the explosives'. By way of contrast, he commended the work of security men at Scotland Yard who noticed that the bolts of the number plates on one of the cars did not fit the holes for them and subsequently were in time to defuse one of the bombs. 'If there were medals for such courage such medals should go to men such as these who, with such nerve and skill, protected other people.' According to the newspapers, the attorney general then gave a detailed account of how, in the view of the prosecution, the IRA operation had been carried out. Catching the defendants had been possible by a 'combination of human error, carelessness and coincidence'. Their guilt was mainly to be established through their use of false names and the fact that they all got up very early on the morning of the bombing 'to catch a plane to be back snug in the republic'. Rhetorically he asked: 'If their purpose was innocent why was it that they were scurrying home on the morning of March 8th?'[119]

During the trial, the prosecution tried to undermine the credibility of the defendants and picture them as callous murderers. The policemen were asked how they had behaved under questioning; their answers revealed that most of them had been unwilling to cooperate. One policeman suspected that the defendants had undergone counter-interrogation training, since when questioned 'they fixed their eyes on an object, clenched their hands and stared at it continuously, as if "appearing to have been hypnotised".' During her first interrogation, Marian Price was said to have 'looked pointedly at [the] watch and smiled' when she was asked about the bombings. A special target was Dolours Price, who was identified by Rawlinson as the leader of the group, and whose human feelings were called into question. Did she avow to feelings of horror, indifference or pleasure, Rawlinson asked, when he showed Price photographs taken after the explosions at Scotland Yard and the Old Bailey and then asked her what kind of person would perpetrate such a crime. To that question she replied 'indifferent'. After establishing that she had been a politically active Republican, which she confirmed, he produced a photograph of her with a British soldier taken at an army checkpoint in Northern Ireland, apparently to diminish her status among Republicans.[120]

In the final summing-up the prosecution reminded the jury, and with it the wider audience, that the huge bombs of great destructive power constituted a concerted attack on selected targets on the day of the plebiscite in Northern Ireland. Going through the evidence step by step, Rawlinson conceded that the Crown's case was founded on a mass of circumstantial evidence. It was difficult, he said, to unravel the 'web of deceit' around 'one of the most serious crimes which had been perpetrated in the capital'. What could be demonstrated beyond doubt is that all the bombs arrived in London during the brief time the defendants were there. Between the arrival of the first car and the explosions, all the cars were parked in one garage, the people involved all stayed nearby in different hotels and all set off for Dublin the next day under false names. All other people travelling that day could identify themselves, while they could not. He then referred to 'coincidence upon coincidence' and to 'chance meetings' which were put forward by the defendants to explain events, adding that they 'had advanced explanations which they [the jury] might think in many cases to be wholly unacceptable'. Comparing the number of coincidences needed to explain the evidence to a pantomime, he attacked the integrity of the defendants mainly by innuendo and inference. After establishing that they were active nationalists he asked the jury: 'Have you any doubt this was an operation planned, organised and financed and controlled by the I.R.A. and executed by those sympathetic with its aims and beliefs?' He had no doubt; in his view they were guilty beyond reasonable doubt. The lack of evidence caused *Republican News* to allege that the prosecutor was motivated by vengeance and 'showed no interest in proving the elements of the crime charged. His main objective was to show the jury the defendants were I.R.A. agents. The defendants were not put on trial. Their political opinions were put on trial.' The certainty evinced by the prosecution appeared to flag when it came to Roisin McNearney, who had cooperated with the police. In her case, he wondered whether she really should be convicted of placing the bomb at Old Bailey, since 'she seemed a bit on the fringe of this'.[121]

The presiding judge, Sebag Shaw, generally attempted to demonstrate impartiality. He was responsible for the extra tables brought in to accommodate the seventeen counsels for the defendants. To help the jury follow proceedings in the noisy courtroom, worsened by poor acoustics, he had loudspeakers installed and called upon all participants to speak loudly.[122] Some of the Irish journalists noticed that this did not always have the desired effect, due to the heavy Irish accents and colloquialisms used by some of the defendants. Paul Holmes, in particular, had a heavy Ardoyne accent and used unfamiliar expressions in his evidence like 'I was under the whip'; 'He said he was brassic'; 'He must have thought I was touch for a tap'; 'he was skippering'.

Shaw clearly did not follow all that was said; at one point he failed to remember a man who had been introduced a couple of times before. In a feature article Eamonn McCann expressed his concern: '"My God", muttered a journalist behind me, "they have not understood a word he has been saying."'[123] Shaw did show he possessed a sense of humour. After one of the police officers had said he was certain of his identification of one of the defendants because he 'had never seen someone looking so much like a villain', one of the lawyers doubted the accuracy of his recollection and referred a couple of times to '"the wickedest-looking, most unshaven villain" that Constable Benson had ever seen.' The judge then told him, 'You have, if I may say so, a splendid gift of sarcasm.' After the same lawyer referred to 'a glorious piece of retrospective ratiocination', the judge asked him to 'have mercy on the shorthand writer'.[124]

Shaw did try to ensure that the jury stuck to the rules. He told them not to discuss the case with others when they went home. That they were allowed to do so at all is quite surprising, considering the security concerns of the authorities. He also warned them not to listen to outside opinion, as 'people seem to know exactly what happened on the basis of second hand knowledge', he urged them to base their judgment solely on what they heard in court.[125] He told them not to be influenced by the guilty plea of the defendant McLarnon and assured one of the defendants that he would not be kept in solitary confinement over the weekend if he did not finish his evidence on a Friday, as his wardens had apparently said he would.[126] He even acknowledged that many people in Ireland may share the ideals of the Republicans. The question, as he put it, was whether the defendants supported violence to further that ideal. Before the jurors started their deliberations on the verdict, he advised them that having Republican views and even having been interned had no bearing on the question of whether or not the defendants were guilty as charged. He told them that because 'a case like this arouses strong horror and resentment', they must resolve not to let emotion play a part in their decision. He also reminded them of the possibility that the police had planted evidence, as was alleged by Michael Mansfield, senior counsel for the Price sisters. During questioning, Shaw told one of the detectives that if he had planted evidence this was the time to say so, and afterwards reminded the jury that being a police officer 'does not necessarily make him an angel of truth or a person who conformed to decent standards'. He also forbade the prosecution from questioning Marian Price on her father's republican views. The *Republican News* nevertheless accused Shaw of allowing the defendants to be questioned on their political beliefs and opined that his tactics reeked of vengeance.[127] He asked the jury not to allow sentiment to intrude on their judgment: 'All the accused were young people not out of their twenties. "Sympathy and chivalry have no place in trying matters such as these."' He also reminded them that there were no special rules for what 'were called political crimes whatever that may mean'.[128]

Nevertheless, Shaw's prejudices occasionally surfaced. Generally, a consequent negative attitude towards the defendants was based on his repudiations of violence and expressions of horror over the bombings. When one of the policemen on the stand tried to undermine the trust between the defendants and their lawyers by stating that he had received information from Michael Mansfield on the time the bomb was planted at the Old Bailey, the judge questioned the need to introduce matters of this kind, but 'pointed out that it might reflect credit to Mr. Mansfield'. What in fact had happened was that Mansfield had parked his car at the Old Bailey and had testified that the car used for the bombing had not been there when he arrived. His own Triumph was apparently severely damaged in the explosion.[129] Shaw also made a special effort to commend for his great courage a journalist who, upon receiving the warning from the IRA, had gone to one of the car bombs and had warned the public there before the police arrived. 'The staff of the Times seemed to be infected with a reckless courage that day—hovering in the vicinity of the explosion.'[130] After the verdict he praised the bomb squad and Special Branch and said that all the police could go home with their integrity untarnished.[131] Another show of feeling on the part of Judge Shaw emerged when one of the defendants refused to give the names of people who could corroborate his version of events. He had been interned, and Loyalists, as he believed, had a policy of assassinating former internees. Moreover, he did not want to say anything at the trial that would get a comrade interned; internment, he said, was like being put in a cage. To which Shaw replied, 'You do understand that at a trial like this these matters have to be brought out. Just as you naturally detest internment, so people walking about the streets detest being blown up.'[132] In his summing up, he reminded the jury members that they should not overlook 'statements made from the dock which failed to deal with matters earlier heard in evidence', subsequently mentioning the 'terse statement' by Walsh to explain how his fingerprints got onto both the rear-view mirror of one of the bomb cars and a parking ticket found in another. '*If* Walsh had been given a lift in the Viva he might have left his print on the mirror but how on earth, the jury might ask themselves, did he leave his fingerprint or did it find its way on to the car park ticket for the Cortina?' Remarks such as these hinted broadly that he did not believe the explanations given by the accused; they almost gave the impression of directing the jury to a guilty verdict.[133] In the *Guardian*, it was also made clear he wanted a 'not guilty verdict' for Roisin McNearney. 'If the jury did convict the other defendants, they would be "wise and just"'; referring to McNearney, he said that 'she was too precariously near the line to say with certainty she was guilty, rather than just ignorant and foolish'.[134]

Mr Justice Shaw also tried to ensure that the defendants would not use the trial as a political platform. In this regard he demonstrated a lack of understanding of the motives of the defendants when he asked William Armstrong, a father of five, how he 'got involved into this kind of affair'. 'Is it money or a misguided notion of patriotism?'[135] He was also unable to conceal his scepticism concerning the way the defendants attempted to explain away one unlikely coincidence after another. 'It might occur to the jury that "no fairy godmother in any fairy tale had ever appeared so opportunely to a protégé, to provide just what was needed, as Dave did for Martin Brady".' Full of irony, he instructed the jury not to swallow the explanations but to test them in the light of good sense. 'If [you] feel [the] case as presented by prosecution is too harsh too inflexible to allow for the contingencies of life [...] you will accept, no not accept, but regard Mr Brady as somebody who, until his unfortunate arrest, had been looked upon benevolently by providence.'[136]

Shaw clearly wanted to portray himself as a defender of society against terrorism. This was apparent from his answer to one of the lawyers, who called upon the judge to take account in his verdict of the growing unrest among the Irish. He had it in his power either to feed that sense of grievance or else to retard the historical cycle of retaliation and reprisal. Shaw's first reaction was to deny the existence of this cycle by stating 'these people kill even people on their own side'. When this was dismissed as rubbish by the defendants, he retorted that he was concerned only with 'offences against this society'.[137] In his verdict he referred to the bombings as a murderous enterprise, to which one of the solicitors objected because the perpetrators had placed warning phone calls intended to save lives. Shaw stood by his use of the qualification 'murderous', but admitted that killing or injuring was not the foremost aim of the attacks. In his effort to protect society against the defendants he initially gave the Price sisters and Hugh Feeney a life sentence on a charge for which the law limited the penalty to 20 years.[138] The *Observer* reported that the combative attitude of the defendants during the sentencing brought Shaw to the verge of tears. 'Passing sentence on people as young as you are is repugnant to me', he professed, eliciting the sarcastic retort: 'Don't worry, we absolve you.'[139]

In dealing with Roisin McNearney, who had been acquitted and given police protection until she was restored to her family, he took it upon himself to present her as an example to society. After reading out the sentences he asked her to sit down and pay heed to a lesson he wished to convey to her and all Irish youngsters: 'You have been in custody since last March and you have nobody but yourself to blame.

You have learnt a bitter lesson and I hope it has taught you and others like you not to dabble in murderous enterprises, and treat it as a frolic, for it brings grave danger to you.' He added that he did 'not know the dangers outside this courtroom that you will face. I hope all will be well with you. I think the jury was right to acquit you. But you came near to the edge of guilt and you may reflect upon that. And if you have friends in Ireland still, you tell them about the experiences here, so they may know what to expect if they follow your example.'[140]

Unlike in the other cases discussed here, the defendants in this case had not admitted membership of the IRA and denied involvement in the bombings. Consequently they recognised the court as legitimate and had themselves defended by English lawyers. The IRA seemed to assent in their taking this stance, even though it contravened general IRA policy. The jurisdiction of the courts was apparently accepted when operating in Britain. Although not an issue in the proceedings itself, the IRA membership of the defendants was not a secret. Immediately after the completion of the trial, the newspapers reported on the activist background of almost all the defendants, including their rank and unit in the IRA. In line with judicial practice this information was not allowed to be reported on during the trial. The first time a previous record in the IRA was mentioned was on the day the verdicts were reported, when the *Irish Independent* stated, 'Dolours Price and her sister, Marian, nicknamed the "Armalite Widow" by the Provisional I.R.A.—smiled and waved from the dock to relatives and friends in the public gallery before the judge entered. Marian is said to have got her nickname from her expertise with the Provos' favourite weapon, the Armalite rifle.'[141] The *Irish Press* said it referred to the large number of widows she had made among army wives. It also cited the Price sisters, who studied at a teacher training college, as examples of the new breed of IRA intellectuals.[142] Because their IRA membership did not have direct bearing on the bombings, the prosecution was not allowed to put it forward during the trial. They did nevertheless refer to a trip to Italy made by Dolours Price to lecture on the Northern Irish situation to left-wing groups. Showing that although Mr Justice Shaw instructed the jury that holding republican beliefs and having been interned should not be taken into consideration in judging guilt or innocence, the prosecution was willing to use an activist background to make the charges stick.

One recurring motif in the defence of the accused was that they were maltreated in custody, a claim that fortified the idea—among Irishmen in particular—that British society was marked by an anti-Irish bias. The *Irish Independent*, which in contrast to the *Irish Times* reported only occasionally on the trial, and generally provided only a simple summary of the evidence, picked up on this issue; the editors must have expected it to be of interest to its readers. Even the *Guardian*, which generally supported the Conservative government's actions against the IRA, reported extensively, in a concurring tone, on the aspersions cast by the defence on the truthfulness of the police evidence. Upon arrest the clothes of the defendants had been taken from them for forensic tests, and it was not until the next day that they were given spare clothes, clothes that the Price sisters and Feeney refused to accept. In the interim they were dressed in blankets, a condition in which their photos were taken. Because Dolours refused to use the blanket, which she claimed was filthy, the photo shows her completely naked. The defendants had been forced to have their fingerprints taken, which was against the law. They also claimed to have been manhandled, and Feeney said he did not get a mattress in his cell. Mansfield alleged that the leading inspector had called Price an 'evil little maniac' and had told her she 'would not be seeing the sunshine again for some time'. He had also taken her crucifix as he felt 'she did not deserve to have it'.[143] All newspapers reported these events fairly dispassionately, but somewhat surprisingly it was the *Irish Independent* that defended the enforced fingerprinting of Dolours Price—an act that technically constituted an assault—on the grounds that police investigations sometimes require desperate measures.[144]

The inspector justified his actions. He denied having said those things to Dolours Price, but admitted that at the end of the first interview he was 'perhaps a little annoyed with her', and had taken a chain and locket as he believed something might be hidden in it. He did not deny that the fingerprints were taken forcibly. He knew that he did not have the right to do so, but said that he needed them for the investigation. The photograph of Price was taken with no clothes on because she unexpectedly did not put on the blanket, as he thought she would. That the prisoners had not been allowed to see a solicitor for four days, the inspector said, was because their identity had not yet been established.[145] When one of the lawyers asked a policeman if he knew that his colleague had ordered what he called 'a criminal assault', the judge forbade him to answer the question, adding, 'The Jury have had quite enough about that.'[146] The defendants considered the maltreatment and the anger it generated explanation enough for their lack of cooperation as well as their lack of distress when confronted with the pictures of the bombings.[147]

During the trial, they presented themselves in an upbeat, unconcerned and innocent manner. When they were first brought to the court many of the defendants, including the Price sisters, gave V-signs through the small windows of the police van. This was later prevented by having the windows blackened. In court the defendants seemed to be in a perfectly good mood. The *Irish Times* reported that the girls had shiny hair and were sprucely dressed when they arrived, accompanied by half a dozen women prison officers. The next day the girls were reported to cause 'heads to turn in the galleries when they arrived in the dock wearing brightly coloured pinafore dresses and blouses'.[148] The other Irish and British papers also made occasional references to the looks of those involved, but the *Observer* stood out for its rapt attention to outward appearances.[149] In a background article entitled 'English justice in all its grandeur for Winchester: 9',[150] details of the physical appearance of some of the men were provided, including Judge Shaw, who came to court carrying his black hat and white gloves, and Gerard Kelly, 'who wears his dark hair shoulder-length and walks with the cheerful swagger known in Belfast as a dander'. The other men in the dock were described as 'rather a square looking bunch'. The paper contradicted the evidence of one of the police witnesses, who had described William Armstrong as the most villainous-looking man he had ever seen, saying that he 'looks as inoffensive as any other window-cleaner [his stated occupation] in a sports jacket'. In another implicitly critical reference, it recounted how Peter Rawlinson, the attorney general, was said to be getting £200 a day for this case. Most space was however given to the women. Roisin McNearney was described as having delicate pretty features; the paper noted that 'at the end of the day she rests her chin on a folded arm and looks dreamily ahead'. The Price sisters attracted the most attention: 'They are handsome rather than pretty, with firm jaw lines, creamy complexions and auburn tint to their chestnut-coloured hair.' They seem to have played on the effect of their appearance by often changing their clothes during the lunch break; 'pinafore dresses and smocks seem to be the favourite'. Somewhat in opposition to the description above, the paper reported how 'everybody in court, police, counsel, reporters—agrees they are an absolute knockout'. ('Dolly birds in the dock', said a headline in the London *Evening News*.) In a retrospective article, somewhat confusingly entitled 'The sisters of terror', the paper recalled how rural policemen were amazed that beauty could be so dangerous.[151] This trivialisation of the defendants gave them a sense of innocence, an unexpected effect coming from a British newspaper.

In their evidence, the defendants accounted for their presence in London in various ways, saying that they were looking for a job, visiting people or that they came simply as tourists. A few of them refused to testify but gave statements through their solicitors. Their use of false names was explained with reference to the situation in Northern Ireland, where it was dangerous to admit having a Republican name or even a name easily identifiable as belonging to a Catholic. Gerry Kelly explained that many, even very respectable, people were giving false names due to the introduction of internment without trial. Hugh Feeney said he had started to use a false name after having been stopped and beaten up by vigilantes of the UDA, the Ulster Defence

Association.[152] The *Irish Independent*, in stressing the credibility of these explanations in a Northern Irish context, contributed to the idea that the suspects were victims of English ignorance.[153] The main argument of the defence lawyers was that the defendants did not have to prove their innocence—the prosecution had to prove guilt; the case, they argued, was based 'upon allegations made by assertion more than anything else'. A bit of consideration, they argued, would reveal that the picture painted by the defendants was not that unlikely. Most people on a short holiday would meet someone they knew who travelled on the same day. This was not a strange coincidence, just something that happened. With the Special Powers Act in force in Ulster, giving a false name was quite logical. That one of them was identified in a line-up was also unsurprising, considering the fact that he was the only one in borrowed clothes and without shoelaces. The fear that their family and friends would be shot if they testified was hard to accept, but was 'reality in Northern Ireland'.[154]

Dolours Price was portrayed as the leader of the IRA bombing team and was singled out for special attention. She came from an active Republican family. Her father had been interned for eight years during the 1940s and had moved to the South after their house had been searched frequently following the reintroduction of internment in August 1971. Dolours admitted to having given lectures in Italy on the Northern Ireland situation. She was in favour of a united Ireland and claimed to understand the aims and principles of the IRA. Yet, as McNearney's lawyer argued, it was no offence in England to be a member of the IRA or to associate with it. And although there was probably 'no organisation in this country at this moment with a more unpopular ring to it than the I.R.A.', the jury should not be led by their feelings.[155] Dolours Price was more assertive in her answers than some of her co-defendants. She had a reasonable explanation for the photograph taken of her with a British soldier. She was held up at a checkpoint with a man who was wanted, she said, and when a soldier asked for a photo with her she agreed so as not to cause suspicion. Distress over her own situation was responsible for her unwillingness to cooperate and her flat reaction when having been shown pictures of the aftermath of the bombings. She was also defiant. When asked by Peter Rawlinson what kind of person would perpetrate a crime like the bombing of the Old Bailey, she said: 'I really don't know. If you saw photographs of Berlin after it was bombed [during World War Two], could you say the person who did it was a maniac?' Being asked whether she supported the use of violence to further her ideals she evaded the question.[156]

The two defendants who pleaded guilty or collaborated with the police were treated somewhat differently by the rest. After William McLarnon had pleaded guilty and was led away, the other defendants showed no reaction.[157] This was quite different for Roisin McNearney, who like the others pleaded not guilty but cooperated with the police. She admitted to having been drafted into the IRA recently on an eleven-month trial, after singing Irish songs in a Belfast bar. A short while before the bombings she was told to go to Dublin, where she met two women and later two men who said she was going to London, which she thought was great as she had never been there. In London she had done a bit of sightseeing, going to Madame Tussaud's and Buckingham Palace, but knew nothing of the bomb in the car. As the attorney general noted pointedly, a statement by her that was read in court contained evidence only against herself, not against the others. She did provide whatever details she knew of the movements of the others. She also offered to show the police the hotels where they had stayed, 'on condition that no one knew or saw her because otherwise she would be shot'. Her fear of deadly reprisal was repeated at least three times.[158]

Until the verdicts were read, there nevertheless seemed to be nothing special about the way she was treated by the others. However, when all the accused stood to hear the verdicts read, McNearney stood back a little from the line of prisoners instead of taking her usual place between Feeney and Brady. Another thing that was noticed immediately was that McNearney's father and eldest sister sat apart from the other relatives, separated from them by three uniformed policewomen. When McNearney was declared not guilty there was a scuffle in the dock. Feeney and Brady had to be restrained while McNearney was taken down the stairs. Feeney threw a coin at her and shouted, 'Here is your blood money.' As she left, several of the defendants started to hum 'Dead March from Saul' intimating she would soon be killed. There was a minor altercation between her father and relatives of the other defendants, after which her family left abruptly. When she was brought up again for the verdict on the other two charges, she returned crying into a white handkerchief.[159] The newspaper that paid most attention to the way McNearney was treated by the other defendants was the *Guardian*. The front page opened with the headline 'Eight bombers chant death as girl is freed.' In a departure from the facts as reported in the other papers, the *Guardian* wrote that she had been ostracised from the beginning and was now effectively sentenced to death by the Provisionals. Although acknowledging that McNearney had been a member of the women's organisation of the IRA, by painting her so pitifully the paper clearly wanted to place the emphasis not on her culpability but on the ruthlessness of the IRA. The single coin Feeney threw at her in the Irish newspapers became a handful of coins in the *Guardian*.[160] The *Irish Press* was the only paper that reported on the death threats from the Loyalist UVF (Ulster Volunteer Force) received by relatives of the two defendants who escaped punishment.[161]

After the verdict the prisoners dropped the pretence of non-involvement in the IRA, determinedly limiting their appeal to their own supporters. To hear the sentences, the defendants were brought in with fifteen prison guards who packed the seats behind them. Before the judge came in, several of the defendants were smiling, waving to public and press, and leaning on the rail. Some continued to do so during the sharp exchanges with Shaw that now ensued. It was as if now that they were condemned, they manifested contempt for the court in retrospective conformity to the traditional Republican refusal to recognise courts that they had not followed during the trial. Even before sentence was passed the defendants announced that they were going on hunger strike to be recognised as political prisoners and to be allowed to serve their time in Northern Ireland. As the sentences were announced, the defendants defiantly shouted IRA slogans and raised clenched fists in the air. None of them asked for leniency, and in their speeches from the dock they admitted membership of, and expressed support for, the Provisional IRA and the ideal of a united Ireland. Feeney, in an impassioned address, said, 'Victory is within the grasp of the Irish nation. She will not bend the knee. England shall realise that we are indeed an arisen people.' Kelly stated that, as a member of the IRA, he would fight until the people of Ireland could decide their own destiny. Holmes concurred and ended with a famous quotation from Republican icon Patrick Pearse: 'Ireland unfree shall never be at peace.' They also claimed that this had been a political trial, and that the real defendant should be the British government. They called for a trial in Strasbourg to judge the actions of the British army in Northern Ireland, whom they called 'uniformed thugs' and who, they claimed, had planted bombs in Dublin and hired criminals to fight Republicans. Even McLarnon, who had admitted guilt from the beginning and was given fifteen years, did not ask for leniency, and when sentenced shouted 'Up the Provisional IRA.'

The proceedings ended in some chaos. Gerry Kelly was removed when the judge decided that the statement he was declaiming was a political speech; six spectators who applauded and shouted support for him were also taken out. The entire audience seemed to consist of—mainly female—relatives and supporters of the defendants. By then none of the defendants was inclined to show respect for the judge. Shaw's order that they keep quiet only brought the defendants to shout 'no' in unison. When he sentenced Feeney and the Price sisters, they interrupted him constantly, stating that they did not want to listen to a lecture from him. The *Guardian* paid a great deal of attention to what it described as 'a series of extraordinary incidents in court'. As the paper saw things, the statements by the other defendants were also blatantly political, even after Kelly was removed. The *Guardian* moreover expressed surprise that the defendants 'were quite unashamed of their deliberate perjury in an attempt to avoid conviction'. When eventually led away, all gave the clenched fist sign to shouts of 'All the best' and 'Cheerio, girls' from their supporters. After their arrival in prison, they issued a written statement in which the eight confirmed their hunger strike and their refusal to wear prison clothes until they were transferred to Northern Ireland and given political status. This would allow open visits, food parcels once a week, the freedom to write and receive as many letters as they wanted and the right to be together. Imprisonment in England, they claimed, would moreover entail financial and emotional hardship for their relatives.[162]

The Provisional IRA did not come out with an official response until after the verdict. As the defendants had previously denied involvement with them, the organisation had so far refused to be drawn into the case. In its initial reaction immediately after the bombing it had announced that the eight operatives who had really carried out the bombings had returned safely to Ireland. This implied that the accused men and women were innocent, while countering Scotland Yard's claim that the car bombs had been planted by splinter groups.[163] In a later article, the *Guardian* reported that the attack had occasioned much argument in the IRA. Former Chief of Staff Sean MacStiofáin was said to have disapproved of the plan. It was only after his imprisonment that the new Belfast-based leaders, who were under pressure in the North and needed a success, pushed it through over lingering opposition in the ranks. According to the *Guardian* this led to a huge row in the IRA Army Council.[164] Disregarding the possible effects of such an action on the defendants' denial that they were members of the IRA, the Republican newspapers organised aid campaigns for them from the beginning. 'People wishing to offer support or give assistance to the Belfast Ten should get in touch with Miss Maureen Maguire.' *Republican News* was also the only paper consistently to report on the support groups emerging in England and Ireland.[165]

In a statement following the conclusion of the case, the Provisionals criticised the harsh sentences, which they claimed betrayed anti-Irish prejudices and hatred and were 'similar to the shooting of the sepoys from the barrels of cannons because they too defied the Empire in defence of freedom'. This belated interjection of the narrative of injustice was followed by threats of revenge: 'The day is long past for Irish people to lie under the lash of British Imperialists. In due course, retribution will be extracted from the people who inflicted such callous punishment on Belfast youth in Winchester today.'[166] They expressed their admiration for the prisoners: 'Undeterred by the coercive atmosphere of the infamous Winchester court, the prisoners asserted the god-given right of the Irish nation to freedom and affirmed that truth and attested it with their liberty. Their heroism will inspire thousands more to drive home the struggle for freedom to a victorious conclusion.' This admiration did not apply to Roisin McNearney, who the Provisionals said was expected after her release to appear before an IRA court of inquiry to explain her actions. For now nobody knew where she was, but the declaration added menacingly that police protection would not last forever. The next day Sinn Fein took defiance a step further. Irish Republicans no longer feared the British, they said. As the sentences showed, it was the British who feared the Irish. They made the specific prediction that 1974 would be the year of 'victory over British imperialism'. In this they took inspiration from the convicted: 'Inspired by their display of dignity and courage in the face of their enemies, we rededicate with recharged enthusiasm to the present resistance struggle in the North. Now, more than ever before, it is essential to conclude the victorious armed struggle undistracted by "political" obstacles. In this victory our comrades will taste the sweet air of freedom.'[167]

The Republican newspapers built on this argument. An analytical article in the *Republican News* positioned Britain as the real loser in the case of the Belfast Ten. The bombs had made millions aware of 'occupied Ireland'. British people had previously been apathetic, it claimed, but now millions asked 'what evils their government had perpetrated in Northern Ireland to induce ten Irish youths to sacrifice their lives and freedom'. The trial only accentuated British repression. The defendants had received unprecedented life terms and had been treated as political enemies, to be put out of commission for a long time to come. 'It was a political trial.' Even the English attorneys representing the defendants admitted to this. The British Tories, said the *Republican News*, had had their vengeance, but their 'blunders have poisoned the well of Anglo-Irish relations for generations to come'. 'Moderate Irishmen were shown what to expect under the British system of justice. Once again, the Crown became the chief recruiting officer for the IRA.'[168] In a special supplement to *An Phoblacht* dedicated to the Winchester hunger strikers, a whole list of allegations was published to back up the accusation that the proceedings were a show trial. The defendants, the paper claimed, were already found guilty before the trial, which was moved to Winchester in the expectation that there would be a more 'pro-Government blood-thirsty jury' there; the defendants had been maltreated; and the press had influenced the trial by a 'wave of hysteria whipped up by [the] Capitalist press'; even before the trial started, the BBC had described the suspects as culprits (a qualification it later withdrew); and, *An Phoblacht* recalled, the sentence by 'blood-thirsty Sebag' initially exceeded the legal maximum.[169]

The government clearly wanted to show that it took up the challenge put to it by the IRA and the defendants. Although Scotland Yard denied any knowledge of an alleged IRA plan to kidnap ten villagers from Essex in retaliation, after the trial a major security operation was put into effect. It was announced that the homes of the judge, prosecutors, senior policemen and jurors were being protected and that public buildings were being watched. The authorities refused to confirm or deny reports that armed guards were posted in the houses of those involved in the trial and of senior government figures.[170]

Public reaction to the attempts to impose a specific narrative by those involved is difficult to measure. Reporting on the trial in the *Irish Times* was much more extensive than in the *Irish Independent* and *Irish Press*, let alone the local Irish papers, but even coverage in the *Irish Times* tapered off after the first couple of weeks. Generally, the paper simply conveyed the evidence that was being presented. The strongest reaction in favour of the defendants seems to have been in England. Immediately after the arrest of the ten suspects a 'Belfast Ten Defence Committee' was set up to help the prisoners and to draw attention to the way they were treated. It brought together Irish, left-wing and student organisations on both sides of the Irish Sea. Supporters included Maura Maguire of the Anti-Internment League, Eamonn McCann of the *International Socialist* and Pat Arrowsmith, a pacifist campaigner. They asserted that the newspapers had condemned the suspects before the trial had begun; castigated the authorities for the maltreatment to which the accused were allegedly subjected; and provided moral and financial support as well as organising an 'international solidarity campaign on the lines of the successful Angela Davis Defence Committee'. English civil rights activists became involved immediately, in reaction to the fact that initially no charges were levied against the defendants and because they were not given access to a lawyer for almost five days. The Council for Civil Liberties and the Prisoner Action Committee described this as 'a blatant and cynical denial of basic human rights', and went to the High Court to demand the prisoners' release on grounds of habeas corpus: 'A system of mental torture, intimidation and total isolation is being used in a case where the police are obviously unable to bring charges.'[171]

Early reactions among the British public were not devoid of sympathy for the Irish in general. Politicians and bystanders expressed the hope that 'God would help the people in Belfast if this is what is going on there.'[172] Occasional hostility was elicited by the protest marches and pickets of government buildings organised by the defence committee, which were manned by up to 200 demonstrators. During one of these demonstrations, which went from Charing Cross to Hyde Park, a few fists were shaken by passers-by but there was generally little response even when shouts of 'Victory to the I.R.A.' went up when passing a recent bombsite. *An Phoblacht* reported similar numbers of protesters as the other papers.[173] Only the *Irish Press* expressed concern for the consequences of the events for Irish people living in Britain and for British–Irish relations. It also feared the security precautions would generate a groundswell of prejudice against the defendants amongst townspeople, and that this might affect the jury. It was the only paper to observe a negative response, epitomised by what the *Irish Press* regarded as an exceptional reaction from an elderly man sitting in the public gallery, who said through clenched teeth, 'They shouldn't waste a trial on these people: they should have just shot them.'[174]

However, Irish supporters did concentrate more on social activities and fundraising than on public protest afterwards. Their weekly collections, he said, were not down; sales of *An Phoblacht* even went up a bit. During the trial Republicans felt strong enough to organise a march through the constituency of a very vocal anti-IRA Tory MP. According to the *Irish Times* this was 'a nose-thumping exercise but also a measure of the Provisionals' confidence that they will be able to operate despite bombs'. A certain downturn in support from left-wing organisations in Britain did appear to develop over time. A picket organised by Official Sinn Fein, in which all Irish, socialists and those believing in justice and democracy were asked to participate, saw a turnout of only a hundred people. This stood in blatant contrast to the thousands who had demonstrated after the events a year before on Bloody Sunday, in which fourteen civilians had been shot dead by security forces in Derry.[175]

The *Guardian*, which had provided most detail on the dangers to the population during the trial, helped to create a sense of threat after sentencing by speculating on possible retaliation by the IRA in Britain: 'There are fears that the IRA may try a novel form of terrorist action for them in an attempt to force the authorities to free the prisoners. It is known that bombings and kidnappings have been considered.' The next day it discussed the possibilities that a plane would be hijacked or a 'daring rescue' by helicopter be undertaken, while adding reassuringly that the IRA would find it difficult to operate in Britain, where it lacked public support. The paper also expressed its faith in the positive effects of the hard government line against prisoners who went on hunger strike in order to acquire political prisoner status: 'The Home Office in this country is unlikely to ever accede to granting any of the IRA prisoners this status in Britain, contrary to the practice of the Republic.' In full realisation that prisoners who once went on hunger strike could not go back without losing face, the paper nonetheless concluded that the prisoner would have to give in.[176]

In Ireland itself, public response to the verdicts was very limited. The *Irish Times* felt that the whole bombing plot, which it claimed had been designed in Dublin, was confused and dangerous. None of those involved was apparently able to keep quiet about the proposed mission. 'Their entire approach was muddle-headed and drawn up with monumental incompetence.' The strongest positive response came from the students of St. Mary's and St. Joseph's Colleges in Belfast, where some of the defendants studied. They put a statement out protesting at the savagery of the sentences, demanding the right to appeal and claiming that the prisoners should be allowed to serve their sentence in Northern Ireland.[177] Although most Irish Catholics and nationalists did not much like the bombings, in the months following the sentence their attitude towards the bombers improved when the press reported on the harsh treatment they were receiving from the British authorities and the British refusal, despite the hunger strike, to transfer the convicts to a prison in Northern Ireland.

The Republican newspapers, which had been fairly quiet during the trial, now tried to mobilise support. *An Phoblacht* and, in particular, *Republican News* detailed the ordeal being endured by the seven hunger strikers, claiming that they were effectively being tortured to death. The five male prisoners, dispersed over the country without access to their relatives, had no clothes and just one blanket; they were kept in windowless, unheated cells where they had to sleep naked on stone floors. On the basis of a letter written by Dolours Price, smuggled out of prison, the paper detailed the mechanics of the forcible feeding to which the seven were subjected and compared the conditions to those in Bergen-Belsen concentration camp. It called upon the Irish people, Amnesty International and the International Red Cross to use their good offices to ensure that their demands were met, asking, 'Must these people die before it is too late?'[178] It highlighted the request to be moved to a prison in Northern Ireland, where it was not unusual for political status to be granted to Republican prisoners. The paper recalled how a Northern Ireland minister had recently referred to eighteen convicted prisoners who had been moved from England to the North. A list of efforts supporting the move was then discussed, including actions by the National Council of Civil Liberties and the Association of Legal Justice. The issue had also been raised at a conference on torture in Paris, where relatives of the prisoners had started a 24-hour fast in protest. The paper called upon everyone to phone or write to people with influence, asking them to have a resolution in favour of the prisoners passed and sent to the Home Office. A further demand was addressed to the Dublin government, urging it to take a case to the European Court of Human Rights.[179] In the middle of January the prisoners finally broke through what *An Phoblacht* called the wall of silence erected around them, when their letters detailing their situation were allowed out. This led to demonstrations, mock forced-feeding sessions outside Wormwood Scrubs and Brixton prison, and open expressions of support from a large array of people and organisations in Ireland. Among them, the paper claimed, were the Gaelic League, the GAA, trade unionists, students, teachers, university professors and lecturers, writers, artists, journalists, actors, actresses and a growing number of local authorities.[180] It also criticised the other papers and politicians of all parties who were too busy putting together a political compromise to bother with the issue.[181]

The plight of the hunger strikers also appeared to generate more support in Britain itself. Even some Labour MPs were willing to associate themselves with the Irish Political Hostages Campaign set up to support their demands. As *An Phoblacht* put it, 'The demands are capable of gaining broad support, and so will cut across the hysteria of the press.'[182] The forcible feeding saw to it that the hunger strike continued for more than two hundred days, generating ever more support among those of a nationalist persuasion and also among sympathisers in Great Britain and abroad. The huge difference in public response between the trial and the hunger strike highlights the distinction people felt between sympathy for the plight of the prisoners and support for their tactics. This was just as true of the Irish as of the English and others.

In the long run, all parties involved appear to have been fairly successful in convincing their own audience of the validity of their narrative. The performative power of the government's attempt to highlight the danger of the IRA to law and order seems to have been successful to the extent that English left-wing organisations became more hesitant to express their support for IRA prisoners; even the *Guardian* supported government policy towards the IRA. At the same time, in the public domain there was no noticeable increase in anti-Irish utterances, a phenomenon that was actually in the interest of the British government. (In private, people may well have been much more critical of the Irish than before.) The IRA, although it succeeded fairly well in the initial phases in mobilising support for the defendants among civil right activists and left-wing groupings in Britain, did not reach the masses either in Britain or Ireland. In the long run, however, they were helped by the hunger strike in generating widespread sympathy, in particular among the population in the Irish Republic. The portrayal of the British government as unfair in its treatment of the Irish appears to have struck a chord with the populace, thereby maintaining a potential support base for the objectives and, to some extent, even for the methods used by the Republicans.

5.5. The Trial of Bobby Sands (1977)

The final case discussed here is the trial of Bobby Sands. While best known for his hunger strike in 1981, Sands had been in prison since October 1976. His trial on 7 September 1977 is included here for the insight it offers into the impact of the abolition of trial by jury for cases of political violence in Northern Ireland. The conviction of paramilitary suspects had proved to be particularly difficult for the authorities ever since the outbreak of the Troubles in 1969. We have seen that early in 1971 a type of covert internment policy had been initiated to deal with known leaders such as Card and McKee. Yet this was ultimately unsatisfactory due to the intimidation of jurors and witnesses, acquittals by biased juries, and the inadmissibility of confessions, which often were the only evidence brought forward by the prosecution. To deal with these difficulties, actual internment was subsequently introduced on 9 August 1971. However, this only led to intensified violence, as a large number of people not associated with the Provisionals were interned. The concomitant raids and arrests, with a large measure of violence against people who were not involved, only abetted the recruiting efforts of the movement. The ranks of the IRA were swelled after the first swoops against Republicans, while most prominent members of the Provisionals, who were largely unknown to the security forces, had evaded arrest. From a public relations point of view, internment had considerable drawbacks. It undermined the legal system and its credibility among Catholics, as most internees came from their community.

The introduction of the Diplock courts on 8 August 1973 was a way of ending the need for internment and the use of the associated label 'political prisoner'. These juryless courts made it much easier to convict known activists, as the introduction of Special Criminal Courts in 1972 had done in the South. In contrast to the latter, on which three judges sat on the bench, the Diplock courts had a single county or High Court judge who presided over political cases. When arms were found, the burden of proof was put upon the suspect, while standards for confessions were lowered. To mitigate the effects of a possible miscarriage of justice, the death sentence could not be meted out. Other changes included the introduction of a 28-day arrest period without charge and a higher threshold for bail. From a British perspective, the Diplock courts appear to have been successful. Their introduction led to many more convictions and a substantial reduction in violence. Even most Catholics seem to have preferred them over internment. The assured right to appeal and the requirement that the judges for the first time had to write out the factual and legal arguments underlying their decision improved chances for a successful appeal. It also benefitted the quality of the judgments, as judges did not like to have their verdicts reversed. The favourable reception of the Diplock courts allowed the authorities to abolish internment on 5 December 1975.[183]

Little is known about Bobby Sands's trial, which took a single day. The only papers to report on it were the *Irish Times* and the *Irish Independent*, and even they were content with not much more than the bare facts. This in itself demonstrates that the simplification of the proceedings under the new legislation lessened the public impact of the trials. Most papers in Ireland and Britain however had reported on the incident that led to his arrest, but, again, stuck to the unadorned details. This was even true of the Republican papers. *An Phoblacht* referred briefly to the arrest in their column 'News from the North', while the northern *Republican News* did not even report on this specific action, only the general IRA policy of targeting business premises, of which the specific incident was an example.[184] Sands and five other men had been arrested on 14 October 1976. Together with two others, a man and a woman who escaped, they had taken over the Balmoral Furniture Company at the Balmoral Industrial Estate, held up the staff and placed two twenty-pound bombs and two drums of petrol. When the raiders left they were confronted by troops and police. The six were captured after a shoot-out. In the meantime the bombs exploded and a fierce fire started. The firemen, who were on strike at the time, made sure the staff was safe and that the fire did not spread, but let the factory burn down, causing about £400,000 worth of damage. Sands and three others were arrested in a car in which a revolver was found on the floor. A short clause in the *Irish Independent* article may explain the lack of attention to this relatively minor case: '[...] meanwhile with assassinations reaching almost a rate of one a day and two explosions per day in the North'.[185]

All the defendants refused to recognise the court and seemingly made no attempt to defend themselves. They were ultimately convicted only for possession of a weapon with intent. No evidence could be produced linking them directly to the fire-bombing of the furniture company. Nevertheless, they each received a fourteen-year sentence, almost three times as long as the penalty meted out to Card and McKee for the same offense only two years earlier. The length of the sentence may well have been influenced by the fact that although there was no evidence, the responsibility of the defendants for the fire was fairly incontrovertible. The authorities may also have hoped that severe sentences would deter others.[186] Except for the element of deterrence, the performative power of the case was very minor. Neither Republicans nor the authorities or the media attempted to use the case to make a particular point. The low-key response to the case was probably due to a combination of factors.

The effects of the Diplock court procedures and the extremely violent context of the Troubles robbed the goings-on in a minor court case of any and all publicity value.

5.6. Conclusion

In all the cases discussed above, the various parties involved seem to have been fairly well aware of the message they wanted to put across about themselves and their opponents. The emphasis and effort put into this were adapted to local conditions. It was generally clear to anyone familiar with the political situation of the moment who was being addressed when. In the three jurisdictions—Northern Ireland, Great Britain and the Irish Republic—the population was highly polarised to begin with, leaving only one group in society that could be swayed to one side or the other. In Northern Ireland, Unionists would not be open to whatever message was put out by Republicans. The primary aim of the latter was to maintain the support of their own constituency and to bring nationalists who were opposed to the use of violence to their side. In the main, they were out to portray the proceedings as unjust and unfair. If they succeeded, all nationalists would feel potentially threatened by the state, a state that was apparently able to lock up any of them. The government and the legal profession in Northern Ireland simply tried to emphasise that they maintained the rule of law and that those who broke it would be punished severely. This simple dichotomy also meant that newspapers generally paid little attention to court cases.

In the South, the 'battleground' was more open. As the IRA objective of a united Ireland was widely shared, there was more to gain. It was relatively easy for the IRA, contrary to the government, to claim that, however counterproductive the use of force might be perceived as being, it was doing something tangible for a united Ireland. This dichotomy also enabled them to use a whole range of damaging narratives to tackle the government and generate support among the populace. One favoured tactic similar to what was used in the North was to accuse the southern Irish courts of denying justice to Republicans and using illegal means to convict them. The IRA also emphasised the apparent lack of independence of the Irish government, which appeared to act in unison with the British, who were portrayed as the eternal enemies of Irish independence. In a sense, the emphasis of the Irish government and the legal system in the court cases on maintaining the rule of law can be explained by the absence of a more effective counter-narrative. The IRA succeeded in generating widespread protest, but at the end of the day people were too apprehensive of anarchy to accept the Republican framing. Their claims were only accepted by those who already questioned the agenda of the Irish government.

In view of the unlikelihood that open support would be forthcoming on the British mainland, the best option available to the IRA was to appeal to liberal and left-wing constituencies. They did this by emphasising the imperialist tendencies of the British government and its lack of respect for civil rights, illustrated by its behaviour towards the prisoners and to Irishmen in general. The IRA did not challenge the legality of the court. On the contrary, the fact that it was legal strengthened their criticism of the procedures and the actions of the various actors within the system, including the police, prosecution and judge. In response, the government stressed the threat to society posed by the actions of the defendants, not just in words but also in the way they staged the proceedings. This tactic was picked up by the judge and prosecution as well. The public impact of the bombs had been great, but the court proceedings did not appear to have much effect. Concerns over civil liberties were initially substantial, but the association of the suspects with the violent politics of the IRA seems in the final analysis to have scared away some of the liberal constituency.

Looking at the reporting in the newspapers, one can only conclude that little use was made by the parties involved of the theatrical potential of court proceedings. The case of the Belfast Ten, in which this did occur, was an exception. The staging of that trial, the security measures outside the courtroom and the placing of the defendants inside sent out a clear message. In Northern Ireland, the news was dominated by the violence taking place on the streets. No court case could command as much public attention as a lethal bomb attack or the killings on the street. To some extent, the same can be said of the South and Great Britain, where coverage of the court cases had to compete with reports on the latest violent incident or attempts to come to a peaceful solution of the conflict. The long history of IRA violence also limited the ability of politicians, the judicial system and the IRA itself to use the court cases for their performative power. The parties involved appear to have known fairly well which message worked and which did nothing for their intended audiences even more so in Ireland than in Britain.

One instructive aspect of this analysis concerns the way various newspapers emphasised different aspects of events. The so-called quality papers tended to pay most attention to the content of the proceedings. They nevertheless each had their own individual slant. The *Guardian*, for instance, stressed the danger emanating from the IRA, possibly in an attempt to justify its support for the policies of the conservative government and to counter criticism from civil rights organisations. Papers like the *Observer* and the *Sunday Independent* felt most comfortable with superficial aspects of the case, such as the appearance and background of the defendants. The local papers in Ireland did not pay any attention to the cases, apart from an occasional obligatory report, but the various national newspapers did cover them, each in keeping with its own political position. The *Irish Times*, which represented a fairly wide range of views, was critical of the governments in relation to civil liberties and press freedom, but tended to side with law and order. The *Irish Independent* was erratic in its reporting. It featured a strong human interest component, but was certainly not swayed by the Republican narrative. The *Irish Press*, which had a close association with the government party in Ireland that contained a faction of relatively hard-line Republicans, was most likely to accept the way the defendants framed their opponents sometimes in opposition to the government.

In general it could be argued that this analysis of court cases against IRA suspects in different jurisdictions has revealed that the parties involved were quite conscious of the narrative they wanted to put out to certain targeted audiences, and explicitly questioned the quality of justice administered ("Is there any justice left in this country?"). The societies in the three jurisdictions were divided by clearly drawn lines of identification and by their past experience with cases like those dealt with here. That and the all dominating violence in Northern Ireland constrained possibilities for exploiting the performative element to the full. Those who implemented it did so mostly to strengthen their own or undermine the opponent's narrative. The public reacted much more strongly to the performative power of the hunger strike, which the IRA preferred over the court case, if only because it had more control over the physical sufferings of IRA prisoners than over the impact and framing of judiciary proceedings. It could nevertheless be argued that the Republican narrative was strengthened by their use of the performative power of the court cases and therefore was a contributing factor in maintaining the Republican campaign of force for such a long time by maintaining the idea that Republicans were more willing to suffer for the shared objective of Irish unity than existing parties and in the process were unjustly treated by the governments involved.

Notes

1 Joost Augusteijn, *Patrick Pearse. The Making of a Revolutionary* (London: MacMillan, 2010), pp. 289–293.

2 These include the *Anglo-Celt, Connacht Sentinel, Connacht Tribune, Irish Farmers Journal, Kerryman, Leitrim Observer, Meath Chronicle, Munster Express, Nenagh Guardian, Southern Star,*

Tuam Herald, *Westmeath Examiner*, all to be accessed through the Irish News, Archives website: http://www.irishnewsarchive.com/index.php.

3 *Irish Times*, 15 April 1971; See also *Irish Press*, 17 June 1971.

4 *Republican News*, May 1971.

5 *Irish Times*, 1 April 1971.

6 *Irish Times*, 1 April 1971.

7 *Irish Times*, 14 May 1971 and 17 June 1971; *Irish Press*, 17 June 1971.

8 *Irish Times*, 17 June 1971; *Irish Press*, 17 June 1971.

9 *Irish Times*, 17 June 1971.

10 *Guardian*, 17 April 1971; *Irish Times*, 17 and 24 April 1971.

11 *Irish Times*, 8 May 1971; *Irish Times*, 17 June 1971.

12 *Irish Times*, 14 May 1971; *Irish Times*, 17 June 1971.

13 *Irish Times*, 24 April 1971.

14 *Guardian*, 17 April 1971; *Irish Times*, 17 April 1971.

15 *Irish Press*, 17 June 1971.

16 *An Phoblacht*, July 1971.

17 *Irish Times*, 26 June 1971; *Irish Press*, 31 May 1971.

18 *Irish Times*, 1 November 1972.

19 *Guardian*, 3 November 1971; *The Observer*, 5 November 1972; *Irish Times*, 20 November 1972.

20 *Irish Times*, 6 November 1972.

21 A name for Republicans using physical force.

22 *Guardian*, 10 November 1972.

23 Dáil Éireann Debates, vol. 263, 'Order of Business' (7 November 1972).

24 *Irish Times*, 20 and 21 November 1972; *Irish Press*, 20 November 1972.

25 *Guardian*, 27 November 1972.

26 *Republican News*, 24 November 1972.

27 *Sunday Independent*, 26 November 1972.

28 *Irish Times*, 25 November 1972.

29 *Republican News*, 24 November 1972.

30 *Irish Press*, 25 November 1972; *Irish Times*, 25 November 1972; *Sunday Independent*, 25 November 1972.

31 *Guardian*, 25 November 1972.

32 *Sunday Independent*, 26 November 1972; *Irish Press*, 27 November 1972.

33 *Irish Times*, 22 November 1972.

34 *Irish Press*, 24 November 1972.

35 *Irish Press*, 27 November 1972.

36 *Irish Times*, 25 November 1972.

37 *Irish Times*, 22 and 25 November 1972; *Guardian*, 22 and 27 November 1972; *Irish Independent*, 26 November 1972.

38 *Irish Press*, 25 and 27 November 1972; *Guardian*, 27 November 1972.

39 *Irish Times*, 20 November 1972.

40 *Irish Times*, 20 November 1972; *Guardian*, 22 November 1972.

41 *An Phoblacht*, 26 November 1972.

42 *Republican News*, 24 November 1972.

43 *The Guardian*, 20 November 1972; *Irish Press*, 21 November 1972.

44 *Republican News*, 24 November 1972.

45 *Irish Independent*, 12 December 1972.

46 The first prime minister of independent Kenya.

47 A prominent Irish activist and socialist.

48 *Irish Times*, 21 November 1972. Similar sentiments were expressed by Bernadette Devlin in the House of Commons, House of Commons Debates, vol. 846 (23 November 1972), pp. 1530–1557.

49 *Republican News*, 24 November and 1 December 1972.

50 *An Phoblacht*, 26 November 1972.

51 *Guardian*, 20 November 1972.

52 *Irish Times*, 23 and 25 November 1972.

53 *Irish Times*, 21 November 1972.

54 *Irish Times*, 25 November 1972; Dáil Éireann Debates, vol. 263, 'Questions' (23 November 1972).

55 *Guardian*, 27 November 1972.

56 *Guardian*, 21 November 1972.

57 *Guardian*, 22 November 1972.

58 *Irish Times*, 20 November 1972.

59 *Irish Times*, 27 November 1972; *Irish Independent*, 26 November 1972; *Guardian*, 25 November 1972; *The Observer*, 26 November 1972.

60 *Irish Times*, 21–27 November 1972. See also *Republican News*, 24 November 1972.

61 *Irish Times*, 25 November 1972.

62 *Irish Times*, 24 November 1972.

63 Sean Mac Stiofáin, *Memoirs of a Revolutionary* (London: Gordon Cremonesi, 1975), p. 348.

64 *Irish Times*, 27 November 1972; *The Observer*, 26 November 1972; *Irish Independent*, 26 November 1972; *Guardian*, 27 November 1972; *Irish Press*, 27 November 1972; *An Phoblacht*, 26 November 1972.

65 *Irish Press*, 27 November 1972.

66 *Irish Times*, 27 November 1972; *The Observer*, 26 November 1972; *Irish Independent*, 26 November 1972; *Guardian*, 27 and 28 November 1972.

67 *Guardian*, 27 November 1972.

68 *Irish Press*, 27 November 1972.

69 Ibid.

70 *Guardian*, 2 December 1972; *Sunday Independent*, 3 December 1972.

71 *Guardian*, 28 November 1972; *Irish Press*, 27 November 1972.

72 *Guardian*, 27 November 1972.

73 *Irish Times*, 27 November 1972; *Irish Press*, 24 November 1972.

74 *Guardian*, 27 November 1972.

75 *Irish Times*, 28 November 1972.

76 *Irish Times*, 27 and 28 November 1972; *Irish Independent*, 26 November 1972; *Irish Press*, 21 November 1972; *Guardian*, 27 November 1972.

77 *Irish Times*, 28 November 1972.

78 Ibid.; *Irish Independent*, 26 November 1972; *Connacht Sentinel*, 29 November 1972; *Guardian*, 1 December 1972; *Guardian*, 29 January 1973; *Munster Sentinel*, 1 December 1972; *Anglo-Celt*, 1 December 1972; *Kerrymen*, 2 December 1972.

79 *Irish Times*, 28 December 1972; *Irish Independent*, 1 December 1972; *Connacht Sentinel*, 1 December 1972; *Guardian*, 29 January 1973 and 1 December 1972; *Munster Sentinel*, 1 December 1972; *Anglo-Celt*, 1 December 1972; *Kerryman*, 2 December 1972; *Irish Independent*, 2, 29 and 30 December 1972; *Anglo-Celt*, 8 December 1972; *Nenagh Guardian*, 9 December 1972.

80 *Kerryman*, 2 December 1972. See also *Republican News*, 15 December 1972.

81 Dáil Éireann Debates, vol. 264, 'Offences against the State (Amendment) Bill, 1972: Second Stage' (29 November 1972).

82 Dáil Éireann Debates, vol. 264, 'Private Notice Question:—Condition of Prisoner' (28 November 1972).

83 *Irish Independent*, 5 and 26 December 1972.

84 *Sunday Independent*, 3 December 1972.

85 *Irish Times*, 16 January 1973.

86 *Irish Independent*, 1 December 1972.

87 *Guardian*, 29 November 1972; *Irish Independent*, 1 December 1972.

88 *Guardian*, 30 November 1972. See also *Guardian*, 1 December 1972.

89 *Sunday Independent*, 10 December 1972; *Irish Independent*, 29 and 30 December 1972.

90 *Guardian*, 1 December 1972; *Irish Independent*, 1 December 1972. This is confirmed in his memoir, Mac Stiofáin, *Memoirs*, pp. 354–355.

91 *The Observer*, 3 December 1972.

92 *Sunday Independent*, 17 and 24 December 1972 and 23 January 1973.

93 *Irish Times*, 2 and 4 December 1972; *Guardian*, 30 November 1972; *Irish Independent*, 2 December 1972; *Sunday Independent*, 3 and 10 December 1972; Mac Stiofáin, *Memoirs*, p. 362; *Irish Independent*, 8 December 1972.

94 *Irish Times*, 9 January 1973.

95 *Irish Times*, 2, 4, 5, 8 and 19 December 1972 and 9 and 11 January 1973.

96 *Irish Times*, 29 November 1972.

97 House of Lords Debates, vol. 355, cc 825–909, Lord Dunleath (12 December 1974).

98 Dáil Éireann Debates, vol. 264, 'Offences against the State (Amendment) Bill, 1972: Second Stage' (29 November 1972).

99 *Irish Times*, 6 May 85.

100 *Irish Times*, 19 June 1972; *Irish Independent*, 7 October 1972.

101 *Irish Independent*, 8 October 1972; *Irish Independent*, 11 October 1972.

102 *Irish Times*, 19 June 1972.

103 *Irish Times*, 4 December 1972; *Guardian*, 2 December 1972; *Observer*, 3 December 1972.

104 *Irish Independent*, 1 December 1973; *Observer*, 3 December 1972.

105 *Irish Independent*, 5 December 1972.

106 *Irish Times*, 22 and 26 February 1973.

107 *Irish Times*, 17 March 1973; *Observer*, 26 November 1972.

108 The defendants were: Roisin McNearney (18) typist from Fort St, Belfast; William Patrick McLarnon (19) unemployed, Finlay Park, Newtownabbey; Robert Martin Walsh (24) roof tiler, Theodore St, Belfast; Gerard Kelly (19) unemployed, Britton's Parade, Belfast; Martin Francis Brady (22) driver, Granville St, Belfast; Paul Joseph Holmes (25) tiler, Butler St, Belfast; William Joseph Armstrong (29) window cleaner, Moyard Crescent, Belfast; Hugh Feeney (21) student teacher, Blacks Rd, Belfast; Marion Magdalene Price (19) student, Slievagallion Drive, Belfast; Dolours Price (22) student, Slievagallion Drive, Belfast.

109 *Irish Times*, 10 March 1973.

110 *Irish Times*, 9 and 13 March 1973.

111 *Irish Times*, 11, 12 and 20 September 1973 and 16 November 1973.

112 *Observer*, 16 September 1973.

113 *Republican News*, 29 September 1973.

114 *Irish Times*, 10 and 11 September 1973.

115 *Irish Times*, 16 November 1973 and 11 and 12 September 1973; *Sunday Independent*, 9 September 1973; *Irish Independent*, 10 and 11 December 1973; *Guardian*, 10 September 1973; *Irish Press*, 10 September 1973.

116 *Irish Independent*, 11 and 12 September 1973.

117 *Irish Times*, 11 and 12 September 1973.

118 *Guardian*, 11 September 1973.

119 *Irish Times*, 11and 12 September 1973.

120 *Irish Times*, 24, 25 and 26 October 1973.

121 *Irish Times*, 30 and 31 October 1973 and 1 November 1973; *Republican News*, 15 December 1973.

122 *Irish Times*, 13 September 1973.

123 *Irish Times*, 24 October 1973.

124 *Irish Times*, 14 September 1973; *Guardian*, 14 September 1973.

125 *Irish Times*, 15 September 1973; *Guardian*, 15 September 1973.

126 *Irish Times*, 20 October 1973; *Irish Press*, 11 September 1973.

127 *Republican News*, 15 December 1973.

128 *Irish Times*, 28 September 1973, 26 October 1973 and 8, 9 and 13 November 1973; *Guardian*, 14 November 1973; *Irish Press*, 24 October 1973.

129 *Irish Times*, 12 October 1973.

130 *Irish Times*, 21 September 1973; *Guardian*, 21 September 1973. See also *Guardian*, 12 September 1973.

131 *Irish Times*, 16 November 1973.

132 *Irish Times*, 21 October 1973.

133 *Irish Independent*, 14 November 1973.

134 *Guardian*, 15 November 1973.

135 *Irish Times*, 16 November 1973.

136 *Irish Times*, 14 November 1973; *Guardian*, 14 November 1973.

137 *Irish Times*, 16 November 1973.

138 Ibid.

139 *Observer*, 18 November 1973.

140 *Irish Times*, 15 November 1973.

141 *Irish Independent*, 15 November 1973; *Observer*, 18 November 1973; *Guardian*, 15 November 1973.

142 *Irish Press*, 15 November 1973.

143 *Irish Times*, 6, 9, 17 and 25 October 1973; *Irish Independent*, 10 October 1973. See also 11, 12 and 28 September 1973; *Irish Press*, 25 October 1973; *Guardian*, 20 September 1973.

144 *Irish Independent*, 16 November 1973.

145 *Irish Times*, 10 October 1973.

146 *Irish Times*, 12 October 1973.

147 *Irish Times*, 25 October 1973; *Irish Press*, 12 October 1973.

148 *Irish Times*, 11 and 13 September 1973; *Observer*, 16 September1973.

149 *Irish Independent*, 24 October 1973; *Guardian*, 13 September 1973; *Irish Press*, 11 September 1973.

150 After one of the defendants had pleaded guilty, some papers refered to them as the 'Winchester 9' instead of the 'Belfast Ten'.

151 *Guardian*, 13 September 1973; *Observer*, 16 September and 18 November 1973. See also *Sunday Independent*, 18 November 1973.

152 *Irish Times*, 9, 16, 18 and 20 October 1973.

153 *Irish Independent*, 1, 7 and 8 November 1973.

154 *Irish Times*, 9, 18 and 25 October 1973 and 1, 2, 6 and 8 November 1973; *Irish Press*, 1, 2 and 6 November 1973.

155 *Irish Times*, 25 October 1973 and 6 November 1973; *Irish Press*, 6 November 1973.

156 *Irish Times*, 24, 25 and 26 October 1973.

157 *Irish Times*, 11 September 1973.

158 *Irish Times*, 11 September 1973 and 6 and 11 October 1973.

159 *Irish Times*, 15 November 1973.

160 *Guardian*, 11 September 1973 and 15 November 1973; *Irish Press*, 15 November 1973.

161 *Irish Press*, 17 November 1973.

162 *Irish Times*, 15 and 16 November 1973; *Guardian*, 16 November 1973; *Irish Independent*, 16 November 1973.

163 *Irish Times*, 9 and 10 March 1973.

164 *Guardian*, 15 November 1973.

165 *Republican News*, 3 and 24 November 1973.

166 *Irish Times*, 16 November 1973; *Guardian*, 16 November 1973; *An Phoblacht*, 14 December 1973; *Republican News*, 22 December 1973.

167 *Irish Times*, 17 November 1973; *Irish Independent*, 17 November 1973.

168 *Republican News*, 15 December 1973.

169 *An Phoblacht*, January and February 1974 and 18 January 1974.

170 *Irish Times*, 17 November 1973; *Irish Independent*, 17 November 1973.

171 *Irish Times*, 9, 12, 13 and 26 March, 24 September and 17 November 1973.

172 *Irish Times*, 9 March 1973.

173 *Republican News*, 3 and 24 November 1973.

174 *Irish Press*, 11 September 1973.

175 *Irish Times*, 24 September 1973, 6 October 1973 and 17 November 1973.

176 *Guardian*, 15 and 16 November 1973. See also *Guardian*, 20 September 1973.

177 *Irish Times*, 16 November 1973; *Irish Independent*, 16 November 1973.

178 *Republican News*, 8 December 1973.

179 *Republican News*, 15 December 1973 and 19 January 1974; *An Phoblacht*, 14 December 1973.

For letters from Dolours Price see: Vancemeros Sisters, *Prison Writings of the Price Sisters* (Cathal Brugha Cumann, Andersonstown 1975). See also *Republican News*, 22 December 1973 and 19 January 1974; *An Phoblacht*, 18 January 1974.

180 *An Phoblacht*, 18 and 25 January 1974.

181 *An Phoblacht*, 25 January 1974.

182 *An Phoblacht*, 14 December 1973.

183 Laura K. Donohue, *The cost of counterterrorism: power, politics, and liberty* (Cambridge: Cambridge University Press, 2008), pp. 42–45; Antonio Vercher, *Terrorism in Europe. An International Comparative Legal Analysis* (Oxford: Clarendon, 1992), pp. 120–121.

184 *Republican News*, 2 October 1976; *An Phoblacht*, 19 October 1976.

185 *Irish Independent*, 15 October 1976.

186 *Irish Independent*, 15 October 1976; *Irish Press*, 15 October 1976; *Guardian*, 15 October 1976; *Irish Times*, 8 September 1977 and 15 October 1976; *Republican News*, 2 October 1976; *An Phoblacht*, 19 October 1976. The defendants were Sean Lavery (28) of Kerrykeel Gardens, Belfast; Robert Gerard Sands (23) Summerhill Gardens, Belfast; Joseph Francis McDonnell (26) Lenadoon Avenue, Belfast; Seamus Finnucane (20) Dungloe Crescent, Suffolk; Gabriel Norman Corbett (19) Cherry Gardens, Twinbrook; Seamus Martin (21) Glasvey Rise, Belfast.

6. Germany Confronts the Baader-Meinhof Group. The Stammheim Trial (1975–1977) and Its Legacies

Jacco Pekelder and Klaus Weinhauer

6.1. Introduction

One of the most remarkable twentieth-century legal confrontations between state and terrorists took place at the trial against the leaders of the Rote Armee Fraktion (RAF, Red Army Faction) at Stammheim, Germany, from 21 May 1975 until 28 April 1977. This trial stands out because of its extraordinary length and the ferocity of the altercations between those present in the courtroom, in particular between the presiding judge and the accused and their defence team. Daily proceedings over the 192 trial days lasted between ten minutes and ten hours, a total of about 1,000 hours. After the trial, 14,000 pages of protocol were typed up, and in early October 1977, the Stammheim judges presented a written verdict of 319 pages.[1] We begin our analysis of this trial with a brief history of the RAF. This is followed by a review of research on German left-wing terrorism in the late twentieth century, and an outline of our analytical perspective.

6.1.1. *History of the Red Army Faction: A Brief Overview*

Between 1970 and 1998, the Red Army Faction (also known as the Baader–Meinhof Group) confronted the Federal Republic of Germany. The RAF was a social-revolutionary terrorist group that began as an offspring of the protest movement of the late 1960s, just as this movement was in the process of disintegrating into various groups. The RAF regarded itself as a left-wing revolutionary urban guerrilla group, and modelled itself on similar organisations in Latin America (Uruguay's Tupamaros) and the United States (the Black Panthers). To continue the struggle for a revolution in West Germany, the RAF opted to take up arms against the state.

The RAF outclassed other left-wing terrorist groups in Germany for several reasons. Firstly, its membership included some of the most prominent people of the protest movement: lawyer Horst Mahler, who had defended many protesters; journalist

Ulrike Meinhof, whose critical columns in the left-wing periodical *Konkret* had earned her respect among Germans of radical and liberal persuasions; and the radical lovers Andreas Baader and Gudrun Ensslin, already convicted of arson against two department stores in Frankfurt in 1968. Secondly, the RAF entered the political stage spectacularly, with the liberation of Baader from captivity on 14 May 1970. Thirdly, the RAF aimed to win the hearts and minds of others on the radical left by publishing declarations and semi-intellectual brochures, including, in 1971, the lengthy essays *The Urban Guerrilla Concept* and *About the Armed Struggle in Western Europe*. Finally, the Baader–Meinhof Group strongly portrayed itself as the vanguard organisation in West Germany for all the radical left-wing groups, action committees and projects, and it emphatically demanded their solidarity and support.

During the first two years of its existence, the RAF concentrated its efforts on building the organisation, with its members only occasionally involved in violent, sometimes fatal, confrontations with the police. Yet even at this stage the RAF caused great upheaval throughout West Germany. On the one hand, there were waves of moral panic in mainstream society, fuelled by anxious press commentaries and politicians demanding tougher anti-terrorist policies. On the other hand, several surveys of public opinion in 1971 found that the RAF enjoyed some sympathy among a number of left-wing intellectuals and youngsters. Partly in reaction to this, state institutions implemented rather radical counter-terrorist policies, not just against the perpetrators of political violence but scrutinising a far wider radical left milieu. The Bundeskriminalamt (BKA, the Federal Criminal Police Office) coordinated counter-terrorist policies, and high hopes were invested in its new president Horst Herold, and the advanced computer-based investigation techniques he introduced. The BKA and other government agencies also mobilised the press in an effort to win over the general public for the fight against terrorism. While genuine support for the RAF remained minimal and decreased over the years even in radical circles, government policies encouraged right-wing politicians and the media to instigate large-scale campaigns against RAF 'sympathisers'.

In May 1972, the RAF launched its first campaign of political violence: six bomb attacks spread over several weeks. On 11 May, the US Army barracks in Frankfurt were attacked, killing one American officer and wounding thirteen. On the following day, explosions in police headquarters in Augsburg and Munich left another ten people wounded. On 15 May a bomb destroyed the car of a federal judge in Karlsruhe, seriously wounding his wife. Four days later, an attack on the Hamburg offices of the conservative Springer Press injured 38 staff members. On 24 May, Heidelberg US military headquarters were targeted in a violent blast that killed three American soldiers and wounded five more. The RAF's triumph at the 'success' of its May offensive was short-lived, and when in June 1972 police arrested its leaders, including Baader, Ensslin and Meinhof (Mahler had already been apprehended in late 1970), it seemed that the RAF had come to an end. Its members faced court trials and lengthy prison terms.

In the crucial period that followed, 1972–1977, events took an unexpected turn. Instead of passively undergoing their detention in custody, most members of the RAF (excluding Mahler who left the organisation) started a prison struggle involving collective hunger strikes. This was intended to create a solidarity campaign within the left-wing radical milieu and to attract new recruits, which led to the formation of new terrorist cells. Violent acts were committed with the aim of forcing the German government to release the prisoners. The first of these acts was the armed occupation of the German embassy in Stockholm, on 24 April 1975, just weeks before the start of the trial against the RAF leaders at Stammheim.

As will become apparent below, however, the RAF and the state saw the Stammheim trial as their most important battleground over the next two years. Only in the spring of 1977, when the trial was nearing its end, did the RAF cells begin another campaign of violence. 'Offensive 77' drove West German society to the brink of a socio-political crisis in the so-called 'German Autumn' of September/October 1977. During these months German business leader Hanns Martin Schleyer was kidnapped (and four security men were shot and killed in cold blood) and a passenger jet was hijacked by Palestinian terrorist comrades of the RAF. On 18–19 October 1977, German GSG-9 Special Forces liberated the abducted plane at Mogadishu airport in Somalia. After hearing this, Baader, Ensslin and Raspe collectively committed suicide in their Stammheim prison cells and, immediately thereafter, Schleyer was murdered by his captors.

Now that its leaders were dead, it seemed the RAF really would come to an end. It proved to be a long goodbye however, lasting more than twenty years despite further RAF arrests and deadly gun battles with the police. All through the 1980s and until 1991, the RAF mounted attacks against NATO-related targets, German business leaders and government representatives. Remarkably, the perception of the RAF as a fundamental threat to German society gradually faded away despite these events. This was in part caused by changing civic attitudes towards the state. Whereas in 1977, extreme measures by police and state against the terrorists and their prospective 'sympathisers' had met with consent from most quarters of German society, it appears that following the 'German Autumn' a period of critical reflection began. In the last years of the 1970s criticism of the police grew markedly, especially of measures electronically to collect and process large quantities of personal data. Trust in state institutions eroded and state officials were subject to increased democratic scrutiny. In view of the traditional regard for the state in Germany's political culture, these were remarkable developments.[2]

In the early 1990s, fragmentary discussions between RAF members (both inside and outside prison) and small conciliatory gestures by government officials led to the final dissolution of the organisation. On 10 April 1992 the RAF announced a unilateral armistice, and in 1993 performed its last, highly symbolic bombing. No physical harm resulted but a new prison facility in the final phase of construction was destroyed (60 million Euros damage). Five years later, on 20 April 1998, the RAF announced its disbanding, proclaiming that in future its members would seek other ways to promote social transformation.

6.1.2. *Theoretical Outlook and Line of Investigation*

'Terrorism' is a contested term.[3] It is often used for political effect: labelling certain acts or organisations as 'terrorism' or 'terrorists' can disqualify political adversaries. We will distinguish between two interrelated meanings of 'terrorism'. Defined narrowly, terrorism is a specific act or threat of political violence through which the perpetrators attempt to influence the behaviour of social actors other than the immediate victims of violence. In their seminal study *Violence as Communication*, Alex Schmid and Janny de Graaf thus frame terrorism as 'a kind of violent language'.[4] On a meta-level terrorism can be interpreted as a 'social construction'; just like any other social problem, the concept of terrorism 'is shaped by social and political processes, by bureaucratic needs and media structures'.[5]

Following this interpretation, we can recognise that the reactions that are provoked by acts of violence, reactions among politicians, the media and the general public, are *constituent* elements of terrorism. While the actual violent attacks cannot be reasoned away, nor the victims discounted, these acts or threats acquire their 'terrorist' quality when other groups in society label them or react to them as 'terrorism'. In this sense, communications and interactions between 'terrorists' and other groups and institutions in society have a considerable influence on the development of 'terrorism' as a social problem. Against this background, we argue that reactions to RAF activities by politicians, social actors and the established media in the FRG in the 1970s co-determined the impact this organisation had on German society at the time. The brief historical introduction to the RAF above has demonstrated some aspects of this notion.

Examining terrorism as both a process of communication and a social construction has important consequences for our approach to the phenomenon. It demands a shift of focus from questions that have usually dominated terrorism research (and research on the RAF)—questions restricted to the emergence of terrorist groups or to their confrontation with the state in violent acts. Broadly-based research is necessary to understand the social, political and cultural dynamics which are set in motion by certain acts or threats of violence that public debate deems to be 'terroristic'. More emphasis on the wider context of events and structures is required.[6] We also need to take a closer look at developments in particular societies *after* specific chains of events (attacks, reprisals, trials etcetera) related to 'terrorism' have taken place. How were the violent acts and the proclamations of the terrorists perceived, interpreted and responded to by state institutions, social actors, the mass media[7] and by other groups in society?[8] The semantic coding which shapes the interpretation of terrorism also requires analysis. Such a broadly-based social and cultural historical approach could not only help to overcome the dichotomous interpretations of terrorism. It could also contribute to opening up some analytically challenging avenues for a general debate about terrorism as a phenomenon which is shaped by the interactions of state, social and media actors on the one hand and militant activists on the other.

Seeing terrorism as an act of communication can help us understand its strong potential for the performative; terrorism is a constructed reality which is shaped and defined by the performances of different actors.[9] From the perspective of communication and performance, the confrontation between the opposing parties can be seen essentially as a clash between different narratives of justice and injustice. This approach is particularly useful for the analysis of terrorist trials, as a recent comparative study into the dynamics around court cases and associated detention conditions (in Germany and the Netherlands in the 1970s) has shown.[10] The courtroom provides a unique stage for the clash of narratives, with its clear division of roles between judge(s), prosecution and defence, as well as the customary procedural court rules and rituals. The various players involved adopt strategies and perform accordingly, with the aim of persuading audiences within and outside the courtroom to endorse their narrative.[11]

Not least because of its extraordinary length and the exceptional vehemence with which the parties involved played out their confrontations, the Stammheim trial against the RAF leaders offers an excellent subject for analysis from the perspective of communication and performance. Of course, ours is not the first attempt to study the trial, and it will not be the last. Following the release of early collections of various documents on the trial,[12] book-length studies first appeared in the mid-1980s. In 1986, the apparently well-informed *Spiegel* magazine journalist Stefan Aust published *Der Baader Meinhof Komplex*. A long and informative chapter on the Stammheim trial is probably based on newspaper reports and trial transcripts (unfortunately Aust does not reveal his sources). In the same year, Dutch lawyer Pieter Herman Bakker Schut published *Stammheim. Die notwendige Korrektur der herrschenden Meinung*, an insider's analysis of the trial. Smaller books or edited volumes were released around the same time, mainly focused on the so-called 'Deutscher Herbst' (German Autumn) of 1977 when the confrontation between the RAF and the state reached its zenith, but also dealing with some aspects of the Stammheim trial.[13]

Thirty years after these events, in 2007, the journalist Ulf G. Stuberger published an eyewitness account of the trial, and in 2009 a well-researched legal study by Christopher R. Tenfelde appeared.[14] Further books written by and about former RAF defence lawyers cover the trial to some degree.[15] With rare exceptions, professional historians avoided the subject of the trial and the RAF in general until the 21st-century. More historians are now studying and writing about the subject of West Germany's left-wing terrorism.[16]

Although these studies about Stammheim have produced valuable information and many interesting viewpoints, they also have some shortcomings. The older publications about the trial tend to focus on personal drama and many exhibit strong political bias and a lack of objectivity. Aust's journalistic approach provides a clear illustration of the first flaw; he also betrays some personal emotional involvement. Bakker Schut's writing, in spite of the legal discourse he uses, is about as politically partisan as one can get. The smaller books and edited volumes were mostly produced to participate in Germany's public debate and are often biased and often provocative.

Not even the most recent publications escape these shortcomings. Stuberger's attempt at a more nuanced approach, combining the unique circumstance of his eyewitness status with the benefit of hindsight, is valuable. Still, his account is too narrow and personalised really to increase our understanding of the trial. Even Tenfelde's monograph fails to deliver, although at first glance it looks like the most promising serious legal analysis of the trial. Central to Tenfelde's examination is the question of whether or not Stammheim was a 'political trial'. Tenfelde clearly aims to criticise and counter the claims by various German officials at the time that politics played no part in the trial or in the confrontation with the RAF in general. By debating this claim, Tenfelde enters into a dialogue with the historical material he studied as if he were himself part of a discussion taking place in the 1970s. From a jurist's perspective this endeavour might make perfect sense. As historians, however, we are far more interested in asking why the trial's (obvious) political character was contested at all. Instead of trying to proclaim a final verdict on this, we present a critical, theoretically informed analysis of the probable intentions and deeds of the trial's actors, and of the social dynamics they were involved in.

In general, the authors who have studied Stammheim to date have consciously or unconsciously embraced a narrow view of the RAF's history, reducing the issue to a two-sided confrontation. Caught up in the moral dilemmas presented by the history of the RAF and the counter-terrorist policies it provoked, these authors are constrained within a 'them versus us' perception of this particular chapter of German history. Because of that, in the end, they feel morally obliged to take sides. It seems to us that academic research about the RAF in general until around the year 2000 still betrayed a similarly view.

We suggest that early historiography about the RAF and other German left-wing terrorist organisations has been flawed in two interrelated ways. Firstly, the authors (be they journalists, political scientists, sociologists or legal experts) interpreted terrorism mainly as a bipolar confrontation between the terrorists and the state. The analytical narrowness of this dichotomy was intensified by a second flaw: while some authors told stories about single actors, others focused on social structures, ignoring actions by individuals. Intellectual exchanges or even communications between researchers from both groups were rare.

This gap was bridged only when historians entered the fray after 2000, and the concept of 'terrorism as communication' (introduced to terrorism studies by Schmid and de Graaf in the early 1980s) was applied to the analysis of German left-wing terrorism.[17] Using a communication-oriented approach, scholars were able to escape the dominance of binary coding and gradually to emphasise the triadic structure of communication on the issue. The actors in this process of communication can be clearly named: the militants and their constituency; the state and its institutions; and society at large, which of course consists of many sub-groups. The media (newspapers, radio and television) play an important role, not only providing channels of communication but also performing as agents with their own political agendas.[18]

A communication-oriented approach helps to address the tendency that many publications on the RAF have of insulating confrontations between left-wing terrorism, the state and society from all other developments of the time. The strong focus on communication enables scholars to re-contextualise the RAF, re-connecting its history to the social and cultural history of state and society. As Klaus Weinhauer proposed earlier, this enables the integration of the study of German left-wing terrorism into a broader social and cultural history of 'Internal Security' (Innere Sicherheit), focusing on the interaction of the three main actors mentioned above.[19]

On this theoretical basis, we aim to present an example of what a new approach to the history of the RAF has to offer. Firstly, using a wide variety of publications and sources, our narrative of the Stammheim trial also focuses on the events leading up to the trial and in court, with attention being paid to the performative aspects of the proceedings. We analyse the legacies of the trial from a similar perspective, and this chapter takes a first step towards an analysis of the political, juridical and social consequences or repercussions of the Stammheim trial. Because a solid social and cultural history of West German terrorism is still lacking, this can be only a modest attempt to analyse the collective memory of the Stammheim trial in West German society and to contextualise it within the general re-evaluation of left-wing terrorism and the counter-terrorist policies it provoked at the time.

We see our chapter, and its openness to criticism, as an important step in breaking free from established patterns of thinking about the trial and related themes. Even after their conclusion, terrorism trials exhibit the semantic coding that structures the interpretation of terrorism as a whole. These codes (and sometimes also the trials) frame public memories. We argue that in 1970s/1980s Germany, the semantics of communication about left-wing terrorism were structured by a binary and highly politicised coding system, built on a clear dichotomy of them (terrorists, supporters) versus us (state, society). In this system 'Stammheim' was an important symbol; it helped to locate the transnational struggle of left-wing militants against imperialism, the state and its institutions, and at the same time it drew attention to the German state and its inhumane arrogance. Or, as the news magazine *Der Spiegel* wrote in 1992, 'Stammheim' was 'a symbol, congealed in concrete, of uncompromising raison d'état'.[20]

6.2. Setting the Stage, Writing the Script

Almost three years passed following the arrests of the leading RAF members, Andreas Baader, Gudrun Ensslin, Ulrike Meinhof and Jan-Carl Raspe, before their trial began in the Oberlandesgericht (Higher Regional Court) in Stuttgart, sitting in the city's Stammheim district, on 21 May 1975. This meant all parties involved had a lengthy period to prepare for this unique courtroom confrontation. This section will elaborate on the pre-trial phase and the various ways the prosecution and the defence tried to influence the setting of the stage and the writing of the script. We will discuss new rules (and laws) drawn up by the state, and the way the RAF and its lawyers responded to, or anticipated, these steps.

6.2.1. *State Trial Strategy and the Introduction of New Legislation*

The various state institutions involved, including the prosecution, regarded the trial as more than just an opportunity to bring the RAF leadership to justice, as the following statement by Bundesgeneralanwalt (Chief Federal Prosecutor) Siegfried Buback shows. 'In this trial', Buback told a radio reporter in June 1976, 'because we were dealing with the leaders of this Baader–Meinhof Gang, we had to prosecute more comprehensively. It was important to present the court with a representative cross-section of their actions.'[21] In effect, politicians and state officials tried to create the preconditions that would turn the trial at Stammheim into a public reckoning with RAF terrorism in particular and German left-wing extremism in general. Firstly, this involved the formulation of the accusations in a bill of indictment against the suspects by which the state hoped to influence the content of the trial proceedings. Secondly, it meant the choice of a stage for the trial; this resulted in the building of a new courthouse. Thirdly, the long period of preparation permitted the state to rewrite laws intended to limit the defence's ability to obstruct trial proceedings.

The Accusation against the RAF Suspects: A Political Trial without Politics

Although no one doubted the political significance of the Stammheim trial, the authorities declared time and again that it was 'ein ganz normaler Strafprozeß gegen Kriminelle' (an absolutely normal trial against criminals).[22] This fitted well with the discursive strategy practised by the authorities in their struggle with the RAF from 1970 onwards. In the eyes of established politics and media in the Federal Republic of Germany (FRG), the RAF's destructive violence automatically disqualified the organisation as a political entity. Instead, the RAF was portrayed as a criminal gang of egotistical maniacs, devoid of any idealism. Rather than using its chosen name Rote Armee Fraktion (RAF—Red Army Faction) or the quasi-neutral Baader–Meinhof Group, politicians, state officials and many journalists preferred the use of 'Baader–Meinhof Bande' (gang), a reference that called up associations with criminals like Bonnie and Clyde, whose story had been made into a successful Hollywood film in 1967.[23]

By denying the RAF's political project, the authorities attempted to isolate the RAF from other critical groups. As Horst Ehmke, Chief of the Office of Chancellor Willy Brandt, declared on 7 June 1972, it was 'one of the most important tasks' to 'deny [the RAF] all solidarity, to isolate it from what other left-wing views there are in this country'.[24] In the bill of indictment, therefore, Baader *cum suis* were not accused of political crimes like 'high treason' (paragraph 81 of the German Criminal Code, StGB[25]) or the preparation thereof (paragraph 83 StGB). Although the option had been discussed within the Bundesanwaltschaft (Federal Prosecutor's Office),[26] this possibility was dismissed as part of an effort of 'de-politicising by selecting the norms', as German legal scholar Christopher Tenfelde writes in his dissertation about the Stammheim trial. At a 'high treason' trial the political character of the confrontation between the armed groups and the state would necessarily have been acknowledged.[27]

Instead, the bill of indictment (354 pages, with an extra 471-page attachment) mainly stressed the ordinary crimes of the RAF leaders: murder (of one policeman, killed during a bank robbery, and four American soldiers, killed in two of the 1972 bombings), attempted murder (71 wounded, also in 1972), robbery, theft and criminal use of explosives.[28] The problem was, however, that in spite of a massive number of 996 witnesses mentioned by name in the indictment and despite some 1,000 additional reports (mostly by criminal experts), the prosecutors were unable to prove conclusively that the suspects had been on the crime scene at any of the bombing sites, although some witnesses had seen them in the immediate surroundings shortly before the explosions. To circumvent this problem, the Federal Prosecutor's Office built the indictment on the notion that the RAF be regarded as a 'Krimineller Verein' (criminal association), of which the accused had been leading members, thus creating a collective responsibility for RAF acts.

Inadvertently, by reverting to paragraph 129 of the German Criminal Code, the prosecutors themselves reintroduced a political element into the prosecution of the RAF. It is important to note in this respect that the legal history of this paragraph goes back to the legislation of German states preceding the establishment of the Federal Republic. In Prussia, the Kaiserreich (empire) and the Weimar Republic, this paragraph was mostly used against political organisations rather than against profit-oriented criminal gangs. During the Bismarck era, social democratic organisations had been suppressed with the help of this paragraph, while in the Weimar years it had been used against Communist organisations. The fact that the accusation against Baader and others was based on paragraph 129 indicates a continuation of a tradition of the German justice system against left-wing adversaries who were portrayed (and subsequently widely perceived) as criminals.[29]

Paragraph 129 made it possible to hold different members of a criminal association responsible for acts of the organisation as a whole without having to prove their actual participation as individuals. There were also other practical juridical benefits. With only 'typical' crimes like murder on the agenda, it would have been necessary for a range of state prosecutors (from different states within the Federal Republic) to prosecute the accused for separate crimes. The use of paragraph 129 made it possible to prosecute the RAF as a whole and place the central management of the prosecution in the hands of the Federal Prosecutor's Office. The added benefit was that one central trial could be organised at an Oberlandesgericht (Higher Regional Court) in one of the eleven German state capitals. This was the only way for the state to achieve the exemplary trial against the RAF it so strongly desired.[30]

Building the Stage and Its Props: A Fortress of Fear

Apart from juridical considerations, security issues were important in discussions about the choice of a location for the trial. Politicians, security officials and administrators feared a repetition of the RAF's first act, the armed liberation of Andreas Baader from captivity in May 1970. The Oberlandesgericht in Stuttgart (the state capital of Baden-Württemberg) was selected, as it was in this state that the bombing with the gravest consequences (the attack on the US Army headquarters in Heidelberg) had taken place. The Stuttgart suburb of Stammheim also hosted a modern prison facility that could easily be upgraded to maximum security level. Stuttgart is also conveniently close to the Federal Prosecutor's Office in Karlsruhe. There were objections to Stuttgart on the ground that it violated legal requirements that called for trials be held in the place in which the accused lived or was arrested. The government took care of this problem in a technical sense by moving the accused to Stammheim prison before the trial began, making them Stuttgart residents.[31]

The Second Senate of the Stuttgart Oberlandesgericht consisted of six voting judges (one of them presiding) and three substitutes. Theodor Prinzing, president of the Second Senate at the time of the trial, was a relatively fresh appointee installed on 4 February 1974. Rumours suggested some behind-the-scenes manoeuvring had side-lined his predecessor and that Prinzing had been hand-picked by the political authorities to conduct the impending trial against the RAF.[32] Prinzing (then president of a youth court) was seen to possess experience with lengthy proceedings (gained in trials against former Nazis), as well as the analytical skills, self-assertiveness and ambition necessary for the job. Prinzing also had the reputation of a judge whose verdicts had never been revised by higher courts, which meant he would probably meet public expectations for the trial against the RAF.[33]

If this is a correct interpretation—this information has not been verified by historical research—a conflict arises with the principle that every accused has the right to a lawful judge—in this case Prinzing's predecessor—without political interference. The impression that a special court was created is reinforced by the state's decision to build, alledgedly for security reasons, a new (12 million D-Mark) courthouse close to the Stuttgart-Stammheim prison, rather than make use of the existing court in the city centre. In an ironic remark, Stefan Aust described this new building as a 'memorial of steel and concrete [which] had been erected to [the RAF leadership] in their lifetime'.[34] In Germany and beyond, concerns were raised that the government was organising a show trial in a special court, which German and international law specifically prohibit. Some RAF lawyers and other critics compared the decision to build the special courthouse to the creation of the Sondergerichte (special courts) by the Nazis to guarantee convictions of perceived enemies of the state.[35]

The law also holds that a fair trial should not take place in prison, because that would be in violation of the presumption of innocence of the accused. Some critics believed that locating the new Stammheim courthouse close to the penitentiary amounted to a pre-trial conviction, or could at least be interpreted as such by the suspects themselves. German authorities reacted to this by declaring that the new concrete hall was part of an older plan to renovate the prison facilities. They described the new structure as a 'Mehrzweckgebäude' (multi-purpose building) that would in future function as a sports facility or workshop for the inmates. Retrospectively, it has become clear that this was mere window dressing, as during the 35 years since its construction the multi-purpose building has been used only for high security trials and has remained the main seat of the Second Senate of Stuttgart's Oberlandesgericht.[36]

Security arrangements around and within the new Stammheim courthouse were extraordinary. This is apparent from a balanced overview written by Ulf Stuberger, a German journalist (who claims to have been the only reporter present on all trial days). Stuberger relates that on his first visit to the trial site the two rows of fencing surrounding the entire facility reminded him of the border with Communist East Germany. The first fence was topped by a roll of barbed wire and the second, twice as high, with military-style NATO razorwire. Between the fences a secure zone was controlled by motion detectors, surveillance cameras and heavily-armed police with watchdogs. Parts of the court building were covered with steel netting to prevent a prisoners' liberation attempt by helicopter. Despite this, and the tight control of airspace above the courthouse, a small aeroplane flew over the site on the first day of the trial and was forced to land by army helicopters. Apparently a photojournalist had hired the plane to take pictures.[37]

Stuberger notes the police presence outside the courthouse, especially on this first day of the trial. Hundreds of police, some on horseback, as well as paramilitary border police, riot police and a special counter-terrorist commando were present to block undesired visitors from approaching the facilities. Physical obstacles such as 'Spanish riders' (knife rests—military-style wire obstacles), road blocks and concrete walls created further barriers around the courthouse. Visitors entered the building through a revolving door of steel and armoured glass, scrutinised by security officers in a bullet-proof glass room with surveillance camera monitors. Identity papers were checked and visitors were searched and personal belongings temporarily removed (reporters were allowed only paper and one ballpoint pen). Finally, visitors passed through a full-height turnstile to reach the courtroom.[38]

Critics have questioned the impact of this high security environment on the independence of judicial decision-making. Such measures not only reinforced the idea of the accused as being extremely dangerous, but also displayed the performative power of the government's RAF trial policies. Press commentary about the opening day of the trial noted that the whole atmosphere around the court undermined both the state's claim that the trial only involved 'ordinary criminals', and the image of a liberal democracy dealing with criminal behaviour in a matter-of-fact and legal manner. Reports of the harsh treatment of some of the journalists created an impression that the authorities had lost their sense of proportion and humanity.[39] According to Aust, however, the security extravaganza at Stammheim 'can also be explained by the fact that no one in government was willing to take personal responsibility for possible risks. A bit too much safety seemed at any rate better than somewhat too little.'[40]

The enormous interior of the courtroom (610 square metres) did little to redress the balance. Walls and floors consisted of raw concrete, the ceiling was an assembly of heating pipes and other utility installations. The general public were seated in rows of yellow plastic chairs (120). Chairs fitted with small foldout tables (81) were to serve the press. At the end of the room, beneath an oversized coat of arms of the state of Baden-Württemberg, the judges sat behind a table. Behind the judges a giant bookcase would store hundreds of ring binders of trial records. In front of the judges' table stood a solitary witness chair and in between a table for the state prosecutors and one for the defence.[41]

One day during the trial, Stuberger visited the office of the presiding judge Prinzing. For Stuberger, the official quarters confirmed the impression of a machine-like state mercilessly seeking revenge; the judge was no more than a pawn in the game. 'A bunker of justice, I thought', Stuberger writes.

> The whole building radiates nothing but coldness, no trace of humanity. Here the naked state is on display, cold and merciless. I was convinced that in these surroundings, reminiscent of an old black-and-white movie version of George Orwell's *Nineteen Eighty-Four*, I [as a judge] would be unable to reach a humane verdict. Behind

> the scenes [Stammheim] appeared to me [...] like a slaughterhouse. Or, to put it in friendlier terms, like the technical area behind the coulisses of a modern theatre: the aim ruled everything, there was no room for human emotions.[42]

Rewriting the Code of Criminal Procedure, Evicting Lawyers

As a third trajectory towards a trial outcome favourable to the wishes of the authorities several changes were introduced into the Code of Criminal Procedure. These changes were intended to restrict the potential for the defence lawyers and the accused to delay or obstruct a trial through the lawful use of petitions, motions and the like. Such precautionary measures were deemed necessary based on several experiences with left-wing suspects and their lawyers since the mid-1960s. During the student rebellions of the 1960s, there had been unprecedented courtroom scenes in the FRG, with left-wing radicals mocking judges and prosecutors and turning trials into farcical political demonstrations.[43]

More shocking to the establishment than the unruly student behaviour was that lawyers, often working collectively,[44] had also begun to reject juridical conventions. These 'Linksanwälte' (a wordplay on 'Rechtsanwälte'—lawyers, and the adjective 'links'—left-wing)[45] had shed the traditional understanding of lawyers as 'Organe der Rechtspflege' (instruments of the justice system). They had distanced themselves from the traditional interpretation of their job as the 'third profession of the law', alongside judges and prosecutors, 'to form a bridge between the justice system and the accused'. Instead, they decided to advocate their clients' interests far more strongly and single-mindedly.[46]

Obviously, this style of 'political defence', as they themselves dubbed it, drew these lawyers into a direct confrontation with the other parties involved in the justice system.[47] A brochure published in 1975 by the Rote Hilfe (Red Aid), an organisation supporting left-wing radicals against the judiciary, presents a clear picture of how these left-wing lawyers saw themselves. 'In principle, at a trial', the list begins, 'left-wing lawyers practise solidarity with their clients. Although they do not have to identify completely with the ideology of their clients, politically they will always side with them and in principle they oppose the same enemy.' On this basis, left-wing lawyers would lend their technical juridical skills to clients to help 'destroy the illusion of an apolitical and impartial justice system'. Apart from that, they would not hesitate to appeal to public opinion by publicising their clients' detention situation or reporting on miscarriages of justice.[48]

In practice, this concept of political defence meant that the lawyers used every opportunity to exploit the Code of Criminal Procedure to stall and obstruct trials by procedural means. Rather than attacking the accusations against their clients, these 'Linksanwälte' seemed determined to undermine the legitimacy of the trial and the justice system that had produced it.[49] Angry and frustrated, judges and prosecutors were forced to listen to the fulminations of the left-wing lawyers as if they themselves were in the dock.

From June 1972 onwards, a campaign against the justice system was initiated; lawyers involved accused the state of subjecting RAF members to torture. One aspect of the campaign immediately raised great concerns for the state. The authorities had already been confronted with the possibility that a lawyer would smuggle handwritten notes (*Kassiber*) between RAF members inside and outside prison to maintain communication. A note by RAF member Gudrun Ensslin (clearly written while she was in custody) had been found among Ulrike Meinhof's papers when she was arrested. Ensslin's lawyer, Otto Schily, was suspected as the middleman, but there was no evidence to convict him.

A corresponding effort to have Schily evicted from Ensslin's legal team also failed when on 14 February 1973 Germany's Bundesverfassungsgericht (Federal Constitutional Court) quashed an eviction order made by a lower court. The constitutional judges considered such an eviction to amount to an unlawful breach of the professional freedom of a lawyer. They declared, however, that this case had highlighted 'ein höchst unbefriedigender Rechtszustand' (a highly unsatisfactory legal situation) and advised the legislator to resolve this by making it legally possible to evict a lawyer from a trial.[50]

The authorities sought to protect *their* trial of the RAF leadership from some of these unexpected outcomes by introducing two sets of anti-terrorism legislation: the First Law for a Reform of Criminal Proceedings of 9 December 1974, and the Law to Amend the First Law for a Reform of Criminal Proceedings of 20 December 1974 (both came into force on 1 January 1975).[51] These changes rolled back attempts to strengthen the rights of the defence that had been part of a wave of liberalisation making its mark on the Code of Criminal Procedure and the Criminal Code since 1964.

The first set of changes abolished the right of the defence to have any final say on the criminal allegation before the arraignment by the prosecution. The second set of changes established extensive restrictions on the legal defence. Two measures specifically targeted the practice of collective 'political defence': the number of lawyers for each accused was limited to a maximum of three (paragraph 137, section 1 StPO[52]) and a ban on the common defence of multiple accused by one lawyer was introduced (paragraph 146 StPO).[53] Until then some lawyers had had power of attorney for several RAF members, which created a tightly coordinated defence team. Under the new law it would be far more difficult to uphold this measure of cooperation. The new laws also prevented an unlimited number of lawyers making use of the defence's rights to petition the court, thus limiting the risk of the obstruction of trial proceedings.

The new legislation created the possibility of evicting a lawyer from a trial (paragraph 138a, 138b StPO). This was the stopgap measure the Federal Constitutional Court had asked for in its verdict in the Schily case. Moreover, the new law made it possible to continue a trial *in absentia* of the accused when a lack of fitness to stand trial was of his or her own doing (paragraph 231a, 231b StPO). Hitherto in West Germany it had been considered taboo to proceed without the defendant, because of experiences during the Third Reich. Finally, the defence's right to make statements during a trial was somewhat restricted (paragraph 257 StPO); and the powers of the presiding judge were expanded to enable the disciplining of unruly participants in a trial, including members of the audience disturbing the proceedings, for example by shouting abuse.[54]

During the Stammheim trial a third set of anti-terrorism legislation was introduced in the form of the Counter-terrorist Law of 18 August 1976 (it entered into force on 20 September 1976 and 1 January 1977).[55] This introduced further restrictive changes to the Code of Criminal Procedure that came into force while the Stammheim trial was underway, as well as changes in the Bundesrechtsanwaltsordnung (the law regarding federal rulings of the legal defence trade) that made it easier to prosecute and punish lawyers who violated their professional code. This ruling provided the authorities with another instrument with which to discipline lawyers who were seen to obstruct normal court proceedings or who assisted imprisoned terrorists in their efforts to maintain links with their organisation.[56]

In his book about the Stammheim trial, Tenfelde reflects upon the mixed reception of the new laws against terrorism. Some authors condemned them as an infringement upon the rights of the defence and as an example of undemocratic ad hoc legislation ('Lex Baader–Meinhof'[57]), while others regarded them as an effective and proportionate response to terrorism within the rule of law. Some even felt the new laws did not go far enough. According to Tenfelde the measures have to be seen as part of a range of responses by the state to the terrorist threat that were directly related to societal reactions to terrorism and to the expectations of state responses held by the general public. This implies there was no 'master plan' behind the legislation, in spite of speculation by some on the left that the new laws were inspired by a totalitarian strategy of pre-emptive counter-revolution that had allegedly engulfed Western societies since the 1950s. Instead, as Uwe Berlitt and Horst Dreier have already proposed in their early analysis of the anti-terrorism laws, the legislation and the activities of the violent terrorist perpetrators are better understood as 'an interactive process' in which societal and state forces mutually influenced the end result.[58]

The fact that the legislative process around the first two sets of anti-terrorist laws suddenly accelerated at the end of 1974 makes this interaction perfectly clear. In November and December 1974 the confrontation with left-wing terrorism reached a high point during the third campaign of collective hunger strikes by RAF prisoners. On 9 November 1974, the death of hunger striker Holger Meins (one of five RAF leaders to be tried at Stammheim) led to a wave of protest by left-wing radicals throughout West Germany. The revenge killing of Berlin's most important judge, Günter von Drenkmann, by another terrorist group on 10 November 1974, in turn triggered a large-scale police operation against left-wing radicals, their organisations and publications.

Influenced by these events, legislators of the Bundestag (Federal Diet) and the Bundesrat (Federal Council) not only hastened their deliberations on the first set of anti-terror legislation (originally presented to them in 1973), but also approved the second set of changes that the government had only recently proposed.[59] These tensions present in late 1974 encouraged the legislative change that the authorities thought they needed, just in time for the scheduled start of the Stammheim trial in May 1975. As might be expected, this speedy legislation process led to some mishaps that had a negative influence on the trial during its first months.

With the option to evict lawyers in place, the authorities started to move against some of them in the early months of 1975. There were risks associated with this course of action, because German law prescribes that a legal defender must always be available for an accused person. To prevent the interruption or even cancellation of the trial, judge Prinzing (of the Second Senate of the Stuttgart Oberlandesgericht) decided to appoint two 'Pflichtverteidiger' (officially commissioned lawyers) for each of the accused. If a 'Wahlverteidiger' (lawyer of choice) acting for the accused was evicted by order of the presiding judge, he or she could be replaced by such commissioned lawyers. The appointment of these substitute lawyers was intended by German law to ensure the continuity of long trials. Of course the Pflichtverteidiger were paid by the state, not by the defendant.[60] RAF members did not want to speak to the substitute lawyers, whom they called 'Zwangsverteidiger' (lawyers forced upon them), because they did not trust them.[61]

Usually, in order to accommodate the rights of the accused and assist with the organisation of the legal defence, the court formally commissioned all or some of the lawyers of choice as Pflichtverteidiger, with the state covering the bills. Many of the lawyers originally chosen by RAF members were also officially commissioned by judge Prinzing. In early 1975, however, Prinzing started to decommission some of them. Klaus Croissant (Stuttgart), Kurt Groenewold (Hamburg) and Hans-Christian Ströbele (Berlin), all three lawyers of Baader's choice, were sacked as Pflichtverteidiger, on suspicion of supporting the (criminal association) RAF. In Ströbele's case the suspicion rested on letters in which he had called his clients 'comrades'; he called himself a 'socialist' and his work that of a 'political defender'. Now that the state would no longer cover their costs, the participation of these three lawyers of choice in the impending trial became precarious.[62]

In the last month before the trial started, Prinzing went even further and actually evicted the three lawyers he had already decommissioned as (state financed) Pflichtverteidiger but who had still been allowed to defend the accused at their own expense, one after the other, on the basis of recent legislation (paragraph 138a StPO).[63] These evictions created enormous problems for Baader's defence, especially when the last remaining lawyer to enjoy Baader's trust, Siegfried Haag (Heidelberg), went underground in early May 1977. The Bundeskriminalamt (Federal Criminal Police Office) had temporarily arrested Haag on suspicion of involvement with the armed occupation of the German embassy in Stockholm by a RAF commando on 24 April 1975. Haag spent the next year and a half organising a new terrorist commando group of the RAF, until he was arrested for a second time at the end of 1976.[64]

With the state and media pressure on left-wing lawyers, and the ban on common defence recently installed, it was clear Baader would have difficulty finding a trustworthy new barrister in time for the trial of his life. The pool of leftist or liberal-minded lawyers was small. On 21 May 1975, the front man of the RAF entered the Stammheim courtroom without a lawyer of choice. This did not reflect well on the trial, and subsequently dented the credibility of the state's narrative of justice at Stammheim.

6.2.2. *The RAF and Its Lawyers: Expanding the Stage*

In complete contrast to the actions of the authorities, the RAF leadership and their lawyers did their utmost to stress the political implications of the impending trial. In the years after their arrests they deliberately expanded the stage for the confrontation with the established order. Firstly, the imprisoned members of the RAF started challenging the conditions of their imprisonment, a struggle intended to inspire a solidarity movement among left-wing radicals (in Germany and abroad). Secondly, the RAF's defence lawyers developed a strategy in line with the style of the late 1960s political defence we discussed above. As will be demonstrated, the RAF leaders directly influenced the formulation and implementation of this defence strategy.

Prison Struggle: Hunger Strikes and the Rise of an RAF Solidarity Movement

In the years after their arrests, the leaders of the RAF did not passively await their impending trial and the lengthy prison sentences that would probably result from it. Baader, Ensslin, Meinhof and their comrades started a prison struggle. They accused the state of using extreme solitary confinement that amounted to torture ('Isolationsfolter'). They claimed this was intended to destroy their identities as 'guerrillas' and to mentally and physically 'annihilate' them (they spoke of 'Vernichtungshaft'). They stressed their plight by staging several collective hunger strikes, the first one lasting from mid-January to mid-February 1973.[65]

It must be acknowledged that there was some truth in these allegations. The West German state kept the imprisoned members of the RAF and other left-wing terrorist groups on a very short leash indeed. Although a general historical overview of the prison conditions of RAF members has yet to be written, it is generally accepted that, initially at least, three female members were held in solitary confinement for exceptionally long periods.[66] In the case of other RAF prisoners there is reason to believe that (less extreme) modes of solitary confinement were applied, although some group members were held under regular prison conditions. The forced feeding of prisoners on hunger strike, a painful and humiliating procedure, lent, in the eyes of some observers, a degree of substance to accusations of state torture.[67]

The notion that the authorities were out to kill the RAF prisoners was, nevertheless, rather far-fetched. In reaction to the hunger strikes, for example, the authorities began granting privileges to RAF members, especially to the leaders, to avoid jeopardizing their participation in the upcoming trial. From late 1974 onwards, the authorities also began accommodating Baader and other RAF leaders, men *and* women, together on the seventh floor of Stammheim prison. Special favours, like the provision of electric hotplates to cook their own meals, were granted to RAF prisoners to help them recover from the hunger strikes. From February 1975 onwards, they were even allowed to spend several hours a day in the corridor of their high security ward in order collectively to prepare for their trial. To prevent eavesdropping on discussions about the defence strategy, the judge ordered the prison guards to keep out of hearing distance.[68]

Regardless of these and other concessions, Baader and others continued to remonstrate against prison conditions. This indicates that the dual purpose of the prison struggle was not only to put pressure on the German government to improve prison conditions, but also to create empathy that would serve as a platform for an

RAF solidarity campaign. In styling themselves as martyrs for the radical left, the RAF prisoners aimed at mobilising support among other radical Germans and recruiting new members from this pool of sympathisers. Apart from that, the prison struggle can also be seen as an effort to hold on to the RAF claim to lead the vanguard of the radical left, a claim that had been stated from the beginning, especially in the 1971 publications.[69]

The RAF lawyers played an essential role in the solidarity campaign. In February 1973, alongside the first collective hunger strike of the RAF, they staged a four-day solidarity hunger strike in front of the Federal Court of Justice in Karlsruhe to attract public attention to the plight of the prisoners.[70] As hinted at above, the lawyers were of central importance for maintaining communications between the RAF prisoners and with their supporters (and probably also with active terrorist cells) in the outside world. In the spring of 1973 the lawyers established an intricate communication system called 'das info'.[71] Instructed by the prisoners, the office of Hamburg lawyer Kurt Groenewold functioned as an information centre and archive. It collated all instructions, (circular) letters, newspaper clippings and other discussion materials provided or requested by RAF leaders. Subsequently, the lawyers circulated these among the imprisoned members of the RAF by using the *Verteidigerpost* (defence mail between lawyers and their clients) which was protected by law.[72]

After a police raid on Groenewold's office on 23 June 1975, a month after the Stammheim trial had started, the information system broke down. Gradually, however, lawyer Klaus Croissant's office in Stuttgart re-established communications among the prisoners and with the outside world. At first, Croissant and his associates used the defence mail as before. However a change in the Code of Criminal Procedure in August 1976 made it possible to control defence mail in those cases where there was a grounded suspicion that it served to establish or continue a terrorist association. After that, lawyers started touring the country, visiting all of the RAF prisoners one after another.[73]

RAF lawyers also initiated special solidarity committees for the imprisoned members of the RAF, the so-called *(Anti-)Folterkomitees* (Committees against Torture). These were founded in many big cities and university towns throughout the FRG, beginning in April 1973. During the second hunger strike of the RAF, in May and June 1973, a national teach-in of Anti-Torture Committees in Frankfurt strengthened the campaign's base, and created material for propaganda, such as the special issue on the torture of 'Political Prisoners' in the influential left-wing intellectual magazine *Kursbuch*.[74] Around 450 activists joined the Anti-Torture Committees in the first year.[75]

Political activism in defence of the RAF peaked during the third hunger strike, which began after a proclamation by Ulrike Meinhof when the trial against her and others started in the West Berlin Schwurgericht (lower regional jury-based court) on 13 September 1974.[76] The RAF leadership had been preparing this third hunger strike with great care since late 1973, and this time they were very determined. In January 1974, Baader had written to RAF activists outside the prison to insist that this time the hunger strike would not be broken. 'Das heißt es werden typen dabei kaputtgehen.' (This means that some types [of people] will die.)[77] And indeed, on 9 November 1974, RAF member Holger Meins did die of starvation. In a declaration distributed by his lawyer Croissant after his demise, Meins blamed the state for his death: 'In case I switch from life to death in prison, it was murder—whatever the pigs might say. Don't believe the lies of these murderers.'[78]

The significance of this hunger strike for the trial at Stammheim that was to begin half a year later lay in the solidarity and support it managed to mobilise in Germany and abroad. After Meins's death, protests and demonstrations in West Berlin attracted 2,500 participants. A resolution circulated amongst those present at a gathering in Berlin's Technical University. The resolution stated that it was clear that the special treatment of 'political prisoners' in the FRG aimed 'to silence them [...], to make them renounce their political beliefs, and, as a necessary step to that end, to destroy their souls and rob them of their identities.'[79]

Many young people subscribed to the RAF framing of the situation. Criticism of the organisation and of the use of political violence in revolutionary politics was temporarily silenced. The revenge murder of Günter von Drenkmann, president of Berlin's Kammergericht (higher regional court), did not change this. While most radical left-wing demonstrators did not endorse this killing, few were having second thoughts about their support for the RAF's prison struggle linked to it.[80]

The third hunger strike also raised solidarity with the RAF to an international level. When the strike began on 27 September 1974, RAF sympathisers in Hamburg, Amsterdam and London staged a series of well-coordinated actions, attracting considerable media attention. A visit by French philosopher Jean-Paul Sartre to Andreas Baader in Stammheim prison on 4 December 1974 was a veritable publicity coup.[81] Only days later, the RAF's lawyers established an international network to muster foreign pressure on the German government.[82] Stories about the treatment of imprisoned members of the RAF had raised anxiety outside Germany, and on 14 December 1974 the 'Comité International de Défense des Prisonniers Politiques en Europe' (International Committee for the Defence of Political Prisoners in Europe) was established in Utrecht. The committee consisted mainly of lawyers and doctors from the Netherlands (where lawyer Bakker Schut was the driving force), Belgium, France and Italy.[83]

The committee was presented as an independent network of foreign professionals, but in reality it was an instrument of the RAF's defence team—as further developments indicated. After the International Committee, known under its German name 'Internationales Verteidigungskomitee' (International Defence Committee, IVK), had reconvened and formulated its programme at a meeting in Paris on 20 January 1975, the secretariat was based in Croissant's office in Stuttgart, where the FRG arm of the committee resided.[84] During the Stammheim trial this bureau helped to coordinate the activities of national committees such as the Dutch Medisch Juridisch Comité Politieke Gevangenen (Medical-Juridical Committee for Political Prisoners, MJC), founded on 19 April 1975.[85] In the following years, the IVK and these national committees published declarations of international solidarity and other kinds of propaganda, including Ulrike Meinhof's last texts in German and other languages[86] as well as a voluminous book documenting prison correspondence by RAF members.[87] The committees were also associated with other international bodies such as the 'independent' research committee that investigated Ulrike Meinhof's suicide in prison on 9 May 1976.[88]

By the time the Stammheim trial began, the RAF had constructed a transnational network able to transmit statements by the accused and their defenders to left-wing supporters they regarded as their first audience, and to the public at large. The operations of this network had already been active during the trial against the only Dutch member of the RAF, Ronald Augustin, at Bückeburg (near Hanover) in mid-February 1975, when activists in the Netherlands vigorously publicised this trial as a dress rehearsal for the Stammheim trial. There were some striking parallels, including the fact that the courtroom was situated on the grounds of Bückeburg prison. The Augustin campaign helped to get the network off to a running start in preparation for the trial at Stammheim.[89]

Guerrilla Tactics: Clients, Lawyers, and the Defence Strategy

As explained above, the RAF had used court cases against its members for propaganda purposes well before the Stammheim trial. RAF members had spoken at length from the dock about their ideology and their plight in prison, hoping to attract the attention of other left-wing radicals and German liberals. Initially there appeared to be some reservations regarding the RAF's defence strategy at the Stammheim trial. 'It is far from certain that there will be a defence in Stammheim', Baader confessed in a circular letter, dated June 1974. 'We are interested in this show only if we can turn it around.'[90] It took some time for the RAF to understand that the media coverage of this trial had the potential to spread their gospel.[91]

Ultimately, however, the RAF leadership saw their performance at the trial as a continuation of guerrilla warfare against the state and its 'counter-insurgency strategy' against the radical left.[92] To understand this we have to go back to the intellectual roots of the RAF's urban guerrilla practice, which was partly inspired by the guerrilla warfare theory of Latin American revolutionary Ernesto 'Che' Guevara in the 1960s, as it was subsequently popularised by the French left-wing journalist Régis Débray. Guevara had explained guerrilla warfare as a strategy operated by small, elusive, armed groups, designed to provoke the state into large-scale repression of the general population, thereby revealing its true, oppressive nature to the masses and inciting revolution.[93]

Analogous to this, the RAF leadership, using secret letters distributed among RAF members within and outside the prison, devised behaviours at the trial by which they hoped to provoke judges and prosecutors into revealing the naked oppressiveness of the West German state. 'What we want', read one circular letter from early November 1975, 'is that the operations of the Federal Prosecutor, in the legal vacuum between the bourgeois rule of law and the open fascism of the state of emergency legislation, are used to reveal the strategies of the state security apparatus.' The RAF wanted to turn the trial at Stammheim into a demonstration of 'the dimension of the domestic repression', and the unveiling of 'fascism as an institutional strategy'.[94]

A circular letter from September 1975 revealed the optimum result the RAF hoped to gain: a failed trial.

> [A] failed trial contradicts the assumption of a normal situation, a normal criminal procedure—the war begins to look like a war—what the state fears most, because it makes it clear that a small group of 20 or 30 fighters can challenge the state—it makes clear that armed struggle is right, possible, and necessary, in spite of the weakness of the left here and because of its weakness.[95]

The RAF's legal defenders were crucial to its goal: to transform the trial into an instrument of propaganda. It was up to the lawyers to enlighten the public with regard to the trial's alleged political function. In a statement from a circular letter on one of the first trial days, 1 July 1975, lawyers were depicted as teachers, 'let's say, with chalk, pointer, and blackboard'. The lawyers, with their legal skills, could point out the weaknesses in the arguments put forward by prosecutors and judges, showing 'the people' the true nature of these functionaries: 'underneath their robes [they are] politicians, [and] as politicians [they are] reactionaries of the darkest hue, virulent anticommunists, bureaucratic collaborators of mass murder'.[96]

In true communist fashion, the RAF regarded its strategy of political defence as a 'popular front strategy', building a coalition of left-wing and liberal forces around a communist core, like the antifascist alliances in Spain, France and elsewhere during the 1930s. The lawyers were important in building this popular front and creating 'democratic public opinion' against the government policies aimed at the radical left. This did not mean the RAF leaders held their lawyers in high esteem. In their view, it was 'grotesque' that socialist lawyers seemed to have become 'the last defenders of bourgeois rule of law'. In fact the RAF leadership ridiculed their efforts to save the bourgeois state. Baader and his comrades nevertheless considered their efforts useful—defending RAF members in court and protesting against restrictive counter-terrorist legislation, which contributed to the mobilisation of opposition against the established order.[97]

The lawyers reacted differently towards efforts to instrumentalise them. Heinrich Hannover (Bremen), who was very experienced in political cases, was one of several lawyers who were too independent to maintain good relationships with RAF clients. Ulrike Meinhof had once sacked Hannover for refusing to comply with her demands, and he finally left in 1974, having defended her since 1970.[98] Other lawyers were more docile. Prominent RAF lawyer Kurt Groenewold, for instance, had acknowledged as early as 1972 that a lawyer's task was to reveal the essence of the justice system as an instrument of the status quo; he also pleaded for the creation of an association of communist lawyers.[99] His colleague Klaus Croissant went further and identified to a large degree with the RAF. Croissant gave up his independence as a legal adviser to comply fully with RAF wishes and demands.[100]

Otto Schily, the sharpest mind and most able orator on the defence team, kept a seigniorial distance from his clients, staunchly addressing them with the formal 'Sie'—instead of 'du'—the informal term for family members, friends and (especially on the left) political comrades.[101] Yet even Schily adhered to the RAF leaders' defence strategy and complied with Baader's conditions, agreeing in a letter he wrote to Klaus Croissant on 17 April 1974 to 'collective defence, the course that has been discussed by the prisoners, [and] final editing of the plea speeches by the prisoners'.[102]

Before we look at the Stammheim trial in detail, it is worth mentioning that the RAF leaders also displayed a kind of stage fright. More than once they seemed to be searching for an emergency exit to evade facing their judges altogether. They had discussed among themselves whether or not a hunger strike that undermined their physical fitness would create plausible grounds not to appear in court. A letter that circulated among RAF prisoners in March 1974 proposed this route to obstruct the efforts of the state to bring them to justice.[103] In the press, however, they denied considering this strategy, dismissing police reports about it as examples of the government's 'Countertaktik, Gegenpropaganda' (counter tactics, counter propaganda).[104]

At an early stage, Andreas Baader had also tried to motivate underground RAF comrades to organise a hostage-taking operation to force the government to swap the imprisoned RAF members for the hostages.[105] The arrests of seven members of an underground cell on 4 February 1974 had initially thwarted this plan, but Meins' death in the hunger strike added momentum to rebuilding the armed struggle. One such RAF sympathiser who decided to take up arms against the state was Susanne Albrecht. She remembered thinking after Meins' death, 'If the justice system won't change the conditions of detention, then we must act. We cannot allow more prisoners to die.'[106]

On 24 April 1975, the RAF commando group 'Holger Meins' stormed the German embassy in Stockholm, taking hostage the ambassador and other personnel. They were clearly inspired by the success of an earlier act of hostage-taking of the West Berlin CDU politician Peter Lorenz by another group that had resulted in the release of five left-wing radical terrorists from custody in late February 1975.[107] In exchange for the lives of their captives, the Stockholm hostage-takers demanded the release of 26 'political prisoners' in order to rescue these comrades from 'isolation torture'. To underline their resolve the commandos killed two German diplomats, but the government in Bonn proved unwilling to give in. That evening, with new deaths seemingly imminent in the Swedish capital, there was a sudden series of explosions when RAF explosives accidentally detonated. One RAF member was killed instantly and another was fatally wounded. In the ensuing turmoil, Stockholm police cleared the burning embassy and arrested the hostage-takers.[108] The RAF's final effort to evade the Stammheim trial, a month before its scheduled start, had resulted in bloody failure.

6.3. 192 Days: From Stammheim Stalemate to Ghost Trial

In the days just before 21 May 1975, the day the trial against the RAF leadership would finally get under way, the media set the stage for the proceedings with great anticipation. Many journalists focused on the scale and cost of the security measures and the collection of evidence. The weekly *Der Spiegel* even entitled its article about the trial's opening 'Materialschlacht' (material battle), comparing the preparation of the opposing forces at Stammheim with the industrialised trench warfare of the First World War.[109] On the one hand this terminology clearly shows, as Andreas Musolff has worked out,[110] that even in liberal newspapers metaphors of warfare were used to describe the confrontation between the RAF and the state, which did not exactly downplay the supposed terrorism threat. On the other hand the WW I comparison became indeed an appropriate metaphor as conflicts over procedural issues sometimes appeared to produce a stalemate. During the 192 days of the trial proceedings, daunting legal complexities and vehement confrontations between the participants combined to confuse and sometimes infuriate observers. We will try to deal with the apparently strictly legal issues and the turbulent theatrics separately to illustrate the performative aspects of the Stammheim trial.

6.3.1. *Strictly Legal? Protracted Proceedings in a 'Normal Criminal Case'*

After months in which the RAF had been confronted with the consequences of the recent changes in the Code of Criminal Procedure, the Stammheim trial finally presented a chance for them to redress the balance.[111] Thus in the first months of the trial, the accused and their lawyers swamped the proceedings with applications on all kinds of procedural issues. The long second phase of the trial began in November 1975, when the court at last was able to proceed to the actual hearing of the evidence. Most of the legal wrangling in this phase concerned the role played by two 'crown witnesses', as the defence dubbed them. The RAF's lawyers also argued for criminal proceedings against their clients to be abandoned altogether. It was argued that the RAF had committed acts of war in resistance to American interference in Vietnam, rather than crimes, and its leaders should therefore be treated not as criminals but as prisoners of war.

Procedural Issues: Evicted Lawyers and Fitness to Stand Trial

Before the Stammheim trial, the judges of the Stuttgart Oberlandesgericht's Second Senate were among the first to implement the legislative changes hastily introduced for trials against the RAF. This had put the judges in an awkward position, and especially their president, whose task it had been to make decisions on the conditions of imprisonment of the accused and the admission of their lawyers. During the opening stages of the trial, this pre-history made discussion about procedural issues highly likely, as already became apparent on the first day when the RAF's defence team tried to prevent the eviction of Baader's lawyers of choice. As we related earlier, judge

Prinzing had evicted all three of them before the trial, a decision based on a recent change in the Code of Criminal Procedure (paragraph 138 StPO). Immediately after the president had opened the trial, the RAF defence team asked the court to re-admit these evicted lawyers to defend Ensslin, Meinhof and Raspe.

At issue was the question whether evicting the lawyers as Baader's representatives meant they were banned from the Stammheim trial for good. Initially judge Prinzing bluntly denied the lawyers' request; however, the prosecutors sided with the defence, warning Prinzing that it would not do to simply deny them access to the courtroom. The text of the law may indeed have left room for the interpretation put forward by the RAF lawyers, namely that a lawyer could legally only be evicted as counsel to one specific defendant. The prosecutors advised a temporary halt to the proceedings until the lawyers in question had been evicted from the defence of all four RAF members facing trial at Stammheim.[112] In effect, the prosecution admitted that the RAF had spotted one of several lacunae that legal authorities in their haste had allowed to enter the new legislation.

Of course the prosecutors were not keen to admit this lacuna, but were worried that a Stammheim verdict could be overturned in future by a higher court disapproving of the non-admittance of lawyers without proper legal grounds. After hours of deliberation, the president suspended the trial until further notice and left the judges of the First Senate to decide on the matter. After two weeks the First Senate decided to back Prinzing's broad interpretation of the law. Given the doubts that even the prosecutors had displayed, this was a controversial decision. Nevertheless it was later upheld by the Federal Court of Justice.[113]

In relation to the first procedural issue, Andreas Baader himself introduced another issue on 5 June 1975, the second trial day. Pointing out that he lacked a lawyer of his own choice, he asked for a five-day adjournment to find one. The president denied this request, arguing that Baader still had two substitute lawyers commissioned by the court at his disposal. Linked to this was the next procedural issue, which arose on 11 June 1975 (the fourth trial day), when a new lawyer of choice for Baader, Hans-Heinz Heldmann (Darmstadt), finally presented himself and asked the Second Senate for a ten-day adjournment for trial preparation (to look at thousands of pages of police documents). The court denied this request despite the fact that it had evicted Baader's three lawyers at such short notice, arguing that Baader had had ample time before the beginning of the trial to find himself a new lawyer of choice. In protest, Heldmann filed a constitutional complaint against this decision with the Federal Constitutional Court in Karlsruhe, but a commission of three constitutional judges decided not to admit the complaint.[114]

In the meantime, on the third trial day, 10 June 1975, the substitute lawyers commissioned by the court had found themselves at the centre of a row between the RAF members and the court. The defence had demanded the court decommission these 'Zwangsverteidiger' (compulsory defence attorneys) as the RAF called these substitute lawyers. When the substitute lawyers tried to speak, Baader and the other accused shouted them down and called them names until the presiding judge ordered the court's guards to lead the accused from the room.[115] The court decided not to comply with the RAF defence's demand and to keep the substitute lawyers. The judges (and the prosecutors) probably feared that without substitute lawyers the risk was simply too great that at some point in time during the proceedings a walk-out by the lawyers of choice would lead to a failed trial. To the court's embarrassment, later that day one of the substitute lawyers fell asleep. When Baader directed the president's attention to the old man, the audience erupted in a roar of laughter.[116]

The following week, the court's president had become the main focus of attack. On 18 and 19 June 1975, Otto Schily, acting on behalf of his client Gudrun Ensslin, questioned the appointment of Prinzing as president of the Second Senate. He portrayed him as a functionary of the national security state, bowing to the officials of the West German security services and denying the RAF prisoners their rights. Schily accused Prinzing of having allowed and defended the conditions of severe detention for RAF prisoners and of co-responsibility for the death of Holger Meins. Against this background, Schily challenged the judge on grounds of bias: the accused could not regard Prinzing as an impartial judge and therefore he should be taken off the case.[117]Six weeks later on 30 July 1975, lawyers acting for Ulrike Meinhof continued the attack on Prinzing, challenging him on similar grounds. They argued that judge Prinzing had shown bias in an interview on German television on the day before the trial started, because he had called the Stammheim trial a 'normalen Straffall' (normal criminal case) rather than a political matter. In a statement before the court, Ulrike Meinhof declared that this denial of the trial's political character was intended to obscure its function as 'a show trial against revolutionaries'. Without this denial, the trial could not fulfil its counter-revolutionary purpose, she added.[118]

Less than a month later, on 20 August 1975 (trial day 27), Schily pleaded for a cancellation of the trial altogether. According to him there was no longer any question of a fair trial because of the total absence of the presumption of innocence of the accused, as required by the European Convention on Human Rights. To make his point he presented a list of about 30 statements by politicians about the accused, including a comment by Federal Chancellor Helmut Schmidt in reaction to the Stockholm hostage crisis that referred to the accused as 'unscrupulously violent criminals [and] bandits'.[119] The defence argued that these statements were based on a conscious campaign by the Federal Prosecutor's Office to influence public opinion against the RAF.[120] The defence also pointed to another indication suggesting the absence of a fair trial: although the RAF leaders were far from being convicted, a high security prison ward obviously meant for them was already under construction in Bruchsal (near Karlsruhe).[121]

The biggest procedural issue, however, concerned the health of the defendants and their presence in court. In the Federal Republic criminal trials were rarely conducted in the absence of the accused, the legal maxim being that nobody should be convicted without having his or her say in court. The Code of Criminal Procedure actually obliged the accused to appear before the court. Yet, as explained earlier, the legislator had changed the Code of Criminal Procedure (paragraph 231a StPO) in reaction to the hunger strikes shortly before the Stammheim trial began. This was to enable a court case to proceed if an accused had deliberately undermined his or her fitness for trial.[122]

From June until November 1975, parties at the court in Stammheim wrestled with two questions: were the accused 'verhandlungsunfähig' (unfit to stand trial) and, if so, was this of their own doing (because of the hunger strikes). Only if the accused themselves were to blame for their lack of fitness could the court decide to continue in their absence; otherwise the only legal options were suspension or cancellation of the trial. On 11 June 1975, Marieluise Becker (Heidelberg), acting for the defence, presented the first motion to stop proceedings because of lack of fitness to stand trial, arguing that the Stammheim prison situation and earlier circumstances of detention were responsible for the poor condition of her client, Gudrun Ensslin. Becker painted a bleak picture of the periods of solitary confinement that her client had endured. Becker claimed the confinement imposed a deprivation of the senses that surpassed human tolerance levels. Referring to propaganda material used during the solidarity campaign, she argued that this sensory deprivation was a scientifically proven torture method, a counter-insurgency strategy used by imperialist states, and she demanded a hearing in court of foreign experts such as the Dutch psychiatrist Sjef Teuns (who had written on political prisoners in 1973 in a special issue of *Kursbuch*).[123] At the end of that day, in a demonstrative gesture, the lawyers of choice requested an early end to the day's proceedings due to the condition their clients were in. After judge Prinzing turned down the request the lawyers walked out of the courtroom collectively, leaving the president fuming about what he called their act of sabotage.[124]

As the law required a medical doctor to be consulted before a judge could decide whether or not an accused person was fit to stand trial, the lawyers repeatedly tried to obtain permission for medical examinations by doctors of their clients' choice (including Teuns). Initially the Second Senate, supported by the prosecutors, refused to comply and was only prepared to consult prison doctors. This led to several accusations of bias against the president and other judges. Later, in a conciliatory gesture, the judges set up a committee of three medical experts from outside the prison system to examine the accused. These doctors diagnosed a limited fitness and advised that proceedings should not exceed three hours a day to enable the accused to follow them with the measure of clarity of mind required by the law. Moreover, the experts listed possible causes of the limited fitness of the accused, explicitly mentioning the tight prison regime.[125]

On the basis of this medical advice, lawyers estimated that just hearing the evidence of the almost 1,000 witnesses would take at least eight years. On 30 September 1975, however, Prinzing announced the decision of the Second Senate to continue as before, because the prisoners themselves were responsible for their weak condition. When the president tried to explain this decision by reading aloud letters by RAF prisoners that clearly indicated their intention to render themselves incapable of standing trial by means of hunger strikes, this led to an uproar in the courtroom among defendants and counsel alike. When the president refused to stop reading, Rupert von Plottnitz (defencelawyer), shouted 'Heil, Dr. Prinzing!'[126]

Although the defendants and especially their defenders reacted with a disturbing degree of emotion, their objections to the court's decision were not wholly irrational. The judges of the Second Senate (and those of the Federal Court of Justice and the Federal Constitutional Court, which later upheld the decision)[127] did indeed stretch the 'limited fitness to stand trial' rule attested to by the medical doctors. This was done in order to be able to fulfil the 'absolute unfitness for trial' ruling that the (recently changed) Code of Criminal Procedure (paragraph 231a, StPO) considered a precondition for continuation of a trial in the absence of an accused. Tenfelde interprets this as an indication of the judges' willingness to serve political purposes and is therefore very critical of their decision.[128] In fairness, though, the judges had a point—it really would have been undesirable to extend the trial by limiting the proceedings as dramatically as the medical doctors had advised. It seems overly principled to demand that the judges accept the ultimate consequences this advice brought with it: a trial in excess of perhaps eight years. This would uphold one specific right of the defendants, but at a huge cost. Such lengthy proceedings would in turn neglect other rights of the defendants, who might then face eight years in custody without a conviction. Moreover, it would have adverse effects on the legitimacy of the trial as such, and for the rule of law in West Germany.

'Crown Witnesses': The Credibility and Legality of Bought Testimony

As we mentioned earlier, the Federal Prosecutor had not succeeded in establishing the individual guilt of the accused. Therefore it was alleged that the criminal organisation 'RAF' had performed the indicted murders and other criminal acts, creating a collective responsibility for all members of the RAF. However, this notion is absent in the German Criminal Code. Individual members of an organisation can only be convicted of certain criminal acts when it is proven that the individuals have actually committed them. The fact that RAF leaders, on 13 and 14 January 1976, taking turns, had read aloud lengthy political statements (in total 200 pages of manuscript)[129] in which they confessed to being members of an urban guerrilla movement and took 'political responsibility' for the bombings they were accused of, did not really change this. Not only did they, at the same time, explicitly deny responsibility 'in a legal sense', they also refrained from making further statements. Thus a time-consuming demonstration to show an 'Indizienkette' (chain of evidence) of their involvement was still necessary. To establish this, the prosecution at Stammheim relied heavily on witnesses whose evidence put the accused close to the scene of the bombings shortly before the bombs went off. The prosecution tried to close the remaining gap by emphasising further indications of the ultimate responsibility of the accused.[130]

In a seemingly endless row of witness hearings, the questioning of two witnesses for the prosecution stood out. Both were deeply implicated in the crimes that were central to the trial. The first of these was the metal sculptor Dierk Hoff, in whose workshop the 1972 bombs had been produced. At the end of January 1976, Hoff testified against the accused, sketching in detail his cooperation with the RAF. Initially, he told the court, he had been making metal objects for them in the belief that these would be used as props in a film by Holger Meins, a former film maker with whom he was vaguely acquainted, and a few other men who visited his shop. Later, when they admitted they were members of the RAF, he had continued his involvement because they had threatened him.[131]

The other witness was Gerhard Müller, an RAF member who had been involved in a shoot-out with the Hamburg police in October 1971 in which an officer had died. After his arrest in 1972, Müller had remained a loyal member of the RAF, keeping in close contact with the other members through his lawyer, Hans-Christian Ströbele. He had also participated in the collective hunger strikes. In the autumn of 1974, however, after numerous confrontations with police interrogators, Müller decided to split from the RAF and share his knowledge of the organisation with the authorities.[132] His evidence closed many gaps in the prosecution's case. On 8 July 1976 (trial day 124), Müller testified on the structure of the RAF, lending support to the view that it was a criminal organisation. He called Baader the head of the organisation and mentioned Meinhof, Meins, Raspe and Ensslin as its core members, separating them from ordinary and marginal members.[133]

In Stammheim the role of these two witnesses triggered enormous controversy, not only because of the suspicion raised about the fact that a witness had a criminal background. Many observers openly suggested that Hoff and Müller were in fact 'crown witnesses', whose testimony against the accused had been bought by the prosecution with promises of money and reduced sentencing for their complicity in the crimes committed by the RAF. This was more problematic because the German justice system did not have a place for crown witnesses; the suggestion of their existence therefore also implied that the Federal Prosecutor was breaking the law.[134]

The suggestion was amplified by the preceding public debate about the use of crown witnesses as a means to address the difficulties of raising evidence in terrorist cases. Since 1975, debates in political circles in Bonn had proposed introducing the legal institution of crown witnesses as part of a larger set of anti-terrorism legislation. Many legal experts, even including Chief Federal Prosecutor Siegfried Buback, however, had objected to this element as too foreign to the German justice system. As is well known, in exchange for a crown witness making statements helpful to the prosecution, some of the crimes he or she is suspected of having committed are to be immune from prosecution. Critics pointed out that such measures would collide with one of the central maxims of German law, the 'Legalitätsprinzip' (legalist principle), which holds that all crimes must be prosecuted.[135]

The persistent suspicion that the prosecution had made a deal with these witnesses was not eliminated by these objections. Witnesses on behalf of the defence, as well as the accused, had contradicted some of the remarks by the 'crown witnesses'. Andreas Baader denied having threatened Hoff to obtain his continued cooperation, arguing that the RAF never used coercion when dealing with its sympathisers.[136] And the imprisoned RAF member Brigitte Mohnhaupt contradicted Müller's statements about the organisation's authoritarian traits, declaring that the 'guerrilla' is a 'hydra, which means it has many heads.'[137]

In the end, however, the defence decided against a detailed denial of all of the statements by the alleged crown witnesses. Instead, the defence lawyers concentrated far more on undermining their credibility, especially Müller's. Not only did they try to portray him as an untrustworthy opportunist, but when they questioned Müller on 22 July 1976 (trial day 129) they also openly suggested his evidence had been bought. Although Müller denied this, the defence managed to get him to admit that his treatment in prison had improved after he broke with the RAF—though he stated that this was also caused by a change in his own behaviour.[138] The defence showed that Müller clearly had much to gain from a deal with the prosecution. They even produced an eyewitness statement by one of the imprisoned members of the RAF, Margrit Schiller, who testified that Müller had shot and killed the Hamburg police officer in 1971.[139] For the RAF's lawyers, this evidence suggested that by acting as a crown witness Müller was evading murder charges and a probable mandatory life sentence.

Federal Prosecutor Heinrich Wunder protested against the accusation that Müller had been bought or brainwashed by members of the Federal Criminal Police Office. Wunder suggested that Müller's earlier criminal behaviour did not lessen his credibility, declaring this would not be 'the first time that a Saul turns into a Paul'.[140] Some journalists, however, suggested that the prosecution had already delivered its part of the deal. Müller had been tried at the Hamburg Schwurgericht during the early stages of the Stammheim trial. He had been sentenced on 11 March 1976 to a mere ten years' imprisonment for membership of a criminal organisation, accessory to murder and some lesser crimes.[141]

Earlier, the authorities had felt it necessary to close a file detailing Müller's early statements to the police. In the autumn of 1975, the file's existence had become public, but the Federal Minister of Justice, Hans-Jochen Vogel, had closed the file citing state security. This added to the suspicions about the quality of Müller's evidence; there were speculations that he had confessed to being the Hamburg shooter and that the state was willing to refrain from prosecuting a possible murderer in exchange for testimony against the RAF. When efforts to obtain the file failed, the defence summoned Chief Federal Prosecutor Buback as a witness in order to question him about its contents. At first, Buback's superior, the Federal Minister of Justice Vogel, refused to grant the necessary permission, but the defence lawyers' efforts led to a new decision by an administrative judge ordering Buback to appear in Stammheim. On 14 October 1976 (trial day 153), Buback was questioned by lawyers Schily and Heldmann, and remarkably also by Baader and Raspe, but he revealed nothing new. He reiterated that the prosecution had not made a deal with Müller or any other witness. Although Buback was composed and answered all questions in a courteous manner, his very brief answers left a bad impression. Vogel had apparently limited his permission to testify.[142]

Just before Buback's appearance, from 5 October 1976, the prosecution had presented its final plea, which took three full days. There was little public interest and of the lawyers of choice only Hans-Heinz Heldmann was present. By now, apparently, many thought the outcome was a foregone conclusion. In Stuberger's account of the Stammheim trial, we can read that in his long career of trial reporting he had rarely heard prosecutors talk so emotionally and at times even irrationally and defamatorily about the accused. Again and again, the prosecution stressed that the three remaining RAF leaders (Ulrike Meinhof had in the meantime committed suicide) were mere ordinary criminals, devoid of political motivations. State Prosecutor Peter Zeis called the RAF's claim to political ideals 'den größten Etikettenschwindel des Jahrzehnts' (the decade's greatest labelling fraud). His colleague Klaus Holland accused the RAF of a mentality 'devoid of human traces'. Baader's behaviour was especially criticised; the prosecutors decried the stark contrast between his luxurious lifestyle and the proclaimed struggle for the underprivileged. Stuberger found it offensive that the prosecutors talked about the absent lawyers of choice, as if they too were facing trial.[143]

Journalist Gerhard Mauz's report, published in *Der Spiegel* at the time, is largely in line with Stuberger's memories, although Mauz gives more credit to the oldest prosecutor, Wunder. According to Mauz, Wunder argued sharply but matter-of-factly and thereby represented a system of justice that showed respect for the procedural and human rights of the accused. Mauz wrote that his younger colleague Zeis, however, manifested 'a scary kind of "system of justice", in which the prosecution aims at annihilation, destruction, elimination. This "system of justice" does not deal with people, but with phlegm.'[144]

Prisoners of War: The RAF *and the Geneva Conventions*

On several occasions during the trial the RAF's lawyers were seen as addressing issues that were not strictly legal. More than once, judges and prosecutors and many outside observers expressed their doubts. They suspected the RAF leaders and their lawyers of political motives and accused the defence of, as they saw it, misusing the trial as a stage for political propaganda. As we have shown, this was in fact what they intended to do. One key argument was mistrusted by observers, and was not regarded as a serious legal point. This was the plea to treat the RAF members as prisoners of war who had been fighting on German soil against the US war effort in Vietnam.

On 28 October 1975, this line of argument was expressed in court for the first time, albeit unsystematically. Judge Prinzing began this (41st) day of the trial with an explanation of how he wished the proceedings to continue, now that it was established that the accused were lacking in fitness. He announced that the accused were allowed to follow the proceedings whenever they felt able. The defence lawyers reacted furiously and, not for the first time, challenged the judge on grounds of bias. Von Plottnitz declared that the president's actions amounted to a 'declaration of war' against the accused. 'However, in war there would always be the Geneva Convention[s], whose provisions would protect the prisoners from something that is to be considered legitimate in consequence of the judge's decision: the deliberate destruction of their health. The risk of the prisoners' health deteriorating if they continue to be kept in isolation, as mentioned in the medical report, does not bother the judges; after all, they long since shifted their responsibility for the destruction of the prisoners' health on the prisoners themselves.'[145]

In the months to come, the 'prisoners of war' argument would return. On 20 January 1976 (trial day 65), Axel Azzola, a law professor from Darmstadt University who had recently joined Meinhof's defence team, brought forward a motion to halt the trial and start treating the accused as prisoners of war. Remarkably, Schily and Heldmann did not endorse this, seemingly because of legal peculiarities. This action broke with the established practice of the RAF lawyers to support each other's motions. Until this time the imprisoned members of the RAF had always demanded to be treated like ordinary prisoners, so Azzola's motion also marked a switch to a plea for special treatment.[146]

The Darmstadt professor based his motion on an intricate analysis of the conflict between the RAF and the West German state. He argued that the two sides were taking part in an international war between the forces of capitalist imperialism and the liberation movements of the third world. At the time international law still considered war to be a matter of nation-states, and excluded members of other organisations from protection as enemy combatants. However since the early 1970s, negotiations about an additional protocol to the Geneva Conventions and the law of war had moved towards including movements of national liberation and their 'soldiers'. Professor Azzola tried to persuade the Stammheim court to accept this impending extension of international law (in the end, the protocol was added to the Geneva conventions in 1977) and to recognise the RAF as a legitimate 'subject of war', being a partner organisation of one of the third world liberation movements, the National Liberation Front of Vietnam (Vietcong). As such, its members should be treated as prisoners of war (to be housed in special, internationally monitored camps) and criminal proceedings against them had to be halted.[147]On this basis, only an investigation into possible war crimes committed by the RAF, and possibly a new trial on the basis of that, still seemed feasible. Azzola also stated that the RAF had legitimately used their constitutionally guaranteed right to resist institutionalised fascism, and, apart from that, had used violence in self-defence, 'not to defend the existing order, but exactly with the aim of its abolishment'.[148]

Federal Prosecutor Wunder was unimpressed by Azzola's inventive analysis, arguing that existing law did not allow for such 'wishful thinking'. According to Wunder this was a preposterous attempt to legitimize the RAF's acts of violence. 'In our country murders are prosecuted as what they are. We live in peace and not in the state of war that the accused have imagined.' Azzola's remarks about the RAF's legitimate use of the right to resist had specifically annoyed Wunder, who called them an offence to the members of the actual resistance during the Nazi era.[149] Wunder thus refrained from an in-depth discussion of the motion. The same applied to the reaction of the court, which swiftly dismissed the motion, concluding that there was 'no legal ground to switch to a treatment of the accused as prisoners of war'.[150] Although these brief reactions may have made good sense from a legal standpoint, they did little to challenge Azzola's faulty reasoning or expose it to the public eye.[151] Azzola's detailed attempt at Stammheim to portray the RAF as Robin Hood-style freedom fighters thus remained untested.[152]

On 4 May 1976, the defence brought forward a large number of motions (among them nine by Schily alone) to summon as witnesses a range of American politicians (among them former President Richard Nixon), military and security service personnel (including former CIA Chief William Colby), various West German politicians (such as former Federal Chancellor Willy Brandt and his successor Helmut Schmidt) as well as experts in international law and other academics. According to the defence their evidence would prove that US forces had committed war crimes in Vietnam, that US military institutions on West German soil had played an important role in these actions, and that members of the Federal government and other leading West German politicians had supported or at least not prevented this. This would lead to the conclusion that the accused members of the RAF should be acquitted, because by bombing American facilities in Frankfurt and Heidelberg they had legitimately made use of the right to resist and the right of self-defence.[153]

With some ceremony, the lawyers declared that their motions at the Stammheim trial would at last introduce the issue of the Vietnam War, which they claimed to be of central importance in the prosecution of the RAF. Axel Azzola, now in full cooperation with the other defence lawyers, even called the RAF 'an answer to Vietnam'. He stated that these motions, finally, put the crucial question on the table as to 'whether the individual, who had put himself up against the murderers of Vietnam and had been prepared to wage this struggle with relatively modest means, must on the basis of existing law be seen as a member of a criminal gang'. Wunder was unmoved. He saw the Vietnam motions as merely another instance of the accused attempting 'to turn the trial against them into a stage for propagandistic self-presentations'. According to him, the motions were not really meant to serve the purpose of finding the truth and he pointed out that they did not even really refer to the allegations in the bill of indictment.[154] Two weeks later, after ample consideration, the court denied a right of resistance and self-defence in this case, and turned down the motions.[155]

6.3.2. *Theatrics: Charming the Audiences*

In the end, these attempts by the defence to derail the trial by repeatedly addressing procedural issues, except when dealing with the issue of crown witnesses, all appeared rather far-fetched and futile. Indirectly, however, the RAF leaders and their lawyers scored some points. They managed to turn the trial into a continual bickering between parties; this considerably undermined its legitimacy. Many observers lost interest in the perceived stalemate at Stammheim. This meant that the trial did not become, as the authorities had hoped, the staged reckoning with the RAF. At least as far as spectators close to the RAF were concerned, the protracted proceedings at Stammheim confirmed the political character of the trial that the defence had always alleged. Contributing to the image of a 'failed' trial were the conscious and unconscious performances of the various participants. Constantly interacting with one another, the players in this drama—including the president and the other judges, the prosecutors, the lawyers and the accused, and even some of the witnesses—modelled their behaviour to appeal to audiences inside and outside the courtroom.

Acting Their Part: An Unavoidable Clash between Judge and Accused

For a first impression of the actual events in court we can rely on Ulf Stuberger's eyewitness account from which we have already quoted several times. When this journalist sat down in the Stammheim courtroom for the first time on 21 May 1975, he could not help smiling to himself: 'I could not suppress the thought that I sat waiting for the chime to announce the beginning of the show.' And indeed, 'Suddenly, a buzzing sound could be heard, just like in a modern theatre.' Ulrike Meinhof and the other accused entered the courtroom first, followed by the Second Senate of the Stuttgart Oberlandesgericht. To Stuberger and some of his colleagues this entrance looked like a ballet performance. 'In their black robes the nine men strutted daintily to their seats', he observed.[156] The beginning of this confrontation between judges and accused and between prosecution and defence had long been anticipated by all present and by many more who followed the trial in the media. The question now was whether the actors would live up to expectations.

The accused and their lawyers, as we have made clear in our discussion of the RAF's defence strategy, had given much thought on how to perform in court. One of the RAF's lawyers, Gerd Temming, had even conceived a 'dramaturgical frame for the defence' as a basis for an internal debate on the matter.[157] From Stuberger's memoirs, however, we gather that the demeanour of the defendants at the trial and their trial strategy mostly reinforced the sceptical attitude towards the RAF with which this left-leaning journalist and probably many other more or less neutral observers had entered the courtroom. 'Baader often looked very nervous', Stuberger writes, 'constantly playing with a plastic lighter, plucking his clothes or browsing through legal papers that he had carried in. He was able to control himself for days and would then erupt in choleric outbursts, visibly sweating and blurting out vulgarities like a little child.' The RAF leader was said to have a high sex appeal, but Baader appeared rather dim-witted to Stuberger because of his constant swearing and a cynical grin that clearly annoyed the other participants in the courtroom. It was Baader's bad luck, Stuberger argues, that his looks made him the perfect example of the terrorist scarecrow. In a way, he seemed to confirm the image that the prosecutors had spread of him as the RAF's ringleader.[158]

Of the other three, neither Gudrun Ensslin nor Jan-Carl Raspe appeared in a good light. To Stuberger, Ensslin seemed 'a particularly aggressive, radical young woman, [who] erupted easily and in her way seemed to imitate Baader's behaviour'. Without hesitation, she rebuked the court, the prosecution and the substitute lawyers. Stuberger's impression was that Ensslin felt able to give orders to the other participants at the trial, totally misjudging her actual status. In contrast, Raspe appeared as 'the great taciturn'. Mocking Azzola's prisoners of war motion, Stuberger and other reporters labelled the subservient Raspe as commandant Baader's 'boot-jack'. Raspe seemed to conceal his real motives and ideas, a negative impression that was amplified (in the eyes of Stuberger) by his deep eye sockets.[159]

However, when confronted with Ulrike Meinhof, Stuberger sometimes needed to remind himself of the crimes for which she was on trial. 'From the first trial day onwards, she seemed to stand out from the other [three]', he writes, '[looking] almost well-behaved with her long pigtails'. Meinhof, herself a journalist before turning terrorist, often seemed to have the impression that the other accused RAF members ignored her, for instance when she indicated to Ensslin that it was not polite to light a cigarette in court. In contrast to Baader and Ensslin, Meinhof hardly spoke and rarely raised her voice in anger. She preferred 'fascist' or other political terms of abuse to the use of gutter language. She looked physically and mentally weaker than the other three, an impression that grew stronger by the day. This was confirmed by stories about tension and arguments between Meinhof and the other RAF members, reported to Stuberger by some of the guards. 'She seemed less and less able to follow the course of [the trial] that would determine her future', he remembers, '[and] she looked more and more absent.'[160]

That there were indeed splits within the group became apparent on 4 May 1976 (trial day 106) when, after the defenders had presented their Vietnam motions, Ensslin addressed the court (in Meinhof's absence) with a remarkable statement:

> If there is one thing about the 1972 affair that depresses us, it is our lack of correlation between head and hands. We would have liked to have been militarily more efficient. To put it simply once again: we are also responsible for the attacks on the CIA headquarters and the headquarters of the Fifth US Army Corps in Frankfurt am Main and the US headquarters in Heidelberg. In so far as we were organised into the RAF from 1970 onwards, fought in it, and were involved in the process of the conception of its policies and structure, we are certainly also responsible to the same degree for operations undertaken by commandos—for instance, against the Springer building [in Hamburg], of which we knew nothing, and disagree with in principle; which we disowned while it was in progress.[161]

Since it is generally assumed that a commando group under Meinhof's leadership was responsible for the Springer bombing, Ensslin's statement basically isolated Meinhof from the other three standing trial, and excluded her from the RAF's central command.[162] It is chilling to note that Meinhof's suicide followed only four days later, during the night of 8/9 May 1976.

To return to the performance of the accused in court, it is clear that they accepted the rules of the trial only to the extent that these enabled them to continue their political struggle from the podium of the courthouse. In this sense their behaviour was typical of the composure of others facing political trials, as analysed by Otto Kirchheimer. According to this German-American jurist and political scientist 'With the political defendant [...] reversal of the roles becomes real; whatever adjustments he is likely to make to the necessities of the situation are of a tactical and narrow nature.'[163] The right to bring forward petitions on all kinds of legal issues (under the Code of Criminal Procedure) created great opportunities for the defence to turn the trial into a platform for the RAF's political communication efforts. Or, as the RAF leaders declared, 'because the Code of Criminal Procedure allows for an explanation of these [motions], they could function as transporters of political argumentation'.[164]

This effort to politicise the trial or, from the RAF point of view, to reveal its political character, made a clash with the court almost inevitable, especially when its president, Theodor Prinzing, appeared to take keeping politics out of the courtroom as one of his most important tasks. From the beginning he displayed an extraordinary eagerness to prevent political speeches, interrupting the accused or their lawyers whenever he felt they were moving away from legal grounds towards political terrain. As a consequence, he repeatedly withdrew their permission to speak when they trespassed beyond the imaginary line in the sand that he had drawn. Prinzing used various disciplinary measures at his disposal to control the proceedings. At an early stage, the lawyers of choice walked out in protest when the court refused to have the defendants' fitness to stand trial tested by independent doctors. The presiding judge warned them that next time he would withdraw their formal court appointment. The lawyers regarded this as a threat, because the state would then no longer cover their costs and they would have to be paid by their clients, who were without means.[165] Over the following months the court would indeed decommission these lawyers, one after the other.[166]

Prinzing tried to soften his strictness with little jokes, but his ironic wit tended to backfire, causing indignation on the defence counsel's bench. Moreover, Prinzing often appeared not to be completely even-handed, thereby confirming the defence's complaint that he was basically working for the state. It left a bad impression, for instance, when he thanked Federal Prosecutor Siegfried Buback for 'his patience' after he had appeared as a witness—*Der Spiegel* clearly found this deference toward a state functionary overdone.[167]

The judge seems not to have been a very good listener. On 28 October 1975 (trial day 41), for example, he lost his patience with Ulrike Meinhof when she was struggling with words, talking in theoretical terms about the difficulties faced by an isolated prisoner. In hindsight, Meinhof's statement could be interpreted as a signal to the authorities that she was contemplating a change of attitude. At the time, though, Prinzing could not be bothered with her theorising and failed to register not only a possible hidden message behind her words, but also how far she had already drifted away from the RAF. After all, for the RAF, a member who openly hinted at leaving the organisation was dangerously close to becoming a traitor. An irritated Prinzing simply interrupted Meinhof several times, finally withdrawing her right to speak altogether.[168]

Prinzing's insensitivity to the defendants reached its nadir with his handling of the trial immediately after Ulrike Meinhof's suicide. On the following trial day the president wanted to continue in a business-as-usual way, as if nothing had happened.

The court turned down a request from the defence for an adjournment of the trial until after Meinhof's burial, even though one of the substitute lawyers, Manfred Künzel (Waiblingen), supported their plea. This decision caused uproar in the crowded public gallery on the day following Ulrike Meinhof's death. Her death had enhanced the motivation of these RAF sympathisers in the gallery to show their support, 'to show, especially today, that there is somebody there [for them]'.[169] After the protesters were led out on the president's orders, others in the room jumped up and chanted abuse: 'Prinzing "raus"', 'Prinzing murderer' and 'Suicide is a lie.' The lawyers of choice collected their files and left in protest, saying they would not return until after the funeral.[170]

Importantly, the court's refusal to allow for an adjournment may have been caused in part by the way the lawyers and defendants argued for it. For example, Hans-Heinz Heldmann, defending, not only pointed to the close ties between the four prisoners torn by Meinhof's sudden and unexpected death, but also remarked that the lawyers saw reason to doubt the official explanation of her death because Meinhof had supposedly not given the slightest hint of suicide plans.[171] Jan-Carl Raspe even went a step further and openly declared:

> We think Ulrike has been executed. We don't know how, but we know by whom. And we can work out the way it was calculated. [...] It was an execution, conceived in cold blood, in the same way as Holger [Meins] was executed.[172]

In fact, prison notes reveal that only hours after having been informed of her death, in a reflex reaction, the remaining leaders of the RAF together with their defence counsel had decided to use Meinhof's death as an opportunity to revive the RAF solidarity campaign.[173]

Et tu, Künzel? Prinzing's Final Challenge and the End of the Trial

The accused RAF leaders regularly erupted in anger against the strictness and formality of the presiding judge and were genuinely frustrated at Prinzing's interruptions, which ruined the effect of statements they had so laboriously drafted in their cells.[174] In part, however, these outbursts were consciously provoked confrontations with the president to show disdain for the court and the established order of the Federal Republic. Other commentators have already cited some of these clashes in detail, so we will only relate one illustrative discussion from the court, taking place on 19 August 1975. On trial day 26 the accused stood up and shouted abuse in an attempt to be removed from court. The ensuing violent exchange mimicked an absurdist play. At first judge Prinzing refused to expel them, then Raspe asked if they should 'make some sort of formal disturbance'. Finally the judge informed the accused that they were 'now causing disruption of the trial'. Later in the day, when the defendants were led back into the courtroom, they repeated their abusive language, calling Prinzing 'a fascist asshole', 'an old pig' and 'a dirty bastard'.[175]

The climax of animosity toward the presiding judge occurred on 28 July 1976 (trial day 131), when Klaus Jünschke, an RAF member who at that time was facing a trial in Kaiserslautern, testified on behalf of the defence. In the middle of a dispute with Prinzing, after he already had called the president 'a fascist' and had received disciplinary punishment, Jünschke suddenly stood up, ran around the witness table and cried, 'Wait, here I come.' In three quick paces he had jumped onto the judges' table and crashed onto the president, so that they fell to the floor together. Several judges, guards and policemen overpowered the enraged witness. As Jünschke shouted, 'For Ulrike, you pig!', the guards tied his hands and feet and carried him out.[176]

Within the parameters of the Code of Criminal Procedure the clearest expression of confrontation from the defence was the torrent of accusations facing Prinzing and other judges on the grounds of bias.[177] In theory, for any such challenge to succeed it was sufficient for the accused to come to a convincing rational conclusion that a certain judge was biased.[178] Within a total of 175 trial days, various lawyers brought a total of 85 challenges against Prinzing, of which only the last was successful.[179] The sheer number of challenges in the Stammheim trial raises the question whether this was a misuse of defendants' rights. This question is further justified because according to the Code of Criminal Procedure these challenges have to be dealt with immediately, making them a powerful tool for trial obstruction.[180]At Stammheim, the prosecutors and the judges did indeed accuse the lawyers of deliberately slowing down the trial with their challenges.[181] Tenfelde's legal study of the Stammheim trial argues that the lawyers, in his opinion, were simply exploiting the rights of their defendants. He criticised the judges' negativity when faced with such challenges, which they considered to be shameful and damaging to their professional honour.[182]

In Prinzing's case it was probably indeed a question of his honour that led to the success of the 85th and final challenge against him. It all began in January 1977 when Otto Schily, defence counsel for Ensslin, received explosive information that revealed Stammheim's presiding judge had been in contact with Federal Judge Albrecht Mayer, of the Third Senate of the Federal Court of Justice in Karlsruhe. This court was not only responsible for dealing with complaints about the judges at Stammheim, but would also have to consider any appeals after the court had reached a verdict. Prinzing regularly spoke to Mayer by phone and once even sent him copies of trial documents through his private mail. Mayer, in turn, forwarded these to the chief editor of the conservative newspaper *Die Welt*, apparently hoping that this might result in an article that could damage Schily.[183]

On 10 January 1977 (trial day 171), Schily challenged the presiding judge over his contact with Mayer, but the other judges of the Second Senate curtly disallowed this challenge. Substitute lawyer Manfred Künzel (Waiblingen), court-appointed counsel for Ensslin, challenged the president again, because he felt that Prinzing's contact with Mayer and Mayer's actions should be openly discussed. This motion was also rejected by the court, but Künzel had obviously hurt the president's feelings, or damaged his honour as Tenfelde suggests, since Prinzing now began to show signs of panic. On the evening of 13 January 1977, he telephoned Künzel, who was still acting as a lawyer in the case he was presiding over.[184] It was an act of desperate disillusion, remotely reminiscent of Julius Caesar's last encounter with his former pupil, the dagger-wielding senator Brutus.

To Künzel's astonishment, the president complained that his challenge had been the worst experience in the two years of the trial, because it came from such an unexpected quarter. Prinzing was hinting at their shared past, when Künzel was a junior in Prinzing's chambers. The lawyer replied that he simply desired a better explanation for Prinzing's contact with a judge of a superior court. In his opinion it was not enough to say, as the president had done, that he would not comment on private conversations, because that nourished the suspicion that such contacts had occurred. 'Put yourself in Frau Ensslin's position', Künzel explained. 'She must now be saying to herself that any future appeal is pointless, since there's been an interchange between the two courts with the aim of ensuring that no appeal against the court's judgment can succeed.' Prinzing replied that Ensslin would not care, and that it was all Schily's doing. Künzel disagreed, whereupon the president told him that he was looking at it 'in the abstract'. The conversation ended with Prinzing complaining about the stress the case put upon the court and on him especially: 'I'm almost at the end of my tether. And if I can't see it through, Herr Künzel ...'[185]

After Prinzing had hung up, Künzel told Baader's lawyer Hans-Heinz Heldmann about the telephone conversation. On 20 January 1977, Heldmann challenged the president again, and this time the Second Senate decided to uphold the challenge. 'Ultimately it does not depend on whether Dr. Prinzing is or feels himself to be biased', they declared. 'The deciding factor is whether, from the defendant's viewpoint, there may be reasonable distrust of the judge's impartiality. Such misgivings cannot be dismissed.' On the basis of this decision Prinzing was discharged from the case. His associate, Dr. Eberhard Foth, replaced him.[186]

All in all, Prinzing had clearly not been in full control of the trial. Stuberger remembers that he was often reminded of Don Quixote as the president engaged in one procedural quarrel after another, as did the man of la Mancha with Spanish windmills.[187] Nevertheless, Stuberger also reminds us that it would be too easy to put the blame for the unfortunate turn of events in the Stammheim trial solely on Prinzing. So much was at stake, and external pressures for a conviction were so demanding that no judge would have been able to preside over the trial without making mistakes.[188]

Still, Prinzing appeared to be lacking both the sovereignty and impartiality required for his role. He appeared to have taken the trial's events and challenges rather personally, missing the point that they were mainly attacks on his function. We can illustrate this by his remarks in a recent interview. The former president confessed to a certain sportsmanlike respect for his most important opponent. 'Baader was capable of cool calculation', Prinzing told the press, 'and for me he was really a highly intelligent desperado, who on account of his failed career up to that moment found a confirmation of himself in this new career as revolutionary'.[189]During the trial, it seemed that the president's pride was hurt that this respect was not returned by the accused. Time and again, the lawyers argued that it was not Prinzing presiding over the proceedings, but the Federal Prosecutor.[190] Psychologically, many of these challenges were rather testing, for instance when Baader sneered just after the president turned off his microphone, 'So maybe you're in charge of the microphones, but you're not in charge of this trial, far from that.'[191]

The constant bickering and legal nitpicking on display at the trial was nearly fatal to the public interest in it. After the first few trial days, media coverage dwindled and the press chairs were left empty. 'Most of the time, I was really lonesome and the only representative of "published opinion" in Stammheim', Stuberger remembers. The court was also less attractive to visit when the RAF leaders were absent. As one visitor concluded, 'The zoo effect is lost.' In the eyes of most observers, the trial took too long and was far too expensive. Nevertheless, Stuberger notes that the visitors' benches were often well occupied and that altogether there were about 30,000 visitors attending one or more sessions of the court.[192]

Most observers agreed that compared to Prinzing the new president was a relief. Eberhard Foth not only reprimanded the lawyers, for example, but also corrected the prosecutors if their statements were too aggressive.[193] In essence, though, Stuberger reveals that president Foth, like Prinzing, kept up the pretence that the trial was a strictly legal affair. He recalls the president's final statement, after reading out the verdict, on 28 April 1977. Foth addressed the audience and the press with a short rhetorical question: 'Some might ask: Where now is politics? There where it belongs, outside this courtroom.' Stuberger wrote that he and other journalists could barely suppress their laughter.[194]

Nevertheless, the Stammheim trial clearly had a better judge in its final stages, although on Foth's watch the going was at times also rough. For instance, in the early months of 1977 the weekly *Der Spiegel* revealed that the German secret service had installed a listening device in the private home of nuclear scientist Klaus Traube when it was discovered that he had been in contact with a left-wing terrorist. Following this revelation, a member of parliament in Bonn asked the government to prevent similar actions in future, adding, as if he knew more, 'including wiretapping in prisons'. As a consequence, on 15 March 1977 (trial day 184), defence lawyer Otto Schily demanded an interruption of the trial proceedings and invited the Federal Minister of the Interior, Werner Maihofer, to the witness stand. Schily wanted to ask him if state security services or other agencies had possibly overheard, taped and analysed conversations among the RAF prisoners, and between them and their lawyers.[195]

Senior Public Prosecutor Zeis reacted strongly, accusing Schily of capitalising on the developing scandal around Traube. However on the next trial day, 17 March 1977 (day 185), Zeis had to tone down his comments, because in the meantime the Baden-Württemberg State Ministers of the Interior and of Justice had confessed that prisoners in Stammheim had been overheard, albeit only during two small intervals.[196] Thereafter, Schily called for a suspension of the trial until further notice, because the affair had uncovered 'a systematic destruction of all constitutional guarantees'. He declared the defence did not feel able to continue to cooperate in the proceedings, 'when it may perhaps seem to offer a kind of alibi by appearing'. All of the substitute defenders, too, asked for an immediate suspension of proceedings.[197]

Zeis distanced himself from the affair, professing that his office had not been informed about the taps. After that statement, president Foth tried to continue the proceedings, but he was interrupted by Schily's announcement that the defence lawyers of choice would leave the courtroom if the trial proceeded. 'I can't stop you', Foth reacted, '[but] I think you must stay'. Schily and his colleagues gathered their files and walked out, leaving the defence of their clients to the substitute lawyers. Remarkably, Künzel also asked for a suspension of the trial, on the grounds that a lawful defence might have been rendered impossible from the moment the taps had been installed. Thereupon, the president closed the proceedings for deliberation.[198]

On 29 March 1977 (trial day 187), president Foth opened by reading a letter of assurance by State Justice Minister Traugott Bender, stating that the taps had had no connection with the Stammheim trial. After this, in what was to be their last trial appearance, the accused spoke one after the other. Baader and Raspe demanded to hear important politicians as witnesses about the wiretaps, while Ensslin announced that the prisoners had just started another hunger strike. When Raspe and Ensslin tried to make political statements, the judge interrupted them and they gave up.[199] Later in the day, several substitute defence lawyers asked for more assurances from the court with regard to an absolute ban on wiretapping. After the court had turned down all the formal requests regarding the wiretaps, Künzel sent a telegram requesting that he be decommissioned as substitute lawyer. He announced that he would no longer cooperate in the proceedings because he thought it demeaned the standards of the legal profession.[200] At that point in time, the Stammheim trial had finally turned into a 'ghost trial', as Stefan Aust calls it.[201]

The impotence of the justice system was made all the more visible by the murder in broad daylight of Chief Federal Prosecutor Siegfried Buback and two employees—the work of a RAF commando group in Karlsruhe, on 7 April 1977. This ruthless assault was the start of a string of violent attacks by the RAF in an effort to force the German government to release its imprisoned leaders. This campaign of violence has since become known as the 'German Autumn' of 1977.

On 21 April 1977 (trial day 191), in the absence of the lawyers of choice, the substitute lawyers made their final pleas, lasting between one minute and three quarters of an hour. Most defence lawyers demanded the cancellation of the trial. Thereafter, the presiding judge instructed a prison guard to ask the accused whether they wanted to use their right to make a final statement. In the presence of four witnesses all three waived this right.[202]

A day before the final trial day, on 27 April 1977, in the Park Hotel in Stuttgart, the lawyers of choice held a press conference at which Schily and Heldmann pronounced their final pleas, which they called 'Bewertung' (evaluation), in the presence of about 100 journalists.[203] On the next day, 28 April 1977 (trial day 192), judge Foth concluded the trial with the oral presentation of the verdict: life sentences for all of the accused.[204]

After this, a long process of appeals before the Federal Court of Justice was to be expected. In the aftermath of Prinzing's dismissal, a disciplinary procedure instigated by Schily had forced the replacement of Judge Mayer. Although most observers expected the higher court to uphold the life sentences, representatives of the prosecution had cautiously informed Stuberger that they were worried that certain aspects of the sentences would be revised. Journalists expected that the lawyers of choice would launch a multitude of challenges against the judges on grounds of bias. They also expected the lawyers to try to petition for a temporary release for their clients. Baader, Ensslin and Raspe had already spent almost five years in custody before a verdict was reached, which could be regarded as a breach of provisions in the European Convention on Human Rights. Legal observers thought that especially Raspe, who had no previous convictions, had a real chance of being released from prison during a second trial. The state thus seemed to have manoeuvred itself into a cul-de-sac. In the end, however, the appeals against the Stammheim verdict were never heard. The collective suicides of Baader, Ensslin and Raspe in their Stammheim prison cells during the night of 18/19 October 1977 made them irrelevant.[205]

6.4. Legacies of the Stammheim Trial

The 'Todesnacht' (night of death) at Stammheim prison not only ended the lives of RAF's triple leadership, but it also propelled the Stammheim trial definitively into the domain of collective memory, which is the topic of this final section of our article.[206] Our analysis of the legacies of the Stammheim trial will present a critical overview of how 'Stammheim' was 'remembered' in German-language academic publications on terrorism and in the West German press. A complicating factor is the fact that in public memory, 'Stammheim' as a trial was soon overshadowed by 'Stammheim' as a symbol for the battle between the state and the RAF. This broader interpretation of 'Stammheim' integrated many elements. These included the debates related to the incarceration of the accused RAF members, and their deaths in October 1977—and the accusation that the state had killed the RAF prisoners rather than that they had committed suicide. 'Stammheim' also stood for the ultimate confrontation between the West German state and the RAF, and as such was a universal code for the climate of fear, anger and state repression during the 'Deutscher Herbst' (German Autumn) of 1977. The initial intense media interest in the Stammheim trial almost completely vanished after 1977. Press articles published in 1987, ten years after the German Autumn, mentioned the trial only in passing, and concentrated mainly on the events triggered by the Hanns Martin Schleyer kidnapping.[207]

6.4.1. Dichotomies Rule: Remembering Stammheim

Media scrutiny at a very early stage after the Stammheim trial led to the expression of serious reservations. *Der Spiegel*, for instance, criticised the over-activity of state institutions during the trial, while political elites had displayed such a lack of interest in earlier trials against Nazi perpetrators.[208] After the verdict in May 1977, both the *Frankfurter Rundschau* (FR) and the *Süddeutsche Zeitung* (SZ) expressed a sense of resignation over the trial and the verdict. In their view, the judiciary had not fully uncovered the truth about the RAF's actions. These newspapers even claimed a lack of dignity on the part of the judges, who had made many 'mistakes' (SZ). The consequences were a sense of 'helplessness' (SZ) and a 'stale feeling' (FR) about a trial that had 'negative consequences for the rule of law' (*Der Spiegel*).[209]

A further consequence that left a bad taste was the introduction of anti-terrorism laws. Some of them have remained in place since their inception in the mid-1970s, including provisions against terrorist associations (tightened up after 9/11) and the restrictions of defence rights for those accused of terrorist acts. For these reasons, legal expert Uwe Wesel deems the Stammheim trial 'a catastrophe of the rule of law' in his 2006 assessment of the criminal proceedings against the RAF in the 1970s and beyond. Moreover, Wesel argued that the trial and conditions of incarcerationof the accused RAF members had violated human dignity, as well as undermined the principle of proportionality.[210] As early as May 1977, *Der Spiegel* journalist Gerhard Mauz had declared somewhat less forcefully that, at the trial, 'the effort to come a little bit closer to the rule of law had failed'. Mauz also identified an atmosphere of 'bitterness' and 'hatred' during the trial.[211]

Counter-intuitively, we will begin our analysis of the social and political effects of Stammheim by examining the few positive effects of the trial. Firstly, it seems clear that after 1977, in general, defence lawyers were motivated by the frustrating experiences of the Stammheim trial to a heightened commitment in confrontations with their counterparts in legal cases. Secondly, in a more general sense, the long view shows that civic attitudes in Germany *were* changed by the experience with the RAF. 'Stammheim' and the 1977 German Autumn marked a historical caesura, a breach with a long tradition of state-centred political culture in Germany (see our earlier historical overview). At least in some sections of West German society, scepticism towards the state and the criticism of police measures became more widespread. Moreover, the last third of the 1970s saw a growth of (new) social movements which addressed many political issues that were first raised around or during the German Autumn.[212]

Despite these positive long-term effects, Stammheim had mainly negative consequences at first. In conjunction with other terrorism trials, Stammheim strongly contributed to a process of growing political radicalisation in West Germany's left-wing milieu and to a polarisation in German politics in general.[213] The major publications about the trial, especially the books published by Aust and Bakker Schut in 1986, did not escape the pitfall of partiality. While the political direction of their criticism differs, both of the trial itself and of the actors involved,[214] each author presents a polarised narrative that uncritically copied the lack of communication between the opposing groups involved, portraying the judiciary and West German state institutions on one side, and the RAF, its lawyers and sympathisers on the other side, fighting each other relentlessly. State officials are depicted as imagining themselves deeply threatened by the activities of the so-called terrorists, while the RAF and its supporters are seen to be convinced that the state was utterly and mercilessly opposed to all left-wing radicals. No matter how accurate this picture may be, Aust's and Bakker Schut's texts help to construct and re-enact an unbridgeable gap, the entrenched lack of communication between these two opposing camps.[215]

Similar dichotomies can be found in the state's documentation (in late 1977) of the Schleyer abduction, and in edited volumes published by radical intellectuals, such as *Ein deutscher Herbst* (1978/1997) and *Der blinde Fleck* (1987).[216] Polarised interpretations also shaped the book written by journalists Oliver Tolmein and Detlef zum Winkel, *Nix gerafft* (1987), and also Tolmein's later publication, *Stammheim vergessen* (1997).[217] In October 1987, ten years after the trial, commemorative issues of the liberal newspapers *Frankfurter Rundschau* and *Süddeutsche Zeitung* were dominated by the polarised interpretations outlined above. This model of analysis can still be found in more recent publications on the RAF.[218] Interpretations claiming that the RAF's activities were an indication of insanity were part of the same problem, as this explanation denied the RAF militants any political purpose and sought to exclude them from West German society.[219]

The weekly newspaper *Die Zeit* observed early in 1986 that there were obvious 'difficulties in coping with our recent past ... the problem has been isolated, the chapter is closed, [we only have] time for the theatre and for the feature pages ...'[220] Indeed, media interpretations usually collided with harsh social realities, as the reception of Reinhard Hauff's film 'Stammheim' demonstrated. Early in 1986 a public debate about the film, scheduled for Hamburg's alternative theatre venue *Kampnagelfabrik*, was cancelled when fistfights and brawling broke out. Once again, the inability of both 'sides' to engage in dialogue was an indication that the radical left's motto still applied: 'Über Stammheim wird nicht gesprochen' (Stammheim is not open for discussion).[221]

6.4.2. Establishing the Individual Victim

A first crack in this entrenched view of the struggle came late in 1986. Gerold von Braunmühl, a German middle-ranking diplomat, was assassinated by the RAF on 10 October 1986. Following his death, von Braunmühl's brothers published an open letter to the militants who killed him in the left-wing daily *taz*.[222] In September 1987, they also released a small book entitled *Ihr habt unseren Bruder ermordet* (You have killed our brother) which included some reactions by *taz* readers and a few short articles.[223]

The von Braunmühl brothers' attempt to initiate a public dialogue with the RAF constructed a clearly recognisable third party, the individual victim,[224] located between the two opposing parties (the state and the RAF). The language of victimhood was by no means new in this field.[225] Siegfried Buback and Hanns Martin Schleyer, assassinated by RAF commando groups in 1977, had also been labelled as victims of the RAF. In the case of Gerold von Braunmühl, however, it was individuals rather than the state who claimed the right to victimhood. In this process it was not the victim's relationship to the state or to structural or social issues which served as the primary point of reference. Instead, the von Braunmühls' letter to the RAF underlined their brother's individuality, his aims and his personal life. Moreover, they stressed the suffering of his family—this was not about von Braunmühl's death as a representative of the state.

This kind of communication between victim and offender, with its strong emphasis on the suffering of human beings, is a very ambivalent process. Firstly, it has the potential to detract attention from a necessary analysis of social interactions between state and social institutions, and the terrorist(s). A focus on victims can also sustain the omnipresent tendency that many commentaries have: to individualise and personify terrorism. On the other hand, defining the victims of terrorism inevitably intervenes in the communicative process between state and society and terrorism. Consciously or not, the von Braunmühls questioned the state's monopoly to claim and define the victims of terrorism. Simultaneously, they cast doubts on the state's ability adequately to protect its citizens against terrorism or to care for the victims of terrorism. The criticism implicit in the initiative of the von Braunmühl brothers may explain the irritated reactions of some politicians and state functionaries to their intervention in the public discourse. From a criminological perspective, the state's monopoly on setting the conditions for the sentencing of offenders can also be challenged when the interests of victims dominate. Victims and their families may have completely different opinions with regard to the length and severity of offenders' sentences. A focus on the victims of terrorism can also be seen as a by-product of new penal policies that have emerged since the late 1970s, which tend to stress the rights of victims above the re-integration of offenders in society.[226]

Considering the discourse around terrorism in West Germany in the 1980s, however, it was victim-led communication that indicated a first step towards breaking down the entrenched interpretative model of them (terrorists), versus us (the state). Further efforts to move away from a polarised pattern of interpretation can be discerned in the attempts by Antje Vollmer and Christa Nickels of the Green party to communicate with (former) terrorists and discuss new exit options for them.[227] At about the same time, plans were made to establish a foundation for terrorists who wished to leave their militant way of life.[228] It took another ten years for the process of victim-focused communication to emerge strongly. The language of victimhood became much more widespread in the late 1990s, and elements of victim-based communication can be found in the films of Heinrich Breloer ('Todesspiel'—1997) and Andres Veiel ('Black Box BRD'—2001).[229]

By the late 1990s, interest had also moved beyond the 'big name' victims of the RAF. Press articles were written about the son of Schleyer's chauffeur, for example, mourning his father who was also killed in 1977, and about the shocked residents of the street where Schleyer and his escort were ambushed.[230] By 1999, former militants and some relatives of their victims began talking to each other.[231] This disruption of entrenched patterns also took place among some former RAF prisoners, creating a platform for changing self-definitions. Former militants spoke of their individually traumatising experiences, their fears and their suffering, eroding the tough fighter image step-by-step. Acceptance of this new image should not be overestimated as widespread, however.[232] Also in the late 1990s, criticism emerged that the state's tactics towards the RAF had been too hard-line and inflexible during the German Autumn.[233] Nevertheless, even as late as the end of the 1990s it remained highly controversial openly to stress the structural roots of West German left-wing terrorism by examining the interactions of the state, society and the media.[234]

In the early 2000s, two parallel and interrelated tendencies could be discerned in discussions about 1970s terrorism. One was an erosion of the established polarised interpretations, which is not to say that this view disappeared altogether. Secondly, the dominant interpretations of left-wing terrorism and the state's responses splintered into several competing narratives. A very strong current among these was the focus on victims, as demonstrated by controversy around plans for an art exhibition on the RAF at the KunstWerke art centre in Berlin in 2003. The exhibition finally opened in early 2005.[235] KunstWerke curator Klaus Biesenbach and his team's main aim was to focus on the terrorists as perpetrators, and on the pre-history of 1970s terrorism. The public debate generated in summer 2003, however, called for the role of victims to be integrated into the concept. At the same time it became obvious that the old dichotomous interpretation of the terrorists versus the state still existed.[236] Against this background, it was no surprise that the early 21st-century saw a wave of popular literature on individual victims of German left-wing terrorism, mostly written by family members of people killed by the RAF.[237] Interestingly the role of victim was only conceded to family members or friends of those killed by the RAF. It was almost unimaginable to write about dead militants as victims, or about the suffering of their families and friends.[238]

But victim-based communication was not the only way of recalling the history of terrorism. Interpretations of certain other aspects of terrorism also began to appear.[239] These published individual accounts still did not focus on the Stammheim trial, but they did comment on related aspects, such as the conditions of imprisonment of RAF members.[240] The old polarised codes dominated biographies about former militants, which appeared from the late 1990s. The same was true for other authors like Butz Peters (who published several popular books on the RAF), although he at least tried to demystify the RAF.

Still, by the early 2000s the dualistic 'them versus us' was less prevalent in the discourse about terrorism. In recent years several narratives have coexisted. As early as 2002, Christopher Roth's film 'Baader' had depoliticised the leading RAF figure, focusing on Andreas Baader's ambivalent personality as other pop cultural interpretations of the Baader–Meinhof Group had in the meantime emerged.[241] This trend becomes even more evident in a series of articles published in the *Frankfurter Allgemeine Zeitung* in 2007, dealing with the experiences of the traumatised passengers and crew of the Lufthansa jet that had been hijacked during the German Autumn (by a Palestinian terrorist group supporting the RAF). In the same year the *Süddeutsche Zeitung* suggested that West German terrorism had contributed to a 'democratisation of society' (*Demokratisierung der Gesellschaft*).[242]

As Thomas Steinfeld pointed out in the *Süddeutsche Zeitung* in April 2007, relatives of the victims of terrorist attacks now played a much more important role in public debates about West German terrorism. Almost no trace of the original political motives of the terrorists can be found in these discourses. As Steinfeld put it, 'in the near future everything that was political about terrorism will fragment into individual fates.'[243] The discourse about 1970s left-wing terrorism was no longer dominated by a polarised political controversy.

There is no easy explanation of why this occurred. Some may relate this change to the end of the Cold War as the black-and-white images of the Cold War enemy dissolved; or to German unification in 1989/1990, as the Federal Republic of Germany developed more self-awareness in its dealings with domestic political opponents. The situation had altered since the 1970s, when at the end of the decade political commentator Alfred Grosser could still detect a lack of self-assurance in West Germany, which 'had not sufficiently realized how stable her state was [and] how stable the foundations of [the] ideological consensus underpinning this state really were'.[244] By 2002, the *Süddeutsche Zeitung* could declare that the West German state had become 'more stable and self-confident than ever before'.[245]

A closer look, however, reveals far more complex and contradictory patterns. First, the perception of the West German state had been changing from the early to mid-1980s, as the importance of the state in people's lives became less central. State services (like unemployment payments) began to be seen as comparable to goods and services offered by the marketplace. As contemporary observers, whose statements also echoed the demise of the welfare state, claimed, citizens used these state payments for individual purposes only. They did not care about articulating feelings of moral obligation or gratitude towards the welfare state.

The public debates about globalisation and its practical consequences may have contributed to assumptions that state power was waning.[246] Remarkably, the latest films and press series mainly focus on the question of how far the state had intercepted the communications between the imprisoned RAF members in Stammheim until their deaths in October 1977.[247] Second, the demise of the radical left at the end of the Cold War made it less problematic for state and police institutions in West Germany to make concessions to the RAF. Third, as the individualisation of society placed more value on individual suffering, the discourse shifted to individual victims of terrorism.[248] Fourth, the scale of the attacks in the United States on 11 September 2001 served to put the RAF into perspective as a terrorist organisation, which led to a more balanced interpretation of its political threats.[249] Three other important developments should be taken into consideration in explaining the changing discourse on 1970s terrorism: the initiative to bring about a 'reconciliation' with RAF prisoners by the liberal Minister of Justice Klaus Kinkel in early 1992,[250] the cease fire declared by the RAF on 10 April 1992, and the RAF's self-dissolution in April 1998.[251]

All in all, the double process of the erosion of the entrenched lack of communication with (1) its hermetic binary political code and (2) the splintering of the memories of 1970s West German left-wing terrorism had unquestionably begun in the last third of the 1980s and saw its breakthrough in the early 21st-century. At that time, remembering 1970s terrorism was mainly structured by victim-based communication and by individualised, often non-political narratives. Even the temporal resurfacing of old dichotomous 'frontline' arguments, such as in the debates about the Berlin RAF exhibition, could not conceal that there was no more space for the highly polarised atmosphere of the 1970s/1980s. As memories finally splintered and the hermetic master narrative became depolarised and depoliticised, Germany's left-wing terrorism of the 1970s had become part of history.

6.5. Conclusion

We have examined the Stammheim trial from the perspective of communication and performance, focusing on the way that different actors (defendants and their lawyers, prosecutors, judges, the media and bystanders) manipulated their behaviour and statements with the aim of mobilising public and political support for their interpretations of politics and justice in post-war Germany. The trial resembled a staged drama, with the players often losing sight of legal issues while leading commentators classified the trial as a 'Justizalbtraum' (justice nightmare).[252] The trial also displayed the enduring negative results a terrorist trial can produce. Partly because of the extraordinary theatricality of the proceedings at Stammheim, we believe the public memory of the trial remained highly politicised and polarised, in a sense reproducing the lack of communication between the parties that was so manifest at the trial itself.

The Stammheim trial turned into a bizarre game of shadow boxing over its purported political character. Even in the lengthy pre-trial phase, it became clear that the question whether this was 'an absolutely normal trial against criminals' as the authorities maintained, or a 'political show trial' as the RAF would have it, would become a major issue. In essence, the RAF leadership saw their performance at Stammheim as a continuation of their guerrilla warfare against the state, meant to undermine its legitimacy by subverting court trial procedures whenever this promised to be to their advantage. The credibility of this RAF strategy was reinforced by the inconsistent pre-trial policies of the government. The Federal Prosecutor's Office itself inadvertently reintroduced a political element into the prosecution of the RAF, building the indictment on the notion that the RAF be regarded as a criminal association, thus creating a collective responsibility for its acts. Numerous other factors, such as the choice of the Stuttgart Oberlandesgericht for the trial and the extreme security arrangements in and around the purpose-built courthouse, the many changes in the criminal code procedure, the appointment of the court president and the use of de facto 'crown witnesses' all created the impression that the state regarded the RAF as political adversaries, in spite of its own rhetoric that they were criminals. These inconsistencies were rooted in the desire of the authorities to achieve more with the Stammheim trial than merely bringing the RAF leadership to justice. We believe the intention was to create the preconditions for a public reckoning with RAF terrorism in particular, and with German left-wing radicalism in general.

By addressing these inconsistencies and legal anomalies at the trial the RAF defenders seem at first glance to have effectively shifted the burden of self-justification away from the RAF, and onto the state representatives (and especially to Stammheim's presiding judge, Theodor Prinzing). The fierce attacks against Prinzing undermined the authority and legitimacy of the court. Both contemporary press reports and historical accounts of Stammheim reflect a high degree of criticism about Prinzing's handling of the trial, and show some understanding for the arguments brought forward by the defence. However one could also argue that the RAF missed a chance to use the trial as a stage to spread its message of dissent, because the protracted wrangling over procedural issues meant that both media and public attention for the trial quickly faded away in the first months. As a result, there was hardly any opportunity for the RAF to directly communicate their radical ideas; they managed only to accuse the state of a miscarriage of justice.

Summing up, we offer some final conclusions regarding the effectiveness of the performance of the different players at Stammheim. Firstly, the aim of the authorities to stage a public reckoning with the RAF leadership largely failed, due to the inconsistencies in their own trial strategy. The problem was twofold: the blatantly unrealistic denial of the RAF's political clout by politicians and state officials lacked credibility from the start, and the special arrangements around the Stammheim trial (location and construction of the court, security, the appointment of officials) indicated that the authorities clearly felt this was a highly political case, in spite of their statements to the contrary. The state thus performed rather poorly, largely because it did not want to discuss the 'political' elephant in the room. The attitude and demeanour of judge Prinzing and many of his peers contributed further to this problem. Their approach resembles a viewer who observes only the puppets at a Wayang theatre, and neglects the shadows that are the crux of this Indonesian art form.

To the state participants, this attitude made perfect sense. It matched the post-war West German tradition of a militant democracy that banned the fundamentally radical opposition forces from the competitive forum of official politics.[253] Or, as Ralf Dahrendorf argues in his seminal article on the social structure of German politics:

> Wherever opposing interests meet in German society, there is a tendency to seek authoritative and substantive rather than tentative and formal solutions. Many institutions of German society have been and still are set up in such a way as to imply that somebody or some group of people is 'the most objective authority in the world', and is therefore capable of finding ultimate solutions for all issues and conflict.[254]

This tendency has fostered a very specific political attitude among West German elites from the 1950s until the 1980s. They have neglected or shown blatant disinterest in extreme political viewpoints, because in their daily lives it has been unnecessary to take these into account (as one does not even come across these voices). At Stammheim, neither the prosecutors nor the judges conceded a semblance of curiosity about the political or other motives that led the accused to their deeds. Yet the urge to discover these motives might reasonably be considered an essential part of establishing the truth (*Wahrheitsfindung*) that the elites themselves would claim to be central to criminal trials. Instead of making an effort to communicate with the defence, prosecutors and judges seemed merely interested in communication with each other, over the heads of the defendants. In our view, this lack of curiosity at Stammheim shown by the prosecutors and judges betrays an underlying insecurity or anxiety on the part of those elites.

For reasons discussed above, the RAF's performance, measured against its aim to use the trial as a platform for its own propaganda, was also poor. The efforts of the leaders of the RAF to enforce their interpretations of reality upon audiences within and outside the courtroom failed. A clear parallel can be discerned here with their campaigns of violence, which never resulted in tangible gains, but occasionally succeeded in scratching the reputation and legitimacy of West German democracy. Ultimately, the RAF was never able to match the achievements and power of its counterparts at the trial, the judges and prosecutors who represented the state.

One of the most striking features of the Stammheim case (and its legacy), finally, was the lack of genuine communication within the court, and within German society as a whole. As an instrument to restore social peace and renegotiate norms and values, the trial was clearly a failure. Rather, our overview of the collective memory of 'Stammheim' suggests that the trial contributed to a continuation of the 'entrenched speechlessness' that had been characteristic of the German government's dealings with contestant militants from the start. In the late 1970s some of these dichotomies between the state and the militants were re-articulated (a menacing fascist state had been replaced by a menacing security state). However, as we have elsewhere stated,[255] the codes for remembering Stammheim both in a narrow sense (focused on the trial) as well as in a broader sense (taking Stammheim as a summary symbol of the battle between the state and the RAF) remained fairly stable until the late 1980s. It seemed unlikely that there was a way out of this interpretative spiral.

The semantics of (the symbolic) 'Stammheim' and of the 1970s terrorist–state confrontation was structured by a highly politicised dualistic master narrative until the late 1990s. As we have explained, two developments played a crucial role in breaching the stasis in the communication between 'them' (terrorists) and 'us' (state and society). The individual victims intervened in this polarised field, and at the same time the collective memory of 1970s terrorism splintered into a variety of co-existing narratives.

In hindsight it seems clear that the early 2000s presented an analytical and methodological turning point. For the first time, historians began writing about the history of the RAF and integrating that story into the general history of the German Federal Republic and its society. This enabled memories and narratives to coexist within a broader framework and time span, and to be re-interpreted against established patterns. We see the present analysis as a contribution to this innovative socio-cultural and historical research agenda.

6.6. Table of actors at the Stammheim trial

Categories	Subcategories	Names and age*	Limitation	Specifics
Suspects**		Andreas Baader (32)		
		Gudrun Ensslin (34)		
		Ulrike Meinhof (40)	Until 9 May 1976	Died in prison
		Jan Carl Raspe (30)		
Court of Judges (Second Senate of the Stuttgart Oberlandesgericht)	*President*	Theodor Prinzing (49)	Until 20 January 1977	Forced to quit by the defence
		Eberhard Foth	From 20 January 1977	
	Other members	Eberhard Foth	*See President*	
		Hubert Maier		
		Kurt Bruecker		
		Ulrich Berroth		
		Otto Vötsch	From 20 January 1977	
	Substitute members (present at the trial no vote in the court)	Otto Vötsch	*See Other members*	
		Heinz Nerlich		
		Werner Meinhold		
		Hans-Jürgen Freuer		

* At the start of trial, if available.

** Originally, Holger Meins was also indicted, but he died on 9 November 1974 after a hunger strike, before the trial started.

Categories	Subcategories	Names and age	Limitation	Specifics
Prosecutors (representing the Federal Prosecutor's Office)	*Chief Prosecutor*	Heinrich Wunder (51)		
	Other team members	Peter Zeis, Oberstaatsanwalt		
		Werner Widera, Regierungsdirektor		
		Klaus Holland, Staatsanwalt		
	Chief Federal Prosecutor	Ludwig Martin	Until 30 April 1974	Only pre-trial phase
		Siegfried Buback	30 April 1974–7 April 1977	Killed by RAF commando
		Kurt Rebmann	From 1 July 1977	
Law	*Lawyers of choice active at the Trial**	Hans-Heinz Heldmann (Darmstadt)	From 11 June 1975	Representing Baader
		Otto Schily (West Berlin)		Representing Ensslin
		Marieluise Becker (Heidelberg)		
		Helmut Riedel (Frankfurt/Main)		Representing Meinhof
		Axel Azzola (Darmstadt)	Late 1975	
		Rupert von Plottnitz (Frankfurt/Main)		Representing Raspe

* There were also other lawyers but they appeared not to have been active at the trial. At the beginning of the trial these were Franz Josef Degenhart (Hamburg), representing Ensslin, Jürgen Lauschner (Heidelberg), representing Raspe, and Rainer Köncke (Hamburg) and Dieter Hoffmann (West Berlin), both representing Meinhof. Apart from that several lawyers and law students worked for the defence team, some of them accredited to the court.

Categories	Subcategories	Names and age	Limitation	Specifics
	Pre-trial evicted lawyers of choice	Klaus Croissant (Stuttgart)	Evicted 22 April 1975	Representing Baader
		Kurt Groenewold (Hamburg)	Evicted 2 May 1975	
		Hans-Christian Ströbele (West Berlin)	Evicted 13 May 1975	
	Substitute Lawyers	Schnabel (Ditzingen)		Representing Baader
		Eberhard Schwarz (Stuttgart)		
		Eggler (Karlsruhe)		Representing Ensslin
		Manfred Künzel (Waiblingen)		
		Karl-Heinz Linke (?)	Until 11 May 1976	Representing Meinhof
		Dieter König(?)	Until 11 May 1976	
		Peter Grigat (Stuttgart)		Representing Raspe
		Stefan Schlägel (Esslingen)		
Witnesses	*'Crown witnesses'*	Dierk Hoff		
		Gerhard Müller		
	Defence witnesses appearing at the trial	Several imprisoned RAF members, the journalist Ulf Stuberger, etc., Siegfried Buback, Generalbundesanwalt		

Categories	Subcategories	Names and age	Limitation	Specifics
	Defence witnesses turned down by the court	Nixon, Brandt etc.		
Media	*Prominent journalists*	Gerhard Mauz		*Der Spiegel*
		Hans Schueler		*Die Zeit*
		Karl-Heinz Krumm		*Frankfurter Rundschau* (FR)
		Renate Faerber		*Frankfurter Rundschau* (FR)
		Hanno Kühnert		*Süddeutsche Zeitung* (SZ)
		Jürgen Busche		*Frankfurter Allgemeine Zeitung* (FAZ)
		Werner Birkenmaier		*Stuttgarter Zeitung*
		Rudolf Gerhard		Algemeine Rundfunk Deutschland (ARD), ex-FAZ
		Ulf G. Stuberger		Reuters, writer of memoirs
Audiences	RAF *sympathisers* *Members of the general public* *Outside protesters*			

Notes

1 Ulf G. Stuberger, *Die Tage von Stammheim. Als Augenzeuge beim RAF-Prozess* (München: F.A. Herbig Verlagsbuchhandlung, 2007), pp. 85, 180 and 183.

2 Nicolas Büchse, 'Von Staatsbürgern und Protestbürgern—Der Deutsche Herbst und die Veränderung der politischen Kultur in Deutschland', in: Habbo Knoch (ed.), *Bürgersinn und Weltgefühl. Politische Moral und solidarischer Protest in den sechziger und siebziger Jahren* (Göttingen: Wallstein Verlag, 2007), pp. 311–332; Cf. Jacco Pekelder, 'Towards Another Concept of the State: Historiography of the 1970s in the USA and Western Europe', in: Cordia Baumann, Sebastian Gehrig, and Nicolas Büchse (eds), *Linksalternative Milieus und Neue Soziale Bewegungen in den 1970er Jahren* (Heidelberg: Winter, 2011), pp. 61–83.

3 A good start for a discussion of the term 'terrorism' is: Rudolf Walther, 'Terror, Terrorismus', in: Otto Brunner, Werner Conze and Reinhart Koselleck (eds), *Geschichtliche Grundbegriffe. Historisches Lexikon zur politisch-sozialen Sprache in Deutschland, Studienausgabe*, 6 (Stuttgart: Klett-Cotta, 2004), pp. 323–444.

4 Alex P. Schmid and Janny de Graaf, *Violence as Communication. Insurgent Terrorism and the Western News Media* (London: Sage, 1982), pp. 1 and 15.

5 Philip Jenkins, *Images of Terror. What We Can and Can't Know about Terrorism* (Hawthorne, N.Y.: Aldine de Gruyter, 2003), p. ix.

6 Klaus Weinhauer, 'Terrorismus in der Bundesrepublik der Siebzigerjahre. Aspekte einer Sozial- und Kulturgeschichte der Inneren Sicherheit', *Archiv für Sozialgeschichte*, 44 (2004), pp. 219–242, is programmatic in this respect.

7 See for the RAF and the media: Martin Steinseifer, 'Zwischen Bombenterror und Baader-Story. Terrorismus als Medienereignis', in: Martin Klimke and Joachim Scharloth (eds), *1968: Handbuch zur Kultur- und Mediengeschichte der Studentenbewegung* (Stuttgart: J.B. Metzler, 2007), pp. 289–301; and Sonja Glaab, 'Die RAF und die Medien in den 1970er Jahren', in: Sonja Glaab (ed.), *Medien und Terrorismus. Auf den Spuren einer symbiotischen Beziehung* (Berlin: Berliner Wissenschaftsverlag, 2007), pp. 31–50.

8 Some of the researchers involved legitimise the change of perspective by referring to modern sociological studies about violence that are based on a triadic approach to violent confrontation: they do not just concern themselves with the confrontations of perpetrators and victims, but also with the role bystanders or onlookers play. See for instance: Trutz von Trotha (ed.), *Soziologie der Gewalt* (Opladen: Westdeutscher Verlag, 1997); and Wilhelm Heitmeyer and Hans-Georg Soeffner (eds), *Gewalt. Entwicklungen, Strukturen, Analyseprobleme* (Frankfurt/Main: Suhrkamp, 2004).

9 On historical aspects of performativity in general see: Jürgen Martschukat and Steffen Patzold (eds), *Geschichtswissenschaft und 'performative turn'. Ritual, Inszenierung und Perfor-*

manz vom Mittelalter bis zur Neuzeit (Cologne: Böhlau, 2003). The performative perspective in terrorism research is highlighted by Beatrice de Graaf, *Evaluating Counterterrorism Performance. A Comparative Study* (Abingdon: Routledge, 2011).

10 Jacco Pekelder, 'Dynamiken des Terrorismus in Deutschland und den Niederlanden', *Geschichte und Gesellschaft*, 35 (2009), pp. 402–428: here pp. 402–403.

11 See the remarks on the performative perspective in the Introduction to this volume.

12 See: Ulf G. Stuberger (ed.), *'In der Strafsache gegen Andreas Baader, Ulrike Meinhof, Jan-Carl Raspe, Gudrun Ensslin wegen Mordes u.a.'* Dokumente aus dem Prozeß (Frankfurt/Main: Syndikat Autoren- und Verlagsgesellschaft, 1977); RAF/BRD, *texte: der* RAF (Lund: Verlag Bo Cavefors, 1977).

13 Oliver Tolmein and Detlef zum Winkel, *Nix gerafft. 10 Jahre Deutscher Herbst und der Konservatismus der Linken* (Hamburg: Konkret Literatur Verlag, 1987); Michael Sontheimer and Otto Kallscheuer (eds), *Einschüsse. Besichtigung eines Frontverlaufs zehn Jahre nach dem Deutschen Herbst* (Berlin: Rotbuch Verlag 1987).

14 Stuberger, *Die Tage von Stammheim*; Christopher R. Tenfelde, *Die Rote Armee Fraktion und die Strafjustiz. Anti-Terror-Gesetze und ihre Umsetzung am Beispiel des Stammheim-Prozesses* (Osnabrück: Julius Jonscher Verlag, 2009).

15 Hellmut Brunn and Thomas Kirn, *Rechtsanwälte, Linksanwälte. 1971–1981—das Rote Jahrzehnt vor Gericht* (Frankfurt/Main: Eichborn, 2004); Peter O. Chotjewitz, *Mein Freund Klaus. Roman* (Berlin: Verbrecher Verlag, 2007); Martin Block and Birgit Schulz, *Die Anwälte. Eine deutsche Geschichte* (Cologne: Fackelträger-Verlag, 2010); Stefan Reinecke, *Otto Schily. Vom* RAF*-Anwalt zum Innenminister* (Hamburg: Hoffmann und Campe, 2003).

16 Recent overviews of the historiography of German left-wing terrorism include: Klaus Weinhauer, 'Einleitung: Die Herausforderung des 'Linksterrorismus'', in: Klaus Weinhauer, Jörg Requate, and Heinz-Gerhard Haupt (eds), *Terrorismus in der Bundesrepublik. Medien, Staat und Subkulturen in den 1970er Jahren* (Frankfurt/Main: Campus, 2006), pp. 9–32; Jacco Pekelder, 'Historisering van de RAF. Geschiedschrijving over dertig jaar links Duits terrorisme, 1968–1998', *Tijdschrift voor Geschiedenis*, 119:2 (2006), pp. 196–217; Wolfgang Kraushaar, 'Einleitung. Zur Topologie des Terrorismus', in: Wolfgang Kraushaar (ed.), *Die* RAF *und der linke Terrorismus* (Hamburg: Hamburger Edition, 2006), pp. 13–61. Recently Gisela Diewald-Kerkmann presented a very short historical overview of the Stammheim trial: 'Der Stammheim-Prozess. Vorgeschichte, Verlauf und Wirkung', in: Johannes Hürter and Gian Enrico Rusconi (eds), *Die bleiernen Jahre. Staat und Terrorismus in der Bundesrepublik Deutschland und Italien 1969–1982* (Munich: R. Oldenbourg Verlag, 2010), pp. 53–62.

17 In Germany Peter Waldman's study *Terrorismus. Provokation der Macht* (Munich: Gerling Alademie Verlag, 1998) was very influential.

18 See as a historical study on the media reports on West German left-wing terrorism: Hanno Balz, *Von Terroristen, Sympathisanten und dem starken Staat. Die öffentliche Debatte Über die RAF in den 70er Jahren* (Frankfurt/New York: Campus, 2008); see also: Andreas Elter, *Propaganda der Tat. Die RAF und die Medien* (Frankfurt/Main: Suhrkamp, 2008).

19 Cf. Klaus Weinhauer, *Terrorismus in der Bundesrepublik. Medien, Staat und Subkulturen in den 1970er Jahren* (Frankfurt am Main: Campus Verlag, 2006).

20 In German: 'ein zu Beton erstarrtes Symbol unbeugsamer Staatsräson'. 'Grundgebot der Versöhnung', *Der Spiegel* (20 April 1992).

21 Quoted in: Pieter H. Bakker Schut, *Stammheim. Der Prozeß gegen die Rote Armee Fraktion* (Kiel: Neuer Malik Verlag, 1986), p. 274.

22 Stuberger, *In der Strafsache*, p. 242.

23 See, for instance, the annual reports on state security published by the Federal Ministry of the Interior: Bundesministerium des Innern (ed.), *betrifft: Verfassungsschutz* (Bonn: Der Bundesminister des Innern, Referat Öffentlichkeitsarbeit, 1970). In the issues from 1971, 1972 and 1973 the RAF was explicitly called 'Baader/Meinhof-Bande'; Cf. N.N., *Der Baader-Meinhof-Report. Dokumente—Analysen—Zusammenhänge. Aus den Akten des Bundeskriminalamtes, der 'Sonderkommission, Bonn' und dem Bundesamt für Verfassungsschutz* (Mainz: Hase & Koehler Verlag, 1972).

24 Quoted in: Bakker Schut, *Stammheim*, p. 44.

25 StGB: Strafgesetzbuch (German Criminal Code).

26 Bundesanwaltschaft is the commonly used unofficial name. Actually the institution is called 'Der Generalbundesanwalt beim Bundesgerichtshof' (the Chief Federal Prosecutor at the Federal Court of Justice). The fact that this name applies both to the institution and its leader creates some semantic confusion, even for Germans, especially when the acting Chief Federal Prosecutor is female (since 2006 this is 'die' Generalbundesanwältin Monika Harms, while the institution remains 'der' Generalbundesanwalt).

27 Tenfelde, *Die Rote Armee Fraktion und die Strafjustiz*, p. 94.

28 Tenfelde, *Die Rote Armee Fraktion und die Strafjustiz*, pp. 19 and 87–89.

29 Karsten Felske, *Kriminelle und terroristische Vereinigungen—§§ 129, 129a StGB. Reformdiskussion und Gesetzgebung seit dem 19. Jahrhundert* (Baden-Baden: Nomos Verlagsgesellschaft, 2002).

30 Tenfelde, *Die Rote Armee Fraktion und die Strafjustiz*, p. 94.

31 Stuberger, *Die Tage von Stammheim*, pp. 267–268.

32 At the time, newspapers reported that the Federal Prosecutor's Office and the Minister of Justice of Baden-Württemberg, Traugott Bender, were not convinced that the ruling president of the Second Senate of the Oberlandesgericht that dealt with state security issues was up to the task of successfully leading the impending RAF trial. They were thought to have conceived of a plan to promote this judge to the presidency of the

First Senate (after clearing this post by appointing his predecessor to a high ranking administrative job) and thereafter nominate their own candidate, Prinzing, to the Second Senate. Tenfelde, *Die Rote Armee Fraktion und die Strafjustiz*, pp. 102–106.

33 Tenfelde, *Die Rote Armee Fraktion und die Strafjustiz*, pp. 102–103.

34 Stefan Aust, *Der Baader-Meinhof-Komplex. Neuausgabe.* (Hamburg: Hoffmann und Campe, 2008), p. 467. [Translation from: Stefan Aust, *Baader-Meinhof. The inside story of the* R.A.F. (Oxford: Oxford University Press, 2009), p. 231.]

35 Stuberger, *Die Tage von Stammheim*, pp. 267–269.

36 Ibid., pp. 53, 267 and 269.

37 Ibid., pp. 52–53 and 66.

38 Ibid., pp. 53–54, 61 and 65.

39 Stories about excessive behaviour by security officials, who forced an English reporter to tear the bandages off his injured leg and a woman to take her sanitary towel out of her underwear during searches, helped confirm this impression. Stuberger, *Die Tage von Stammheim*, p. 62.

40 Aust, *Der Baader-Meinhof-Komplex*, p. 469.

41 Stuberger, *Die Tage von Stammheim*, p. 54; Bakker Schut, *Stammheim*, pp. 184–188; Aust, *Der Baader-Meinhof-Komplex*, p. 476.

42 Stuberger, *Die Tage von Stammheim*, p. 120.

43 Cf. Sandra Kraft, *Vom Hörsaal auf die Anklagebank. Die 68er und das Establishment in Deutschland und den* USA (Frankfurt/Main: Campus, 2010).

44 Klaus Eschen, 'Das Sozialistische Anwaltskollektiv', in: Kraushaar (ed.), *Die* RAF *und der linke Terrorismus*, pp. 957–972.

45 See: Brunn and Kirn, *Rechtsanwälte, Linksanwälte.*

46 Stefan Reinecke, 'Die linken Anwälte. Eine Typologie', in: Kraushaar (ed.), *Die* RAF *und der linke Terrorismus*, pp. 948–956, here: p. 949.

47 Otto Schily and Christian Ströbele, *Plädoyers einer politischen Verteidigung. Reden und Mitschriften aus dem Mahler-Prozeß, Rote Hilfe, Internationale Marxistische Diskussion Arbeitspapiere*, 11 (Berlin: Merve Verlag, 1973).

48 N.N., *Ausschluß der Verteidiger—wie und warum? Dokumente und Analysen zur politischen Strafjustiz seit 1945, Internationale Marxistische Diskussion, Arbeitspapiere*, 17 (Berlin: Merve Verlag, 1975), p. 75.

49 Reinecke, 'Die linken Anwälte', pp. 950–953.

50 Tenfelde, *Die Rote Armee Fraktion und die Strafjustiz*, pp. 74–75.

51 In German: 'das Erste Gesetz zur Reform des Strafverfahrensgesetz vom 9.12.1974' (1. StVRG) and 'das Gesetz zur Änderung des Ersten Gesetz zur Reform des Strafverfahrensgesetz vom 20.12.1974' (1. StVRGErgG).

52 StPO: Strafprozessordnung (German Code of Criminal Procedure).

53 Tenfelde, *Die Rote Armee Fraktion und die Strafjustiz*, pp. 72–73.

54 Ibidim.

55 In German: 'das Terrorismusbekämpfungsgesetz vom 18.8.1976' (this is the official, abbreviated law title).

56 Changes in the Criminal Code, including the introduction of the 'terroristische Vereinigung' (terrorist association) (§ 129a StGB), were obviously not relevant for the Stammheim trial (*nulla poena sine lege*). Tenfelde, *Die Rote Armee Fraktion und die Strafjustiz*, p. 73.

57 The term is mentioned in several publications such as: Frits Rüter, 'Lex Baader Meinhof?', *Delikt en Delinkwent* (June 1975), and 'A la Klettermaxe', *Der Spiegel* (9 June 1975).

58 Tenfelde, *Die Rote Armee Fraktion und die Strafjustiz*, p. 77; Uwe Berlit and Horst Dreier, 'Die legislative Auseinandersetzung mit dem Terrorismus', in: Fritz Sack and Heinz Steinert (eds), *Protest und Reaktion. Analysen zum Terrorismus, Band 4/2* (Opladen: Westdeutscher Verlag, 1984), pp. 227–318. Here: p. 229.

59 Tenfelde, *Die Rote Armee Fraktion und die Strafjustiz*, pp. 74–75; Stuberger, *Die Tage von Stammheim*, pp. 11 and 13.

60 Stuberger, *Die Tage von Stammheim*, p. 85. According to Stuberger, their participation at Stammheim would in the end set the state back about 100,000 D-Mark per lawyer.

61 Tenfelde, *Die Rote Armee Fraktion und die Strafjustiz*, pp. 146–149.

62 Stuberger, *Die Tage von Stammheim*, pp. 13 and 19.

63 Stuberger, *In der Strafsache*, pp. 13, 19.

64 After his arrest, Haag had successfully appealed with the Bundesgerichtshof (Federal Court of Justice), which ordered his immediate release. Butz Peters, *Tödlicher Irrtum. Die Geschichte der RAF* (Berlin: Argon Verlag, 2004), pp. 371–372.

65 Wolfgang Kraushaar, *1968 als Mythos, Chiffre und Zäsur* (Hamburg: Hamburger Edition, 2000), pp. 163–171; Jeremy Varon, *Bringing the War Home. The Weather Underground, the Red Army Faction, and Revolutionary Violence in the Sixties and Seventies* (Berkeley: University of California Press, 2004), pp. 196–253; Sebastian Scheerer, ''Folter ist kein revolutionärer Kampfbegriff' Zur Geschichte des Foltervorwurfs in der Bundesrepublik Deutschland'; in: Jan Philipp Reemtsma (ed.), *Folter. Zur Analyse eines Herrschaftsmittels* (Hamburg: Junius Verlag, 1991), pp. 209–237; Martin Jander, 'Isolation. Zu den Haftbedingungen der RAF-Gefangenen', in: Kraushaar (ed.), *Die RAF und der linke Terrorismus*, pp. 973–993.

66 This took place in the prison of Cologne-Ossendorf, where Astrid Proll spent a total of 119 days in solitary confinement from late 1971. Ulrike Meinhof was held there in similar circumstances for 237 days in a row, from 16 June 1972 to 9 February 1973, and during two

shorter intervals: two weeks in December 1973 and between 5 February and 20 April 1974. During that last period Gudrun Ensslin was also held in isolation in the same prison. Scheerer, 'Folter ist kein revolutionärer Kampfbegriff', pp. 215 and 218.

67 Some authorities might have been aware of this adverse public relations effect of forced feeding, but they nevertheless stuck to the policy. According to the Social Democrat Federal Minister of Justice Hans-Jochen Vogel, there was no legal way around the obligation to do everything to keep the prisoners alive, if necessary against their will. The state was obliged by law to take care of people in its custody and was bound by constitutional provisions to safeguard their lives and corporeal integrity. Appeals by members of the Christian Democrat opposition to stop forced feeding, because of the financial burden caused by the number of personnel and the specially processed food that was required, failed to change his position. Vogel is quoted in: Peters, *Tödlicher Irrtum*, p. 318.

68 Aust, *Der Baader-Meinhof-Komplex*, p. 435 ff.; Kurt Oesterle, *Stammheim. Die Geschichte des Vollzugsbeamten Horst Bubeck* (Tübingen: Klöpfer & Meyer, 2003).

69 Jacco Pekelder, 'Links slachtofferschap. De RAF als afrekening met de Duitse schuld', in: Patrick Dassen, Krijn Thijs, and Ton Nijhuis (eds), *Duitsers als slachtoffers. Het einde van een taboe?* (Amsterdam: Mets & Schilt, 2007), pp. 305–335. Here: pp. 312–321.

70 See the documentation published by the Rote Hilfe (Red Aid): Wienke Zitzlaff (ed.), *Hungerstreik vor dem BGH gegen Psychoterror in deutschen Gefängnissen, Freitag 9.11. bis 12.11.1973* (Gießen: Prolit-Buchvertrieb, 1973). Zitzlaff was Ulrike Meinhof's sister.

71 Pieter H. Bakker Schut (ed.), *Das info. Briefe der Gefangenen aus der RAF 1973–1977* (Kiel: Neuer Malik Verlag, 1987); Olaf Gäthje, 'Das 'info'-System der RAF von 1973 bis 1977 in sprachwissenschaftlicher Perspektive', in: Kraushaar (ed.), *Die RAF und der linke Terrorismus*, pp. 714–733.

72 Alfred Klaus, *Aktivitäten und Verhalten inhaftierter Terroristen* (Bonn: Bundesministerium des Innern, 1985), pp. 16–18.

73 Ibid., p. 20.

74 N.N., *Kursbuch 31. Folter in der BRD. Zur Situation der Politischen Gefangenen*, n.d.; *Der Kampf gegen die Vernichtungshaft* (Komitees gegen Folter an politischen Gefangenen in der BRD, 1974).

75 Peters, *Tödlicher Irrtum*, p. 314.

76 Together with Mahler and other companions Meinhof was tried because of her role in the armed liberation of Baader in 1970.

77 Andreas Baader, *Kassiber* [prison letter] (January 1974), available via labourhistory.net.

78 Quoted in: Peters, *Tödlicher Irrtum*, p. 320.

79 Varon, *Bringing the War Home*, p. 220.

80 Pekelder, 'Links slachtofferschap', p. 317.

81 Sartre had accepted an invitation written by Meinhof and Baader and delivered to Paris by their lawyer Croissant. The ageing philosopher and the imprisoned terrorist conferred for an hour in a visitor's cell, accompanied by former student leader Daniel Cohn-Bendit, who acted as interpreter. Afterwards, Sartre explained Baader's inhumane treatment to the international media at a press conference in Stuttgart organised by the RAF's lawyers, and later again at a press conference in Paris. See Klaus Croissant, 'Bericht zur Pressekonferenz in Paris am 10.12.1974' (10 December 1974), RA 02/039, 011, HIS.

82 This transnational RAF solidarity network is explored in: Jacco Pekelder, 'The RAF Solidarity Movement from a European Perspective', in: Martin Klimke, Jacco Pekelder, and Joachim Scharloth (eds), *Between Prague Spring and French May. Opposition and Revolt in Europe, 1960–1980* (New York and Oxford: Berghahn Books, 2011), pp. 251–266.

83 In its press communiqué, the committee expressed its 'concern about the development of new forms of repression in Western Europe, especially in the Federal Republic of Germany, where prisoners of the Red Army Faction [were] submitted to murderous prison conditions [...].' Its first task was therefore to ensure the legal defence of the German 'political prisoners'. As the legal foundation for its work the committee referred to the European Convention on Human Rights, article 3, which stated that '[n]o one shall be subjected to torture or to inhuman or degrading treatment or punishment'. Press Communiqué, Niederlande, *International Institute for Social History, Amsterdam* (IISH), *Ronald Augustin Collection* (14 December 1974), Folder 14.

84 The International Committee reconvened under a slightly different name: *Comité International de Défense des Prisonniers Politique en Europe-occidentale.* There had been no mention of 'occidentale' (Western) in the earlier statement—it might be suspected that some members had succeeded in excluding Eastern Europe from the International Committee's activities. See P.H. Bakker Schut, 'Politieke justitie in de Bondsrepubliek Duitsland', *Nederlands Juristenblad* (15 February 1975), pp. 203–212.

85 'ANP-Persbericht', *Knipsels en persberichten betreffende het proces tegen de Amsterdammer Ronald Augustin, 1975–1976, Deel II, 8/3/75-28-4-75, Collectie Willem de Haan,* IISH. (19 April 1975), Folder 3.

86 Ulrike Meinhof, *Letzte Texte von Ulrike* (Internationalen Komitee zur Verteidigung politischer Gefangener in Westeuropa, 1976).

87 RAF/BRD, *texte: der* RAF.

88 *Der Tod Ulrike Meinhofs. Bericht der Internationalen Untersuchungskommission. 2. Überarbeitete Auflage* (Tübingen: IVA-Verlag, 1979).

89 Jacco Pekelder, *Sympathie voor de* RAF. *De Rote Armee Fraktion in Nederland, 1970–1980* (Amsterdam: Mets & Schilt, 2007), p. 137 ff.

90 Baader's opinion was quoted in a decision by the Second Senate of Stuttgart Oberlandesgericht (30 September 1975), reprinted in: Stuberger, *In der Strafsache*, p. 112.

91 In contrast, Baader wrote, 'trials that could not support anything [no political messages], that don't have public resonance, won't be conducted. They only get a statement, afterwards no defender + no accused.' Andreas Baader, *Kassiber* (June 1974), available via labourhistory.net.

92 '"Wir werden in den Durststreik treten" SPIEGEL-Fragen an Andreas Baader, Ulrike Meinhof, Gudrun Ensslin und Jan-Carl Raspe', *Der Spiegel* (20 January 1975).

93 John Shy and Thomas W. Collier, 'Revolutionary War', in: Peter Paret (ed.), *Makers of Modern Strategy from Machiavelli to the Nuclear Age* (Princeton, N.J.: Princeton University Press, 1986), pp. 815–862.

94 RAF/BRD, *texte: der* RAF, p. 547.

95 Ibid., p. 541.

96 Ibid., p. 149.

97 RAF/BRD, *texte: der* RAF, p. 149.

98 Note, by Ulrike Meinhof (9 February 1974), RA, J/001, 005, HIS, and Letter by Hannover to Klaus Croissant a.o. (of 18 February 1974), J/RA, J/002, 001, HIS. With this letter Hannover resigned as lawyer for Meinhof and Raspe. On the one hand, he judged the measures taken by the state as too intrusive for the activities of the defenders and, on the other, he noticed that there was a lack of trust between Meinhof and himself. 'Ihr Kommentar in ihrem Rundschreiben vom 9.2. reicht mir nun wirklich. Es hat keinen Zweck, darüber zu diskutieren. Eine Identifizierung mit Faschisten lasse ich mir von niemandem vorwerfen, auch von U.M. nicht' (Your commentary in your circular letter of February 9th is really not sufficient. There is no use, discussing it. Nobody can accuse me of being a fascist, not even U.M. [Ulrike Meinhof].) Cf. Heinrich Hannover, *Die Republik vor Gericht 1954–1995. Erinnerungen eines unbequemen Rechtsanwalts* (Berlin: Aufbau Taschenbuch Verlag, 2005), p. 370 ff.

99 Klaus, *Aktivitäten und Verhalten inhaftierter Terroristen*, p. 52.

100 Chotjewitz, *Mein Freund Klaus*.

101 Reinecke, *Otto Schily*.

102 Peters, *Tödlicher Irrtum*, p. 345.

103 Klaus, *Aktivitäten und Verhalten inhaftierter Terroristen*, pp. 141–143.

104 '"Wir werden in den Durststreik treten" SPIEGEL-Fragen an Andreas Baader, Ulrike Meinhof, Gudrun Ensslin und Jan-Carl Raspe', *Der Spiegel* (20 January 1975).

105 Andreas Baader, *Kassiber* (January 1974), available via labourhistory.net.

106 Peters, *Tödlicher Irrtum*, pp. 322–323.

107 About these connected actions: Michael März, *Die Machtprobe 1975. Wie RAF und Bewegung 2. Juni den Staat erpressten.* (Leipzig: Forum Verlag Leipzig, 2007).

108 Peters, *Tödlicher Irrtum*, p. 364 ff.

109 'BM: die Materialschlacht', *Der Spiegel* (19 May 1975). This comparison had been introduced by BKA president Horst Herold: 'Große Schlacht', *Der Spiegel* (14 January 1974).

110 Andreas Musolff, 'Terrorismus im öffentlichen Diskurs der BRD. Seine Deutung als Kriegsgeschehen und die Folgen', in Weinhauer, Requate and Haupt (eds), *Terrorismus in der Bundesrepublik*, pp. 302–319.

111 Bakker Schut, *Stammheim*, p. 190.

112 It seems this reasoning was also behind the plea, a few weeks later, by Federal Minister of Justice Hans-Jochen Vogel for a re-writing of the law to broaden its scope.

113 Stuberger, *In der Strafsache*, pp. 28–31.

114 Ibid., pp. 54, 59.

115 Aust, *Der Baader-Meinhof-Komplex*, p. 473 ff.

116 Ibid., p. 478. According to Stuberger the sleepy lawyer was Eggler (Karlsruhe). He told Stuberger that he had not read the documents of the trial. See Stuberger, *Die Tage von Stammheim*, p. 68.

117 Stuberger, *In der Strafsache*, p. 154 ff.

118 Ibid., pp. 181 ff. and 195 ff.

119 Ibid., pp. 81–82.

120 Tenfelde, *Die Rote Armee Fraktion und die Strafjustiz*, pp. 115–116.

121 Stuberger, *Die Tage von Stammheim*, p. 82.

122 Stuberger, *In der Strafsache*, pp. 71–72.

123 Stuberger, *In der Strafsache*, pp. 72–73; *Kursbuch*, p. 32.

124 Aust, *Der Baader-Meinhof-Komplex*, p. 480.

125 Stuberger, *In der Strafsache*, pp. 101–104.

126 Stuberger, *Die Tage von Stammheim*, pp. 76–77.

127 Stuberger, *In der Strafsache*, pp. 104–114, 119–120 and 130–132.

128 Tenfelde, *Die Rote Armee Fraktion und die Strafjustiz*, pp. 138–139.

129 Bakker Schut, *Stammheim*, p. 382.

130 Stuberger, *Die Tage von Stammheim*, pp. 85–87.

131 Aust, *Der Baader-Meinhof-Komplex*, pp. 310–312, 318–322 and 516.

132 The lawyer Heinrich Hannover is very critical about the use of this 'crown witness' by the Federal Prosecutor in: Heinrich Hannover, *Terroristenprozesse. Erfahrungen und Erkenntnisse eines Strafverteidigers. Terroristen & Richter*, 1 (Hamburg: VSA-Verlag, 1991), p. 144 ff. According to him in cooperation with the Federal Minister of Justice the prosecution suppressed

documents that could have led to the condemnation of Müller for the murder of a Hamburg police officer and for his contribution to the building of bombs for the RAF. In Hannover's opinion, in effect, this means that Müller's testimony has been bought.

133 Aust, *Der Baader-Meinhof-Komplex*, pp. 550–552. This statement was also important, because in the bill of indictment, the prosecution had initially placed much emphasis on Baader's alleged 'Rädelsführerschaft' (ring leadership). Later on, the prosecutors largely dropped this point, because it was hard to prove as it was practically only based on the statements of the two 'crown witnesses' and on an offhand remark of Meinhof comparing Baader to other revolutionary leaders (such as Fidel Castro and Ernesto 'Che' Guevara). In the end more emphasis was put on the idea of collective leadership. Cf. Tenfelde, *Die Rote Armee Fraktion und die Strafjustiz*, pp. 94–95.

134 'Singen um die Wette', *Der Spiegel* (26 January 1976).

135 'A la Klettermaxe', *Der Spiegel* (9 June 1975).

136 Gerhard Mauz, 'Herr Schily, zu welchem Behufe?', *Der Spiegel* (2 February 1976).

137 Aust, *Der Baader-Meinhof-Komplex*, pp. 552–554.

138 Ibid., pp. 562–565.

139 "Müller schoß, Schmid fiel", *Der Spiegel* (12 July 1976).

140 Aust, *Der Baader-Meinhof-Komplex*, pp. 562–565.

141 Stuberger, *Die Tage von Stammheim*, p. 114. See also: 'BM-Prozesse. Sprengstoff brühwarm', *Der Spiegel* (19 July 1976); '"Heute diene ich mit der reinen Wahrheit." Gesetzwidrige Manipulationen mit "Kronzeugen" in Terroristenprozessen', *Der Spiegel* (14 May 1979). The 1976 *Spiegel* article also highlighted how precarious Müller's position was as a crown witness in a jurisdiction in which crown witnesses did not officially exist. In contrast to the US, where a crown witness could always rely on an official deal with the prosecution, in Germany he constantly had to heed the danger of implicating himself by his statements. According to the article, this also explained why Müller answered questions by the judges and prosecutors far more easily and openly than questions by the RAF's lawyers.

142 Gerhard Mauz, 'Wir danken Ihnen für Ihre Geduld', *Der Spiegel* (18 October 1976); Stuberger, *Die Tage von Stammheim*, p. 92.

143 Stuberger, *Die Tage von Stammheim*, pp. 167–168.

144 Mauz, 'Wir danken Ihnen für Ihre Geduld', *Der Spiegel* (18 October 1976).

145 Aust, *Der Baader-Meinhof-Komplex*, p. 512. English translation: Stefan Aust, *Baader-Meinhof. The Inside Story of the RAF* (Oxford: Oxford University Press, 2008), pp. 249–250.

146 Bakker Schut, *Stammheim*, p. 329.

147 Bakker Schut, *Stammheim*, p. 329 ff.; Hannes Breucker, *Verteidigungsfremdes Verhalten. Anträge und Erklärungen im 'Baader-Meinhof-Prozeß'* (Berlin: Duncker & Humblot, 1993), p. 134 ff.

148 Bakker Schut, *Stammheim*, p. 336.

149 Bakker Schut, *Stammheim*, p. 337; Breucker, *Verteidigungsfremdes Verhalten*, p. 149.

150 Breucker, *Verteidigungsfremdes Verhalten*, p. 149.

151 Azzola, for instance, had only referred to the attacks on US army buildings in Frankfurt and Heidelberg in May 1972 in his motion. As legal expert Hannes Breucker rightly pointed out, he had not made it clear to what extent the bombings of a judge's car in Karlsruhe, two police stations in Augsburg and Munich, and the Hamburg offices of the Springer media concern were also legitimate targets in a 'war' against American involvement in Vietnam. Cf. Breucker, *Verteidigungsfremdes Verhalten*, pp. 143–144.

152 It should be noted that the media, judging by the trial reports in the weeklies *Die Zeit* and *Der Spiegel*, seems not to have reported on this attempt to change the legal framework to any significant extent.

153 Breucker, *Verteidigungsfremdes Verhalten*, pp. 150–151.

154 Indeed, as noted earlier, there were only vague references to the attacks on the American facilities and again no mention was made of the other four strictly German bombings of May 1972.

155 Breucker, *Verteidigungsfremdes Verhalten*, pp. 150–153; Bakker Schut, *Stammheim*, pp. 326–327. On 28 June 1976 (trial day 121), there was another attempt by the defence to introduce Vietnam into the proceedings. The lawyers had brought five Americans who had been employed at US military facilities in West Germany to testify about the use of these in the performance of the supposed war crimes in Vietnam. After prolonged discussions and deliberations the court decided not to allow the questioning of these witnesses: 'The Vietnam War is not the subject of this trial'; Aust, *Der Baader-Meinhof-Komplex*, pp. 541–544.

156 Stuberger, *Die Tage von Stammheim*, pp. 64 and 68–69.

157 Bakker Schut, *Stammheim*, p. 311. Alas, this book does not quote Temming's note at length and does not mention its archival whereabouts.

158 Stuberger, *Die Tage von Stammheim*, pp. 94–95.

159 Ibid., pp. 96–99.

160 Ibid., pp. 99–100.

161 Aust, *Der Baader-Meinhof-Komplex*, p. 526.

162 Ibid., pp. 523–525.

163 Tenfelde, *Die Rote Armee Fraktion und die Strafjustiz*, pp. 143–145; Otto Kircheimer, *Political*

Justice. The Use of Legal Procedure for Political Ends (Princeton, NJ: Princeton University Press, 1961), p. 19.

164 Breucker, *Verteidigungsfremdes Verhalten*, p. 145; RAF/BRD, *texte: der* RAF, p. 140.

165 Aust, *Der Baader-Meinhof-Komplex*, p. 481. The Federal Prosecutor had asked the judge to decommission the lawyers of choice.

166 Stuberger, *In der Strafsache*, pp. 61, 63. Apart from that, various disciplinary procedures and libel actions were set in motion against RAF lawyers such as Hans-Heinz Heldmann and Otto Schily as a consequence of some of their statements or petitions during the Stammheim trial. Some of the legal actions lasted well into the 1990s. Hannover, *Die Republik vor Gericht*, p. 559 ff..

167 Mauz, 'Wir danken für Ihre Geduld', *Der Spiegel* (18 October 1976).

168 Aust, *Der Baader-Meinhof-Komplex*, pp. 513–514.

169 'Dienstag Morgen—Prozess in Stammheim', *Fuzzy Extra* (9 May 1976).

170 Aust, *Der Baader-Meinhof-Komplex*, p. 530 ff.

171 Ibid., pp. 530–531.

172 Aust, *Der Baader-Meinhof-Komplex*, pp. 531–532. Translation from: Aust, *Baader-Meinhof. The inside story of the* R.A.F., pp. 260–261.

173 Small notice, without date [May 1976], by one of the prisoners [probably Gudrun Ensslin], HIS: Me, U/015, 005; Notice, 'am 9.5.76 nach der pk [Pressekonferenz] zu ulrike' (9 May 1976), HIS: Me, U/015, 006.

174 Aust, *Der Baader-Meinhof-Komplex*, p. 494.

175 Aust, *Der Baader-Meinhof-Komplex*, p. 496 ff. Translation from: Aust, *Baader-Meinhof. The inside story of the* R.A.F., p. 244.

176 Aust, *Der Baader-Meinhof-Komplex*, pp. 565–566.

177 The correct German term is 'Antrag zur Ablehnung wegen Besorgnis der Befangenheit'.

178 Tenfelde, *Die Rote Armee Fraktion und die Strafjustiz*, p. 107.

179 Stuberger, *Die Tage von Stammheim*, p. 129. There were also a number of similar challenges against other judges. Tenfelde, *Die Rote Armee Fraktion und die Strafjustiz*, p. 108.

180 Aust, *Der Baader-Meinhof-Komplex*, p. 492.

181 Stuberger, *Die Tage von Stammheim*, p. 74.

182 Tenfelde, *Die Rote Armee Fraktion und die Strafjustiz*, pp. 108–109.

183 The documents in question concerned protocols of the interrogation of Gerhard Müller by the criminal police and trial protocols of his evidence in court. Mayer had hoped that this journalist would use the material to address a report by the liberal weekly *Der Spiegel* of 4 September 1972 that dismissed the possible smuggling by Schily of a letter written by Ensslin out of prison, an affair we alluded to with earlier in this chapter. Aust, *Der Baader-Meinhof-Komplex*, pp. 578–579.

184 Aust, *Der Baader-Meinhof-Komplex*, pp. 579–580.

185 Ibidim. Translation from: Aust, *Baader-Meinhof. The Inside Story of the* RAF, p. 275.

186 Aust, *Der Baader-Meinhof-Komplex*, pp. 580–581. Translation from: Aust, *Baader-Meinhof. The Inside Story of the* RAF, p. 276.

187 Stuberger, *Die Tage von Stammheim*, pp. 128–129.

188 Stuberger, *Die Tage von Stammheim*, p. 127.

189 Quoted in: Aust, *Der Baader-Meinhof-Komplex*, pp. 467–468.

190 Stuberger, *In der Strafsache*, p. 145 ff.

191 Aust, *Der Baader-Meinhof-Komplex*, pp. 494–496. Translation from: Aust, *Baader-Meinhof. The Inside Story of the* RAF, p. 240.

192 Stuberger, *Die Tage von Stammheim*, pp. 74, 78–79 and 83–85.

193 Aust, *Der Baader-Meinhof-Komplex*, pp. 593–594.

194 Stuberger, *Die Tage von Stammheim*, pp. 177–178.

195 Aust, *Der Baader-Meinhof-Komplex*, pp. 593–594. The court did not summon Maihofer.

196 Ibidem. It remained uncertain whether these ministers had spoken the full truth—some newspapers doubted this. For factual details about the affair: ibid., pp. 451, 458–460. It is clear that during at least two hostage takings probably some conversations between the RAF prisoners and their lawyers were overheard.

197 Aust, *Der Baader-Meinhof-Komplex*, pp. 595–597. Translation from: Aust, *Baader-Meinhof. The inside story of the* R.A.F., pp. 281–282.

198 Aust, *Der Baader-Meinhof-Komplex*, pp. 596–597.

199 Ibid., pp. 608–610.

200 Ibid., pp. 610–611.

201 Ibid., p. 288.

202 Ibid., pp. 615–616.

203 Stuberger, *Die Tage von Stammheim*, pp. 168, 172 ff.

204 The accused were found guilty of having collectively committed three murders and six attempted murders as well as of one additional murder and a murder attempt. Next to that, they were also found guilty of 27 attempted murders resulting from bomb attacks. Moreover, all three were found guilty of forming a criminal organisation. Baader and Raspe were found guilty of two further attempted murders and Ensslin of one. Aust, *Der Baader-Meinhof-Komplex*, pp. 616–617.

205 Stuberger, *Die Tage von Stammheim*, pp. 182–183.

206 Of course, since the trial we deal with in this article there have been several other RAF related trials in Stammheim. In an ironic twist of fate, from late September 2010, the *Mehrzweckhalle* even hosted yet another RAF trial, this time against Verena Becker, who was accused of participation in the 1977 killing of Chief Federal Prosecutor Buback. Cf.

Michael Sontheimer, 'Der Stammheim-Komplex. Prozess gegen Verena Becker', *Spiegel Online* (29 September 2010).

207 'Der wichtigste Hinweis ist übersehen worden', FR (17 October 1987); 'Die Tode von Stammheim und die Annehmlichkeiten des Ungewissen', *Die Tageszeitung* (*taz*) (17 October 1987); 'Tage des Zorns, Tage der Trauer', *Zeit* (16 October 1987). This last article at least deals (in some paragraphs) with elements of the Stammheim trial.

208 'Das verlangt das Recht von ihm', *Der Spiegel* (2 May 1977).

209 'Ende in Stammheim', FR (29 April 1977); 'Urteil, aber kein Ende', SZ (29 April 1977); 'Früher hätte man sie als Hexen verbrannt', *Spiegel* (2 May 1977). In 2005 even the conservative *Frankfurter Allgemeine Zeitung* (FAZ) wrote about 'pecularities and blunders' (*Merkwürdigkeiten und Patzer*) of the trial: 'Test auf Rechtstaatlichkeit', FAZ (22 May 2005).

210 Cf. Uwe Wesel, 'Strafverfahren, Menschenwürde und Rechtsstaatsprinzip. Versuch einer Bilanz der RAF-Prozesse', in: Kraushaar (ed.), *Die RAF und der linke Terrorismus*, pp. 1048–1057. Here: p. 1057 (quote).

211 'Das verlangt das Recht von ihm', *Der Spiegel* (2 May 1977).

212 See Klaus Weinhauer, 'Terrorismus und Kommunikation: Forschungsstand und -perspektiven zum bundesdeutschen Linksterrorismus der 1970er Jahre', in: Nicole Colin, Beatrice de Graaf, Jacco Pekelder, Johachim Umlauf (eds), *Der 'Deutsche Herbst' und die RAF in Politik, Medien und Kunst. Nationale und internationale Perspektiven* (Bielefeld: transcript, 2008), pp. 109–123. Here: p. 121 f.

213 See Wesel, 'Strafverfahren', p. 1057; Weinhauer, *Terrorismus in der Bundesrepublik*, p. 227 ff.

214 Bakker Schut, for example, underlines the communicative structure of that trial. With other authors, he emphasises one important fact: that in Germany of the 1970s a political climate existed that lacked a 'culture of conflict' (Eschen) in which controversies between the state and its opponents could be acted out. See Klaus Eschen, 'Rechtsstaat ohne Konfliktkultur. Die RAF-Prozesse im politischen Ausnahmezustand', in: Michael Sontheimer and Otto Kallscheuer (eds), *Einschüsse. Besichtigungen eines Frontverlaufs zehn Jahre nach dem Deutschen Herbst* (Berlin: Rotbuch, 1987), pp. 78–98.

215 These perceptions are discussed in more detail in: Weinhauer, *Terrorismus in der Bundesrepublik*; Heinz Steinert, 'Sozialstrukturelle Bedingungen des 'linken' Terrorismus der 70er Jahre', in: Bundesministerium des Innern (ed.), *Analysen zum Terrorismus*, 4:2 (Opladen: Westdeutscher Verlag, 1984), pp. 387–603.

216 Presse- und Informationsamt der Bundesregierung (ed.), *Dokumentation zu den Ereignissen und Entscheidungen im Zusammenhang mit der Entführung von Hanns Martin Schleyer und der Lufthansa-Maschine 'Landshut'* (Cologne: Druckhaus Deutz, 1977); Tatjana Botzat, Elisabeth Kiderlen, Frank Wolff, *Ein Deutscher Herbst. Zustände, Dokumente, Berichte,*

Kommentare (Frankfurt: Verlag Neue Kritik, 1978); Tatjana Botzat, Elisabeth Kiderlen, Frank Wolff, Wolfgang Kraushaar, *Ein Deutscher Herbst. Zustände 1977* (Frankfurt: Verlag Neue Kritik 1997); Klaus Hartung, Christiane Ensslin, Gert Schneider, *Der blinde Fleck. Die Linke und die RAF* (Frankfurt: Verlag Neue Kritik, 1987) (this was also partly published in a special issue of the *Tageszeitung* at the ten year anniversary of the German Autumn, *taz*, 5 October 1987). See also Karl Kopp, Rainer Kreuzer, and Peter Maroldt (eds), *Die Mythen knacken. Materialien wieder ein Tabu. Neue Linke—RAF—Deutscher Herbst—Amnestie* (Frankfurt/Main: Linke Liste an der Universität Frankfurt (a/M), 1987).

217 Tolmein and Zum Winkel, *Nix gerafft*; Oliver Tolmein, *Stammheim vergessen. Deutschlands Aufbruch und die RAF* (Hamburg: Konkret, 1992).

218 See Willi Winkler, *Die Geschichte der RAF* (Berlin: Rowohlt, 2007); Butz Peters, *Tödlicher Irrtum. Die Geschichte der RAF* (Frankfurt/M.: Fischer-Taschenbuch Verlag, 2007).

219 'Das Wahnsystem RAF', FR (18 October 1997).

220 'Die Wunde Stammheim', *Zeit* (7 February 1986).

221 'Die Wunde Stammheim', *Zeit* (7 February 1986). See also 'Das Gefühl, es platzt einem der Kopf', *Der Spiegel* (27 January 1986); 'Wie kommt ihr dazu?', *Zeit* (19 June 1987).

222 'An die Mörder unseres Bruders', *taz* (7 November 1986).

223 N.N., *'Ihr habt unseren Bruder ermordet'. Die Antwort der Brüder des Gerold von Braunmühl an die RAF* (Reinbek bei Hamburg: Rowohlt, 1987).

224 The German language does not differentiate between 'sacrifice' and 'victim', using the word 'Opfer' for both terms. On the one hand, victims can be people, whose passive death is turned into an interpretation of an active process of dying *for* something or someone. On the other hand, referring to victims can serve to underline the suffering of these victims, their relatives and families; see Sabine Behrenbeck, *Der Kult um die toten Helden. Nationalsozialistische Mythen, Riten und Symbole* (Vierow: SH-Verlag, 1996).

225 See Nicole Colin, 'Täter- versus Opferdiskurs: Eine *andere* Geschichte des deutschen Terrorismus', in: Colin, De Graaf, Pekelder, Umlauf (eds), *Der 'Deutsche Herbst' und die RAF in Politik, Medien und Kunst*, pp. 187–194.

226 See David Garland, *The Culture of Control. Crime and Social Order in Contemporary Society* (Oxford: Oxford University Press, 2001), pp. 11 f. and 179. 'The new political imperative is that victims must be protected, their voices must be heard, their memory honoured, their anger expressed, their fears addressed. [...] The victim is now, in a certain sense, a much more representative character, whose experience is taken to be common and collective, rather than individual and atypical. Whoever speaks on behalf of victims speaks on behalf of us all.' (p. 11).

227 See Grünen im Bundestag (eds), *Ende der bleiernen Zeit? Versuch eines Dialogs zwischen Gesellschaft und RAF* (Bonn: Die Grünen, 1989).

228 See 'Wie kommt ihr dazu?' *Zeit* (19 June 1987); 'Die Ausgrenzung ist für beide Seiten tödlich', *Der Spiegel* (19 October 1987). See also 'Dein Vater ist ein Mörder', *Der Spiegel* (24 June 1991).

229 'Todesspiel' is about the kidnapping of Hanns Martin Schleyer and related events such as the hijacking of the Lufthansa airliner 'Landshut' and about the death of the imprisoned RAF members in October 1977. It was broadcast on 24 and 25 June 1997. See 'Spiel mir den Film vom Tod', SZ (19 June 1997); 'Harter Staat, Schleyers Not', *Der Spiegel* (30 June 1997); 'Der heisse Herbst' and 'Schleyers Stimme', FAZ (18 and 26 June 1997 respectively). 'Black Box BRD' (2001) tells the life stories of the banker Alfred Herrhausen, assassinated by the RAF in November 1991, and the militant Wolfgang Grams, who died in a (still controversial) shoot-out with the police in Bad Kleinen in June 1993.

230 'Ich bin derjenige, der weiter leidet', *Zeit* (1 August 1997); 'Wenn die Erinnerung nicht loslässt', SZ (5 September 2002). See also 'Eine Kindheit zwischen Schickeria und Untergrund' [about the daughter of Ulrike Meinhof], *Brigitte* (12 November 1997).

231 See the report about a conference held at the Evangelische Akademie Bad Boll, where former militants met relatives of their victims 'Die Zeit ist reif oder: überall ist Oldenburg', FR (22 February 1999); 'Kein wohliges Gefühl linker Selbstgerechtigkeit', FAZ (6 March 1999).

232 See Angelika Holderberg, *Nach dem bewaffneten Kampf. Ehemalige Mitglieder der RAF und Bewegung 2. Juni sprechen mit Therapeuten über ihre Vergangenheit* (Giessen: Psychosozial-Verlag, 2007); 'Endlos im Käfig einer Zwischenzeit', SZ (10 March 2007). In the 1997 meeting of former militant activists no traces of a victim-based communication could be discerned; see 'Ich habe dieses Land gehasst', *Der Spiegel* (26 May 1997); 'Talkshow für taube Terroristen', SZ (21 May 1997).

233 See 'Bist du verrückt?', *Der Spiegel*, 29 September 1997, where Alfred Klaus, a policeman of the Bundeskriminamt, mentions his doubts about the effectiveness of the official hard-line tactics against the RAF. See also 'Bleierne Zeit—bleierne Schuld', SZ, 11 October 1997; 'Wie aus Schutzrechten für Bürger Staatsschutzrechte wurden', *Zeit* (17 October 1997).

234 See 'Sie fielen nicht vom Himmel', *Zeit* (17 October 1997).

235 See the catalogue Klaus Biesenbach (ed.), *Zur Vorstellung des Terrors. Die RAF-Ausstellung*. 2 volumes (Göttingen: Steidl, 2005).

236 See 'Zwischen Historie und Hysterie', *taz* (23 July 2003); 'Auf dem Grund der Geschichte der Republik', and 'Protest gegen RAF-Ausstellung', SZ (both 24 July 2003); 'Auch Schily hat Vorbehalte gegen RAF-Ausstellung', and 'Rituale der Labilität', FR (25 and 26 July 2003 respectively); 'Ausstellung mit blutrotem Faden', FAZ (29 July 2003); 'Kunstwärts', FR (16 September 2003); 'Engel der Geschichte', SZ (11 December 2004).

237 See as a personal account of a relative of the assassinated Alfred Herrhausen: Carolin Emcke, *"Stumme Gewalt". Nachdenken über die RAF* (Frankfurt/M: S. Fischer Verlag, 2008); analytically weak is Anne Siemens, *Für die RAF war er das System, für mich der Vater* (Munich: Piper, 2007). Julia Albrecht and Corinna Ponto, *Patentöchter. Im Schatten der RAF—ein Dialog* (Cologne: Kiepenheuer & Witsch, 2011). See for more literature and for a detailed critique of such 'Befindlichkeitsbeschreibungen' (descriptions of empathy): Colin, 'Täter- versus Opferdiskurs', p. 194.

238 With one exception: the book about an RAF member who died in a bomb blast, by his mother: Ulrike Thimme, *Eine Bombe für die RAF. Das Leben und Sterben des Johannes Thimme von seiner Mutter erzählt* (Munich: C.H. Beck, 2004).

239 Some of these biographies are quoted in Weinhauer, *Terrorismus in der Bundesrepublik*; see also Diewald-Kerkmann, *Frauen, Terrorismus und Justiz. Prozesse gegen weibliche Mitglieder der RAF und der Bewegung 2. Juni* (Düsseldorf: Droste Verlag, 2009), p. 16 f.

240 On Stammheim, see Oesterle, *Stammheim*. This book was based on interviews published in the *tageszeitung* ('Nur für Stammheim spreche ich', 27 April 2002). Another individual account is Alfred Klaus, *Sie nannten mich Familienbulle. Meine Jahre als Sonderermittler gegen die RAF* (Hamburg: Hoffmann und Campe, 2008).

241 See 'Die Prada-Meinhof-Bande', *Der Spiegel* (25 February 2002); 'Der Che-Guevara-Effekt', FAZ (16 February 2002); 'Sohn der Angst', *FAZ Sonntagszeitung* (17 February 2002); 'Die Söhne Stammheims' and 'Der kalte Schmerz', SZ (both 17 October 2002); 'Das Wesentliche am Terrorismus ist die Inszenierung', FAZ (17 October 2002).

242 Butz Peters, 'Die Legenden der RAF', FAZ (6 May 2007); 'Zu wütend, um Angst zu haben', FAZ, (8 August 2007); 'Das stille Einvernehmen mit dem Terror', SZ (5 April 2007).

243 'RAF privat', SZ (24 April 2007).

244 Alfred Grosser, 'Die innere und die äussere Sicherheit', in Walter Scheel (ed.), *Nach dreissig Jahren. Die Bundesrepublik Deutschland Vergangenheit, Gegenwart, Zukunft* (Stuttgart: Kohlhammer, 1979), pp. 47–75. Here: p. 54.

245 'Der kalte Schmerz', SZ (17 October 2002). See for the following paragraph: *Der Spiegel* (10 September 1980), pp. 32–47.

246 See Klaus Weinhauer, 'Terrorismus und Kommunikation', p. 119.

247 See the film by Stefan Aust and Helmar Büchel 'Der Baader Meinhof Komplex' (2007) and the related series of articles published in: 'Der letzte Akt der Rebellion' and 'Dann gibt es Tote', *Der Spiegel* (10 and 17 September 2007 respectively). As the FAZ underlined, it was a film mainly about the perpetrators; 'Wissen wir jetzt, wer Schleyer erschoss?', FAZ (8 September 2007). See also 'Die Stimmen von Stammheim', *FAZ Sonntagszeitung* (9 September 2007); 'Die Namen der Mörder', FAZ (10 September 2007); 'Suche nach dem Tonband der Todesnacht', SZ (11 September 2007); 'Eine Überwachung hätte uns viele

Tote erspart' [interview with former BKA president Horst Herold], SZ (12 September 2007).

248 See as the solid historical overview on the main trends in German history of the 1970s/1980s by Anselm Doering-Manteuffel and Lutz Raphael, *Nach dem Boom. Perspektiven auf die Zeitgeschichte seit 1970* (Göttingen: Vandenhoeck & Ruprecht, 2008).

249 See '45 Tage im Herbst', SZ (11 August 2007).

250 See 'Grundgebot der Versöhnung' and 'Eine ehrliche Chance', *Der Spiegel* (both 20 April 1992).

251 See 'RAF: Abschied vom bewaffneten Kampf' and 'RAF bekennt sich zum eigenen Scheitern', *taz* (14 April 1992); 'RAF erklärt sich zu Geschichte' and 'Die RAF macht Schluss' (21 and 22 April 1998 respectively); 'Etwas loslassen', FAZ (22 April 1998).

252 Peters, *Tödlicher Irrtum*, p. 336.

253 For a discussion of the emergence of this specific post-war (and post Weimar), political culture of the FRG, see Sebastian Ulrich, *Der Weimar-Komplex. Das Scheitern der ersten deutschen Demokratie und die politische Kultur der frühen Bundesrepublik* (Göttingen: Wallstein Verlag, 2009). See also Stephan Scheiper, *Innere Sicherheit. Politische Anti-Terror-Gesetze in der Bundesrepublik Deutschland während der 1970er Jahre* (Paderborn: Ferdinand Schöningh, 2010).

254 Ralf Dahrendorf, 'Conflict and Liberty: Some Remarks on the Social Structure of German Politics', *The British Journal of Sociology*, 14:3 (1963), pp. 197–211. Here: p. 198. Interestingly, Dahrendorf uses the example of the German judge.

255 Weinhauer, *Terrorismus in der Bundesrepublik*.

7. National Security on Trial: The Case of Zacarias Moussaoui, 2001–2006

Geert-Jan Knoops

7.1. Introduction

Criminal prosecutions of terrorism suspects are perhaps the most controversial trials within (international) criminal law. The juxtaposition between the nature of the charges and the level of fair trial rights bestowed upon terrorist suspects raises a recurring question in public debate: should such rights also be granted to terrorist suspects? A derivative question pertains to which judicial forum should be most competent to hear terrorism cases—a military commission or federal (civilian) court? The choice of forum is contingent upon security concerns as well as on the political strategies to be performed by the government and the defendants. The Moussaoui trial is perhaps the most illustrative example of this juxtaposition; it serves as a good example of showcasing how national security threats are sentenced in ordinary district courts.

The federal trial before the United States (US) District Court for the Eastern District of Virginia, which took place in the period from August 2001 to May 2006, against Zacarias Moussaoui illustrated both the advantages and deficiencies of the criminal law system in dealing with terrorism. Despite the US government's political preference for subjecting prominent terrorist suspects, such as Salim Hamdan (Osama Bin Laden's driver) and Khalid Sheikh Mohammed and his four co-defendants (the alleged organisers of 9/11), to the US Military Commission's proceedings at Guantánamo Bay, Zacarias Moussaoui's trial was held before a federal (civilian) court.

Whilst the US government, evidenced by Moussaoui's conviction and sentencing to life imprisonment on 4 May 2006, demonstrated its capacity to prosecute terrorist suspects before US federal courts, it almost simultaneously pursued similar prosecutions before military commissions. What rationale underlays this duality?

This article covers the performance of the terrorist suspects and their opponents, but relates this performance predominantly to the fundamental question, why Zacarias Moussaoui—contrary to other 9/11 terror suspects—was brought before a US federal (civilian) court instead of before a military commission. Did this choice pertain to a genuine belief that the federal justice system was more suitable to try terrorism cases? Secondly, it examines whether and how this type of trial was—either procedurally or politically—more legitimate from the perspective of the accused as opposed to military commission proceedings (sections 2 and 6). Section 3 delves into the particulars of the Moussaoui case: the events preceding and during the trial. Section 4 examines the prosecutorial theory underlying the Moussaoui case. Section 5 addresses the performative strategies pursued by the prosecution and especially by Moussaoui, as well as their effects on the fairness of the trial.

7.2. The 9/11 Legacy

7.2.1. *Ever-expanding Anti-terrorism Legislation*

It has been said that the terrorist attacks of 9/11, 2001, when two planes crashed into the World Trade Center, another hit the US Pentagon and one crashed in the fields of Pennsylvania, changed the international legal order.[1] Significantly, after 9/11 a series of new US laws expanding the possibilities of investigating (terrorist) crimes entered into force. Just over a week after the attacks, on 18 September 2001 President George W. Bush signed into law the 'Authorization for Use of Military Force Against Terrorists' (AUMF) Bill; an Act allowing for the use of military force against those held responsible for the 9/11 attacks.[2] Two days thereafter, President Bush announced the 'War on Terror', stating that 'loosely affiliated terrorist organisations' operating under the name of Al Qaeda were responsible for the 9/11 attacks.[3] Al Qaeda is a terrorist organisation that was established around 1989 under the leadership of Osama Bin Laden.[4] Al Qaeda—a terrorist group with connections across the world—violently opposed non-Islamic governments. The roots of this group can be traced back to Afghanistan and Pakistan, particularly Peshawar; subsequently Al Qaeda was headquartered in Sudan from 1991 until 1996, before moving back to Afghanistan.[5]

President Bush claimed that Al Qaeda had a great deal of influence in Afghanistan through its support for the Taliban regime; a regime that he accused of repressing its own people and of housing, supplying and sponsoring terrorists.[6] Bush demanded that the Taliban hand over Al Qaeda operatives who were hiding in Afghanistan and close all terrorist training camps; yet to no avail.[7] On 7 October 2001, Operation Enduring Freedom was launched and the first bombs were dropped on Afghan soil.[8] On 26 October 2001, the so-called US Patriot Act was signed into law. With the advent and expansion of US anti-terrorism legislation, the powers of law enforcement agencies to gather intelligence, to detain and deport immigrants suspected of terrorism and the penalties for those committing and supporting terrorist crimes all increased.[9] These developments impacted on the international legal order in a manner that is still evident today.

Less than three weeks after the enactment of the US Patriot Act, President George W. Bush signed an executive order establishing the Military Commissions.[10] This order was heavily criticised by the media, fuelling a debate on the legitimacy of the military commissions promulgated by Bush without authorisation of the US Congress. The last time that military commissions of this nature became operative within the United States dated back to the Second World War; they had been established to prosecute illegal immigrants from Nazi Germany;[11] at that time the United States was engaged in an officially declared conventional war. The 9/11 events did not trigger a traditional war but rather a 'war on terror' against non-state parties like Al Qaeda.[12]

7.2.2. *Prosecuting 9/11 Suspects: Realpolitik Effects*

The ramifications of the 9/11 events on the legal order were not limited to a spate of security laws; they also affected the way terrorism trials were to be conducted. In the aftermath of 9/11 the US Administration expanded the boundaries of law enforcement and international (criminal) law principles. The criminal case against Zacarias Moussaoui, who was tried before a US federal court, illustrates this phenomenon. Moussaoui, whose case will be described below, was arrested *before* the 9/11 attacks for violating US immigration laws and was subsequently charged with not disclosing to federal agents information on the impending 9/11 attacks which could have prevented them happening. As a result Moussaoui was given a life sentence.

The influx of *realpolitik*, exacerbated by the 9/11 events, was manifest in a second high-profile case, namely the case against Khalid Sheikh Mohammed (KSM), the alleged mastermind of the 9/11 attacks whose evidence played an essential role in the case of Moussaoui. KSM was captured in 2002 in Pakistan by CIA and Pakistani intelligence forces. He was detained at various CIA 'black sites' before he was transferred to the Guantánamo Bay detention camp in 2006.[13] The case of KSM is particularly controversial since it turned out that he had been repeatedly subjected to waterboarding at Guantánamo Bay, where he—in 2013—has been held for six years and eleven months.[14] Due to security considerations the KSM case was ultimately referred from the federal court system to the military commission system. Initially the Obama Administration intended to prosecute KSM and his four co-defendants before a federal court in New York City. If this were to happen, evidence obtained from torture would probably be barred while the security costs would be exceedingly high.[15] This led to opposition on the part of the US Congress and ultimately to a bill in December 2010 prohibiting Obama from using government funds to transfer Guantánamo Bay detainees to US courts.[16]

Military commissions are said to be designed specifically for wartime situations; differences with federal courts include the admissibility of hearsay evidence, the use of protective orders that may require disclosure of attorney–client communications and broad classified information rules that obstruct verifying the prosecution's sources for some information.[17] Furthermore, evidence obtained outside the US is not barred even if it is obtained without a preceding search warrant; similarly, use of statements made by the defendant without a preceding Miranda warning is permissible.[18] According to the US government, these differences between military commissions and civilian courts are justified since military commissions take into account 'the reality of the battlefield'.[19]

The legal basis for military commissions' trials after 9/11 can be found in the Military Order of 13 November 2001, signed into law by President Bush.[20] This order provided for prosecuting a non-US citizen before military commissions if there was 'reason to believe' that the person was a member of Al Qaeda or had engaged in terrorist activities harming the US.[21] This Order was replaced by the Military Commissions Act of 2006 after the US Supreme Court ruled in *Hamdan v. Rumsfeld* that the Commissions violated the Geneva Conventions and the Uniform Code of Military Justice (UMCJ).[22]

7.2.3. Prosecuting 9/11 Suspects: Legal Effects

The criteria promulgated by the US Administration in order for the military commission to assume jurisdiction are indicative of its political purpose. Military commission trials can only be initiated when the suspects are:

- non-US citizens;
- affiliated with Al Qaeda; and
- persons ('unlawful enemy combatants') who have engaged in hostilities against the US or its coalition partners or persons who have purposefully and materially supported such hostilities.[23]

Next to the limitation regarding whom to prosecute, only certain types of offences can be brought to these commissions: the alleged crimes should qualify as 'violations of the laws of war'. The US government has pursued a broad interpretation of what can be subsumed under 'violating laws of war'; e.g. throwing one grenade at a US soldier in Afghanistan was deemed to meet this definition. That particular act was at the heart of the Omar Khadr case, that of a Canadian boy who was captured by US Special Forces at the age of 15 and tried before the Military Commission at Guantánamo Bay. No-one actually saw whether or not Khadr threw the grenade.[24] Omar Khadr ultimately entered into a plea agreement with the prosecution.[25]

These limitations are yet balanced by a quite extensive prosecutorial tool under US law, namely the insertion of the concept of conspiracy into penal law. Unlike several jurisdictions in civil-continental law systems, common law accepts that a simple 'meeting of minds' without any crime actually taking place can constitute a criminal offence, i.e. that of conspiracy. One can prosecute a person on the basis of this liability concept simply when there is proof of an agreement between two or more persons to commit a crime, irrespective of whether it subsequently materialises. The agreement itself constitutes the crime. Mere knowledge of the agreement, however, does not suffice; the intent should be materialised in acts which reveal the criminal objective, inferred from sufficiently significant circumstances.[26] Or, as put by the South Carolina Court:

> It is sufficient that the minds of the parties meet understandingly, so as to bring about an intelligent and deliberate agreement, to do the act and commit the offense charged, although such agreement be not manifested by any formal words.[27]

The conspiracy concept may perhaps have been one of the decisive factors in determining why Zacarias Moussaoui was not tried before a military commission. Under the laws of war, conspiracy is not deemed to be a separate crime—which deserves some elucidation at this stage. As far as prosecutions for violations of the laws of war are concerned, the International Criminal Tribunal for the former Yugoslavia (ICTY) Appeals Chamber in the *Tadic* case differentiated between the concept of Joint Criminal Enterprise (JCE) and conspiracy, the latter not being a violation of the laws of war.[28] The *Tadic* judgment emphasised the proper nature of criminal liability: that of individual participation and responsibility. The ICTY Appeals Chamber held that 'nobody may be held criminally responsible for acts or transactions in which he has not personally engaged or in some other way participated'.[29] These words must not be interpreted as creating a means of international collective responsibility—comprising the act of conspiracy—as opposed to the classic individual responsibility. The Appeals Chamber specified which type of scenario JCE refers to. Actually the Chamber referred to a scenario of JCE in which 'the participation and the contribution of the other members of the group is often vital in facilitating the commission of the offence in question'.[30] The participation has of course to be voluntary and intentional, and must be made in full knowledge both of the gravity of the acts planned to be committed and of their foreseeable consequences. On its face this seems similar to the definition of the offence of conspiracy; yet, JCE can be distinguished by the nature of the 'participation' in the commission of the crime. Within this concept, the Appeals Chamber held that 'participation' need 'not involve commission of a specific crime under one of those provisions (for example, murder, extermination, torture, rape, etc.), but may take the form of assistance in, or contribution to, the execution of the common plan or purpose'.[31] There is no such requirement in the crime of conspiracy, which relies more on the intent of the conspirator than his or her effective participation in the commission of the crime.

This differentiation was affirmed by the US Supreme Court in *Hamdan v. Rumsfeld*.[32] The Court endorsed the argument that 'international sources confirm that the crime charged here [i.e. conspiracy; GJK] is not a recognized violation of the law of war'.[33] Thus, in hindsight it might have been a prudent choice to have the Moussaoui case referred to a federal court, since the conspiracy charge would most likely have been quashed, as happened in the *Hamdan* case. However, the US Supreme Court's decision in *Hamdan v. Rumsfeld* has been superseded by the Military Commissions Acts (MCA) of 2006 and 2009 which do include conspiracy.[34]

Unlike the KSM case, which was barred from the Federal Court system, Moussaoui was put on trial before a federal court, which case commenced in January 2002 and lasted until his conviction in May 2006. Following an analysis of Moussaoui's history and the particulars of his case, this chapter focusses on the political and defence strategies of his trial.

7.3. Zacarias Moussaoui: A Personal History

For defence barristers, probably one of the most problematic clients is a defendant who is uncooperative, especially one who challenges the competence of the court to hear his case. Zacarias Moussaoui turned out to be such a defendant. The reasons for his (strategic) position in court had probably much to do with his personal history.

Zacarias Moussaoui was born on 30 May 1968. His mother was only 14 years old when she married. Five years later she and her husband moved from Morocco to France where Moussaoui was born and brought up without much of a religious education. Moussaoui's parents divorced in 1972. During his childhood Moussaoui was confronted with violence, particularly by his father, and racism; he grew up partly with his family and partly in different orphanages.[35]

Zacarias Moussaoui and his family followed different religious paths. Whereas he and his brother were both believers in Islam, though in different forms, his sister found her faith in Judaism and his mother did not practise her religion in public, although she did identify with Islam.[36] The Moussaoui household thus turned out to be a synthesis of different religions, underlining the freedom of choice of the family members.[37] Surprisingly, unlike his brother and sister (having more or less the same socio-cultural background) Zacarias Moussaoui radicalised. Apparently, a shared socio-cultural background does not fully account for the choices an individual makes, as the example of the Moussaoui family shows.[38] Moussaoui's radicalisation process must thus have had a different cause.

7.3.1. *Moussaoui's Radicalisation Process*

The Moussaoui family, being first generation immigrants from Morocco, was often confronted with racism in France, as was also testified to by a witness for the defence during the sentencing phase of the Moussaoui trial.[39] In France, Moussaoui and his brother were discriminated against because of their Arab descent, had fights at nightclubs for the same reason and did not meet the approval of the parents of Moussaoui's girlfriend.[40] In 1992 Zacarias Moussaoui moved to London to learn English where he obtained a Master's degree in international business from Southbank University in London in 1995.[41] While in London, Moussaoui's family started noticing Moussaoui's transformation. He started wearing a beard and made comments on his sister's clothing, calling her a whore because she was too Western.[42] As a student Moussaoui started to attend prayers at different mosques, among which were the Brixton Mosque and later the more radical Finsbury Mosque. The imam of the Brixton Mosque noticed that Moussaoui was growing more militant.[43] After showing up in military fatigues, wearing a backpack and demanding information about joining the jihad, Moussaoui was suspended from the Brixton Mosque.[44] In the meantime he was approached by more extremist groups, such as Al Muhajiroun ('the emigrants').[45] According to some, perhaps due to his experiences with racism in France and his inability to find a proper job despite his Master's degree, he was drawn into this militant branch of Islamism.[46] As of 1996, the French authorities became interested in him after Moussaoui was seen with Islamic extremists in London. The French authorities noticed his growing affinity with Islamic radicalism and they started monitoring him.[47] Moussaoui had already started to sever ties with his family, returning to France only once, in 1997. In 1998, he went to the Khalden training camp in Afghanistan, a training camp tied to Al Qaeda, at the same time as Mohamed Atta.[48] Atta hijacked and piloted American Airlines Flight 11, the first plane that flew into the World Trade Center on 9/11.[49] In 2002 Moussaoui saw his mother again, when she appeared at his trial hearings in Alexandria, Virginia.[50] At trial, Moussaoui's defence team presented evidence outlining his ongoing mental health problems, indicating that Moussaoui was suffering from paranoid schizophrenia.[51] Furthermore, the vulnerable relationship with his French girlfriend, and more particularly the rejection of Moussaoui by her parents, was put before the jury in an effort to obtain a reduced sentence.[52]

7.3.2. Moussaoui's Arrest

Moussaoui returned to London after he attended the Khalden training camp. Clearly, this strengthened his opposition to non-Islamic governments and his desire to fight for the jihad, since he continued and intensified his activities for Al Qaeda.[53] In 2000 he was sent to Malaysia by Khalid Sheikh Mohammed, the alleged mastermind of the 9/11 attacks, to take flying lessons.[54] Moussaoui, who could not find a flying school of his choice in Malaysia, started with other terrorist activities, such as buying materials to produce bombs. When Khalid Sheikh Mohammed found out about this, he ordered Moussaoui to take flying lessons in the US.[55] He started at the Airman Flight School in Norman, Oklahoma, in February 2001.[56] After a break from late May onwards, he made inquiries about taking Boeing 747 lessons at the Pan Am International Flight Academy in Eagan, Minnesota. On 10 July 2001, Moussaoui deposited US$ 1,500 for training at that flight academy, after which he received a training schedule for 13–20 August.[57] It was never revealed how Moussaoui had obtained the large sums of money that were in his possession during his time in the US. No explanation was found for the US$ 32,000 that Moussaoui had deposited in a bank account in Norman upon his arrival in the US, and it was not believed that Moussaoui's self-declared job as a freelance telemarketer brought in enough money to pay US$ 8,300 for flying lessons. Mohamed Atta, a friend of Moussaoui, who was also allegedly involved in the 9/11 complot, indicated that Moussaoui received money from overseas; yet he was unable to say how he knew this.[58]

Moussaoui's flight instructor, Clarence Prevost, became suspicious because Moussaoui had paid his tuition fee in cash and, unlike the other students, he focused his training specifically on piloting a Boeing 747 in mid-air. He was not interested in learning to take off and land the plane.[59] The flight school warned the FBI. On 16 August 2001, the FBI arrested Moussaoui because his visa had expired, just a month before the 9/11 attacks.[60] After Moussaoui was arrested, the FBI had difficulty researching Moussaoui's assets; the FBI headquarters in Washington were reluctant to issue either a criminal warrant or a Foreign Intelligence Surveillance Act warrant, because they believed there were insufficient grounds to justify the warrants.[61] Prior to 9/11, the US government was limited in its ability to collect and share intelligence inside the US. This legislative situation within the US changed dramatically after the 9/11 attacks, as outlined in the preceding section.

Although Moussaoui's activities subsequently raised the suspicion that he might have been selected to be one of the 9/11 hijackers, were it not that he was detained at that time, Khalid Sheikh Mohammed revealed in one of his interviews with the US intelligence services that Moussaoui was not part of this plot.[62] Another important question raised was whether the attacks could have been prevented if Moussaoui had told the FBI in August 2001 everything he knew. The prosecution argued that this was indeed the case, whilst the defence argued that Moussaoui had no specific knowledge of the 9/11 attacks.[63]

Few contested that Moussaoui was linked to Al Qaeda. He had attended Al Qaeda training camps, he could be linked to several other Al Qaeda members and when FBI officials searched Moussaoui's house after 9/11 a note was found with the mobile phone number of an Al Qaeda cell member in Germany. This person turned out to have dealt with the financial arrangements for all nineteen 9/11 hijackers. It was established that Moussaoui's flying lessons were paid for with money wired by this German cell of jihadist comrades.[64]

From a legal perspective, it was questionable whether this link was sufficient to sustain the conviction of Moussaoui for conspiring in the 9/11 attacks. When taking into account the evidence that was released during the trial, one could well ask why Moussaoui entered a guilty plea. From KSM's written evidence previously obtained by the US—Moussaoui's defence was not allowed to call this witness at trial—it could be derived that Moussaoui was not involved in the 9/11 attacks. According to KSM, Moussaoui was supposed to participate in a second follow-up attack.[65] Moreover, because 'Moussaoui was supposed to be in flight school and was not supposed to be in contact with him or anyone until after graduating',[66] KSM was reportedly unaware that he was captured before the 9/11 attacks. Later, at the sentencing stage, Moussaoui testified that he was supposed to fly a plane into the White House on 9/11 together with shoe bomber Richard Reid. But no evidentiary link was ever established between Reid and Moussaoui in relation to a White House attack on 9/11.[67] It seems that—aware of the evidentiary weakness of the prosecution's case—Moussaoui deliberately entered a guilty plea as part of an overall trial strategy, which included his tactic to die as a martyr (see below).

7.4. The Prosecution's Theory as regards the Moussaoui Case

As mentioned, Zacarias Moussaoui was initially arrested on immigration charges in August 2001; yet ultimately he was prosecuted on the basis of conspiring in the 9/11 attacks, particularly for not disclosing the impending attacks. Notably, at the time of the attacks, Moussaoui was already detained and had been interrogated on the basis of these immigration charges. The 'conspiracy' element was based on the assumption that in August 2001, at the time of his arrest, Zacarias Moussaoui was already aware of the impending twin tower attacks, whilst withholding this information from US federal officials. This conspiracy charge arose from suspicious acts surrounding Moussaoui's flying lessons, his connections to other Al Qaeda members who were allegedly involved in the plot and the fact that he had attended an Al Qaeda training camp. The notion that Moussaoui was aware of the 9/11 plot might also have been fuelled by his personal history, as illustrated above.

Yet, no conclusive evidence existed in August 2001 that Moussaoui materially contributed to the 9/11 attacks other than lying to federal authorities about his contacts and flying lessons, with the apparent aim of preventing the attacks from being revealed. It might even have been the case that in the absence of a guilty plea on Moussaoui's part (which he entered in 2002, but which was refused by the court, yet successfully re-entered on 22 April 2005),[68] he could have been acquitted.[69]

On 11 December 2001, the French-Moroccan was charged by a Federal Grand Jury in the US District Court for the Eastern District of Virginia with six conspiracy counts: conspiracy to commit acts of extra-territorial terrorism, conspiracy to commit aircraft piracy, conspiracy to destroy aircraft, conspiracy to use weapons of mass destruction, conspiracy to murder US employees and conspiracy to destroy property.[70] The indictment included overt acts such as providing guesthouses and training camps for Al Qaeda, providing military and intelligence training and attempting to obtain nuclear weapons.[71] Many acts did not explicitly refer to Moussaoui, but were targeted more broadly by naming 'Usama Bin Laden, and others known and unknown' or 'unindicted co-conspirators, known and unknown'.[72] Furthermore, the time-frame included in the indictment was rather extensive, using terminology such as 'at various times from at least as early as 1989'.[73] The acts leading up to the 'conspiracy to commit terrorism' charge that did explicitly refer to Moussaoui consisted of his alleged attendance at an Al Qaeda training camp in 1998, his inquiries about flying training (i.e. an e-mail to the Norman Flight School in Oklahoma and letters from his employer indicating that he would earn a monthly income of US$ 2,500 as a marketing consultant), flight logs that indicated that Moussaoui flew from London to Pakistan, from Pakistan to London, from London to Chicago—where he declared at least US$ 35,000 cash at customs—and from Chicago to Oklahoma. In Norman, Oklahoma, Moussaoui opened a bank account where he deposited US$ 32,000 in cash. Moussaoui took flying lessons in Norman from February 2001 until he stopped his classes early in May 2001.[74] Curiously, Moussaoui's membership of a gym in Oklahoma was also brought up as one of the acts in the indictment.[75] With regard to the allegation that Moussaoui withheld vital information about the impending 9/11 attacks, the prosecution alleged that Moussaoui 'while being interviewed by federal agents in Minneapolis, attempted to explain his presence in the United States by falsely stating that he was simply interested in learning to fly'.[76] The five other conspiracy counts in the indictment all made reference to the acts mentioned in the first count (i.e. conspiracy to commit terrorism). Taken together, the acts were meant to demonstrate that Moussaoui used the same preparatory *modus operandi* as the nineteen co-conspirators who conducted the 9/11 hijackings.[77]

7.5. Prosecution and Defence Trial Strategies within the Moussaoui Case

7.5.1. *Introduction*

The Moussaoui case illustrates the level of legal randomness involved, inasmuch as it concerns the places where the 9/11 and other major terrorism suspects were prosecuted. Moussaoui and Ahmed Ghailani were tried before a federal (civilian court). Ghailani was indicted before a federal court in New York in 2010 for conspiring in the 1998 bomb attacks on the US embassies in Kenya and Tanzania.[78] Yet other terrorist suspects such as KSM and his four co-defendants were subjected to the military commissions system, created through the aforementioned Military Order.[79]

In general, terrorism trials may serve as legal mechanisms both for governments and defendants to pursue (political) strategies. The legal arena, in which the government, the terrorist suspects, possible witnesses, victims and the media all have a role to play, may encourage such strategies.[80] Unlike military commissions, whose proceedings are held in closed session, public federal trials enable terrorist suspects to elevate them into 'show trials', i.e. using the public trial to advocate the ideological message of their terrorist organisation. Similarly, the public nature of a federal trial can serve the political agenda of the government, i.e. the message conveyed by the US government that it endorses the rule of law by showing the world the fairness of the US criminal law system.

In what follows we will discuss how both the US government and Moussaoui tried to instrumentalise the trial in pursuit of their respective political strategies.

7.5.2. *Trial Strategy of the US Government*

Security considerations were increasingly factored in when dealing with legal-procedural questions. Section 2 touched on some of the differences between federal courts and military commissions relating to jurisdictional and evidentiary issues. Once such differences exist, a government can anticipate them by opting for either the civil court system or the military commission's system. In a military commission context the defence does not have the same access to witnesses or other evidence as it has in a federal court; hearsay evidence is more easily admissible before military commissions and there are few options available to challenge its source; and rules protecting the use of classified information transform military commissions trials into proceedings entrenched in secrecy.[81] Proponents of military commissions point to the security and disclosure risks accompanying a federal trial, arguing that a federal trial could (more easily) result in acquittals of guilty persons.[82] On the other hand, federal trials are generally seen as able to produce fair verdicts; an important perception factor within the US and abroad.[83] The possibility of undue delay may also be part of a prosecution strategy to opt for federal trials which are, time-wise, most often conducted more efficiently. Federal courts have not only processed a far greater number of terrorism cases than military commissions, but also concluded them more swiftly.[84] Whereas military commissions had completed seven cases in the ten years after the 9/11 attacks, federal courts had completed 578 terrorism-related cases in the same timeframe.[85] Yet, at the time Moussaoui was tried in a US federal court, the prosecution could not have foreseen this.

It is instructive to ascertain why the US Administration made the legal-political choices that it did between a federal court trial and that of a military commission. In a public speech at Northwestern University near Chicago in 2012, US Attorney General Eric Holder set out the policy and preference of the Obama Administration for prosecuting terrorism suspects before federal criminal courts. Holder proffered the view that there '[is] no inherent contradiction between using military commissions in appropriate cases while still prosecuting other terrorists in civilian courts'.[86] The US Attorney General advocated that the 'reformed commissions' (in 2009—under the Obama Administration—the Military Commissions' rules were amended supposedly in favour of the defendant) guaranteed the same fair trial rights as within the civil court system; for example, that 'statements obtained through torture, inhuman or degrading treatment' are prohibited, suspects have the right to legal counsel, and that these commissions too 'provide a presumption of innocence and require proof of guilt beyond a reasonable doubt'. Yet the US Attorney General acknowledged that there is one fundamental difference between these two types of trials; some of the evidentiary rules at the military commission level do reflect the 'reality of the battlefield', in that statements obtained from suspects and witnesses 'may be admissible even in the absence of Miranda warnings, because we cannot expect military personnel to administer warnings to an enemy captured in battle'.[87]

Holder's statement regarding the fair trial equality between the two types of trial does not, however, hold for when the Moussaoui case was first dealt with in court in January 2002. At that time military commissions proceedings did allow evidence obtained through coercion. A slightly augmented Military Commissions Act (MCA) was enacted by the US Congress and signed into law by the Bush Administration following the US Supreme Court's ruling of 29 June 2006 in *Hamdan v. Rumsfeld*.[88] In this five-to three majority judgment, the justices ruled that the military commissions established without congressional approval by President Bush in November 2001 were unconstitutional because the executive branch of government did not have the power to create judicial organs with special jurisdiction. They also deemed that such military proceedings violated Common Article 3 of the Geneva Conventions. In particular, the admission of evidence at trial in the absence of the defendant was ruled out of order by the US Supreme Court. In 2009, under the Obama Administration, the MCA was revised, amending some of the 2006 rules. And yet, as of this writing, the defence lawyers for KSM and his four co-defendants still face court hearings at Guantánamo Bay in which the defendants are not allowed to participate, the reason given being that they may not share the results of these hearings with them.[89]

While balancing these arguments pro and contra military commission proceedings, it may have been the case that the US government under the Bush Administration was willing to put Moussaoui on trial before a federal court in order to test the resilience of the federal criminal law system in prosecuting terrorism suspects. After all, Moussaoui did not have an active part in the 9/11 attacks; from this point of view, he was only 'a small fish'. The US government was able to demonstrate 'good faith' to the international community by subjecting terrorism suspects to a swift and expedient federal trial. Clearly, the objective that the US government pursued in the Moussaoui case was to show the world the transparency of its system, a 'strategy' that the trial judge Ms. Leonie Brinkema was eager to implement. Her intention was to admit all of the victims into the courtroom and to organise simultaneous video casts in other places in order to provide extensive live coverage of the proceedings. Furthermore she had these screenings set up in other courtrooms akin to the 'real' one.[90] Therefore, the choice to try Moussaoui before a federal court had direct consequences for the families of the victims, offering them a forum to ease their pain and to seek justice. Despite the fact that many members of the victims' families were willing to testify in court (relatively soon after the attacks), the Moussaoui trial ultimately did not turn into a public forum for the victims. Only some of the family members of the victims testified at trial, and these appearances did not turn into a media circus as was feared.[91]

One could say that the success of the prosecution's strategy was evidenced by the jury convicting Moussaoui and sentencing him to six consecutive life sentences, without the possibility of parole.[92] On the other hand, the prosecution had sought the death penalty, which Judge Brinkema tried to prevent.[93] Be this as it may, in the Moussaoui trial the US government was able to demonstrate that it could produce guilty verdicts against 9/11 suspects through its federal court system while upholding fair trial guarantees as provided for in the US constitution. This observation does not negate the criticism that revolved around the Moussaoui trial; namely that it offered a 'stage' for Moussaoui to express his radical ideas. This performative perspective is addressed in the next section.

7.5.3. Moussaoui's Performative Trial Strategies

The Plea Agreement 'Battle'

At the start of the trial, Moussaoui proclaimed, 'In the name of Allah, I do not have anything to plead, and I enter no plea'.[94] From the outset of the trial—which began on 2 January 2002—Zacarias Moussaoui intended to steer the proceedings in his own direction by refusing legal counsel and insisting on representing himself, by refusing to plead to the charges (as a result of which federal judge Ms. Brinkema entered a not guilty plea 'on his behalf') and to petition to hear several detained Al Qaeda leaders as potential witnesses, including Khalid Sheikh Mohammed. At the outset, Moussaoui staged more aggressive tactics, in that he challenged the court's competence to try him and indeed the very competence of the US court system as a whole. His refusal to accept any legal assistance from court-appointed lawyers is illustrative of this. In response, on 22 April 2002, a hearing was held to assess Moussaoui's demand to represent himself without counsel. To clarify his reasons for declining court-appointed counsel and to underpin his view that he was subjected to a 'corrupted' legal system, Moussaoui recited several surahs of the Koran.[95] On 13 June 2002—after a mental evaluation by experts—the federal judge considered him competent to represent himself whilst at the same time ordering the previously court-appointed counsel to stay on as a standby.[96]

Moussaoui changed his legal defence strategy several times. When the trial began in January 2002, Moussaoui refused to enter a plea.[97] As mentioned above, in April 2002 Moussaoui asked to represent himself, occasioning Judge Brinkema's request that he be mentally evaluated.[98] On 13 June 2002, Moussaoui, once he had been permitted to represent himself, pleaded not guilty. On 18 July 2002, after the indictment was amended by the prosecution to strengthen its case for the death penalty, Moussaoui announced his intention to plead guilty. He then told the court, 'I have knowledge and I participated in Al Qaeda. [...] I am a member of Al Qaeda [...] I pledge *bayat* to Osama Bin Laden'.[99] On 25 July 2002, Judge Brinkema—after giving Moussaoui one week to reconsider—rejected his plea as disingenuous and equivocal, not being convinced that Moussaoui fully understood the consequences of his actions. On 14 November 2003, Judge Brinkema terminated Moussaoui's self-representation due to his repeated unprofessional and dishonourable interventions.[100] Between 2002 and 2004 several important procedural aspects were litigated at trial, such as access to certain Al Qaeda witnesses (including KSM) and the admissibility of the death penalty. In April 2005 Moussaoui again expressed his intention to plead guilty, a plea Judge Brinkema accepted on 22 April 2005 for all six conspiracy charges. Hence, the trial entered the sentencing stage.[101] Opening statements were delivered on 6 March 2006. On 3 April 2006 the twelve-person jury ruled that Moussaoui was eligible for the death penalty since his lying to federal agents implicated him in the 9/11 attacks.[102] After a month of deliberations the jury—unable to reach unanimity on the death penalty—recommended a sentence of life imprisonment on 3 May 2006. This recommendation was formally accepted by Judge Brinkema on 4 May 2006.[103] One day after Moussaoui was sentenced to life imprisonment, he announced to his lawyers his intention to withdraw his guilty plea; on 6 May 2006 a motion was filed to that effect.[104] Judge Brinkema denied Moussaoui's motion on 8 May 2006, ruling that federal law does not provide for withdrawing a guilty plea after sentencing.[105]

Moussaoui's Main Strategy: Putting the Trial 'on Trial'

Moussaoui's changing attitude during the trial makes it difficult to detect his exact strategy. The most likely strategy he pursued was to disrupt the actual trial and question the legitimacy of the trial itself, an explicit strategy of rupture. From this perspective, it might have been a deliberate choice to switch tactics (such as his inconsistent approach vis-à-vis pleading to the charges) in order to discredit the US criminal justice system. It is unlikely that Moussaoui was unconscious of the implications of his strategy due to his mental state. On the one hand, Moussaoui's lawyers argued that Moussaoui's actions—e.g. firing his lawyers—showed his disturbed state of mind, while he invented conspiracy theories.[106] Judge Brinkema had Moussaoui mentally examined during the trial phase.[107] Moussaoui's mother, Aicha el-Wafi, stated in an interview on 21 June 2002—when she was in the US to visit her son in jail—that Moussaoui had made a mistake by firing his lawyers. In her view, her son did this due to the fact that he had been 'shut up and closed away from the world for the past nine months, that he doesn't eat well. He is not sleeping well. He has light above his head 24 hours a day. He doesn't see anyone.'[108] Yet, these factors do not support the notion that Moussaoui was insane.

On the other hand, Moussaoui appeared to have deliberately targeted the US legal system and the person of the presiding judge, Ms. Brinkema, transforming the courtroom into an arena of open lawfare (see Introduction), with the intention of undermining the integrity of the judge. On 11 June 2002, Moussaoui submitted a self-written motion, entitled 'Motion for pre-contempt of Leonie Brinkema order to declare Zacarias Moussaoui crazy'. Clearly this action attacked the impartiality of the federal judge since she had earlier ordered the psychiatric assessment of the defendant. Moussaoui's strategyto undermine the legitimacy of the trial as such was illustrated in his 'own' psychological analysis of the federal judge, embedded in that motion, reading:

> *Mental Status Examination*
> Axis 1: Acute symptom of Islamaphobia with complex of gender inferiority.
>
> *Diagnostic Impression*
> Legal pathological killer instinct with ego boosting dementia to become Supreme.
>
> *Conclusion and Recommendations*
> Immediate psychiatric hospitalization to specialist unit. (Propose unit. UBL Treatment Center, of course UBL stand for Unique Best Location)[109]

Another example was Moussaoui's motion filed on 22 February 2003 entitled:

> In the Name of Allah: Censured by the United Sodom of America
>
> Slave of Allah v. Slave of Satan
> Zacarias Moussaoui John Ashcroft[110]

John Ashcroft, the US Attorney General at the time of the Moussaoui case, is thus referred to as 'Slave of Satan', while Judge Leonie Brinkema is referred therein as 'Death Judge Leonie'. The power struggle between the court and the defendant continued until 14 November 2003, when Judge Brinkema's tolerance was exhausted; citing the continued recurrence of several inflammatory briefs from the defendant, she annulled Moussaoui's right to self-representation and appointed counsel.[111]

Moussaoui's strategy of rupture to discredit the US legal system was also visible during the battle at the trial when it came to disclosing evidence. Moussaoui must have been aware that under the US criminal legal system the prosecution bears the absolute obligation to disclose to the defence upon request all exculpatory evidence in its possession and other discovery materials. This obligation originates from a US Supreme Court ruling in *Brady v. Maryland*: 'Suppression by the prosecution of evidence favorable to an accused who has requested it violates due process where the evidence is material either to guilt or to punishment, irrespective of the good faith or bad faith of the prosecution',[112] as well as from Rule 16 of the Federal Rules of Criminal Procedure. This provision obligates the government to disclose to a defendant copies of relevant statements made by the defendant as well as of photographs, documents, books, etc., relevant to the trial when these are within the government's possession, custody or control.[113]

As a result, in the Moussaoui case, due to these strict disclosure obligations, the prosecution—assisted by experts from the Counter-Terrorism Section of the Criminal Division of the Justice Department—was forced to invest 'hundreds of hours in reviewing thousands of documents' in the possession of the US intelligence services.[114] Subsequently, in July 2003, Moussaoui asked the court for access to Al Qaeda detainees, including KSM, in order to interview them. Moussaoui and his appointed lawyers also relied on the Fifth Amendment (due process protections) and the Sixth Amendment (fair trial rights).[115] Moussaoui's actions triggered an intense and fundamental legal debate and opinions, revealing a dichotomy between the judiciary and executive branch within the US as to the scope of fair trial rights that terrorism suspects should have. The disclosure battle also resulted in a debate on the admissibility of the death penalty, which the prosecution sought. On 2 October 2003, Judge Brinkema barred the US government from seeking the death penalty because Moussaoui was denied access to certain Al Qaeda witnesses.[116] This decision was overturned by a federal court of appeals on 22 April 2004; the government was allowed to seek the death penalty. It was also argued that national security provided satisfactory grounds for refusing the right to interview certain witnesses prior to or during the trial, and that Moussaoui would have to manage with government-prepared summaries of the statements by the Al Qaeda witnesses that were requested.[117]

All of these actions by Moussaoui indicate that he had deliberately chosen to put the trial and the judge 'on trial', and as such they also contradict the suggestion that he was insane. In addition, more tacit indications confirm that Moussaoui's strategy was intentional. These include his legal battle to represent himself without counsel as well as his filing of all sorts of motions in an effort to discredit, delegitimise and delay the trial; providing a catalyst for journalists to refer to the case as *Moussaoui v. the United States* instead of the other way around.[118] It is thus fair to say that, given Moussaoui's legal performances, his approach was indeed defined by a well-chosen strategy of rupture, which turned the courtroom in a theatre of lawfare.

Moussaoui's Secondary Strategy: Putting the Western World on Trial

It is also likely that a secondary goal of his strategy of putting western civilisation as such 'on trial' was to become a martyr within the Islamic society. Several examples illustrate this aim.

First, from the outset of the trial, the French-Moroccan prayed for the annihilation of several states, including Israel, Russia, Canada, the United Kingdom, Australia and the US, as well as for the liberation of Palestine, Chechnya and Afghanistan.

Second, two specific tactics can be disentangled from Moussaoui's 2002 guilty plea. Moussaoui made it known at the trial in no uncertain terms that he wanted to die as a martyr in his fight for the jihad.[119] Two days before Moussaoui announced his decision to plead guilty, the government had strengthened its case in order to support the request for the death penalty.[120] If Moussaoui wanted to die as a martyr, he had to act accordingly at trial in order to 'convince' the jury to impose the death penalty. Yet, he was unsuccessful in pursuing this strategy; in the end the death penalty was not imposed. Three weeks after Moussaoui was sentenced to life imprisonment, Osama Bin Laden released a video denying Moussaoui's involvement in the 9/11 attacks.[121] Analysts concluded that Al Qaeda was probably trying to distance itself from 'a lunatic', for many considered Moussaoui to be erratic during his trial. This message from Osama Bin Laden must have been a setback in Moussaoui's 'martyrdom strategy'.[122]

Still, some analysts have argued that Bin Laden's video was released to demonstrate the flaws of the US criminal justice system; one that was willing to convict someone for conspiracy in a plot in which, according to high-ranking Al Qaeda leaders, the defendant was not even involved.[123]

Moussaoui's Sentencing Strategy: The Battle for the Death Penalty

The opening statement of Moussaoui's defence attorney, Edward MacMahon, at the sentencing stage raised the question whether the trial could have produced a guilty verdict had Moussaoui not entered this plea. On 6 March 2006 MacMahon proclaimed that Moussaoui had not admitted involvement in the 9/11 attacks, while those attacks formed 'the heart of this case'.[124] MacMahon contended that:

> What the Statement of Facts contains is mostly historical admissions of a general nature about al Qaeda and its training and other plans that Moussaoui, as an admitted al Qaeda member, was in a position to know, including, yes, the existence of a plane's operation. The reason Mr. Spencer [lead prosecutor, GJK] declines to tell you that he is going to prove what role Moussaoui played in the 9/11 attacks is because there is no evidence to support it. There is no evidence as to what he did in these attacks, and the government would surely come forward with that evidence if it existed.[125]

The defence statement contended that Moussaoui did not lie to federal agents, since he simply did not know about the impending 9/11 attacks.

At the end of the trial, Moussaoui's defence attorney concluded that a verdict would give Moussaoui exactly what he was longing for, namely, martyrdom. MacMahon stated, 'the only way he can achieve that dream and then live on as some smiling face on a recruiting poster for Usama Bin Laden is by your verdict. Please don't make him a hero.'[126] However, against the advice of his lawyers Moussaoui, on 27 March 2006, alleged that he was supposed to fly a fifth plane into the White House on 9/11, although—as said—no evidence of that was found.[127] On 13 April 2006 Moussaoui stated that he did not regret the 9/11 attacks. Five days later a psychologist on behalf of the defence testified that Moussaoui suffered from paranoid schizophrenia with delusions.[128] On 24 April the jury started its deliberations and on 3 May 2006 recommended a life sentence, which was accepted by Judge Brinkema on 4 May 2006.[129]

As mentioned, the appropriateness of imposing the death penalty was both legally and politically one of the most axiomatic issues. Provoking the death penalty most likely served as an additional trial strategy for both the prosecution and for Moussaoui in terms of his becoming a martyr.

The prosecution's adamantly seeking to impose the death penalty on Zacarias Moussaoui raised one of the most controversial issues of dispute. Ironically, by pursuing the death penalty the prosecution was obliged to meet a higher standard of proof, namely that Moussaoui 'intentionally participated in an act [...] and the victim died as a direct result of the act'.[130] Yet, Moussaoui only conceded that he knew about the plot and did not do anything to prevent it from taking place.

Why then did the prosecution ask for the death penalty? Radsan notes that 'the justice department's decision to seek the death penalty in the Moussaoui case was political', since 'the American public was outraged after the attacks on our soil'.[131] Here, as observed, one may find the reason why Judge Brinkema was relatively lenient in favour of the defendant in terms of the disclosure of exculpatory evidence, namely 'the looming threat of the death penalty over Moussaoui.'[132] Had the death penalty not been on the table, the prosecution would probably not have been put under legal pressure to disclose classified materials to the defence, or at the least would have been authorised extensively to redact such documents.[133]

On 3 May 2006, the federal jury—after having found Moussaoui guilty—sentenced him, not to death, but to life imprisonment without the possibility of parole. The irony lies in the fact that because, on one charge, a single juror voted against the death penalty, it was the US jury system itself that saved Moussaoui's life. Three of the six charges were punishable by the death penalty, yet required a unanimous jury. But, as the foreman of the 12-member jury revealed to the *Washington Post*, the jury was not unanimous; it voted 11–1, 10–2 and 10–2 in favour of the death penalty.[134]

Judge Brinkema, in her sentencing order, sentenced Moussaoui to six consecutive terms of life imprisonment which, as observed, deprived Moussaoui of 'martyrdom in a great big bang of glory'[135]—words chosen by Judge Brinkema. Needless to say, Mr. Moussaoui must have been surprised to receive life imprisonment instead of the death penalty. He apparently never anticipated that outcome.[136]

For the international community though, the fact that federal prosecutors were pursuing the death penalty could have endangered international cooperation in criminal matters, for example in extradition cases between the European Union and the US.[137]

In conclusion, Moussaoui's performance suggests a fourfold strategy:

1) Discredit the judge;
2) Discredit the US legal system
3) Put western society as such on trial;
4) Provoke the use of the death penalty and die as a martyr.

Unlike KSM and his four co-defendants who face the death penalty before the Military Commission, Moussaoui was not put on death row. It is doubtful whether this was due to this fourfold strategy. It seems more likely that his escaping death row was due to the functioning of the federal (jury) system.

7.6. Conclusion: Past and Future Legislative (Political) Lessons

7.6.1. *The Aftermath*

Aicha El-Wafi, Moussaoui's mother, responded after the trial by stating that her son was 'being judged for the things he says, the things he believes, the convictions he has that shock us all, but not for his involvement in the attacks'.[138] Indeed, as analysed before, the evidence was not persuasive as to the actual knowledge Moussaoui had before 9/11; what exactly did he know about the 9/11 plots? Both Khalid Sheikh Mohammed and Osama Bin Laden denied that Moussaoui was to be the 20th hijacker. Two other Al Qaeda operatives—detained at Guantánamo Bay—declared in their interviews conducted by US authorities that Moussaoui was not involved in the 9/11 conspiracy; rather, the government would come to suspect that the 20th hijacker was an Al Qaeda detainee at Guantánamo Bay.[139]

The question triggered by Mrs. El Wafi's remark is whether the outcome of the Moussaoui trial was justified from a legal and political perspective. From the perspective of law enforcement, the Moussaoui trial made clear that disclosure obligations in the federal court system put intelligence agencies at a disadvantage, whereas military commission proceedings provide the government with more mechanisms of secrecy to submit classified documents required for a conviction while securing its sources.[140] As John Radsan put it, Zacarias Moussaoui 'should have been dealt with as we are dealing with Khalid Sheikh Mohammed and other members of the Al Qaeda terrorist network; through non-criminal detention. [...] Placing him in a federal district court for a criminal trial was a mistake.'[141] Indeed, the criminal law paradigm in dealing with terrorist suspects (the tension between the secrecy of counter-terrorism operations and the defendants' fair trial rights) is at the heart of the political reluctance to prosecute terrorist suspects in civilian courts. Proponents of pursuing the line of military commissions, as being the appropriate forum to try terrorist suspects (affiliated with Al Qaeda), tend to rely on pragmatic arguments such as the costs, complications, risks to intelligence sources and agencies.[142] They will also point to trial performances akin to Moussaoui's tactics.

However true these arguments may be, they negate the fact that by submitting these cases to civilian courts the incentive for law enforcement and intelligence officers to comply with the law and fair trial standards is strong. In other words, they will be more inclined to abstain from illegal methods lest the federal judges hold such methods against them. Thus, the quality of their fact-finding and ultimately the quality of the criminal evidence submitted could be reinforced. Potential disruptive trial performances should not weigh against the advantages of allowing the rule of law to prevail.

7.6.2. Political Choices Revisited

Following the Moussaoui trial, several terrorism trials, such as the case against KSM, have been referred to a military commission. Was this due to Moussaoui's performances at his trial? The ten years since 9/11 have demonstrated that terrorism trials in federal courts seem a more viable option in terms of efficiency: quantitatively more trials can be concluded, and in a shorter period of time. Moreover, the judgments rendered by federal courts are likely to be more widely accepted because of adherence to international fair trial standards. Yet, at a federal trial the government faces more legal risks, and cannot satisfy all national security demands or meet all security risks involved.

In this regard, it is interesting to focus on post-Moussaoui trials held before the revised Military Commissions, specifically the Omar Khadr and the Ghailani trials which took place in 2010. Like Moussaoui, Ghailani was tried before a federal court and sentenced to life imprisonment. Yet, unlike the French-Moroccan Al Qaeda member, Ghailani cooperated with his counsel and pleaded not guilty, launching an effective defence. The question of Ghailani's right to a fair trial arose during the proceedings, as it appeared that he had been tortured by the CIA during his detention in Guantánamo Bay. The New York federal judge, Judge Kaplan, ruled in favour of Ghailani's right to a fair trial—as Judge Brinkema had done in the Moussaoui case. The US district Judge Lewis Kaplan admonished the US government for torturing Ghailani (which led to the disclosure of the name of the person who allegedly delivered the explosives to him). Hence, Judge Kaplan precluded the evidence of this witness.[143] Although both federal courts gave preference to the fair trial rights of the accused, Moussaoui was ultimately denied access to key witnesses at his trial, such as KSM. At the end of the day, the result was the same: both Moussaoui and Ghailani received a life term in prison.

Terrorism trials are lost or won on procedural and evidentiary issues. The US federal courts and actually the criminal justice system in its entirety are predominantly created for ordinary crimes, not for crimes allegedly committed on the battlefield. The choice to try terrorists before a civilian court may inevitably lead to a distortion of common procedural mechanisms. The Moussaoui trial illustrated this tension: national security interests clashed with the defendant's fundamental rights, and no actor in the legal arena was able to unequivocally demonstrate the superiority of either of them. Hence, trying a national security threat in an ordinary district court remains a balancing act for the presiding judge and jury.

However, it seems that Moussaoui did benefit from a trial before a federal court. In the aftermath of the Moussaoui case, the policy pursued by the US government in countering terrorism through (criminal) trials remains ambiguous. Its policy for deciding between US civilian courts and military commissions seems arbitrary and subject to amendments (i.e. laws have been frequently amended to keep all options open for the US government). The 9/11 events were instrumental in transforming the international legal order, in terms of security policies but also as to the political choices to prosecute terrorism suspects before civil courts or military commissions. The trial strategies performed in the Moussaoui case may have exacerbated the current preference within US policy for bringing high-profile 9/11 suspects such as KSM to justice before military commissions and for allowing security considerations to prevail over open and fair trial standards.

Notes

1 See for example: Mathias Borgers and Elies van Sliedregt, 'The Meaning of the Precautionary Principle for the Assessment of Criminal Measures in the Fight against Terrorism', *Erasmus Law Review*, 2:2 (2009), pp. 171–195; Oliver Kessler, 'Is Risk Changing the Politics of Legal Argumentation?', *Leiden Journal of International Law*, 21:4 (2008), pp. 863–884; Jude McCulloch and Sharon Pickering. 'Precrime and Counter-terrorism: Imagining future crime in the "War on Terror"', *British Journal of Criminology*, 49:5 (2009), pp. 628–645; Marieke de Goede and Beatrice de Graaf, 'Sentencing Risk. Temporality and precaution in terrorism trials', *International Political Sociology*, 7:3 (2013), pp. 313–331.

2 Public Law 107-140—sept. 18, 2001, S.J. Res. 23; the Act authorises the President to 'use all necessary and appropriate force against those nations, organizations, or persons he determines planned, authorised, committed, or aided the terrorist attacks that occurred on September 11, 2001, or harbored such organizations or persons, in order to prevent any future acts of international terrorism against the United States by such nations, organizations or persons'.

3 'President Bush Declares "War on Terror"', *Speech to a Joint Session of Congress* (20 September 2001), http://middleeast.about.com/od/usmideastpolicy/a/bush-war-on-terror-speech.htm. Retrieved 2 July 2013.

4 *United States of America* v. *Zacarias Moussaoui*, US District Court for the Eastern District of Virginia (December 2001), http://www.justice.gov/ag/moussaouiindictment.htm. Retrieved 2 July 2013; 'Al-Qaeda's origins and links', BBC *News* (20 July 2004), http://news.bbc.co.uk/2/hi/1670089.stm. Retrieved 2 July 2013.

5 *United States of America* v. *Zacarias Moussaoui*, US District Court for the Eastern District of Virginia (December 2001), http://www.justice.gov/ag/moussaouiindictment.htm. Retrieved 2 July 2013.

6 'President Bush Declares "War on Terror"', *Speech to a Joint Session of Congress* (20 September 2001), http://middleeast.about.com/od/usmideastpolicy/a/bush-war-on-terror-speech.htm Retrieved 2 July 2013.

7 Ibid.

8 'U.S. War in Afghanistan', *Council on Foreign Relations* (no date), http://www.cfr.org/afghanistan/us-war-afghanistan/p20018. Retrieved 2 July 2013.

9 'Uniting and Strengthening America by Providing Appropriate Tools Required to Intercept and Obstruct Terrorism (USA PATRIOT Act) Act of 2001', *Public Law 107-156—Oct. 26, 2001*, http://www.gpo.gov/fdsys/pkg/PLAW-107publ56/pdf/PLAW-107publ56.pdf. Retrieved 2 July 2013.

10 'President Bush's Order on Trial of Terrorists by Military', *New York Times* (14 November 2001), http://www.nytimes.com/2001/11/14/national/14DTEX.html?pagewanted=all. Retrieved 22 August 2013; 'Military Order of 13 November 2001—Detention, Treatment, and Trial of Certain Non-Citizens in the War Against Terrorism', *Federal Register, 66:22* (2001).

11 Nada Mourtada, 'Les Tribunaux Militaires Aux Etats-Unis: Inter arma silent leges?', AFRI: *Annuaire Français de Relations Internationales*, 4 (2003), pp. 115–147, there p. 115.

12 At the time, the Taliban was the government of Afghanistan. However, it was recognised by only three countries.

13 Krishna Andavolu, 'Strange Things Are Happening at Khalid Sheikh Mohammed's Trial', *Vice* (3 February 2013), http://www.vice.com/read/strange-things-are-happening-at-khalid-sheikh-mohammeds-trial. Retrieved 2 July 2013.

14 'The Guantánamo Docket, Khalid Sheikh Mohammed', *New York Times* (22 August 2013), http://projects.nytimes.com/guantanamo/detainees/10024-khalid-shaikh-mohammed. Retrieved 23 August 2013.

15 The Military Commissions Act of 2009 in principle prohibits the use of statements elicited through torture, yet not 'against a person accused of torture or such treatment

[...]'. The MCA furthermore provides that 'No statement of the accused is admissible at trial unless the military judge finds that the statement is reliable and sufficiently probative; and that the statement was made "incident to lawful conduct during military operations at the point of capture or during closely related active combat engagement" and the interests of justice would best be served by admission of the statement into evidence; or that the statement was voluntarily given, taking into consideration all relevant circumstances, including military and intelligence operations during hostilities; the accused's age, education level, military training; and the change in place or identity of interrogator between that statement and any prior questioning of the accused.' See Jennifer K. Elsea, 'Comparison of Rights in Military Commissions Trials and Trials in Federal Criminal Court', *Congressional Research Service* (28 February 2013), http://www.fas.org/sgp/crs/natsec/R40932.pdf. Retrieved 23 August 2013.

16 'House Blocks US trial of Guantánamo detainees', *The Guardian* (9 December 2010), http://www.theguardian.com/world/2010/dec/09/guantanamo-bay-criminal-courts-barack-obama. Retrieved 5 September 2013.

17 'Some Key Facts on Military Commissions v. Federal Courts', *Human Rights First* (no date), http://www.humanrightsfirst.org/wp-content/uploads/pdf/Fact_Sheet-Key_Facts_Military_Commissions_vs_Federal_Courts.pdf. Retrieved 5 September 2013.

18 Ibid.

19 'How Military Commissions Work', *Website of the Office of Military Commissions* (no date), http://www.mc.mil/ABOUTUS.aspx. Retrieved 15 August 2013.

20 'Military Order of 13 November 2001—Detention, Treatment, and Trial of Certain Non-Citizens in the War Against Terrorism', *Federal Register*, 66: 22 (2001).

21 Ibid; 'U.S. Court of Military Commissions Review (USCMCR) History', *Website of the Office of Military Commissions* (no date), http://www.mc.mil/ABOUTUS/USCMCRHistory.aspx. Retrieved 15 August 2013.

22 *Hamdan v. Rumsfeld*, 548 U.S. 557, 635 (2006); Military Commissions Act (MCA) (2006); G.G.J. Knoops, 'The Proliferation of the Law of International Criminal Tribunals Within Terrorism and "unlawful" combatancy trials after Hamdan v. Rumsfeld', *Fordham International Law Journal*, 30:3 (2007), pp. 599–641.

23 J.K. Elsea, 'The Military Commissions Act of 2009: Overview and legal issues', *Congressional Research Service* (6 April 2012), p. 7.

24 Michele Shepard, *Guantánamo's Child* (Ontario: Wiley & Sons Canada, 2008).

25 *United States of America v. Omar Ahmed Khadr*, Offer for Pre-trial agreement (12 October 2010), http://www.law.utoronto.ca/documents/Mackin/Khadr_PreTrialAgree.pdf. Retrieved at 9 September 2013; Jennifer Turner, 'Khadr Accepts Plea Deal, Trial Averted',

American Civil Liberties Union (25 October 2010), https://www.aclu.org/blog/national-security/khadr-accepts-plea-deal-trial-averted. Retrieved 9 September 2013.

26 *State v. Cole*, 107 S.C. 285, 288–289, S.E. 624, 625 (1917), in: Rollin Perkins and Ronald Boyce (eds), *Criminal Law*. 3rd ed. (Mineola, NY: Foundation Press, 1982), p. 684.

27 Ibid.

28 '*Prosecutor v. Duško Tadić*', ICTY IT-94-1-A (15 July 1999).

29 Ibid., paragraph 186.

30 Ibid., par. 191.

31 Ibid., par. 227.

32 Knoops, 'The proliferation of the law of international criminal tribunals within terrorism and "unlawful" combatancy trials after Hamdan v. Rumsfeld', p. 625.

33 *Hamdan v. Rumsfeld*, 'Secretary of Defence, et al.', No. 05–184 (29 June 2006), http://caselaw.lp.findlaw.com/scripts/getcase.pl?court=us&vol=000&invol=05-184. Retrieved 9 September 2013.

34 National Defence Authorization Act for the Fiscal Year 2010, Title XVIII—Military Commissions, §950t. Crimes triable by military commission (29); Military Commissions Act 2006, §950v, Crimes triable by military commissions (28).

35 Phil Hirschkorn, 'Moussaoui Is Mentally Ill', CNN *Law Centre* (17 April 2006).

36 Katherine Donahue, 'The Religious Trajectories of the Moussaoui Family', ISIM *Review*, 21 (2008).

37 Ibid.

38 Ibid.

39 Michael J. Sniffen, '"America, You Lost—I Won": Moussaoui sentenced to life in prison', *Chicago Sun Times* (5 April 2006); see also Phil Hirschkom, 'Lawyers: Moussaoui possibly schizophrenic', CNN (25 January 2006).

40 Katherine Donahue, 'The Religious Trajectories of the Moussaoui Family', ISIM *Review*, 21 (2008), pp. 18–19; Neil. A. Lewis, 'Moussaoui's Childhood Is Presented as Mitigating Factor', *New York Times* (18 April 2006).

41 Ibid.

42 'Psychologist: Moussaoui schizophrenic', NBC *News* (17 April 2006), http://www.nbcnews.com/id/12348153/ns/us_news-security/t/psychologist-moussaoui-schizophrenic/. Retrieved 9 September 2013.

43 Donahue, 'The Religious Trajectories', pp. 18–19.

44 'A Profile of Zacarias Moussaoui', CNN *Justice* (22 April 2005), http://articles.cnn.com/2005-04-22/justice/moussaoui.profile_1_airman-flight-school-zacarias-moussaoui-ramzi-binalshibh?_s=PM:LAW.Retrieved 27 June 2012.

45 Donahue, 'The Religious Trajectories', pp. 18–19.

46 Ibid.

47 'A Profile of Zacarias Moussaoui', CNN *Justice* (22 April 2005).

48 *United States of America* v. *Zacarias Moussaoui*, US District Court for the Eastern District of Virginia (December 2001), http://www.justice.gov/ag/moussaouiindictment.htm. Retrieved 14 June 2012; Stephen E. Atkins, *The 9/11 Encyclopedia*. 2nd ed. (Santa Barbara, CA: ABC-CLIO, 2011), p. 311.

49 'The 9/11 Commission Report', *Final Report of the National Commission on Terrorist Attacks Upon the United States* (22 July 2004), p. 2, http://www.911commission.gov/report/911Report.pdf. Retrieved 12 June 2012.

50 Donahue, 'The Religious Trajectories', pp. 18–19.

51 Neil A. Lewis, 'Moussaoui's Childhood Is Presented as Mitigating Factor', *New York Times* (18 April 2006).

52 Ibid.

53 Or possibly he thought there was no way back; yet this option seems less likely, given his attitude in court as will be discussed throughout this chapter.

54 'The 9/11 Commission Report', *Final Report*, p. 225.

55 Ibid.

56 'Request from Minneapolis FBI to Washington for Search Warrant for Zacarias Moussaoui', UMKC: *University of Missouri-Kansas city* (24 August 2001), http://law2.umkc.edu/faculty/projects/ftrials/moussaoui/zmfbi8-24.html. Retrieved 9 September 2013.

57 'The 9/11 Commission Report', *Final Report*, pp. 246–247.

58 'Request from Minneapolis FBI to Washington for Search Warrant for Zacarias Moussaoui', UMKC: *University of Missouri-Kansas city* (24 August 2001), http://law2.umkc.edu/faculty/projects/ftrials/moussaoui/zmfbi8-24.html. Retrieved 9 September 2013.

59 'Private email from Harry Samit to W. Jay Abbot' (15 August 2001), http://en.wikisource.org/wiki/FBI_eMails_concerning_Moussaoui. Retrieved 21 June 2012; Office of the Inspector General, 'A Review of the FBI's Handling of Intelligence Information Related to the September 11 Attacks', *Special Report—November 2004* (June 2006), p. 1.

60 T. Dwyer and J. Markon, 'Flight Instructor Recalls Unease with Moussaoui', *Washington Post* (10 March 2006).

61 Stephen E. Atkins, *The 9/11 Encyclopedia* (2011), p. 311; Office of the Inspector General, 'A Review of the FBI's Handling of Intelligence Information Related to the September 11 Attacks', *Special Report—November 2004* (June 2006), p. 2.

62 'The 9/11 Commission Report', *Final Report*, p. 247.

63 Timothy Dwyer and Jerry Markon, 'Flight Instructor Recalls Unease with Moussaoui', *Washington Post* (10 March 2006).

64 Douglas O. Linder, 'The Trial of Zacarias Moussaoui: An account' (2006), p. 4., http://

law2.umkc.edu/faculty/projects/ftrials/moussaoui/moussaouihome.html. Retrieved 22 August 2013.

65 'Substitution for the testimony of Khalid Sheikh Mohammed' (date unkown), p. 3, http://law2.umkc.edu/faculty/projects/ftrials/moussaoui/sheikhstmt.pdf. Retrieved 22 August 2013.

66 Ibid.

67 *United States of America v. Zacarias Moussaoui*, Stipulation regarding Richard Reid, Crim. No. 01-455-A,http://law2.umkc.edu/faculty/projects/ftrials/moussaoui/reidstipulation.pdf. Retrieved 22 August 2013.

68 See section 11.5.2.

69 John Rosenthal, 'Doing Justice to Zacarias Moussaoui', *Policy Review*, 146 (2007), p. 2, http://www.hoover.org/publications/policy-review/article/5870. Retrieved 31 August 2012.

70 *United States of America* v. *Zacarias Moussaoui*, US District Court for the Eastern District of Virginia (December 2001), available at: http://www.justice.gov/ag/moussaouiindictment.htm. Retrieved 14 June 2012.

71 Ibid.

72 Ibid.

73 Ibid.

74 Ibid.

75 Ibid.

76 Ibid.

77 Attorney General Transcript, News Conference regarding Zacarias Moussaoui (11 December 2001), https://www.fas.org/irp/news/2001/12/agremarks12_11.htm. Retrieved 3 September 2012.

78 United States Attorney Southern District of New York, 'Ahmed Khalfan Ghailani found guilty in Manhattan Federal Court of conspiring in the 1998 destruction of United States embassies in East Africa resulting in death', *Press release* (17 November 2010), http://www.justice.gov/usao/nys/pressreleases/November10/ghailaniahmedkhalfanverdictpr.pdf Retrieved 3 September 2012.

79 Department of Defence, Military Commission Order No. 1 (21 March 2002), http://www.defence.gov/news/Mar2002/d20020321ord.pdf. Retrieved 3 September 2012.

80 Beatrice de Graaf, 'Terrorists on Trial: A performative perspective', ICCT *Expert Meeting Paper* (2011).

81 Jennifer K. Elsea, 'Comparison of Rights in Military Commission Trials and Trials in Federal Criminal Court', *Congressional Research Service* (28 February 2013); Human Rights First, Fact Sheet, http://www.humanrightsfirst.org/wp-content/uploads/pdf/

Fact_Sheet-Key_Facts_Military_Commissions_vs_Federal_Courts.pdf. Retrieved 22 August 2013.

82 Elsea, 'Comparison of Rights in Military Commission Trials and Trials in Federal Criminal Court'.

83 Ibid.

84 On average 1.4 years before completion at a federal court against 7.6 years before completion at a military commission. See 'Facts and Figures: Military Commissions v. Federal Courts', *Human Rights Watch* (last updated 12 June 2014), http://www.hrw.org/features/guantanamo-facts-figures, Retrieved 22 August 2013.

85 The terrorism-related cases pertain to crimes inspired by jihadist ideas, see Karen J. Greenberg (ed.), 'Terrorist Trial Report Card: September 11, 2001-September 11, 2011', *Centre on Law and Security, New York University School of Law* (2011), p. 7, http://www.lawandsecurity.org/Portals/0/Documents/TTRC%20Ten%20Year%20Issue.pdf. Retrieved 22 Augustus 2013; 'Facts and Figures: Military Commissions v. Federal Courts', *Human Rights Watch* (12 June 2014), http://www.hrw.org/features/guantanamo-facts-figures. Retrieved 22 August 2013.

86 Eric Holder, 'Attorney General Eric Holder Speaks at Northwestern University School of Law' (5 March 2012), http://www.justice.gov/iso/opa/ag/speeches/2012/ag-speech-1203051.html. Retrieved 26 June 2012.

87 Ibid.

88 *Hamdan v. Rumsfeld* (No. 05–184) 548 U.S. 557, Argued March 28, 2006—Decided June 29, 2006.

89 Guus Valk, 'Een Gitmo-proces is geen normaal proces', NRC *Handelsblad* (21 August 2013).

90 See ICCT Seminar The Hague on 'Zacarias Moussaoui', (25 January 2012).

91 Larry Abramson, 'Sept. 11 Victim Testimony Given at Moussaoui Trial' (11 April 2006), http://www.npr.org/templates/story/story.php?storyId=5335748. Retrieved 9 September 2013.

92 Moussaoui was formally sentenced by Judge Brinkema to consecutive life sentences on 4 May 2006, after the jury had recommended this sentence on 3 May 2006; see Jerry Markon and Timothy Dwyer, 'Jurors Reject Death Penalty for Moussaoui', *Washington Post* (4 May 2006).

93 On 13 July 2003 the Justice Department announced that Moussaoui was not allowed to question detained Al Qaeda leaders. Citing this stance, Judge Brinkema tried to prevent the government from seeking the death penalty. Yet, on 22 April 2004, the possibility of imposing the death penalty was reinstated by a federal court of appeals. Moussaoui was allowed to use government prepared summaries of detained Al Qaeda leaders, but—due to national security reasons—not allowed to question them at trial; see 'Timeline: Major

Events in the Zacarias Moussaoui Case', *New York Times* (2001), http://www.nytimes.com/ref/us/mouss-timeline.html?ref=zacariasmoussaoui. Retrieved 9 September 2013.

94 *United States of America v. Zacarias Moussaoui*, United States District Court for the Eastern District of Virginia, 01-455-A, Memorandum of Law Regarding Defendant's Motion to Proceed *Pro Se* and Status of Counsel, p. 2, referring to 2 January 2002 Tr. at 4.

95 Matthew Engel, 'Drama in court as Moussaoui fires lawyers', *The Guardian* (23 April 2002); Phil Hirschkom, 'Stand-by Lawyer for Moussaoui Named', CNN (18 June 2002).

96 Phil Hirschkom, 'Judge Rules Moussaoui can Represent Self', CNN (13 June 2002).

97 Information in this section is derived from different timelines and news articles on the Moussaoui case, see for example: 'The Zacarias Moussaoui (September 11) Trial: A chronology', http://law2.umkc.edu/faculty/projects/ftrials/moussaoui/zmchronology.html. Retrieved 15 August 2013; 'Timeline: The Case Against Zacarias Moussaoui', NPR (3 May 2006), http://www.npr.org/templates/story/story.php?storyId=5243788. Retrieved 15 August 2013; 'Zacarias Moussaoui Fast Facts', CNN *Library* (3 April 2013), http://edition.cnn.com/2013/04/03/us/zacarias-moussaoui-fast-facts/index.html?iref=allsearch. Retrieved 15 August 2013.

98 See also paragraph 11.4; 'The Zacarias Moussaoui (September 11) Trial: A chronology', http://law2.umkc.edu/faculty/projects/ftrials/moussaoui/zmchronology.html. Retrieved 15 August 2013; Timeline: The Case Against Zacarias Moussaoui, NPR, http://www.npr.org/templates/story/story.php?storyId=5243788. Retrieved 15 August 2013; Zacarias Moussaoui Fast Facts, CNN *Library* (3 April 2013), http://edition.cnn.com/2013/04/03/us/zacarias-moussaoui-fast-facts/index.html?iref=allsearch. Retrieved 15 August 2013.

99 Philip Shenon, 'Traces of Terror: The terror suspect', *New York Times* (19 July 2002), http://www.nytimes.com/2002/07/19/us/traces-terror-terror-suspect-9-11-defendant-guilty-plea-judge-rejects-it.html. Retrieved 29 August 2014; *bayat* is an Arabic oath of allegiance.

100 'Timeline: Major Events in the Zacarias Moussaoui Case', *Associated Press / New York Times* (2001), http://www.nytimes.com/ref/us/mouss-timeline.html?ref=zacariasmoussaoui. Retrieved 22 August 2002.

101 Ibid.

102 Ibid.

103 Phil Hirschkorn, 'Moussaoui curses America but judge gets final word', CNN (5 May 2006).

104 *United States of America v. Zacarias Moussaoui*, 'Defendants Motion to Withdraw a Guilty Plea', Criminal No. 01-455-A (6 May 2006), http://law2.umkc.edu/faculty/projects/ftrials/moussaoui/withdrawguilty.pdf. Retrieved 23 August 2006.

105 Neil A. Lewis, 'Moussaoui's Move to Recant Guilty Plea is Denied', *New York Times* (9 May 2006).

106 Margaret Warner interviewing Aicha el-Wafi: 'Mother of Sept. 11 Suspect', PBS *Newshour* (21 June 2002), http://www.pbs.org/newshour/bb/terrorism/jan-june02/moussaoui_6-21.html. Retrieved 23 August 2013.

107 'Timeline: Major Events in the Zacarias Moussaoui Case', *Associated Press / New York Times* (2001), http://www.nytimes.com/ref/us/mouss-timeline.html?ref=zacariasmoussaoui. Retrieved 22 August 2002.

108 'Mother of Sept. 11 Suspect, Margaret Warner interviewing Aicha el-Wafi', PBS *Newshour* (21 June 2002), http://www.pbs.org/newshour/bb/terrorism/jan-june02/moussaoui_6-21.html.

109 'Moussaoui Questions Judge's Mental State', *The Smoking Gun* (no date), http://www.thesmokinggun.com/file/moussaoui-questions-judges-mental-state?page=1. Retrieved 3 September 2012; note that the abbreviation UBL is used by federal prosecutors to refer to (U)sama Bin Laden.

110 'Moussaoui Prepares Quiz for Ashcroft', *The Smoking Gun* (no date), p. 1, http://www.thesmokinggun.com/file/moussaoui-prepares-quiz-ashcroft. Retrieved 3 September 2012.

111 'Timeline: Major Events in the Zacarias Moussaoui Case', *Associated Press / New York Times* (2001), http://www.nytimes.com/ref/us/mouss-timeline.html?ref=zacariasmoussaoui. Retrieved 22 August 2002.

112 Brady v. Maryland, US Supreme Court, 373 US 83, 87 (1963); see https://supreme.justia.com/cases/federal/us/373/83/case.html.

113 Federal Rules of Criminal Procedure, Rule 16: Discovery and Inspection; see also J. Radsan, 'The Moussaoui Case: The mess from Minnesota', *William Mitchell Law Review*, 31:4 (2005), p. 1428, http://www.ilnd.uscourts.gov/LEGAL/FRCrPWeb/fcr00020.htm. Retrieved 22 August 2013.

114 Ibid., pp. 1432–1434.

115 Ibid., p. 1432.

116 'Timeline: Major Events in the Zacarias Moussaoui Case', *Associated Press / New York Times* (2001), http://www.nytimes.com/ref/us/mouss-timeline.html?ref=zacariasmoussaoui. Retrieved 22 August 2002.

117 Ibid.

118 Edward A. Adams, 'Moussaoui v. the United States: How due process thwarted a courtroom jihad', ABA *Journal* (1 September 2007), http://www.abajournal.com/magazine/article/moussaoui_v_the_united_states/. Retrieved 23 August 2013.

119 Jasper Mortimer, 'New Bin Laden Tape May Be Bid for Status', *Associated Press / Washington*

Post (24 May 2006), http://www.washingtonpost.com/wp-dyn/content/article/2006/05/24/AR2006052400603.html. Retrieved 22 August 2013.

120 'Timeline: Major Events in the Zacarias Moussaoui Case', *Associated Press / New York Times* (2001), http://www.nytimes.com/ref/us/mouss-timeline.html?ref=zacariasmoussaoui. Retrieved 22 August 2002.

121 Jasper Mortimer, 'New Bin Laden Tape May Be Bid for Status', *Associated Press / Washington Post* (24 May 2006), http://www.washingtonpost.com/wp-dyn/content/article/2006/05/24/AR2006052400603.html. Retrieved 22 August 2013.

122 Ibid.

123 Ibid.

124 'Opening Statement of Defence Attorney Edward MacMahon in the Zacarias Moussaoui Trial' (6 March 2006), p. 49. http://law2.umkc.edu/faculty/projects/ftrials/moussaoui/zmmacmahon.html. Retrieved 23 August 2013.

125 Ibid.

126 Ibid., p. 76.

127 'Timeline: Major Events in the Zacarias Moussaoui Case', *Associated Press / New York Times* (2001), http://www.nytimes.com/ref/us/mouss-timeline.html?ref=zacariasmoussaoui. Retrieved 22 August 2002.

128 Ibid.

129 Ibid.

130 18 USC, Part II, Chapter 228, paragraph 3591—Sentence of Death.

131 Radsan, 'The Moussaoui Case', pp. 1438–1439.

132 Ibid.

133 Ibid., p. 1440.

134 Timothy Dwyer, 'One Juror Between Terrorist And Death', *Washington Post* (12 May 2006).

135 See Order 4 May 2006, 'Moussaoui Formally Sentenced, Still Defiant', *Associated Press* (4 May 2006), http://www.msnbc.msn.com/id/12615601. Retrieved 9 September 2013.

136 Linder, 'The Trial of Zacarias Moussaoui: An account' (2006), p. 9.

137 Radsan, 'The Moussaoui Case', pp. 1441–1442.

138 Olivier Douliery, 'Moussaoui's Mother: "This Is a Show Trial"', *Time US* (20 April 2006), http://www.time.com/time/nation/article/0,8599,1185866,00.html. Retrieved 27 June 2012.

139 Linder, 'The Trial of Zacarias Moussaoui: An account' (2006), p. 7.

140 Radsan, 'The Moussaoui Case', p. 1450.

141 Ibid., p. 1458.

142 Ibid., pp. 1458–1459.

143 *United States of America v. Ahmed Khalfan Ghailani*, United States District Court for the

Southern District of New York, Memorandum and Order (6 October 2010), http://www.lawfareblog.com/wp-content/uploads/2010/10/GhailaniMemo.pdf. Retrieved 9 September 2013.

8. Guantánamo as Theatre: Military Commissions as a Performance in the Court of Public Opinion, 2003–2004[1]

Fred L. Borch

Chief Prosecutor for Military Commissions:
'Mr. Secretary, I can win these cases. But convictions are not what is important.
Rather, the only important trial is the trial in the court of public opinion.'

Deputy Defence Secretary Wolfowitz:
'Do you really believe that?'[2]

8.1. Introduction

The decision to use military commissions to prosecute terrorists held at Guantánamo Bay was premised on the idea that these men had committed war crimes that should be tried by 'war courts'.[3] But the decision did not ignore the fact that the trials would be a performance on the world stage in that, for the judicial proceedings to be a success, the world must be persuaded that the terrorists received fair trials—and that justice was done.

This chapter explores the 'script' written by the prosecution in order to win its military commission cases in the court of public opinion. It focuses almost exclusively on events in the military commission process between May 2003 and May 2004, because during this twelve-month period public interest in military commissions was greatest, if for no other reason than that military trials for terrorists appeared to be imminent. It first 'sets the stage' by looking at the events leading up to the decision by President George Bush to use military commissions to try Al Qaeda members. It then discusses the 'actors' and 'stage' in the Guantánamo 'play' before examining the audience for the 'performance', i.e. the news media and public opinion.[4] The chapter then looks at the first cases selected for prosecution and the prosecution's theory of criminal liability, and how these were part of the effort to shape public opinion. A discussion of the death penalty as a possible sentence follows. Finally, this chapter raises a number of performance mistakes that occurred in the Guantánamo process in the period under consideration, and concludes with a brief analysis and critique of these early military commissions as theatre, including some comments on their judicial, political and social impact.

8.2. Setting the Stage

Early in the morning on 11 September 2001, fifteen Saudi Arabians and four Egyptians boarded four commercial airliners. Two of the aircraft took off from Boston. The third flight departed from Newark, and the fourth flight left from Washington, DC, for Los Angeles. At 8:46 a.m. and 9:03 a.m., the two Boston aircraft crashed into the north and south towers, respectively, of the World Trade Center in New York City. At 9:38 a.m., the Washington, DC, flight struck the Pentagon, destroying a portion of the building. The remaining Newark flight crashed into a rural area southeast of Pittsburgh, Pennsylvania, at 10:10 a.m. By mid-morning, when both World Trade Center towers had collapsed, the death toll—including the airline passengers—was 2,753 killed in Manhattan and 189 killed in Washington, DC. The victims came from more than ninety countries from around the world.[5]

Within days of the terrorist attacks, the US government had identified Osama bin Laden and his Al Qaeda ('the Base') network as responsible for the 9/11 attacks. The nineteen Al Qaeda hijackers had entered the United States legally (on student or tourist visas) and, while they kept to themselves, tried to fit in as Americans to avoid any suspicion (e.g. they drank alcoholic beverages in bars). In formulating their plan of attack over a period of years, some of the terrorists took flying training at civilian schools. This rudimentary instruction was sufficient to allow them to pilot the American and United Airlines planes after they killed the commercial pilots or otherwise overpowered the crews. While bin Laden did not claim immediate responsibility, he released videotapes praising the 9/11 hijackers, and also threatened more attacks against America.[6]

After the Taliban as the *de facto* government of Afghanistan refused US demands to surrender Osama bin Laden and Al Qaeda operatives, the United States launched air strikes against Afghanistan in October 2001. These air operations were followed by ground combat involving US and Allied soldiers and marines. By mid-2002, Taliban and Al Qaeda forces had been driven from most areas of Afghanistan.[7]

In the meantime, one month after hostilities in Afghanistan had commenced, President George W. Bush announced that Al Qaeda's attacks on the United States had 'created a state of armed conflict' and that the 'extraordinary emergency' arising out of this new 'war against terrorism' required a number of extraordinary decisions. Consequently, the president proclaimed in his 'Military Order of November 13, 2011', that he was taking the following actions. First, any Al Qaeda member or international terrorist falling into US hands would 'be detained at an appropriate location'. Second, President Bush announced that, having determined that a state of armed conflict existed, these detainees would 'be tried by military commission for any and all offenses ... that such individual is alleged to have committed'.[8] According to Bush's military order, these terrorists must be prosecuted by a military commission because only trial by a military tribunal would 'protect the United States and its citizens', ensure 'effective conduct of military operations' and prevent future terrorist attacks.[9]

This view—that a military commission was the only appropriate tribunal at which to prosecute Al Qaeda terrorists—was a radical change in the US government's perspective on terrorist acts. Prior to 9/11, the United States had insisted that attacks by international terrorists were criminal acts, and that the United States would prosecute these crimes in federal civilian court.[10] The magnitude of damage and loss of life on 9/11, however, caused President Bush to decide that these terrorist attacks against America and its citizens could no longer be categorised as criminal offences to be prosecuted in civilian courts. Rather, the nature of Al Qaeda's attack[11] meant that the United States was engaged in a 'war against terrorism', and that terrorist acts were war crimes that should be prosecuted by a special war court, i.e.the military commission.[12]

While President Bush personally decided that the military commission would now be the proper forum at which to prosecute Al Qaeda and other international terrorists, it is unlikely that he had the idea of using a military legal framework. What is known is that the idea for the Military Order of 13 November 2001 originated in the White House, and that the principal author was on the president's or vice-president's staff. This person was also familiar with American legal history, as key language used in Bush's order was borrowed from the procedural rules for a military commission created by President Franklin D. Roosevelt in the early months of World War II.

To recall: on 2 July 1942, after eight Germans who had landed by submarine in New Jersey and Florida were caught before they could accomplish a sabotage mission on American soil, Roosevelt proclaimed that 'all persons who are subjects ... of any nation at war with the United States' and who set foot in the United States in an attempt to commit 'acts of sabotage, espionage, hostile or warlike acts', would be tried by a military commission.[13] While Roosevelt also announced that same day in a related military order that the commission had the power to make its own rules 'for the conduct of the proceedings', and that the commission might consider any evidence that had 'probative value to a reasonable man', Roosevelt also stated that the German defendants must receive a 'full and fair trial'.[14] Since this same evidentiary standard and the 'full and fair trial' language appears in Bush's Military Order of 13 November 2001,[15] there is little doubt that the author of the military order was using the trial of the German U-boat saboteurs as a template.

The White House saw the U-boat military commission as an attractive model for at least three reasons. First, Roosevelt (relying on his authority as commander-in-chief) had created a military commission that had met in secret, determined the guilt of eight Germans defendants, and sentenced most of them to death—all in less than five weeks.[16] This speedy process appealed to President Bush and his advisors because it ensured that Al Qaeda members and other terrorists who attacked the United States could expect swift and certain punishment. A speedy process would also deter others contemplating a future attack on America.

The second reason that the Roosevelt model was an attractive precedent was that it was a sort of 'rough justice'. Terrorists would get a trial that would be 'full and fair' but justice would not be perverted by evidentiary and procedural safeguards that, while appropriate for civilian defendants, had no place in a trial of international terrorists who were guilty of war crimes. This explains why, in announcing that Al Qaeda members and other terrorists would be prosecuted at a military commission, Bush expressly stated that 'given the danger to the safety of the United States and the nature of international terrorism', he had personally determined that it was not 'practicable to apply in military commissions ... the principles of law and the rules of evidence generally recognized in the trial of criminal cases in the United States district courts'.[17]

Third and finally, the creation of a military tribunal by the president—using his powers as commander in chief under Article II of the Constitution[18]—meant that the commission's work would be unfettered by legal precedent that had developed in US civilian courts governed by Article III of the Constitution and the Bill of Rights contained in the first ten Amendments.[19] For example, evidence obtained by coercion was admissible, as was hearsay, even though these would be barred in a civilian court. The defendant had a right to be represented by legal counsel at the commission, but only after that defence lawyer had been approved by the government. That same defendant could be convicted and sentenced to life in jail on a vote of two-thirds of the commission members; the unanimous vote required in American civilian criminal proceedings was not applicable to a tribunal created under Article II.[20] Finally, there was no appeal to a civilian court; President Bush personally would review the record and make any final decision, unless he delegated this authority to the Secretary of Defence.[21]

8.3. The Actors and the Stage

Since Bush's Military Order required that he personally approve the prosecution of a terrorist at the military commission, the President himself was a key 'actor', with a leading role in the Guantánamo performance. So, too, was Secretary of Defence Donald Rumsfeld, who was given considerable authority in the military commission framework created by the Military Order. But, when Rumsfeld later delegated his responsibilities in the legal process to Deputy Secretary of Defence Dr. Paul D. Wolfowitz, the latter became a key player, since Wolfowitz was now required to decide on a number of key issues.[22] These included issuing orders and regulations that would establish procedures for a commission to follow in any trial of any alleged terrorist; determining the number and identity of Guantánamo detainees to be recommended for prosecution; after the president had approved the trial of one or more detainees, when the trials should start; and which military officers would be appointed to serve as jurors to decide guilt or innocence and determine an appropriate sentence.[23]

At the direction of Secretary Rumsfeld (and later Secretary Wolfowitz), Mr William J. 'Jim' Haynes II,[24] the Department of Defence's top lawyer, began working on various orders that would govern the operation of the military commission. Haynes also began searching for Army, Navy, Air Force and Marine Corps lawyers to take part in the new military commission framework. While senior uniformed lawyers from all the services were considered, Haynes ultimately chose Army Colonel Frederic L. 'Fred' Borch to be the Chief Prosecutor, and Air Force Colonel William 'Will' Gunn to serve as Chief Defense Counsel for the military commissions. Both Borch and Gunn then began selecting military lawyers for their staffs. While these men and women were selected for their top-notch legal skills, both Colonels Borch and Gunn recognised that the lawyers selected to join their respective teams would be performing in the courtroom and would be the 'face' of their respective efforts. Borch, for example, selected Navy Commander Scott Lang as the Deputy Chief Prosecutor, in part because Lang had obtained a special advanced university degree in trial advocacy that included acting lessons. In the Anglo-American judicial system, the requirement to convince a jury of non-legally trained people that a defendant is guilty requires a prosecutor to present a narrative of the crime and the events surrounding it—and telling such a story is best done by a prosecutor who develops a theme and presents his evidence in a compelling and persuasive manner. Lang's special trial advocacy training would ensure that the prosecution's performance was first-rate.[25]

There were six more actors in the Guantánamo performance: Salim Hamdan, Ibrahim al Qosi, Ali Hamza al Bahlul, David Hicks, Moazzam Begg, Feroz Abbasi. They joined the troupe when President Bush selected them as the first defendants on 3 July 2003.[26] More on why these six men were chosen for the play can be learned below, in the discussion about choosing the first cases for prosecution.

Finally, although not on the Guantánamo stage, Osama bin Laden must be considered an actor in the Guantánamo play, since his efforts had caused 9/11 and he was present in the minds of everyone participating in the military commission process. The fact that bin Laden was off-stage did not make him any less important to the Guantánamo performance,[27] especially as one of the prosecution's aims was to educate the public about the evil caused by international terrorism generally and Al Qaeda in particular.

As for the location of the stage, it soon became clear that it would be in Cuba, where the United States had 'perpetual' possession of a small area of land.[28] This was because shortly after the publication of the 'Military Order of November 13, 2001', the United States announced that it would detain those individuals covered by the order at Guantánamo Bay, Cuba; the first twenty detainees arrived in January 2002.[29] With the individuals subject to the jurisdiction of the Military Order located in Cuba, it only made sense to hold the impending trials there. Moreover, this location also ensured that there was adequate security for all parties to the proceedings, as Guantánamo's geographic isolation made it difficult, if not impossible, for people wanting to disrupt the trials to travel there. At the same time, Guantánamo's location outside the United States meant that the US Article III civilian judges probably would not have jurisdiction over the military commission proceedings. As a result, the judges could not entertain petitions from the terrorist defendants or hear actions filed by civil libertarians desiring to halt or disrupt the process.

8.4. Audience: Media and Public Opinion

From the first day he reported for duty as Chief Prosecutor, Borch began preparing to speak to the news media. As the public face of the prosecution efforts, he knew that he would soon be asked by magazine, newspaper, radio and television reporters to sit for interviews, and that the Defence Department expected him to be able to explain to the American people and the world at large that the trial of the terrorists by a military commission was the right thing to do—both morally and legally.

To assist Borch in his public role, the Public Affairs Office at the Department of Defense (DoD) arranged for him to have media training ordinarily reserved for high profile DoD officials. This included classes on how to develop a theme for each interview, and mock question-and-answer sessions with intentionally aggressive questioners. The focus was on finding the right message for the prosecution efforts, and then getting that message out to the public through the news media.[30]

Borch decided that the principal theme of the prosecution would be 'full and fair trial' and he wanted these four words to be a 'Greek Chorus'[31] that would be picked up by the general public and the media in particular. But there were five other messages—of varying importance—that Borch wanted to deliver to the public, too. First, that Al Qaeda members should be tried by a military commission rather than in civilian courts because the United States was at war with Al Qaeda and its attacks were war crimes that should be tried in war tribunals. Second, that military commissions would be useful because they would educate the public about the dangers of terrorism. Third, that the military commission would serve the criminal justice purposes of retribution, punishment and deterrence. Those tried and punished by a military commission would satisfy a desire, if not a need, for revenge for the evil that befell the United States on 9/11; quick and severe punishment also would deter other terrorists from attacking Americans. Fourth, that military commissions would provide an alternative legal and moral basis for long-term detention of terrorists. Fifth and finally, that the military tribunals held in Cuba would support intelligence collection efforts (and therefore the war effort against Al Qaeda).

8.5. Selecting the First Cases for Prosecution

While the message for the military commission process was 'full and fair trial', the theme for the first cases for prosecution was that each defendant was a 'true believer'[32] who was fanatically committed to the depths of his soul to either Al Qaeda or its terrorist goals, or both. The prosecution ultimately recommended to Secretary Wolfowitz that he request President Bush to designate six Guantánamo detainees as defendants in the first military commissions. Each of the six men selected for prosecution fitted into the true believer theme; all had met with bin Laden or were his close associates, or else had met bin Laden and supported his terrorist goals.

Salim Ahmed Hamdan was a Yemeni citizen whose close personal association with bin Laden made him an ideal defendant. Hamdan had joined Al Qaeda in 1996, when he travelled to Afghanistan with the express purpose of joining bin Laden's military group of holy warriors. Hamdan ultimately took an oath of personal loyalty ('bayat') to bin Laden, picked up and delivered weapons, and finally joined bin Laden's inner circle as a chauffeur, mechanic and bodyguard. In late November 2001, Hamdan was captured by a group of Afghan warlords near the Pakistani border and turned over to the United States for a $5,000 bounty.

While these facts alone were sufficient to convict Salim Hamdan in a trial, Borch immediately saw that Hamdan was the perfect first case for the government. Unlike many Al Qaeda members, who had never met, Hamdan was intimately familiar with him, and had freely admitted during questioning at Guantánamo that he had worked directly for bin Laden. Additionally, unlike many jihadists, who had joined Al Qaeda after 1999, Hamdan had served bin Laden since 1996—which meant that Hamdan was a member of bin Laden's inner sanctum during the 1998 attacks on the US embassies in Kenya and Tanzania, the 2000 bombing of the USS *Cole*, and the 9/11 attacks. Hamdan's should be the first case to be prosecuted because his trial would allow the United States to tell the story of Al Qaeda's evil-doing through the narrative of a man who not only had Osama bin Laden's trust and confidence, but had breathed the same air and eaten the same food as the 'prince of darkness'. Since one of the prosecution's goals was to educate the public about Al Qaeda as a force for evil, Hamdan's narrative was ideal.[33]

Ali Hamza Ahmad Sulayman al Bahlul, also a Yemeni citizen, was selected as one of the six defendants because his misdeeds likewise fitted into the prosecution's overall theme. Under questioning at Guantánamo, al Bahlul had boasted that he worked as bin Laden's bodyguard and as his media secretary. From late 1999 to December 2001, al Bahlul had used his computer skills to create 'instructional and motivational recruiting video tapes' for Al Qaeda, and thereby act as a mouthpiece for bin Laden's evil designs.[34] One of these tapes was an internet-based video that glorified the October 2000 suicide attack on the USS *Cole*, which had killed 17 American sailors. The video combined film footage of the damaged warship with calls by bin Laden for jihad against America.

Like Hamdan, al Bahlul also was a trusted member of bin Laden's inner circle, and had been with him on 11 September 2001. During questioning, al Bahlul revealed that bin Laden had asked him to set up a satellite connection on 11 September so that he and other Al Qaeda members 'could see news reports'.[35] In the weeks immediately following the 9/11 attacks, bin Laden tasked al Bahlul with obtaining media reports about the attacks, and 'gather[ing] data concerning the economic damage caused by these attacks'.[36]

Al Bahlul was proud of his affiliation with Al Qaeda and, as he later proclaimed, 'I will never deny any actions I did along with bin Laden fighting you and your allies, the Jews.'[37] While in custody in Cuba, al Bahlul also continued to insist that, if given the opportunity, he would kill innocent Christians and Jews. Perhaps the best proof of his evil intent was the statement he made to interrogators at Guantánamo Bay:

> I wish it had been me as the hijacker who went into the World Trade Center. I hope you Americans kill me as this will anger Usama bin Laden and there will be greater retribution. I can be a double martyr.[38]

The entire prosecution team believed that when a military commission jury heard this statement, any feelings of sympathy they might have for al Bahlul—or concerns about his guilt—would evaporate instantly.

Born in Sudan, Ibrahim Ahmed Mahmoud al Qosi also was a good choice for an early trial. He, too, was a long time bin Laden lieutenant; al Qosi had joined Al Qaeda in 1989 while the organisation was located in Sudan. Initially, al Qosi had served as a messenger, and passed information between members of terrorist cells operating in that country; al Qosi also provided food, shelter and clothing for these terrorists.

In 1990, al Qosi travelled from Sudan to Afghanistan, where he received training in military tactics and weapons. After participating for a period of time in the fighting in Afghanistan, al Qosi became an accountant in Al Qaeda's *Mektabh al Muhassiba* (accounting office) in Pakistan. From 1992 until 1994, he was put in charge of managing donated money and distributing it for salaries, travel and support of Al Qaeda operations, including terrorist training camps in Afghanistan. In the mid-1990s, after a failed assassination attempt on bin Laden in Sudan, al Qosi was handpicked to serve as a member of bin Laden's newly formed bodyguard.[39]

As for Australian-born David Matthew Hicks, his case was attractive because English was his mother tongue and he was cooperative. Although Hicks insisted that he had never been an Al Qaeda member (he admitted only to membership of Lashkar-e-Tayyiba ('Army of the Righteous')), there was proof that he had attended an Al Qaeda-run camp in Afghanistan, where he 'trained in weapons familiarization and firing, land mines, topography, field movements, and basic explosives'.[40] Hicks claimed to have engaged in hostile military operations against India and, after the 9/11 attacks, he had returned to Afghanistan to rejoin his Al Qaeda associates. Hicks was captured by Northern Alliance forces and turned over to US personnel for a $1,000 bounty.[41]

While Borch believed there was sufficient evidence to convict Hicks at a military commission, and recommended that Hicks be one of the first six defendants, Borch rejected the idea of bringing Hicks to trial quickly. His chief reason was that Hicks' was not the face of terrorism. As a white Australian with very fair skin and blue eyes, Hicks did not look like what the American public considered a typical Al Qaeda member and, if a goal of the prosecution was to educate the public about the danger posed by terrorists, a defendant at this stage of the process needed to look like the men responsible for hijacking and mass murder on September 11.

In contrast to Hicks, Moazzem Begg and Feroz Abbasi were good first cases for trial because both defendants spoke fluent English and, as men of Pakistani descent, looked like the typical Al Qaeda member.

Both men had admitted under interrogation at Guantánamo that they had trained at Al Qaeda-run military camps in Afghanistan, and had received training in close combat tactics, individual and crew-served weapons, and explosives. Begg and Abbasi also freely admitted that they were Al Qaeda members and supported that organisation's goal of carrying out terrorist attacks on Western targets. But, as will be explained, the selection of Abbasi and Begg was a mistake, because their UK citizenship would later cause significant disruptions in the prosecution's performance strategy.

One other possible defendant who, like Hicks, Abbasi and Begg, spoke English was Canadian-born Omar Khadr. Khadr admitted that he had killed a US Special Forces soldier and was unrepentant about this homicide. This made him an attractive candidate for prosecution. But Borch decided that he would not try Khadr because Khadr had been fifteen years old at the time of the killing and his legal status as a juvenile almost certainly would cause the Canadian government to oppose the prosecution. Ultimately, it was a cost-benefit analysis, and Colonel Borch decided that Canadian resistance and possible negative publicity in the court of public opinion was not worth the value of bringing Khadr before a Guantánamo tribunal, at least during Act I of the play.

8.6. Prosecution Strategy and Theory of Criminal Liability

As soon as the prosecutorial cast was selected and assembled, the prosecutors developed their trial strategy.[42] This included the details of the trials themselves, such as determining which terrorists detained in Cuba should be tried first (and in what order), which offences should be charged, and whether the death penalty was appropriate. Of paramount concern was articulating a theory of criminal liability that would permit the military commission to find the terrorists guilty of war crimes. Additionally, it was imperative that this theory of liability be conveyed to the commission's panel members and the public if the tribunals were to win in the court of public opinion.

After some discussion, the prosecutors adopted this basic theory of criminal liability: (1) that each of the six defendants had participated in a common criminal enterprise to attack civilians, destroy civilian property, commit murder while concealing themselves amongst the population, and terrorise governments and peoples with the aim of acquiring power and changing the political order and; (2) that each of the defendants had committed one or more acts in furtherance of this enterprise.

While President Bush's Military Order was a direct result of Al Qaeda attacks on New York City and Washington, DC, the prosecution team was careful to adopt a theory of criminal liability that did not require a defendant to be an Al Qaeda member in order to participate in the conspiracy. While it was probable that most defendants who would ultimately appear before a military commission would be affiliated in some way with bin Laden, Bush's Military Order clearly stated that *any* non-US citizen who 'engaged in, aided or abetted, or conspired to commit acts of international terrorism' could be prosecuted.[43] By way of example, the fact that David Hicks denied being a member of Al Qaeda, but admitted receiving extensive training in marksmanship, small team tactics, and intelligence gathering in training camps run by Al Qaeda in Afghanistan meant that any comprehensive theory of criminal liability must be built around a conspiracy that was *larger* than Al Qaeda, i.e. that could include Al Qaeda without being limited to it.

A diagram (see figure 8.1 on page 356) illustrating the prosecution theory of liability showed the scope of the conspiracy theory as a dotted line, with bin Laden ('UBL') and his associates ('Shura Council/UBL Inner Circle') as full participants in the conspiracy. Members of other terrorist organisations—the Abu Sayyaf Group,[44] Jemaah Islamiyah,[45] Lashkar-e-Tayyiba,[46] Egyptian Islamic Jihad,[47] Armed Islamic Group (GIA)[48] and the Taliban—could be part of the conspiracy too.[49] However, the diagram showed that not *all* members of Al Qaeda or other terrorist organisations necessarily were part of the conspiracy; this was an intentional decision on the part of Borch, who wanted to avoid making mere membership a crime. Borch's decision reflected the strong precedent in Anglo-American jurisprudence against 'guilt by association', i.e., status alone is not a criminal offence.[50]

Of almost equal importance to formulating a conspiracy theory was selecting the actual crimes with which the Al Qaeda terrorists would be charged. While Military

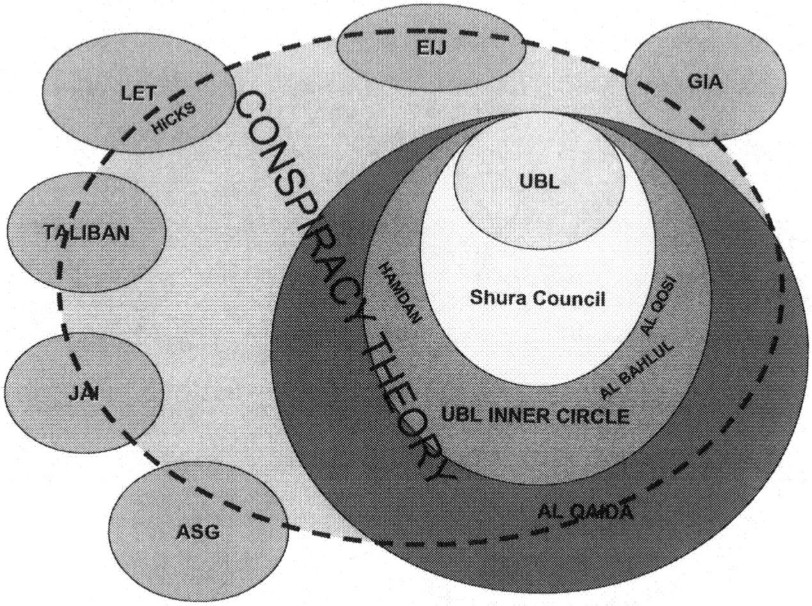

Figure 8.1: Diagram showing prosecution theory of terrorist conspiracy

Commission Instruction No. 2, *Crimes and Elements for Trials by Military Commission*,[51] listed more than thirty possible offences, the prosecutors decided to charge each defendant with conspiracy to commit five offences: attacking civilians, attacking civilian targets, murder, destruction of property, and terrorism.

Al Bahlul, for example, was charged with 'willfully and knowingly' joining 'an enterprise of persons' consisting of bin Laden, Dr. Ayman al Zawahari,[52] and other 'associates of the Al Qaeda organisation, known and unknown'. Al Bahlul then conspired with the persons in this enterprise and shared 'a common criminal purpose' to commit the five offences listed above.

What followed in the text of the charging document (or indictment) was a list of overt acts that al Bahlul and other conspirators had committed in order to bring about the aims of their criminal enterprise. These included training at Al Qaeda-sponsored training camps in Afghanistan and taking an oath of allegiance to bin Laden, which affirmed a willingness to perform any act requested by bin Laden. For al Bahlul specifically, overt acts performed by him included creating a USS *Cole* video to recruit, motivate and inspire Al Qaeda members and others to commit violent attacks against the United States and serving as a bodyguard for Osama bin Laden.

The theme in the al Bahlul case was that he was a true believer who had protected evil (as bin Laden's bodyguard), spread evil (through his media work) and continued to want to do evil (as evidenced by his statement that he wished he had participated in the 9/11 attacks). In presenting its case against al Bahlul, the prosecution's 'script'—the way it would present its evidence to the jury—would be written to support and develop these themes.

A final point: the criminal enterprise that al Bahlul and the other defendants had joined was prosecutable as a war crime because the men were engaged in an armed conflict, yet had no lawful basis for their actions under international humanitarian law or other the laws of war. As Professor Gary D. Solis explains in his authoritative treatise *The Law of Armed Conflict*, there are 'only two categories of individuals on the battlefield: combatants and civilians'. The law gives immunity from criminal liability only to combatants who are members of the armed forces of a nation-state; civilians who take part in hostilities have no immunity 'for their violent conduct and can be tried and punished under civil law for their belligerent acts'. It follows that terrorists belonging to groups like Al Qaeda, having no association with any nation-state, enjoy no combatant privilege, and a terrorist who kills a soldier is an unprivileged belligerent or unlawful combatant who is guilty of murder.[53]

8.7. Desisting from Asking for Death Penalties

Early in the military commission process, Borch informed Secretary Wolfowitz that he would not seek the death penalty for the first six defendants. This was Borch's decision to make as the top prosecutor, and no one attempted to change his mind. While Borch personally believed that the death penalty was an appropriate punishment—and that some of the defendants might deserve it—he understood that much of the world, especially European public opinion, was hostile to the death penalty. If the prosecution announced that the defendants faced a capital sentence, the risk was that the military commission process would become an argument about the morality of the death sentence instead of a discussion about the evils of terrorism and the guilt of those being prosecuted for war crimes. Not willing to run this risk—and perhaps damage his chances of winning in the court of public opinion—Borch took the death penalty off the table.

There were other reasons to avoid the death penalty in the first six cases. There was every reason to think that some of the defendants desired martyrdom, and consequently wanted to be put to death. It follows that removing capital punishment from the process would undercut public sympathy for Al Qaeda by depriving the defendants of any prestige that might be gained from a death sentence. There was also another, albeit less important, reason to remove the death penalty from consideration: Borch believed that Colonel Gunn and his defence counsel would fight much harder if their clients faced a death sentence; taking the ultimate punishment away might encourage a more cooperative attitude and even a willingness to advise their clients to plead guilty in return for an agreed upon sentence.

8.8. Performance Mistakes

The prosecution made three major performance mistakes between May 2003 and May 2004, all of which affected the timing of the 'opening' of the play.[54] First, it failed to understand the depth of British government opposition to the trial of two British citizens, Moazzam Begg and Feroz Abbasi. Attempts to overcome this opposition delayed the trial of all defendants for months—thus damaging the overall prosecution efforts. Second, the prosecution was never able to overcome opposition from those within the Bush administration who believed that there was no good reason to prosecute Al Qaeda terrorists at military commissions. This opposition delayed the start of the trials—ensuring that there was no performance for months. Third and finally, Borch failed to convince Secretary Wolfowitz and others that the actual results of the trial in the courtroom, while important, paled in significance when balanced against the need to win in the court of public opinion.[55]

While Abbasi and Begg were ideal defendants because they spoke English and their trial would have proceeded without the aid of a translator, Lord Peter Goldsmith, the United Kingdom's Attorney General, decided that the two men could not be tried at a military commission because there were not sufficient guarantees that they would receive a fair trial. At first, Goldsmith voiced these concerns privately, but he then began making public statements about his unhappiness with the military commission process. The Defence Department General Counsel, Jim Haynes, tried to convince Goldsmith that Abbasi and Begg would enjoy a fair trial, and Haynes and a team of lawyers even flew to London to meet face-to-face with Goldsmith. But it was to no avail. Nothing Haynes said satisfied the British government's concerns. Goldsmith would not compromise and his public pronouncement that a military commission 'did not offer sufficient guarantees of a fair trial'[56] for the two UK citizens, meant that American efforts to prosecute Abbasi and Begg collapsed. For political reasons, the United States could not prosecute the men in the face of official British opposition, and ultimately both Abbasi and Begg were released from Guantánamo (and returned to the United Kingdom). While this left four defendants still facing trial, valuable time had been lost.

A further shortcoming in the performance was the failure to convince Secretary Wolfowitz and others in leadership roles that military commissions needed to start soon or the United States risked 'losing' the trial in the court of public opinion. While the Chief Prosecutor repeatedly argued that the trial should go forward as soon as possible, others with great credibility argued the opposite. Former US Attorney General William 'Bill' Barr,[57] for example, argued vociferously against the trials—more than once in the presence of Borch. Barr insisted that there was no reason to try the detainees and advised Secretary Wolfowitz that he and the Bush administration should simply detain these alleged terrorists for the duration of the war—just as the United States had done with German and Italian prisoners of war in World War II. Given Barr's stature in the government—as a first class lawyer who had been the country's Attorney General—it was perhaps to be expected that Barr had more credibility with Paul Wolfowitz than did a career military lawyer with whom both Wolfowitz and the public were less familiar.

Particularly telling was a Pentagon conversation between Borch and Wolfowitz in late July 2003, after Rumsfeld had delegated his responsibilities as Appointing Authority to Wolfowitz and after the president had selected the first six defendants for prosecution. Secretary Wolfowitz began by asking if Borch could guarantee that the prosecution would win every case it brought to trial. Colonel Borch answered 'no', in that victory at trial could not be assured because of the nature of the process and the unpredictability of any jury. But Borch told Wolfowitz that the prosecution had selected good solid cases and that there was every reason to expect good results. Then Borch said, 'Mr. Secretary, I can win these cases. But convictions are not what is important. Rather, the only important trial is the trial in the court of public opinion.' This provoked a sceptical look from Wolfowitz, and the response, 'Colonel, do you really believe that?'[58]

How can Wolfowitz's reticence to move forward with the military commissions be explained? A producer wants to be certain of 'good reviews' from the critics before launching a play. Paul Wolfowitz was no different: he was ultimately accountable to both Rumsfeld and Bush for the success of the Guantánamo performance. Just as a producer is ultimately responsible for what happens in the theatre when the lights go out and the actors take the stage, politicians too are accountable for their decisions. It is likely that Wolfowitz decided that the uncertainty surrounding the process made it too risky to move ahead, despite the urgings of the Chief Prosecutor.

8.9. Denouement: Comments, Criticisms and 'Loose Ends'

In 2004, Salim Hamdan's defence counsel filed a writ of habeas corpus in the US District Court in Washington, DC, challenging the lawfulness of his detention in Guantánamo Bay, Cuba. Ultimately, *Hamdan v. Rumsfeld*[59] reached the US Supreme Court, which decided in June 2006 that the military commission process created by Bush's Military Order of 13 November violated both US and international law. While the court was careful not to rule that the President lacked authority under Article II of the US Constitution to create a military commission framework, it did decide that the process created by Bush's Military Order was deficient because it violated both the Uniform Code of Military Justice (created by the US Congress to govern courts martial) and the Geneva Conventions.

The decision in *Hamdan v. Rumsfeld* meant the end of the legal framework created by the President using his authority as commander-in-chief and resulted in the US Congress creating an entirely new military commission process by statute in the Military Commissions Act of 2006.[60] That legislation, amended by Congress in 2009,[61] now controls the structure of military commissions taking place in Guantánamo today.

This legislative response to *Hamdan v. Rumsfeld* has completely remade the process. The legal basis for its existence flows from Article I of the Constitution rather than from Article II. Significant changes adopted by Congress—in order to satisfy the Supreme Court ruling in *Hamdan v. Rumsfeld*—include: the creation of pre-trial, trial, and post-trial procedures, including elements of proof (other than the requirement for a full and fair trial, there were relatively few procedural rules in the Bush military commission process); the creation of a military judge (there was no judge in the original military commission); and the right to appeal to the US Supreme Court (after appealing to a newly created Court of Military Commission Review and District of Columbia Circuit Court of Appeals). A newly created *Manual for Military Commissions, United States (2010 edition)*, consisting of more than 250 pages of text, and modelled closely on the *Manual for Courts-Martial, United States*, also had been created by the Defense Department to ensure that the new military commissions operate more like ordinary courts martial.[62]

Was the performance in Guantánamo Bay from 2003 to 2004 a 'hit' or a 'miss'? Let us hear from the critics. Given the Supreme Court's ruling in *Hamdan v. Rumsfeld*, it was a 'miss' in terms of how many terrorists were convicted of war crimes during the period. It was also a 'flop' in the sense that the military commission process created by President Bush was declared to be legally deficient. Was the performance a victory in the court of public opinion? The jury are still out and the answer to this question will have to wait until more commissions are completed at Guantánamo Bay.

Despite these theatrical failures, however, it is clear that the Guantánamo performance succeeded in at least three areas. First, the selection of Hamdan, al Bahlul, al Qosi and Hicks as defendants was a success, in that all four men were eventually tried and convicted. Second, the theory of liability adopted by the prosecution remains intact. Third and finally, the United States government continues to support the legality of military commission trials for terrorists who attack the United States and its allies; the administration of President Barack Obama appears just as committed as its Republican predecessor to holding military tribunals for terrorists (albeit not at Guantánamo Bay).

What happened to the defendants initially selected for prosecution? In March 2007, David Hicks pleaded guilty and was sentenced to seven years in jail. He served nine months in Australia and was released.[63] In August 2008, Salim Hamdan was convicted by a military commission of providing material support to terrorism and sentenced to five and a half years' imprisonment. He returned to Yemen to serve his sentence and was released in 2009.[64] Al Bahlul was convicted by a military commission in 2008, and sentenced to life imprisonment.[65] As for al Qosi, he pleaded guilty in July 2008 and was sentenced the following month to fourteen years in jail.[66] Finally, in October 2010, Canadian citizen Omar Khadr pleaded guilty to murder in violation of the law of war and other related offences and was sentenced to forty years' imprisonment. He will serve all but one year of his sentence in Canada.[67]

Colonel Borch was dismissed from his position after one year in the job. Two Air Force lawyers, Major Rob Preston and Captain John Carr, convinced that the military commission process was unfair and mismanaged, accused Borch of wrongdoing. In an email message sent to the Chief Prosecutor, the two attorneys 'accused fellow prosecutors of ignoring torture allegations, failing to protect exculpatory information, and withholding information from superiors'.[68] An investigation into their allegations concluded that their claims were without merit, but retired Major General John D. Altenburg, Jr., who had recently replaced Wolfowitz as the Appointing Authority, decided that it would be best for the prosecution team if Preston, Carr and Borch went elsewhere.[69] Colonel Borch retired from active duty the following year.

Some final thoughts about 'Guantánamo as Theatre'. Regardless of what happened between 2003 and 2004, the basic questions remain: how do we balance freedom with safety? How do we design a legal system that balances the requirement for full and fair trials with national security needs in an on-going war on terrorism? The new commissions created by the US Congress will have to wrestle with these questions and try to arrive at a satisfactory answer.

Notes

1 This article is an expanded version of a lecture presented on 30 March 2011, at the University of Leiden's Centre for Terrorism and Counterterrorism in Den Haag, Netherlands. The author thanks Prof. Dr. Beatrice A. de Graaf for suggesting to him that the Guantanamo Bay terrorist prosecutions have much in common with a theatre performance, and Colonel Patrick D. O'Hare for improving this article with his insightful comments and suggestions.

2 Conversation between Deputy Secretary of Defence Paul Wolfowitz and Chief Prosecutor Fred Borch, Office of the Deputy Secretary of Defence, Pentagon, Washington, DC, July 2003.

3 Military commissions are war courts, and have been the traditional tribunal for the trial of the enemy for war crimes. After World War II, for example, Australia, Canada, France, Great Britain, the Netherlands, Norway, Poland, and the United States convened 2,116 military commissions or similar war courts to try German, Italian and Japanese defendants for war crimes committed during the war. John A. Appleman, *Military Tribunals and International Crimes* (Westport/Connecticut: Greenwood Press, 1971), p. x.—In contemporary American jurisprudence, a military commission is a war court with extremely narrow subject matter jurisdiction, in that it has cognizance only over violations of the law of war that occur during armed conflict. Additionally, the US military commission established by President George W. Bush in the aftermath of the 9/11 attacks had very narrow *in personam* jurisdiction, in that only non-US citizens could be tried by it. For an exhaustive historical examination of the military commission in US legal history, see David Glazier, 'Precedents Law: The Neglected History of the Military Commission', *Virginia Journal of International Law*, 46:1 (2005), pp. 5–82. See also: Wigall Green, 'The Military Commission', *American Journal of International Law*, 42:1 (1948), p. 832.

4 While the relationship between the news media and public opinion is important to a discussion of the Guantanamo 'audience', it is beyond the scope of this article to delineate where the news media stops reporting and starts creating public opinion.

5 For a comprehensive history of 9/11, see Stephen E. Atkins, *The 9/11 Encyclopedia* (Westport, Connecticut: Praeger, 2008). For casualties, see Jesse Green, 'Accounting of the Dead', *The Encyclopedia of 9/11* (date unkown), http://nymag.com/news/9-11/10th-anniversary/number-of-deaths/. Retrieved 10 January 2012.

6 Even prior to 9/11, Osama bin Laden was 'the public face of anti-American terrorism'. He and Al Qaeda were responsible for the terrorist bombings of the US embassies in Dar-es-Salam and Nairobi that occurred in August 1998; 224 people were killed and more than 5,500 injured. See: Michael Grunwald and Vernon Loeb, 'Charges Filed Against bin Laden', *Washington Post* (5 November 1998), p. A17.

7 While Taliban elements continue to wage 'jihad' against US and North Atlantic Treaty Organisation forces in Afghanistan, the country is no longer a major haven for terrorists waging war against the United States.

8 Military Order of 13 November 2001, 'Detention, Treatment, and Trial of Certain Non-U.S. Citizens in the War Against Terrorism', *Federal Register*, 66:222 (16 November 2001) 57833. In the preamble to this order, Bush stated that he derived his authority for ordering the detention and trial of terrorists from his powers under the US constitution as commander in chief and from the joint resolution enacted by the US Congress authorising him to use military force against those responsible for the 9/11 attacks on the World Trade Centre and Pentagon.

9 Ibid., Section 1(e). Note that only non-US citizens were subject to the Military Order of 13 November 2001; the rights guaranteed American citizens under the US Constitution made it problematic for them to be detained by the military and tried by a military commission.

10 For example, Sheik Omar Abdel Rahmen, along with several other men, was convicted in a US District Court in New York City of conspiring to wage war against the United States in bombing the World Trade Center in 1993. *United States v. Rahmen*, 189 Federal Reporter 3d 88 (2d Circuit, 1999), *certiorari denied*, 528 United States 1094 (2000). Similarly, those responsible for the bombings of the US embassies in Tanzania and Kenya were tried for murder in federal courts. *United States v. Bin Laden*, 92 Federal Supplement 2d 189 (Southern District New York, 2000). Note also that even after Bush's decision to prosecute Al Qaeda members at military tribunals, one high-profile Al Qaeda member, Zacharias Moussaoui, was indicted in December 2001 and subsequently tried and convicted in a U. civilian court. See *United States v. Moussaoui*, 333 Federal Reporter 3d.509 (2003). See also: Seymour M. Hersh, 'The Twentieth Man', *The New Yorker* (30 September 2002), p. 64.

11 The scope of the 9/11 attacks was so great that all serious legal scholars believe they qualified as an 'armed attack', permitting self-defence under Article 51 of the United Nations Charter. See generally: Yoram Dinstein, *War, Aggression and Self Defence*. 3rd ed. (New York: Cambridge University Press, 2001), pp. 165–183.

12 For a good discussion of 'some of the legal and practical implications of treating terrorist acts as war crimes', see Jennifer Elsea, *Terrorism and the Law of War: Trying Terrorists as War*

Criminals before Military Commissions (Washington, DC: Congressional Research Service Report for Congress, 2001).

13 Proclamation 2561, 'Denying Certain Enemies Access to the Courts', *Federal Register*, 7: 5101 (1942).

14 Order Establishing a Military Commission to Try Eight Captured German Saboteurs, *Federal Register*, 7: 5103 (2 July 1942).

15 Military Order of 13 November 2001, Sec. 4(c) (1) & (2).

16 Roosevelt created the military commission on 2 July; the military commission met from 8 July 1942 until 1 August 1942; the commission members sentenced all eight defendants to death on 1 August; six of the eight were executed on 8 August 1942 (Roosevelt commuted the sentences of two of the eight German accused to life imprisonment). For more on the trial of the U-boat saboteurs, see *Ex parte Quirin*, 317 United States 1 (1942). See also Louis Fisher, *Nazi Saboteurs on Trial: A Military Tribunal and American Law*. 2nd ed. (Lawrence: University of Kansas Press, 2003).

17 Supra, note 15, Section 1(f).

18 U.S. Constitution, Article II, Sec. 2 ('The President shall be Commander in Chief of the Army and Navy of the United States, and of the Militia of the several States, when called into actual Service of the United States ...').

19 The U.S. Constitution creates a three-part government. Article I sets out the authority of Congress. Article II creates an Executive Branch headed by the president. Article III establishes the Judiciary, with the Supreme Court at the top and 'such inferior Courts as the Congress may ... establish'. As a general proposition, the *co-equal* and *independent* status of each of the three branches means that court decisions arising out of Article III courts have no applicability to a military court created by the President under Article II. For a discussion of this 'separation of powers', see generally Pauline Maier, *Ratification: The People Debate the Constitution* (New York: Simon & Schuster, 2010). Perhaps even more importantly, the Bill of Rights contained in the first ten Amendments to the Constitution arguably applies only to courts operating under Article I and Article III, and not to the military commissions established by Bush under Article II. The extent to which the Bill of Rights applies outside Article III tribunals is uncertain. See Frederic Lederer and Frederic Borch, 'Does the Fourth Amendment Apply to the Armed Forces?', *William and Mary Bill of Rights Journal*, 3:1 (1994), p. 219.

20 Two thirds of the panel members at a military commission had to agree that an accused was guilty for him to be convicted, and a two-thirds vote was required for any sentence, including death. Military Order, Sec. 4.(c)(7).

21 Military Order, Sec. 4.(c)(8).

22 Rumsfeld delegated his authority to Wolfowitz on 21 June 2003. Department of Defence,

Military Commission Order No. 2, subj.: Designation of Deputy Secretary of Defence as Appointing Authority (21 June 2003).

23 Under Military Order, Sec. 4.(b), Secretary Rumsfeld was required to promulgate 'orders and regulations' governing the operation of any tribunal that would prosecute Al Qaeda members, to include 'orders for the appointment of one or more military commissions'. After a short period of time, however, Rumsfeld decided that his work as Defence Secretary left him with insufficient time to perform as the 'Appointing Authority'. Consequently, as permitted by Sec. 6.(b), he delegated his appointing authority powers to the Deputy Secretary of Defense.

24 For more on Haynes and his role in military commissions, see Vanessa Blum, 'Pentagon's Law Man', *Legal Times* (10 December 2001). For a decidedly negative view of Haynes' role as Defence Department General Counsel, see Scott Horton, 'Jim Haynes's Long Twilight Struggle', *Harper's Magazine* (8 February 2008), http://harpers.org/blog/2008/02/jim-hayness-long-twilight-struggle/. Retrieved 13 January 2012.

25 Lang's master of laws degree in advanced litigation techniques was from Temple University's Beasley School of Law, Philadelphia, Pennsylvania.

26 Neil A. Lewis, 'Threats and Responses: The Tribunals, Six Detainees May Soon Face Trial', *New York Times* (4 July 2003), p. A1. Another potential actor, Canadian Omar Ahmed Khadr, was considered by the prosecution for the role of defendant in the Guantanamo play but, as will be explained, was ultimately rejected as unsuitable because his trial would not further the goals of the performance.

27 Just as Godot is a central character in Samuel Beckett's absurdist play *Waiting for Godot*, despite the fact that he never appears on the stage. Samuel Beckett, *Waiting for Godot: A Tragicomedy in Two Acts* (New York: Grove Press, 1994).

28 In 1903, the Government of Cuba granted the United States a *perpetual* lease of territory for a naval station at Guantanamo Bay, Cuba. Agreement Between the United States and Cuba for the Lease of Lands for Coaling and Naval Stations (23 February 1903), http://avalon.law.yale.edu/20th_century/dip_cuba002.asp. Retrieved 27 December 2011.

29 'A Guantanamo Timeline', *The Washington Post* (date unkown) http://www.washingtonpost.com/wp-srv/world/daily/graphics/guantanomotime_050104.htm. Retrieved 23 November 2011.

30 The Chief Defense Counsel also received the same public affairs training, and developed a theme for his defence efforts. Colonel Gunn's theme was that the defence of these men was both legally and morally correct, and that his defence counsel should be applauded for agreeing to defend unpopular (if not despised) defendants. For an example of Gunn's use of the media to get his theme out, see Jeffrey Toobin, 'Annals of Law: Inside the Wire: Can an Air Force colonel help the detainees at Guantanamo?', *The New Yorker* (4 February 2004), pp. 36–52.

31 In ancient Greek drama, a group of actors who 'served as … commentators on … the main action of the drama', *Webster's Unabridged Dictionary*. 2nd ed. (New York: Random House, 1998), p. 367. In terms of the Guantanamo drama, the idea was that all prosecutors and other actors supporting the prosecution would include the words 'full and fair trial' in every public pronouncement they made to the news media.

32 The term 'true believer' comes from Eric Hoffer's treatise on the psychological causes of fanaticism and explores why individuals enthusiastically embrace a group's ideology. Eric Hoffer, *The True Believer: Thoughts on the Nature of Mass Movements* (New York: Harper & Row, 1951).

33 For more on Hamdan, see Jonathan Mahler, 'The Journey of Salim Hamdan', *New York Times Magazine* (8 January 2006), p. 44.

34 Indictment, United States v. Ali Hamza Ahmad Sulayman Al Bahlul, See also, Stephen Hodges, 'Military indicts 2 Guantanamo terror suspects', *Chicago Tribune* (25 February 2004), p. 1.

35 'Indictment of al Bahlul', *Office of military commissions* (23 February 2004), http://www.mc.mil/CASES/MilitaryCommissions.aspx. Retrieved 31 December 2011.

36 Ibid.

37 'Alleged al-Qaida video maker's trial opens at Guantanamo Bay', *The Guardian* UK (28 October 2008), p. 1.

38 Notes, Statement by Ali Hamza al Bahlul, Chief Prosecutor's files.

39 Indictment, *United States v. Ibrahim Ahmed Mahmoud al Qosi*, Charge: Conspiracy. See also Department of Defence News Release No. 0179–08, *Charges Referred Against Detainee Al Qosi* (5 March 2008), www.defence.gov/Releases/Release.aspx?ReleaseID=11735. Retrieved 12 December 2011.

40 Indictment, *United States v. David Matthew Hicks*, June 2004, reprinted in Leigh Sales, *Detainee 002: The Case of David Hicks* (Melbourne: Melbourne University Press 2007), Appendix II, pp. 256–260.

41 Sales, *Detainee 002*, pp. 26–27.

42 The members of the Office of the Chief Prosecutor who were chiefly involved in formulating the prosecution strategy were Navy Commander Scott M. Lang (serving as Deputy Chief Prosecutor), Marine Corps Majors Kurt J. Brubaker and Stuart Couch, Air Force Majors Thomas A. Dukes and Robert J. Preston, and Army Captain Ronald Sullivan.

43 Military Order, sec. 2(a)(1)(ii).

44 The Abu Sayyaf Group (ASG) is located in the Philippines and emerged in the 1990s when it split off from the larger Moro National Liberation Front. The ASG's goal is to establish an independent Islamic state in areas of the southern Philippines heavily populated by Muslims. The group carries out kidnappings, bombings and assassinations to further its aims.

45 Jemaah Islamiya ('Islamic Congregation') was founded in Indonesia in 1993. Its goal is to establish an Islamic caliphate in Southeast Asia. Jemaah Islamiya is best known for carrying out a terrorist car bombing on the island of Bali in October 2002; this attack killed more than 200 people.

46 Lashkar-e-Tayyiba (LET) operates mainly from Pakistan and has training camps in Pakistan-controlled Kashmir. LET's primary goal is to liberate Muslims living in Indian Kashmir; its members have carried out numerous terrorist attacks against India.

47 Formed in Egypt as the Islamic Jihad (EIJ), the group was created to overthrow the Egyptian government and replace it with an Islamic state. In the 1990s, the EIJ was led by Dr. Ayman al-Zawahiri, a surgeon who later became bin Laden's personal physician. After the death of bin Laden, Al Zawahiri took command of Al Qaeda.

48 The Armed Islamic Group (GIA) was organised to overthrow the government of Algeria and replace it with an Islamic state. Between 1992 and 1998, the GIA killed hundreds of civilians by assassination and bombings in Algeria.

49 The terrorist groups identified here were representative only; other groups (not known or in existence) could be members of the conspiracy, or join it.

50 In Anglo-American jurisprudence, criminal liability generally requires *mens rea* (intent), plus an act; mere status is insufficient. For example, the US Supreme Court has held that while it is lawful to make using drugs a crime, it is not lawful to make it a crime to be addicted to drugs. See *Robinson v. California*, 370 United States 666 (1962). Similarly, at the Nuremberg war crimes prosecutions, while the United States concurred with the Soviets and others that the Nazi Schutzstaffel (SS) was a 'criminal organisation', it resisted efforts to punish individual SS members simply for membership of the SS and instead looked for a criminal act or acts by an SS member as a predicate for criminal liability.

51 Military Commission Instruction No. 2 specified the offences triable by a military commission created pursuant to Bush's Military Order of 13 November 2001. The instruction was published on 30 April 2003.

52 Al-Zawahari, also known as 'The Doctor' was born in Egypt in 1951. He merged his Egyptian Islamic Jihad organisation with bin Laden's Al Qaeda in 1998 and is sometimes described as the 'brains' of Al Qaeda. After the death of bin Laden in May 2011, Zawahari took command of Al Qaeda.

53 Gary D. Solis, *The Law of Armed Conflict: International Humanitarian Law in War* (New York: Cambridge University Press, 2010), p. 206.

54 No one knows better than William Shakespeare that bad timing can cause an actor, director or producer to miss his moment:

We at the height are ready to decline.
There is a tide in the affairs of men
Which, taken at the flood, leads on to fortune;
Omitted, all the voyage of their life
Is bound in shallows and in miseries.
On such a full sea are we now afloat,
And we must take the current when it serves,
Or lose our ventures.

Julius Caesar, Act IV, Scene iii, lines 215–221.

55 This failure to convince Wolfowitz and others in authority that the Guantanamo performance must start without delay if public opinion was going to accept both the legal and moral correctness of having military commissions was a performance mistake from which the Guantanamo play has yet to recover.

56 Joshua Rozenberg, 'Guantanamo Bay trials unfair, says Attorney General', *The Telegraph* (26 June 2004), p. 1.

57 William Pelham Barr served as U.S. Attorney General from 1991 to 1993. He served under President George H.W. Bush.

58 Conversation between Deputy Secretary of Defence Paul Wolfowitz and Chief Prosecutor Fred Borch, Office of the Deputy Secretary of Defence, Pentagon, Washington, D.C., July 2003.

59 *Hamdan v. Rumsfeld*, 548 United States 557 (2006).

60 Military Commissions Act of 2006 (17 October 2006), Public Law 109–336, Title 10, United States Code, Sections pp. 948–949.

61 Military Commissions Act of 2009 (8 October 2009), Public Law 111-84, Title 10, United States Code, Sections pp. 948–949.

62 Department of Defence, *Manual for Military Commissions*. 2010 edition, www.mc.mil/Portals/0/2010 Manual for Military Commissions.pdf. Retrieved 27 December 2011.

63 Sales, *Detainee 002*, pp. 254–255.

64 Jerry Markon, 'Hamdan Guilty of Terror Support', *Washington Post* (7 August 2008), p. A1.

65 On 9 February 2008, al Bahlul was re-charged under the military commission process created by Congress; he was convicted in November 2008 of conspiring with Al Qaeda, soliciting murder and providing material support for terrorism, and sentenced to life in prison. Al Bahlul remains incarcerated at Guantanamo Bay, Cuba. see Peter Finn, 'Guantanamo Jury Sentences bin Laden Aide to Life Term', *Washington Post* (4 November 2008), p. A1.

66 Department of Defence, 'News Release No. 718–10; 'Al Qosi Sentence Announced'' (11 Augustus 2010), http://www.defence.gov/utility/printitem.aspx?print=http://www.defence.gov/releases/release.aspx?releaseid=13792. Retrieved 16 December 2011.

67 Department of Defence, 'News Release No. 1002–10, "DoD Announces Sentence for Detainee Omar Khadr"' (31 October 2010), http://www.defence.gov/utility/printitem.aspx?print=http://www.defence.gov/releases/release.aspx?releaseid=14023. Retrieved 16 December 2011.

68 Jess Bravin, 'Two Prosecutors At Guantanamo Quit in Protest', *Wall Street Journal* (1 August 2005), p. B 1.

69 For more on Borch's firing, see Sales, *Detainee 002*, pp. 157–165.

9. The Hofstad Group on Trial: Sentencing the Terrorist Risk, 2005–2014[1]

Beatrice de Graaf

9.1. Introduction

'Our legal system is the "sharia". That is the only system we acknowledge', one of the defendants stated during the trial of Dutch jihadi radicals, a network the secret service internally dubbed the 'Hofstad Group'. At that time, the defendants wore *djellabas*, refused to stand up in court and were visibly encouraged by a number of burqa-clad friends from the public gallery.[2] A distinct performative strategy aimed at rejecting the democratic rule of law guided their behaviour. In terrorism trials, the actors involved often deploy performative strategies intended to mobilise or convince their target audience(s) of their vision of justice and injustice. While the public prosecutors try to invoke the reality of potential terror as allegedly inflicted by the defendants, the defendants may adhere to a completely different set of beliefs, directed against the democratic society or rule of law as such.

In this chapter, we will analyse how conflicting strategies, performances and outcomes of the three subsequent trials against the so-called 'Hofstad Group', between 2005 and 2006 (appeals are included up to 2014) developed over time. While the trial avoids easy characterisation, we discern elements of (1) a virtual trial, (2) a show run by the prosecution, and (3) a media show (with sideshows) that evolved over the years. In this analysis, three trials are discussed, which were closely linked through 'fictive kinship', friendship and the prosecution's projections of guilt: the trial against Mohammed Bouyeri, the trial against the first set of Hofstad Group defendants (the 'Arles' case) and the trial against the second group of suspects (the 'Piranha' case).

9.2. Theory and Method[3]

The trial against the Hofstad Group turned out, for most of the suspects, to be a protracted battle between defendants and public prosecutors about the meaning of texts, the nature of the Hofstad associates' network, the future possibility of terror attacks and the level of radicalisation, rather than about actual acts of terrorism (Mohammed Bouyeri's murder of Theo van Gogh was the only violent act actually committed). Taking centre stage was not a concrete terrorist attack, nor even a defined plot of preparation, but the question of jihadi innuendo in speech and in writings, in phone calls, in chats and in text messages as well as the question of the organisational nature of jihadist activities in the Netherlands. Therefore, large parts of the trial could be defined as 'virtual trials'. To elaborate on this element of 'virtual reality'—i.e. simulated or imagined reality—it is necessary to point to the concept of 'premediation', that, in the words of Marieke de Goede, enables the virtual or precautionary turn when trying suspects of terrorism.[4]

De Goede and De Graaf have argued[5] that new anti-terrorism legislation since 9/11 has propelled the development of 'anticipatory prosecution',[6] the phenomenon of anticipating and preparing cases based on indication, allegations or even rumours of preparatory deeds, far in advance of projected attacks.[7] This tendency has been identified and analysed before from legal,[8] criminological[9] and political[10] perspectives. We added to that body of literature the observation that *terrorism trials* function as a highly effective performative space where the 'spectre of catastrophe'[11] is invoked, where potential future deeds of terror are projected, contested and adjudicated on—and hence made real.[12]

Here we will analyse the court cases of Mohammed Bouyeri and the two trials against the Hofstad Groupdefendants from the perspective of premediation, as described above and introduced before by Richard Grusin.[13] De Goede (see references above) and Grusin have analysed some of the techniques that have been used to imagine potential future scenarios, to bring them into the present and to make them 'real'. Although these mediated future attacks will never become reality, since the suspects have already been apprehended, and the status of the anticipated attacks will remain virtual forever, they are configured into charges and turned into judgments. Thus, the trials against the Hofstad Group present exceptional cases of virtual adjudication; or, as Claudia Aradau and Rens van Munster have coined it, theatres of a 'conjectural style of reasoning' which 'constructs an explanation out of apparently insignificant details. It links the smallest and most inconsequential facts to a larger context that cannot be directly observed or experienced.'[14]

We will describe and identify how during these trials real or future terror scenarios were mobilised and visualised, how evidence was used, and how these bits, pieces and imaginations were incorporated in the charges and final verdict. At the same time, we will address how the audience, the media, other stakeholders (victims or victims' relatives), and the defendants themselves responded to this virtual or premediative turn in the criminal justice system. Was this premediated scenario accepted, did the defendants resist it, and in what ways did they try to argue against a strategy that deals with allegations and associations projected onto (merely) future scenarios? In short, we will discuss how these terrorism trials functioned as a site for terrorism risk management such that, in the latter two Hofstad trials, not the attack but the premediated risk of an attack stood trial.

In asking and responding to these questions, we pay tribute to the 'productive power of legal arguments' and the manner in which 'legal arguments are embedded in and reproduce deeper-lying social and symbolic structures'.[15] Terrorism trials are key opportunities to legitimise the scope and substance of post-9/11 terrorism legislation, which is simultaneously implemented, contested and performed. By distinguishing instruments and techniques in courtroom proceedings, we are able to contribute to wider debates on precaution in counter-terrorism, and to analyse the ways in which the logic of what Michael Power calls 'secondary risk management' can function. This kind of risk management strategy is not geared towards actually preventing a calculated catastrophe, but towards addressing explicitly or implicitly the question of political responsibility. Secondary risk management techniques are intended to avert or displace the responsibility and to prevent reputation damage in cases of 'decisions which must be made in potentially undecidable situations'.[16] We will see how the three trials discussed here could indeed be considered sites of anticipatory prosecution and secondary risk management techniques.

9.3. Context of the Trial: The Emergence of the Hofstad Group

9.3.1. The Emergence of the 'Hofstad Group' as a Threat to National Security

From 2002 on, the Dutch intelligence and security agency, AIVD (Algemene Inlichtingen- en Veiligheidsdienst), monitored a group of jihadi radicals; a network which the service dubbed internally 'the Hofstad Group', since it operated partly in the nation's capital, The Hague (*Hofstad* translates as 'capital city'). Except for Mohammed, the murderer of the journalist Theo van Gogh, whose case is discussed later, its alleged core members were under surveillance. Even before December 2001, the AIVD had kept a close eye on the radical Salafist El Tawheed Mosque in Amsterdam-West, looking for any suspicious Egyptian or Saudi influences (the mosque had financial relations with a Saudi non-governmental organisation, Al Haramein International).[17] In the summer of 2002 the secret service identified a group of Muslim young people who met in and around the mosque and gathered around Redouan al-Issa (then 43 years old), also named 'Abu Khaled' or 'the Sheikh', who had ties to radical Muslims in Spain and Belgium.

Abu Khaled, a former member of the Syrian Muslim Brotherhood, came to the Netherlands in 1995 as an illegal immigrant from Syria. He became a mentor to a number of radical Muslims.[18] He inspired, amongst others, 17-year-old high school student Samir Azzouz, of Moroccan origin, but born and raised in the Netherlands. Samir Azzouz came to the attention of the AIVD in January 2003 when he, together with his friend Khalid (or Hussam, age 17), took the train to Berlin, bound for Chechnya, to join local jihadists in their fight against the Russian forces. At the Ukrainian border, they were arrested and put back on a train to Western Europe. The media described their adventurous journey as an amateurish endeavour, but the two young Islamists had prepared for their trip thoroughly. The police found night vision goggles and a GPS system (which turned out to have been used in Russia) at Samir's residence after their return. The police suspected that the two students were recruited by Redouan al Issa. After his return Azzouz's status rose; he started his own Islamic book company and began only associating with Moroccan young people.[19]

Ismail Akhnikh was another alleged core member of the Hofstad Group, who had international aspirations. The Dutch-Moroccan Akhnikh, born in Amsterdam in 1982, regularly attended the El Tawheed Mosque in Amsterdam where he became acquainted with Azzouz and was believed to have helped him establish the Hofstad network in the autumn of 2002. In the summer of 2003, he may have travelled with Azzouz to Barcelona to meet there with Abdeladim Akoudad for guidance and instructions. This Abdeladim Akoudad (or 'Naoufel'), a Moroccan national living in Spain, was suspected by the Moroccan security services to be involved in the Casablanca terror attacks of 16 March 2003.[20]

In October 2003, Akoudad and Azzouz discussed over the phone 'shoes, first and second rate, coming from Greece or Italy and that will do well in Spain', and 'documents'. At this point, the Spanish authorities intervened and arrested Akoudad on 14 October 2003.[21] Two days later, the AIVD alerted the National Terrorism Prosecutor that Azzouz and other members of the Hofstad Group, all regular visitors to the El Tawheed Mosque and a phone shop in Schiedam which also functioned as a place to meet were probably preparing a terrorist attack. On 17 October arrests were made in several Dutch cities: Samir Azzouz, the Syrian 'Abu Kahled' (or Redouan al-Issa), Jason Walters, Ismail Akhnikh and Mohamed Fahmi Boughaba were apprehended. Apartments, including the house of Mohammed Bouyeri in Amsterdam, were raided.[22]

However, because the allegation of terrorism could not be substantiated, the Hofstad Group members were released after eleven days. Even though a supermarket bag, filled with goods resembling ingredients for constructing explosive devices, including six security glasses, fertiliser, power tape, distilled water, liquid ammonia, hydrochloric acid, batteries, a timer, kitchen gloves, halogen bulbs and chemical cleaner, was retrieved by the police from Mohamed Fahmi Boughaba's apartment, where he had allegedly kept it on Azzouz's instructions, this was not enough evidence to keep the men in custody. Neither a direct link to a terrorist organisation nor any specific terrorist intent could be substantiated.[23]

After their temporary detention in October 2003, Akhnikh, Azzouz and Walters continued to collaborate and urged other Muslims to go abroad to wage jihad.[24] Akhnikh went to Pakistan that year, as did Zakaria Taybi and Jason Walters (who went twice, in July and December 2003). Walters and Akhnikh even bragged about contacts with Maulana Masood Azhar, a core Al Qaeda member—something they later downplayed in court. In June 2004, Nouriddin el Fatmi went to Portugal with other members of the group, among whom was Mohamed El M. The AIVD warned the Portuguese authorities, out of fear that the members were planning to kill José Manuel Durao Barroso (the then president-designate of the European Commission) and other guests during a reception in Oporto, which was organised in honour of the European Soccer Championship that took place in Portugal. The three were arrested and sent back to the Netherlands, where the AIVD and the special anti-terrorism unit of the National Police Services Agencies (KLPD) interrogated them. It finding no evidence of concrete preparations, the men were released.[25] Only when they felt that the security forces in Pakistan, Portugal and the Netherlands were closing in on them did they presumably begin to conspire and confine their scope to their local environment. The next time the security forces intervened to arrest them was after the murder of Van Gogh in November 2004.

The international inspiration and the impulse to organise were believed to have come from their mentor, Redouan al-Issa, who also acted as Bouyeri's mentor until October 2003. With his alleged experience as a martyr, he seemed to have functioned as the charismatic 'magnet' that bound the group together in the beginning, from 2002 onwards. In his seminal study *Leaderless Jihad*, Marc Sageman dismisses Al-Issa's role because 'he seemed to have simply disappeared from his group' and 'the remaining members of the Hofstad Group rarely mentioned him'.[26] Sageman correctly warns against viewing people like Al-Issa as hierarchical leaders or recruiters in the traditional sense of the word. However, precisely because terrorist networks are not static organisations, we should be careful not to dismiss him too soon from the picture.

Moreover, it is only logical that the remaining Hofstad Group members did not mention Al-Issa after their arrests in 2004, since all of them tried to escape conviction and did not confess to terrorist crimes. On the contrary, they denied being part of a terrorist organisation altogether.[27] It would therefore have been rather foolish to comment on their relationship with Al-Issa or to dwell on his role as inspirer of the Hofstad Group. There is another explanation for his disappearance from the scene as well. After the first arrests in October 2003, Al-Issa, as an illegal immigrant, was declared an 'unwanted alien' and deported. His role of inspirer, ideologist and proselytiser was assumed by other leader personalities such as Azzouz and Bouyeri.[28] Al-Issa did return in the course of 2004 (and had contacts with Mohammed Bouyeri), but had too little time to regain his former position or build another network. He fled the Netherlands again on the morning of 2 November when Bouyeri assassinated Theo van Gogh.

Al-Issa's real role within the network still remains vague (because group members remained silent and did not want to compromise their defence strategy) and changed over time (because of counterterrorism efforts). Nonetheless, he should not be underestimated. He was wanted by Morocco and by Spain for involvement in the 2003 Casablanca and the 2004 Madrid bombings. Additionally, he brought the Hofstad Group members together, first through meetings in the El Tawheed Mosque in Amsterdam and subsequently on a more informal basis, at Mohammed Bouyeri's apartment, where he inspired them with stories of international jihad and conducted Islamic marriages.[29] After his apprehension in October 2003, Abu Khaled compared himself to a 'Christian evangelist'. A witness in court, who attended the living room meetings at Bouyeri's home, saw him as a 'priest' and the young people surrounding him as 'disciples'.[30] Only in the course of 2004 did the remaining Dutch members of the network take over his role.[31]

In short, the Hofstad network was organised locally, without any demonstrable direction from an Al Qaeda command centre or from any other identifiable, pre-existing terrorist organisation.[32] It started with some individuals prone to radical jihadist philosophy. But they actively sought inspiration from international contacts, from a foreign preacher and from international Salafist texts. Some members were subsequently recruited to contribute to international jihad in Chechnya and established contacts with terrorists abroad. Only when these attempts in 2002–2003 were thwarted by the intelligence services and their mentor was expelled did they, in 2004, allegedly began to conspire against Dutch targets.[33]

9.3.2. *The Murder of Theo van Gogh*

On the early morning of 2 November 2004, Mohammed Bouyeri, a 26-year old Dutch-Moroccan, born and raised in Amsterdam, awaited journalist Theo van Gogh in an Amsterdam street, shot him off his bicycle and slaughtered him with a knife in the middle of the street in front of many witnesses.[34] This murder would tremendously affect governmental counter-terrorism efforts.

Bouyeri's action had taken the security services by surprise. From 2002, the AIVD had monitored 'the Hofstad Group', the network of jihadi radicals that Bouyeri was acquainted with.[35] Its core members were under surveillance, but Bouyeri was not viewed as one of them. He did not take part in the foreign trips made by some members and was not considered a main actor in the Dutch jihadi scene.[36] Bouyeri's radical texts calling for violent jihad, disseminated under the name 'Abu Zubair', were noticed only after the police and the AIVD stepped up their investigation into the Hofstad Group after the murder of Van Gogh on 2 November 2004.[37]

However, Bouyeri's radicalisation process had taken some time and was not a solitary process. He grew up in a dreary area in Amsterdam-West as the eldest son (after his sister Saïda) of eight children, but was able to pursue higher education and engaged himself in community development. From 1999 onwards, he rented his own apartment at the Marianne Philipsstraat and studied an accounting course at a college. He became more fundamental and aggressive; for example, he held his sister captive for having an affair. In the summer of 2000 he was involved in a pub brawl, and in the spring of 2001 he attacked his sister's boyfriend. In October, he was sentenced to 12 weeks in prison, where he studied the Koran intensively.[38]

At the end of 2001, when he was released, his father was declared disabled and his mother died of cancer. In 2002, Bouyeri's plans to set up a youth centre in his neighbourhood collapsed. He left college and began to live on unemployment insurance. He now devoted his time completely to studying radical Islamic texts and started wearing fundamentalist clothes. In the El Tawheed Mosque, which he visited frequently, he met with similar radicalising Muslim young people, and a preacher of Syrian descent, Redouan al-Issa, or Abu Khaled.[39]

Bouyeri invited his new soulmates to his apartment, where he organised so-called living-room meetings and listened to lectures by Abu Khaled. He also provided lodgings for one of the alleged key Hofstad Group members: Nouriddin el Fatmi. His mentor, Abu Khaled, taught him and the other members of the Hofstad Group about 'Tawheed' (the unity of Allah), and instructed them on how to live as radical Salafist Muslims. Bouyeri embraced these ideas.[40] After Abu Khaled was expelled from the

Netherlands in October 2003 as an illegal immigrant, Bouyeri took over Khaled's role as spiritual leader. As the ideologue of the Hofstad Group, Bouyeri wrote, translated and disseminated via the internet more than 50 texts, in which he increasingly called his brothers to arms against Dutch society, rather than on behalf of international jihad elsewhere.[41]

In May 2004 he abused an employee of the Social Services, and on 29 September 2004 the police arrested him because he resisted being fined for fare-dodging. The law enforcement officials found on him notes with telephone numbers and e-mail addresses of Hofstad Group members, which they sent to the AIVD. Since he had committed only a minor offence and was not on the list of approximately 150 jihadi radicals the AIVD had identified as a risk to security, Bouyeriwas released. At the time, neither the police nor the AIVD considered Bouyeri to be a serious threat, nor did they take seriously his participation in the jihadi network of the Hofstad Group.[42]

Secondly, although Bouyeri carried out the immediate preparations for his attack on his own initiative, he was continually surrounded by his jihadi associates during this preparatory stage. On 19 May 2004, Bouyeri received his last unemployment cheque. Between 19 May and 28 October he withdrew only €200 from his bank account (not an amount someone can live on for five months). On 28 October, he withdrew the rest of his savings, €930, and reached his maximum overdraft. That same day, he handed Rachid B. an envelope containing €1,650, intended for his family. Where did he find the additional €720? And how could he have afforded his firearm, a HS 2000 pistol, which costs approximately €1,000 to €1,500? It is therefore not unlikely that others—possibly the defendants—were involved in one way or another. No evidence, however, was found that supports this assumption.[43]

On Monday evening, 1 November 2004, during Ramadan, Bouyeri had a late supper together with his friends from the Hofstad Group. He also left behind some letters, discovered later to be his will. Early in the morning, Bouyeri prayed with his associates, had breakfast with them and left the house on his bicycle with his gun, a ritual Kukri Machete and a fillet knife in his backpack. His housemates denied having known anything about these weapons, despite the fact that they lived together in his cramped two-room flat (the living room measured 15 square metres, the single bedroom only ten), nor could they provide explanations about how Bouyeri could have purchased the gun.[44]

Bouyeri carefully planned the attack on the controversial publicist and film maker Theo van Gogh. Van Gogh was known, among other things, for his anti-Islamist statements for producing the provocative documentary *Submission* (an attempt to liberate Muslim women from their oppressive religion, broadcast in August 2004), together with the Somali-born Member of Parliament Ayaan Hirsi Ali. Hirsi Ali was protected by Dutch security agencies at that time, but Van Gogh, who had rejected protection, seemed a good alternative. For weeks, Bouyeri observed Van Gogh's house and daily cycling routine and, in one of the most crowded streets on the route, spotted the place where he would kill his target. At 8:40 on Tuesday morning 2 November Bouyeri overtook Van Gogh on the Linnaeusstraat, shot him from his bicycle, followed him to the other side of the street, fired another round of bullets (eight in total), then slashed his throat with the machete, in front of 53 witnesses. With the smaller knife, he pinned an 'Open Letter to Hirsi Ali' to Van Gogh's chest and then fled the scene, fruitlessly shooting at some passers-by before engaging in gunfire with the police. He tried to kill the police officers that pursued him, planning to be killed himself in the process and become a martyr, but was shot in the leg and overpowered.[45]

The police found a farewell letter on him, entitled 'Drenched in blood'. This versed text read as an incitement to holy war and was signed Saifu Deen al-Muwahhied. At least according to Ruud Peters, a Dutch Islam expert and witness for the prosecution, these words are a combination of two Arabic terms 'sword of religion' (Saif al-Din) and 'confessor of Tawheed' (al-Muwahhid).[46] In the 'Open Letter', he directly threatened Dutch-Somali liberal politician Ayaan Hirsi Ali, and blamed politicians for allowing Jewish influences in politics. According to Norwegian researcher Petter Nesser, the conclusion of the letter reflects 'the essence of al-Qaedaism' by prophesying the defeat of the enemy on the individual, local, regional and global levels in order of priority:

> And like a great prophet once said: 'I deem thee lost, O Pharaoh.' (17:102) And so we want to use similar words and send these before us, so that the heavens and the stars will gather this news and spread it over the corners of the universe like a tidal wave. 'I deem thee lost, O America.' 'I deem thee lost, O Europe.' 'I deem thee lost, O Holland.' 'I deem thee lost, O Hirsi Ali' 'I deem thee lost, O unbelieving fundamentalist.'[47]

Since Bouyeri wrote these texts to provide spiritual support for this network, these two texts suggest that Bouyeri's attack was the result of an ideological turn to violent jihad against the Netherlands, which may have inspired the Hofstad Group network. One of Bouyeri's last writings was the 'Open Letter to the Dutch Population' dated 12 August 2004 (which he left on a USB stick for other Hofstad Group members to disseminate). For 'the Umma',[48] he announced attacks against Dutch public places, justifying the attacks by the support of the Dutch government for the United States and Israel. His argument echoed a fatwa announced by dissident Saudi Sheikh Hamoud bin Oqlaa' al Sjou'abi, legitimising the September 11 attacks.[49] A translation of these and other texts was found on the computers of other members of the Hofstad Group.[50]

9.3.3. *The Arrest*

Bouyeri was arrested on the spot, but not before he tried to shoot some eyewitnesses and tried to carry out a 'suicide by cop' attempt. The public prosecutor charged him on 11 November with murder, attempted murder (of a police officer), attempted manslaughter (of by-standers and police officers), violation of the law on gun-control, suspicion of participating in a criminal organisation with terrorist aims and conspiracy with a terrorist purpose to murder Van Gogh, Hirsi Ali and others who were mentioned in his open letter and demanded a life sentence.[51]

The public prosecutor also set out to arrest the other members of the Hofstad network for taking part in a conspiracy to wage terrorism in the Netherlands. Most of the arrests went smoothly, but on 10 November 2004, a special arrest squad entered the apartment in The Hague where Ismail Akhnikh and Jason Walters resided. Walters threw a hand grenade, wounding four law enforcement officers, turning the arrest into a 14-hour siege and a national spectacle.[52]

9.3.4. *The Remaining Hofstad Network Continues*

In the meantime, two other leaders, Abu Khaled (who had illegally entered the country again) and Nouriddin el Fatmi, fled the country. Samir Azzouz, one of the other core members of the group, had been arrested on 30 June 2004 for his alleged participation in a shop robbery. While picking him up, the Special Forces retrieved a number of weapons, chemicals and maps from his apartment, signalling that he seemed to be preparing for a terrorist attack.[53] When Bouyeri committed his attack, Azzouz was thus stored away and could not be implicated in this first trial.

However, Azzouz and El Fatmi continued their attempts when Azzouz was released after his acquittal in April 2005. The judge had ruled, in a rather short trial, that the chemicals found in his apartment were not sufficient to assemble an explosive device.[54] Despite strong protests by a number of conservative and right-wing politicians, Azzouz was acquitted. As a law enforcement official who was involved in the case stated in an interview, 'From the moment Azzouz was acquitted due to lack of evidence, we were tasked to carry out an autonomous investigation. We knew there had to be more guns. We also found out that Nouriddin and possibly Azzouz had been in Brussels, probably to purchase weapons. We tapped their telephones, did observations.'[55] Thus, in April 2005, the police immediately launched a second investigation, called 'Paling' (Eel), and later 'Piranha'. The police immediately started a new investigation.[56] Two months later, was spotted in The Hague and was arrested together with his wife Soumaya S. and friend Martine van den O. (a native Dutch Islamist convert) at Amsterdam Lelylaan railway station. After their arrest an automatic gun (a Croatian Agram 2000) with an unleashed firing pin (safety) lock was taken from El Fatmi's backpack.[57]

Together with two others, Azzouz continued his efforts to purchase arms; they made observations in and around Schiphol Airport and chatted about waging jihad.[58] According to the criminal intelligence units of the Utrecht and Amsterdam police forces, Azzouz and his comrades had set out to find ten AK-47 rifles, two guns with silencers and ten explosive belts.[59] The police and secret service also found recordings of a video 'will' or farewell message by Azzouz, in which he, with a 'baby Uzi' in the background, said goodbye to his family and friends and addressed the Dutch population, all in Arabic: 'We will spill your blood like you spilled the blood of our Muslim citizens in Iraq.' The will was not (yet?) intended for dissemination and was only later revealed to the public. For the police and intelligence services, this video triggered their arrest.[60] On 14 October 2005, Azzouz and Jermaine Walters (the brother of the aforementioned Jason Walters), who were suspects in the first Hofstad case but not detained, and five other co-conspirators were arrested on suspicion of preparing an attack against unnamed national politicians, the AIVD and other targets.[61]

9.4. Performative Strategies during the Three Hofstad Group Trials

9.4.1. The Trial against Mohammed Bouyeri, 11–26 July 2005 (the 'Fakir' case)

The Hearing

The trial against Bouyeri started on 11 July 2005 under massive media attention. The public prosecutor, Frits van Straelen, charged him with murder with terrorist intent, attempted murder (of eyewitnesses and police officers) and obstructing the work of a member of parliament (Ayaan Hirsi Ali). He demanded a life sentence and the withdrawal of his active and passive voting rights. For the prosecution the case was straightforward. The only question was how Bouyeri would defend himself. That answer proved to be anticlimactic.

Apart from using his right to the 'last word', Mohammed Bouyeri remained silent from 11 until 24 July (he spoke only during the last two days of the trial). During this first trial, Bouyeri instructed his defence counsel[62] to be present in court but to remain silent. As he did not recognise the jurisdiction of the court, he did not want them to pursue an active defence on his behalf.[63] Even though the defence counsel obeyed his instructions, one of his attorneys, Mr. Plasman, did comment on the case in the media, thereby triggering a response from the judges: They felt that he/they should defend their client in court.[64]

Bouyeri's defence strategy basically entailed ignoring the court. He refused to appear and after being forced to be present he remained silent. From a perfomative perspective his refusal to engage was successful. It provoked a response from the court: The judges ordered him to be present. This inspired all sorts of legal debates. Were there actually legal grounds for this in Dutch—or international—law?[65] Furthermore, even though he remained silent, he expressed himself non-verbally; for instance, by appearing in a black-and-white 'keffiyeh' (a traditional Arab headdress), a long *djellaba* and holding a Koran.[66]

On 26 July, he demonstrated his contempt for the court by openly addressing his last word (which is a right of the defendant before the presiding judges close the trial) to the mother of his victim; this, while stressing that he did not feel obliged to address the court. He made his speech only, or so it seemed, to fend off the allegations that he was personally insulted by Van Gogh (and that the murder had thus been a personal vendetta rather than a religious statement in general), and to offer some sort of consolation to Van Gogh's mother. She was the only person in the courtroom to whom Bouyeri paid some respect, while acknowledging her grief and offering some apologies.[67]

By exercising his right to the last word in the manner that he did, one can conclude that he tried to persuade his target audience of the legitimacy of his cause. Among other things, he said:

> So the whole story that I was offended as a Moroccan because he called us 'Geitenneukers'[68] is in no way the truth. I did what I did because of what I believe. Even if it had been my father or my little brother I would have done the same thing .... I can ensure you that if I were released I would do it again .... The same law that obliges me to behead anyone who insults Allah or the Prophet does not oblige me to live in a country where, as the public prosecutor said, the 'freedom of expression' is preached.[69]

Thus he justified his crimes on the basis of his religion. His religious arguments were predominately inspired by several Salafist sources, which included the conviction that true jihadists should hate those who threaten the Islam and should isolate themselves from the non-Muslim world.[70]

After challenging the judiciary so openly and stating that he, if given the chance, would do it again, the life sentence he received came as no surprise.[71] His behaviour seemed to suggest that this had been his aim all along. When he failed in committing suicide by cop and becoming a martyr in death, he now showed himself willing to become a martyr in life, thus possibly mobilising his sympathisers or other adherents to follow his steps, to renounce the laws and the institutes of 'non-believers' and to wage jihad against them.[72]

He might have succeeded in persuading a few regarding his (in)justice perspective and his religious motives. From a qualitative study done in Amsterdam we know that some radicalised young people described the murder of Van Gogh as a heroic and positive deed and argued that the violent Jihad was indeed the apt response to perceived injustices carried out against Muslims.[73] However, apart from the group of sympathisers on the court's public gallery (there were only a handful), Bouyeri did not seem to attract a crowd of followers at all; not at that time and not since. On the major religious social sites that were frequently visited by religious Muslim young people (notably marokko.nl), his trial was not a major topic of debate at all.[74]

Media Response

From the attack onwards, the nature and character of the terrorist threat captured Dutch public debate for many months to come. The attacks by Al Qaeda in New York had, of course, already shocked the Dutch government and sensitised the general public which, until then, had been rather indifferent to international terrorism. The murder of Van Gogh, however, triggered public and political vigilance vis-à-vis the terrorist threat within Dutch society. For example, the Minister of Finance, Gerrit Zalm, declared 'War' on Muslim terrorists.[75] The terrorist threat was enhanced by emerging fears of globalisation, immigration and Islam and transformed these fears into a state of moral panic. From that moment onwards, policy efforts, research projects and public debate centred on the question: was Bouyeri a lone wolf, or was it more likely that he was but one of the many more radicalised Muslim young people who were being recruited and organised to inflict more damage to Dutch society?[76]

However, it was significant that Bouyeri's murder was hardly cited or appraised on the dominant internet sites and fora on which Dutch Muslim youth expressed themselves.[77] Sections of his oral pleadings were taped by a tele-journalist of NOVA. As he had not given permission for this it caused a stir. The media focused on his background, his radicalisation process, on the other Muslim youngsters that formed part of the group, and—during the last hearing—on the relatives of Van Gogh, his sister, parents and 15-year-old son who were present in the courtroom. Van Gogh's mother summed the national sentiment up in describing and dismissing Bouyeri as a 'loser' (*stakker*).[78]

The Verdict and the Aftermath

On 26 July, the judge issued the verdict.[79] Bouyeri received a life sentence, without parole—unusually harsh in Dutch judicial history.[80]

Neither the public prosecutor nor the defence counsel appealed the verdict. The judicial process was not over yet for Bouyeri. The national prosecutor announced that he would continue the prosecution of Bouyeri regarding his membership of the so-called 'Hofstad Group' organisation. That meant that Bouyeri would be heard as a witness and accused in a new trial that was scheduled for the autumn of that same year.

One particular consequence of this straightforward trial and verdict was the shift in attention of some of the public and commercial media from Bouyeri to the question whether Van Gogh's murder could have been prevented. Who was to blame? The AIVD revealed that Bouyeri did belong to a group of a few dozen young people that they considered to be radical Salafists. Why, then, for example, did a documentary presented by a national celebrity reveal that the security services had allowed Bouyeri roam freely? At this point, a conspiracy theory was introduced that surfaced from time to time: Bouyeri had been an agent of the AIVD and 'the government'. And that the 'government', e.g. the AIVD, had willingly sacrificed Van Gogh.[81]

9.4.2. The Hofstad Group Trial, February 2005–10 March 2006 (the 'Arles' Case)

The Hofstad (and Piranha) case in the Netherlands offers a set of conspicuous new premediation and risk management techniques, made possible by the implementation of the European Framework Decision within the Dutch legal framework in July 2004. Previously, Dutch legislation had not referred to or address any special terrorism-related criminal acts. The Act on Terrorism Crimes, proclaimed in the official government paper *Het Staatsblad* in June 2004,[82] added several new articles to the Dutch Criminal Code, namely articles 140a, 83a, and 96^2: an article penalising membership of a terrorist organisation (140b), an article on 'terrorist aim' (83a) and an article on conspiring to commit terrorist crimes (96^2).[83] The Hofstad and Piranha cases were the first overlapping cases in which these criminal offences were tested. Among others, the six defendants were charged with belonging to and participating in a terrorist organisation (article 140a), recruiting for terrorist activities (article 205), possessing firearms and monitoring, preparing and conspiring (articles 96 and 46) to commit terrorist crimes (article 83a). The prosecution demanded considerable prison sentences: between eight and fifteen years.[84]

The case was highly interesting because of the risk management techniques applied. The first and most contested one, both by defence counsel and in the judicial commentaries on the case, pertained to the admission of *intelligence evidence* in court. As Eijkman and Van Ginkel point out:

> Traditionally, a distinction exists between collecting intelligence for national security purposes and gathering evidence for criminal investigations, as they serve different purposes. This distinction also translates into the allocation of powers to law enforcement officials and the specific powers allotted to the intelligence services. For the latter, it is crucial that the sources of the intelligence are kept secret, whereas the fair trial principle demands that during a criminal trial, the public prosecutor and defencecounsel enjoy equal access to the evidence. However, in specific circumstances, such as the prosecution of terrorist crimes, these two worlds meet and intelligence information is shared.[85]

Since 2004, terrorism cases have been carried out on an 'inverse investigation' basis. Not proof of evidence, but intelligence reports act as immediate cause to start the investigation. The use of intelligence material was thoroughly expanded. These reports made up for the lack of concrete evidence (a common element with preventive arrests) and furthermore admitted into the investigative process telephone taps, hearsay and other information the origin of which remained in the dark. Possible deeds and alleged future attacks that only exist in preparatory actions, such as conversations, telephone conversations or the purchase of completely legal goods, were accepted as evidence in court. Only the premediated use of these legal goods turned them into bona fide evidence of illegal conspiratorial acts.

This risk management technique reduced the discretionary competencies of the public prosecutor. After the perceived intelligence failure surrounding Van Gogh's death, where the murderer had been on an AIVD-list of second-rank jihadists, the service started to divulge a continuous stream of intelligence reports to the prosecution. Although public prosecutors have discretionary competences in deciding to launch an investigation, order an arrest or run a second check on the AIVD material, in terrorism cases they felt pressured to act much more quickly. In these instances the highest counsel of the Prosecution Office, often also including the Minister of Justice, has a say in the matter, thereby reducing the autonomous function of the prosecutor of an individual case to one (lower) link in a set of politically sensitive deliberations. This centralised and politicised handling of terrorism cases went hand in glove with the tendency of the Dutch AIVD to dispatch their alerts much more quickly and based on much less evidence. In short, since Bouyeri's attack, the public prosecutors felt the pressure to act immediately after an official written report entered their e-mailbox.[86]

A conspicuous consequence of this risk management assemblage, dictating an increasingly heated prosecution cycle once the terrorism alert was signalled, was that the deliberations for commencing an investigation were shielded from the public. Intelligence briefs were characterised by their brevity, and more often than not did not reveal much about the background or the reliability of the sources. Defence counsel in the Hofstad and Piranha trials consequently accused the prosecution of discriminatory and selective investigation praxis. Why were some individuals subpoenaed? Were some merely interrogated as potential witnesses and others charged with jihadist crimes?[87] The reasons for incriminating some individuals and leaving others out remains hidden in the secret chambers of the security agencies.

In short, we will see that the new laws, the heated political climate and the pervasive sense of fear and terror (deliberately created by the defendants themselves, according to the prosecution) spurred the prosecution to follow a strategy of projecting 'virtual realities' into the trial.[88]

The Public Prosecutor's Strategy

In the 'Arles' investigation (the name that the national investigation squad gave the investigation into the Hofstad members after 2 November), contrary to the case, no defendant had committed or accomplished a physical attack, murder or other violent act. Therefore, the prosecution relied on the new legislation adopted after 2004 to charge the defendants with the crime of belonging to a terrorist organisation, preparing for a terrorist attack, recruiting others, inciting hatred and terrorism.[89] This indicated a completely different approach. The prosecution had to invoke the possible terrorist future based on preparations, intentions and associations only. That made the trial a highly interesting and novel proceeding; it was cutting-edge jurisprudence, also according to the prosecutors.[90]

In February and May 2005, two preliminary (*pro forma*) hearings took place in which the prosecutors, Koos Plooy and Alexander van Dam, announced that the twelve (later thirteen) defendants were charged with being members of a terrorist organisation and that their custody would be extended by ninety days.[91] During the summer, the national investigation squad concluded its searches and observations and heard a number of witnesses, in particular female friends and (ex-)partners of the defendants. Rumours and stories about 'seduced' young girls, manipulated and recruited by Hofstad Group members to join their alleged jihadist cause, started to spread.[92] The spectacular arrest of El Fatmi (see below) and his wife Soumaya S. on 22 June 2005 further sparked the national debate and expectations as to the true terrorist nature of the defendants.

In September a fourth *pro forma* hearing was organised, after which two defendants were released due to lack of evidence. The prosecution further announced that they would also prosecute Mohammed Bouyeri for participating in the Hofstad Group. Bouyeri's counsel, Peter Plasman, accused the prosecution of turning the trial into a 'show trial'. 'The point is that the public prosecutor wants to mete out additional punishment to Mohammed B, although he has already received a maximum sentence. This only serves to make Bouyeri suffer more. That is something the criminal law does not allow for.'[93]

Notwithstanding these protests, on 5 December the trial against the 13 defendants commenced in the heavily guarded Amsterdam-Osdorp courtroom, 'the Bunker', a venue far from the city centre, in an industrial area that is very difficult to access by public transport. The group of defendants consisted of Mohammed Bouyeri, three other alleged core group members (Nouriddin el Fatmi, Jason Walters and Ismail Akhnikh) and nine others. Jason Walters and Ismail Akhnikh had been arrested after heavy resistance (Walters threw a hand grenade at the police on 10 November 2004), which gave them special status, since they could be charged under the regular criminal law with attempted murder as well.

The prosecution initiated the hearing with Professor Ruud Peters, an Islam expert from the University of Amsterdam, who commented on the ideology that the Hofstad Group adhered to, as deduced from the numerous texts and videos the police and security services had found on the members' computers. Although Peters made clear that such an ideology, albeit fundamentalist and radical, need not necessarily lead to concrete acts of jihadism, the prosecutor took his statements as an argument to underpin the innate violent character of the Hofstad Group. Other witnesses were summoned to substantiate this allegation. Sixteen-year-old 'Malika', who had left home to enter into an 'Islamist marriage' with Nouriddin el Fatmi and who had spilt the beans on how El Fatmi and the group recruited new members, was summoned to explain her experiences to the court. She however refused to talk in court; it turned out that she had received threatening letters. Her story as it leaked out to the press, however, made a great impression on the public and the court.

In his final plea on 23 January 2006, public prosecutor Alexander van Dam made it clear that it was his aim to identify the network as a terrorist organisation, based on two arguments:

> Step 1: The binding agent [of the group] is the radical political ideology [...], characterised by hatred against the western, in particular also the Dutch democratic rule of law, directed against people who think differently, who may and must be killed as apostates and nonbelievers. It is an ideology aimed at the violent destruction necessary to erect an Islamist state.
>
> Step 2: What is pursued from that ideology (the intent) are criminal acts. We have seen with Bouyeri, Walters, Akhnikh, El Fatmi and Azzouz, based on the evidence, that their convictions cannot have another outcome than to commit *acts of violence*. Their ideology *obliges* them to violence against anyone who insults their prophet, against non-believers and apostates. There is no room for a peaceful way. Since voting is prohibited according to various writings, a political movement that disseminates its principles through dialogue or legal action is thus unthinkable. The writings, videos and recordings found at their places glorify and call to violence, as a means to reach the ultimate goal. And thus, we have proved the criminal intent for the core members of this organisation.[94]

With this argument, the public prosecutors invited the judges and the public at large to take into account the potential future if the suspects had *not* been disrupted and apprehended (which happened shortly after the murder in 2004). Later on in the trial, the prosecutors posed the rhetorical question: who knows where this group of suspects would have stood if [Mohammed Bouyeri] had not murdered Van Gogh but had continued its ideological and practical formation? And the briefing went on to speculate:

> Fanaticism and extremism make one blind. Driven by a strong sense of connection people can be moved to conquer heaven. By limiting themselves to talking, sometimes open recruitment, and doing very little substantially to come to an attack, their intent developed itself insidiously and perhaps all the more dangerously .... It is our conviction that this group of and around the core members was undergoing this transformation.[95]

Through these speculative moves that were repeated in the appeals sessions, the potential terrorist scenario of the Hofstad Group became configured into the court documents and was a basis for evidence.

Moreover, the defendants were charged not only with participating in a terrorist organisation, aimed at committing violent attacks, but also with aiming *to commit preparatory activities for enabling such attacks in the future*. 'It may seem strange, an organisation that has the commitment of preparatory acts as its aim. However, it is feasible that a group occupies itself on a frequent basis with the preparation of crimes that might be committed by others, or by that same organisation, but in a later stage. [...] Although we claim enough evidence for the aim of concrete violent or other acts, the ancillary acts or preparatory aim can be determined as well.'[96]

The artefacts supporting these precautionary charges were mainly evidence from the aforementioned female friends and texts and recordings, as interpreted by Islam expert Ruud Peters. The other charges, murder and attempted murder, against Walters and Akhnikh weres much more straightforward, and based on solid evidence of the thrown hand grenade.

The Defence Strategies

Overall, the performative strategies differed from defendant to defendant during the successive Hofstad trials and changed over time.[97] Some clear strategic positions were visible. First of all, the most important difference existed between Bouyeri's trial and those of the rest. Bouyeri had of course accomplished his acts, but while the prosecutors tried to argue that the accused had together committed major acts of preparing for terror attacks themselves, they all, except for Bouyeri, categorically rejected this charge.

The second issue on which the defendants showed different strategies was their attitude towards the court and the rule of law as such. Some engaged with the court, while others refused to show 'respect for the laws of non-believers'.[98] This refusal was symbolised by not rising when the magistrates entered the courtroom, which is a custom in the Netherlands. Key Hofstad Group suspects such as Bouyeri, Akhnikh and Jason Walters refused to rise before the judges, thereby signalling that they indeed did cherish other opinions on justice and injustice. Although Walters, Azzouz and Akhnikh did not plead guilty to terrorist attacks, they did accept the radical Islamist attribution as formulated by the prosecution. Others, including Rachid B. and Nadir A., seemed to distance themselves not only from the charges but also from the alleged ideology the group supposedly adhered to, and they showed every conformity and deference in responding to the court.[99]

During the first trial, the court dealt with the fourteen defendants (one at a time), commencing with Bouyeri, whom the prosecution identified as the leader of the group.[100] As in his first trial he was ordered by the court to be present. Even though on the first day he wore a red-and-white 'keffiyeh', this changed over the course of the trial. He began to wear western-style clothing.[101] This time he reluctantly responded when questioned by the judges and the public prosecutor. Furthermore, instead of his defence counsel, who were present in court, he delivered his oral pleadings in person. To do so is uncommon in the Netherlands. His oral pleadings lasted three hours, during which he confessed he was filled with 'joy and pride' that the prosecution compared him to Osama bin Laden. He also explained that he had killed Theo van Gogh because he had insulted 'the Prophet'.[102]

Most of the other defendants distanced themselves from Mohammed Bouyeri's violent act and the association with terrorism. Stating that although they—occasionally—had visited his house, received religious instruction and watched videos of beheadings, they had been unaware of his plan to kill Van Gogh. Rachid B., for example, a childhood friend, who met with him the night before the murder, and approximately one week before had been given some personal belongings (four letters), stated that he had been ignorant of Mohammed Bouyeri's intentions.[103] He also made clear that he was not an extremist, was cooperative in responding to the questions of the judges, emphasised he held a steady job and did not share the radical ideology of some of the other defendants.[104] In the context of the Hofstad Group trial this strategy of showing respect for the court was distinctive. It communicated that Rachid B., in contrast to some of the others, wanted to communicate that he was an ordinary person who due an unfortunate course of events was mixed up in the Hofstad Group affair. Additionally, most suspects denied being terrorists. Jason Walters, for example, defended himself by explaining that he only acted with the Hofstad Group to 'look cool' (for social status).[105]

Because radical and/or extremist religious ideology and activities played an important role in the allegation that the Hofstad Group was a terrorist organisation, several defendants were cross-examined by either the judges or the public prosecutor about their extremist or radical convictions. Some, like Bouyeri and Jason Walters, were explicit about their orthodox beliefs; others including Rachid B. and Mohammed el B. emphasised that although they were 'Muslim' they were not extremists.[106]

Nonetheless, among those with extremist religious beliefs there were differences in defence strategies. Even though both Bouyeri and Jason Walters explicitly renounced the Dutch legal system, Walters, in contrast to Bouyeri, stressed that he would defend himself. Jason Walters stated, 'Our legal system is the "sharia". That is the only system we acknowledge.' Subsequently a judge verified whether or not he would defend himself. He then responded with the words, 'I will defend myself, because this is a non-Muslim state ... and there is no "sharia".'[107]

As noted earlier, the performative strategies differed for each successive Hofstad trial and were not static.[108] Jason Walters, for instance, adapted his defence strategy a number of times. During his first trial he engaged to some extent; he would not rise before the judges, but responded to their cross-examination. Yet in appeal he refused to respond to the judges' questions.[109] During the partial retrial, however, he explicitly stated that he was convinced he would receive a fair trial and remained engaged.[110] Furthermore, he first appealed his case and then filled a request not to, but ultimately had to because the public prosecutor stuck to his request for an appeal.[111] During his second appeal, he changed his performative strategy again; expressing a revolutionary turn in his behaviour and speech and affirming his belief that his trial would be fair and just.[112]

Finally yet importantly, defence counsel played a crucial role in the performative strategies of the defendants. Some were extremely vocal, both in court and in the media. For example, a prominent Dutch newspaper, the NRC *Handelsblad*, quoted Ms. Böhler and Mr. Koppe, who represented Ahmed A. and Zakaria T., as saying 'this trial is a classical witch-hunt'.[113] In the same interview, both criticised the public prosecutor and the judges for focussing too much on religion rather than on concrete activities.

In court, defence counsel's strategy differed from client to client. However, at times they did collaborate with each other. In an effort to emphasise that the Hofstad Group trial was severely politicised, suggestions of conspiracies, including the possibility that the police and secret service had set their clients up, were inserted in their pleas and communicated to the press. During the first trial, the lawyers requested to hear in person the law enforcement officials who had taken statements from their clients; a highly unusual request in the Netherlands because it suggests that the law enforcement officials might have been biased in their interrogations.[114] Moreover, on appeal, two defence counsel questioned the neutrality of the judges and demanded a *wraking*, a special request to replace one or more trial judges. Their rationale was that by hearing a witness behind closed doors, the judges had given the impression of no longer being objective and were giving in to the whims of the prosecution and intelligence services.[115]

Although the particular request was denied, it fuelled suspicions of a tainted investigative procedure. Counsel's strategy was obviously intended to discredit the security and police forces, to raise suspicion as to their integrity and thus to raise doubts about the defendants' access to a fair trial as such. However, contrary to some of their defendants (Bouyeri, Walters and Akhnikh), and contrary to strategies adopted by their forebears in the 1970s, the defence lawyers did not reject the legal system as a whole. On the contrary, they operated according to the same core principles of Dutch and human rights law (fair trial, *habeas corpus*, freedom of speech and religion) that they claimed the judicial and police forces were denying their clients.

The Verdict

On 10 March 2006, the District Court of Rotterdam convicted Jason Walters, Akhnikh and El Fatmi and sentenced them respectively to fifteen, thirteen and five years in prison. Nine suspects were convicted of being members of a criminal terrorist organisation, whereas five others were acquitted of that charge. The Hofstad Group was also placed on the European Union's blacklist of terrorist organisations.[116]

However, on 23 January 2008 the Appeals Court of The Hague overturned the sentences of seven defendants in the Hofstad Group case who had appealed the verdict at first instance. They ruled that there was too little evidence to define the Hofstad Group as a terrorist organisation that shared an ideological viewpoint, and that conspired and associated on a regular basis.[117] According to the judge, 'the Hofstad Group displayed insufficient organisational substance to conclude the existence of an organisation as laid out in articles 140 and 140a of the Criminal Code'.[118] Only the sentences of Jason Walters (fifteen years for attempted murder for throwing the hand grenade), Akhnikh (fifteen months for possession of illegal firearms and munitions), El Fatmi (five years for possession of illegal firearms) and his wife Soumaya S. (nine months, same charge) were upheld on appeal.[119]

The Dutch court acquitted the Hofstad Group in reference to articles 9 and 10 of the European Convention on Human Rights (freedom of religion and freedom of speech). The court concluded that the prosecution's dependence on ideological writing did not provide sufficient evidence for labelling the Hofstad Group as a terrorist organisation. It also underlined that it attached great importance to religious pluralism and the freedom of speech, even if this pluralism included fundamentalist and anti-democratic opinions, such as expressed by the members of the Hofstad Group.[120]

This verdict, however, did not mark the end of the Hofstad Group saga. The public prosecution filed for cassation and on 2 February 2010 the Dutch Supreme Court, which only overturns the decisions of lower courts when their judgment is not in accordance with the applicable law or on procedural concerns, ruled that a partial retrial should be held.[121] According to the Supreme Court's judgment, the Appeals Court of The Hague had too narrowly interpreted the legal definition of what constitutes a terrorist organisation and should bring the definition more in line with jurisprudence on cases of group coherence of criminal organisations engaged in stock fraud of money laundering.[122] Henceforth the suspects' organisation might not be too loosely structured to merit the conviction Therefore, the case was referred to the Amsterdam Appeals Court for partial retrial.[123]

In December 2010, the Appeals Court ruled that the Hofstad Group was a terrorist organisation and sentenced seven defendants for participating in a terrorist and criminal organisation; five of them received a fifteen-month sentence, one 38 months and one thirteen years.[124] Henceforth, the Hofstad Group network was labelled as a terrorist organisation, aimed at inciting hatred, violence and intimidation, partly with a terrorist intent.[125] This ruling of the Amsterdam Court of Appeals had a strong effect on legal counterterrorism instruments, since it legitimised the lowering of the standards to classify a group as a terrorist organisation.

Public Debate

The defence strategies and verdicts differed during the successive Hofstad trials, a shift that was also linked to the waxing and waning tides of media attention. The initial setting of the trial in 2005 was polarised—the prosecution opened with an exposé on fear and intimidation on the one hand, and defence counsel claimed that the trial was a show trial or witch-hunt. The tension was caused in part by the extraordinary socio-political context of the trials and the extensive media coverage in the immediate aftermath of the Van Gogh murder, and the revelations about 'Islamic lover boys' within the Hofstad Group during the first half of 2005. Moreover, the Hofstad trial was the first one that made great use of the new terrorism legislation, involving suspects charged with non-violent preparatory crimes.

The heavy public, political and judicial pressure put the defendants in a very defensive position. It was hard to argue against 'conjectural reasoning' and invoked and premediated terrorist futures; the London bombings of July 2005 and other terrorist attacks carried out by 'home-grown radicals' elsewhere in Europe made it all sound so feasible. Defence counsel had to argue to contradict these fearful images and associations. They did so by explaining to the media how their defendants, in their view, were already demonised in the press and were being sentenced based on public fears and anti-Muslim sentiments alone. The only crimes the prosecution held against them were their religious convictions, according to defence counsel, Ms. Böhler, Mr. Plasman and Mr. Koppe.[126]

Initially, these pleas were not well received in mainstream Dutch society. Increasingly, however, their calls on behalf of their clients for freedom of religion, tolerance for extremist religious ideologies and the phenomenon of immigrant youth culture became part of the public and political debate.[127] Their arguments were to some extent supported by the emerging conspiracy theory mentioned above. If one were to accept these conspiracy theories, the prosecution was thus busy shifting the blame from the AIVD by implicating defendants in omissions committed by the government. Thus, the debate evolved from a discussion about the intrinsic violent nature of Islam or Salafism to whether the notion of a 'War on Terror' itself constituted a threat to the rule of law and to the principle of a fair trial.[128]

In later years, when the Hofstad Group trial was rehearsed in a first and second appeal, not the purported future attacks, but the boundaries of freedom of expression were what was subjected to greater scrutiny. Politicians, journalists and social media websites alike commented on the trial, and it appeared to some as if the defendants, especially those who had not committed acts of violence, were primarily convicted on the basis of their radical beliefs. National celebrity, parliamentary representative and the addressee of Bouyeri's warning letter, Ayaan Hirsi Ali herself stated that radical ideologies such as those of the Hofstad Group defendants formed part of the freedom of expression, and should be engaged through debate and not by the criminal justice system.[129]

9.4.3. The Second Hofstad Group Trial: The Piranha Case, 2005–2006

The Prosecution's Strategy

While the Hofstad Group trial was already under way with the first preliminary hearings, a second investigation started in April 2005 against the remaining members of the group. This investigation, called the 'Piranha' case by the police forces, came out in the open through the arrest of Nouriddin el Fatmi, who had been a fugitive since 2 November 2004.

On 22 June 2005, a Special Intervention Unit rushed onto the platform of the Amsterdam Lelylaan railway station and fought two jihadist suspects to the ground, Nouriddin el Fatmi, aged 22, and his wife Soumaya S., aged 21. Both were connected to the Hofstad Group network to which Mohammed Bouyeri, the murderer of Theo van Gogh, belonged. El Fatmi had a firearm, an Agram 2000, in his backpack. In the end, El F. was sentenced to five years in prison for illegal possession of a firearm and membership of a terrorist organisation. Soumaya S. spent six months in jail for complicity in the possession of the weapon and was released on 20 December 2005.[130]

Meanwhile, on 14 October 2005, Samir Azzouz (who had been released in April 2005) and two others were arrested and charged with preparing to commit an attack on politicians, government buildings and an El-Al aeroplane. In August 2006, Soumaya S.

was thought to belong to this group and was taken into custody again. Apparently, new evidence had emerged.[131] All in all, the group of defendants included five young males and one female (all of Dutch-Moroccan descent), connected in some way or another to the defendants of the Hofstad Group trial.

For the prosecution, this time represented by Alexander van Dam and Bart den Hartigh, this case was much easier to make. In the Piranha case, the prosecutors could prove that the suspects possessed illegal firearms and munitions and had collected names and addresses of politicians and were therefore in a much later stage of preparation than the suspects in the Hofstad case.[132] However, in April 2004, Azzouz had been acquitted of a terrorist crime because the preparations were found to lack focus and the chemical ingredients did not yet make for a real bomb. This time, the prosecution did not want to obtain convictions based on the Weapons and Munitions Act only, but intended to get Azzouz for terrorism as well. Therefore, they presented some convincing attempts at conjectural reasoning.

Van Dam had already made the connection between the murder of Van Gogh, the Arles case and the Piranha case. In his statement during the Arles trial in February 2006 (before the Piranha trial had started), he invoked the potential disastrous future towards which Samir Azzouz (who was not a defendant in that trial at all, but who was called as a witness) was heading:

> The intended crimes [of the Hofstad Group, including both the defendants in the Arles and the Piranha investigation] are located in the future. The group of defendants was heading toward something, they felt they had to do it. Azzouz was probably the first (at least according to the OM) to capitalise on this future; despite his acquittal [in April 2005] his behaviour was drenched in a terrorist ideology. But Bouyeri [Van Gogh's murderer] set the tone, as host and (co-)director of the meetings and by his writings in which he was writing towards a violent climax. Then by embarking upon the road towards jihad and martyrdom. A road that begged for future imitation.[133]

Thus, the murder of Theo van Gogh on 2 November 2004 (when Samir Azzouz was still in detention) was viewed as the inevitable outcome of a process of home-grown radicalisation in which also the other defendants, both in the Arles and the Piranha cases, were involved.

In the Piranha trial, which started in April 2006, AIVD intelligence information constituted the hard core of the evidence presented by the public prosecutor. One of the most convincing and vivid pieces of evidence was a CD-ROM, collected by the AIVD, on which Samir Azzouz had videotaped several versions of a farewell message. Azzouz had not dispatched this video 'will' to his friends, relatives or the media. The various versions were retrieved from his home computer. However, the prosecutor argued that the will was concrete proof of a pending attack. During the trial, the public prosecutor gave a presentation of thirteen minutes in which he first showed a message by Bin Laden, followed by footage of Al Zawahiri, and some parts from the suicide message of a Pakistani suicide terrorist responsible for the London attacks. Then again a message by Al Zawahiri and finally (a version of) Samir Azzouz's taped will (in Arabic)—all provided with Dutch subtitles. The prosecutor wanted to demonstrate that this was no 'joke', that Azzouz' will resembled other jihadist messages *broadcast after an attack*, and it was thus immediate proof of 'a deed that was to be carried out in the Netherlands'. The will, furthermore, was 'obviously intended to be made public after Azzouz had committed this act'.[134] By showing the videotape and images from the websites maintained by the defendants, the prosecution effectively coloured the mind-set of the audience in and outside court and made it almost impossible to refute the power of this sequential imagery (Bin Laden—Al Zawahiri—the London Bombings—*Samir Azzouz*—Al Zawahiri).[135]

This very visual and compelling premediation technique was flanked by a subtler one. Apart from Samir Azzouz, four other male suspects, including Nouriddin el Fatmi, were included, and after some months one female suspect, Soumaya S. She was implicated in the charge based on intelligence evidence as well. In her case, it became plain how intelligence evidence can be transformed into incriminating evidence by lifting snippets of conversation out of their original context, thereby stripping it of its original meaning and opening the door to other, more sinister meanings. In the Piranha case, one of the two key arguments for charging the female defendant, Soumaya S., with membership of a terrorist organisation and conspiring to commit terrorist crimes was supported by playing excerpts of a taped telephone conversation with her sister Hanan. In the recordings, the defendant asked the sister, who worked at a pharmacy close to the Dutch parliament buildings, for addresses of centre-right and liberal politicians. According to the defendant, she only meant 'to make dawah to them'—as stated in the phone conversation.[136]

For the prosecution, the conversation implied a target-identifying process; the remarks on 'dawah' were only meant to deceive the sister. By lifting the conversation out of its context and connecting it to a jihadist website maintained by another group member and to jihadist texts stored on their computers, the prosecution used the technique of premediation: the defendants were already suspected of being members of a terrorist group, therefore inquiring after names and addresses of Dutch politicians could only have been made for that reason, notwithstanding other explanations being available.[137] By omitting the conversation's context defence counsel turned an innocent exchange into a threatening phone call. To be sure, the prosecution did in fact ask the AIVD for more contextual information, but it drew a blank.[138] The AIVD refused to meet the demand. The prosecution therefore stuck to its charge. (Note, exactly this refusal of the AIVD to disclose the rest of the conversation prompted the Dutch Supreme Court in 2011 to overrule this verdict and to call for a new trial. In March 2014, the Amsterdam Court confirmed the terrorismsentence of three years for Soumaya S.)[139]

A final way in which potential violent futures were interpolated into the present terrorist trial revolved around introducing a vignette of the brainwashed female jihadist into public discourse. In February 2005, just before the investigation into the Piranha case started, two prominent Dutch journalists published a book on 'Female Warriors of Allah',[140] in which they stated that the Dutch judicial and intelligence authorities had severely underestimated the threat of female jihadists within the Islamist networks in the Netherlands. The tabloid press branded the converted jihadist women as seduced, brainwashed and repressed by the male terrorist suspects in supporting their radical activities. *De Telegraaf* wrote about 'Preaching and porn: Young women abused by Islamic "lover boys"'. The 'Hofstad Group network'—the name an invention by the AIVD connecting a disparate group of individuals and friends surrounding Mohammed Bouyeri—had been extended to include 'mentally unstable young women falling for the lures of radical "lover boys"'. The handful of women were even described as 'Muslim groupies'.[141] Debates on television, in parliament and plenty of research projects followed. The defendants' counsel condemned the trial as political justice; anti-Islam parties complained about police and judicial indolence, raising the stakes for trials to come.

The defendant Soumaya S. did not quite fit into this passive frame, since she impressed the prosecution and the audience alike with her eloquence, intelligence and bravado in court and during her arrest. She was arrested twice, first for co-possession of a firearm with her husband (in October 2005) and secondly for conspiring to commit a terrorist attack. Already during the first trial, on 18 and 19 October 2005, public prosecutor Koos Plooy deplored the fact that he could not charge her with membership of a terrorist organisation, even though she was assumed to be 'a potential instrument in the hands of her husband'. He motivated his demand for a twelve month prison sentence accordingly:

> She followed him [her husband] blindly, but with eyes wide open. That turned her into a *potential instrument* in the hands of this man.[142]

In other words, although public prosecutor Plooy was only able to charge her with co-possession of a firearm, admitting that he could not file a terrorism charge against her based on her association with her husband and the conversational stub mentioned above, he positively identified her as a 'ticking bomb', a potential, powerful and willing instrument in the hands of a bunch of terrorists. In August 2006, Soumaya was arrested a second time, based on roughly the same evidence as before, but this time the prosecutor felt he could charge her with membership of a terrorist organisation. This second time, the prosecutor rejuvenated his 'old' evidence by reminding the public of the London bombings and Al Qaeda videos:

> Fanaticism and extremism make blind. Driven by a common basic feeling people can turn into zealots, sparing nothing and no one. And that might lead to bizarre offences, from unexpected angles. No one had expected the perpetrators of the London attacks [7 July 2005] to carry out such acts. Likewise, no one would possibly expect some of the defendants here today capable of participating or carrying out an attack. However, this has been proven. There is therefore no room for underestimation.[143]

The Defendants' Strategy

Like Mohammed Bouyeri, Samir Azzouz also explicitly rejected the Dutch rule of law. Since 2003, he had been suffering from a chronic illness and inflammation of his intestines, but often he did not receive his medication and was not allowed transport to the hospital. His lawyer, Victor Koppe, wanted to enforce his treatment through a court order. Azzouz, however, refused to use the Dutch legal system, because he only respected the laws of Allah. 'We reject you', he stated on 21 December 2005 during the Hofstad Group trial, where he was summoned as a witness, 'we denounce your system. We hate you. That's about it.'[144]

On the other hand, Azzouz vigorously denied being a terrorist or having prepared for terrorist attacks, and together with his co-defendants aggressively countered the prosecution's charges. He tried to discredit some key witnesses by implying that they were even more fundamentalist in their beliefs than he was. His defence counsel also tried to trivialise the farewell video by portraying it as try-outs during some severe feelings of frustration.[145] Nouriddin el Fatmi also played down his radical behaviour, even claiming the he only carried the Agram 2000 with him to protect himself against Soumaya's angry ex-husband.

The only female suspect, Soumaya, followed a different performative strategy. She tried to tone down her image as a 'dangerous woman'. She did not deny that the other defendants, notably Samir and Nouriddin, might have been radicalised, but she clung to her statement that she had more or less tumbled into the whole affair; explaining that she became affiliated with Nouriddin in the spring of 2005 and had only spent six weeks with him before they were arrested, not knowing what he was up to. She claimed ignorance regarding the gun he was carrying with him. Soumaya also felt that her lawyers held her hostage within this group of defendants, lest she make incriminating statements about Nouriddin and the others. She felt caught between two stools. Her angry ex-husband sat in the public gallery accompanied by her relatives.[146] The public prosecutor wanted to get her convicted for terrorism this time.[147] And she was flanked by her co-defendants, including her Islamic husband, and lawyers who were pressuring her to adhere to their performative strategy of rejecting the charges as a collective.[148]

Soumaya, however, initiated attempts to detach herself from the group. On 20 October, she testified against Imam Fawaz Jneid, revealing that he had delivered a sermon a few weeks before Bouyeri's attack in which he had cursed Van Gogh and others. Bouyeri was in attendance as well. 'It was awful what I heard', she confessed. 'Fawaz constantly makes you feel that you are lacking in zeal and activity on behalf of the defence of Islam'. With this confession, she detached herself from the 'father figure' who had drawn her into Salafism's lure. Fawaz, who was heard as a witness, protested and provided the opposite story. He had 'rapped Soumaya's knuckles' and had warned her against continuing down a 'path of mortal peril,' only to see her 'throw dirt' at him now. Soumaya started sobbing. 'He only warned me about the secret service. He is denying everything now, I feel betrayed.' In addition, a copy of the sermon surfaced, confirming Soumaya's earlier testimony.[149]

On 1 November, she took the stage again and proclaimed her divorce from El Fatmi. Her father, another defendant and her counsel had acted as witnesses, as was required under Islamic law for undoing a marriage. The presiding judge Koning questioned Soumaya on her relations with Fatmi. Had she been obedient to him, followed him on his paths? 'I am not good at obeying a man, so we just had to let that go', Soumaya explained. 'You seem so cheerful and spry when saying that', remarked the judge. 'Did your father not say "no" to you often enough? ... Were you spoiled as a girl? I can see your mother and sister nodding vigorously.'[150] Despite this almost fatherly conversation, the court was not impressed by Soumaya's performance, as she acted erratically and capriciously in their eyes. 'Did Soumaya do this [the divorce] to belatedly distance herself from her "God-fearing" husband, who made her a radical, and, in doing so, from the remaining defendants as well?', the public prosecutor wondered in his oral pleadings. 'We believe that this gesture comes too late. For us, it is beyond doubt that she belongs to the same organisation as her now ex-husband.'[151]

On 6 November 2006, the public prosecutor, Alexander van Dam, submitted the sentences he was requesting to the court. Fatmi, Azzouz and another defendant, Mohammed C., were believed to have been the 'core members', 'inspirators and initiators', and 'Soumaya S. and Mohammed H. allowed themselves to be inspired by them and actively got involved in their activities'. And what did these activities involve? 'It is our conviction that only through intervention of the police and judicial authorities has an actual terrorist attack been prevented. Although this attack was still in a preparatory stage, the plans and means were abundantly present.' Since the 'danger of recurrence was very high', the prosecutor demanded heavy sentences. Against Azzouz, the public prosecutor demanded fifteen years, against Nouriddin twelve (since he already had been sentenced in the first Hofstad trial for five years) and against Soumaya ten years.[152]

The requested sentence for Soumaya startled most of the spectators. According to her defence counsel, Yasser Özdemir, it was 'absurd' that the public prosecutor had hardly made any distinction between core members and the others, like Soumaya. In the fifty or so investigation files, her name did not appear in connection with any of the preparatory activities for terrorist attacks. Soumaya was 'shocked to pieces'. According to the defence counsel 'the Zeitgeist [i.e. the prevailing culture of fear, caused by the terrorist attacks] had driven this trial' and its severe sentences. During the final hearing, on 10 November, Soumaya addressed the court one last time. In her view, 'the blind hatred against Muslims' from the crusaders' times had returned in this trial and in the anti-terrorism campaigns the Dutch government was waging. She compared the special unit for terrorism suspects in the high security prison in Vught with the Nazi concentration camp that had been located on that same spot during the times of the German occupation. She wished the court good luck and wisdom in deciding upon the sentence, although, ultimately, what would happen to her was 'Allah's will'. Samir Azzouz also proclaimed his 'surprise' over the severe demands by the prosecution; he felt he 'was being punished for being a Muslim and hating the democratic rule of law'.[153]

The Verdict

A note of caution has to be added to the above-mentioned techniques of risk management and premediation deployed by the prosecutors. Although their pleas sometimes made for an impressive display of conjectural reasoning and compelling images, the Dutch inquisitorial system as such does not make for a 'good show'. The oral pleadings of the public prosecutor and defence counsel are rather lengthy, very detailed and difficult to understand for those without legal training. No television coverage is allowed in court either to record their arguments. Moreover, the prosecutor's risk management techniques were new to the Dutch judicial system. They gained credibility through the context of the heightened awareness for terrorist attacks in 2004 and 2005, but when no new attacks occurred, the waves of public indignation and outrage over the Hofstad Group's purported terrorist intentions waned a little.

On 1 December 2006, the court reached its verdict. In his verdict the judge accepted some of the prosecution's charges, but not all. The court acquitted the defendants of membership of a terrorist organisation out of lack of evidence of a structured association. The charge of inciting hatred and recruiting for jihad was dismissed as well.[154] The activities of the group had not been structured enough to meet the conditions for constituting a real terrorist organisation. The judge moreover criticised the way the prosecution had based its case on official notifications of the AIVD (the so-called *ambtsberichten*); the judge even excluded some reports from the case altogether. He also expressed his doubts about the evidence of the prosecution's crown witnesses.

However, the judge accepted the prosecution's argument that Azzouz and the others had planned for a terrorist attack in the near future, on an individual basis. He especially saw Azzouz as someone 'who wanted to attack the heart of the Dutch democracy and inflict fear on the Dutch population by committing attacks that might kill numerous persons'. Azzouz' videotaped message to his next of kin and to the Dutch population proved that intent.[155] The imagery was hard to reject and impossible to downplay, even if it had only been a private attempt. Moreover, Azzouz had a track record of strange behaviour; he had tried to purchase arms and amassed a number of maps and details on critical infrastructure. According to the judge, the prosecution had rendered plausible that the defendant had conspired to bomb the headquarters of the Dutch security service, thereby killing many people or harming high-ranking politicians.[156] Even if the preparation had been insufficient and amateurish, the court took into account the purchase of a number of professional firearms, the use of which could have resulted in a high number of casualties.[157]

Ultimately, the six defendants were thus convicted of conspiring to commit a terrorist offence, but not of constituting a terrorist organisation. They received lesser sentences than the prosecutors had argued for: Soumaya S. received a prison sentence of three years, her husband Nouriddin four years, Samir Azzouz eight years[158] and the three others some minor sentences.[159]

Response and Aftermath

In the media, criticism came from all parts of the political spectrum. 'Frustrated youngster, but terrorist?', the Amsterdam newspaper *Het Parool* wondered.[160] 'Bunch of guys or terrorist organisation', doubted the regional papers. *Trouw* suggested that the defendants had been convicted on their extreme convictions rather than on their actual deeds. Soumaya was portrayed as a 'frail young woman', devastated by the verdict.[161] Even Ayaan Hirsi Ali, who had been on a list of alleged targets, came to the rescue. Hirsi Ali described Soumaya as our 'hope for the future'. Clever girls like Soumaya, who could think for themselves, were sorely needed in the struggle against radicalisation.[162]

Many politicians, ranging from social-democrats, Christian-democrats to liberals, were glad Samir Azzouz had been convicted. 'It is good news that the court managed to convict Samir this time, before an attack occurred', according to CDA representative Sybrand van Haersma Buma. 'This shows our legislation is in order.' Right-wing Member of Parliament Geert Wilders, who participated in the elections for the Second Chamber for the first time with his new 'Party for Freedom', thought otherwise, finding the prison sentences 'ridiculously' short. The defence counsel and the prosecution were dissatisfied as well. The defence counsel Mr. Koppe characterised the verdict as 'shoddy'; the public prosecution held the same opinion, but for opposite reasons: they would file an appeal to question the acquittal of being a terrorist organisation.[163]

Around that time, Samir Azzouz' Dutch-Moroccan wife, Abida, started to campaign in the media for her husband's plight. She tried to raise sympathy for the severe circumstances under which he was held prisoner. On 14 October 2006, in a television documentary about Azzouz, she characterised the charges as 'bizarre'. She suggested that his case was used by the authorities 'to terrorise the Dutch population'.[164] Her mother, a Dutch female convert, also gave her opinion: 'They scare the population with terror threats to push their repressive measures in parliament.' Abida: 'They would have preferred an attack in the Netherlands. The secret service tried to sell weapons to Samir via an informer, but he refused. After an attack they could have further tightened the laws.' Samir was treated 'inhumanely', he was held in isolated captivity even in youth detention (during his first arrest, he had been only sixteen or seventeen-years-old). She was not allowed to visit him at first and only after heavy public pressure did he receive the right medication. 'We are heading in the direction of a Guantánamo Bay.'[165] Abida's main argument was, however, that Samir and she did indeed adhere to the sharia and believed in solidarity for the 'oppressed ummah', even if that required the use of violence, and that the Dutch freedom of speech and expression allowed for that. She compared their fate to the Dutch resistance to Nazi rule. Fighting jihad from a defensive position was legitimate. Confronted with the question whether she and her husband renounced violence in the Netherlands, she evaded a straightforward answer, although she tried to make a distinction between living in a peaceful society and joining the jihad elsewhere—a more quantitative and gradual distinction than a qualitative one.[166]

In March 2008 the appeal commenced. Under heavy security and blindfolded, the defendants were escorted to the Osdorp court in Amsterdam. Media attention was high for a last time. Defence counsel Bart Nooitgedagt stated on television that the trial was 'false and constructed'. In June 2008, a member of the European Committee for Prevention of Torture (CPT), who had visited the terrorist high security wing in Vught and De Schie the year before, criticised the 'irresponsible' circumstances under which the youthful detainees were held in prison, especially pointing to the plight of the sole female detainee, Soumaya S. She had been in total isolation for ten months now, and her health was deteriorating. 'We will call upon the Dutch government to deal with this', according to CPT member Marc Nève.[167]

This international criticism regarding the circumstances of the detention had its effect. Soumaya was relocated to a regular women's prison in Zwolle. She enjoyed the advantage of all the social contacts there, engaged in a dialogue with the prison's rabbi, Aryeh Heintz, whom she had met during her first detention in 2005 and joined an Evangelical church choir. In August 2008, Heintz wrote the court a letter, wanting to 'counterbalance, as a sort of *character witness*, the negative image the prosecution had projected of Soumaya'. 'To me, she appears honest and reliable.' Soumaya had been drawn into 'the wrong circles', by a 'hate mongering imam'. While that imam, Fawaz Jneid, is still allowed to incite hatred, this 'orthodox, but tolerant Muslima' is being held in captivity. 'I believe that she can act as a role model for other girls that are on the verge of radicalisation. She can show them how to be an orthodox Muslim without having to turn against society.'[168]

This was to no avail. On 18 September 2008, the court issued its shocking verdict. This time, the judge identified the 'Piranha' group as a real terrorist organisation. The judge hardly responded to Soumaya's pleas, nor did the arguments put forward by defence counsel regarding the conjectural reasoning based on intelligence reports that lacked context impress him. The judge recognised that the AIVD might have tampered with the telephone conversations of Soumaya and her sister, but he did not draw any consequences from that, apart from warning the prosecution to treat such evidence 'carefully'. The court moreover acknowledged some 'irregularities' during the investigation, but found that the prosecution had put them right during the hearings. On 2 October, the Appeals Court of The Hague pronounced the sentences.[169] Azzouz was sentenced to nine years' imprisonment, Nouriddin el Fahtmi to eight years, Mohammed C. to six years, Soumaya S. four years (one year in addition to the initial sentence) and Mohammed H. to three months. The sentences were higher, since the judge included their involvement in real criminal acts (possession of firearms, etc.) in the criminal act of constituting a terrorist organisation.[170]

Samir applauded upon hearing that the court considered him the 'leader of a terrorist organisation'.[171] Soumaya's counsel, Bart Nooitgedagt, was 'livid', branding it 'political justice'. Soumaya had, 'bluntly stated, been screwed'.[172] The lawyers immediately announced their intention to refer the case to the Supreme Court. Advocate General Leo Hollander did not see their problem. 'In terrorist cases we operate with relatively new legislation, causing prosecutors to test its boundaries.' For the public prosecutors, the verdict was 'a boost'. The newspapers were hesitant. 'A terror group after all?' the regional media asked, or rather 'a political verdict'? *De Telegraaf* called Soumaya a 'terrorist sweetheart'. Even conservative *Elsevier* warned that the rule of law was balancing on a thin line. 'In the end, it boils down to the difference between thought and action', a difference which was increasingly difficult to distinguish with the new antiterrorism legislation. The Supreme Court therefore first had to check carefully 'whether the trials functioned according to the rules', and to establish 'how tight a group had to be organised to justify a conviction [as a terrorist organisation]'.[173]

The extent to which the perceived terrorist threat had been a product of the imminent post-Van Gogh years became clear after 2008. Azzouz' wife Abida was invited to share her story on national talk shows.[174] In 2011, the Supreme Court critically reviewed the Piranha case: the Appeals Court of The Hague had not sufficiently reasoned its refusal to question the context and content of intelligence reports that were used as evidence, and had to partly re-try the case in 2012.[175]

9.5. Conclusion

In this chapter, we have tried to analyse the trials against Bouyeri and the Hofstad Group defendants from a performative perspective, thereby focusing upon how future terror scenarios were mobilised and visualised and on the extent to which they were incorporated in the judgments (terrorist risk sentencing). It has become clear that only Bouyeri followed a clear strategy aimed at mobilising his perceived target audience to accept his vision of justice and injustice. To a lesser extent Samir Azzouz also stuck to his extreme perspective, ventilating in court and (via his wife) on television, that waging jihad on behalf of oppressed Muslims was a noble and righteous cause. He, however, rejected the charges of preparing a terrorist attack. In his case, the line between legitimate war and non-violent protest was not as clear-cut as he portrayed it to be. Neither he nor his wife renounced violence as such; for them, their Islamic consciousness and solidarity with the oppressed ummah had priority over protecting the Dutch rule of law.

On the other hand, the prosecution made clear that between 2004 and 2006 the willingness to charge potential terrorists based on projected risk scenarios increased. We maintain that since 2004 the appetite for sentencing 'individuals at risk to become involved in terrorism' (terrorist risk sentencing) increased in the Netherlands. Courts showed significant willingness to entertain the likely and possible effects of inchoate plots and they delivered sentences based on potential violence. We have established that performative strategies by the prosecution, where pre-emption and premediation replace retribution, challenged basic fair trial standards. We have identified and examined various ways in which the public prosecutors interpolated potential disastrous scenarios as a reality in court and made full use of the associative, preparatory and precautionary elements in the new Dutch anti-terrorism legislation; this, even though the Dutch inquisitorial system does not offer the best opportunities for this.

More than a purely judicial shift, these findings can be related to shifting notions of public and political responsibility. They can be understood in terms of what Michael Power has called 'secondary risk management'. For Power, risk management professionals are not solely concerned with managing the primary risk they are responsible for—this being, in our cases, the risks of terrorism and grave security threat. They are also and in fact increasingly so, according to Power, 'preoccupied with managing their own risks'.[176] Secondary risk management, as discussed by Power, arises as an asymmetry appears between risk appetite on the one hand, with the authorities more prone to act on future risks, and a responsibility-taking aversion on the other, with authorities more worried about being held responsible for actual disasters by the media, their constituencies, parliament, etc.[177] As such, Power's argument has affinities with that of Aradau and Van Munster,[178] for whom 'The rationality of catastrophic risk translates into policies that actively seek to prevent situations from becoming catastrophic at some indefinite point in the future' (emphasis in the original). In Aradau and Van Munster's formulation, however, the responsibility aversion of secondary risk management itself becomes an important knowledge practice and spur to action.

The cases analysed in this chapter illustrate how practices of primary and secondary risk management have entered the judicial domain. The incorporation of precautionary counterterrorism into criminal legislation is not just a matter of juridical change, but plays out in the performative dynamic between the police, the public prosecutor, defence counsel and the judges. After the Van Gogh murder, the security and intelligence services were quick to provide their early warnings, prompting public prosecutors to launch investigations into possible terrorist attacks before actual preparations had begun and based only on fragmented and inconclusive evidence. Security agencies and politicians responsible for these 'inverse investigations' (initiated with a highly condensed intelligence alert, focussing on a certain individual, and then developing into the search for a corresponding crime) legitimised it on the basis of 'the will of the people' and 'dangerous times'.

In the Dutch Hofstad case, the implementation of significant legal reform, and the increasingly active role of the security services in bringing cases to prosecutors' attention, produced a situation in which public prosecutors were not satisfied with the acquittal of a suspect, felt heavy political and public pressure and proactively made use of sparse intelligence alerts to launch pre-emptive investigative operations. They subsequently rehearsed the AIVD evidence to demonstrate the potential volatility of the suspects (by showing a home-made video 'will' or by referring to the new vignette of the brainwashed female terrorist). They moreover actively sought to test and expand the reach of new terrorism laws.

For the defendants, it was very hard to argue against such instances of precautionary and premediated charges that could very well have been true in their anticipative dimension. In the cases discussed above, only Bouyeri—who did commit a murder—accepted the charges. Although all other defendants rejected the terrorist charges, the mediated nature of the trial, the broadcast farewell video, the lively images of burqa-clad female friends and partners and the lists of chemicals presented by the prosecutors made it very hard, if not impossible, to counter these projected terrorist associations. Some of them, including Bouyeri and Azzouz, tried to raise their own radical narratives of injustice (oppression of the Ummah; the Dutch democratic rule of law) and justice (legitimate jihad). Lack of sympathisers within the larger Muslim community and of an organised 'Umfeld' meant that they were not able to mobilise much support. The strategy of their defence counsel, however, in pointing to the inherent contradictions to compliance with human rights in the adjudication and investigative process, achieved some results, not leading to acquittals, but in the case of Soumaya S. to a partial retrial.

After a number of years the assessment of the Hofstad Group's activities boiled down to what they really were: chats, boasts and flawed attempts to draw maps and to purchase weapons. Since then, Soumaya S. and Jason Walters have distanced themselves completely from the rest and proclaimed their belief in the rule of law.

The terrorist intent, their membership of a terrorist organisation, was overturned in appeal, then upheld again, overruled by a higher court, confirmed by another, and some defendants in this process still have appeals filed as of September 2014. In large part, the Hofstad Group trials thus have been virtual, invoking possible futures and transforming security considerations and risk management approaches into acts of adjudication. For Bouyeri and Azzouz the trials were about conflicting systems of justice, whereas the other defendants were nailed down and locked up in their own nightmarish but inchoate deliberations. Performing and sentencing with imagined reality remains a risky business for the public prosecutors, but even more so for the defendants.

Notes

1 The author wants to thank Quirine Eijkman, Bart Schuurman and Marieke de Goede for their advice and input into this chapter.

2 Emerson Vermaat, *De Nederlandse Jihad: Het proces tegen de Hofstadgroep* (Soesterberg: Aspekt, 2006), p. 33.

3 This paragraph is based on the methodological paragraphs in: Marieke de Goede and Beatrice de Graaf, 'Sentencing Risk: Temporality and precaution in terrorism trials', *International Political Sociology*, 7:3 (2013), pp. 313–331.

4 Marieke de Goede, 'Beyond Risk: Premediation and the post-9/11 security imagination', *Security Dialogue*, 39:2/3 (2008), pp. 155–176.

5 De Goede and De Graaf, 'Sentencing Risk', pp. 313–331.

6 Robert Chesney, 'Beyond Conspiracy? Anticipatory prosecution and the challenge of unaffiliated terrorism', *Southern California Law Review*, 80:3 (2007), pp. 425–502.

7 Matthias Borgers and Elies van Sliedregt, 'The meaning of the precautionary principle for the assessment of criminal measures in the fight against terrorism', *Erasmus Law Review*, 2:2 (2009), pp. 171–195.

8 E.g. Robert Chesney, 'The Sleeper Scenario: Terrorism-support laws and the demands of prevention', *Harvard Journal of Legislation*, 42:1 (2005), pp. 40–44; Maartje van der Woude, *Wetgeving in een Veiligheidscultuur: Totstandkoming van antiterrorismewetgeving bezien van maatschappelijke en (rechts)politieke context* (Den Haag: Boom Juridische Uitgevers, 2010); Laura K. Donohue, 'Terrorism and Trial by Jury: The vices and virtues of British and American criminal law', *Stanford Law Review*, 59 (2007), pp. 1321–1364.

9 Lucia Zedner, 'Security, the State, and the Citizen: The changing architecture of crime control', *New Criminal Law Review*, 13 (2010), pp. 379–403; J. McCulloch and S.J. Pickering,

'Pre-crime and Counter-terrorism: Imagining future crime in the "War on Terror"', *British Journal of Criminology*, 49:5 (2009), pp. 628–645.

10 Ronald Kessler, *The Terrorist Watch: Inside the desperate race to stop the next attack* (New York: Crown, 2007).

11 Lawrence Douglas, Austin Sarat and Martha Merrill Umphrey, *Law and Catastrophe* (Stanford: Stanford University Press, 2007), p. 7.

12 De Goede and De Graaf, 'Sentencing Risk', pp. 313–331.

13 Richard Grusin, *Premediation: Affect and mediality after 9/11* (London: Palgrave 2010); Richard Grusin, 'Premediation', *Criticism*, 46:1 (2004), pp. 17–39.

14 Claudia Aradau and Rens van Munster, *Politics of Catastrophe: Genealogies of the unknown* (London and New York: Routledge, 2011), p. 31.

15 Wouter Werner, 'The Use of Law in International Political Sociology', *International Political Sociology*, 3:4 (2010), pp. 304–307, there 305.

16 Michael Power, *The Risk Management of Everything: Rethinking the politics of uncertainty* (London: Demos, 2004), p. 10.

17 NCTb [Nationaal Coördinator Terrorismebestrijding], *Salafisme in Nederland* (The Hague: NCTb, 2008), p. 25; 'De omstreden El Tawheed-Moskee', Nova broadcast (9 November 2004), http://www.novatv.nl/page/detail/uitzendingen/3011. Retrieved 1 June 2009. According to Nova, Saudi businessman Aqeel Alaqeel financed the El Tawheed Mosque with 1.3 million Euro. Al Haramein was blacklisted as an Al Qaeda charity, but the accusations were not substantiated, and the mosque continued to operate. I am grateful to Dennis de Widt for these references.

18 'Feitenrelaas', attachment to the Letter to Parliament (ministers of the Interior and Justice), 10 November 2004, Handelingen van de Tweede Kamer, No. 29854.

19 For an account of this story, see 'Samir A.: Staatsvijand nr. 1', KRO *Reporter* (1 October 2006), http://reporter.incontxt.nl/seizoenen/reporter-2006/afleveringen/01-10-2006. Retrieved 1 June 2009. The documentary includes interviews with Azzouz and his wife; Eric Vrijsen, 'Hofstadgroep: Van Samir A. tot Marad J.', *Elsevier* (5 July 2005); Arjan Erkel, *Samir* (Amsterdam: Balans, 2007).

20 Petter Nesser, *The Slaying of the Dutch Filmmaker: Religiously motivated violence or Islamist terrorism in the name of global jihad? FFI report* (Kjeller: FFI, 2005), pp. 17–19.

21 Nesser, 'Slaying of the Dutch Filmmaker', 17–19; 'Spanish link to Dutch film-maker's killing is probed', *El País* (9 November 2004); Craig S. Smith, 'Dutch Look for Qaeda Link After Killing of Filmmaker', *New York Times* (8 November 2004); 'Muslims arrested in Van Gogh murder belong to militant group', *Haaretz* (13 November 2004).

22 Emerson Vermaat, *De Hofstadgroep: Portret van een radicaal-islamitisch netwerk* (Soesterberg: Aspekt, 2005), pp. 76–77.

23 Siem Eikelenboom, *Niet bang om te sterven: Dertig jaar terrorisme in Nederland* (Amsterdam: Nieuw Amsterdam, 2007), pp. 81–83; National Prosecutor's Office, *Requisitoir in de strafzaak tegen de verdachten van de Hofstadgroep*, Part I, Amsterdam (23 and 25 January 2006); interview with the national terrorism prosecutor Polyan Spoon (Rotterdam, 7 September 2009).

24 National Prosecutor's Office, *Repliek van de officier van justitie in de strafzaken tegen Nadir A.*, p. 7, 13.

25 'Dutch radical Islamic group planned Euro 2004 attack in Portugal', AFP press release (15 November 2004); 'Dutch Islamists Planned Barroso Attack,' *Reuters* press release (15 November 2004); Ministry of Justice, *Letter to Parliament, With a Report on the Assassination of Theo van Gogh* (10 November 2004). Handelingen van de Tweede Kamer (HTK) 2004–2005, 29,854, No. 3; see also the parliamentary debate on this report on November 11, 2004. HTK 2004–2005, No. 22, pp. 1278–1332.

26 Marc Sageman, *Leaderless Jihad: Terror networks in the twenty-first century* (Philadelphia: University of Pennsylvania Press, 2008), p. 79; see also Lorenzo Vidino, 'The Hofstad Group: The new face of terrorist networks in Europe', *Studies in Conflict and Terrorism*, 30:7 (2007), pp. 579–592, there pp. 585–587; Sageman, 'Hofstad Case Study & The Blob Theory', *Theoretical Frames on Pathways to Violent Radicalization*. Artis Research and Risk Modelling (August 2009), p. 14; http://www.artisresearch.com/articles/ARTIS_Theoretical_Frames_August_2009.pdf. Retrieved 1 June 2009.

27 See their defence in the court cases in Rotterdam and Amsterdam, 2006; 'Hofstadgroep bestaat helemaal niet', NRC *Handelsblad* (1 February 2006).

28 National Prosecutor's Office, *Requisitoir van de officier van justitie*, pp. 44–45. For the role of Al-Issa see also Vermaat, *De Hofstadgroep*, pp. 69–74.

29 Ruud Peters, 'Dutch extremist Islamism: Van Gogh's murderer and his ideas', in: Rik Coolsaet (ed.), *Jihadi terrorism and the radicalisation challenge in Europe* (London: Ashgate, 2008), pp. 115–130, here: p. 118.

30 Verdict in the case of the Hofstad group, paragraph 109.

31 At present, Al-Issa is supposedly detained in Syria.

32 See also Vidino, 'The Hofstad Group', p. 585.

33 National Prosecutor's Office, *Requisitoir van de officier van justitie*; *Verdict in the Hofstad Group case*; 'The "Hofstad Group"'.

34 A highly informative account of the assassination of Van Gogh and the development of the Hofstad Group can be found in Albert Benschop, 'Jihad in the Netherlands: Chronicle of a political murder foretold', *Universiteit van Amsterdam* (2 November 2004) http://www.sociosite.org/jihad_nl_en.php. Retrieved June 2009.

35 The description of this case is based, amongst others, on the oral pleadings of the National

Prosecution in the Hofstad Group case. National Prosecutor's Office, *Requisitoir van de officier van justitie*, part I, 23 January 2006 and part II, 25 January 2006; District Court of Amsterdam, *Verdict against Bouyeri*, LJN AU0025, 13/129227-04, 26 July 2005. Verdict, LJN AV5108, District Court of Rotterdam, 10/000322-04;10/000328-04;10/000396-04;10/000393-04;10000325-04;10/000323-04;10/000395-04, 10 March 2006; LJN: BC2576, Appeals Court of The Hague, 23 January, 2008 (appeal). Verdict in appeal, Appeals Court of The Hague, 2 October 2008, no.2200734906; LJN: BK5172, Supreme Court, 2 February 2010 (cassation); LJN: BO7690, Amsterdam Court of Appeals, 17 December 2010 (retrial on appeal); 'The "Hofstadgroep"', *Transnational Terrorism, Security & the Rule of Law*, Working Paper (April 2008) www.transnationalterrorism.eu/tekst/publications/Hofstadgroep.pdf. Retrieved 1 June 2009.

36 The Review Committee on the Intelligence and Security Services officially concluded in March 2008 that this had been a serious intelligence failure, as evidence surfaced prior to the attack that Bouyeri was at least affiliated with Dutch jihadist groups. See the official report: 'Toezichtsrapport inzake de afwegingsprocessen van de AIVD met betrekking tot Mohammed B.', *Commissie van Toezicht betreffende de Inlichtingen- en Veiligheidsdiensten* (CTIVD), 17 (March 2008).

37 Siem Eikelenboom, *Niet bang om te sterven: Dertig jaar terrorisme in Nederland* (Amsterdam: Nieuw Amsterdam, 2007), pp. 23–27; see also National Prosecutor's Office, *Repliek van de officier van justitie in de strafzaken tegen* Nadir A. etc., Amsterdam (6 February 2005), pp. 4–5, 9–10, 17–23.

38 'De wereld van Mohammed B.', NRC *Handelsblad* (9 July 2005).

39 Jutta Chorus and Ahmet Olgun, *In godsnaam: Het jaar van Theo van Gogh* (Amsterdam/Antwerpen: Contact, 2005), p. 64, 200.

40 Ruud Peters, 'De ideologische en religieuze ontwikkeling van Mohammed B.: Deskundigenrapport in de strafzaak tegen Mohammed B. in opdracht van het Openbaar Ministerie opgesteld voor de arrondissementsrechtbank Amsterdam' (2005), p. 8; see also 'Verdict in the Hofstad Group case', paragraph 109, p. 116.

41 For his religious and ideological ideas and their development, see the report of Ruud Peters, who was an expert witness for the prosecution during the trial, http://www.sociosite.org/jihad/peters_rapport.pdf. Retrieved June 2009.

42 Statement of the Minister of the Interior and Kingdom Relations, Johan Remkes, during the parliamentary debate on the murder of Theo van Gogh. House of Representatives of the States General, 11 November 2004, Parliamentary Papers, No. 22–1303, 11 November 2004; Chorus and Olgun, *In godsnaam: Het jaar van Theo van Gogh*, p. 200.

43 National Prosecutor's Office, *Requisitoir van de officier van justitie in de strafzaak tegen Mohammed* B. (Amsterdam, 12 July 2005), pp. 7–8.

44 Ibid., p. 7.

45 Ibid., pp. 10–26.

46 Peters, 'Dutch Extremist Islamism', in: Rik Coolsaet (ed.), *Jihadi terrorism and the radicalisation challenge in Europe: European and American Experiences* (London: Ashgate, 2011), pp. 115–130.

47 Nesser, *The Slaying of the Dutch Filmmaker*, p. 25.

48 National Prosecutor's Office, *Repliek van de officier van justitie in de strafzaken tegen Nadir A.*, pp. 31–32.

49 A Dutch biography of this Sheikh is available on the website of 'Marokko Community', in which references to the 11 September fatwa are found: 'Sheikh Hamoud bin Uqla as-Shu'aybi. De levensloop van een groot geleerde' (24 July 2008) http://forums.marokko.nl/showthread.php?t=2092457. Retrieved 11 July 2009.

50 National Prosecutor's Office, *Requisitoir van de officier van justitie in de strafzaak tegen Mohammed B.*, p. 43.

51 Ibid., p. 49; District Court of Amsterdam, *Verdict against Bouyeri*, LJN AU0025, 13/129227-04 (26 July 2005).

52 'Gewonden bij politieactie in Den Haag', *De Telegraaf* (10 November 2004).

53 National Criminal Investigation Service ('Dienst Nationale Recherche'), RL 8026; KRO-Reporter, 'Samir A.: staatsvijand nr. 1' (broadcast on 1 October 2006).

54 'Het vonnis in de zaak-Samir A. verklaard', *Elsevier* (16 April 2005).

55 Interview team leader National Criminal Investigation Service (Houten, 16 August 2011).

56 Interview team leader National Criminal Investigation Service (Houten, 16 August 2011).

57 'Een afgeluisterd gesprek over VVD'ers', *NRC Handelsblad* (20 July 2005).

58 'Terreurverdachte Samir A. schrijft boek', NOVA (24 January 2006). http://www.novatv.nl/page/detail/uitzendingen/4069/Terreurverdachte+Samir+A.+schrijft+boek. Retrieved June 2009.

59 Politieverslagen; interview met de teamleider van de Nationale Recherche (Houten, 16 augustus 2011); KRO-Reporter, 'Samir A.: staatsvijand nr. 1' (1 October 2006).

60 Janny Groen and Annieke Kranenberg, *Strijdsters van Allah: Radicale moslima's en het Hofstadnetwerk* (Amsterdam: Meulenhoff/De Volkskrant, 2006), p. 208.

61 Verdict on appeal, Appeals Court of The Hague, 2 October 2008, no. 2200734906.

62 He had two defence counsel: Mr. Plasman and Mr. Sarikaya.

63 *Netwerk* (28 July 2005), http://www.netwerk.tv/node/2723#. Retrieved 27 August 2012.

64 'Mohammed B. spreekt in de rechtzaal', NOVA (12 July 2005); 'Laatste Woord Mohammed B.', *De Volkskrant* (9 August 2005).

65 Hattum, W.F., van and Jong, de, W.H. 'Twee Kwesties Naar Aanleiding van het Vonnis Tegen Mohammed B.', *Nederlands Juristenblad*, 8 (2005), pp. 246–252.

66 'Eerste dag rechtzaak tegen Mohammed B.', *ÉénVandaag* (11 July 2005).

67 District Court of Amsterdam, *Verdict against Bouyeri*, LJN AU0025, 13/129227-04, July 26, 2005; 'Laatste Woord Mohammed B.', *De Volkskrant* (9 August 2005).

68 Term of abuse, literally translated 'goat fuckers'.

69 District Court of Amsterdam, *Verdict against Bouyeri*, LJN AU0025, 13/129227-04, July 26, 2005; 'Laatste Woord Mohammed B.', *De Volkskrant* (9 August 2005).

70 Beatrice de Graaf. 'The Nexus between Salafism and Jihadism in the Netherlands', *CTC Sentinel*, 3:3 (2010), pp. 17–22; Joas Wagemakers, 'A Purist Jihadi-Salafi: The ideology of Abu Muhammad al-Maqdisi', *British Journal of Middle Eastern Studies*, 36:2 (2009), pp. 287–297; Joas Wagemakers, 'Framing the "Threat to Islam": Al-wala' wa-l-bara' in Salafi Discourse', *Arab Studies Quarterly*, 30:4 (2008), pp. 1–22; Joas Wagemakers, 'Abu Muhammad al-Maqdisi: A counter-terrorism asset?', *CTC Sentinel*, 1:6 (2008), pp. 7–9.

71 District Court of Amsterdam, *Verdict against Bouyeri*, LJN AU0025, 13/129227-04, 26 July 2005.

72 'Hofstadgroep de dag voor de moord vooral bezig met trouwerij', *De Volkskrant* (25 July 2005); 'De bode wordt er kwaad om, de rechter niet', *Trouw* (5 January 2006).

73 Marieke Slootman and Jean Tillie, *Processes of Radicalisation: Why some Amsterdam Muslims become radicals* (Amsterdam: Institute for Migration and Ethnic Studies, 2006), p. 99.

74 Martijn de Koning, *Zoeken naar een 'zuivere' Islam: Geloofsbeleving en identitietsvorming van jonge Marokaanse-Nederlandse Moslims* (Amsterdam: Bert Bakker, 2008), pp. 379–386.

75 'Zalm: we zijn in oorlog! Regering: terrorisme met wortel en tak uitroeien', *Algemeen Dagblad* (6 November 2004); 'Terroristen met dubbele nationaliteit raken Nederlands paspoort kwijt. Kabinet verklaart de oorlog aan terreur', *Het Parool* (6 November 2004); 'Overheid wil meer armslag: anti-terreurmaatregelen', *Trouw* (6 November 2004).

76 See, for example, Ron Eyerman, *The Assassination of Theo van Gogh: From social drama to cultural trauma* (Durham/London: Duke University Press, 2008); Ian Buruma, *Murder in Amsterdam: The death of Theo van Gogh and the limits of tolerance* (New York: Penguin, 2006).

77 De Koning, *Zoeken naar en 'zuivere' Islam*, pp. 379–386.

78 'Mohammed Bouyeri wil de doodstraf', *Elsevier* (11 July 2005).

79 District Court of Amsterdam, *Verdict against Bouyeri*, Case Number LJN: AU0025, 13/129227-04, 26 July 2005.

80 In the Netherlands, life sentences are very rare. Bouyeri was the 28th person to receive such a sentence since 1945, war criminals included. Capital felonies, such as murder, usually result in sentences of ten to fifteen years. The new terrorism law, however, states that if there is a terrorist motive for a crime the sentence may be increased by half. Imprisonments ordinarily in excess of fifteen years can be upgraded to life imprisonment, as was the case with Bouyeri.

81 Stan de Jong, *Prettig weekend ondanks alles* (Amsterdam: Xtra, 2005); Stan de Jong, 'De moord op Theo van Gogh: wie wist wat', *De Nieuwe Revu*, 44 (2006), pp. 18–23.

82 'Wet Terroristische Misdrijven', *Staatsblad* (24 June 2004).

83 Cf. for the decision making process and parliamentary discussion regarding this new law: Maartje van der Woude, *Wetgeving in een veiligheidscultuur: totstandkoming van antiterrorismewetgeving in Nederland bezien vanuit maatschappelijke en (rechts)politieke context*. Leiden University Docteral Thesis (2010), pp. 204–231.

84 Public Prosecution (OM), *Requisitoir van de Officier van Justitie in de zaak 'Piranha'*, Part I & II, 3 & 6 November 2006, here: Part II, 'Eisen'.

85 Q.A.M. Eijkman and B. van Ginkel, 'Compatible or Incompatible: Intelligence and human rights in terrorist trials', *Amsterdam Law Forum*, 3:4 (2011), pp. 3–16, here: p. 4.

86 Interviews with public prosecutor Koos Plooij (Schiphol: 5 October 2011).

87 'Pleitnota' (Defence) in the Piranha-case, 8 November 2006; interview with defence counsel Bart Nooitgedagt (October 2011).

88 National Prosecutor's Office, Requisitoir van de officier van justitie in de 'Arles' zaak, Part I (23 January 2006), pp. 2–4.

89 Cf. for the new Dutch anti-terrorism legislation Maartje van der Woude, Wetgeving in een Veiligheidscultuur; Marianne Hirsch Ballin, *Anticipative Criminal Investigation: Theory and counterterrorism practice in the Netherlands and the United States* (The Hague: T.M.C. Asser Press and Springer, 2012).

90 Interview with Koos Plooy (Schiphol, 5 October 2011).

91 'Leden Hofstadgroep blijven vastzitten', *Elsevier* (7 February 2005).

92 'Bewijs tegen Hofstadgroep stapelt zich op', *Elsevier* (20 September 2005).

93 Ibid.

94 National Prosecutor's Office, *Requisitoir van de officier van justitie* (Part 1), 'Arles' case (23 January 2006), p. 47.

95 Verdict in appeal, Appeals Court of The Hague, 23 January 2008, LJN BC 2576 no. 22006189706.

96 National Prosecutor's Office, *Requisitoir van de officier van justitie* (Part 1), 'Arles' case, 23 January 2006, pp. 47–48.

97 At first instance in 2005 and 2006, on appeal 2007, and during the partial retrial in 2011. The 'cassation' procedure at the Supreme Court is mostly a written procedure in the Netherlands. Sometimes, as was the case with Piranha, defence counsel plead their case orally before the Supreme Court, but this is an exception.

98 'Hofstadgroep de dag voor de moord vooral bezig met trouwerij', *De Volkskrant* (25 July 2005); 'De bode wordt er kwaad om, de rechter niet' *Trouw* (5 January 2006).

99 Groen and Kranenberg, *Strijdsters van Allah*; 'Hofstadgroep de dag voor de moord vooral

bezig met trouwerij', *De Volkskrant* (25 July 2005); Maurits Berger, 'Nieuwe Spelers, nieuwe regels', *Tijdschrift voor Religie, Recht en Beleid*, 1:1 (2010), pp. 3–4; 'Je bent als Hofstadter een held in de gevangenis', *De Volkskrant* (27 January 2006); Vermaat, *De Nederlandse Jihad*, p. 137.

100 On appeal he was a witness and no longer a defendant.

101 'Bouyeri: Mijn ideologie is niet van belang', *Elsevier* (2 December 2005); Vermaat, *De Nederlandse Jihad*, pp. 23–24.

102 'Bouyeri: Vergelijking met Bin Laden te veel eer', *Elsevier* (2 February 2006).

103 Vermaat, *De Nederlandse Jihad*, pp. 137–146; 'Rechter laat weer Hofstadverdachte vrij', *Elsevier* (22 December 2005).

104 Vermaat, *De Nederlandse Jihad*, pp. 137–146.

105 'Jason W.: Ik wilde interessant doen', *Elsevier* (9 December 2005); Vermaat, *De Nederlandse Jihad*, pp. 35–36.

106 Vermaat, *De Nederlandse Jihad*, pp. 170–173.

107 Ibid., p. 33.

108 In first instance, nine of the fourteen defendants were convicted. In seven cases the verdict of the District Court of Rotterdam was appealed (both by the defendants and the public prosecutor).

109 'Hofstadverdachte Jason W. wil niet meewerken', *Trouw* (23 July 2007); 'Jason W. zwijgt in hoger beroep' *Trouw* (24 July 2007).

110 'Jason W. werkt mee aan berechting', *De Telegraaf* (16 July 2011), author was present on 16 July 2011 in the Appeals Court of Amsterdam.

111 'Advocaat Jason W. niet in beroep, Openbaar Ministerie wel om helderheid terroristisch oogmerk', *Nederlands Juridisch Dagblad* (9 February 2007).

112 'Jason W. zwijgt in hoger beroep' *Trouw* (24 July 2007); 'De bode wordt er kwaad om, de rechter niet' *Trouw* (5 January 2006).

113 'Dit proces is een klassieke heksenjacht', NRC *Handelsblad* (7 January 2006).

114 'Hofstad-advocaten willen verhoor verbalisanten' *Trouw* (6 December 2005).

115 'Rechters hoger-beroep Hofstad niet vervangen' *Trouw* (8 November 2007).

116 Verdict, LJN AV5108, District Court of Rotterdam, 10/000322-04;10/000328-04;10/000396-04;10/000393-04;10000325-04;10/000323-04;10/000395-04, 10 March 2006.

117 'Hofstadgroep vrijgesproken van terrorisme', *De Volkskrant* (23 January 2008).

118 Appeals Court of The Hague's decision in the appeal of Jason Walters, LJN: BC2576, 2200189706, 23 January 2008.

119 Interview with Polyan Spoon (Rotterdam, 7 September 2009).

120 Verdict in the Piranha case. LJN: AZ3589, 10/600052-05, 10/600108-05, 10/600134-05, 10/600109-05, 10/600122-05, 10/600023-06, 10/600100-06.

121 'Hoge Raad vernietigt vrijspraken in de Hofstadgroep zaken', Press Statement *Hoge Raad* (2 February 2010).

122 Verdict, LJN BK5196, Supreme Court of the Netherlands, 08/00740, 2 February 2010.

123 'Hoge Raad vernietigt vrijspraak Hofstadgroep', NRC *Handelsblad* (2 February 2010).

124 Verdict, LJN: BO7690, Court of Appeals Amsterdam, nr. 23-000751-10, 17 December 2010.

125 Verdict, LJN: BO9018, BO9017, BO9016, BO9015, BO9014, Court of Appeals Amsterdam, 23-000748-10, December 17, 2010; LJN: BO8032, Court of Appeals Amsterdam, 23-000747-10; 17 December 2010; LJN: BO7690, Court of Appeals Amsterdam, 23-000751-10; 17 December 2010.

126 Irene Frankhuijzen, 'The Hofstadgroep in beeld', Student Master thesis (Rotterdam: Faculty of History and Art, Erasmus University Rotterdam, 2006); Britta Böhler, *Crisis in de rechtsstaat: Spraakmakende zaken, verborgen processen* (Utrecht: Arbeiderspers, 2004).

127 Vermaat, De *Nederlandse Jihad*, pp. 291–377; Groen and Kranenberg, *Strijdsters van Allah*, pp. 233–235, 251–254; lecture by Bart Nooitgedagt, *De rol van de advocaat* (The Hague: Leiden University, 15 September 2011). The author was present.

128 *Netwerk*, 'Verdachten Hofstad: Beweren: AIVD-informant leverde handgranaat Laakkwartier' (28 October 2005); 'Samir A: Saleh B. was wel informant van de AIVD', *Elsevier* (21 December 2005); Vermaat, De *Nederlandse Jihad*, pp. 63–65; 'Dit proces is een klassieke heksenjacht', NRC *Handelsblad* (7 January 2006); For more information see Quirine A.M. Eijkman and Bibi van Ginkel, 'Compatible or Incompatible: Intelligence and human rights in terrorist trials', *Amsterdam Law Forum*, 3:4 (2011), pp. 3–16.

129 Groen and Kranenberg, *Strijdsters van Allah*, pp. 255–259; 'Radicale Moslims woedend over de uitspraak Hofstad-zaak', *De Volkskrant* (13 March 2006); 'Breedveld/Politici begrijpen niets van eigen anti-terrorisme wet', *Trouw* (14 March 2006).

130 Rotterdam District Court, Verdict LJN: AU4531, 19 October 2005.

131 National Prosecutor's Office, *Requisitoir van de officier van justitie in de zaak 'Piranha'*. Part I & Part II (3 and 6 November 2006), Amsterdam-Osdorp.

132 Interview with Polyan Spoon, the public prosecutor for terrorism (Rotterdam, 7 September 2009).

133 National Prosecutor's Office / Koos Plooy and Alexander van Dam, *Repliek van de officier van justitie in de zaak 'Arles'* (24 February 2006), p. 10.

134 National Prosecutor's Office /Alexander van Dam and Bart den Hartigh, *Requisitoir van de officier van justitie in de zaak 'Piranha'*. Part I (3 November 2006), pp. 84–85.

135 The video had already been broadcast on a national news show; *De Volkskrant* (14 September 2006), http://www.volkskrant.nl/vk/nl/2686/Binnenland/article/detail/814966/2006/09/14/Video-testament-Samir-A-op-televisie.dhtml. Retrieved July 2009.

136 Cf. Requisitoir Part I, p. 61. While still in custody, the defendant phoned a radio

programme to refute the allegations made by the prosecution; 'Terreurverdachte Soumaya S. ontkent aantijgingen', *Business News Radio* (3 Augustus 2005).

137 See the excerpt and argument of the prosecution: (Oral pleadings) Requisitoir in the Piranha case, Part I, pp. 59–63.

138 Interview with Alexander van Dam, public prosecutor in that particular case (28 January 2011).

139 See verdict of the Amsterdam Court against Soumaya S., 25 March 2014. Case no. 23-005455-11. http://uitspraken.rechtspraak.nl/inziendocument?id=ECLI:NL:GHAMS:2014:905&keyword=jihad Retrieved 2 September 2014.

140 Groen and Kranenberg, *Strijdsters van Allah*.

141 'Preken en porno', *De Telegraaf* (16 July 2005).

142 'Soumaya weet niets van jihad', BN/*De Stem* (5 October 2005); interview with Dutch Federal Prosecutor Koos Plooy (Schiphol/Amsterdam, 5 October 2011).

143 Requisitoir, Part II, pp. 45–46.

144 'Samir A. ernstig ziek en sterft van de pijn', *Elsevier* (22 December 2005).

145 'Terreurgroep doet aangifte tegen rechercheur', *Elsevier* (31 October 2006).

146 Interview with Soumaya S. (9 June 2011).

147 Interview with the team leader of the Nationale Recherche (Houten, 16 August 2011).

148 Interview with Soumaya S., The Hague (9 June 2011).

149 'Imam vervloekte Van Gogh vóór moord', *De Volkskrant* (31 October 2006); Report of the hearings, 30 October 2006, Rotterdam; cf. for the text of the sermon Groen and Kranenberg, *Strijdsters van Allah*, pp. 331–332.

150 'Justitie pakt ons vanwege ons geloof', *Trouw* (1 December 2006).

151 National Prosecutor's Office, *Requisitoir van de officier van justitie in de zaak 'Piranha'*, Part II, 6 November 2006.

152 Ibid.

153 'OM eist tot vijftien jaar tegen terreurverdachten', *Het Parool* (7 November 2006); 'Terreurverdachte Samir A. wil snel "weg uit dit zieke land"', *Trouw* (11 November 2006).

154 'Netwerk rond Samir A. geen terreurorganisatie', *Elsevier* (1 December 2006).

155 National Prosecutor's Office /Alexander van Dam and Bart den Hartigh, *Requisitoir van de officier van justitie in de zaak 'Piranha'*. Part I, 3 November 2006, pp. 84–85; The video was broadcast on television: 'Videotestament Samir A. op televisie', *De Volkskrant* (14 September 2006).

156 LJN:AZ3589, District Court of Rotterdam, 10/600052-05, 10/600108-05, 10/600134-05, 10/600109-05, 10/600122-05, 10/600023-06, 10/600100-06; 1 December 2006, 'Samir A.: acht jaar cel voor terreurplannen', *Elsevier* (1 December 2006).

157 LJN: AZ3589, District Court of Rotterdam, 10/600052-05, 10/600108-05, 10/600134-05, 10/600109-05, 10/600122-05, 10/600023-06, 10/600100-06; 1 December 2006.

158 'Samir A.: acht jaar cel voor terreurplannen', *Elsevier* (1 December 2006).

159 Verdict in the Piranha-case, LJN: AZ3589, Rotterdam District Court, 10/600052-05, 10/600108-05, 10/600134-05, 10/600109-05, 10/600122-05, 10/600023-06, 10/600100-06, 1 December 2006; 'Samir A. veroordeeld tot 8 jaar cel', *De Volkskrant* (2 December 2006).

160 'Gefrustreerde jongere, maar terrorist?', *Het Parool* (28 November 2006).

161 'Justitie pakt ons vanwege ons geloof', *Trouw* (1 December 2006).

162 'Hirsi Ali: Soumaya S. biedt hoop', *De Volkskrant* (18 November 2006).

163 'Kamer blij met vonnis', *De Volkskrant* (2 December 2006).

164 KRO-Reporter, 'Samir A.: staatsvijand nr. 1' (1 October 2006).

165 'Wat heeft mijn zoon nou misdaan?', NRC *Handelsblad* (14 October 2006).

166 Marion van San, Stijn Sieckelinck en Micha de Winter, *Idealen op drift: Een pedagogische kijk op radicaliserende jongeren* (Amsterdam 2010), pp. 50–51; 'Wat heeft mijn zoon nou misdaan', NRC *Handelsblad* (14 October 2006); KRO-Reporter, 'Samir A.: staatsvijand nr. 1', broadcast 1 October 2006; interview with Abida at the daily show De Wereld Draait Door (9 September 2011).

167 'Nederland in de fout met isoleren terreurverdachte', *De Volkskrant* (5 June 2008); cf. Council of Europe, *Report to the authorities of the Kingdom of the Netherlands on the visits carried out to the Kingdom in Europe, Aruba, and the Netherlands Antilles by the European Committee for the Prevention of Torture and Inhuman or Degrading Treatment or Punishment* (CPT) *in June 2007*, Strasbourg (5 February 2008), pp. 24–30.

168 'Rabbijn steekt nek uit voor verdachte moslima', *De Volkskrant* (19 August 2008).

169 LJN: BF3987, Appeals Court of The Hague, no.2200734906, 2 October 2008/ LJN: BF5225, Appeals Court of The Hague, no.2200735006, October 2, 2008/ LJN: BF4814, Appeals Court of The Hague, no.2200735106, 2 October 2008/ LJN: BF5180, Appeals Court of The Hague, no.2200738406, 2 October 2008.

170 Appeals Court of The Hague's decision in the appeal in the Piranha case (2 October 2008), no.2200734906.

171 'Samir A. veroordeeld tot 9 jaar', NOS-item (2 October 2008); Gerechtshof 's-Gravenhage, LJN: BF5225, 2 October 2008.

172 'Advocaat woest over arrest "Piranha"', ANP (2 October 2008); 'Verbijsterde advocaten, glunderend OM', *De Volkskrant* (3 October 2008); 'Veroordeling van terroristenvrouw is politiek vonnis', *Algemeen Dagblad* (3 October 2008).

173 'Advocaat woest over arrest "Piranha"', ANP (2 October 2008); 'Verbijsterde advocaten, glunderend OM', *De Volkskrant* (3 October 2008); 'Veroordeling van terroristenvrouw is

politiek vonnis', *Algemeen Dagblad* (3 October 2008); 'Beleefdheid', *De Telegraaf* (9 October 2008); 'Koorddansen', *Elsevier* (11 October 2008).

174 Interview with Abida at *EenVandaag* (6 Augustus 2011); interview with Abida at the daily show *De Wereld Draait Door* (9 September 2011).

175 LJN: BP7544, Supreme Court, CPG 08/04418, 15 March 2011; LJN: BP7585, Supreme Court, CPG 08/04272 15 March 2011; Supreme Court, 'Hoge Raad beslist in de terroristenzaken Nouriddin el F. en Soumaya S.' (15 November 2011).

176 Power, *The Risk Management of Everything*, p. 14.

177 ibidem, p. 10.

178 Claudia Aradau and Rens van Munster, 'Taming the future. The dispositif of risk in the war on terror'. In: Louise Amoore and Marieke de Goede (eds), *Risk and the War on Terror* (London: Routledge, 2008), pp. 23–40, here: p. 32.

10. Supporting Prisoners or Supporting Terrorists: The 2008 Trial of Gestoras Pro Amnistía in Spain

Carolijn Terwindt

'This is a political trial. It is a disfraz jurídico (legal farce). It ...'
The defendant was interrupted by the judge:
'This is not what the right to a last word means.
You have no blanket permit to offend the court.
You cannot call me a disfraz jurídico.'
A woman in the audience commented softly:
'She cannot interrupt a last word!'
The defendant responded:
'I had no intention to offend.'
The judge:
'We have already heard this discourse, this history, it is already very clear'.[1]

10.1. Introduction

On 18 June 2008, these were the last words of the last defendant in a trial that was characterised by a battle between different narratives of justice and injustice and competing demands for respect and recognition. As in the quotation above, the narratives and their confrontation found expression in the interactions between the actors in the trial—the defendants, judge and public—who all 'perform' in a way that constitutes, confirms or rejects their specific role. Thus, the actors in the courtroom stage a 'show' that in its idealised form becomes a 'performance of justice', which Beatrice de Graaf, in her introduction to the present volume, describes as

> A show where the verdict educates the public about the importance of the rule of law in a democratic society, creates a collective memory and sets standards for future conduct by states and society. This type of show is run by the judge/jury, but the

> performative strategy is based on a (perceived) neutral application of the law, not on partisan politicisation of justice.[2]

From the words of the defendant above it is abundantly clear that in his perception he did not think he was being tried under a 'neutral application of the law'. In order to understand why the trial under study failed to become generally accepted as a 'performance of justice', this chapter argues that it can most fruitfully be understood as the staging of competing shows in the same venue at the same time. In her analysis of the dynamics in operation between the different actors and their audiences, the author applies the typology developed by De Graaf and demonstrates that while the trial defies easy characterisation, it is possible to discern elements of (1) a virtual show, (2) a show run by the defendants and their lawyers and (3) a media show (with sideshows).

The trial against the defendants of the Basque organisations Gestoras pro Amnistía and Askatasuna (in short, the 'Gestoras trial') is one of the 'macro-juicios' (macro-trials), called such given the large number of defendants. The macro-trials started in Spain at the end of the 1990s and prosecuted members of left-nationalist groups[3] as members of the terrorist organisation Euskadi Ta Askatasuna (ETA). Significant in these trials is the new conceptualisation of ETA as a broad 'entramado' (network) rather than, more narrowly, as the military wing alone. This innovative perspective and its usage in criminal proceedings will be explored in more detail below. The targets in the macro-trials were a Basque youth organisation, a certain newspaper, a number of bars, a language institution, and Gestoras pro Amnistía, an organisation engaged in prisoner support work. The prosecution claimed that these apparently socio-political bodies were actually part of the broader ETA 'network' and thus constituted subgroups in a terrorist organisation. The Gestoras trial was thus a terrorist trial in the sense that the defendants were charged with membership of a terrorist organisation, which they all denied.

The macrotrials against the alleged ETA network form an important transition in the Spanish repertoire of contentious terrorism trials.[4] The performance strategies in the trials against ETA defendants during the 1980s and 1990s had been very different from the interaction in the macro-trials. ETA defendants traditionally refused to defend themselves. While they rejected the jurisdiction of the Spanish state, they generally did not dispute the charges and often openly claimed their ETA militancy in the courtroom. The earlier trials had generally belonged to the category of the 'not-so-dramatic show' in De Graaf's typology.[5] Part of the reason for this is that during the 1980s the battle between ETA and the Spanish state tended to be viewed from a military perspective.[6] It took place in the streets, not in the courtrooms. Illustrative of this war-oriented way of thinking were the confessions by former President Felipe González, who told a reporter from newspaper El *País* that in 1989 or 1990 he once had the opportunity to have the entire leadership of ETA killed during a meeting in France. At the time, he rejected the option, but in 2010 was still wondering whether that had been the right decision.[7]

Taking the Gestoras trial as illustrative of the new dynamics in the macrotrials, this chapter describes the battle between the different narratives and performative strategies employed by the prosecutors, the court, the defendants, the victims and sympathisers on both sides. Because Spanish-Basque society is so polarised, it is impossible to fit the trial into a single typological category as developed by De Graaf in her introduction to this volume. The show was run by both the defendants *and* the prosecutors, but each only for their own audience. They could not or did not reach out to the constituency of the other side. The trial thus only confirmed pre-existing divisions and pre-existing 'narratives of (in)justice'.[8] At the same time though, this trial, along with the other macrotrials, effectively established the notion that ETA is a network and that criminal responsibility lies upon the shoulders of all who are part of that network.

In the Gestoras trial, the accusation that the defendants were part of that network was based on their engagement in activities that they described as 'prisoner support'. The analysis presented here, therefore, explores competing narratives that defend and challenge this description of the activities of Gestoras pro Amnistía, as the trial called into question the distinction between legal support for prisoners and illegal support for (imprisoned) terrorists.

This chapter describes the Gestoras trial in four parts: before the trial, during the trial, outside the courtroom, and after the trial. But first the data that were used will be briefly described.

10.2. Data

The argument in this chapter relies on the author's fieldwork in the Basque Country and in Madrid, where she attended a large part of the seven-week proceedings in the Gestoras trial. The author also gained access to many court documents, the oral tapes of proceedings, court verdicts and other documentary materials. The author was further present at several activities of what she has called 'prisoner support mobilization',[9] both in Madrid and the Basque Country. In addition, the collected data included in-depth interviews with several of the defendants, their supporters, representatives of organisations of victims of ETA and their families,[10] and the lawyer executing the popular accusation on behalf of these victim organisations (a Spanish legal procedure allowing citizens to act as prosecutors). Unfortunately, the state prosecutor of this particular trial refused to be interviewed,[11] but the author did interview the chief prosecutor of the Audiencia Nacional[12] as well as one of the investigative judges. Finally, the collected data included newspaper accounts across the political spectrum that covered this trial as well as reports written by organisations sympathising with the defendants or with victim organisations.

The research for this chapter was completed in 2008. ETA announced to lay down its arms in 2011.

10.3. Before the Trial

This section first describes some of the key features of the Spanish criminal justice system, specifically in relation to terrorism prosecutions. Then the 'ETA network' concept and the related macrotrials will be described in more detail. The section goes on to describe the place assigned to Gestoras pro Amnistía within the ETA network and its prisoner support activities. Lastly, the Gestoras trial and its chronology are presented.

10.3.1. *The Spanish Criminal Justice System in Relation to Terrorism Offences*

Terrorism proceedings in Spain should be understood within the context of a long battle by the state against various terrorist groups. Especially in the early 1980s, quite a few organisations were employing violence and threatening the young Spanish democracy. ETA was just one of them; others were the Comandos Autónomos (CCAA, perceived as a radical split from ETA), Terra Lliure (for the independence of Catalonia), the anti-Fascist GRAPO, MPAIAC (for the independence of the Canary Islands), and the right-wing groups Triple A and Batallón Vasco Español. Spanish laws against terrorism therefore have a long history. The period from 1975 to 1985 saw many legal reforms and attempts to bolster the judicial institutions so that they could deal effectively with the threat of continuing terrorist attacks. In 1995 a new penal code was written into which the special terrorism laws were integrated as separate offences. The code has been revised several times since.[13] The terrorism provisions have authorised solitary confinement and limiting or suspending some constitutional rights.[14] Membership of a terrorist organisation is criminalised in articles 516 and 515 sub 2 of the penal code.

Until the reform of 1978, terrorism crimes fell under the jurisdiction of the military courts. Under the new laws, terrorist offences were to be tried by a new court, the Audiencia Nacional, which had been founded in 1977.[15] Critics pointed out that this court was an all too obvious successor to the 'Tribunal de Orden Publico' (Public Order Tribunal), a heavily criticised instrument used by the former dictator Franco to detain political opponents. The Audiencia Nacional was founded by executive decision, adding to its illegitimacy in the eyes of its critics.[16] Years of legal proceedings followed, until in 1987 the Spanish Constitutional Tribunal ruled that the European Commission of Human Rights had declared the Audiencia Nacional to be a normal court. That decision effectively ended the dispute in strictly legal terms, but to this day the court is criticised both within the Basque movement and outside the Basque Country.[17]

The jurisdiction of the Audiencia Nacional is restricted to certain areas, of which terrorism is only one (the other areas are money laundering, tax fraud, corruption and the drug trade). In the words of one of the investigative judges, it is not a special court—as its critics say—but a specialised court.[18] Proponents of the Audiencia Nacional argue that physical distance from the Basque Country—the court sits in Madrid—is needed to guarantee the safety and neutrality of judges. In 2003 a law was adopted that created an appeals chamber in the Audiencia Nacional. Previously, appeals were possible only in a limited review at the Tribunal Supremo, the highest Spanish court. In 2001, the United Nations Human Rights Committee ruled that this was not an adequate measure.[19] At the time of the Gestoras trial, however, the appeals chamber was still not operational, making the Tribunal Supremo the instance for appeal and the last domestic resort.

The Audiencia Nacional is thus a separate judicial organ, with its own judges and prosecutors. Operating as they do in a continental legal system, Spanish prosecutors work in cooperation with so-called instruction judges or investigative judges. In Spain, investigative judges occupy an especially important role in criminal proceedings, as they prepare a case and make the crucial decisions regarding who is charged with what. Only when the investigative phase is closed and the case goes to trial does the prosecutor take over the dossier.

In recent decades, there has been an important shift within the criminal justice system and its perceived capacity to deal with terrorism.[20] In the period immediately after the transition to democracy, the criminal justice system was deemed to be inappropriate to respond to terrorist offences. In 1979, the Attorney General wrote,

'Let's be honest: in the face of the terrorist phenomenon the normal operation of judging, applying a penalty and taking care of its execution, is like writing in the sea.'[21] Doubts about the ability of the criminal justice system to deal with terrorist offences have vanished over the years, and by 2007 the Attorney General asserted that judicial activity against terrorism was in 'good health' and that the work that had been done was 'firm, resounding, and according to strict fulfilment of the principle of legality'.[22] Indeed, the trial after the Al Qaeda-linked attack in March 2004 was showcased as an example for the international community in employing criminal justice in response to terrorism. The NGO Human Rights Watch asserted that 'the Spanish government sees itself as a leader in the effort to combine effective counter-terrorism measures with full respect for internationally recognised human rights'.[23]

10.3.2. *The ETA Network and the Macro-trials*

The simple question 'What is ETA?' proved to be far more complicated than I could imagine when I embarked on my fieldwork. Not only is the legal nature of the group in dispute—is it a *terrorist* organisation or an *armed* organisation?—but so is its membership. It is not at all clear who belongs to ETA and who does not. During the Gestoras trial even the prosecutor got confused. The charge brought against the defendants was membership of ETA, but during his argument he talked about the relationship *between* one of the defendants and ETA, as if ETA were actually external to the defendants. He corrected himself quickly.[24]

Another example serves to illustrate the discrepancies plaguing our understanding of ETA. During a trial regarding the legality of a Basque political party, the defence lawyer interrogated one of the police expert witnesses. The policeman claimed that in a public speech a mayor of that particular party had openly called for support for two ETA members who were detained and allegedly tortured. The defence lawyer asked, 'Did she use the word "ETA"?' The expert witness responded: 'she said "Basque political prisoners" which *everyone* understands to mean ETA prisoners'.[25] During the Gestoras trial this question and the competing answers—whether Basque political prisoners are the equivalent of ETA militants—became one of the core issues. Whereas the Gestoras defendants steadfastly referred to the collective they supported as 'Basque political prisoners', the verdict of the Audiencia Nacional talked about the 'mobilisation campaign in favour of the prisoner collective of E.T.A.'.[26]

In the macro-trials, the prosecutors' narrative was an important voice in this debate concerning the character of ETA and who belongs to it. The prosecutor's investigation and charges were based upon the premise that ETA consisted of more than just 'gunmen' and that the socio-political and media activities of the defendants were therefore to be construed as 'functions' within the ETA network. Several victim organisations strongly supported and advocated this notion of the ETA network.[27] In order to understand these assumptions and situate the Gestoras trial in the context of the other macro-trials, it is important to describe in more detail the emergence of the notion that ETA is a network.

'If the environment didn't exist, terrorism would be much more marginal; it is the breeding ground', said the chief prosecutor of the Audiencia Nacional in the interview in 2008.[28] This is a common perception in Spanish society and it explains the law enforcement focus on the previously so-called '*entorno de* ETA' (ETA environment). Interestingly, the image of ETA (both the structure and the concept[29])—specifically in relation to its 'environment'—has changed significantly during recent decades, leading to a very different kind of criminal prosecution. In the 1980s and the beginning of the 1990s, the prosecutorial focus was on the ETA commandos, their direct support structure and the armed attacks they committed.[30] During the 1990s, the focus of criminal justice efforts has shifted from the commandos and their support structure to include what was called the ETA 'environment'. Since then, it has become the practice to accuse members of organisations in the Basque left-nationalist movement of 'membership of a terrorist organisation'.

By May 2008, 302 people had already been indicted in the macrotrials, many of whom had spent time in pre-trial detention.[31] The defendants were not suspected of membership of an ETA commando or direct involvement in armed attacks (e.g. providing logistical support, such as housing to fugitives or stealing a car used for a car bomb). Because of their activities in left-nationalist socio-political organisations, they were alleged to be part of the 'ETA network'. People who in the 1980s and 1990s would have been situated in the 'ETA environment'—loosely described by the Director of Public Prosecutions in 1991 as those 'political sectors with goals similar to the terrorist organisation ETA'[32]—were then, in the 2000s, prosecuted as 'members of ETA'.

Investigative judge Baltasar Garzón played an important role in this re-conceptualisation of ETA.[33] Garzón redefined the military wing as a political organisation, and in doing so considered that in turn the political wing formed part of the violent strategy of the military wing. He argued that 'a terrorist organisation was something more complex than a mere collection of persons that kills, plants bombs, kidnaps and engages in extortion to achieve its political objectives'.[34] During the macro-trials, prosecutors had to fight against the old image of terrorism that they themselves had helped to create. In the Gestoras trial the prosecutor repeated over and over again that 'a terrorist organisation is *not* just a group of gunmen'. He was trying to subvert the stubborn notion that terrorists, as a matter of course, were 'pistoleros' (gunmen).

In the indictments, socio-political organisations alleged to be part of the ETA network were linked to ETA by way of the 'funciones' (functions) they were said to fulfil within a broader strategy aimed at subverting the Spanish constitution. The macro-trials were directed against both individuals and their organisations, because an important goal was to suspend and outlaw these socio-political organisations in order to make it more difficult for the network to operate.[35]

To bolster the argument that organisations such as Gestoras pro Amnistía were in fact part of the ETA network, the prosecutor in all of the macro-trials sketched the history of ETA since the end of the Franco regime in 1975, when ETA decided to put into effect a process called 'desdoblamiento' (split identity). This process was a response to the fact that with the emergence of democratic structures, many cultural and political organisations that had been prohibited under the dictatorship could start to work above ground; only the military wing of ETA would stay underground. In order to maintain cohesion between the various organisations, ETA decided that its members would perform their illegal tasks within the underground armed organisation and simultaneously sit on the above-ground boards of various socio-political organisations.

Further, ETA developed a theory of different 'frentes' (fronts). The armed struggle was just one of the fronts in the fight for an independent Euskal Herria (the larger Basque Country, including Navarra and the French parts); other battlefields were the 'frente politico' (political front) and the 'frente de masas' (front of the masses). Gestoras pro Amnistía, as a popular grassroots organisation, belonged to the front of the masses. More specifically, Gestoras was said to be active within the 'frente de makos' or 'frente de cárceles' (prison front). The coordination between Gestoras and ETA allegedly took place in committees called ASK; these were dissolved in 1995, after which coordination was carried out without intermediaries. Underlying the ETA network was therefore the assumption of the complementarity of different forms of struggle: the institutional struggle within political parties, the struggle of the masses by means of multiple socio-political organisations and the armed struggle by (the military wing of) ETA.

10.3.3. *Gestoras Pro Amnistía and Prisoner Support*

Many of the details regarding the historical relations as well as the communication between the military wing of ETA and the socio-political organisations in the left-wing nationalist movement had thus been given during each of the macrotrials and were essentially undisputed. As the Audiencia Nacional put it in its verdict of September 2008, and the defendants would probably have agreed, ETA and Gestoras pro Amnistía were struggling for the same political project, namely Euskal Herria.[36] The issues that remained contested concerned the nature and extent of the communication and coordination. The Gestoras defendants particularly criticised the leading role in the hierarchy allotted to the military wing of ETA, a role that would have denied autonomous decision-making and independent initiative to individual members of Gestoras. Whereas the defendants asserted that they chose to perform certain activities as part and parcel of their main task, which was to assist prisoners and their families, the prosecutor claimed that their activities were coordinated with ETA and in line with ETA's strategic goals and its armed struggle. In its verdict, the court explicitly addressed this tension between different perspectives. It found that what *seems* to be personal or legal assistance can be something else entirely if it fits into the logic of maintaining cohesion within the collective of ETA prisoners.[37] At issue therefore in the Gestoras trial was the question: when does support for prisoners turn into support for terrorists?

Gestoras pro Amnistía was founded in 1976 out of solidarity with the political prisoners of the Franco regime.[38] As its name implies, the main goal of Gestoras pro Amnistía was to bring about an amnesty for those prisoners. In 1977, the Spanish government indeed adopted a broad amnesty law (Law 46/1977) covering all political prisoners who were detained under the Franco regime, to promote 'the pacification of spirits, reconciliation and national concord'.[39] ETA prisoners and others, for example members of GRAPO, were recognised as 'political' prisoners and released. The amnesty did not put an end to Gestoras, which continued its solidarity with what it called 'personas represaliadas' (repressed persons), i.e. prisoners, refugees and deportees. Later, in a process named 'construcción nacional' (national construction), a merger was effectuated between Basque left-wing nationalist organisations in northern Spain and in southern France. Thus, in 2001 Gestoras pro Amnistía merged with Iparralde Koordinateka to become Askatasuna.

Gestoras/Askatasuna (*hereafter* Gestoras) has been engaged in prisoner support since its foundation. Many of its members dedicated a full-time working week to this commitment, paid for by the left-wing nationalist movement.[40] It monitored and reported incidents of repression, published lists of 'political prisoners' and organised ceremonies honouring ex-prisoners.[41] A lawyers' collective provided legal assistance. Prisoner support is given in many countries where people express concerns about state repression and politics justice. Because the Gestoras trial questioned the distinction between the (legal) support for prisoners and the (illegal) support for terrorists, the prosecutorial narrative in this trial is relevant beyond the immediate case concerned.

For our analysis, four different kinds of prisoner support and supporters can be distinguished: (1) personal support, (2) innocence support, (3) liberal support and (4) political support. Family and friends often engage in 'personal support' intended to alleviate the suffering of the imprisoned person. This is the kind of support that is given regardless of the definition of the criminal facts, regardless of innocence or guilt, and regardless of the political cause. The defendant/prisoner is simply recognised as a human being worthy of human treatment.

A second form of support is extended only to those defendants or prisoners that the supporters think are innocent of the charges. These supporters stand behind a defendant because they believe his or her denial of the charges. A special strategy to persuade the public of the innocence of prisoners, employed also by Gestoras pro Amnistía, is to criticise the court's decisions as pre-determined and politically motivated or based on faulty evidence, such as confessions extracted under torture. Such criticisms do not necessarily address any defendant in particular. They rather disrupt the general belief (prevalent in liberal democracies) that there is a good reason for everyone in prison to be there. The message sent by Gestoras frequently encourages the larger public to identify with the prisoners, as anyone might be the next victim of the alleged politically motivated persecution.

'Liberal' support is given, for example, by human rights organisations who criticise torture, long preventive detention, disproportionate sentences or the lack of due process. Such groups draw a distinction between 'formal' support (for the legal case) and 'substantive' support (for the political cause). Liberal supporters limit their efforts to formal support, generally insisting on the right to a fair trial. They typically demand that the state should play according to its own rules.

Finally, defendants or prisoners can try to be recognised as 'political' by receiving support from a broader movement that agrees with their political claims.[42] 'Political' prisoners and their political supporters generally defy the state's legitimacy to condemn their actions. Legal scholars hold that the possibility of punishment involves a claim to legitimacy.[43] Real punishment presupposes an agreement between the parties. Similarly, anthropologist Max Gluckman once wrote that 'If the litigants have rules of rightdoing different from those of the judges, the judges can punish them, but not convict them.'[44] Self-identification as a 'political' prisoner may be a strategy to advance the collective political cause. Such a decision is not, however, taken lightly. It can be prejudicial to the individual criminal case. For example, if defendants commit themselves to a solution in the political cause, they may decide to waive chances of individual leniency from judges.

Of course, while some supporters may limit their support to one of these kinds, the different forms of support can and do also often overlap and interact. Thus, Gestoras pro Amnistía is mainly a political support group, which also engages in the other forms of support. And as will be addressed below in the analysis of performative strategies, it also seeks different kinds of support from specific target audiences.

Support groups often come into existence in response to the practical needs of a given defendant or convict, such as money to pay for legal counsel. A support group may help with letter writing or visits to the jail, or gather reliable information about trial dates and the treatment of the prisoner. As a case drags on, and during the term of imprisonment, many moments lend themselves to public outcry and mass rally. Common activities include demonstrations in front of the prison or the courthouse, benefit concerts to raise money, ceremonies honouring prisoners and in some cases hunger strikes for better prison conditions. Indeed, scholars have recognised that prisoner support activity can become 'a social movement activity in its own right'[45] and can attract the involvement of moderate civil society representatives when the state is perceived to be 'overreacting'.[46] Criminal justice issues can even come to replace or overshadow the original political claims.[47] A successful prisoner solidarity effort can turn prisoners into a political issue. Indeed, the many activities of Gestoras pro Amnistía have contributed to public debate in Spain regarding the amnesty, reintegration and dispersion of Basque 'political' prisoners.

Political solidarity efforts aim to transform the intended effects of criminal prosecution: incapacitation, deterrence, rehabilitation, retaliation. Many prisoner support activities, for example, challenge the stigmatising function of criminal proceedings and the distance they create between the 'ordinary citizen' and convicts; insofar as criminal proceedings manifest the character of what Garfinkel called a 'status degradation ceremony',[48] well-designed activism can reduce that effect. Prisoner support may even result in the elevation of a 'political prisoner' into a hero. This can reverse the costs of repression into an asset.[49] This is not always the case though. There is always the danger of internal disagreement among 'political' prisoners and their solidarity groups or with the movement as such. Arguments about the means of struggle or the question whether or not to negotiate with the government can lead prisoners to cut ties with the movement as a whole or with their specific support group. Instances of hero formation and internal splits were also part of the dynamics of the 'Basque political prisoners'. As the official prisoner support group, Gestoras pro Amnistía has been deeply involved in these developments.

The prosecution's charge that Gestoras and the military wing of ETA formed a single organic whole was based on the alleged communication, cooperation and coordination between them, in combination with their historical relationship and shared support for armed struggle. The prosecutor relied on the non-juridical concept of 'functions' in order to link the defendants to armed attacks executed by ETA commandos. These functions of Gestoras would include: control over the collective of ETA prisoners; facilitating contact between ETA prisoners and the ETA leadership; collecting information vital for the security of ETA; identifying targets and legitimating their assassination; the publication of pamphlets; the de-legitimation of the Spanish state and the recruitment of militants. For example, Gestoras pro Amnistía launched a campaign called 'Alde Hemendik' (Get out of here), which called upon the Guardia Civil to leave the Basque Country. The prosecutor interpreted this campaign as one of the functions that Gestoras performed within the ETA network.

10.3.4. *The Gestoras Proceedings*

On 31 October 2001 twelve members of Gestoras pro Amnistía were detained at the instructions of judge Garzón. Later another defendant was arrested and extradited from France. The case is known as Sumario 33/01. On 19 December 2001, Garzón declared the organisation illegal, suspending its activities. On 27 December 2001, the European Council adopted its Common Position regarding terrorists, terrorist groups and measures such as the freezing of funds. Gestoras pro Amnistía, together with other alleged parts of the ETA network, were included on the list.[50] These thirteen defendants were held in pre-trial detention for four years until they were released after paying large amounts of bail. In 2003, five Askatasuna representatives who had continued the activities of so-called 'support to ETA' were detained.[51] They were also among the 27 defendants tried between April and June 2008 at the Audiencia Nacional.

Two of the defendants were active not in Gestoras pro Amnistía or Askatasuna but in Etxerat, an organisation of family members of prisoners (i.e. more in line with the category of 'personal' support). Etxerat organised and coordinated visits to far-away prisons.[52] Another defendant was the driver of the bus that took family members to dispersed prisoners. Notably, at the end of the trial the prosecutor dropped the charges against the two Etxerat defendants. He apparently did not consider this organisation and its type of support to be part of the ETA network.

This notwithstanding, their inclusion in the indictment led the defendants to claim that it meant a persecution of the entire Basque amnesty movement. Indeed, the defendants and their lawyers interpreted the dropping of the charges as a subtle strategy to lend an air of fairness to a trial the verdict of which—in their view—had been written before the trial had even started.[53] In similar strategic reasoning, the defendants argued, the court would only acquit those few defendants who had not spent time in pre-trial detention. Acquitting defendants who had spent the full maximum four pre-trial years in jail would amount to an admission of the failure of the justice system to correctly decide on the need for such detention.[54]

On 17 September 2008, the judges of the Audiencia Nacional convicted 21 people for membership of a terrorist organisation, based on article 515.2 of the penal code. Gestoras pro Amnistía and Askatasuna were designated as illegal terrorist organisations and their dissolution was ordered. Two of the accused, Juan Mari Olano and Julen Zelarain, received the highest penalty, ten years, because they were regarded as leaders (envisaged in a separate sentencing provision in the penal code). The other 18 defendants were sentenced to eight years' imprisonment. On 13 October 2009 the Tribunal Supremo broadly confirmed the decision of the Audiencia Nacional. One other defendant was acquitted by the Tribunal Supremo.

The following analysis, while taking into account the entire proceedings, is focussed on the 2008 trial before the Audiencia Nacional. It turned into a battle between competing narratives of (in)justice. Prosecutors, defendants, judges and victims all employed performative strategies aimed at targeted audiences. Our discussion will first focus on the dynamics inside the courtroom as part of the official proceedings and then turn to performative strategies outside the courtroom.

10.4. During the Trial

The Gestoras trial took place not in the courtroom in the centre of Madrid normally used for sessions of the Audiencia Nacional, but in a larger building on the outskirts that was equipped to hold the large number of accused and where the necessary security measures were easier to effectuate. Indeed, those security measures communicated without words the message that the defendants in this trial were suspected of being related to a terrorist network. Everyone entering the building was screened for metal objects.[55]

In the following section the prosecutorial performative strategy during the trial will be analysed as a specific kind of 'virtual show'. In the succeeding passage, we will look at the way defendants and their lawyers tried to turn the show to their advantage in order to expose their grievances.

10.4.1. *Virtual Show*

Unlike previous trials against ETA members, the macro-trials were not triggered by specific violent events. The decisions to launch these prosecutions were pro-active. The lack of a specific attack for which the defendants were held responsible gave these trials the character of a 'virtual' show. In the introduction to this volume, Beatrice de Graaf describes such trials as 'a tool of risk management', in which 'crimes under consideration deal with conspiracies and preparations rather than actual attacks'. What turns the Gestoras trial into a virtual show is not that terrorist actions have not yet taken place. The virtual aspect lies rather in the fact that no specific terrorist action or event is attributed to any of the defendants. In the words of the Audiencia Nacional, their wrongdoing is a 'permanent crime'.[56] As 'membership' can be seen as a status crime, it remains unclear exactly what constitutes the individual criminal conduct. During the trial, the prosecutor had to counter this virtual aspect of the charge in order to enact a 'performance of justice'. Specifically, the performance strategy had to compensate for the absence of a 'smoking gun' as evidence, the absence of direct victims of a terrorist attack, and the fact that criminal liability was not based on any personal or direct involvement in a terrorist event.

Evidence

For several weeks the prosecutors presented evidence aimed at proving undisputed aspects of the charge. For example, even though the defendants did not deny their membership of Gestoras pro Amnistía, the prosecutor presented the confiscated agenda of one of the defendants to demonstrate his participation in Gestoras meetings. There was no disagreement about most of the activities organised by Gestoras, such as ceremonies honouring ex-prisoners.[57] At the core, the question was not what the defendants did or did not do, but whether their actions constituted a crime. Thus, the questions posed by the trial were whether those activities were coordinated with the military wing of ETA, whether they had the goal of furthering and supporting the armed struggle and, if so, whether this implied criminal liability for Gestoras members. Proof of such 'coordination' or entertaining the goal to 'support the armed struggle' does not come in the form of a smoking gun. Instead, the evidence consisted for a large part of the expert testimony of police officers about the history of ETA, making the courtroom appear to be a history class.[58] Another source of evidence consisted of public documents—their content undisputed by the defendants—like Gestoras pro Amnistía press releases.

Further, the prosecutorial narrative relied on documents found after raids on underground ETA offices and after the detention of high-level members of the military wing of ETA in 1993, 1999 and 2001. In the main, they dealt with internal relations and structures for communication. The apparent use of code words in these documents (for example, Gestoras was allegedly referred to as 'Adidas') was interpreted as an indication that the communication was criminal in nature. A further source of suspicion was that some documents found at the Gestoras office in Bilbo-Bilbao were marked 'read and burn', which the police experts considered to be a characteristic of ETA communications. While the documents and police evidence may have demonstrated that the military wing of ETA was secretive in its communication, they provided no evidence that the content of the communications concerned specific terrorist actions. Given, however, that the prosecutor only intended to prove that Gestoras formed part of the ETA network, that was not necessary.

The virtual character of the offence, as opposed to an actual terrorist attack, created insecurity in the Basque left-nationalist movement about what exactly constituted the criminal conduct. One interviewee expressed concern that Basques might be prosecuted because of 'who they talk to in a bar'.[59] In each of the macro-trials the defendants argued that they were working above ground: they assumed that what they were doing fell squarely within the boundaries of the law. The switch to prosecutions based on the concept of an ETA network was often claimed to have been necessitated precisely by this perceived abuse, by members of ETA and their sympathisers, of legal spaces offered by the Spanish democracy. For example, investigative judge Juan del Olmo, in his indictment of a Basque newspaper, clarified that the ETA network

> takes advantage of the democratic framework and the establishment in Spain of a democratic *Rechtsstaat*, with a foundation in a constitution and a rights-based legal order and protection of fundamental rights and liberties. This terrorist organisation has thus generated a plural structure, legal and alegal, in which it has embedded instruments that are indispensable and serviceable for the strengthening and support of its terrorist strategy.[60]

The distinction between legal and illegal had thus become blurred since judge Garzón introduced the concept 'alegal' which he used to denote the space between legality and illegality. For example, the fact that Gestoras pro Amnistía did not reject the armed struggle was not a crime in itself. It was, however, presented in the courtroom in order to support the argument that Gestoras formed part of the ETA network.[61] Also, even though attending an honouring ceremony of an ex-prisoner is not a crime, the way in which the court construed it as evidence of ETA membership created insecurity among Basque left-wing nationalists.

Thus, the evidence for the prosecutorial narrative largely confirmed undisputed historic relations or public activities, which were interpreted as proof of membership of the ETA network.

Victim Organisations as Popular Accusers

The lack of a specific violent event also meant that the Gestoras trial did not involve direct victims. This was the case in all the macro-trials, where defendants were accused of ETA membership, not of a specific crime against identified victims. This stands in contrast to a trial such as that against two members of an armed ETA commando, during which a kidnapped businessman testified at length about his experiences throughout his captivity.[62]

This does not mean that victims of ETA did not play a role during the macro-trials. On the contrary, victim organisations were very actively involved. Representatives of one particular victim organisation, Asociación Dignidad y Justicia (Dignity and Justice), attended some days of the trial against the Gestoras defendants, one of them with the name of the organisation printed on his T-shirt, another accompanied by bodyguards because of death threats from ETA.[63]

The most important form of participation by victim organisations, however, was the employment of the legal instrument of 'acusación popular' (popular accusation). In Spain, victims of a crime have two formal ways in which they can assume a prosecutorial role in a criminal trial. A direct victim can claim the role of an 'acusador privado' (private accuser). Popular accusation can only be invoked by an organisation representing a class of victims. Popular accusation is the only form of victim involvement in those trials where there are no direct victims.[64]

Since the beginning of the 1990s, the Asociación de Víctimas del Terrorismo (Association of Victims of Terrorism; AVT) has employed the instrument of popular accusation in order to promote the interest of victims of ETA. A spokesperson told me that, due to the initial lack of government attention for victims of ETA in those early days, this was merely a way to ensure that the victim would be notified of the date of the trial.[65] Now the AVT and Dignity and Justice routinely participate in criminal trials as popular accusers. In all the macro-trials, the prosecutors of the Audiencia Nacional were joined by a lawyer representing the popular accusation.[66] Even though the prosecutorial performance lacked a direct victim testifying about a concrete terrorist event, the victims and their families were visibly present in the courtroom.

Selection of the Defendants and Establishing Individual Liability

At the time of the trial, Gestoras pro Amnistía had been around for three decades. It was a grassroots organisation in which many people were active. Picture a context in which many Basque cafés sport pictures of 'Basque political prisoners' above the bar and the balconies in villages are decorated with flags demanding the return of dispersed prisoners to the Basque Country. This raised questions about the individual defendants and their relation to Gestoras. Why did the prosecution select these particular people? And what did the trial mean for the criminal liability of all those who were or still are a part of it, but were not indicted? One interviewee, for example, expressed his surprise that he had *not* been indicted, despite his long record of commitment as a Gestoras pro Amnistía lawyer.[67] Indeed, he was amazed that among the defendants were people who had only joined Gestoras or Askatasuna very recently and therefore had little to do with the early history of Gestoras. He wondered if younger members could be held responsible for relations that existed in the past.

Applying the concept of the network to ETA, in combination with the charge 'membership of a terrorist organisation', had an important consequence. Once the court considered it proven that Gestoras pro Amnistía was an organic part of ETA, it only had to be proven that a given defendant was indeed a member of Gestoras in order to get a criminal conviction. Since the defendants acknowledged their membership in their opening words, it followed as a matter of course that they would be found guilty.

For the defendants, this contradicted the imperative that each individual was to be judged for his or her own actions. Still, the prosecutor strategically discussed details that showed the activities of each defendant to indicate their membership of the ETA network, such as presence during a specific meeting of the left-wing nationalist movement or attendance at an honouring ceremony for ETA militants. It was also argued that the defendants had specific responsibilities, such as territorial coordination for a given province (Gipuzkoa, Bizkaia, Araba or Nafarroa) or for special functions or fields (law, finance, communication, international relations, relations with fugitives or prisoners).[68]

The Gestoras trial risked becoming a 'virtual show' as it was not the adjudication of criminal responsibility for a specific terrorist event. The prosecutorial performative strategy seemingly relied on the quantity of evidence it presented to compensate for the fact that it mostly proved undisputed activities of Gestoras. In the absence of direct victims whose evidence could form part of the performance, the presence of victim organisations as popular accusers reminded the audience that many victims of ETA were interested in the outcome of the trial. Finally, the prosecutors paid attention to the particular roles and responsibilities of each of the defendants as they individualised the evidence showing the specific conduct warranting individual liability.

The defendants did not, however, view the trial as a 'performance of justice'. Together with their lawyers, they used the trial to justify and explain the work of Gestoras pro Amnistía. Doing so, they defied the roles ascribed to them as defendants on trial. Instead of defending themselves against the charges, they used the courtroom to communicate their grievances. Their performative strategies are explored in the next sections.

10.4.2. *Defendants and Their Lawyers Running the Show*

In response to what the defendants perceived as 'pure theory',[69] the defendants and their lawyers also tried to run the show. Claiming that the verdict was already written in advance, they explicitly rejected a juridical defence. Instead they chose to defend themselves 'politically', as they called it.[70] This section describes the performative strategies they employed to persuade their target audience of their narrative of (in)justice. The defendants did not bring any evidence to refute the charges. Instead, the defendants chose to use the speaking time allowed to them and their witnesses to express their grievances. The defendants subverted the proceedings and refused to play the role that they were allotted as 'defendants' in a criminal trial. They redefined the trial as a prosecution of the entire amnesty movement and used the courtroom and sideshows outside the courtroom to present their narrative of (in)justice. The sideshows are the topic of the next section. Here, the focus is on their performative strategy during the proceedings inside the courtroom.

The defendants coordinated their performance collectively. For example, during their evidence on the first day, each of the defendants took up a different aspect of state repression.[71] Significantly, the judge allowed the defendants to complete their speeches on this day, even though they did not respond to the charges or questions posed by the prosecutor and lawyer of the popular accusation. At the end of their speeches, most defendants said that they did 'not expect justice; the verdict and the punishment are already written. I will not defend myself legally, this trial is a farce and I will not participate in that. These are my last words.'[72] The defendants also posted online a declaration explaining their posture.[73]

The decision not to defend themselves legally was a departure from the performative strategy in earlier macro-trials. The defendants in those trials had taken the legal defence very seriously. This also meant that they accepted the Spanish criminal justice system. The Gestoras defendants decided to stick to their long-time criticism of the Audiencia Nacional and collectively rejected the jurisdiction of the court.[74] Their team of defence lawyers—from the Gestoras collective—supported that decision. In taking this stance, the Gestoras defendants came closer to the position usually taken by ETA militants who had always rejected any defence. After declaring 'I am an ETA militant and I do not recognise this court', ETA militants routinely asked their lawyers to be silent.[75] To avoid being associated with ETA just for this reason,[76] the Gestoras defendants explained their decision to their constituency in a publication in a Basque newspaper.[77] Gestoras's position did differ from the general attitude of ETA militants though, as these would not usually make the sustained effort to use their time in court for a 'political' defence. The Gestoras defendants deliberately staged a show to communicate their grievances. They chose not, however, to seek open confrontation with the judges or insult them: not out of respect or fear, but because the court was 'their playing field'.[78] One of the defendants pointed out, for example, that everything is filmed and the media can choose what they cut and what they show.[79]

The defendants staged a show by calling upon witnesses who represented their criticisms of the Spanish state, not witnesses who could disprove the charges. Thus, an alleged torture victim, Unai Romano, made a declaration[80] as did the relative of a judicially proven victim of torture by the Guardia Civil. Twelve other victims of state repression gave testimonies before the Audiencia Nacional. While the court allowed the witnesses time to speak, they were cut short and were asked to come to the point. In its verdict, the court rejected and discredited the witness testimonies presented by the defendants as 'biased'.[81]

The rejection of a juridical defence ignited a tense battle between defendants, their lawyers, the prosecutors and the judges. The defendants drew attention to the longstanding grievances of Gestoras pro Amnistía, such as the perceived illegitimacy of the Audiencia Nacional, the use of solitary confinement and the torture allegations. The presiding judge was not receptive to the complaints expressed by the defendants and their witnesses. Instead, she swiftly and snappily drew the boundaries of acceptable legal arguments and showed her authority over her courtroom. She also demanded from the defendants a respectful attitude towards the court, at one point telling a defendant to take his hands out of his pockets while he was speaking.[82] Thus, the trial turned into a competition for recognition and respect. This conflict was played out in minute detail, for example, as defendants with a perfect command of the

Spanish language insisted on making their declarations in Euskara, while at the same time publicly correcting the interpreter if they perceived a mistake in the Spanish translation.[83]

The judge thus excluded the grievances of the defendants from the courtroom. For example, she told a lawyer to refrain from using certain arguments:

> Ms. Attorney, [...] you can't say that there are convictions without evidence. [...] You can't be gratuitous. [...] You can't offend ... [...] I don't like to intervene in your remarks. Here we are not trying the Audiencia Nacional as a tribunal. That is not the trial.[84]

The attorney had to speak on the topic of the trial and the judge defined the boundaries of what belonged to that discussion and what did not. At a later point the judge warned: 'Don't talk about torture again, that is not what we are judging here.'[85]

Thus, the defendants and their lawyers tried to use the platform of the courtroom as a way to communicate their narrative of (in)justice. The defendants used their speaking time to explain and defend their activities as members of Gestoras pro Amnistía. Instead of denying the charges, they claimed pride in their work.[86] The judges were not receptive to this narrative. The performative strategy, however, aimed to reach a larger public through the media, a fact which is explored in more detail in the next section.

10.5. Outside the Courtroom

The media play an important role broadcasting the events in the courtroom to a larger public. But the actors involved in the proceedings also made additional efforts to bring their perspective to their target audiences in a variety of sideshows.

10.5.1. *The Media Show*

The media turned up in large numbers for the first day of the trial with at least eight cameras and twenty journalists.[87] Most of the press, however, only attended the first and last days of the hearings. The press in Spain has clear political affiliations which was evident in the reporting choices. Thus, the newspaper seen as closest to the left-wing nationalist movement (*Gara*) described in detail the evidence and grievances expressed by the defendants,[88] whereas other newspapers conveyed a different perspective. For example, *El País*, the newspaper most closely associated with the Spanish socialists, argued that Gestoras had chosen 'victimismo' (victimhood) and that the Gestoras defendants had chosen to present themselves as victims. *El País* called their evidence propaganda without elaborating much on the content of the expressed grievances.[89] *El Mundo*, a right-wing newspaper, concluded that the defendants 'showed the same uniformity that they, according to the prosecutor, imposed on the ETA prisoners as the leaders of the prison front'.[90]

While the media were the most official and constant factor in bringing the trial into the public debate, the different trial actors also engaged in 'sideshows' to influence public opinion in the form of press releases, public talks, demonstrations and petitions. Victim organisations staged their performance mainly through participating as the popular accusation. In addition, they commented on the trial in press releases and publications.[91] Also ETA reached out to the media. In its communiqués, ETA warned the Spanish state to stop harassing the left-wing nationalist movement in criminal proceedings, particularly mentioning the imprisonment of members of the 'amnesty movement'.[92] Most active in the strategic organisation of sideshows were the defendants. What follows therefore focuses on the efforts of the defendants and their sympathisers to persuade their target audiences of the veracity and legitimacy of their narrative.

10.5.2. *Sideshows*

Defendant Madariaga, in his last word in the Gestoras trial, said that 'any injustice creates an antidote which is solidarity. Solidarity is real.'[93] Indeed, the sideshows were an expression of solidarity. For example, during the trial, on 17 May 2008, there was a demonstration in support of the defendants in the city centre of Bilbo-Bilbao in the Basque Country. During the march, Askatasuna stickers were distributed and many people on the march put the stickers on their chests. In front of the march demonstrators carried pictures of prisoners. A newspaper reported later that more than 16,000 people had attended the demonstration.[94] In the speech of one of the key Gestoras defendants during the march on 17 May, the message of their narrative was taken to the target audience. The speaker emphasised that the struggle should be continued. If the enemy was chasing them in this way, it showed that Gestoras was doing good work. He compared the Gestoras trial to the trial of Burgos, a well-known example of a Franco show trial in 1970 against alleged members of ETA. He further claimed that the only difference between the trials was that with Burgos it had been a military tribunal and now the judges were wearing robes. Those defendants were executed; he said, 'we will receive life imprisonment'.[95]

As to their motivation to attend the event, someone on the march said that even though this demonstration might not change anything, '*hay que ir*' (one had to go). His friend commented that a demonstration with so many people would at least be mentioned in the newspapers.[96] Media coverage of an event can thus spread the message of a sideshow. This demonstration was just one of the many sideshows that were organised by and for sympathisers of the defendants. On 28 June 2008, after the final trial hearings, there was another demonstration.

Such sideshows sometimes lead to a showdown between the different actors. As both Gestoras pro Amnistía and Askatasuna had been declared illegal by judge Garzón in the preliminary proceedings and their activities suspended, victim organisation Dignity and Justice demanded that a demonstration announced by Askatasuna for 14 September 2008 should be declared illegal.[97] The demonstration was indeed prohibited, which subsequently led to confrontations between demonstrators and the police and various detentions.[98]

These sideshows aimed to elicit support for the Gestoras defendants in particular and the collective of 'Basque political prisoners' in general. Their enactment and the vocabulary for their messages were often strategically adapted to the different target audiences in an effort to maximise support. Different kinds of support were sought and given, including liberal support demanding fair proceedings and political support recognising the defendants as political prisoners.

Typical liberal support was provided, for example, by the Association of European Democratic Lawyers. Just before the trial started, on 19 April 2008, this organisation sent a letter from Amsterdam expressing its concern regarding the macro-trials. It denounced the entrance of Spanish investigators into the offices of defence lawyers, thus violating the right to professional confidentiality, and the extensive use of pre-trial detention.[99] The Gestoras defendants also strategically reached out for liberal support by inviting Martin Scheinin, the United Nations Special Rapporteur on the promotion and protection of human rights and fundamental freedoms while countering terrorism. He attended the trial for one day. Liberal support for defendants and prisoners is generally regarded as legitimate. A journalist of the newspaper *El País*, however, criticised international human rights organisations such as Amnesty International. According to him, their one-sided commitment to human rights is naïve and counterproductive when their informants are ETA militants. He called these human rights organisations 'Ambassadors of ETA'.[100]

While liberal support accepts the Spanish state and challenges a specific trial within the framework of the rule of law, 'political' support challenges the Spanish state more fundamentally, rejecting its legitimacy. The Gestoras defendants frequently said that the court could 'judge' them, but not 'condemn' them for their activities and thus self-identified as political prisoners. Many sympathisers from the Basque Country and Madrid attended the trial in solidarity with the defendants, accepting this identification as 'political' prisoners.[101] As a sign of their political solidarity, an activist group in Madrid organised a dinner for the defendants after one of the trial days.[102] They also co-organised a forum in Madrid with different speakers, including one of the defendants.[103] The trial was further brought back home to the Basque Country where defendants visited different villages to provide their target audience with an update. In these talks, the defendants explained to the audience, for example, why they had chosen to reject a juridical defence.[104]

The Gestoras trial thus provided an occasion for the different media outlets to make public their competing interpretations of the proceedings. This media show was complemented with sideshows outside the courtroom, in which the defendants and their sympathisers drew on a broad repertoire of support mobilisation activities.

10.6. After the Trial

The trial against the defendants of Gestoras pro Amnistía lasted seven weeks. Three months after the trial, the Audiencia Nacional issued its verdict. It convicted most of the defendants of membership of a terrorist organisation. The terrorist organisation in this case was Gestoras pro Amnistía as part of the ETA network.

10.6.1. The Verdict

In its verdict, the court clearly aimed to enact a 'performance of justice'. Just like the prosecutor, it diligently countered the elements that had the potential to turn this trial into a virtual show. For example, even though the court pointed repeatedly to ideological similarities between documents from the military wing of ETA and documents found at the Gestoras headquarters,[105] at the same time, the court explicitly declared that it is not resemblance in ideas nor the aspiration of independence that turns the actions of defendants into a crime.[106] Instead, the court argued that the shared struggle was expressed in a 'shared operation', with a clear division of tasks linked to ETA.

The court further made it clear that it cared about individual responsibility. Just like the prosecutor had done during the trial, the court emphasised the personal conduct that demonstrated membership of Gestoras pro Amnistía and support for the armed struggle. Proof of this was, for example, that some of the defendants had attended an honouring ceremony where two unknown people with their faces covered appeared on a stage and held a placard with the symbol of ETA.

To justify the selection of the defendants, the court drew a distinction between the leaders, who were indicted, and those who worked at the 'basis' in the larger movement for amnesty.[107] The court attributed to the leaders knowledge of the ETA network (but not of particular attacks) and thus *mens rea* (criminal intent) that those at the margins of the movement did not possess. In a clear example that mere membership of Gestoras did *not* automatically lead to criminal liability, the court argued that while the membership of Gestoras pro Amnistía of defendant Julen Arzuaga had been proven, there was no further evidence of his involvement 'in favour of ETA' apart from the 'exercise of his profession' as a lawyer. He was acquitted.[108] The court also recognised the distinction between individual criminal liability and membership liability when it adjudicated that recruitment for ETA was an individual crime and not a structural function of Gestoras pro Amnistía as an organisation.

In several instances the court thus specified particular reasons for accusing a defendant of criminal liability. At the same time, however, the court defended the logic that membership in Gestoras automatically created criminal liability. This was implied in its insistence that there was no need to go into detail regarding the ways in which specific defendants had participated in Gestoras and its criminal connections and activities as part of the ETA network.[109] Indeed, the court added that not punishing people only because proof of concrete action was lacking would amount to impunity, as then only those who engaged in the most visible activities would be punished.[110]

10.6.2. *Supporting Prisoners or Supporting Terrorists?*

At the core of the charge was the argument that as a prisoner support group Gestoras pro Amnistía fulfilled a function in ETA's strategy complementary to the armed struggle and in subordination to the military wing. The court's verdict decided how Gestoras's prisoner support activities contributed to the ETA network.

The charge raised the question which kinds of communication and coordination can be considered 'criminal' or constitutive of a terrorist organisation. It says a lot in this regard that no proof was established as to the most obvious forms of criminal cooperation. Unsubstantiated allegations of financial support were not even addressed in the final verdict, despite the importance of this claim in the dossier produced by investigative judge Garzón that ETA financed Gestoras pro Amnistía at least until 1991.[111] The court further judged that the alleged structural recruitment of new ETA militants by Gestoras had not been demonstrated. The proven instances of such recruitment were not an integral task of Gestoras within the 'global strategy' of the organisation and should therefore be prosecuted as separate offences of 'individual conduct'.[112] Even the facilitation of communication between ETA and its prisoners could not be proven.[113] Lastly, the court judged that it could not be proven that Gestoras organised specific days of street violence in coordination with ETA.

Four alleged functions of Gestoras, however, were considered proven by the court: (1) maintaining cohesion in the prisoners' collective; (2) signalling potential targets to ETA; (3) awareness-raising and agitation within the Basque populace; (4) delegitimation of the Spanish state. These four functions were further deemed sufficient to consider Gestoras part of the ETA network. The argumentation of the court will be discussed in slightly more detail.

First, Gestoras worked to keep the collective of prisoners together and to dissuade prisoners from accepting offers of rehabilitation in exchange for repentance.[114] According to the court, if Gestoras pro Amnistía really cared about the well-being of the prisoners and their families they would not qualify such repentance as an 'abandoning of the interests of the collective'.[115] Gestoras thus played a role in the disciplining of the prisoners. Such control aimed to prevent 'individual ways out', meaning that prisoners put their own fate above that of the entire collective and the future of an independent Basque Country. As an example of other forms of control given by the court, prisoners were not allowed to give interviews without the prior permission of ETA and certainly not about political subjects. The ETA leadership further sometimes took the decision to expel a prisoner from the collective, for example, when a prisoner had chosen to accept an offer by the Spanish state. Gestoras, as the guardian of the prisoner collective, would then enforce those decisions.

A peculiar second task of Gestoras pro Amnistía was found to be the activity of 'señalamiento' (signalling): pointing to potential targets for ETA. In the prosecutorial narrative, the denunciation of perceived state repression thus obtained a different meaning. For example, one Gestoras campaign called attention to the so-called 'judicialisation of the repression', criticising judges for their rulings. In 2001, ETA killed judge José Lidón after Gestoras had expressed such criticism. The prosecutor claimed that Gestoras not only 'signalled' to ETA to kill the judge, but also 'prepared' the population by providing a justification.[116] The court did not accept that the judge was killed because of Gestoras's criticism. It did consider proven, however, that Gestoras had the task of signalling to ETA whom to attack.

Third, Gestoras was found to be responsible for awareness-raising. According to the prosecutor, as the 'prison front' Gestoras had an 'internal' and 'external' function. Internally, it was responsible for prisoners and their families. Externally, it had to persuade the Basque population that prisoners were 'Basque political prisoners' and that their repression was due only to their ideological convictions.[117] When ETA members perished, they were portrayed as 'patriots' who had fallen 'in defence of the rights of Euskal Herria'. The court declared this to be a 'distorting message' and part of the ETA strategy of 'awareness-raising'.[118] Thus, Gestoras was said to have a function in the maintenance of ETA: because ETA members were depicted as heroes, new militants were always ready to replace the captured or dead.

A final function attributed to Gestoras was the de-legitimation of the Spanish state. One of the major 'tools' for such discrediting was found to be the allegations of torture in solitary confinement.[119] The prosecutor argued that ETA's 'yellow manual' obliged its members to denounce torture.[120] The court held that Gestoras's reports on torture did not represent facts, but rather fitted with ETA's claim that prisons were centres of torture.[121] Thus, according to the court, Gestoras executed ETA's strategy to use torture allegations to discredit the Spanish state. In relation to Gestoras's critique on the Guardia Civil's presence in the Basque Country, the court rejected the possibility that Gestoras voiced the opinion of a significant part of the Basque population. Instead, it was said to be part of a strategy to portray the Spanish state as repressive.[122] Similarly, Gestoras's criticisms that the Audiencia Nacional was a 'foreign' and 'exceptional' court were interpreted as part of ETA's strategy. Evidence of this was found in a passage in a document seized from an underground ETA member in 1993. The document addressed 'Adidas', the supposed code name of Gestoras pro Amnistía: 'We believe that we need to revisit our focus in relation to the trials: the Basque citizen is judged in foreign courts. We think we need to revisit the profound significance of not recognising the court.'[123] According to the court, Gestoras criticised the state in order to uphold the perception that there was a need for armed struggle.[124] Thus, the court dismissed all criticisms expressed by the defendants and classified them as instruments in a larger strategy ordered by ETA.

Ultimately, the court was unsuccessful in establishing the Gestoras trial as a 'performance of justice'. The defendants did not feel recognised and they as well as many of their supporters did not perceive a neutral application of the law. Moreover, they maintained fundamental disagreement about the legal interpretation of Gestoras's prisoner support activities. Many of the abovementioned activities are typical of prisoner support groups elsewhere. This makes the battle between the narratives relevant beyond this single case.

10.6.3. *The Aftermath*

A year after the court's verdict, it was largely confirmed by the Tribunal Supremo. Those who were not already detained were arrested to serve their sentences. In the eyes of members of the left-wing nationalist movement, the trial and the convictions simply confirmed the existing injustice narrative and the perceived 'judicialisation of the repression'. Outside the left-nationalist movement, this trial was simply one more episode in the macro-trials.[125]

Legally, the trial confirmed that ETA is a network. It also contributed to viewing terrorism as something that involves more than just guns and bombs. During the Gestoras trial, the prosecutor built on what had been considered proven during the previous macro-trials. These trials thus helped to establish a new regime of truth. A representative of a victim organisation emphasised that this was their significance.[126] The trials expanded the reach of criminal law to include socio-political organisations from the left-nationalist movement. The prosecutor's office and representatives of victim organisations further viewed the macro-trials as an important instrument to destroy ETA.[127]

Indeed, three years after the Gestoras trial, ETA released a communiqué declaring the end of the armed struggle.[128] Pressure by older ETA members in the prisoner collective had been a major factor in bringing this about. The fate of 703 ETA-related prisoners has since become one of the main issues at the negotiation table.[129] Already during the previous negotiations in 2006, the government studied the options of bringing the prisoners closer to the Basque Country and even considered releasing some of the prisoners.[130] Victim associations, however, strongly oppose such lenient measures.[131] On 7 January 2012, a demonstration in the Basque Country in solidarity with the prisoners attracted 110,000 people.[132] Thus, the battle between the competing narratives of (in)justice continues.

10.7. Conclusion

The performative strategies during the Gestoras trial featured elements of three shows: a virtual show; a show run by the defendants and their lawyers; and a media show augmented by sideshows.

Firstly, the trial displayed elements of a 'virtual' show. The charge was membership of a terrorist organisation. There was no mention of individual involvement in a concrete terrorist attack. The tasks of the members of Gestoras pro Amnistía were said to fit into a broader ETA strategy. The defendants were said to be subordinated to the military wing of ETA. Specific 'functions' of Gestoras—the signalling of potential targets, the disciplining of the prisoner collective, awareness-raising among the Basque population and the de-legitimation of the Spanish state—would promote ETA's maintenance and facilitate armed attacks.

The prosecutor's performative strategy aimed to compensate for the virtual character of the charges. Individualised evidence was brought to prove that the defendants were members of Gestoras, even though this was never disputed. Evidence was also brought in to prove Gestoras's functions. Thus, for many days, the audience was presented with evidence from police experts, telephone interceptions, documents seized from ETA militants or Gestoras offices, and press declarations. This evidence narrated the largely undisputed historic relations between ETA and Gestoras as well as public Gestoras activities. The trial thus raised two important questions: when does communication or coordination with members of a terrorist group become a criminal activity? And how would that be proven without de facto criminalising otherwise legal activities?

Secondly, the defendants attempted to run the show by rejecting a juridical defence. Instead, they used the podium to bring their grievances into the courtroom. For example, they called upon witnesses that emphasised the role of the Audiencia Nacional judges in facilitating torture by allowing for solitary confinement. This performative strategy turned the trial into a battle for mutual respect and recognition between the defendants and the judges.

Thirdly, the trial displayed elements of a media show. It offered different media outlets the opportunity to publish their narratives of the ETA network and the role of prisoner support. In addition, the trial event led to the enactment of sideshows. The defendants and their sympathisers drew upon a repertoire of prisoner support activities to persuade their target audiences of their narrative of (in)justice.

The Gestoras trial did not become a generally accepted 'performance of justice'. Instead, multiple and competing shows were staged in- and outside the courtroom. Because the Spanish-Basque society is so polarised, the show was run by both the defendants and the prosecutors (including the popular accusation), but each only for their own audience. During the sideshows, the defendants were mostly preaching to the choir, i.e. to their own constituency—a sector in society that 'fears the Spanish state more than it fears ETA'.[133] According to one of the defendants, the target audience was the 'Basque and international society'.[134] The prosecutors did not make any particular efforts either to reach out to the left-wing nationalist movement. Without outreach beyond their own constituencies, the trial confirmed pre-existing divisions and pre-existing narratives of (in)justice. The judges allowed the defendants the opportunity to stage their show and express their grievances. At the same time, they did not accept the grievances as legitimate and dismissed their criticisms. Obviously, the defendants and also the victims of ETA have a particular constituency. However, it is the tragedy of the Spanish justice system that the judges were not able to reach out to all parts of the Spanish and Basque societies.

Notes

1 Field notes of author during observations at the Gestoras trial, Audiencia Nacional, Madrid (18 June 2008). All translations from Spanish to English by the author.

2 Beatrice de Graaf, 'Introduction: A Performative Perspective on Terrorism Trials' (Chapter 1 of this volume).

3 The left-nationalist movement (also referred to as the *izquierda abertzale*, leftist patriots in the Basque language, Euskara) or Basque National Liberation Movement shares the same goals as ETA.

4 For a more detailed description of this transition see; Carolijn Terwindt, *Ethnographies of Contentious Criminalization: Expansion, ambivalence, marginalization* (New York, 2012). Submitted in partial fulfilment of the Requirements for the degree of Doctor of the Science of Law at Columbia Law School Columbia University. Available at: http://hdl.handle.net/10022/AC:P:14864.

5 Indeed, trials against members of armed ETA commandos continued in that same manner also in the 2000s, as observed by the author during the two-hour-long trial against 'Lola' and 'Kantauri' (11th of June 2008, Audiencia Nacional, Madrid).

6 The state viewed ETA as an opponent in a war (Fiscalía General del Estado [Office of the Director of Public Prosecutions], 'Memoria Annual'. 1979, p. 65, on file with author). Criminal prosecutions during the 1990s revealed that the Spanish government was deeply involved in the so-called 'Dirty War' between 1983 and 1987. In this period, the paramilitary group 'GAL' (*Grupos Antiterroristas de Liberación* or Anti-terrorist Groups of Liberation) killed 27 people (Calleja, José, and Ignacio Sanchez-Cuenca, *La derrota de ETA; de la primera a la última víctima* (Madrid: Adhara Publicaciones, 2006), p. 97). The judicial investigations revealed that government officials hired mercenaries in order to kill ETA militants who had sought refuge in France. See Paddy Woodworth, *Dirty War, Clean Hands: ETA, the GAL and Spanish democracy* (New Haven and London: Yale University Press, 2002).

7 Juan José Millás, 'Entrevista: Felipe González: "Tuve que decidir si se volaba a la cúpula

de ETA. Dije no. Y no sé si hice lo correcto"', *El País*, (7 November 2010), http://www.elpais.com/articulo/reportajes/Tuve/decidir/volaba/cupula/ETA/Dije/hice/correcto/elpepusocdmg/20101107elpdmgrep_2/Tes. Retrieved 11 September 2011.

8 The concept 'narratives of (in)justice' is a key element of the performative perspective which is adopted in this volume. According to De Graaf this perspective means that 'trials are viewed as a stage of *lawfare* where the different actors adopt and act out strategies with the aim of convincing their target audience(s) in and outside the courtroom of the validity of their narrative of (in)justice'. In narratives of (in)justice actors share their specific account of justice while denouncing perceived injustices.

9 Carolijn Eva Terwindt, *Ethnographies of Contentious Criminalization: Expansion, Ambivalence, Marginalization*. Colombia University Academic Commons (2012), http://hdl.handle.net/10022/AC:P:14864. Retrieved 11 September 2011.

10 This chapter refers to these organisations simply as 'victim organisations'. While there are also organisations within the Basque Left Nationalist Movement that claim victimhood, the organisations representing victims of ETA and their families were most successful in having their account of victimhood recognised in the courtroom.

11 Ostensibly because he feared the author was somehow affiliated with the defendants. 'Did you come with *them*?' he asked while moving his head in the direction of the defendants, as the author approached him to request an interview on the last day of the trial.

12 The Audiencia Nacional is the specialised court in Madrid which has exclusive jurisdiction over terrorism charges.

13 For an in-depth discussion of the legal reform and the provisions on terrorism see Mariángeles Catalina Benavente and Teresa Manso Porto, 'Combating the terrorism of ETA with the penal model', *Crime, Law and Social Change*, 62:3 (2013), pp. 269–288.

14 Article 55:2 of the constitution allows for the suspension of rights with respect to length of detention, protection of home privacy and secrecy of communication 'as regards specific persons in connection with investigations of the activities of armed bands or terrorist groups'.

15 Decreto Ley 1/1977 (4 January 1977).

16 Manuel J. Pérez Lorenzo, *Los Pecados de la Audiencia Nacional* (Barcelona: Arcopress, 2005).

17 For example, the Spanish lawyer Lorenzo disputes the interpretation of the Constitutional Tribunal. See Lorenzo, *Los Pecados de la Audiencia Nacional*, p. 38.

18 Interview with an investigative judge at the Audiencia Nacional, (Madrid, 12 May 2008).

19 Human Rights Watch, 'Setting an Example? Counter-terrorism measures in Spain', *Human Right Watch Reports*, 17:1 (2005), p. 17, http://www.hrw.org/reports/2005/spain0105/spain0105.pdf. Retrieved 9 September 2011.

20 For more information about the Audiencia Nacional and the Spanish approach to terrorism see Antonio Vercher Noguera, *Antiterrorismo en el Ulster y en el Pais Vasco* (Barcelona: PPU, 1991); Esteban Mestre Delgado, *Delincuencia terrorista y Audiencia Nacional* (Madrid: Ministerio de Justicia Centro de Publicaciones, 1987); Juan Moral de la Rosa, *Aspectos penales y criminológicos del terrorismo* (Madrid: Centro de Estudios Financieros, 2005); and Juan Carlos Moreno Campo, *Represión del terrorismo, una visión jurisprudencial* (Sedaví: Editorial General de Derecho, S.L., 1997).

21 Fiscalía General del Estado (Office of the Director of Public Prosecutions) 'Memoria Annual' (1979), p. 66, on file with author.

22 Fiscalía General del Estado (Office of the Director of Public Prosecutions), 'Memoria Annual' (2007), p. 161, on file with author.

23 Human Rights Watch, 'Setting an Example?', p. 2.

24 Field notes, Gestoras trial, Audiencia Nacional (June 2008).

25 Field notes, illegalisation ANV/PCTV, Tribunal Supremo, Sala 61, (Madrid, 19 June 2008).

26 Verdict Audiencia Nacional, Madrid, Chamber Section 4a (15 September 2008), p. 64, see also p. 80. Part of the 'Basque political prisoner collective' are also those convicted of collaboration with ETA, youth convicted of acts of street violence (*Kale Borroka*) and prisoners accused in one of the macro-trials.

27 For example, the director of Dignity and Justice wrote about the ETA network, D. Portero, *La Trama Civil de ETA. El fin está muy cerca* (Barcelona: Arcopress, 2007).

28 Interview with the Chief Prosecutor of the Audiencia Nacional, Madrid (May 2008).

29 Douglass and Zulaika distinguished between ETA as a concept and ETA as a structure. Joseba Zulaika and William A. Douglas, *Terror and Taboo: The Follies, Fables, and Faces of Terrorism* (New York: Routledge, 1996).

30 The list of crimes committed by ETA in 1992 in the Memoria Annual contains only armed attacks. Fiscalía General del Estado (Office of the Director of Public Prosecutions), 'Memoria Annual' (1993), p. 252. The chief prosecutor confirmed that in the 1980s the 'vision regarding terrorism was much more limited' (Interview S-21).

31 Asociación Dignidad y Justicia, 'Total de implicados' (no date), http://www.macrojuicio.com/implicados.asp. Retrieved 9 September 2011.

32 Fiscalía General del Estado (Office of the Director of Public Prosecutions), 'Memoria Annual' (1991), p. 197, on file with author.

33 Baltasar Garzón, *La lucha contra el terrorismo y sus límites* (Madrid: Adhara Publicaciones, 2005); Baltasar Garzón, *Un mundo sin miedo*, 2nd ed. (Barcelona: De Bolsillo, 2006).

34 Ibid., p. 297.

35 Personal conversation with the director of victim organisation Dignidad y Justicia (Madrid, April 2008).

36 Verdict Audiencia Nacional 15 September 2008. Euskal Herria is how left-nationalists call the Basque Country, which includes the Basque autonomous community, Navarra, and the Basque provinces in France.

37 Ibid., p. 47.

38 In 1976 it was called the Comisión pro Amnistía and in 1979 Gestoras pro Amnistía was formed. Interviews with a lawyer with Gestoras pro Amnistía and the Basque human rights organisation Behatokia, defendant in the Case Gestoras pro Amnistía, Bilbo-Bilbao (January and April 2008).

39 Fiscalía General del Estado (Office of the Director of Public Prosecutions). 'Memoria Annual' (1978), p. 114, on file with author.

40 Interviews with a lawyer with Gestoras pro Amnistía and the Basque human rights organisation Behatokia, defendant in the Case Gestoras pro Amnistía, Bilbo-Bilbao (January and April 2008).

41 Gestoras also published various pamphlets, such as Gestoras pro Amnistía, and Koordinaketa, 'Amnistía ta Askatasuna. Amnistie et liberté', Hernani, Basque Country, and EPPK (no date) 'PRES.O.S. Basque Political Prisoners Situation and Prospects'.

42 Of course, the definition of who counts as a 'political' prisoner is fundamentally contested. Political prisoners are generally contrasted to 'common' prisoners often referred to by Basque left-nationalist activists as 'social' prisoners.

43 Louk Hulsman, *Afscheid van het strafrecht. Een pleidooi voor zelfregulering* (Houten: Het Wereldvenster, 1986); G.P. Fletcher, *The Grammar of Criminal Law* (Oxford: Oxford University Press, 2007).

44 Gluckman, in: A. Norrie, *Crime, Reason and History: A critical introduction to criminal law*. 2nd ed. (London: Butterworths, 1993), p. 59.

45 G. Zwerman and P. Steinhoff, 'When Activists Ask for Trouble: State-dissident interactions and the New Left cycle of resistance in the United States and Japan', in: C. Davenport, C.H. Johnston, C. Mueller (eds), *Repression and Mobilization* (Minneapolis and London: University of Minnesota Press, 2005), p. 96.

46 D. della Porta and H. Reiter, *Policing Protest: The control of mass demonstrations in Western democracies* (Minneapolis and London: University of Minnesota Press, 1998), p. 18.

47 Armory Starr, Luis A. Fernandez, Randall Amster, Lesley J. Wood and Manuel J. Caro, 'The Impacts of State Surveillance on Political Assembly and Association: A socio-legal analysis', *Qualitative Sociology*, 31 (2008), pp. 251–270, there p. 265.

48 René van Swaaningen, 'Kritische criminologie', in: E. Lissenberg, S.V. Ruller and R. van Swaaningen (eds), *Tegen de regels III. Een inleiding in de criminologie* (Nijmegen, Ars Aequi Libri, 1999), p. 204; G.B. Vold, T.J. Bernard (et al.), *Theoretical Criminology* (New York: Oxford University Press, 1998), p. 213.

49 K.D. Opp, and W. Roehl, 'Repression, Micromobilization, and Political Protest', *Social Forces*, 69:2 (1990), pp. 521–547.

50 Council Common Position of 27 December 2001 on the application of specific measures to combat terrorism, Official Journal L 344, 28/12/2001 P. 0093–0096, http://eur-lex.europa.eu/LexUriServ/LexUriServ.do?uri=CELEX:32001E0931:EN:HTML. Retrieved 2 January 2012.

51 Europa Press, 'Detenidas cinco personas en el País Vasco vinculadas a la reorganización de Gestoras', *El Mundo* (5 February 2003), http://www.elmundo.es/elmundo/2003/02/05/espana/1044433135.html. Retrieved 29 September 2013.

52 After the suspicion was raised in 1989 that ETA kept organising meetings and planning attacks in the prisons, the Spanish state started the 'dispersion policy'. This policy entails that ETA prisoners are kept separate in jails all over Spain (and France). In addition, ETA prisoners frequently have to change prison after several years. It has been claimed as necessary to split 'hardliners' and 'soft liners'. It is criticised by the left-nationalist movement and families of prisoners.

53 Field notes (June 2008).

54 Personal conversation (Madrid, 29 April 2008).

55 Field notes (Madrid, April-June 2008).

56 Verdict Audiencia Nacional, Madrid, Chamber Section 4a (15 September 2008), p. 23.

57 Some alleged Gestoras activities were disputed. There was, for example, disagreement about whether it was a structural function of Gestoras to recruit new members for ETA's military commandos. In its verdict, the court did not consider this to be proven.

58 One of the defendants commented after the evidence of the police expert about the history of ETA that 90 per cent of what he had declared had been true. Personal conversation, Audiencia Nacional (Madrid, 13 May 2008).

59 Interview with author, Bilbo-Bilbao (June 2008). Many interviewees from the left-nationalist movement mentioned this as an important aspect of the macro-trials. In Basque society, it is not an academic question to ask under what conditions contacts with a member of ETA turn criminal. This question is on the mind of friends and family members of ETA members, but also of people who are not so intimately connected to ETA, voicing their concern that they may be prosecuted. Arguing the absurdity of simply criminalising contact with ETA, left-nationalists pointed out that the Spanish government also had entered into contact with ETA militants for negotiations, indicating that the mere evidence of contact cannot be sufficient to prove 'criminal' cooperation.

60 Auto de procedimiento, Case Egunkaria, Sumario 44/2004, instruction judge J. del Olmo Gálvez, Juzgado Central de Instrucción Nº 6, Audiencia Nacional, Madrid, Auto de procesamiento (4 November 2004), p. 3, on file with author.

61 Verdict Audiencia Nacional, Madrid, Chamber Section 4a (15 September 2008), p. 33.

62 Observations of author during the trial against ETA militants known as "Lola" and "Kantauri", Audiencia Nacional (Madrid, 11 June 2008).

63 Field notes (Madrid April 2008).

64 The legal figure of the popular accusation obviously raises the question of representation. Who does the Asociación de Víctimas del Terrorismo (AVT) represent? How much support do they have among all victims of ETA? How is the 'class of victims' defined? Surprisingly, these issues were hardly debated.

65 Interview with the spokesperson of victim organisation Asociación de Víctimas del Terrorismo, Madrid (May 2008).

66 In the macro-trial against a Basque newspaper, the surreal situation arose that the state prosecutor withdrew his case after examination of the evidence while Dignity and Justice continued alone to pursue its popular accusation. This is quite extraordinary and the right to continue the popular accusation without the backing of a state prosecutor was questioned by left-wing nationalists. On 15 April 2010, while most of the macro-trials ended in (partial) convictions, the Audiencia Nacional acquitted all the defendants in this trial against the newspaper.

67 Interview with the lawyer of the Basque lawyer's collective in the case 18/98, Jarrai/Haika/Segi and many others, Hernani (February 2008).

68 Auto de procedimiento, Case Gestoras pro Amnistía Sumario 33/2001, Juzgado central de instrucción No. 5 (29 October 2002).

69 Conversation with defendants during the Gestoras trial, field notes (Madrid, June 2008).

70 Interview with a lawyer with Gestoras pro Amnistía and the Basque human rights organisation Behatokia, defendant in the Case Gestoras pro Amnistía (Bilbo-Bilbao, April 2008).

71 This performance strategy was explained by one of the defendants during a public talk in the village Amurrio on 12 June 2008.

72 Field notes (28 April 2008): these were the words of one of the defendants.

73 On the website www.askatu.org. Altuna, Manex, 'Los procesados afirman que la AN carece de legitimidad para juzgarles', *Gara* (22 April 2008), http://www.gara.net/paperezkoa/20080422/74079/es/Los-procesados-afirman-que-AN-carece-legitimidad-para-juzgarles. Retrieved 3 January 2012.

74 Interview with a lawyer with Gestoras pro Amnistía and the Basque human rights organisation Behatokia, defendant in the Case Gestoras pro Amnistía, Bilbo-Bilbao (Jan/April 2008) and interview with another defendant in the trial Gestoras pro Amnistía and a previous prisoner because of a Kale Borroka conviction (Bilbo-Bilbao, May/ Jun 2008).

75 Field notes of author during the trial against 'Lola' and 'Kantauri' (11 June 2008), Audiencia Nacional, Madrid. Lola declared 'as you know, I am a Catalan, I am from ETA, I do not recognise this tribunal, I will not answer any question'. (She had belonged to the Barcelona commando and spoke in Catalan, but her words were translated by an interpreter). Kantauri stated that he had three things to say: '(1) I was declared a militant of ETA; (2) I will not participate in this theatre; (3) I ask my lawyer not to do my defence'. While he refused to answer any questions, when the police came to take him away, he voluntarily put his hands behind his back, to enable them to put on the handcuffs. This indicates a subtle difference between a selective refusal to cooperate in the trial as a 'performance of justice' versus a more generalised refusal to cooperate. A journalist covering this trial commented to the author that the trial was quite representative of other ETA trials. He added that sometimes they shouted 'Gora ETA' (Long live ETA) or 'lucha armada' (armed struggle).

76 Conversation with a defendant during the Gestoras trial, field notes (Madrid, April 2008).

77 Julen Arzuaga, 'Torres más altas', *Gara* (6 April 2008), available at: http://www.gara.net/paperezkoa/20080406/71266/es/Torres-mas-altas. Accessed 9 January 2012.

78 A more visible disturbance of the trial proceedings (e.g. throwing chairs) had been a topic of discussion in the group of defendants, but this was rejected. An alternative option that was considered was to maintain total silence and to refrain from the political defence. Conversation with a defendant during the Gestoras trial, field notes (Madrid, 29 April 2008).

79 This was explained by one of the defendants during a public talk in the village Amurrio on 12 June 2008.

80 For his evidence see TAT, *Torture in the Basque Country* (Torturaren: Aurkako Taldea, 2002).

81 Verdict Audiencia Nacional, Madrid, Chamber Section 4a (15 September 2008), p. 48.

82 Field notes, Gestoras trial (Madrid, June 2008).

83 Ibid.

84 Ibid.

85 Ibid.

86 This was explained by one of the defendants during a public talk in the village Amurrio on 12 June 2008.

87 Field notes (Madrid, April 2008).

88 Manex Altuna, 'Los procesados afirman que la AN carece de legitimidad para juzgarles', *Gara* (22 April 2008), http://www.gara.net/paperezkoa/20080422/74079/es/Los-procesados-afirman-que-AN-carece-legitimidad-para-juzgarles. Retrieved 3 January 2012.

89 José Yoldi, 'Gestoras opta por el victimismo: Los 27 procesados del aparato de presos de ETA renuncian a su defensa', *El País* (22 April 2008).

90 'Los 27 acusados de Gestoras renuncian a casi todas las pruebas propuestas por su defensa', *El Mundo* (22 April 2008).

91 For example, victim organisation AVT published a picture of a trial hearing of the Gestoras trial in its magazine, *El Mirador*, 2:3 (July 2008), p. 5.

92 See for example, "ETA no se cruzará de brazos ante el ataque terrorista a Euskal Herria", *Gara* (6 November 2008), http://www.gara.net/paperezkoa/20081106/105173/es/ETA-no-cruzara-brazos-ante-ataque-terrorista-Euskal-Herria. Retrieved 2 January 2012.

93 Field notes Audiencia Nacional, (18 June 2008).

94 Newspaper *Gara* (18 May 2008).

95 Field notes (Bilbo-Bilbao, 17 May 2008).

96 Personal conversations during the march. (Bilbo-Bilbao, 17 May 2008).

97 'Dignidad y Justicia pide se prohíba manifestación de Askatasuna en Donostia', EFE (3 September 2008), http://www.macrojuicio.com/index_noticia.asp?id=2121. Retrieved 10 January 2012.

98 'La Ertzaintza aplica mano dura frente a los proetarras', *El País* (15 September 2008), http://www.macrojuicio.com/index_noticia.asp?id=2156. Retrieved 10 January 2012.

99 Letter on file with author.

100 José Luis Barbería, 'Las "embajadas" de ETA', *El País* (1 June 2008), http://www.elpais.com/articulo/reportajes/embajadas/ETA/elpepusocdmg/20080601elpdmgrep_1/Tes. Retrieved 13 January 2011.

101 Personal conversations with people who attended the trial in support of the defendants.

102 Madrid (17 June 2008).

103 This event took place in the Club de Amigos de la UNESCO de Madrid (CAUM) on 9 June 2008.

104 The author attended one such event in the village of Amurrio on 12 June 2008. A small village of 10,000 people, only 10–15 people attended the event. Later more people joined; they had just arrived from Madrid, where the mayor of Amurrio had faced prosecution because of his involvement in the organisation of an honouring ceremony in his village for an ex-prisoner.

105 Verdict Audiencia Nacional, Madrid, Chamber Section 4a (15 September 2008), pp. 34, 55.

106 Ibid., p. 70.

107 Ibid.

108 Ibid., p. 22.

109 The court referred, for example, to a verdict from the Tribunal Supremo on 17 June 2002 in which membership of a terrorist organisation was further discussed (p. 69). The court argued that the defendants were akin to an ideologue of a terrorist organisation. See also p. 68 from the verdict and p. 82.

110 Verdict Audiencia Nacional, Madrid, Chamber Section 4a (15 September 2008), p. 69.

111 Auto de procedimiento, Case Gestoras pro Amnistía Sumario 33/2001, *Juzgado central de instrucción*, No. 5 (29 October 2002), p. 5. Instruction judges produce 'autos de procedimiento' which are the dossiers or judicial orders declaring the investigative phase of the process closed.

112 Verdict Audiencia Nacional, Madrid, Chamber Section 4a (15 September 2008), p. 54.

113 Ibid., p. 70.

114 Inspired by similar practices in Italy, in 1980 the Spanish government launched a project to motivate ETA prisoners to accept the rules for an 'arrepentido' (repenting prisoner). Even though in the beginning various prisoners did accept the proposal, ETA reacted harshly against some of the people who accepted such a deal with the state. For example, ETA assassinated the very well-known former ETA member 'Yoyes' in broad daylight in her own village, while she was tending her daughter. The anti-ETA organisation Basta Ya pointed out that between 1989 and 1995 the dispersion policy (and thus decreased cohesion within the collective) led 112 ETA prisoners to take advantage of the reinsertion-policy; 'La Dispersión de los Presos de ETA', *Basta Ya* (no date), p. 2, http://www.bastaya.org/actualidad/Violencia/InformeTorturas/Ladispersiondelospresosdeeta.pdf. Retrieved 11 September 2011.

115 Verdict Audiencia Nacional, Madrid, Chamber Section 4a (15 September 2008), p. 50.

116 In the case against Basque journalist Pepe Rei this phenomenon of 'signalling' was also discussed (Sumario 18/98). There, the judge ruled that 'signalling is not a juridical-penal entity' and 'alone it is not penally relevant' ('[E]l señalamiento no es una entidad jurídica-penal ...] por sí sólo no es penalmente relevante'), *Euskal Herria Watch* (2008), pp. 2–3. Signalling is thus not a criminal offence in itself. However, it played a role in describing the so-called 'organic relations' between Gestoras and ETA.

117 Verdict Audiencia Nacional, Madrid, Chamber Section 4a (15 September 2008), pp. 47–48.

118 Ibid., p. 86.

119 See also Carolijn Terwindt, 'Were They Tortured or Did They Make That Up? Ethnographic reflections on torture allegations in the Basque Country in Spain', *Oñati Socio-Legal Series*, 1:2 (2011).

120 Field notes, Gestoras trial (June 2008).

121 Verdict Audiencia Nacional, Madrid, Chamber Section 4a (15 September 2008), p. 50.

122 The criticism of Gestoras in this regard is part of a campaign called 'Alde Hemendik', which can be translated as 'Get out of here'. See also: Ibid., p. 60.

123 'Creemos que hay necesidad de retomar el concepto enfoque a lo que se refiere a los juicios: al ciudadano vasco lo juzgan los tribunales extranjeros. Pensamos que tenemos

la necesidad de retomar el profundo significado de no reconocer al tribunal.' (Anexo 13, tomo 34), in: ibid., p. 61.

124 Ibid., p. 49.

125 The media had covered more closely the case known as 'Sumario 18/98' which had lasted sixteen months, leading to the conviction of 47 defendants (Case Sumario 18/98, Audiencia Nacional, Madrid, 19 December 2007) and the case against the Basque newspaper *Egunkaria* (which ended in acquittals).

126 Personal conversation during the trial (28 April 2008).

127 Daniel Portero, *La Trama Civil de* ETA. *El fin está muy cerca* (Arcopress, 2008); personal conversation with the Director of victim organisation Dignidad y Justicia (Madrid, April 2008); Memoria elevada al gobierno de s.m. (Madrid: Ministerio de Justicia, 2010). p. 262, https://www.fiscal.es/fiscal/PA_WebApp_SGNTJ_NFIS/descarga/MEMFIS10.pdf?idFile=7124a2c1-d69e-44d1-8e96-1b05037f6f9f. Retrieved 1 September 2011.

128 'Basque group Eta says armed campaign is over', BBC *News* (20 October 2011), http://www.bbc.co.uk/news/world-europe-15393014. Retrieved 2 January 2012.

129 Mónica Ceberio Belaza, 'Las 700 "consecuencias del conflicto"', *El País* (20 October 2011), available at: http://politica.elpais.com/politica/2011/10/20/actualidad/1319144401_806536.html. Retrieved 2 January 2012.

130 Luis R. Aizpeolea, 'El futuro de los presos: "No es posible un indulto a todos los presos"', *El País* (4 December 2011), http://politica.elpais.com/politica/2011/12/04/actualidad/1323024854_010561.html. Retrieved 2 January 2012.

131 Mónica Ceberio Belaza, 'Las 700 "consecuencias del conflicto"', *El País* (20 October 2011), http://politica.elpais.com/politica/2011/10/20/actualidad/1319144401_806536.html. Retrieved 2 January 2012.

132 'Apuntes de una movilización nueva para un nuevo tiempo', *Gara* (9 January 2012), http://www.gara.net/paperezkoa/20120109/314235/es/Apuntes-una-movilizacion-nueva-para-nuevo-tiempo. Retrieved 12 January 2012.

133 These were the words of a sympathiser attending the Gestoras trial, field notes (17 June 2008).

134 Julen Arzuaga, 'Torres más altas', *Gara* (6 April 2008), http://gara.naiz.eus/paperezkoa/20080406/71266/es/Torres-mas-altas. Retrieved 9 January 2012.

11. Performing Justice, Coping with Trauma: The Trial of Anders Breivik, 2012

Tore Bjørgo, Beatrice de Graaf, Liesbeth van der Heide, Cato Hemmingby and Daan Weggemans

11.1. Introduction

The sophistication behind the attacks, the extreme brutality, the number of victims and the fact that 33 of the 77 people killed were under the age of 18, made the 22 July 2011 attacks in Norway one of the major terrorist incidents in the history of terrorism. Compared to other acts of terrorism conducted by a single actor, they were unique in their destructiveness. The subsequent trial was also unique for the Norwegian judicial system and court administration.

At the same time, this was also a highly dramatic and explicit example of a terrorist suspect's attempt to turn his trial into a theatre. In the 1,500-page manifesto that Anders Behring Breivik posted on the internet, he wrote 'your trial will offer you a stage to the world'.[1] In addition, the Norwegian newspaper *Verdens Gang* published extracts of a letter Breivik sent from his cell in which he stated that the court case looked like a circus; 'it is an absolutely unique opportunity to explain the idea of 2083 [the manifesto] to the world'.[2] He described the attacks in Oslo and Utøya as only the first part of his 'operation'. With his trial, or what he called the 'propaganda phase', the time had come to convince the public of his narrative.

This chapter elaborates on the different strategies of some of the main actors in the Breivik trial, particularly the defendant and his defence team, and the Attorney General and the prosecution's team. The main sources are Breivik's compendium *2083: A European Declaration of Independence*, an accurate word-for-word transcript of the court proceedings, the sentence handed down on 24 August 2012, as well as selected literature and media sources. The authors were also present in court during parts of the trial, conducted a survey amongst the population in- and outside the courtroom regarding their perception of the trial and the strategies of the actors involved and interviewed the main actors (but not Breivik himself).[3] One of the authors of this chapter (Tore Bjørgo) also appeared as an expert witness in court.[4]

We will focus first on the attacks in Oslo and Utøya, Breivik's early life and the events leading up to these attacks. Important information on this pre-history has been gleaned from Breivik's manifesto and other open sources. The manifesto provides valuable insights into Breivik's underlying motives and the pathway to his atrocities. Then, we will discuss the course of the trial. Thirdly, we will focus on what happened outside the trial; for instance, what happened in Norwegian society after the attacks and during the trial. How did the population in- and outside the courtroom respond to the performative strategies of the actors involved? We will discuss the extent to which the trial affected coping mechanisms within Norwegian society and what classical goals of justice were served by it.

11.2. Before the Trial (the Attacks and the Manifesto)

11.2.1. The Attacks

The attacks on 22 July 2011 were the most extreme manifestation of violence in Norway since the Second World War. The fact that an act of terrorism of this magnitude could happen in a small, homogeneous, highly affluent and stable society of five million inhabitants was for many incomprehensible.

At 15.25 hours a bomb exploded in Oslo's government district. The blast damaged buildings and blew out windows over more than a half-mile radius.[5] Closest to the blast was the 17-storey building where the Prime Minister had his offices. The explosion killed eight people and injured at least 209. At about 16.57, approximately 38 kilometres north west of Oslo city centre, a person dressed as a policeman asked a ferryman to transport him to Utøya Island where an annual youth camp organised by the youth wing of the Norwegian Labour Party was taking place. At that moment there were 564 people on the island. The 'policeman' told everybody that he had been sent there following the attacks in Oslo. But after coming ashore on the island, he opened fire, eventually killing 69 people. People panicked and fled into the woods or jumped into the cold water, trying to swim to the shore some 600 metres away. One of the survivors, who had been spared by the shooter because he resembled a right-wing supporter,[6] reported the killer shouting 'I will kill you all' and 'today it is your time to die' when he was aiming at the swimming youths.[7] The youngest victim was 14 years old.[8]

During the shooting the killer called the police saying, 'My name is Anders Behring Breivik, of the Norwegian anti-communistic resistance movement. I am at Utøya and

I wish to surrender.'[9] The police arrived only after half an hour on the landside. It took another 35 minutes, and another phone call by Breivik himself, before the first police ct-team came ashore on the island. Breivik then surrendered, was arrested and his 'operation' brought to an end.[10]

For years, Breivik had been planning the attacks. He claimed to have studied over 600 bomb-making manuals,[11] among them al Qaeda's tactics manuals (accessed by means of Google Translate). Breivik considered different scenarios for spreading his ideas. In the first instance, he intended to raise three million Euros in order to publish and disseminate his 1,500-page manifesto, '2083: A European Declaration of Independence'. After getting into financial difficulties, he embraced a much more violent 'plan B'.[12] This plan involved detonating three car bombs at different locations in Oslo (amongst these the government district, the Labour Party's office and the Royal Palace).[13] Then, if he survived the explosions, he would carry out a shooting spree. This plan was discarded since building a bomb 'took much more time than he expected'.[14]

Instead, he decided to deploy a vehicle-borne explosive device, containing a self-constructed fertiliser bomb, in Oslo's governmental district, close to the offices of the Norwegian Prime Minister. The idea was 'to bring the building down', to destroy the ministry office and kill all those present there. When this did not happen, he chose to proceed with the shooting spree at Utøya. Breivik said, 'If the building had collapsed then going onto Utøya would have been unnecessary and I would have driven straight to a police station and surrendered. I had thought of this in advance.' At Utøya, his goal was to kill all the leftist youth politicians present at the political youth camp as well as the former Prime Minister, Gro Harlem Brundtland, who was visiting the camp on that day.[15] His aim was to decapitate Brundtland while filming her, achieving maximum impact with his killings. However, the former Prime Minister had already left when he arrived.

11.2.2. *Manifesto and Motive*

Previously, Breivik had been a prolific internet debater, initiating discussions on the dangers of Islam and immigration. But only hours in advance of the attack, he announced his actions by sending his manifesto, written under the pseudonym 'Andrew Berwick', to thousands of people.[16] He disseminated it amongst sympathisers and people whom he had randomly found on Facebook,[17] and posted a twelve-minute video called 'Knights Templar 2083' on YouTube as well. The video presented an analysis of the imminent multiculturalist 'threat'.

The manifesto offers some insight into what motivated Breivik.[18] The manuscript contains a diagnosis of everything Breivik considered perverted in Western society, and at the same time offers a road map to overcome these ills. In his 'compendium' of documents, mainly composed by others, he first of all tried to demonstrate the rationality behind his fear of Muslim immigration. Islam, he wrote, posed a direct threat to the humanistic, Jewish and Christian cultural heritage of Europe, and European social democracy did nothing to prevent this, throwing the doors wide open instead. Hence, the whole European political system had failed in protecting the core values. Breivik then proceeded to outline a radical reform plan. In historical analogy to the Battle of Vienna of 1683, when the European powers joined forces against the Ottoman Empire and started the Great Turkish War, he proposes a similar campaign to fight the islamisation of Europe. An elite order called the 'Poor Fellow-Soldiers of Christ and of the Temple of Solomon', which he more often refers to as 'The Knights Templar', was to act as a vanguard force.[19] Based on the crusader myth, Breivik claimed to have founded this order anew in 2002, and devised it to act as 'leaderless network, made to be self-driven cells'. His Knights Templar were 'to defeat the cultural Marxist/Multiculturalist Alliance of Europe, seize political and military control of Western European countries and implement a cultural conservative political agenda'.[20]

According to the manifesto, the campaign consisted of three phases. The first phase (from 2009 to 2030) aimed 'to take the "anti-Jihad movements" to a second level, approach, cooperate with and/or merge with Christian movements and other cultural conservative movements (who agree on a set point of principles)'.[21] By means of 'open source warfare', combined with 'military shock attacks by clandestine cell systems', social unrest was to be fomented, leading to citizens questioning the state of their societies[22]—a classical right-wing 'strategy of tension' approach. The second phase (2030–2070) projected an advanced status for the Knights Templars' resistance front. Around this time, when 15 to 60 per cent of the European population would already consist of Muslims, resistance groups were to join forces with regular armies while preparing for 'pan-European coup d' états'.[23] The third phase (2070–2083) would culminate in the actual execution of multiple coups d' état. A cultural conservative agenda was to be implemented. Deportation of Muslims would be initiated, and category A (political, media, cultural and industrial leaders) and category B (people who have actively supported or stimulated multiculturalism) traitors would be executed.[24] Breivik described his envisaged utopian end state as a society bearing a resemblance to the—in his words—monocultural, but highly developed and progressive 'Japanese' or 'South

Korean' system.[25] Politically, a 'European Federation' should be created, based on national sovereignty and completely sanitised of 'multiculturalism or Marxist principles'.[26]

11.2.3. *Breivik's Life and Pathway towards the Attacks*

The manifesto also contained autobiographical sketches. Breivik was born in Oslo on 13 February 1979 and lived the first year of his life in London. His father, Jens Breivik, worked as a diplomat at the Norwegian embassy in London (and later in Paris); his mother was a nurse. When Breivik was one year old, his parents divorced and he moved back to Oslo with his mother and half-sister. He visited his father and stepmother frequently until he was fifteen, when the contact was broken. According to Breivik, his father 'wasn't very happy about my graffiti phase from 13–16'.[27] Breivik's father, however, contends that Breivik himself broke off contact.[28]

Although Breivik stated that he had not 'really had any negative experiences in my childhood in any way', psychiatrists concluded that he must have felt emotionally abandoned, and therefore missed an important part of childhood and adolescence.[29] In *A Norwegian Tragedy*, publicist Aage Borchgrevink revealed the conclusions of different reports from (child) psychiatrists who observed Breivik in 1983 after his mother had asked for their help. One expert noticed the peculiar way in which the four-year-old Breivik smiled, as if he understood how and when to smile, but without the actual emotional basis of joy.[30] Specialists also diagnosed his mother, Wenche Behring, as having an 'unstable personality'. She frequently hit her son, while at the same time sleeping in the same bed.[31] Therefore, in 1983, psychiatrists advised the authorities to transfer Breivik to a different environment, advice that was ignored by the child protection services.

At a later stage in his life, Breivik attended the Hartvig Nissen High School in Oslo where he was described as an intelligent student. During this period, he developed his graffiti skills, which led to an arrest by the police when he was fifteen. He also started working out and used anabolic steroids.[32] Since he was teased for having an 'Arab nose', he underwent a corrective nose operation when he was twenty.[33] In 1997 he joined the youth league of the *Fremskrittpartiet* (FrP), a conservative liberal political party known for its anti-immigration campaigns, and stood as a candidate in the local elections in Oslo. Breivik said, 'FrP appealed to me because I had experienced the hypocrisy in society first hand and I knew already then that they were the only party who opposed multiculturalism.'[34] Breivik was active for the FrP until 2006. He left when he realised that a 'democratic struggle against the Islamisation of Europe [...] was lost':

> It is simply not possible to compete democratically with regimes who import millions of voters. 40 years of dialogue with the cultural Marxists/multiculturalists had ended up as a disaster. It would now only take 50–70 years before we, the Europeans are in a minority. As soon as I realised this I decided to explore alternative forms of opposition. Protesting is saying that you disagree. Resistance is saying you will put a stop to this. I decided I wanted to join the resistance movement. However, the main problem then was that there weren't any alternatives for me at all.[35]

After dropping out from the Oslo Commerce School (1995–1998), he found a job at a customer service company before he started his own business in computer programming, allegedly in 2002. In his manifesto he claims to have expanded his firm to six employees and registered several offshore bank accounts. The money he made, and the funds he salvaged after his bankruptcy, were already at that stage intended to be spent 'on both writing the book and [...] the operation,' so he says.[36] All in all, he allegedly spent '130,000 Euros from his own pocket and 187,500 Euros for loss of income during three years'.[37]

Breivik also went travelling, and describes how he (allegedly) visited the opening meeting of his Knights Templar in London, in April 2002—a meeting that could not be corroborated by any evidence:

> There were only 5 people in London re-founding the order and tribunal (1 by proxy) but there were around 25–30 attending in Balticum during the two sessions, individuals from all over Europe; Germany, France, Sweden, the UK, Denmark, Balticum, Benelux, Spain, Italy, Greece, Hungary, Austria, Armenia, Lebanon and Russia. Electronic or telephonic communication was completely prohibited, before, during and after the meetings. On our last meeting it was emphasised clearly that we cut off contact indefinitely. [...] This was not a stereotypical 'right wing' meeting full of underprivileged racist skinheads with a short temper, but quite the opposite. Most of them were successful entrepreneurs, business or political leaders, some with families, most of them Christian conservatives but also some agnostics and even atheists [...] I was asked, not only once but twice, by my mentor; let's call him Richard, to write a second edition of his compendium about the new European Knighthood.[38]

Data from the customs authority confirmed Breivik's visit to the United Kingdom, but the existence of this network could not be proven by anyone.[39] Breivik also went to Liberia, by his own account to meet a 'Serbian crusader and war hero who had killed many Muslims in battle.' According to the prosecution, Breivik went there only to buy 'blood diamonds', and possibly even fell 'prey to a Nigerian internet scam'.[40] As for the other 24 countries, he allegedly visited several other countries (including China, Mexico, Malta, Cyprus and Nigeria), but not much information is available apart from his own statements. Flight records, for example, show that Breivik went to Malta with his mother for a holiday, although he himself claims to have gone there to study the forefront of 'Europe's defence from North Africa'.

In 2006, he moved back to live with his mother in Oslo to write his compendium while saving money for the attacks. During this period, friends testified, Breivik became more and more isolated, and addicted to Internet gaming.[41] Breivik indeed considered his skills at 'Call of Duty: Modern Warfare 2' as 'part of [his] training-simulation', while 'World of Warcraft' helped him to detach him from his 'old life', most of his network and prepare him for his campaign.[42]

In May 2009 he set up a new company, 'Breivik Geofarm', intended as a 'credible cover for [his] activities'.[43] Through this entity he would be able to obtain the supplies for the explosives he wanted to fabricate, such as fertiliser. Two years later, in April 2011, he rented a farm in a village called Åsta, about 2 1/2 hours from Oslo, to cultivate sugar beet. He started purchasing fertiliser, some six tons in total. During preparations he came close to the Norwegian Police Security Service's radar only once, after acquiring a 15-metre powder fuse worth less than 20 Euros through a Polish website.[44] The Norwegian custom authorities, participating in a transnational customs watch programme, sent a list of 41 names and suspicious money transactions (what the people had bought was not revealed) to the security service in December 2010, but this was not followed up.[45] In late August 2010 he went to Prague to buy weapons, stayed there for six days, but returned empty-handed. He then decided to register for a weapons permit in Norway and obtained both a Glock pistol and a .223-calibre Ruger Mini-14 semi-automatic carbine. According to the manifesto, he now entered the final preparatory stage, which lasted a few weeks, in which he read, wrote, radicalised further, collected supplies for the attacks, studied history, trained himself in shooting and learned how to manufacture a bomb.[46]

After the massacres in Oslo and Utøya on 22 July Breivik was arrested and taken, through angry crowds, to a holding cell in Oslo. During one of the first interrogations he called 22 July 'the worst day of [his] life'.[47] He furthermore expressed surprise that he was not being tortured. 'It ought to be introduced in Norway', he added.[48] However, he did opt for making good use of the Norwegian legal order and prerogatives. Breivik specifically asked for and got lawyer Geir Lippestad.[49] The reason for this is probably connected to the fact that Lippestad ten years earlier had defended the neo-Nazi Ole Nicolai Kvisler who, together with two others, committed the racist murder of

15-year-old Benjamin Hermansen in 2001.[50] Breivik had then followed the attorney's performance and he actually, by coincidence, worked in the same building as Lippestad at the time.[51] What Breivik probably did not know was that Lippestad as late as in 2010 was an active, leading member of a local branch of the Labour Party in Oslo, and as such a representative of the Cultural-Marxists that Breivik so very much hated and wanted to kill.[52] When Lippestad in mid-August 2011 told Breivik about his affiliation with the Labour Party, Breivik responded very calmly, without surprise or anger.[53]

Upon accepting Breivik's request, Lippestad himself received numerous threats. However, according to Lippestad, 'No matter how horrible the crime, a defendant has to be represented. This is just a vital brick in the wall of democracy, and I would say that 99 per cent of Norway understands that this is absolutely essential to a sound justice system.'[54]

11.3. The Indictment

On 7 March 2012 the indictment was formally read out to Breivik in his cell at the Ila Prison, just outside the city of Oslo.[55] After some debate and pressure from the Norwegian public, the director of public prosecutions also included the full names of the victims and the details of their deaths.[56] The statement held Breivik responsible for:

> Having committed a terrorist act in [...] bringing about an explosion whereby loss of human life or extensive damage to the property of others could easily be caused [... and] premeditated murder where particularly aggravating circumstances prevail [...] with the intention of seriously disrupting a function of vital importance to society, such as the executive authority or seriously intimidating a population.[57]

Norway had not experienced an offence of this magnitude since the Second World War, nor a perpetrator so fully committed to his crime as Breivik. The prosecutor therefore felt that 'new serious offences of the same nature may recur'.[58] The indictment further reiterated a forensic psychiatric statement from 29 November 2011 by Torgeir Husby and Synne Sørheim who had diagnosed Breivik as psychotic at the time of the criminal actions and during their observation after his arrest.[59] The prosecution adopted their conclusions that Breivik was suffering from the delusion that he was 'participating in a civil war where he is responsible for deciding who shall live and die, and that he expects a power takeover in Europe'.[60] Given this diagnosis, the experts assumed 'that a similar scenario might unfold in the future, and believe that there is a significant risk that people in the subject's proximity, like prison or hospital employees, may also become part of his paranoid delusional world and included in his homicidal thoughts'.[61] Breivik himself did not seem to have any insight into his illness.[62] Consequently, 'the requirement that he be judged sane has not been fulfilled',[63] and the prosecution required 'a sentence ordering his transfer to compulsory mental health care'.[64]

This conclusion became a bone of contention during the next weeks and throughout the period of the trial. Due to heavy criticism from many experts on forensic psychiatry as well as from experts on terrorism and right-wing extremism, the appointed judges decided in mid-January 2012 to order a second opinion, appointing a new team of psychiatrists to assess Breivik's sanity. They reached the opposite conclusion to the first psychiatric assessment, finding Breivik to be suffering from serious personality disorders but not insane. With two conflicting psychiatric assessments, it became up to the court to decide. Contrary to Breivik's wishes and strategy, it was not the attacks or his manifesto that was centre stage, but the trial gravitated around the question of his sanity.

11.4. The 22 July Trial

The extraordinary dimensions of the trial—the number of victims and relatives, and the global span of the media attention—took a heavy toll on the authorities. Presiding judge Wenche E. Arntzen admitted that the case raised both practical and legal dilemmas for the court system; the court had to acknowledge and illuminate the gruesome and brutal details, did not want to compromise the legal rights of the perpetrator, all while being respectful and considerate towards the victims and their relatives present. An almost impossible combination of objectives.[65]

The trial started on 16 April 2012, lasting until 22 June. The main actors present were the court administration, the defendant and his defence team, the prosecutors, the two court-appointed psychiatric teams, as well as the legal representatives of the victims. Expert witnesses, police witnesses, victims and other witnesses prepared their performance, and both victims and national and international media institutions were given a number of seats in Courtroom 250 in the Oslo Court House, or in a number of television-linked courtrooms in Oslo and elsewhere in Norway. Parts of the proceedings were also broadcast on national television—unusual openness even by Norwegian standards.

As explained in this book's introduction and elsewhere, terrorist trials are often more about the performance than the verdict.[66] This was certainly true of the '22 July trial'—as the court sessions were labelled in public, in order to avoid honouring Breivik's name. Public tension and expectations around the trial did not relate to the question of guilt (contrary to other terrorism trials), as Breivik's culpability was undisputed. The debates and often emotional interventions concerned rather the organisation of the trial, the possible behaviour of the defendant in court, and the plight of the victims and relatives. Public debate, however, focussed predominantly on the question of Breivik's mental state. Would the defendant be found mentally accountable, or would he be ruled insane, and hence sentenced to compulsory mental health care—a prospect that inspired quite some public indignation?

The trial attracted massive attention, not only in Norway, but all over the world. Apart from Breivik's evidence and that of his witnesses and details about the individual killings, much of the court proceedings were broadcast live. Only the newspaper *Dagbladet* offered a 'Breivik free zone', where a click on a black button would conceal all Breivik related articles.[67] The Oslo District Court had estimated that the trial would attract 1,000–1,400 people on a daily basis and built a new high-security courtroom. In the main courtroom 190 places were reserved for the victims. About 2,500 people were able to follow the trial via a live-streamed video broadcast in 18 courts around the country.[68] In addition, facilities were provided for about 1,500 journalists. The total cost of these arrangements was estimated at 76 million Kroner (€10.5 million).[69] Breivik got the stage he was expecting.

11.5. Strategies in Court

On 16 April 2012 Breivik entered the courtroom, clenched his right fist, touched his heart and extended his arm. The salute was described in his manifesto:

> The military salutation of the [...] Knights Templar is the clenched fist salute. The raised fist salute consists of raising the right arm with a clenched fist (preferably with a white glove). The clenched fist symbolizes strength, honour and defiance against the Marxist tyrants of Europe while the white glove symbolizes purity, duty, kinship and martyrdom. Using the right arm symbolizes the tradition of the 'Right Opposition'.[70]

Public prosecutor Inga Bejer Engh responded by walking towards him and merely shaking his hand.[71] Later that day Breivik made it clear that he did not acknowledge the legitimacy of the court. 'I do not recognise the Norwegian courts. You have received your mandate from political parties which support multiculturalism.'[72] He specifically denied the authority of presiding judge Wenche Elizabeth Arntzen, whom Breivik accused of partiality. Arntzen was close friends with the former Norwegian Prime Minister Gro Harlem Brundtland's sister, the same Brundtland whom Breivik had wanted to kill at Utøya. He however refrained from making a formal assertion. All in all, the first day already saw a number of highly performative strategies in the courtroom. We will discuss below the strategies adopted by the prosecution and the defence team, including Breivik's own performance.

11.5.1. *The Prosecution's Strategy*

The prosecution's strategy was threefold. First and foremost, Breivik's atrocious deeds had to be put before the judges in full detail. Second, justice should be administered as normal. And, third, Breivik had to be found insane and sentenced to mental health care.

The handshakes with Breivik initiated by prosecutors Engh and Holden illustrate the second point. Whereas international media reported it as 'a bizarre protocol',[73] a 'rare sight in the U.S., as well as in neighbouring Sweden and other Nordic nations',[74] Bejer Engh defended her gesture. 'My goal has been to treat him like any other criminal, and I think that's important', she said.[75]

The prosecution's first goal, however, was to do justice to the victims, their relatives and their emotions as well. Therefore, a highly detailed account of the course of events was presented.[76] On the first day the names and causes of death of all of the 77 victims as well as the names and the injuries of the wounded were read out in court by prosecutor Inga Bejer Engh. Parts of this record were repeated and included by the judges in the final verdict. Engh and her colleague Svein Holden described the horrible circumstances of the attacks in full detail: 'He shot at people who were fleeing or hiding, or whom he lured out by saying he was a policeman.'[77]

After that, security-camera footage and recorded mobile phone calls from victims in Oslo and Utøya were produced, such as the phone call Renate Tårnes made while hiding in the toilets and whispering to the emergency services, 'Come quickly [...] There's shooting all the time.'[78] Some of the victims and relatives left the courtroom; Holden himself later admitted that it had been almost unbearable to listen to these recordings. The prosecution asked different survivors and family members of victims to describe what they had endured and what the consequences of the attacks had been for them. Other stories were read out by the prosecution themselves.

The third aspect of the prosecution's strategy proved to be the most controversial. From the first days onwards, the prosecutors did everything to identify flaws and errors within Breivik's stories. By portraying his 'militant ultra-nationalist' narrative as a delusion, the prosecution wanted to convince the 'mainstream' Norwegian public of its point of view, while at the same time undermining Breivik's possible future martyr status for other right-wing radicals.[79]

In line with this, the prosecutors repeatedly tried to refute the existence of the Knights Templar organisation. When Breivik refused to produce any detail of the founding session of the organisation in London in 2002, Bejer Engh questioned the whole meeting:

> Engh: '[...] but what I think is important that you have in mind now is that you explain to the court what is true and how you have experienced it. That is what is important to get, not what you may remember and have told the police [or] not told the police, but you have to make a choice now to tell what you believe is true and how you experienced these events'.
>
> Breivik:—'Mm. But ...'
>
> Engh:—'This is your chance ...'
>
> Breivik:—'I also understand the role of the police, versus my role. It's not my job to investigate this matter. It's not my job to provide information that leads to arrests. It is the police's job. And I do not want to contribute to that happening. And another thing that I also react to, I know how you and Holden have put up examination, and that is very special, then, that you and Holden ignore radicalisation points ... [inaudible] that you have found the reason why this has happened, rather then you have chosen a strategy of delegitimisation to try to strip me [of my] credibility. Instead of trying to find out the reasons ... you see, or what?'[80]

Breivik's trip to Liberia, allegedly to meet a Serbian warlord, was questioned as well. According to the prosecutors, the only reason the defendant went to Liberia was to purchase so-called 'blood diamonds':

> Breivik:—'I do not want to comment on Liberia or London.'
>
> Engh:—'No ... Why did you try?'
>
> Breivik:—'I'm not going to comment on it.'
>
> Engh:—'What is the risk in saying something about this now, Breivik?'
>
> Breivik:—'No, well, I do not want to make your [delegitimisation] efforts easier. But I may well help to clarify points related to radicalisation points.'

Engh:—'We did a little bit yesterday, we walked a bit through it yesterday, and we can certainly come back to it later.'

Breivik:—'It is well that it is essential in this case.'

Engh:—'Yes, of course. It's an important part.'

Breivik:—'Do not try to ridicule me.'

Engh:—'No, not trying to ridicule you. I am trying to shed light on the matter'.[81]

These two quotations illustrate that Breivik did see through the strategy of the prosecutors, and resisted their attempts. The prosecutors put him in a defensive position though, e.g. when Svein Holden revealed how Breivik sold fake diplomas and degree certificates and how he lost his long-term job.[82] The question, however, remained whether Breivik really considered himself 'master over life and death' and believed in his own phantasies, or whether he was playing a game and following his own strategy of mobilising a potential core of followers.

Interestingly, Professor Einar Kringlen, one of the grand old men in Norwegian psychiatry who for months supported the first report, changed his view after seeing Breivik in court, concluding that he did not display any signs of being psychotic.[83] The first team of forensic psychiatrists who had found Breivik psychotic and suffering from paranoid schizophrenia did not change their assessment during the trial. When challenged by the judges on why they had not consulted external experts on right-wing extremism and terrorism when they, admittedly, had no knowledge of this, they stated, 'If someone had claimed that he was Jesus or Napoleon, we would not have seen any need to consult a theologian or a historian.'[84]

In their closing statement, the prosecution argued for a sentence of compulsory mental health care. They acknowledged that evidence presented during the trial could support the argument that Breivik was not psychotic on 22 July.[85] However, they reasoned that *the doubt* about his mental state, seen in the light of the existing legislation and practice, ruled out punishment, and so they called for compulsory mental health care. They argued that it would be far worse to give one psychotic preventive detention than force a non-psychotic to have psychiatric treatment.[86]

11.5.2. *Breivik's Strategy*

Before carrying out his attacks, Breivik was aware that a trial could provide him with a stage to the world. He wrote in his manifesto, 'If you for some reason survive the operation you will be apprehended and arrested. This is the point where most heroic Knights would call it a day. However, this is not the case for a Justiciar Knight. Your arrest will mark the initiation of the propaganda phase. [...] Your trial offers you a stage to the world.'[87]

For his 'propaganda phase' it was not only the attacks, but even more so a subsequent trial that would enable him to communicate with like-minded people from all over the globe. Illustrative of this intention was his request to wear his self-made uniform covered with medals of honour, portraying himself as a military war-hero.[88] Breivik did not try to 'win' the trial in terms of avoiding imprisonment—after all, he did not deny perpetrating the attacks—but used the trial to win over more sympathisers to his mission. He wanted to generate a 'maximum amount of sympathisers and supporters'.[89] The newspaper *Verdens Gang* published extracts of a letter Breivik sent from his cell in which the defendant underscored this point: 'The process looks like a circus with 450 accredited journalists from all over the whole world. I cannot say I look forward to it, but it is certainly a unique opportunity to explain the idea of 2083.'[90]

This was also reflected in the letter Breivik sent to Beate Zschäpe, who stood accused of acting as an accessory on ten right-wing extremist murder counts in Germany, in May 2012. The letter was intercepted by the authorities and was obtained by the German magazine *Der Spiegel*. It opened with 'Dear sister Beate!', and discussed what Breivik thought were the political motives behind the acts of which Zschäpe was being accused. In this letter he advised her to 'reveal [her] political motives to the population' and that she should use her impending trial 'to spread right-wing propaganda' as he had done as well.[91]

A Ruthless Hardliner with a Pompous Posture Meeting Psychiatry

For Breivik to use his trial as a podium he needed to avoid being labelled 'insane'. From the moment Breivik was arrested he sought to reinforce the fear that he had caused by his gruesome actions. He did so by claiming that two other cells were ready to strike and that he was a Justiciar Knight Commander of the European Knights Templar network; presenting it as an elitist initiative for militant ultra-nationalists against the Cultural Marxists and the threat from Islam.

Breivik did nothing to moderate this impression for the following weeks and months. In the first remand hearing on 25 July he demanded that he be allowed to wear his self-made Commander uniform, but this was refused by the judge due to the seriousness of the case and because it would be disturbing, provocative and offensive.[92]

His defence team, led by attorney Geir Lippestad, from the start had an agreement with Breivik that they would take care of the legal issues, while Breivik could do whatever he wanted with everything else, including the political dimensions.[93] Following this, the defence planned a strategy to go for a delusion plea that Breivik was mentally ill and not responsible for his actions, with compulsory mental health care as the outcome of the forthcoming trial. The defendant initially had no objections to this. At the same time, the court initiated a psychiatric evaluation of the perpetrator, and on 28 July the forensic psychiatrics Torgeir Husby and Synne Sørheim were given the task. Not surprisingly, the question of the mental condition of the perpetrator was of great public interest and it was widely covered in the media.

The two psychiatrists delivered their report on 29 November 2011, concluding that Breivik was suffering from *paranoid schizophrenia*, and that he was *psychotic* during the attacks and the period of observation afterwards. This assessment had a profound impact on the strategies of Breivik and his defence; as well as the Attorney General and the prosecution, represented in court by Svein Holden and Inga Bejer Engh.

For the prosecution, the report became the basis for the indictment drafted by the Attorney General, who concluded that they had no other alternative than to go for an insanity plea and that he should be sentenced to compulsory mental health care, which also meant that Breivik could not be held accountable or be punished for his acts.

For Breivik the report came as a disastrous shock. Even though he knew that the defence team was working for a compulsory mental health care verdict without objection on his part, he immediately characterised the first report as *the ultimate humiliation*.[94] This fear of being regarded as mentally ill is not uncommon in terrorists eager to communicate an ideological message. The Unabomber Theodore Kaczynski is another example in this regard.[95]

Breivik was outraged by the first psychiatric report's conclusion that he was a paranoid schizophrenic. In a 38-page letter he wrote that it was the 'worst that could happen [...] as it would be the ultimate humiliation. [...] Sending a political activist to a mental hospital is more sadistic and cruel than killing him! It is a fate worse than death.'[96] If he wanted to inspire future generations of violent right-wing extremists he needed to be perceived not as a loony who should be locked up in a mental hospital but as a rational being who was not afraid to rise from the passive masses and express a widely-shared belief. Breivik therefore requested his lawyer Geir Lippestad from now on not to plead insanity as a strategy for escaping a long prison sentence. On the contrary, refuting the insanity imputation should be one of the main goals of the defence.

In response to the first psychiatric report Breivik claimed that 80 per cent of the information regarding the interviews which formed the basis of the report was 'fictional, malicious or very sophisticated lies'.[97] He claimed to have found 200 errors in the report and questioned the integrity of the researchers, stating that 'their political views made them obfuscate the accounts of their sessions [...]. Their aim was quite clearly to create the premises that support the diagnosis they reached early on.'[98]

In addition to the first psychiatric report there were two other important factors that made a considerable impact on Breivik. Firstly, he was granted access to newspapers two weeks after the report, effective from 13 December 2011 onwards. The defence had collected newspapers from the time after the attacks and it is most likely that the news media's description of him did not live up to his expectations. Secondly, he started receiving letters from sympathisers around the world who made the point that an insanity verdict would destroy his chances of being taken seriously and make him only a parenthesis in the history books. So in a few weeks the psychiatric report, the media access and letters from sympathisers affected Breivik profoundly. As stated by attorney Lippestad, to Breivik the insanity issue now became a question about politics and not his own personality.[99] He therefore decided to change the defence strategy; a message that Lippestad received on 23 December.[100] It seems that the strategy for a delusion plea was abandoned at this point, although the defence waited to announce this fact.

Towards a Second Psychiatric Evaluation

The first forensic psychiatric report was controversial from the day the main conclusions were made public in late November 2011. The report was highly confidential but was soon leaked to journalists who gave experts, and later the public, access to it. The report and its conclusions came under heavy fire from two different groups of experts. On one side, leading psychiatrists and psychologists claimed that the diagnosis of paranoid schizophrenia and psychosis was wrong and not documented in the material presented. From another perspective, experts on right-wing extremism (including Tore Bjørgo, one of the authors of this chapter) claimed that the psychiatrists clearly had no knowledge about the ideological context of Breivik's acts and statements, and misinterpreted them as expressions of paranoid misconceptions, although they were quite mainstream among militant right-wing extremists.

In an newspaper article, Tore Bjørgo stated that the report reminded him of two Norwegian psychiatrists who went into the jungles of New Guinea to assess the sanity of the locals without any cultural knowledge.[101] Both Breivik's terminology and his world view were of a typical right-extremist nature. Lacking knowledge about this ideological context, the forensic psychiatrists misinterpreted many of Breivik statements, such as assessing his claims that he was engaging in a civil war as 'expressions of paranoid misconceptions'. Likewise, his suspicion that he was under security service surveillance, and the measures he took to avoid such surveillance, was interpreted as 'expressions of paranoid misconceptions'. However, in this respect, Breivik was more reality-oriented than his psychiatrists—he *should* have been under surveillance by the security services and had every reason to believe that he was. The psychiatrists relied solely on a psychiatric frame of reference and did not consider any alternative hypotheses or interpretations.[102] These points were later repeated and elaborated in Bjørgo's evidence as an expert witness during the trial.[103]

The fierce public debate and the professional disagreement among leading psychiatrists in Norway about Breivik's mental health led to an uncertainty the court was uncomfortable with. The judges in the case had also noted that the experienced staff at Ila Prison, who included one of Norway's leading experts on forensic psychiatry, had not observed any signs of psychosis. The judges found no strong arguments against getting a second opinion, and in mid-January 2012 the court appointed psychiatrists Agnar Aspaas and Terje Tørrisen for a second evaluation and report.[104]

However, this unusual move was not well received by the main parties, by the defence or the prosecution. The Attorney General and the prosecutors had already stated that the psychiatric report was 'very thorough' and had apparently committed themselves strongly to its conclusions. They saw no point in having a second psychiatric assessment. Even if it came to the opposite conclusion, the first assessment had already established sufficient doubt about Breivik's mental health state for the court to have no other option than to sentence him to compulsory mental health care. The defendant should have the benefit of the doubt, and compulsory psychiatric treatment was considered lighter than a prison sentence and preventive detention. Breivik's attorneys appealed the order for a second psychiatric evaluation all the way to the High Court, not knowing then that the result of the report would ultimately become one of their best arguments. The defence lost in the High Court on 15 February, and two days later Lippestad stated that they had abandoned the insanity plea strategy, and instead were going for a *criminally responsible plea*.[105] By the end of February the new psychiatric team had initiated a three-week long compulsory observation period of Breivik, who at this point had decided to cooperate, probably realising he had nothing to lose.

Another thing to note from this period is that the police team interviewing Breivik noted a clear shift from early March onwards in the way that he spoke about the Knights Templar and the compendium.[106] He altered the time when he started planning the attacks, he changed parts of the terminology he used and he played down the importance of the Knights Templar during police interrogation.[107]

In their report delivered on 10 April, less than a week before the trial began, Aspaas and Tørrisen concluded that Breivik was sane at the time of the attacks; in other words, that he was *not* suffering from paranoid schizophrenia and that he was *not* psychotic during the attacks. They found him to have a *dissocial personality disorder* and a *narcissistic personality disorder*, and concluded that Breivik was fit for a prison sentence.[108] This report was far better received in the media and among most experts.[109] Breivik was said to be 'satisfied with the findings and had counted on it'.[110] He felt, however, compelled to attune his previous 'pompous' posture to these new findings, as became clear during the first day of his stage performance.

Following the debate after the first report and the appointment of the second psychiatric evaluation team, the Attorney General and the prosecution *could* have changed their strategy. The Attorney General stated they would be open and dynamic in the process towards the trial, but stuck to the original path of an insanity plea anyway, partly in order to avoid a delay in the trial.[111] Critics claimed that the prosecution had put so much stock on the first psychiatric assessment and the delusion plea that it could not afford to change its position.

Breivik's Performance in Court

Breivik started his first day in court by making a form of fascist style salute.[112] He also took an hour for his opening statement (twice the time allocated to him), very much annoying the lawyers representing the victims. The speech was, however, not as offensive and far-fetched with regard to its content as what he had earlier produced for the police and in the remand hearings during the first months after his arrest. For example, he mentioned the Knights Templar network just once during the opening statement, clearly trying to play down its importance.[113] Later during the trial he continued to downplay the elite impression of the network, although continuing to claim that it existed.

In general, Breivik tried hard to appear less fanatical and 'pompous'—that was the word he used frequently—in the trial than he did earlier in the process, following a strategy that aimed to avoid being found deluded and sent to the 'madhouse'. He explained why he previously had used a more pompous style:

> If, let us say, you represent a group and want to communicate in a way that will optimise the propaganda effect, you communicate in a pompous way. Rather than telling about four sweaty guys in a cellar, you use other ways to describe it.[114]

He openly admitted that what he now said in court was influenced by the fact that there were four psychiatrists present in the courtroom. He wanted to avoid being sent to a madhouse.[115] He argued that the prosecution wanted to make him look ridiculous, and he got irritated when titles and uniforms of the KT network were brought up again and again, as he wanted to play down this dimension.[116] He also admitted that he initially *did* want to use the uniform in court, but that he realised it would be unwise due to the psychiatric assessment.[117] In general, Breivik stayed calm throughout the trial, also during the only sequence with some drama, when an Iraqi present in the courtroom threw a shoe at him, hitting his assistant defence attorney.[118] One of the few times he did seem disturbed was when victims and their families stood and marched out of the courtroom when he started giving his closing statement on 22 June.[119] Another rare occasion was early in the trial, when he was moved to tears as his YouTube film was played. According to judge Arntzen, his ability to keep focus actually proved to be beneficial for him, because seeing his performance and hearing him speak and argue gave the court valuable information as to whether he was psychotic or not.[120]

As described, the psychiatric evaluation and the fear of a delusion verdict were the main constraining factors for Breivik during the trial process; they are the most likely explanation for the change of behaviour compared to his posture during the autumn of 2011. We must also remember that Breivik had media access during the trial and that he could play to that as well.

In court, psychiatric experts testified and debated their findings. One of them, Professor Ulrik Fredrik Malt, told the court that Breivik did not appear to be suffering from the kind of delusions or hallucinations that indicate schizophrenia, therewith refuting the conclusions of the first report. However, he agreed that Breivik could not be treated as a criminal responsible for his actions. He said that he believed that '[Breivik] is suffering from something other than just political extremism'.[121] Hearing this evidence, Breivik was clearly insulted. But at the end of the day when he was given the opportunity to comment he said that he 'want[ed] to congratulate Malt with a well-executed character assassination. At first I thought it was offensive, but eventually it was just ridiculous.'[122] As with others who tried to validate his insanity, Breivik responded by questioning their professionalism.

Breivik lost much time and energy fighting the insanity charges, which inhibited his real aim, of presenting himself as a right-wing vanguard in 'the battle against Islamism and its defenders'. He felt compelled to upgrade his status as a political activist by calling upon different far-right activists as witnesses, like Tore Tvedt (Vigrid Group), Arne Tumyr (Stop Islamisation of Norway) and anti-Islamist blogger

Fjordman. Through these witnesses the defence tried to demonstrate that Breivik was not a lone lunatic, but indeed represented a broader current of political extremism.

It had become apparent that Breivik's strategy would consist of two intertwined parts. As described above, the psychiatric inquiry forced him to focus on convincing people of his sanity. But his primary aim was to convince as many people as possible to consider the plausibility of the ideas he had described in his manifesto, i.e. to convince others of the dangers of invading enemy Muslims and the ruling of spineless multiculturalists.[123] In other words, to be viewed as sane—by the judges but also by the general audience—was an important precondition for using his trial as a stage.

How exactly did he try to use the stage and reach his audience? A central part of this strategy consisted of repeatedly proclaiming the significance of the (future) number of adherents to his ideology. This tied in with his manifesto, in which he had constructed an audience, real or imaginative, to whom he could address his message. For example, Breivik frequently used the collective 'we' in his manifesto, and during his trial to refer to those who shared his right-wing ideas.[124] At the same time, he portrayed people he disagreed with as ignorant or weak. Breivik's narrative offered people an opportunity to belong to an alliance which would eventually win the 'European culture war'. In his final statement in court, Breivik once again appealed to his imaginary audience of potential supporters and sympathisers. With his statement of regret—cut short halfway through by an irritated judge Arntzen—he wanted to apologise to 'all militant nationalists in Norway and in Europe for not having killed more traitors'.[125]

During the trial, Breivik regularly illustrated this point as well. His statements on, and direct salutations to, the Knights Templar are perhaps the most prominent examples. This alleged secret and exclusive organisation, with members' cells all across Europe, would stand by Breivik's side and would be responsible for future attacks. In the letter to Zschäpe he wrote for example:

> If it is clear that you are indeed a militant nationalist that chose to contribute this way than you will be regarded in a lot of people's eyes as a courageous nationalist resistance hero who did everything you could and sacrificed everything to stop multiculturalism and the Islamisation of Germany. [...] We are both among the first rain drops which indicate that there is a massive purifying storm approaching Europe. And within the next decades more and more Europeans will acknowledge our sacrifice. Western European prisons will be filled by anti-communist/anti-Islamic resistance fighters like us. The treacherous cultural Marxists and multiculturalists will eventually lose

> this European culture-war. In fact, they have already lost, they don't know it yet, because multiculturalism is in fact a self-defeating ideology. We are both martyrs for the conservative revolution and you should be extremely proud of your sacrifice and efforts. Know your sacrifice is being celebrated in northern-Europe by tens of thousands of cultural conservatives.[126]

Breivik presented himself over and over again as the European hero who came to the rescue on behalf of a suppressed European people. He defended his attacks as the only way to prevent the Islamisation of the continent, saying he would do it all again, because he was 'trying to prevent civil war in Norway in the future. I and others in Europe are convinced we can avert a major civil war. If we wait another 20–30 years, ethnic Europeans will be in the minority'. In Breivik's opinion, his actions were 'based on goodness, not evil',[127] and he was acting 'out of necessity'.[128] Breivik acknowledged that the 22 July attacks were barbarian—but on only a limited scale compared to the acts of a future civil war as caused by Europe's inevitable Islamisation. He even went as far as to describe his deeds as 'gruesome but necessary'. He had 'acted against human nature', and he apologised for innocent casualties, referring to those without political connections. He also said that he understood the loss inflicted on the victims' families, as he had lost his friends and family after the attack as well.[129] At the same time, however, he did not show any emotion or remorse. During the first days of the trial, Breivik described his attacks as 'the most spectacular sophisticated political acts in Europe since the Second World War'.

Another example of Breivik's lack of anxiety in court was when he commented on the possible future verdict on the first day of the trial. In his opinion his trial could have only two possible outcomes: the death penalty or acquittal. A maximum sentence of 21 years would be 'pathetic'. The only exception to this posture of aloofness was his breakdown during the projection of the propaganda video he had made himself. When asked why he wept, he replied, 'Because I think that my country is dying and that my ethnic group is dying.'[130]

Although the victims' and survivors' lawyers received many messages of protest from people who felt Breivik's statements were extremely offensive, and despite the fact that the judges tried to limit his rampages, Breivik demanded to continue in order to explain his motives. His legal counsel Geir Lippestad, acknowledged the victims' suffering, and understood that they did not want the court to turn into a theatrical performance. However, the defence team did not inhibit their defendant in voicing his claims, saying, 'he has a right as a defendant in Norwegian law to give a statement, and also a human right'.[131]

In his final statement Breivik again reiterated that he did not recognise the court because of its 'mandate from political parties that support multiculturalism'. He added that:

> By discarding my allegations of the principle of necessity and sentencing a representative of the Norwegian resistance movement you have sided with the multicultural majority in parliament and therefore you also expressed support for the multiculturalist ideology. Since I do not recognise this court I cannot legitimize the Oslo district court by accepting this sentence. In my view this sentence and judgment is illegitimate and at the same time I cannot appeal against the judgment because by appealing I would legitimize the court.[132]

Based on his statements and behaviour in court, Breivik's performative strategy was to rebel against the Norwegian judicial system in which he was forced to participate by means of his own trial. It seems clear therefore that delegitimising this system had become an integral part of his right-wing extremist communications.

Breivik's Strategy: A 'Self-evaluation'

After describing some features of the trial, it is interesting to have a look at what Breivik wrote in his compendium about trial proceedings and defence attorneys. There he states that a trial is an excellent opportunity and a well-suited arena the Justiciar Knight can use to propagate his case.[133] As such, he clearly sees the court as a theatre, where the defendant is playing the key role with a unique opportunity to present his ideology and views to a wider audience. In the compendium, Breivik is quite detailed about how the defendant should behave and present demands to the court, presenting the audience with a given scenario, and in so doing prepare both enemies and the public for what lies ahead, in what he describes as a not too distant future.[134] He especially gives a great deal of attention to the opening statement and the closing statement, and he provides ready-to-use scripts that any ultra-nationalist could use if arrested.[135]

Breivik also devoted more than two pages to finding the right defence attorney for a trial, stressing that the defendant should reject any appointed public attorney and search for a patriotic-oriented one.[136] He lists three primary tasks with regard to what to expect from a well-suited defence attorney:[137]

1. Willingness to facilitate you logistically.
2. Willingness to facilitate you ideologically.
3. Willingness to facilitate you to build a case against the regime.

As described, Breivik's priority was to find a lawyer who shared his ideas and ideology, rather than focusing on professional skills. He acknowledged that finding such a lawyer might be difficult, but emphasised that it was absolutely necessary in order to achieve a proper defence.

This begs the question: did Breivik himself act in accordance with the compendium? In some ways he did and in some ways he did not. First of all, even after declaring that he did not recognise the legitimacy of the court in itself, the defendant gave a great deal of attention to the proceedings, was well prepared for the meetings, following every sequence closely and made use of his right to comment on statements made by witnesses and expert witnesses. He used the opening and closing statement rounds as expected, but the content was not the same as in the compendium, but rather adjusted to his situation. As such, the static and descriptive nature of the manuscripts in the compendium did not work, due to the dynamics of the trial. It is like wars, they tend to take on a life of their own when first set in motion. Likewise, he did not foresee that he would have to concentrate on avoiding a delusion verdict, and this constrained him significantly in court.

Secondly, Breivik also recommended in his compendium appointing a defence attorney who endorses the defendant's political agenda. Indeed, Lippestad performed his duty as a defence attorney in a highly professional manner, actually receiving a good deal of public credit for his handling of the difficult task, even from the surviving victims and family members. Very much so because he did not defend the actions of the perpetrator, but focused on his legal rights in a clinical fashion, in order to uphold the values of a society governed by law and justice—precisely the values Breivik tried to defeat. In other words, Breivik did not at all get the collaborating type of lawyer he described and recommended in his compendium. The only thing that really corresponded is that he could choose his own lawyer, but the irony was, as mentioned earlier, that Lippestad turned out to be an active member of the Labour Party.

Another irony: one of Breivik's first demands when he was arrested at Utøya was that torture and the death penalty should be reinstated in Norway. A couple of months after he started serving his prison term, he complained about the prison conditions, among other things that he had to write with a soft rubber pen. According to him, this pen he was given was 'an almost indescribable manifestation of sadism', and that it represented a breach of the European Convention on Human Rights and the UN Convention against Torture.[138]

11.5.3. *The Verdict*

As for the court itself, presiding judge Arntzen kept the leash tight from day one, signalling authority over the courtroom and the parties. She continued to do so for the duration of the trial and succeeded in keeping an independent and objective position, not afraid of correcting or asking critical questions to any of the parties involved, including correcting the media. Her firm and focused performance probably contributed to the public acceptance of the trial process and final verdict and sentencing as being just and credible.

The court found Breivik guilty of the attacks carried out on 22 July. He was sentenced to 21 years' preventive detention in August 2012, with 10 years minimum. In practice this sentence of 21 years may mean that Breivik will be in prison for the rest of his life. His sentence will be reviewed for the first time after ten years but could last his life out (*forvaring*: preventive detention) if he is still deemed to be a danger to society, in which case a sentence can be extended every five years. There is no limit to the number of times the five-year timeframe can be extended. In general, detention can be prolonged by an unlimited number of additional five-year periods as long as the court finds that the convicted person still constitutes a danger to society. In the end, Anders Behring Breivik got the result he hoped for, as his status as a political militant was confirmed, and he avoided the 'madhouse' he feared. It was not an option for him to appeal, since he would then risk a different outcome in a subsequent trial. Accordingly, he had to forego a second chance to hold an ideological show-down in court.

11.6. Outside the Courtroom and the Aftermath of the Trial

De Graaf has argued that terrorism trials offer an exceptional opportunity for understanding and countering terrorism, because they are the only place where all actors involved meet: terrorists, state representatives, the judiciary, the audience, surviving victims, terrorist sympathisers, etc.[139] Furthermore, the media will analyse and broadcast their performances. As a nexus of terrorism violence, law enforcement and public opinion, terrorism trials thus offer an ideal opportunity to showcase justice in progress and demonstrate how the laws of the country deal with terrorist suspects. A trial provides a theatre, inviting various actors to play out their roles and convince and mobilise the public to advance their narratives of (in)justice.

The judicial objectives refer to the classic principles of a fair trial: doing justice and upholding the rule of law, as laid down in the two penal goals of 1) rehabilitation, 2) prevention[140]—and the three informal goals of a trial: 3) truth finding, 4) re-establishing stability in society and restoring the democratic rule of law and 5) providing the need for closure. There are many reasons for this research to focus on the 'performative effect'—particularly the various performances of the actors in the courtroom—on public opinion. Breivik's trial provided him with a global stage and was a media spectacle which involved and mobilised many Norwegians as well as spectators abroad.

It would therefore be relevant not only to map the strategies of different actors, but also to investigate how these strategies affected the coping mechanisms in society. Coping is defined as the thoughts and behaviour that people use to manage the internal and external demands of situations that are appraised as stressful.[141] Coping is a complex, multidimensional process that is sensitive to the environment and its demands and resources, to personality dispositions that influence the appraisal of stress and resources for coping, and the relationship between these. A trial is thought to assist coping mechanisms as it is a means of truth finding; it also helps to re-establish stability and helps those involved to come to terms with the legal offence perpetrated. It is thus justified to explore how a trial like this affects coping mechanisms within the public domain. The Breivik trial is an excellent example to test this hypothesis as it was clear from the start what happened, how it happened and who the perpetrator was. For research purposes, the public space was narrowed down to the participants present in and around the courtroom in Oslo during the days before and after the trial.[142]

First, for this chapter, quantitative research was undertaken by distributing surveys inquiring about people's opinions and attitudes towards the Breivik trial. The surveys were distributed on the streets of Oslo for two days, 23 and 25 August 2012, the day before and the day after the final verdict in the trial.[143] The total number of respondents was 246 of which 124 (50 per cent) were female and 91 (37 per cent) were male (the remaining 13 per cent did not specify gender). The participants' average age was 30 and they were approached at several locations: in a central square in Oslo, at a subway station, at the central railway station, in a mall, in a park and on the campus of Oslo University. Qualitative interviews with parties directly involved in the trial, such as victims, expert witnesses, members of the 22 July Commission,[144] which was set up to review and learn from the attacks, and journalists were also conducted. We selected these respondents based upon their expertise either from our own networks or via a snowball-sampling methodology. During these interviews, a number of general questions relating to the strategies in court and the effects of the trial on society were asked.

Those surveyed were asked to indicate whether they were present at Utøya or in Oslo or whether they knew friends/family who were present (most involved) or whether they learned about the attacks through the media (least involved) to establish their level of involvement. The results indicate how intensely penetrating the Breivik attacks were for the respondents in our sample. But also from a macro perspective: a country with a relatively small population (5 million) had to deal with so many people being killed (77) or injured (242) in the attacks. The responses indicate that many people in our sample personally knew someone who was present at and/or suffered as a result of the attacks.

11.6.1. *Perceptions regarding the Prosecution's Strategy*

The respondents in our sample did not appear to accept the prosecution's insanity plea strategy: a large proportion of the respondents disagreed with the idea that Breivik should receive psychiatric treatment instead of a prison sentence (see table 11.1).

	Agree	Disagree
I believe Breivik is sane.	24 per cent	42 per cent
I believe Breivik is accountable.	60 per cent	30 per cent
I agree with the prosecution's strategy	16 per cent	59 per cent

Table 11.1. Opinion on Breivik's sanity/Accountability

In an interview with journalist Ben McPherson, editor of the newspaper *The Foreigner*, prosecutor Bejer Engh responded to this public sentiment by saying that she understood that people had strong feelings about how to react to Breivik, but that the prosecution's strategy needed to relate to the Norwegian legal framework: 'Otherwise he's won. And you know, he wanted to change Norwegian society and I'm sure he'd feel it was a victory if we gave up our principles. Right at the moment we're being tested—can we hold on to our principles?'[145] She also suggested that even though many

Norwegians disagreed with the prosecutors about how Breivik should be punished, that should not influence their work, saying, 'then we could just as easily have put it to a public vote'.[146] Therefore, selling this idea to the public had become a part of the strategy. Bejer Engh, one of the prosecutors, argued, 'We have murderers who have been sentenced to a psychiatric facility who will probably never get out again.'[147] The prosecutors, however, also emphasised that they were committed to human rights and that serious doubt as to a defendant's mental health should not lead to a prison sentence. The prosecution thus stuck to their argument that Breivik was a delusional lone operator and should be convicted accordingly.

The prosecutors felt that they had sufficiently responded to the victims' needs and the gravity of the attacks by positioning the victims' stories centrally in their arguments. Although 59 per cent of the respondents did not agree with the prosecutors' final argument (the insanity plea), an impressive 74 per cent of the participants surveyed indicated they felt the general prosecutors functioned well.

In short, when relating the prosecution's strategy back to the goals of a fair trial, it can be argued that the prosecution adhered to the goal of truth finding, spending much time reconstructing Breivik's crimes. Concerning the goal of retribution, an interesting tension emerged: in a way, trying to have Breivik declared insane and sent to a mental institution would have been 'the ultimate humiliation', as Breivik himself admitted. Thus, the insanity strategy could have served the goal of retribution in the sense that Breivik would have received exactly what he did not want. However, Norwegian society strongly objected to the insanity claim and most people felt Breivik knew exactly what he was doing when he carried out his acts and therefore deserved the longest sentence possible, carrying full responsibility for his actions. As for the goal of restoring social peace, the prosecution seemed not to consider this, given the widespread objection in Norwegian society to the insanity plea strategy. However, regarding the goal of upholding the democratic rule of law, the prosecution's adherence to fair trial standards was shared and respected by the majority of the respondents in our sample. In the end, the collective feeling was that despite the prosecution's strategy, the trial itself and the way in which Breivik was treated were the ultimate counter-narrative to Breivik's acts of violence.

11.6.2. Perception of Breivik's Strategy

The survey asked participants whether they thought the media paid too much, enough or too little attention to Breivik during the. The results (see table 11.2) indicate that most people in this research felt that the media paid enough attention to Breivik's perspective. Nonetheless, almost a third of respondents felt they paid too much attention to his perspective.

The media paid ...	
Too little attention	0 per cent
Little attention	2 per cent
Enough attention	32 per cent
Much attention	35 per cent
Too much attention	31 per cent

Table 11.2. Opinion on the media attention to Breivik's perspective

One specific response to Breivik's performative strategy was the reaction of the public in the square in front of the court building. During the trial, many people gathered to sing the Rainbow Song,[148] a song that Breivik had referred to in court as an example of how Norwegian students were being brainwashed by Marxist propaganda.[149] Displays of collective mourning and the direct response by the general public to Breivik's statements during the trial also demonstrated the involvement of the Norwegian public in the trial. This could be interpreted as society trying to send a message to the government, Breivik and his possible (future) followers. It seemed to stress, in line with the argument put forward by Prime Minister Jens Stoltenberg, the need for a democratic response to the attacks. Similarly, the survey indicated that respondents wanted a structured and inclusive debate about the Norwegian democratic system and refuted the exclusion of certain extremist groups from society or from public debate.

Breivik's aim to use the trial to further his own extremist motives was recognised by the public present in and outside the courtroom. Throughout the trial, the amount of time Breivik was given to make his own statements was a contested issue in the Norwegian media. The discussion centred on the possible effect: it could both inspire and put off potential followers or adherents to right-wing extremism. The copycat effect of Breivik's performative strategy became apparent in the aftermath of the trial when a series of events were in one way or another connected to Breivik. First of all, Breivik's manifesto was translated into many languages, including Russian, Dutch and German. Also, 13 months after Breivik's attacks, a 'Russian Breivik' was arrested in Moscow for shooting and killing six colleagues and releasing a hate manifesto online.[150] Only a week later, a 29-year-old man in the Czech Republic was charged over a Breivik-style plot, using the name Breivik online and planning a major attack with explosives.[151] In November of that same year, Polish authorities arrested a radical nationalist who was planning to blow up the Polish parliament building and who linked himself to Breivik.[152]

Finally, Breivik received many love letters,[153] as well as correspondence and drawings from children.[154] In a letter he wrote to Tania, a woman who had written to him, he says, 'A lot of people around the world have expressed their support for me, in summary, I have received over 250 letters, most of which are bills, LOL [laughing out loud, social media speak]. About 60% of the letters is positive, 10% is from people who want me to find Jesus, and 30% from those who hate me.'[155]

However, overall it seems Breivik's propaganda has led to different outcomes. Major newspapers rejected his articles, and several anti-Islamic ideologues he admired, such as Peder Are Nøstvold Jensen (known as Fjordman), refused his proposals for cooperation.[156] Also, rather than inspiring a new generation of followers or sparking a far-right-extremist revolution in Europe, his public performance during the trial appears to have had the opposite effect. Although European white nationalist movements, of which Breivik represents an extreme fringe, have been on the rise in recent years, the popular backlash against Breivik and his ideology has put them on the defensive. Far-right movements such as the English Defence League denied links to Breivik and dismissed any alleged ideological connections or overlap.[157] When far-right parties held a mass rally in Denmark in April 2012, opposing protesters actually outnumbered them.[158]

Finally, the trial was viewed by many as not sending Breivik's message but, instead, effectively demonstrating the quality of the Norwegian criminal justice system to the world. Professor Thomas Mathiesen of Oslo University was quoted as saying that 'the Norwegian system is not about revenge, but sober, dignified treatment' of even the worst criminals.[159]

In short, Breivik's performative strategy was immediately recognised as such and vehemently rejected by society at large. The singing of the Rainbow Song and national discussion in the media regarding the amount of attention focussed on Breivik during the trial underscored and defended the importance the Norwegian people ascribe to the democratic system and the rule of law. Both respect for a fair trial, as a cornerstone to a functioning democratic system, and for an inclusive debate demonstrated the Norwegian public's prioritisation of the judicial goals of stabilisation and upholding the democratic rule of law, much more than a plain yearning for retribution or general prevention.

11.6.3. *The Breivik Trial as a Coping Mechanism?*

How has the trial helped the Norwegian people present in and outside the courtroom in coping with the grief and stress caused by Breivik's attacks?

Our questionnaire asked which goals of a fair trial people find important, and whether they feel these were attained in the Breivik trial. The hypothesis is that if an important goal has been attained by the trial that this then may have helped respondents to cope better. The goals listed in the survey were more detailed than the five classical (formal and informal) goals of criminal justice with additional specifications added:

1. Revenge;
2. Preventing the suspect from committing another crime (specific prevention);
3. Preventing others from committing such a crime (general prevention);
4. Truth-finding;
5. Enabling all the involved parties to present their perspectives;
6. Restoring stability in society;
7. Reaffirming the rule of law and democratic values; and
8. Providing closure.

The outcomes are presented in table 11.3.

	Important	Attained
Revenge	8 per cent	4 per cent
Prevention	75 per cent	56 per cent
Symbolic function	56 per cent	22 per cent
Truth finding	49 per cent	39 per cent
Present perspectives	40 per cent	49 per cent
Restore stability	43 per cent	29 per cent
Democratic values	61 per cent	57 per cent
Provide closure	56 per cent	44 per cent

Table 11.3. Judicial goals: important and attained

One interesting result is the very small number of 18 participants (8 per cent) who viewed *revenge* as an important goal in a fair trial. Even though revenge, or retribution, is one of the classical goals upon which criminal justice in the Western world is based, it appears that for most of the participants in this research, this judicial goal was not that important. Laila Bokhari, a member of the 22 July Commission[160] that investigated the Breivik attacks and the government's performance, commented upon this lack of a perceived need for revenge in Norwegian society:

> If you look at the wording in court from the victims, it is not about him [Breivik] or about revenge. In a sense, this is not about Breivik himself. People do not want him to have a role in society. The word revenge has very seldom come out. So retribution in this trial is not so much about revenge, but more about putting back what is right and wrong and focussing on how can we prevent something like this from happening again in the future. And that is also part, I think, of the coping mechanism: looking forward, and not looking back.[161]

Specific prevention (preventing Breivik from committing another crime) and *democratic values* (restoring the rule of law and democratic values) were viewed as the most important goals of a fair trial. The latter was also confirmed by many of the interviewees. In general, the trial itself was viewed as society's answer to Breivik's (undemocratic) principles and worldview. Most participants (57 per cent) felt that the goal of upholding democratic values through the trial had been achieved. The trial ended with a verdict that declared Breivik sane and legally responsible for his acts. He was sentenced to 21 years in prison but with a 'preventive detention' clause allowing for his time in jail to be extended as long as he is deemed a threat to society.

Regarding *general prevention*, the trial also served an important purpose. On a (inter-)national policy level, the developments and the concerns relating to 'lone-wolf' terrorists like Breivik revealed the need for serious scrutiny of national security strategies. The 22 July Commission had already concluded before the end of the trial that 'All in all, 22 July revealed serious shortfalls in society's emergency preparedness and ability to avert threats [...] The challenges turned out to be ascribable to leadership and communication to a far greater extent than to the lack of response personnel.'[162]

The idea that (right-wing) lone wolf terrorism posed a new serious threat led to an increased emphasis, both inside and outside Norway, on communication in times of crisis, the monitoring of right-wing extremists, but also on the policies that relate to the purchasing and possessing of certain accessories that could be used for terrorist attacks. Janne Kristiansen, former head of the Police Security Service—Norway's domestic intelligence branch—said that Breivik represented a new paradigm, 'A lone wolf who has been very intent on staying under the radar of the security services by leading a lawful life', adding that the unconnected terrorist is 'one of their biggest worries'.[163] In the United Kingdom, public figures like Home Secretary Theresa May and one of the founders of the Centre for Fascist, Anti-Fascist and Post-Fascist Studies at Teesside University, Matthew Feldman, highlighted the growing threat of a Breivik-style attack in Britain. May stated that there had been an 'increased focus on Right-wing groups in the last year or so, particularly since the Breivik incident in Norway. [...] It's still the case that we're likely to see a lone actor on the basis of Right-wing extremism.'[164] Feldman concluded that someone like Anders Breivik will be on the radar 'sooner or later'.[165]

However, the most important goal the trial appeared to serve in the eyes of the respondents—something corroborated by reporting in the media—was the goal of *closure*, closely connected to the trial as a symbol for the defence of the Norwegian democratic system. One of the interviewees, Laila Bokhari, said:

> There has been a lot of discussion in the media whether Breivik's trial was actually preventing or inspiring others and about the role the media has played. What words did they use to describe him, what pictures did they show, etc. In a way, a lot of people argued that just by hearing his words, he would actually fall from his platform because everyone could see for themselves that his statements do not make sense. At the same time, there has been a rising awareness that we as citizens need to be engaged in that discussion, in the media, in political parties, in youth groups, to counter his principles. For example: he used the children's song, the Rainbow Song, to show his disgust with multiculturalism and what was our reaction? Everyone met up in the square and sang that song. Maybe that is a crazy thing for people to do but I think it is also part of our coping mechanism and saying: ok, we have given him his platform but at the same time, that demands us to be active citizens and respond to his views.[166]

So, the trial did produce closure, but did not end the debate. Some open questions as to the quality of the Norwegian approach to right-wing extremism and terrorism remained.

First of all, several experts on right-wing extremism pointed to Breivik's growing status of hero within right-wing extremists groups, especially if he were allowed to communicate his ideas by writing books and corresponding with like-minded extremists from his prison cell. For example, this was illustrated by the praise Breivik received during a neo-Nazi march in Germany[167] and at several right-wing extremist festivals.[168] Breivik indeed continued to communicate from his cell. Various letters sent from his prison cell to sympathisers have been published,[169] and in February 2013 he filed a complaint over the prison conditions, which he said were akin to 'aggravated torture'—prolonged isolation, limited time outside his cell and lack of movement opportunities.[170] From a performative perspective this could be explained as an attempt to fuel support for his case from other right-wing extremists.

Secondly, on a (inter-)national policy level, the developments and the concerns about lone wolf terrorists like Breivik revealed the need for serious scrutiny of national security strategies. In the short run, justice minister Knut Storberget and chief of security services (PST) Janne Kristiansen, both in charge at the time, resigned—but for reasons other than their responsibilities for the 22 July failures. In the longer run, the trial, its ensuing discussions and conclusions led to an increased emphasis, both inside and outside Norway, on effective crisis communications, the monitoring of right-wing extremists, but also on the policies that relate to the purchasing and possession of certain materials and substances that can be used for preparing terrorist attacks. One example is the European regulation which obliges citizens to obtain a permit for purchasing materials like fertiliser and nail polish remover that could be used for making explosives.[171] The risk of right-wing extremism, or other brands of lone wolf terrorism, was placed higher on the political agenda, but at the same time many feared that the outcome of this renewed political interest could have a major impact on their privacy and personal freedoms.

11.7. Conclusion

This chapter analysed how the Breivik trial was used by the parties involved to further their performative strategies. All in all, Breivik and his defence team achieved only partial success. The defendant avoided being sent for compulsory mental health treatment and managed to regain his position as a militant activist (terrorist). To some extent he was also able to use the courtroom as a stage, but in a more limited way than he initially thought would be possible. Breivik also missed the opportunity for a second trial show, as he then again would run the risk of being sentenced to compulsory mental health treatment. This illustrates that the static strategy regarding trials and defence procedures prepared in Breivik's compendium did not foresee the dynamics of a terrorist trial.

The prosecution apparently put too much stock on the first psychiatric report, and did not adjust its strategy significantly in the months before or during the trial. The prosecution's firm stance did not lead to a conviction in accordance with their primary view, but at the same time the prosecutors did acknowledge in their closing statement the difficult nature of the case and that there were numerous complicating factors to take into consideration. They claimed they were in serious doubt about his sanity and this doubt necessitated that they went for an insanity verdict. Regarding forensic psychiatry, the court clearly put more trust in the second report. An extensive debate on the subject ensued, both inside and outside the professional circles of psychiatry and psychology.

In our survey, we also asked how these strategies related to classical judicial goals, how this relationship was perceived within Norwegian society and how the trial helped society in coming to terms with what had happened on 22 July. It can be concluded that the trial did indeed influence the coping mechanisms of our respondents in a positive way and that most viewed the trial as part of their answer to Breivik's acts, perceiving the trial as a counter-narrative to Breivik's story. Overall, the trial was viewed as an example of a quality performance of justice and as a trial that focussed on the democratic values of Norwegian society—contrary to Breivik's values. One survey respondent summarised this in the following words, 'Don't let one terrorist take our rights.'[172] Paradoxically, Norwegians largely supported the prosecution's strategy, with the major proviso that they did not want Breivik to be declared insane.

The prosecution's strategy to try and have Breivik declared insane and be sent to a mental institution provoked a variety of reactions in Norwegian society and revealed a tension between the prosecution's strategy and the goals of retribution and/or truth-finding. As Breivik himself had said, having him declared insane would have been 'the ultimate humiliation', and therefore that strategy could have served the goal of retribution in the sense that Breivik would have received exactly what he did not want. However, despite the prosecution's strategy, the collective feeling was that the trial itself was fair, as was the way in which Breivik was treated—this being the ultimate answer to Breivik's acts. In spite of their diverging opinions, the prosecution's adherence to fair trial standards was respected by the majority of the respondents to this research. Norway's open and respectful attitude was reflected in the respondents' views on the importance of judicial goals: prevention and democratic goals were seen as the most important objectives of the trial, while rehabilitation was the least important goal for the respondents. The reaction of media around the world to the trial and in particular to the prosecutor's handshake with Breivik showed that Norway may be a unique country in this respect.

Breivik's strategies received widespread attention in the media: both the defence's initial plea for insanity, to escape a lengthy prison sentence, and his strategy to escape the insanity label in order to be perceived as a rational role model for right-wing extremists were covered by news media. Many (international) commentators questioned whether Breivik exerted too much communicative power during the trial. A substantial number of our respondents (37 per cent) agreed that Breivik received too much attention—in terms both of the amount of time he was given to present his perspective in court and the attention he received from the media. On the other hand, many respondents felt that this attention did not elevate his status, but in fact undermined his position in the sense that anyone could now see that his statements were incoherent and nonsensical, as Laila Bokhari has argued. These results again show that Norwegians trusted that Breivik's opinions would be overruled by moderate opinions and behaviour, leading terrorism researcher Tore Bjørgo to say in an overall assessment of the trial that 'we don't think that the trial has or will produce copy-cats, but we hope that it will instead produce copy-cat trials'.[173]

The influence of a criminal trial on coping is a highly under-researched topic in general, but the influence of a *terrorism* trial on coping with the initial attack is a virtually unexplored issue. Our survey provides some preliminary evidence for a positive relationship between a fair trial—with respect to classical judicial standards—and coping mechanisms in society. When focussing on individuals, a mild positive influence was found: 32 per cent of the interviewees responded that the trial helped them to cope better with their feelings. This might constitute an under-estimation because people are not aware of a direct positive influence of the trial on their feelings, whilst a negative impact would probably have caused a much higher negative result. It can be concluded, therefore, that a fair and transparent trial with enough opportunities for all actors to demonstrate their viewpoints is a necessary condition for strong coping mechanisms in society. However, more research is needed to verify these preliminary findings.

All in all, the Breivik trial could be considered a 'performance of justice', in the broadest, not just formal, but also social sense of the word. As Bokhari points out:

> It helped us in the process of understanding what really happened. It put things in perspective. In one way the trial gives Norwegian society a chance to show its values as a response to Breivik and in another way it gives people a chance to understand, gain insight and deal with what happened. In a way we have been forced to ask—and answer—the question of guilt.[174]

Notes

1 A.B. Breivik, '2083: A European declaration of independence' (2011), p. 947, https://publicintelligence.net/anders-behring-breiviks-complete-manifesto-2083-a-european-declaration-of-independence/ Retrieved 20 June 2013.

2 'Breiviks egne ord fra fengselscellen', *Verdens Gang* (27 March 2012), http://www.vg.no/nyheter/innenriks/22-juli/artikkel.php?artid=10064799. Retrieved 27 August 2012.

3 These parts are based on the following article: Beatrice de Graaf, Liesbeth van der Heide, Sabine Wanmaker and Daan Weggemans, *The Anders Behring Breivik Trial: Performing justice, defending democracy*. ICCT-research paper. (The Hague: ICCT, June 2013), pp. 1–20.

4 Based on his statements as an expert witness in the trial, Tore Bjørgo published the article 'Højreekstreme voldsideologier og terroristisk rationalitet: Hvordan kan man forstå Behring Breiviks udsagn og handlinger?' *Social Kritik*, 131 (2012).

5 'Norway attacks: Oslo hit by bomb explosion and youth shot at camp', *The Guardian* (22 July 2011), http://www.guardian.co.uk/world/2011/jul/22/norway-attacks-oslo-bomb-explosion. Retrieved 3 October 2012.

6 'Adrian Pracon: At han ser noe så grusomt i meg vil jeg ikke ta innover meg', *Verdens Gang* (25 May 2011), http://www.vg.no/nyheter/innenriks/22-juli/rettssaken/artikkel.php?artid=10070690. Retrieved 19 October 2012.

7 'At jeg lever er like tilfeldig som at andre døde', NRK (23 April 2012), http://www.nrk.no/227/dag-for-dag/breivik-husket-adrian-pracon-1.8092843. Retrieved 19 October 2012.

8 '"There's someone shooting just outside. He's coming in": Terrifying phone call of survivor of Breivik's massacre is played to court', *Daily Mail* (16 April 2012), http://www.dailymail.co.uk/news/article-2130757/Anders-Behring-Breivik-trial-Terrifying-phone-survivor-Norway-massacre-played-court.html. Retrieved 3 October 2012.

9 'Tape of Anders Behring Breivik's phone call to police after mass murder on Utøya released', *Telegraph* (24 November 2011), http://www.telegraph.co.uk/news/worldnews/europe/norway/8913536/Tape-of-Anders-Behring-Breiviks-phone-call-to-police-after-mass-murder-on-Utøya-released.html. Retrieved 3 October 2012.

10 'Anders Behring Breivik describes Utøya massacre at Oslo court', *Guardian* (20 April 2012), http://www.guardian.co.uk/world/2012/apr/20/anders-behring-breivik-massacre-court. Retrieved 3 October 2012.

11 'Anders Behring Breivik Googled 600 guides to help build bomb', *Metro* (20 April 2012), http://www.metro.co.uk/news/896783-anders-behring-breivik-googled-600-guides-to-help-build-norway-bomb. Retrieved 3 October 2012.

12 'How many I murder? Gunman asks what toll was and talks of "60-year war"', *Daily*

Mail (27 July 2012), http://www.dailymail.co.uk/news/article-2018917/Norway-shooting-victims-Anders-Behring-Breivik-asks-did-I-murder.html. Retrieved 3 October 2012.

13 'Anders Behring Breivik trial, day four: Thursday 19 April', *Guardian* (21 May 2012), http://www.guardian.co.uk/world/2012/apr/19/anders-behring-breivik-trial-live. Retrieved 3 October 2012.

14 'Anders Behring Breivik spent years training and plotting for massacre', *Guardian* (24 August 2012), http://www.guardian.co.uk/world/2012/aug/24/anders-behring-breivik-profile-oslo. Retrieved 3 October 2012.

15 'Victims were paralysed by fear as I fired: Breivik recounts island youth camp massacre in horrifying detail', *Daily Mail* (20 April 2012), http://www.dailymail.co.uk/news/article-2132656/Anders-Behring-Breivik-trial-Norway-killer-recounts-Utøya-island-massacre-horrifying-detail.html. Retrieved 3 October 2012.

16 Breivik, '2083', p. 1462.

17 'Manifest Breivik: fascinerende kijk in het hoofd van een terrorist', *De Volkskrant* (25 July 2011).

18 Ibid.

19 'Why does Norway's Breivik invoke the Knights Templar?', *Christian Science Monitor* (18 April 2012), http://www.csmonitor.com/World/Global-News/2012/0418/Why-does-Norway-s-Breivik-invoke-the-Knights-Templar-video. Retrieved 3 October 2012.

20 Breivik, '2083', p. 831.

21 Ibid., p. 661.

22 Ibid., p. 827.

23 Ibid., p. 812.

24 Ibid., pp. 938–939.

25 Ibid., p. 1072.

26 Ibid., p. 842.

27 Ibid., p. 1387.

28 'Breiviks far vurderer å besøke sønnen i fengsel', *Abc Nyheter* (12 May 2011), http://www.abcnyheter.no/nyheter/2011/12/05/breiviks-far-vurderer-besoeke-soennen-i-fengsel. Retrieved 15 October 2012.

29 A. Borchgrevink, *En Norsk Tragedie: Anders Behring Breivik og veiene til Utøya* (Gylendal: Oslo, 2012); A. Falk, 'Mass Murder as Unconscious Liberation: Reflections on the Norwegian tragedy of 2011' (20 April 2012), https://www.document.no/2012/04/massemord-som-ubevisst-frigjoring/. Retrieved 17 October 2012; 'Psykiater Finn Skå rderud: Ekstremt Viktig å forstå mer av Breivik', *Ostlendigen* (26 April 2012), http://www.ostlendingen.no/nyheter/psykiater-finn-skarderud-ekstremt-viktig-a-forsta-mer-av-breivik-1.7201624. Retrieved 17 October 2012.

30 Ibid.

31 'Slik var Breiviks barndom', *Nettavisen* (4 October 2012), http://www.nettavisen.no/nyheter/article3485836.ece. Retrieved 10 October 2012.

32 'Skrøt av egen briljans, utseende, kjærester og penger', *Dagbladet* (27 July 2011).

33 'Breivik's ex-friends suspected he was depressed, possibly gay', *The Associated Press* (29 May 2012), http://www.cbc.ca/news/world/story/2012/05/29/breivik-trial-depression.html. Retrieved 29 May 2012.

34 Breivik, '2083', p. 1378.

35 Ibid., p. 1378.

36 Ibid., p. 1381.

37 Ibid., p. 15; 'Anders Behring Breivik Trial- Monday 16 April', *The Guardian* (16 April 2012), http://www.guardian.co.uk/world/blog/2012/apr/16/anders-behring-breivik-trial-live. Retrieved 17 October 2012.

38 Breivik, '2083', p. 1379.

39 'A rational being and the insanity', *The Foreigner* (13 June 2012), http://m.theforeigner.no/pages/columns/a-rational-being-and-the-insanity/. Retrieved 15 October 2012.

40 'Norway mass killer Breivik was victim of "blood diamond" scam, court hears', *New York Post* (31 May 2012), http://nypost.com/2012/05/31/norway-mass-killer-breivik-was-victim-of-blood-diamond-scam-court-hears/. See also: 'Anders Breivik was victim of "blood diamond" scam', *The Telegraph* (30 May 2012) http://www.telegraph.co.uk/news/worldnews/europe/norway/9301539/Anders-Breivik-was-victim-of-blood-diamond-scam.html. Retrieved 10 October 2012.

41 'Breivik's ex-friends suspected he was depressed, possibly gay', *The Associated Press* (29 May 2012), http://www.cbc.ca/news/world/story/2012/05/29/breivik-trial-depression.html. Retrieved 29 May 2012.

42 Breivik, '2083', p. 1418.

43 Ibid., p. 1416.

44 NOU 2012: 14 *Rapport fra 22. Juli-kommisjonen*, p. 353.

45 NOU 2012: 14 *Rapport fra 22. Juli-kommisjonen*, p. 375.

46 R. Spaaij, *Understanding Lone Wolf Terrorism. Global patterns, motivations and prevention* (Springer: New York, 2012), p. 71.

47 Ibid.

48 Anders Behring Breivik Psychiatric Report (29 November 2011), Paragraph 2.5.2, https://sites.google.com/site/breivikreport/documents/anders-breivik-psychiatric-report-of-2011. Retrieved 2 October 2012.

49 Later in the courtroom Lippestad would be accompanied by Vibeke Hein Bæra, a former public prosecutor. They were supported by Tord Jordet and Odd Ivar Grøn, two of Lippestad's employees.

50 The case of a neo-Nazi, Ole Nicolai Kvisler, who was convicted of the murder of a young Norwegian-Ghanaian teenager and sentenced to 17 years' imprisonment: 'The lawyer "defending the indefensible"', *Independent* (15 April 2012), http://www.independent.co.uk/news/world/europe/the-lawyer-defending-the-indefensible-7645968.html. Retrieved 10 October 2012.

51 G. Lippestad, *Det kan vi stå for* (Oslo: Aschehoug, 2013), p. 40.

52 'Breivik erkjenner massedrap', NRK (23 July 2011), www.nrk.no/nyheter/norge/1.7724809. Retrieved 2 February 2012.

53 Lippestad, *Det kan vi stå for*, p. 89.

54 Ibid.

55 'Anders Behring Breivik indicted for the "worst crime in modern Norwegian history"', *The Telegraph* (7 March 2012), http://www.telegraph.co.uk/news/worldnews/europe/norway/9128687/Anders-Behring-Breivik-indicted-for-worst-crime-in-modern-Norwegian-history.html. Retrieved 10 October 2012.

56 'Sladder ikke tiltalen', *An* (2 March 2012), http://www.an.no/Innenriks/article5954609.ece. Retrieved 14 October 2012.

57 Indictment against Breivik, Complaint No.: 11762579 10094/11–115 / SHO017 (2012), http://upload.wikimedia.org/wikipedia/commons/2/2b/Indictment,_Anders_Behring_Breivik.pdf. Retrieved 2 October 2012.

58 Ibid.

59 Anders Behring Breivik Psychiatric Report (29 November 2011), Paragraph 8–9.

60 Ibid., Paragraph 5–9.

61 Ibid.

62 Ibid.

63 'Anders Behring Breivik indicted for "worst crime in modern Norwegian history"', *The Telegraph* (7 March 2012).

64 Indictment against Breivik, Complaint No.: 11762579 10094/11–115 / SHO017 (2012); see also 'Anders Behring Breivik indicted for "worst crime in modern Norwegian history"', *The Telegraph* (7 March 2012).

65 'Jon Even Andersen (NTB): Derfor oppnevnte retten nye terrorsakkyndige', *Aftenposten* (16 March 2013).

66 B. de Graaf, *Evaluating Counterterrorism Performance* (London and New York: Routledge, 2011), p. 226.

67 *Dagbladet.no* (2012).

68 A. Leer, 'Norway readies for its trial of the century', BBC *News Europe* (14 April 2012), http://www.bbc.co.uk/news/world-europe-17710355. Retrieved 9 August 2012.

69 A. Reed, K. Myers, J. Kremer, 'Breivik claims Self-Defence as Oslo Terror Trial Starts',

Bloomberg (16 April 2012), http://www.bloomberg.com/news/2012-04-16/breivik-defends-massacre-as-norway-s-saddest-trial-starts.html. Retrieved 9 August 2012.

70 Breivik, '2083', p. 1092.

71 'Chief prosecutor, in the trial of Norwegian killer, Anders Breivik, Inga Bejer Engh on Newsnight', BBC *Newsnight* (2 June 2012), http://www.youtube.com/watch?v=K2bbpXXvbFc. Retrieved 12 October 2012.

72 'Breivik trial: Key moments of opening day', BBC (16 April 2012), http://www.bbc.co.uk/news/world-europe-17733869. Retrieved 7 October 2012.

73 'Self-pity of a Killer: Anders Breivik sobs in court after admitting murderous "acts, but not the criminal guilt"', *Mirror* (16 April 2012), http://www.mirror.co.uk/news/world-news/anders-breivik-trial-killer-sobs-796517. Retrieved 7 October 2012.

74 'Anders Breivik Trial: Suspect defends Norway massacre, insists he would do it again', *Huffington Post* (17 April 2012), http://www.huffingtonpost.com/2012/04/17/anders-behring-breivik-thomas-indreboe_n_1430483.html. Retrieved 7 October 2012.

75 Ibid.

76 'Anders Breivik pleads not guilty at Norway murder trial', BBC *News Europe* (16 April 2012), http://www.bbc.co.uk/news/world-europe-17724535. Retrieved 12 October 2012.

77 Ibid.

78 'Norwegian Man Claims Self-defence in Killings', *New York Times* (2012), http://www.nytimes.com/2012/04/17/world/europe/trial-of-anders-behring-breivik-opens-in-norway.html?pagewanted=all. Retrieved 12 October 2012.

79 'Prosecution Chips Away at Breivik's Claim of Militant Network', *The Epoch Times* (18 April 2012), http://www.theepochtimes.com/n2/world/prosecution-chips-away-at-breivik-s-claim-of-militant-network-222845.html. Retrieved 12 October 2012.

80 22 July Court Transcripts, 'Transcript 2012-04-18', *Oslo District Court* (18 April 2012) https://sites.google.com/site/breivikreport/transcripts/anders-breivik-court-transcript-2012-04-18-live-report.

81 Ibid.

82 'Breivik trial: Key moments of opening day', BBC *News Europe* (16 April 2012), http://www.bbc.co.uk/news/world-europe-17733869. Retrieved 5 November 2013.

83 'Oppsiktsvekkende helomvending', *Aftenposten* (27 April 2013), http://www.aftenposten.no/nyheter/iriks/22juli/-Oppsiktsvekkende-helomvending-6816248.html. Retrieved 5 November 2013.

84 The quotation is based on Tore Bjørgo's notes from the court proceedings.

85 'The closing statement from the prosecution in the Breivik-trial', NRK (21 June 2012), www.nrk.no. Retrieved 22 June 2012.

86 Ibid.; see also: 'Lippestad: Breivik ikke overrasket over aktors påstand', *Aftenbladet* (21

June 2012), www.aftenbladet.no/nyheter/innenriks/Lippestad-Breivik-ikke-overrasket-over-aktors-pastand-2992045.html. Retrieved 22 June 2012.

87 Breivik, '2083', p. 947.

88 'Breivik i avhør:—Slik var min pompøse uniformsbløff', *Dagbladet* (15 April 2012).

89 Breivik, '2083', p. 1104.

90 'Breiviks egne ord fra fengselscellen', *Verdens Gang* (27 March 2012).

91 '"Martyrs for the Conservative Revolution": Mass-Murderer Breivik writes neo-Nazi Zschäpe', *Der Spiegel* (19 November 2012), http://www.spiegel.de/international/europe/anders-behring-breivik-writes-neo-nazi-terrorist-suspect-beate-zschaepe-a-868042.html. Retrieved 5 November 2013; 'Breivik skriver til "kjære søster Beate"', *Dagbladet Nyheter* (18 November 2012); and 'Murderer Breivik gushes to German "Nazi killer"', *The Sun* (18 November 2012), [http://www.thesun.co.uk/sol/homepage/news/4651225/Murderer-Breivik-gushes-to-German-Nazi-killer.html]. Retrieved 5 November 2013.

92 'Anders Behring Breivik vil bruke uniform i rette under fengslingsmøte', VG *Nett* (25 July 2011), http://www.vg.no/nyheter/innenriks/terrorangrepet-22-juli-anders-behring-breivik/anders-behring-breivik-vil-bruke-uniform-under-fengslingsmoetet/a/10080740/. Retrieved 15 March 2012.

93 Lippestad, *Det kan vi stå for*, p. 42.

94 'Kamp om Breiviks psyke', *Dagavisen* (NTB) (10 April 2012), www.dagsavisen.no/samfunn/kamp-om-breiviks-psyke/. Retrieved 28 March 2013.

95 S.C. Johnson, *Psychological Evaluation of Theodore Kaczynski* (1998), www.paulcooijmans.com/psychology/unabombreport2.html. Retrieved 20 February 2013.

96 'Breivik i protestbrev fra cellen: "Verste som kunne rammet meg": Massedrapsmannen om å bli erklært utilregnelig', VG *Nyheter* (4 April 2012), http://www.vg.no/nyheter/innenriks/22-juli/artikkel.php?artid=10049584. Retrieved 3 February 2013.

97 'Les deler av innledningen i Breivik-brev', VG *Nyheter* (4 April 2012), http://www.vg.no/nyheter/innenriks/22-juli/artikkel.php?artid=10049578. Retrieved 3 February 2013.

98 Ibid.

99 Lippestad, *Det kan vi stå for*, p. 103.

100 'Jeg har ikke snakket med Breivik siden vi avsluttet saken', *Dagbladet* (21 November 2012), [http://www.dagbladet.no/2012/11/21/nyheter/innenriks/geir_lippestad/terrorangrepet/terror/24469707/]. Retrieved 3 February 2013.

101 'Tore Bjørgo: Med monopol på vrangforestillinger', *Chronicle Aftenposten*, (7 December 2012), http://www.aftenposten.no/meninger/kronikker/Med-monopol-pa-vrangforestillinger-6715050.html. Retrieved 2 June 2013.

102 Ibid.

103 'Breiviks strategi: oppskrift på fiasko', *Aftenposten nettavis* (31 May 2012), http://www

.aftenposten.no/nyheter/iriks/22juli/Breiviks-strategi-Oppskrift-pa-fiasko-6840568.html. Retrieved 2 June 2013.

104 'Jon Even Andersen (NTB): Derfor oppnevnte retten nye terrorsakkyndige', *Aftenposten* (16 March 2013).

105 'Sindre Granly Meldalen og Tomm W. Christiansen—Det er ting vi angrer på', *Dagbladet* (17 June 2012), [http://www.dagbladet.no/2012/06/17/nyheter/innenriks/terror/anders_behring_breivik/breivik/22101895/]. Retrieved 11 March 2013.

106 'Breivik endret forklaring', *Hamar Arbeiderblad* (31 May 2012), http://h-a.no/nyheter/breivik-endret-forklaring. Retrieved 11 March 2013.

107 'Slik har han endret forklaring', *Aftenposten* (2 May 2012), www.aftenposten.no/nyheter/iriks/22juli/Slik-har-han-endret-sin-forklaring-6818661.html Retrieved 5 May 2013.

108 Both psychiatric evaluation reports of Anders Behring Breivik can be found at http://www.vg.no/nyheter/innenriks/22-juli/psykiatrisk_vurdering/.

109 However, the Commission for Forensic Psychiatry, which had accepted the first, controversial report without any comments in spite of its obvious shortcomings, had a number of critical questions regarding the second report. The Commission came under heavy fire for its role in the process. It was claimed that it was unable to accept the second report because it had put too much stock in accepting the first report, which had come to the opposite conclusion.

110 'Lippestad:—Slik Breivik trodde', *Nettavisen* (10 April 2012) http://www.nettavisen.no/nyheter/article3372425.ece. Retrieved 28 March 2013.

111 'Kamp om Breiviks psyke', *Dagsavisen* NTB (10 April 2012).

112 'En type høyreekstrem hilsen', *Dagbladet* (6 February 2012), [http://www.dagbladet.no/2012/02/06/nyheter/innenriks/fengslingsmote/terror/anders_behring_breivik/20104331/]. Retrieved 16 March 2013.

113 22 July Court Transcripts, 'Transcript 2012-04-17', *Oslo District Court* (17 April 2012), p. 21, https://sites.google.com/site/breivikreport/transcripts/anders-breivik-court-transcript-2012-04-17-live-report.

114 VG's minutes from court, 17 April 2012.

115 22 July Court Transcripts, 'Transcript 2012-04-17', *Oslo District Court* (17 April 2012), p. 21, https://sites.google.com/site/breivikreport/transcripts/anders-breivik-court-transcript-2012-04-17-live-report. p. 349.

116 Ibid., p. 349.

117 Ibid., p. 351.

118 'Mann kastet sko og ropte mot Breivik', *Aftenposten* (11 May 2012), http://www.aftenposten.no/nyheter/iriks/22juli/Mann-kastet-sko-og-ropte-mot-Breivik-6826502.html#.UVc3djkdhDU. Retrieved 3 March 2013.

119 'Breivik trial closes, victims' relatives walk out', *Reuters* (22 June 2012), www.reuters.com/article/2012/06/22/us-breivik-trial-idUSBRE85LoCM20120622. Retrieved 10 March 2013.

120 'Jon Even Andersen (NTB): Derfor oppnevnte retten nye terrorsakkyndige', *Aftenposten* (16 March 2013).

121 22 July Court Transcripts, 'Transcript 2012-08-06', *Oslo District Court* (8 June 2012), https://sites.google.com/site/breivikreport/transcripts/anders-breivik-court-transcript-2012-06-08-live-report.

122 Ibid.

123 Sociologist Professor Thomas Hylland Eriksen, interviewed by ITN's Sam Datta-Paulin.

124 This idea of belonging to a specific 'in-group' might function as a pull-factor for adjusting one's (social) identity. See for instance M. Sageman, *Understanding Terror Networks* (Philadelphia: University of Pennsylvania Press, 2004); T. Bjorgo, and J. Horgan, (eds), *Leaving Terrorism Behind: Disengagement from political violence* (New York: Routledge, 2009); J. Horgan, 'Psychological factors related to disengaging from terrorism: Some preliminary assumptions and assertions', in: C. Benard, (Ed.), *A Future for the Young: Options for helping Middle Eastern youth escape the trap of radicalization* (Santa Monica, CA: RAND Corporation, 2005), http://www.rand.org/pubs/working_papers/WR354/.

125 22 July Court Transcripts, 'Transcript 2012-08-24', *Oslo District Court* (24 August 2012), https://sites.google.com/site/breivikreport/transcripts/anders-breivik-court-transcript-2012-08-24-live-report.

126 '"Martyrs for the Conservative Revolution": Mass-Murderer Breivik writes neo-Nazi Zschäpe', *Der Spiegel* (19 November 2012), http://www.spiegel.de/international/europe/anders-behring-breivik-writes-neo-nazi-terrorist-suspect-beate-zschaepe-a-868042.html. Retrieved 5 November 2013.

127 Ibid.

128 22 July Court Transcript, 'Transcript 2012-06-22', *Oslo District Court* (22 June 2012), https://sites.google.com/site/breivikreport/documents/anders-breivik-court-statement-2012-06-22 [Note: in the transcript 'necessity' is wrongly translated as 'self-defence'].

129 22 July Court Transcript, 'Transcript 2012-04-23', *Oslo District Court* (23 April 2012), https://sites.google.com/site/breivikreport/transcripts/anders-breivik-court-transcript-2012-04-23-live-report.

130 22 July Court Transcripts, 'Transcript 2012-04-17', *Oslo District Court* (17 April 2012), https://sites.google.com/site/breivikreport/transcripts/anders-breivik-court-transcript-2012-04-17-live-report.

131 'Lippestad: Vurderer å be om utsettelse av saken', NRK (16 April 2012), http://www.nrk.no/227/dag-for-dag/forsvarerne-vil-kanskje-utsette-1.8076216. Retrieved 22 February 2013.

132 22 July Court Transcript, 'Transcript 2012-08-24', *Oslo District Court* (24 August 2012),

https://sites.google.com/site/breivikreport/transcripts/anders-breivik-court-transcript-2012-08-24-live-report.

133 Breivik, '2083', p. 1107.

134 Ibid.

135 Ibid., pp. 1107–1114.

136 Ibid., p. 1115.

137 Ibid., pp. 1115–1116.

138 'Breiviks egne ord om livet i fengsel: Sadisme satt i system', VG (09 November 2012), http://www.vg.no/nyheter/innenriks/22-juli/artikkel.php?artid=10055585. Retrieved 5 March 2013.

139 B. de Graaf, 'Terrorists on Trial: A performative perspective', ICCT *Expert Meeting Report* (2011), http://www.icct.nl/download/file/ICCT-de-Graaf-EM-Paper-Terrorism-Trials-as-Theatre.pdf.

140 C. Kelk, *Studieboek materiel strafrecht* (Deventer: Kluwer, 2005), p. 21.

141 R.S. Lazarus and S. Folkman, *Stress, Appraisal, and Coping* (New York: Springer, 1984), p. 150.

142 Hence the generalisability of the results is limited to the respondents in our sample. It concerns mainly inhabitants from Oslo; our sample was on average younger, poorer and from more diverse ethnic backgrounds than the Norwegian population as a whole. Data from: http://www.indexmundi.com/norway/demographics_profile.html, http://www.zillow.com/local-info/MN-Oslo-people/r_19786/ and our survey.

143 The trial of Anders Behring Breivik started on 16 April and lasted until 22 June 2012. The trial was named after the day of Breivik's attacks: the 22 July trial. The final verdict was read on 24 August 2012 in Oslo district court.

144 Independent commission mandated to review and learn from the terrorist attacks on the Government Complex in Oslo and on Utøya Island on 22 July 2011. The commission submitted its final report to Norwegian Prime Minister Jens Stoltenberg on Monday, 13 August 2012. See for more information: https://www.regjeringen.no/html/smk/22julikommisjonen/22JULIKOMMISJONEN_NO/EN.HTM. Retrieved 5 March 2013.

145 B. McPherson, 'Prosecuting Breivik', *The Foreigner* (7 July 2012), http://theforeigner.no/pages/columns/prosecuting-breivik/. Retrieved 5 March 2013.

146 Ibid.

147 Ibid.

148 Originally a song by the US folk singer and peace activist Pete Seeger, entitled "My Rainbow Race" (1967), translated into Norwegian and popularised by Lillebjørn Nilsen.

149 Breivik Trial Court Transcript, 'Transcript 2012-04-20', *Oslo District Court* (20 April 2012), https://sites.google.com/site/breivikreport/transcripts/anders-breivik-court-transcript-2012-04-20-live-report.

150 A. Lobzina, '"Russia's Breivik" suspect charged with mass murder', *The Moscow News* (11 August 2012), http://themoscownews.com/local/20121108/190828279.html. Retrieved 5 March 2013.

151 'Czech police charge man over "Breivik-style" plot', BBC (18 August 2012), http://www.bbc.co.uk/news/world-europe-19304814. Retrieved 5 March 2013.

152 'Poland arrests bomb plotter linked to Norway's Breivik', *Reuters* (20 November 2012), http://www.reuters.com/article/2012/11/20/us-poland-attack-idUSBRE8AJ0HQ20121120. Retrieved 5 March 2013.

153 'Breivik gets love letters from 16-year old girls', *The Local* (18 June 2012), http://www.thelocal.no/20120618/breivik-gets-love-letters-from-16-year-old-girls. Retrieved 5 March 2013.

154 'Children write letters to Breivik', *The Nordic Page* (18 December 2012), http://www.tnp.no/norway/panorama/3443-children-write-letters-to-breivik. Retrieved 5 March 2013.

155 The Breivik Archive, 'Anders Behring Breivik Letter 15-01-12 to Tania' (15 January 2012), https://breivikreport.wordpress.com/category/breivik/breivik-prison-letters/page/3/. Retrieved 5 March 2013.

156 J.A. Ravndal, 'A Post-Trial of Anders Behring Breivik' (29 October 2012), http://www.ctc.usma.edu/posts/a-post-trial-profile-of-anders-behring-breivik. Retrieved 5 March 2013.

157 M. Fisher, 'What America can learn from Norway's Anders Breivik trial', *The Atlantic* (18 April 2012), http://www.theatlantic.com/international/archive/2012/04/what-america-can-learn-from-norways-anders-breivik-trial/256066/. Retrieved 13 March 2013.

158 'European far-right groups seek to build anti-Islamic network, meet protests', *Reuters* (2 April 2012), http://blogs.reuters.com/faithworld/2012/04/02/european-far-right-groups-seek-to-build-anti-islamic-network-meet-protests/. Retrieved 13 March 2013.

159 'Anders Breivik trial displays Norway's formal legal system', *Washington Post* (17 April 2012), http://www.washingtonpost.com/world/anders-breivik-trial-displays-norways-formal-legal-system-as-confessed-killer-gets-to-explain-fanatical-views/2012/04/17/gIQA5t8kOT_story.html. Retrieved 13 March 2013.

160 Independent commission mandated to review and learn from the terrorist attacks on the Government Complex in Oslo and on Utøya Island on 22 July 2011. The commission submitted its final report to Norwegian Prime Minister Jens Stoltenberg on 13 August 2012. See for more information: https://www.regjeringen.no/html/smk/22julikommisjonen/22JULIKOMMISJONEN_NO/EN.HTM.

161 Interview with Laila Bokhari, member of the 22 July Kommisjonen (Oslo, 23 August 2012).

162 B. Koranyi, 'Norway could have prevented Breivik massacre, says commission', *Reuters* (13 August 2012).

163 W. Boston, 'Norway Attacks: The worrying rise of the lone-wolf terrorist', *Time* (28 July 2011), http://www.time.com/time/world/article/0,8599,2085658,00.html. Retrieved 13 March 2013.

164 R.J. Ford Rojas, 'Risk of "lone wolf" terrorist attack growing', *The Daily Telegraph* (14 January 2013), http://www.telegraph.co.uk/news/uknews/terrorism-in-the-uk/9799192/Anders-Breivik-style-attacker-will-slip-under-the-radar-in-Britain-sooner-or-later-expert-warns.html. Retrieved 13 March 2013.

165 Ibid.

166 Interview with Laila Bokhari, member of the 22 July Kommisjonen (Oslo, 23 August 2012).

167 'Breivik is een held voor extreem rechts', *De Morgen* (14 January 2013).

168 'BNP chief's Hitler salute to Breivik heroine', *The Sun* (4 August 2011), http://www.thesun.co.uk/sol/homepage/news/3732148/BNP-chiefs-Hitler-salute-to-Breivik-heroine.html. Retrieved 20 March 2013.

169 Letters are available online: https://sites.google.com/site/breivikreport/letters.

170 'Breivik anmelder Ila fengsel og Grete Faremo', VG (31 January 2013), http://www.vg.no/nyheter/innenriks/22-juli/artikkel.php?artid=10119534. Retrieved 20 March 2013.

171 'Vergunning nodig voor grondstof explosief', ANP (20 november 2012).

172 L. van der Heide, S. Wanmaker, D. Weggemans and B. de Graaf, 'The 22nd of July Trial reaches its final stage', ICCT *Commentaries* (12 September 2012), http://icct.nl/publications/icct-commentaries/the-22nd-of-july-trial-reaches-its-final-stage. Retrieved 20 March 2013.

173 'Past Events: Terrorists on Trial: The case of Anders Behring Breivik', ICCT—*The Hague Meeting Report* (11 April 2013), http://www.icct.nl/activities/past-events/terrorists-on-trial-the-case-of-anders-behring-breivik.

174 Interview with Laila Bokhari, member of the 22 July Kommisjonen, Oslo, 23 August 2012.

12. Conclusion

Beatrice de Graaf [1]

In this volume, the intricacies of various terrorism trials have been reconstructed and analysed at various levels of depth and from a performative perspective. The idea of looking at terrorism trials as quasi-theatrical performances has led to new insights with regard to both terrorist and counterterrorist performances and strategies in the courtroom. Yet to adhere to performative, or even theatrical concepts remains an uneasy undertaking to those who are accustomed to unquestioningly accepting existing communicative frames of reference, or to seeing 'the law' and 'courts' as solemn institutions and not as objects of *lawfare* and subject to *performance*. At the end of this volume, some reflections on the contested nature of communicatice frames and performative aspects of terrorism trials are offered. First, the widespread unease of governments to put terrorists on trial needs to be addressed. Second, a tentative outline of a typology of terrorism trials will be presented which may serve as a stepping-stone for further research in this field. This tentative typology is developed, to gain deeper insight into how terrorism trials are perceived as and configured into socially and politically relevant categories, leaving aside for the moment the legal questions involved. Since this volume is not intended as a contribution to legal theory, but written from a historic-political perspective on the phenomenon of terrorism trials, this approach might benefit from further categorising and operationalising.

12.1. Why the Unease?

Seeing performative acts in trial as a performance and identifying communicative strategies requires a specific mindset. In carrying out this research project and interviewing various actors involved in terrorism trials, the editors and authors initially were often confronted with scepticism or even resistance to this approach. This reluctance can be explained by pointing to the unease regarding the question of putting terrorists on trial under civilian, criminal law. Why are governments often not at ease with the idea of putting terrorists before civilian courts?

In the US, after President Barack Obama expressed his preference for trials in federal civilian courts and promised to close down the Guantánamo military tribunals in 2009, congressional obstruction forced him to back down from this decision. In early March 2011, the White House announced that it would resume military trials for detainees at Guantánamo Bay, Cuba. 'I strongly believe that the American system of justice is a key part of our arsenal in the war against al Qaida and its affiliates, and we will continue to draw on all aspects of our justice system—including (federal) courts—to ensure that our security and our values are strengthened', Obama stated.[2] Yet, congressional concern relating to the security risks involved in these terrorism trials, given that detainees would have to be transferred to and tried in the 'homeland', prevailed.[3] Former Vice-President Cheney's objection to such trials has already been mentioned in the opening chapter of this volume. In the *Wall Street Journal*, columnist James Taranto also invoked the association of a 'show trial', although he was more nuanced: 'These trials will differ from an ordinary show trial in that the process will be fair even though the verdict is predetermined.' However, even if it were a fair trial with just formal proceedings, it would nevertheless contain an element of show: 'The answer seems to be that the administration is conducting a limited number of civilian trials of high-profile terrorists for show, so as to win "credibility" with the international left.'[4]

Taranto was right in at least one regard: even with legality intact, terrorism trials are highly likely to turn into a spectacle, because either the prosecution or the defendants or both cannot resist adopting communicative strategies (compare the chapters on Breivik and the RAF in this volume for example). As indicated above, the outcome of the first trial against Guantánamo 'ghost prisoner' Ahmed Khalfan Ghailani sparked off a similar debate. Not the final verdict as such, but the use of civilian courts in combating terrorism, became heavily contested. The opposition argued that terrorists should never be granted civilian trials, with all the communicative space and security risks involved, but should be treated and detained as military prisoners. The administration, on the other hand, claimed that the system had shown that a terrorist could be convicted even after a judge excluded evidence gained by coercive interrogations during the Bush administration and by acquitting one defendant on a number of related charges. The sentence meted out—20 years—was probably even stiffer than a military court would have given.

In response to this case, Jack Goldsmith, a high-ranking Justice Department official during the Bush administration, argued that the verdict showed that terrorism suspects should be held without any trial at all, not even a military one. Indefinite military detention, he said, 'is a tradition-sanctioned, Congressionally authorised, court-blessed, resource-saving, security-preserving, easier-than-trial option for long-term terrorist incapacitation. And this morning it looks more appealing than ever.'[5] Since the attacks of 9/11, this new line of thinking became dominant amongst executives and was reinvigorated after every new attack and in the wake of military campaigns in Afghanistan and Iraq.[6] There is a certain logic to it: in war prisoners are usually held until the end of the war, and since the war Al Qaeda declared on the United States twice in the second half of the 1990s is continuing, release would be premature and, in the case of proven charges of war crimes, might result in a military court verdict rather than release at the end of the war.

The tendency to resort to measures other than criminal law is not solely reserved for US officials. In the Netherlands, for instance, the government arranged for other measures in dealing with terrorism than through criminal law alone. Dutch government officials may pick and choose whether they apply intelligence measures (observation), immigration law, control orders and other administrative law instruments (or a combination thereof) before deciding whether or not a criminal investigation should be pursued.[7]

The explanation for governments' unease regarding civilian terrorism trials is twofold. First of all, one has to consider the element of risk in relation to the outcome of the trial. In performative language, this is the aspect of unpredictability and spontaneity involved in so-called 'simultaneous dramaturgy' settings, implying 'techniques designed to involve spectators in a scene without requiring their physical presence onstage.'[8] From the executive's perspective—which is often dominated by national security considerations—handing the suspect over to an independent court is a risky business. Terrorist suspects can be acquitted, sometimes not because they are innocent but because certain crucial pieces of evidence are deemed inadmissible, as was the case in the Ghailani trial. This risk cannot be excluded, at least not at the cost of turning the trial into a farce for the government. This element of uncertainty runs against the grain of the principal goal of counter-terrorism actors: eliminating the terrorist threat. Thus, the executive's rationale behind an *à la carte* treatment of terrorists lies not in contempt for criminal law, but in the priority given to other (legal) obligations, such as protecting the right to life and the security of the citizen. This weighing of rights is known as the *balance or proportionality response thesis*; notable politicians and scholars such as Michael Ignatieff assume that in order to protect security public interest must be weighed against human rights. If this means that the rights of terror suspects are suspended or restricted, according to him that is just an unfortunate side-effect of protecting national security.[9] Critics such as the 2009 Eminent Jurists Panel in its report on Terrorism, Counter-terrorism and Human

Rights, however, contend that this suspension of terrorists' rights normalises the state of exception—thereby one-sidedly strengthening executive powers—and pleaded for reasserting the value of the criminal justice system, especially in the case of citizens' rights.[10]

A second explanation for a government's difficulty with relying on criminal law in dealing with terrorists is the fact that the courtroom trial may turn into a 'political show', with the terrorists dominating the scene or even succeeding in breaking existing communicative frames and presenting new ones. The main functions of the criminal justice system are exerting social control, settling disputes and confirming society's norms.[11] Counter-terrorism verdicts, however, do not necessarily affirm society's shared values. Many terror suspects come from minority groups that oppose a government they consider oppressive; they are not likely to perceive criminal law or its implementation by the judiciary as neutral or legitimate at all. Their (perception of) truth cannot simply be 'tried away' in court. Take for example the trial against Nelson Mandela. During the Apartheid regime in South Africa, Nelson Mandela, who publicly supported violent political struggle, was labelled a terrorist partly due to his conviction in 1964 for conspiracy. Although the trial ended in a legal victory for the prosecution, it was a political disaster for the regime in the court of national and international public opinion. The trial was a communicative defeat; it undermined the legal basis of the adjudication, and even that of the government's legitimacy as such. This is exactly what governments are afraid of: although criminal law may serve immediate political ends (detaining political opponents by sentencing them as terrorists), the intermediate and long-term communicative and political effects can be unforeseeable and potentially devastating. Given the possibility of these kinds of deferred aversive consequences, the element of risk once again enters the courtroom. Mandela's trial became a show of injustice; its reverberations undermined the political credibility and legitimacy of the Apartheid regime, although it managed to survive for nearly three more decades.[12]

The events resulting in the killing of Osama bin Laden underscore the salience of these two points. Indeed, governments are in most cases uneasy about staging major terrorism trials, both because of the security risks and due to the unpredictable communicative 'show' element involved. At the same time, this show element is sometimes consciously used by the prosecuting authorities themselves as an opportunity to showcase to the world that the rule of law has been upheld. Under the right conditions of legality and with adequate performative strategies, terrorism trials (like any other trial) confirm the underlying communicative mode of rules and procedures, and thus may result in a triumph of justice. We will come to this later, but first it is necessary to explore what the 'show' element in terrorism trials actually entails and how this element relates to the concept of 'show trials', a category loaded with heavy historical associations.

12.2. The 'Show Element' in Criminal Trials

In this volume we have introduced the concepts of lawfare and performativity (to be defined below) to enable a broader perspective to be taken on the legal, but also social and political implications of a terrorism trial. This is warranted since 'the Law' is in itself broader than a mere summary of legal norms and principles; it incorporates, amongst other things, social norms, values, power relations and social processes—and offers a constitutive communicative framework in disseminating these. Then, by applying law, one sets in motion a communicative process. In the words of Mark van Hoecke, a legal scholar, 'Law cannot any more be correctly understood within a paradigm of one-dimensional rationality. [...] The dramatic rise of complexity, both of law and of society, have made such a scheme obsolete.'[13] Many legal theorists of the twentieth century held that facts and norms could be separated, but this positivist view of the law has come under attack.[14] Acknowledging today's multi-layered, complex, but also vulnerable societies has unearthed the weakness of a purely positivist approach to law.[15] Law is not (solely) about sifting facts from opinions or about establishing objective truth; it is also about social control, communication and the perception of social norms. Trials are one instance in which the broader public can see law in action. Trials communicate that law is not just in the books but is implemented in practice. In the narrowest perspective, courts interpret and apply legal rules. Yet by doing so they contribute to strengthening certain concepts of justice and inculcate norms and standards to the general public. In addition, by enforcing the law, courts are linked to the state's legitimacy as well as to the elaboration of policy goals.[16] Trials thus communicate publicly and ceremonially to society what a state's norms and principles are (or ought to be).[17]

The law in action *is* a communicative process, but at the same time also *offers* a framework with which to interpret human actions and communication. Trials are the medium through which this communication process takes place, involving, as Mark van Hoecke put it, 'communication between legislators and citizens, between courts and litigants, between the legislator and the judiciary, communication between contracting parties, communication within a trial'.[18] More importantly, exactly this communicational aspect, within the confines of the court and amongst the legal actors involved, can serve 'as the ultimate safeguard for a "correct" interpretation and adjudication of the law', and in so doing thus legitimises the law.[19]

Since this communicational process is the principal foundation underlying the legitimacy of the justice applied, a trial ought to be heavily protected against political interference and manipulation. A fair trial is a basic human right, protected not only by criminal law, but also by international and constitutional law. The principle of fair trial is recognised in numerous international instruments and treaties, such as the Universal Declaration of Human Rights (Article 10 UDHR), the International Covenant on Civil and Political Rights (Article 14 ICCPR) and the European Convention on Human Rights (Article 6 ECHR). Besides serving other functions, the fair trial principle ensures the right of an individual to be informed of the measures taken, to be informed about the case against him or her, the right to be heard within a reasonable period of time, the right to a fair and public hearing by a competent and independent review mechanism, the right to counsel with respect to all proceedings and the right to have his or her conviction and sentence reviewed by a higher tribunal according to the law. However, international law does recognise restrictions in criminal justice for reasons of national security.[20] However, such deviations from the ordinary practice of adjudication must always be temporary and meet standards of legality, necessity and proportionality.[21] The principle of fair trial assures individuals that they have a place to turn to, should the state or others fail to honour their human rights.[22]

The relevance of this normative framework that is meant to safeguard the right to a fair trial can only be understood against the context of its mirror image: the historical reminiscence of the Stalinist (and, to a lesser, extent National-Socialist) show trials; these were the very opposite of fair trials, not in the least because of their one-sidedly executive dominance of the communicative process. 'Show trials' and 'political trials' are often mixed up in public discourse. The overriding characteristics of a classical show trial in the Stalinist sense are 1) the total exclusion of the element of chance and/or risk from the trial and 2) the predominant function of the trial as a tool in 'educating' the public at home and abroad in order to strengthen ideological power. Sometimes such trials are not strictly Stalinist, in the sense that they do not primarily serve to demonstrate and confirm totalitarian rule behind a façade of justice administered. However, we do call them *political* as soon as the executive branch of a government uses criminal law predominantly to further its own political agenda. Otto Kirchheimer, in his classic study *Political Justice*, defines political trials as attempts by regimes to control opponents by using legal procedure for political ends (Alex P. Schmid has extensively covered this in chapters 2 and 4).[23] Authorities deploy criminal law to maintain their dominant power; they eliminate political opponents by outlawing oppositional voices, making them illegal. In such cases, courts only serve political powers, not justice.

However, this type of state-controlled show trial is not the association that was invoked by American comments on the Ghailani case quoted earlier. The show element in the trial they referred to was the risk that the terrorist suspects would manage to dominate the courtroom with their narratives of injustice, thereby turning the trial into a second 'terrorist show'—the first being the attack they had perpetrated.

There is however even a third type of show imaginable: a show in which the authorities demonstrate, through the way in which sentences are meted out, that modern democracies are fully capable of performing a show of justice in a positive sense. The Nuremberg trials may be regarded as a modern model for how a trial can be a communicative masterpiece and performance of justice. They did so by revealing the genocidal dimensions of the holocaust, establishing a historical narrative that stood the test of time and one that is accepted by large majorities of the public in Germany and in most of the rest of the world. Nuremberg created a collective memory, fixed responsibility on Germany and set standards for adjudicating on future misconduct by states and social groups. Indeed, the Nuremberg trial was *the* example of a convincing performance by the victorious powers in using criminal law—rather than mere revengeful force—to deal with war criminals and state terrorists.

In fact, the concept of show trial can refer to totally different types of politicised trials, depending on the normative charge. In the words of legal scholar Awol Kassim Allo, 'What counts is not that a trial is labelled a 'show trial', it is rather the end that the "show" serves.'[24] This brings us to the core question of this volume: which performative strategies were used by the actors in court to convince audiences of the validity of a specific narrative of (in)justice?

12.3. Performative Strategies in Court: What Kind of 'Show' can Terrorism Trials Offer?

It has been stated by various experts that terrorism is a form of communication.[25] Terrorism expert Brian M. Jenkins noted as early as 1975 that 'terrorism is theatre'.[26] Peter Waldmann added to these observations the statement that most terrorists explicitly want theatre, since they are bent on provoking state power.[27] With their deeds, terrorists seek to communicate their visions of justice and injustice, visions on the rearrangement of power relations and attempts to rebalance them. However, there is another side to this coin: counter-terrorism also involves a form of communication, it is performative as well.[28] In court, the prosecutor has a story to tell as well. After an attack, or an attempted one, perpetrators are, if and when apprehended, usually brought to trial. In the courtroom, all parties involved in the drama are brought together. Within the narrow confinements of this stage, issues of (in)justice are addressed, retribution is demanded and justice is carried out—at least that is the theory, to which reality does not always live up. Sometimes terrorists are tried behind closed doors in secret courts; in some cases, trials are so heavily politicised or even tampered with that they resemble more the classic show trial in the Stalinist sense than any display of justice.[29]

The question, then, is what strategy do the actors in this theatre of lawfare, which often amounts to a public drama, follow and what are the legal, political and social consequences of their strategies? Does politicising a trial, putting on a show, rule out the risks referred to earlier? Or, on the contrary, does it incite sectors of the public by violating their sense of justice? Can it placate the public, restore social peace and prevent further radicalisation? Following the provocation-repression theory,[30] a trial controlled and run by the prosecution without counter-balance from judges could provide terrorists with new proof of state oppression, strengthening injustice frames of reference that enable the recruitment of new members and initiate new violent campaigns.

In the introduction, we presented our working definition of the concept of performativity. This definition, however open-ended it may be, refers to discursive efforts and actions to construct social realities,[31] as applied to terrorism trials:[32]

> Performativity in terrorism trials refers to acts or strategies (coherently or incoherently) adopted by parties with a stake in the to try to persuade their target audience(s) in (and outside) the courtroom of the justice of their narrative(s) and the injustice of the one on the opposite side of the bar.

We have seen that these strategies were restricted by the different historical contexts, which provided the dramaturgical framework for the trials.

The first element in every stage play was the script, which was to provide for a plot and for the different narratives and storylines to be heard. The initial script was triggered by the suspect's crime, and drafted by the charge(s) brought by the prosecutor against the accused. Criminal law functioned as a set of guiding principles, dictating how this script should be written. Were intelligence reports accepted as evidence in court? Could witnesses give evidence behind closed doors? The script, or the 'director's clues', provided the legal rules of the game. By bending or changing these rules, the authorities could influence the outcome of the trial. At the same time, manipulating the rules of adjudication during a trial could 'spoil' the game and could undermine confidence in the law.

Secondly, an important question with regard to this dramaturgical element was the nature of the script: Was it a script within a civil law or within a common law system? In other words, was the trial inquisitorial in nature or adversarial? Did the defence need to convince a jury, or was it the judge who heard and weighed the material? Another structural element that mattered was the amount of evidence that needed to be presented in court, which impacted on the length of the trial. In the Netherlands, for example, the charges, evidence and defence's response were mainly exchanged and worked out on paper before the actual trial began.

Third, the way the stage was set also affected the unfolding of the drama. Did a trial take place in a regular court building, or were the defendants transported to a fortified location where the visitors had to go through heavy security checks? Were the defendants placed on regular benches or locked in cages, as was the case in several Italian trials? The courtroom/building could thus enhance or downplay the dramatic quality of a trial as well.

Fourthly, the play itself was performed by actors, who adopted different strategies, which will be discussed below. Actors were the prosecution, the defence, the judges, the witnesses and sometimes also the victims or their families. The play developed through a contest between the prosecution and the defence over the writing of the script. Each side attempted to offer its own script as the way to go and try to arrange its performance so as to advance its truth. Judges often acted both as directors and audience, depending on the type of criminal justice system of the country involved.

Lastly, we have seen that every play was in need of an audience. In terrorism trials, as in other trials, the audience was constituted by the judge (in a civil law system) or jury (in a common law system), but also by the public (including journalists) in the courtroom and the public outside. What the public saw and heard was, however, sometimes filtered, if not controlled, by the media's reporting of the trial. Or it was broadcast directly to the public in and outside the courtroom itself. This gave the media, especially the social media, an important, often crucial, role in the play as well.

Within these dramaturgical frames the terrorism trials unfolded, and resulted in different types of 'show', depending on the relative success of the performative and communicative strategies adopted by the various actors, and on the question which communicative mode of negotiating legality and justice dominated the trial.

12.4. A Communicatively Oriented Typology of Terrorism Trials

A highly defining characteristic of terrorism trials is the struggle for communicative dominance, the contest for the communicative mode in which questions of legality, legitimacy and justice are negotiated. A 'fair trial' is usually characterised by the confirmation and correct and transparant application of legal norms and rules. However, in case of terrorism trials, more often than not turn into a site of severe contestation. The parties involved adopt communicative strategies, execute performative acts; all in order to appropriate, impose and disseminate their version of justice and legitimacy. Based on the definition of performative strategies in terrorism trials, we could now try to place the various terrorism trials discussed in this volume in a graph. The question of positioning is defined by a horizontal axis and a vertical one, and guided by three questions: 1) To what extent did the actors involved accept and uphold the legal system as mutual mode of communication in and outside the courtroom? 2) To what extent did the actors involved tried and succeeded to dominate the communicative space and impose their version of justice and injustice? 3) To what extent did the trial attract media attentation and perhaps even resulted in a 'trial by media'? By answering these question, admittedly in a highly qualitative and associative way, we have placed the trials in the graph below. The horizontal axis delineates the different communicative strategies in court. At the left end of the axis, the executive powers/authorities dominate the communicative mode and turn the trial into a one-sided 'show' of executive prerogatives. This restriction of the communicative space of the defendants is often justified by security considerations. On the right end of the pole the terrorist defendants follow a strategy of rupture, reject the existing modes of communication and law and turn the legal proceedings into a communicative continuation of their struggle. The vertical axis depicts the level of media attention generated by the trial, ranging from nothing to a total take-over of the communicative process by outside forces in the media. Based on a number of cases that we looked into, the following typology can be developed (the trials' position is assessed based on the communicative dominance during the last stage of the trial):

- A *status-quo-trial* where everyone complies with the existing communicative framework of applicable law and legal conventions, such as in the Dutch Piranha and Hofstad group cases. This trial can be positioned in the centre of the horizontal axis and low on the vertical axis. Both sides refrained from adopting explicit performative strategies. Such trials do not score high on the lawfare scale, and

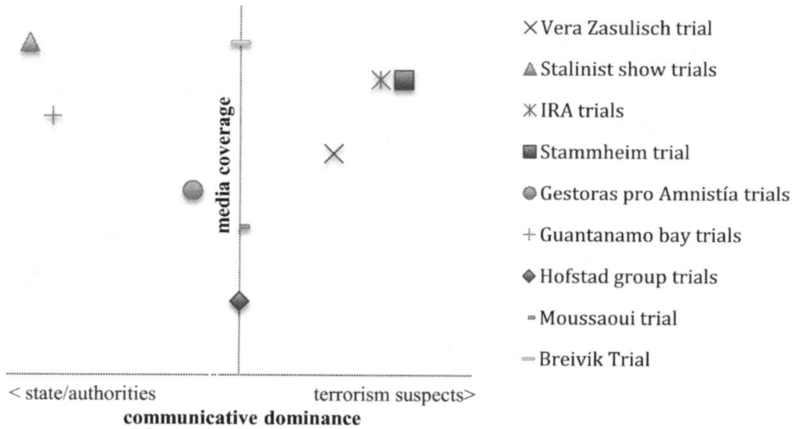

Figure 12.1: A communicatively oriented typology of terrorism trials

often indeed offer closure rather than rupture for society at large, if not always for those accused of serious political crimes.

- A *trial as the continuation of the terrorist struggle* by legal and communicative means. The defendants break through existing modes of communications, reject legal conventions and challenge the legitimacy of the system as such. They often generate a good deal of media attention and inspire new rounds of violence by terrorist sympathisers. The German Stammheim trial (see Chapter 6) in its final stage would be an example of such a significant performative effort by the defence lawyers and their clients. Such trials are a theatre of open lawfare, involving rupture and leading to some kind of closure perhaps only in the long run.
- A *trial as continuation of executive counterterrorism practice*. Not law, but security offers the underlying framework and restricts the open, communicative space in which proceedings take place. Such executive 'shows' are in their extreme form exemplified by the classical Stalinist show trials. Here, the prosecution dominates the show, sometimes even hand-in-glove with the judge or the jury. This show can also be a de facto non-show-like trial, closed to the public or the media, but organised by the state to serve its security agenda. The trial may, however, also be staged as a virtual show: the trial serves as a tool of risk management, when justice is subordinated to principles of national security, turning the trial into a site of 'actuarial justice'. When crimes under consideration deal with conspiracies and terrorist preparations rather than actual attacks, it is difficult to draw the line between *habeas corpus* and imagination—since without an attack, or 'smoking gun', often only inferences can be drawn, and possible future attack be imagined,

rather than proven with statistical evidence. The lawfare element depends on the degree of secrecy involved, but the risk of rupture can be significant.

- A trial may turn into a *media show*—not run so much by the terrorists or the prosecution, but dramatised in the media, often capitalising on public feelings of vengeance and outrage—often helped by *sideshows* staged by audiences and groups outside the courtroom (victims, sympathisers, etc.). Starting point is not the law, 'revolution' or security, but the communicative mode has been taken over in advance by outside forces in the media. The lawfare element is difficult to assess here, since media reporting may fuel the conflict at stake. Closure/rupture strategies may both be possible, rupture being defined as above as the rejection, obstruction or undermining of the legal system.
- A *performance of justice*: a show where the verdict educates the public about the importance of the rule of law in a democratic society creates a collective memory and sets standards for future conduct by states and society. This type of show is run by the judge/jury, but the performative strategy is based on a (perceived) neutral application of the law, not on partisan politicisation of justice. In the ideal world, such a theatre of lawfare provides closure for all parties involved, if not immediately then in the long run. The law as mutual mode of communication has been confirmed or recaptured.

Nota bene: The trial may change in type during the course of its proceedings. It may, for instance, begin as a not so dramatic show but develop into a media show. Other transformations are also possible. We will elaborate on these types below.

12.4.1. *First Type: A Status-Quo-Trial*

The first type of trial is not that dramatic at all. A terrorist trial does not always have to be a social drama. There are indeed instances when terrorism trials created little spectacle. In the Netherlands, the trial against the Moluccan activists who raided and occupied the Indonesian Ambassador's residence in 1970 in order to further their separatist cause, killing a police officer in the process, proceeded very smoothly. The defendants pleaded guilty, complied with the court's demands and raised only one moral question: they wanted their plight to be heard. They wanted to tell their story of expulsion from the Moluccan islands, of the apparent promise made by the Dutch authorities to lobby for their independence from Indonesia and to highlight the discrimination they suffered in Dutch postcolonial society.[33] In this particular case, those accused of terrorism did address a social grievance, but both the judge and the general audience were receptive to their narrative and acknowledged it in their responses. The defendants' communicative space was wide enough and their cause was recognised. The judge, himself a former colonial officer, paid tribute to the sufferings of the Moluccans, their plight after 1950 and their loss of homeland. This, in turn, appeased the defendants and made them accept the verdict based on Dutch laws. They did so without protest—the sentence was lenient considering the fact that it had involved the killing of a policeman.[34] If there was a show at all, it showed the Moluccans' tragic fate and Dutch society's feelings of guilt about having let them down in 1950 and beyond. The law had been violated, yes; a policeman had been killed as the Indonesian residence was occupied. Nevertheless, there was no clash of incompatible ethical or communicative frameworks. On the contrary, the Moluccan activists appealed to their families' shared history with the Dutch people, recalling their parents' loyal service to the Queen, demanding only that the government live up to its own standards and promises.[35]

Another example of remarkably little theatre was the latest hearings in the Hofstad group case, staged in late 2010. When the trial started, following the murder of Theo van Gogh in November 2004, the defendants, all of whom belonged to a group around Van Gogh's murderer Mohammed Bouyeri who were charged with participating in a terrorist organisation and inciting hatred, refused every form of cooperation with the court. They argued that, first of all, the man-made Dutch judicial system was not in line with the divine rule of law and violated *hakimiyyat Allah* (the sovereignty of God). Secondly, they claimed that public and political pressure prevented them from getting a fair hearing in any case. In the heated and anxious climate of the months following Van Gogh's murder, this second complaint had some merit. Government officials had proclaimed a 'war' against Dutch terrorists, public vigilance campaigns against terrorist attacks were launched, radicalised Muslims were spotted everywhere and revenge-fuelled attacks against mosques and other Muslim sites took place.[36] Seven suspects were arrested and charged with being part of a terrorist and criminal organisation engaged in inciting hatred and preparing for terrorist attacks. In 2006, they were convicted on the counts of attempting to murder police officers, the possession of hand grenades and membership of a terrorist organisation. One suspect, Jason Walters, who threw the hand grenade, was sentenced to 15 years in prison.[37]

However, as years passed without any further jihadist attack on Dutch soil, the Dutch political and social climate changed. In 2008, the Court of Appeal in The Hague acquitted those belonging to the Hofstad group on the count of membership of a criminal terrorist organisation.[38] The court hearings in 2010 proceeded almost unnoticed, until Jason Walters stood up to announce his faith in the Dutch democratic system and the rule of law. He demonstrated his abandonment of extremist behaviour by conforming to the norms in court, wearing ordinary clothes and sporting a modern haircut. 'I am certain that I will receive a fair trial', he stated at the end of the pre-trial hearing in the High-Security Court in Amsterdam on 16 July 2010, thereby following a strategy of signalling trust in and conformation to the law.[39] Although this story is an exceptional instance of a terrorist's public conversion, it provides a valuable insight: a change of times, demonstration of reflective justice and a terrorist conversion caused the trial to normalise. The charge of membership of a terrorist organisation was later reconfirmed, but the trial hardly presented a show any more: no party involved tried to turn it into a drama of conflicting ethical frameworks.

Another example of a rather undramatic case of mutual compliance to applicable law and legal conventions is the trial of the first and only Dutch female terrorism suspect, Soumaya S. On 15 March 2011, the Dutch Attorney-General submitted an advisory opinion to the Supreme Court that stated that the verdict against Soumaya S., who had been arrested in 2005 and convicted of participating in a terrorist organisation, had to be annulled. Soumaya S. had already been sentenced for carrying an Agram 2000 machine gun, but had been put on trial a second time for being a member of a terrorist group.[40] Strangely enough, almost no public attention was paid to all of this. No front-page newspaper headlines, no interviews with disgruntled politicians or a disappointed public prosecutor were seen or heard in the national media. No audience outside or inside the courtroom explicitly applauded the verdict, drew attention to the outcome or rallied against it. No public outrage was discernible. This terrorism trial thus ended with a whimper, rather than with a bang.

As has been stated above, the undramatic character of this trial can be explained in part by the brevity of the trial, the inquisitorial nature of the Dutch criminal justice system, and the lack of historical precedent. But more importantly: the terrorist suspects themselves did not follow a strategy of rupture, but of total compliance. Neither were there enough sympathisers willing to stage sideshows, probably due to the lack of support for home-grown jihadist terrorism in the years between 2004 and 2010 within the Dutch Muslim community.

12.4.2. *Second Type: A Continuation of the Terrorist Struggle*

Instances like the Moluccan trials in the 1970s, where those accused of terrorism remain within the boundaries set by the legal system's rules of court procedures and share society's moral values and principles, where the magistrates and general public act low key and are receptive to the terrorists' story, are rare. They mostly depend on the attacks' low level of lethality, the short duration of a terrorist campaign and on the shared historical context in which terrorists and host society operate. Peaceful debates in court are an exception, rather than the rule. More often than not, terrorists challenge and contest society's moral principles in court. This is the second type of terrorism trial we have identified: the show is staged by those accused of acts of terrorism, where the *suspects and their lawyers* play up their version of reality. To be sure, those accused of an act of terrorism have already made their first point with the physical attack. Due to the terrorist attack (assuming they were not arrested for preparatory actions beforehand) they moved to the national stage and into the limelight of mass media and public opinion. The terrorist attack itself on a prominent victim was a kind of kangaroo trial, their own primitive form of justice. Once arrested and confined to the narrow space of the courtroom, they themselves had to stand trial.

A major example of an intended show trial staged by terrorists as continuation of their struggle by legal and communicative means can be found in the history of the Red Army Faction (RAF) in Germany. One of the largest successes of the founders of the RAF (Andreas Baader, Gudrun Ensslin, Ulrike Meinhof and Jan-Carl Raspe) was that, together with their lawyers, they succeeded in portraying their trial—which lasted from May 1975 to April 1977—as a political one, conjuring up an image of political justice in Germany. They tried to portray themselves as political warriors, and in the end as the ultimate martyrs for the revolution's cause. As Jacco Pekelder and Klaus Weinhauer (see Chapter 6) have written elsewhere, their lawyers sought a direct confrontation with the other parties involved in the criminal justice system and carried out a 'political defence': 'More than attacking the actual accusations against their clients these *Linksanwälte* [left-wing lawyers—a play on words in German] seemed to aim at undermining the legitimacy of the trial and the justice system that had produced it.'[41] Although in the end justice prevailed, the West German judiciary damaged its own image of impartiality by reacting so nervously during the trial. The RAF suspects used the court to stage their own play, which served their own revolutionary agenda. They used the long-drawn-out period in which the Stammheim trial unravelled to radicalise and mobilise a second and third generation of new recruits to their cause. These newcomers in turn initiated a second round of violence, the aim of which was the liberation of their historical leaders from jail. When this backfired, climaxing in the raid on the hijacked Landshut aeroplane in Mogadishu in October 1977, the Stammheim prisoners' play moved to its final act: they committed suicide, but staged it in such a way that it looked like politically-motivated murders by the German authorities. With this final act of vengeance, they wrote their own ending to the state's judicial script and turned it upside down. As a consequence, in the eyes of a sizeable segment of the public, both at home and abroad, it was not the suicidal terrorists, but the West German authorities who stood accused in the court of public opinion. With the indispensable help of the mass media, the RAF was able to instrumentalise the Stammheim trial for its own ends and turn it into a veritable show—with far-reaching consequences.[42]

12.4.3. *Third Type: The State is Running the Show*

However, in many cases terrorism trials are a stage performance by the state, which leads us to the third type of terrorist show trial: a continuation of executive counterterrorism practice. Authorities bring terrorists to justice in order to show that there is a terrorist threat but while assuring the public that they can manage to contain and control it. Terrorism trials serve to show that the executive brings peace to society: the perpetrators are caught, law and order are in good hands but further vigilance is called for. Sometimes, substantive law and procedural rules are modified to suit the state's security needs. The executive selects a particular legal tool to ensure that the risk of acquittal is minimal. Hence, the authorities may resort to rewriting the script as well: they sometimes wait until the curtain falls on the criminal trial and then stage their final punishment beyond the eye of the public. The acquitted suspect is sometimes expelled from the country or made subject to permanent surveillance and control orders the moment he or she leaves the courthouse.[43] Some people argue that the Guantánamo tribunals represent a type of trial where the government one-sidedly runs and rules the show, without much media presence, totally restricting the defendant's communicative space.

A variation within this type of state-dominated performance is the terrorist trial organised as a site of 'actuarial justice'. Here the prosecution turns a terrorism trial into a quasi-virtual trial because more and more often such a trial takes place *before* an alleged terrorist attack has been carried out. The trial is a site where not crime, but risk is being sentenced.[44] Contrary to what Foucault stated, it is not the case that 'law recedes'.[45] In fact, as Louise Amoore stipulates, 'as risk advances [...] law itself authorizes a specific and particular mode of risk management' which entails that '[...] evidence, the judgment of the expert witness, and the legal subject as bearer of rights are all reoriented in a risk regime that acts pre-emptively and authorizes with indefinite and indeterminate limits'.[46] Competences, provisions and measures are adapted to make sure the judges (are likely to) render a conviction; either by using criminal law, or via administrative or immigration law (control orders, administrative rule or alien's rights).

Those trials that involve suspects arrested based merely on preparatory actions, on allegations, suspicions or intentions can be termed *virtual* or 'what if' trials. An act is put under judicial scrutiny that may only exist in an imagined future—as (pre- or re-)constructed by the prosecuting authorities. Conspiracy trials, thought crimes, incitement to hatred: such crimes involve possible deeds in the future, based on vague plans and/or allegations only. Depending on the assessment of preparatory evidence, the moment of culpability and the moment of the actual deed are severed. The relationship between offence and punishment becomes much more indirect. Pre-emption and premediation replace retribution inquiries, thereby raising new human rights issues. Rather than assessing different versions of the 'truth' about an incident, judges have to deal with techniques of imagining possible future incidents. Premediation and security imagination replace responsibility for concrete actions. This type of terrorism trial serves to placate virtual threats; they have become instruments in risk management. The sword of justice has been 'securitised'. Deterrence, retribution for present dangers or restoration of social peace—the main functions of criminal law—give way to a secondary function: meting out sentences to pre-empt future risks. Under such circumstances, the trial becomes a theatre of imagined terrorist futures, where the defendants' communicative space is severely limited.[47]

12.4.4. *Fourth Type: The Media are Running the Show*

Terrorism trials may turn into show trials through media saturation coverage but also because the public considers some of these trials to be a spectacle in themselves. Not law, security or 'revolution', but the dramatic potential of the trial becomes the mode of communication and dominates the narrative. Going back to the pre-modern age, trials always were often also theatrical performances. The perpetrator was put on a scaffold and physically punished in full view of all the spectators. The aim of this performance was not just the carrying out of worldly justice, but demonstrating the fate of sinners. Public punishments and executions were a direct *memento mori*, demonstrating how the gates of hell would open for anyone who dared to violate divine and human laws. Such trials were often a theatre of horror. Since those days, most trials have lost such dramatic quality. At their best, they became a theatre of common sense and civility. Trials should ideally be theatres to stage examples of objectivity and prudence, based on well-established criteria and procedures. However, terrorism and war crimes trials have the tendency to slip back into pre-modern theatres of terror. Hannah Arendt followed the trial of Eichmann in the 1960s and concluded that he was tried more for the suffering of the Jewish people than for his individual deeds.[48] In public opinion, as voiced by the media, terrorists should also be punished for the fear and shock they inflict upon society. In this way, adjudication based on concrete criminal acts, individually attributed, disappears behind the front of public indignation. Public opinion takes over the role of prosecutor, judge and jury alike. The trial becomes a show of public vengeance and outrage. In fact, those accused of terrorism are in many cases already sentenced by the media, leaving the judges often hardly any room for manoeuvre, let alone to issue less severe sentences or even acquittals. If they acted otherwise, they might even run the risk of being (virtually) lynched by an outraged public.[49]

A media show can also be created by sideshows, as staged by groups outside the courtroom. The audience—including the victims—has to make sense of the competing narratives as well. They sit and listen; or, like a Greek *chorus*, they comment. They sometimes have their own agendas. Sympathisers for the defendants may stage sideshows, organise picket lines outside the court building, submit petitions and protests in the media against the treatment of those in jail. On the other hand, victims may get together and protest against the court's perceived leniency. Prisoners may initiate hunger strikes and defendants may start an (international) lobby effort to win support for their cause, as the IRA did in the case of Bobby Sands. The defendants may inspire or even appeal to their comrades and followers outside the courtroom to act on their behalf and initiate new rounds of violence, the aim being to put extra pressure on the state, blackmailing the authorities to release the suspects or taking vengeance on the judges, as happened in Germany and Italy in the 1970s when second and third generation terrorists 'punished' judicial representatives for the verdicts being issued against their leaders.

12.4.5. *The Fifth Type: A Persuasive Performance of Justice*

The fifth type involves a show where equality of arms exist, where law and legal procedures offer all parties free communicative space. In these cases, the trial might come to reveal violations of justice, and the verdict might educate the public about the importance of upholding the rule of law in a democratic society. As in the Breivik trial, the verdict shapes a collective memory and sets standards for the future conduct of both government and society. This type of show is run by the judge or the jury, whose performative strategy is based on a (perceived) neutral application of the law, whereby they refuse to bow to a partisan politicisation. Amongst the competing narratives of (in)justice, the *judges* have to try to reconstruct an accurate version of the facts of the case under consideration and interpret and apply the law to it. They have to probe deeply into opposing narratives, diverse testimonies and partisan accounts to discover the various motives and intentions behind the terrorist actions.

From this point of view, judges have first of all an obligation to establish a thorough, accurate and wide-ranging account of the facts pertaining to the incident before the court. Secondly, they have to reveal the underlying motives and strategies, and relate these to the context in which the incident occurred. In carrying out such a penetrating inquiry, they can make a valuable contribution to the general understanding of the facts and their background. They can more or less write history. They may hear the victims, speak on behalf of a terrorised population and thereby give them back their agency.

Of course, reconstructing the truth is an especially troublesome endeavour when it concerns a preventive arrest, based on preparatory actions only. Judges are not there to make up for the authorities' shortcoming or failures in gathering enough compelling evidence; they do not have to protect another branch of government. They have to settle the issue that falls under their jurisdiction, have to throw new light on the affair,[50] which is difficult when an offence exists only as a *possibility*. Carrying out justice in a situation of security risks, of allegations, presumptions and guilt-by-association runs the gauntlet of turning the trial into a virtual show. The judges may face severe criticism from an enraged public and security officials if they acquit the suspects. On the other hand, if they do not, they may face condemnation by the constituency of the terrorists.

In those cases when the judges manage to keep the balance, a fair trial can become a performative act in itself. The verdict will not only be perceived as legally justified, the narrative of guilt and injustice emerging from such a trial can make history, change existing norms and impact on the prevailing values in a given society. At the interface of terrorism, law enforcement and public opinion, terrorism trials can offer an ideal opportunity to showcase justice in progress and demonstrate how terrorist suspects can be dealt with by the laws of the land.

A convincing performance of justice can, moreover, restore the information asymmetry that allowed terrorists to win the (tacit) approval of radical constituencies and can also undermine the narrative utilised to attract support. Most importantly, terrorism trials are also platforms where victims may regain their voice and where their fate, as a consequence of the terrorist's offence, is put centre stage. According to Tom Parker, the former policy director for Terrorism, Counterterrorism and Human

Rights at Amnesty International USA, it is time to redress the balance and to use victim narratives to confront the violence of armed groups. Parker specifically refers to human rights defenders and NGOs, but the same contention can be made regarding terrorism trials: such trials offer a powerful platform for revealing and challenging the terrorists' narratives by confronting them with the messages of horror, pain and destruction they inflicted upon their victims.[51]

12.5. Terrorism Trials as Catharsis

We have extensively described *how* terrorism trials more often than not involve show elements. We would like to argue, however, that they *have* to be theatre as well—in the sense that they present a performance of justice. As noted earlier, 'What counts is not that a trial is labelled a "show trial", it is rather the end that the "show" serves.'[52] The trial is the nexus where countervailing narratives meet, where moral frameworks clash and where society addresses, confirms and possibly repairs a fundamental breach. A trial can demonstrate that trespassers will be convicted and that victims are heard. It may repair the information asymmetry caused by the terrorists' hold on their constituents. The trial and the verdict can undermine the terrorists' claim to justice and reveal the horror and destruction they inflicted upon their victims and upon society. In this sense, it is important that as many people as possible are able to watch the spectacle unfold.

The question thus becomes: what does it take for a terrorism trial to be considered a performance of justice in the eyes of the public? First of all, the authorities should stick to the script. In a structural sense, the script does of course depend on the nature of the criminal law system; whether it is an inquisitorial or an adversarial system, whether evidence should be presented in the courtroom at full length, or can be dealt with on paper before the trial starts. Nevertheless, in both systems—the civil law and the common law—performative strategies matter. Judges in particular have the responsibility to take care that a trial does not resemble a 'Pirandello play',[53] where each actor follows his own account of events, where the most powerful one decides what the truth has to be and where the spectator is left totally powerless when trying to judge what the underlying narrative is, let alone to assess the truth about the plot. To preserve the integrity of the judiciary, the executive should refrain completely from tampering with procedural rules during the trial; it should be extremely careful not to be perceived as trying to exert political control over the conduct and outcome of a trial.

Secondly, terrorism trials should not be based on premediation, virtualities, or seen as a tool of risk management. Magistrates and prosecutors have to make sure the trial does not develop into a demonstration of maximum security and all-encompassing risk management, as the trial at Stammheim did in part, or as the military tribunals in Guantánamo have done fully. The insatiable desire for security should not trump justice; underlying political conflicts cannot be solved through security measures alone. Judicial catharsis should not be sacrificed to secure risk management.

Thirdly, transparency matters. In the case of the Indonesian trial against Abu Bakar Ba'asyir, the court decided to relocate the hearings from the South Jakarta district court to the larger Agriculture Ministry's compound in Central Jakarta, so as to provide more space for the expected number of people. Against critics who feared that this decision would turn the trial into a media circus, the court contended that an open prosecution, visible to as many spectators as possible, demonstrated justice in progress, underscored confidence in the state's counter-terrorism efforts and showed how new laws were put in practice. Thus, the trial would support Indonesia's rule of law *vis-à-vis* extremist challenges.[54]

Fourthly, a trial should leave room for conflicting narratives of truth and injustice. Judges should make sure that the ongoing transformation of a political conflict into a legal dispute takes into account all the narratives. Amongst all these competing narratives of justice/injustice, the judges have to try to re-establish an accurate version of the facts and interpret and apply the appropriate law to them. They have to probe deeply into the differing narratives, evidence and accounts to discover the various motives and intentions behind acts of terrorism. From this performative point of view, judges have first of all an obligation to establish a thorough, accurate and comprehensive account of the facts pertaining to the incident before the court. Secondly, they have to reveal the underlying motives and strategies, and relate them to the context in which the incident happened. They may hear the victims, speak on behalf of the terrorised population and give them back their agency. Responding to all this with unemotional adjudication subsequently provides the best meta-narrative of social and legal resilience thinkable. In this sense, judges have to be aware of sideshows too, where sympathisers, victims, and other target audiences voice their version of justice.

The late Judge Cassese's reflections on the Achille Lauro Affair support this argument. In his seminal discussion of the lessons the international community of states could draw from this incident, Cassese pointed to the fact that there are long-term, mid-term and short-term policy objectives involved in dealing with terrorism. In the short run, governments may give preference to order and stability, viewing terrorism essentially as an attack on the public order and choosing to deal with this attack with repressive military or intelligence instruments. However, he argued, terrorism may also reflect a 'desire for social change, innovation and the adaptation of international relations to changing needs, even when, alas, these are expressed in such perverted and destructive ways'.[55] In the mid- and long term, intransigence to or even denial of this political narrative may alienate the terrorists' broader constituencies from the political system they are operating in. This is not to say that the terrorists' narrative should be accepted or even agreed to, but it should be countered and responded to rather than silenced by repressive means only. Judges or juries can have a role in unveiling these minority narratives by paying attention to the deeper motives or social grievances (without needing to view these as legitimate or rightful 'root causes' for terrorism). Revealing such narratives of social change can do justice to the political conflict at hand. Denying or *only* criminalising these narratives and reducing the trial to a mere dichotomy of legal/illegal narrows reality and could in the end both backfire against the 'order and stability' paradigm of the executive and undermine criminal law's legitimacy in the eyes of aggrieved minorities.

When these four conditions are met, a trial will offer a platform on which narratives of injustice confront each other. A trial not only metes out justice to those suspected of acts of terrorism, but also assesses their intentions, their motives and their legitimations. It reveals the ideas terrorists have to offer on questions of rights and righteousness. If an attack has taken place, or if suspects are arrested in a context of heavy political conflicts, law cannot fix this situation of political division. But glossing over the competing narratives, storing them away in indefinite detention does not serve to solve these conflicts either. Not bringing terrorists to justice out of short term security considerations may in fact further deepen the political antagonisms. If the terrorists represent only a tiny faction within a social movement, or even if they represent hardly anyone at all, letting them tell their story in court may just expose this narrative as the hysterical, nihilistic or illegitimate argument it is.

After shocking incidents of terror and destruction, society needs to regain a greater degree of balance. Terrorism trials, well-prepared and properly conducted, can help to repair the damage by offering a secure, communicative space where clashing narratives of justice and injustice can be discussed and balanced, where facts and culpability can be assessed. Such trials can help to prevent a schism from opening up and to assist the immediate victims of terrorism attacks and society at large to come to terms with loss, grievances and grief. An open and transparent trial is crucial for re-establishing what happened and why, and will serve to institutionalise or mitigate the need for vengeance and retribution. Inevitably, terrorism trials are show trials, staging a social drama, revealing narratives of injustice and grievances. They show how law and legal proceedings—although often lengthy and tiresome—can serve as mode of communicating and negotiating these narratives. Sometimes, at their best, they can even provide some kind of judicial catharsis for most, if not all, actors and audiences involved. Only then may the curtain fall.

Notes

1 Many thanks to Alex P. Schmid for his comments on this conclusion. An earlier, different but overlapping version of this concluding chapter was drafted as internet publication: Beatrice de Graaf, 'Terrorists on Trial: A Performative Perspective'. ICCT-Research Paper, 2011. http://www.icct.nl/download/file/ICCT-de-Graaf-EM-Paper-Terrorism-Trials-as-Theatre.pdf (accessed 25 February 2016).

2 'New Military Trials at Guantanamo Bay Could Include 9/11 Suspects', *Fox News* (8 March 2011); 'Obama billigt neue Militärverfahren in Guantánamo', DPA (16 March 2011).

3 Ibid.

4 James Taranto, 'Obama's Show Trials', *The Wall Street Journal* (13 November 2009), http://online.wsj.com/article/SB10001424052748703683804574533833220552624.html. Retrieved 18 March 2011.

5 Charlie Savage, 'Ghailani Verdict Reignites Debate Over the Proper Court for Terrorism Trials', *New York Times* (18 November 2010).

6 Committee on the Evaluation of Counterterrorism Policy (Suyver Committee), *Naar een integrale evaluatie van antiterrorisme maatregelen [Towards an Integrated Evaluation of Counterterrorism Policies]. Report no.* IBIS-13174. (The Hague: Dutch Government, May 2009), pp. 16–23.

7 Dutch Government, 'Antiterrorisme Maatregelen in Nederland in het Eerste Decennium de 21e Eeuw' [Counterterrorism Measures in the Netherlands in the First Decade of the 21st Century]. *Report no. 04126-6359*. (The Hague: Dutch Government, January 2011), pp. 87/91.

8 Bell, theories of performance, p. 208.

9 M. Ignatieff, *The Lesser Evil: Political ethics in an age of terror* (Princeton: Princeton University Press, 2004), p. 46; cf. Andrew Asworth, 'Security, Terrorism and the Value of Human Rights', in: B.J. Goold, and L. Lazarus (eds), *Security and Human Rights* (Oxford and Portland, Oregon: Hart Publishing, 2007), pp. 207–209, 224.

10 ICJ, *Assessing Damage, Urging Action: Report of the Eminent Jurists Panel on Terrorism, Counter-*

terrorism and Human Rights (Geneva: International Commission of Jurists, 2009), pp. 156–157, 165–167.

11 Steven Vago, *Law and Society* (Upper Saddle River, NJ: Prentice Hall, 2009), pp. 19–21.

12 Linder, 'The Nelson Mandela (Rivonia) Trial: An account', 2011.

13 Mark van Hoecke, *Law as Communication* (Oxford/Portland, OR: Hart, 2002), p. 10.

14 Ibid., p. 8.

15 Ibid., p. 10.

16 H. Bredemeier quoted in R. Cotterrell, *The Sociology of Law*, pp. 89–92.

17 Edward A. Ross quoted in Mathieu Deflem, *Sociology of Law: Visions of a scholarly tradition* (Cambridge: Cambridge University Press, 2008), p. 102.

18 Van Hoecke, *Law as Communication*, p. 7.

19 Ibid.

20 See, for example, European Convention of Human Rights, Article 6. http://www.echr.coe.int/Documents/Convention_ENG.pdf.

21 OHCHR (Office of the High Commissioner for Human Rights), *Human Rights, Terrorism and Counter-Terrorism*. Factsheet No.32, GE.08–41872, (Geneva/New York: Office of the United Nations High Commissioner for Human Rights/ United Nations, 2008), pp. 28–29.

22 Bryan S. Turner, 'Outline on a Theory of Human Rights', *Sociology*, 27:3 (1993), pp. 489–512.

23 Otto Kirchheimer, *Political Justice: The use of legal procedure for political ends* (Princeton: Princeton University Press, 1961).

24 Allo, 'The "Show" in the Show Trials', p. 72.

25 Alex P. Schmid and Janny de Graaf, *Violence as Communication: Insurgent terrorism and the Western news media* (London: SAGE, 1982), p. 175.

26 Brian M. Jenkins, 'International Terrorism: A new mode of conflict', in: David Carlton and Carlo Schaerf (eds), *International Terrorism and World Security* (London: Croom Helm, 1975), p. 16.

27 Cf. Peter Waldmann, *Terrorismus: Provokation der Macht* (Hamburg: Murmann Verlag, 2005); Louise Richardson, *What Terrorists Want. Understanding the Enemy, Containing the Threat* (New York: Random House, 2006).

28 Cf. Beatrice de Graaf, *Evaluating Counterterrorism Performance: A comparative study* (London/Routledge, 2011), pp. 8–10; Beatrice de Graaf, 'Terrorismus als performativer Akt. Die Bundesrepublik, Italien und die Niederlande im Vergleich', in: Johannes Hürter (ed.), *Terrorismusbekämpfung in Westeuropa—Demokratie und Sicherheit in den 1970er und 1980er Jahren* (Berlin/München/Boston: De Gruyter Oldenbourg, 2015), pp. 93–115.

29 Ibid., chapter 9, 'Terrorists on Trial: The courtroom as a stage'.

30 'By attacking the establishment and the security forces, the insurgents provoke the state into mass repression which alienates the general public, and increases support

for the rebels', as Hewitt defines it. Christopher Hewitt, *Consequences of Political Violence* (Aldershot et al.: Dartmouth, 1993), p. 61.

31 J.L. Austin, *How To Do Things with Words* (Cambridge, MA: Harvard UP, 1962); Malcolm Coulthard, *An Introduction to Discourse Analysis*. 2nd edition, (New York: Longman, 1985); Judith Butler, *Excitable Speech: A politics of the performative* (New York: Routledge, 1997). Cf. also De Graaf, *Evaluating Counterterrorism Performance*, pp. 11–13.

32 Historically, this definition should only be applied to the modern period of the late nineteenth century and onwards, when the modern state managed to claim for itself the monopoly of (legitimate use of) violence, when a criminal justice system based on a parliament-approved penal code came to maturity at the same time as modern mass media emerged.

33 Peter Bootsma, *De Molukse acties. Treinkapingen en gijzelingen 1970–1978* (Amsterdam: Boom, 2000).

34 Interview with Henk Droessen, the lawyer of the South Moluccan youngsters who were tried for their actions in 1970 and 1975, Roermond, 14 March 2008; 11 May 2011, Utrecht; M. Rasser, 'The Dutch Response to Moluccan Terrorism, 1970–1978', *Studies in Conflict and Terrorism*, 28:6 (2005), pp. 481–492.

35 A.P. Schmid, J.F.A. de Graaf, F. Bovenkerk, L.M. Bovenkerk-Teerink, L. Brunt, *Zuidmoluks terrorisme, de media en de publieke opinie* (Amsterdam: Intermediair, 1982). See also Beatrice de Graaf and Froukje Demant, 'How to Counter Radical Narratives: Dutch deradicalization policy in the case of Moluccan and Islamic radicals', *Studies in Conflict & Terrorism*, 33:5 (2010), pp. 408–428.

36 'Zalm: we zijn in oorlog! Regering: terrorisme met wortel en tak uitroeien', *Algemeen Dagblad* (6 November 2004); 'Terroristen met dubbele nationaliteit raken Nederlands paspoort kwijt. Kabinet verklaart de oorlog aan terreur', *Het Parool* (6 November 2004); 'Overheid wil meer armslag: anti-terreurmaatregelen', *Trouw* (6 November 2004).

37 The Hague Court, verdict, 10 March 2006. Jason Walters has in the meantime been released.

38 Court of Appeal in the Hague, verdict, 23 January 2008, LJN: BC2576, Gerechtshof 's-Gravenhage, 2200189706. http://zoeken.rechtspraak.nl/resultpage.aspx?snelzoeken=true&searchtype=ljn&ljn=BC2576&u_ljn=BC2576.

39 The author attended the hearing; cf. 'Jason werkt nu wel mee aan proces', *De Volkskrant* (17 July 2010).

40 Hoge Raad (High Council), 'Conclusie advocaat-generaal in terrorismezaken', The Hague (15 March 2011).

41 Cf. the Chapter on the Stammheim Trial in this volume, by Jacco Pekelder and Klaus Weinhauer.

42 Cf. Ulf G. Stuberger, *Die Tage von Stammheim. Als Augenzeuge beim RAF-Prozess* (München: F.A. Herbig Verlagsbuchhandlung, 2007); Christopher R. Tenfelde, *Die Rote Armee Fraktion und die Strafjustiz. Anti-Terror-Gesetze und ihre Umsetzung am Beispiel des Stammheim-Prozesses* (Osnabrück: Julius Jonscher Verlag, 2009); Pieter H. Bakker Schut, *Stammheim. Der Prozeß gegen die Rote Armee Fraktion* (Kiel: Neuer Malik Verlag, 1986).

43 Cf. also Marieke De Goede, 'The Politics of Preemption and the War on Terror in Europe', *European Journal of International Relations*, 14:1 (2008), pp. 161–185.

44 Marieke de Goede and Beatrice de Graaf, 'Sentencing Risk. Temporality and Precaution in Terrorism Trials', *International Political Sociology* (2013) 7:3, pp. 313–331.

45 Michel Foucault, *Security, Territory, Population: Lectures at the College de France 1977–1978*. Translated by G. Burchell (New York: Palgrave Macmillan, 2007), p. 99.

46 Louise Amoore, 'Risk before Justice: When the law contests its own suspension', *Leiden Journal of International Law*, 21 (2008), pp. 847–861, here: p. 850.

47 For an analysis of premediation as a new security technique see Marieke de Goede, 'Beyond Risk: Premediation and the post-9/11 security imagination', *Security Dialogue*, 39:2/3 (2008), pp. 155–176.

48 Hannah Arendt, *Eichmann in Jerusalem: A report on the banality of evil* (New York: Viking Press, 1963); see also Antoine Hol, 'The Theatre of Justice. On the Educational Meaning of Criminal Trials', in: Chrisje Brants, Antoine Hol and Dina Siegel (eds), *Transitional Justice. Images and Memories* (Ashgate: Farnham/Burlington, 2013), pp. 71–86.

49 Cf. for effects of media coverage about terrorism: Gabriel Weimann, 'The Theater of Terror: Effects of Press Coverage', *Journal of Communication*, 33:1 (1983), pp. 38–45; Brigitte L. Nacos and Oscar Torres-Reyna, *Fuelling Our Fears. Stereotyping, media coverage, and public opinion of Muslim Americans* (Lanham et al.: Rowman and Littlefield, 2007).

50 Cassese, *Terrorism*, p. 138.

51 Cf. Thomas Parker, 'Redressing the Balance: How human rights defenders can use victim narratives to confront the violence of armed groups', draft., 2011. Tom Parker was subsequently working for the CTITF of the United Nations in New York.

52 Allo, 'The "Show" in the Show Trials', p. 72.

53 Cf. Luigi Pirandello. *Sei personaggi in cerca d' autore* (1921).

54 Sulastri Osman, 'Indonesia's Trials and Tribulations: The case of Abu Bakar Ba'asyir', *RSIS Commentary*, 15 (10 Februrary 2011).

55 Antonio Cassese, *Terrorism, Politics and Law: The Achille Lauro Affair* (Princeton: Princeton University Press, 1989), p. 131.

13. Literature on Terrorism Trials—A Selective Bibliography

Compiled by Jaclyn A. Peterson[1]

13.1. Books and Book Chapters

Addicott, J. (2009). *Terrorism law: Materials, cases, comments*. 5th ed. Tucson, AZ: Lawyers and Judges Publishing.

Allen, T. (2006). *Trial justice: The international criminal court and the Lord's Resistance Army*. London: Zed Books.

Anderson, D. (2005). *Histories of the hanged: Britain's dirty war in Kenya and the end of empire*. London: Weidenfeld and Nicolson.

Andrain, C. (2008). *Political justice and religious values*. New York; London: Routledge.

Aradau, C. and Munster, R. van (2008). Taming the future. The dispositif of risk in the war on terror. In: Amoore, L. and Goede, M. de (eds), *Risk and the war on terror*. (pp. 23–40). London: Routledge.

Aust, A. (2011). *Handbook of International Law*. 2nd ed. Cambridge: Cambridge University Press.

Austin, J.L. (1962). *How to do things with words*. Cambridge, MA: Harvard UP.

Barry, B. (1973). *The liberal theory of justice: A critical examination of the principal doctrines in 'A Theory of Justice' by John Rawls*. Oxford: Clarendon Press.

——— (1989). *Democracy, power and justice: Essays in political theory*. Oxford: Clarendon Press.

——— (1989). *Theories of justice*. London: Harvester Wheatsheaf.

——— (1995). *Justice as impartiality*. Oxford: Clarendon Press.

Bennett, J.R. (1995). *Political prisoners and trials: A worldwide annotated bibliography, 1990–1993*. Jefferson, NC: McFarland.

Berger, F.R. (1984). *Happiness, justice, and freedom: The moral and political philosophy of John Stuart Mill*. Berkeley; London: University of California Press.

Bhargava, R., Dusche, M. and Reifeld, H. (2008). *Justice: Political, social, juridical*. New Delhi; London: SAGE Publications.

Bianchi, H. (1992). *Politiek en Criminaliteit*. Kampen: J.H. Kok.

Bloxham, D. and Gerwarth, R. (eds) (2011). *Political violence in twentieth century Europe*. Cambridge: Cambridge University Press.

Boudouris, K. (2007). *Values and justice in the global era*. Athens: Ionia Publications.

Bovard, J. (2003). *Terrorism and tyranny: Trampling freedom, justice and peace to rid the world of evil*. London: Macmillan.

Brighouse, H. (2004). *Justice*. Cambridge: Polity Press.

Brown, C. (2002). *Sovereignty, rights, and justice: International political theory today*. Cambridge: Polity Press.

Buckle, S.R.T. and Buckle, L.G. (1977). *Bargaining for justice: Case disposition and reform in the criminal courts*. New York; London: Praeger.

Burnham, D. (1996). *Above the law: Secret deals, political fixes and other misadventures of the U.S. Department of Justice*. New York; London: Scribner.

Butler, J. (1997). *Excitable Speech: A politics of the performative*. New York: Routledge.

Campbell, D.S. (1994). *Free press v. fair trial: Supreme Court decisions since 1807*. Westport, CT, London: Praeger.

Campbell, T. (2009). *Justice*. Basingstoke: Palgrave Macmillan.

Carr, M. (2006). *Unknown soldiers: How terrorism transformed the modern world*. London: Profile Books.

Cassese, A. (1989). *Terrorism, politics and law*. Princeton, NJ: Princeton University Press.

Chadwick, E. (1996). *Self-determination, terrorism and the international humanitarian law of armed conflict*. The Hague: Nijhoff.

Cherif Bassiouni, M. (ed.) (1975). *International terrorism and political crimes*. Springfield, IL: Charles C. Thomas Publisher.

Chesney, R.M. (2007). Anticipatory prosecution in terrorism-related cases. In: Worrall, J.L. and Nugent-Borakove, M.E. (eds), *The changing role of the American prosecutor*. New York: State University of New York Press.

Christenson, R. (1989). *Political trials. Gordian knots in the law*. New Brunswick: Transaction Publishers.

Clarke, R.V.G. and Newman, G.R. (2006). *Outsmarting the terrorists*. Westport, CT; London: Praeger Security International.

Clausewitz, C. von (1972). *Vom Kriege: Hinterlassenes Werk des Generals Carl von Clausewitz*. Bonn: Dümmler Verlag.

Cohen, R.L. (1986). *Justice: Views from the social sciences*. New York, NY: Plenum Press.

Connolly, W.E. (1993) *The terms of discourse*. 3rd ed. Princeton: Princeton University Press

Conquest, R. (1968). *The great terror*. Harmondsworth: Penguin.

Cotterrell, R. (1992). *The Sociology of Law: An Introduction*. London: Butterworths.

Coulthard, M. (1985). *An introduction to discourse analysis*. 2nd ed. New York: Longman.

Crank, J.P. and Gregor, P.E. (2005). *Counter-terrorism after 9/11—Justice, security and ethics revisited.* Ohio: Anderson Publishing.

Crenshaw, M. (ed.) (1983). *Terrorism, legitimacy, and power: The consequences of political violence.* Middletown: Wesleyan University Press.

Cryer, R., Friman, H., Robinson, D. and Wilmshurst, E. (2010). *An introduction to international criminal law and procedure.* 2nd ed. Cambridge: Cambridge University Press.

Daniels, N. (1989). *Reading Rawls: Critical studies on Rawls' a theory of justice.* Stanford, CA: Stanford University Press.

Danner, M. (2005). *Torture and truth: Abu Ghraib and America in Iraq.* New York: Review Books.

Denbeaux, M. and Hafetz, J. (eds) (2009). *The Guantánamo lawyers: Inside a prison outside the law.* New York: New York University Press.

Deutsch, M. (1985). *Distributive justice: A social-psychological perspective.* New Haven, CT: Yale University Press.

Dijk, J.J. van (2008). *The world of crime: Breaking the silence on problems of security, justice, and development across the world.* Thousand Oaks, CA; London: Sage.

Donohue, L.A. (2008). *The cost of counterterrorism: Power, politics, and liberty.* Cambridge: Cambridge University Press.

——— (2001). *Counter-terrorism law and emergency powers in the United Kingdom, 1922–2000.* Dublin; Portland, OR: Irish Academic Press.

Douzinas, C. and Gearey, A. (2005). *Critical jurisprudence: The political philosophy of justice.* Oxford: Hart.

Duffy, H. (2005). *The 'war on terror' and the framework of international law.* Cambridge: Cambridge University Press.

Eisenstein, J. and Jacob, H. (1997). *Felony justice: An organizational analysis of criminal courts.* Boston: Little, Brown and Co.

Ellis, L. and Walsh, A. (2000). *Criminology. A global perspective.* Boston: Allyn and Bacon.

Emerson, S. (2008). Prosecuting homegrown extremists: Case study of the Virginia 'paintball jihad' cell. In: Norwitz, J.H. (ed.), *Armed groups: Studies in national security, counterterrorism, and counterinsurgency.* Washington: Government Printing Office.

Feifer, G. (1964). *Justice in Moscow.* New York, NY: Simon and Schuster.

Fields, L.G. (1981). Bringing terrorists to justice—The shifting sands of the political offence exception. In: Lillich, R.B. (ed.). *International Aspects of Criminal Law Enforcing United States Law in the World Community.* Charlotteville, VA: Michie Co.

Fischer-Lichte, E. (2003). Performance, Inszenierung, Ritual. Zur Klärung kulturwissenschaftlicher Schlüsselbegriffe, in: Martschukat, J. and Patzold, S. (eds),

Geschichtswissenschaft und 'performative turn'. Ritual, Inszenierung und Performance vom Mittelalter bis zur Neuzeit (pp. 34–54). Cologne; Weimar; Vienna: Böhlau Verlag.

Fletcher, G.P. (2002). *Romantics at war: Glory and guilt in the age of terrorism.* Princeton, NJ: Princeton University Press.

Fleurbaey, M., Salles, M. and Weymack, J.A. (2008). *Justice, political liberalism, and utilitarianism: Themes from Harsanyi and Rawls.* Cambridge: Cambridge University Press.

Forst, R. (2002). *Contexts of justice: Political philosophy beyond liberalism and communitarianism.* Berkeley, CA; London: University of California Press.

Freeman, M. (2005). Order, rights, and threats: Terrorism and global Justice. In: Wilson, R.A. (ed.), *Human rights in the 'war on terror'* (pp. 37–56). New York: Cambridge University Press.

Friedrich, C.J. and Chapman, J.W. (1963). *Justice.* New York: Atherton Press.

Frohlich, N. and Oppenheimer, J.A. (1992). *Choosing justice: An experimental approach to ethical theory.* Berekley, CA; London: University of California Press.

Godwin, W.K. (et al.) (1971). *Enquiry concerning political justice, with selections from Godwin's other writings.* Oxford: Clarendon Press.

Graaf, B.A. de (2011). *Evaluating counterterrorist performance: A comparative study.* Oxford; New York: Routledge/Francis and Taylor.

——— (2011). Terrorists on trial: A performative perspective, ICCT *Expert Paper.* ICCT: The Hague.

——— (2012). Terroristen vor Gericht. Terrorismusprozesse als Fortsetzung des Kampfes um die Kommunikationshoheit. Eine Typologie. In Weinhauer, K. and Requate, J. (eds), *Terrorismus als Kommunikationsprozess. Eskalation und Deeskalation in historischer Perspektive* (pp. 281–298). Frankfurt; New York: Campus Verlag.

——— and Härter, K. (eds) (2012). *Vom Majestätsverbrechen zum Terrorismus. Politische Kriminalität, Recht, Justiz und Polizei zwischen Früher Neuzeit und 20. Jahrhundert.* Schriftenreihe des Max Planck Instituts für europäische Rechtsgeschichte. Frankfurt am Main: Vittorio Klostermann.

——— (2013). Terrorist trials as a stage. Some notes on performativity. In: Staal, J. (ed.), *New world academy reader 1. Towards a people's culture* (pp. 109–121). Utrecht: BAK.

———, Heide, E.J. van der, Wanmaker, S. and Weggemans, D.J. (2013). The Anders Behring Breivik trial: Performing justice, defending democracy. ICCT-*research paper* (pp. 1–20). The Hague: ICCT.

——— (2014). The Van Gogh murder and beyond. In: Hoffman, B. and Reinares, F. (eds), *Evolving global terrorism threat: Cases from 9/11 to Osama Bin Laden's death* (pp. 144–187). New York: Columbia University Press.

——— (2015). Terrorismus als performativer Akt. Die Bundesrepublik, Italien und die Niederlande im Vergleich. In: Johannes Hürter (ed.), *Terrorismusbekämpfung in Westeuropa—Demokratie und Sicherheit in den 1970er und 1980er Jahren* (pp. 93–115). Berlin; München; Boston: De Gruyter Oldenbourg.

Greer, S.C. (1995). *Supergrasses: A study in anti-terrorist law enforcement in Northern Ireland*. Oxford: Oxford University Press.

Grossman, J.B. (1974). *Political justice and system maintenance: An overview of some major variables*. Madison, WI: University of Wisconsin-Madison.

Guthrie, C. and Quinlan, M. (2007). *Just war: The just war tradition. Ethics in modern warfare*. London: Bloombury Publishing.

Hagan, F.E. (1997). *Political crime: Ideology and criminality*. Boston, MA; London: Allyn and Bacon.

Hall, W.G.C. (1923). *Political crime: A critical essay on the law and its administration in cases of a certain type*. London: G. Allen and Unwin.

Halverson, J.R., Goodall, H.L., Jr. and Corman, S.R. (2011). *Master narratives of Islamist extremism*. New York: Palgrave Macmillan.

Hanif, N. (1999). *Islamic concept of crime and justice*. New Delhi: Sarup and Sons.

Heitkamp, S. *Terrorism as ethnic antagonism and violence: A view from sociology*. Manuscript.

Henderson, H. (2001). *Global terrorism: The complete reference guide*. New York, NY: Checkmark Books.

Hersh, S.M. (2004). *Chain of command: The road from 9/11 to Abu Ghraib*. New York, NY: Harper Collins.

Heyman, P.B. (1998). *Terrorism and America. A commonsense strategy for a democratic society*. Cambridge, MA: MIT Press.

Hoffe, O. (1995). *Political justice: Foundations for critical philosophy of law and the state*. Cambridge, MA: Polity Press.

Honderich, T. (2002). *After the terror*. Edinburgh: Edinburgh University Press.

Human Security Network (2003). *Understanding human rights. Manual on human rights education*. Graz: Human Security Network.

Ignatieff, M. (2004). *The lesser evil: Political ethics in an age of terrorism*. Princeton, NJ: Princeton University Press.

Ingraham, B.L. (1979). *Political crime in Europe: A comparative study of France, Germany, and England*. Berkeley, CA: University of California Press.

Kaplan, M.A. (1976). *Justice, human nature and political obligation*. New York: Free Press.

Kee, R. (1986). *Trial and error: The Maguires, the Guildford Pub bombings and British justice*. London: Hamish Hamilton.

Keenan, A. (2003). *Democracy in question: Democratic openness in a time of political closure.* Stanford: Stanford University Press.

Kelk, C. (2005). *Studieboek materieel strafrecht.* Deventer: Kluwer.

Kennedy, D. (2006). *Of war and law.* Princeton: Princeton University Press.

Kennedy, L.W. and McGarrell, E.F. (eds) (2011). *Crime and terrorism risk: Studies in criminology and criminal justice.* New York, NY: Routledge.

Kirchheimer, O. (1961). *Political Justice. The use of legal procedures for political ends.* Princeton: Princeton University Press.

Kittrie, N.N. and Wedlock, E.D. (1998). *The tree of liberty: A documentary history of rebellion and political crime in America.* Baltimore, MD: John Hopkins University.

Knight, J. (2001). Social norms and the rule of law: Fostering trust in a socially diverse society. In: Cook, K.S. (ed.). *Trust in society.* New York: Russell Sage Foundation.

Koch, H.W. (1989). *In the name of the volk: Political justice in Hitler's Germany.* London: Tauris.

Krieken, P. (2002). *Terrorism and the international legal order.* The Hague: T.M.C. Asser Press.

Kukathas, C. and Pettit, P. (1990). *Rawls: A theory of justice and its critics.* Cambridge, MA: Polity Press.

Kushner, H.W. (2002). *Essential readings on political terrorism: Analyses of problems and prospects for the 21st century.* Lincoln, NE: Gordian Knot Books.

Laqueur, W. (2004). *Voices of terror: Manifestos, writings, and manuals of Al Qaeda, Hamas, and other terrorists from around the world and throughout the ages.* New York, NY: Reed Press.

Law, R.D. (ed.) (2015). *The Routledge history of terrorism.* Oxon/New York: Routledge.

Luthringer, C. (2000). *So what is justice anyway?* New York: Rosen Publishing Group.

Lynch, A. and Williams, G. (2006). *What price security? Taking stock of Australia's anti-terrorism laws.* Sydney: University of New South Wales Press.

Mackie, J.L. (1977). *Ethics: Inventing right and wrong.* Harmondsworth: Penguin Books.

Mandle, J. (2009). *Rawls' a theory of justice: An introduction.* Cambridge, MA: Cambridge University Press.

Marongiu, P. and Newman, G.R. (1987). *Vengeance: The fight against injustice.* Totowa, NJ: Rowman and Littlefield.

McCarthy, A. (2008). *Willful blindness: A memoir of jihad.* New York, NY: Encounter Books.

McWilliams, J.P. and Cooper, J.F.A. (1972). *Political justice in a republic: James Fenimore Cooper's America.* Berkley, CA: University of California Press.

Meisels, T. (2011). *The Trouble with terror. Liberty, security, and the response to terrorism.* Cambridge: Cambridge University Press.

Midlarsky, M.I. (1949). *Origins of Political Extremism. Mass Violence in the Twentieth Century and Beyond.* Cambridge: Cambridge University Press.

Mitchell, R.H. (1992). *Janus-faced justice: Political criminals in imperial Japan.* Honolulu, HI: University of Hawaii Press.

Montesquieu, C. (1949). *The spirit of the laws.* Hafner Classics.

Moore, B. (1978). *The social bases of obedience and revolt.* London: Macmillan.

Mueller, J. (2012). *Terrorism since 9/11: The American cases.* [http://psweb.sbs.ohio-state.edu/faculty/jmueller/SINCE.pdf].

Musloff, A. (1996). *Krieg gegen die Oeffentlichkeit. Terrorismus und politischer Sprachgebrauch.* Opladen: Westdeutscher Verlag.

Nadelmann, E.A. (1993). *Cops across borders: The internationalization of U.S. criminal law enforcement.* University Park, PA: Pennsylvania State University Press.

O'Brien, W.V. (1991). *Law and morality in Israel's war with the P.L.O.* New York, NY: Routledge.

O'Keefe, M.P. and Coady, C.A.J. (2002). *Terrorism and justice: Moral arguments in a threatened world.* Carlton South, Vic.: Melbourne University Press.

Olwig, K. and Mitchell, D. (2009). *Justice, power and the political landscape.* London: Routledge.

Ostrom, B.J., Ostrom Jr., C.W., Hanson, R.A. and Kleiman, M. (2007). *Trial courts as organizations.* Philadelphia: Temple University Press.

Peden, C.E. and Hudson, Y.E. (1990). *Terrorism, justice and social values.* Lewiston, NY: Edwin Mellen Press.

Pettit, P. (1980). *Judging justice: An introduction to contemporary political philosophy.* London: Routledge and Kegan Paul.

Pitkin, H.F. and Wittgenstein, L. (1972). *Wittgenstein and justice: On the significance of Ludwig Wittgenstein for social and political thought.* Berkley, CA: University of California Press.

Post, J.M. (2002). Terrorist on trial: The context of political crime. In: Kushner, H.W. *Essential readings in political terrorism.* Lincoln: Gordon Knot Books.

Proal, L. (2009). *Political crime.* Holmes Beach, FL: Gaunt, Inc.

Prost, K. (2003). Extradition: The practical challenges. In: Yepes-Enriquez, R. and Tabassi, L. (eds), *Treaty enforcement and international cooperation in criminal matters. With special reference to the chemical weapons convention.* The Hague: T.M.C. Asser Press.

Pruzan, E.R. (1989). *The concept of justice in Marx.* New York: Peter Lang.

Quinn, G.E. (et al.) (1995). *Justice and legal theory in Ireland.* Dublin: Oak Tree Press.

Ratnapala, S. (2009). *Jurisprudence*. Cambridge: Cambridge University Press.

Rawls, J. (1999). *A theory of justice*. Revised ed. Oxford: Oxford University Press.

Reichel, P.L. (2002). *Comparative criminal justice systems: A topical approach*. Upper Saddle River: Prentice Hall.

Revon, C. (1978). *Terrorism and political defense. Deviance et societé*. Geneva: Faculte de Droit.

Richardson, L. (2006). *What terrorists want. Understanding the enemy, Containing the threat*. New York: Random House.

Rishikof, H., Baker, S. and Horowitz, B. (eds) (2012). *Patriots debate: Contemporary issues in national security*. American Bar Association Standing Committee on Law and National Security.

Roberts, J.V. and Stalans, L.J. (1997). *Public Opinion, Crime, and Criminal Justice*. Boulder: Westview.

Robertson, G. (2007). Fair Trials for Terrorists? In: Wilson, R.A. (ed.). *Human Rights in the 'War on Terror'*. Cambridge: Cambridge University Press.

Roche, D. (1999). *Bread not bombs: A political agenda for social justice*. Edmonton: University of Alberta Press.

Roebuck, J.B. and Weeber, S.C. (1978). *Political crime in the United States: Analyzing crime by and against government*. New York: Praeger.

Ross, J.I. (2003). *The dynamics of political crime*. Thousand Oaks, CA: SAGE.

Ruggiero, V. (2006). *Understanding political violence: A criminological approach*. Maidenhead, Berkshire: Open University Press.

Saul, B. (2006). *Defining terrorism in international law*. Oxford: Oxford University Press.

Schaefer, D.L. (1979). *Justice or tyranny? A critique of John Rawls's 'a theory of justice.'* Port Washington: Kennikat Press.

Schafer, S. (1974). *The political criminal: The problem of morality and crime*. New York: Free Press.

Schmid, A.P. (ed.) (2011). *The Routledge handbook of terrorism research*. London; New York: Routledge.

——— (2001). The concept of rule of law. In: Schmid, A.P. and Boland, E. (eds), *The rule of law in the global village: Issues of sovereignty and universality*. Milan: ISPAC.

Seery, J.E. (1996). *Political theory for mortals: Shades of justice, images, of death*. Ithaca, NY: Cornell University Press.

Sen, A. (2009). *The idea of justice*. London: Penguin Books.

Shawcross, W. (2011). *Justice and the enemy: Nuremberg, 9/11, and the trial of Khalid Sheikh Mohammed*. New York, NY: Public Affairs.

Shields, C.A., Damphousse, K.R. and Smith, B.L. (2008). *Assessment of defense and prosecutorial strategies in terrorism trials: Implications for state and federal prosecutors.* Rockville, MD: NCJRS.

Smelser, N.J. and Baltes, P.B. (eds) (2001). *International encyclopedia of the social and behavioral sciences*, 12. Amsterdam: Elsevier.

Sofaer, A.D. (1985). The Political offence exception and terrorism, *Current policy*, no. 762. Washington, D.C.: U.S. Department of State.

Sterba, J.P. (2003). *Justice: Alternative political perspectives.* Australia: Thomas Wadsworth.

Teubner, G. (1997). 'Global Bukowina': Legal pluralism in the world society. In: Teubner, G. (ed.), *Global Law Without a State.* Dartmouth: Aldershot.

Tunnell, K.D. (1993). *Political crime in contemporary America: A critical approach.* New York: Garland Publishing.

Van Dyke, V. (1995). *Ideology and political choice: The search for freedom, justice and virtue.* Chatham, NJ: Chatham House.

Verma, V. (2000). *Justice, equality and community: An essay in Marxist political theory.* New Delhi: SAGE.

Walker, C. and Starmer, K. (eds) (1993). *Justice in error.* London: Blackstone Press.

Walker, C. (1999). Miscarriages of justice in principle and practice. In: Walker, C. and Starmer, K. *Miscarriages of justice: A review of justice in error.* London: Blackstone Press.

Weggemans, D.J., en Graaf, B.A. de (2015). *Na de Vrijlating. Een exploratieve studie naar recidive en re-integratie van jihadistische ex-gedetineerden.* Amsterdam: Stapel & De Koning.

Wilson, C. (2004). *The history of murder.* Edison, N.J.: Castle Books.

13.1.1. Interrogation and Torture Debate

Alexander, M. (2008). *How to break a terrorist: The US interrogators who used brains, not brutality, to take down the deadliest man in Iraq.* New York, NY: Free Press.

Carle, G. (2011). *The interrogator: An education.* New York, NY: Nation Books.

Conrow, J. (2001). *Unspeakable acts, ordinary people: The dynamics of torture.* Oakland: University of California Press.

Greenberg, K.J. (ed.) (2006). *The torture debate in America.* New York, NY: Cambridge University Press.

——— and Dratel, J.L. (eds) (2005). *The torture papers: The road to Abu Ghraib.* Cambridge: Cambridge University Press.

Levinson, S. (ed.) (2004). *Torture: A collection.* Oxford: Oxford University Press.

Mackey, C. and Miller, G. (2004). *The interrogators: Inside the secret war against Al-Qaeda.* New York, NY: Little, Brown and Company.

——— (2005). *The interrogators: Task Force 500 and America's secret war against Al-Qaeda.* New York, NY: Back Bay Books/Little, Brown and Company.

McCoy, A. (2006). *A question of torture: CIA interrogation from the Cold War to the war on terror.* New York, NY: Metropolitan Publishing.

Miniter, R. (2011). *Mastermind: The many faces of the 9/11 architect, Khalid Shaikh Mohammed.* New York, NY: Sentinel.

Office of the Director of National Intelligence (2011). *Intelligence interviewing: Teaching papers and case studies (with accompanying CD-ROM: "report on educing information").* New York: Nova Science Publishers.

Peters, E. (1999). *Torture.* Expanded Edition. Philadelphia, PA: University of Pennsylvania Press.

Rodriguez, Jr., J.A. (2012). *Hard measures: How aggressive CIA actions after 9/11 saved American lives.* New York, NY: Threshold Editions.

Skerker, M. (2010). *An ethics of interrogation.* Chicago, IL: University of Chicago Press.

Soufan, A. (2011). *The black banners: The inside story of 9/11 and the war against Al-Qaeda.* New York, NY: W.W. Norton and Company.

Thiessen, M. (2010). *Courting disaster: How the CIA kept America safe and how Barack Obama is inviting the next attack.* Washington, DC: Regnery Publishing.

Toliver, R.T. and Scharff, H.J. (1997). *The interrogator: The story of Hanns Joachim Scharff: Master interrogator of the Luftwaffe.* Updated Edition. Atglen, PA: Schiffer Publishing.

Williamson, T., Milne, B., and Savage, S. (eds) (2009). *International developments in investigative interviewing.* Portland, OR: Willan Publishing.

13.1.2. Media

Hachten, W.A. and Scotton, J.F. (2002). *The world news prism: Global media in an era of terrorism.* 6th ed. Ames: Wiley-Blackwell.

Hess, S. and Kalb, M.L. (eds) (2003). *The media and the war on terrorism.* Washington D.C.: Brookings Institution Press.

Kavoori, A.P. and Fraley, T. (2006). *Media terrorism and theory: A reader.* Lanham, MD: Rowman and Littlefield Publishers.

Nacos, B.L. (2007). *Mass-mediated terrorism: The central role of the media in terrorism and counterterrorism.* 2nd ed. Plymouth, UK: Rowman and Littlefield Publishers.

——— (1996). *Terrorism and the media.* New York, NY: Colombia University Press.

Norris, P., Kern, M. and Just, M. (eds) (2003). *Framing terrorism: The news media, the government, and the public.* New York; London: Routledge.

Palmer, N. (ed.) (2003). *Terrorism, war, and the press.* Hollis, NH: Puritan Press.

13.1.3. *State Terrorism*

Byman, D. (2005). *Deadly connections: States that sponsor terrorism.* New York: Cambridge University Press.

Dror, Y. (1980). *Crazy States: A counterconventional strategic problem.* New York: Kraus, Milwood.

Mann, M. (2005). *The dark side of democracy: Explaining ethnic cleansing.* New York: Cambridge University Press.

McSherry, J.P. (2005). *Predatory states: Operation Condor and covert war in Latin America.* Lanham, MD: Rowman and Littlefield Publishers.

O'Sullivan, M.L. (2003). *Shrewd sanctions: Statecraft and state sponsors of terrorism.* Washington, DC: Brookings Institution Press.

Stohl, M. and Lopez, G. (eds) (1984). *The state as terrorist: The dynamics of governmental violence and repression.* Westport, CT: Greenwood.

Wright, T.C. (2007). *State terrorism in Latin America: Chile, Argentina, and international human rights.* Lanham, MD: Rowman and Littlefield Publishers.

13.2. Periodicals

Abrahms, M. (2006). Why terrorism does not work. *International Security*, 31:2, pp. 42–78.

Addicott, J.F. (2004). Into the Star Chamber: Does the United States engage in the use of torture or similar illegal practices in the war on terror? *Kentucky Law Journal*, 92:4, pp. 849–912.

Ahmad, M.I. (2009). Resisting Guantanamo: Rights at the brink of dehumanization. *Northwestern University Law Review*, 103:4, pp. 1683–1764. [http://www.law.northwestern.edu/lawreview/v103/n4/1683/LR103n4Ahmad.pdf].

Aldana-Pindell, R. (2002). The 9/11 'national security' cases: Three principles guiding judges' decision-making. *Oregon Law Review*, 81:4, pp. 985–1049.

Algardi, Z.O. (1990). Political trials of the postwar era. *Ponte*, 46:7, pp. 145–450.

Ali, S.S. and Rehman, S. (2005). The concept of jihad in Islamic international law. *Journal of Conflict and Security Law*, 10:3, pp. 321–343.

Allo, A.K. (2010). The "show" in the show trials: Contextualizing the politicization of the courtroom. *Barry Law Review*, 15:1, pp. 41–72.

Alvarez, J.E. (2006). Torturing the law. *Case Western Reserve Journal of International Law*, 37:2–3, pp. 175–223.

Ambos, K. (2008). May a state torture suspects to save the life of innocents? *Journal of International Criminal Justice*, 6:2, pp. 261–287.

Anderlini, L. (1993). Hide-and-seekers-parties and criminal-trials (political). *Il Ponte*, 49:1, pp. 12–16.

Anderson, J.F. (2006). Reflections on standing: Challenges to searches and seizures in a high technology world. *Mississippi Law Journal*, 75:4, pp. 1099–1141. [http://papers.ssrn.com/sol3/papers.cfm?abstract_id=1344516].

Andrews, D.R. (2004). A Thorn on the tulip—A Scottish trial in the Netherlands: The story behind the Lockerbie trial. *Case Western Reserve Journal of International Law*, 36:2–3, pp. 307–318.

Anzenbacher, A. (2001). Cooperation, conflict and recognition—The systematic development of a concept of justice. *Zeitschrift Fur Evangelische Ethik*, 45:3, pp. 168–180.

Aptel, C. (2007). Some innovations in the statute of the special tribunal for Lebanon. *Journal of International Criminal Justice*, 5:5, pp. 1107–1124.

Arrigo, J.M. (2004). A utilitarian argument against torture interrogation of terrorists. *Science and Engineering Ethics*, 10:3, pp. 543–572.

Athey, S. (2007). The terrorist we torture: The case of Abdul Hakim Murad. *South Central Review*, 24:1, pp. 73–90.

Bagaric, M. and Clarke, J. (2005). Not enough official torture in the world? The circumstances in which torture is morally justifiable. *University of South Florida Law Review*, 39:3, pp. 581–616.

Bahar, M. (2007). Attaining optimal deterrence at sea: A legal and strategic theory for naval anti-piracy operations. *Vanderbilt Journal of Transnational Law*, 40:1, pp. 1–85.

Ballin, M.H. (2008). Inside view of Dutch counterterrorism strategy: Countering terrorism through criminal law and the presumption innocence. *The Journal of the Institute of Justice and International Studies*, 8:1, pp. 139–151.

Barkin, A.A. (2003). Corporate America—Making a killing: An analysis of why it is appropriate to hold American corporations who fund terrorist organizations liable for aiding and abetting terrorism. *California Western Law Review*, 40:1, pp. 169–193.

Başoğlu, M., Livanou, M. and Crnobarić, C. (2007). Torture vs. other cruel, inhuman, and degrading treatment: Is the distinction real or apparent? *Archives of General Psychiatry*, 64:3, pp. 277–285. [http://archpsyc.jamanetwork.com/article.aspx?articleid=482225].

Bassiouni, M.C. (2006). The institutionalization of torture under the Bush administration. *Case Western Reserve Journal of International Law*, 37:2–3, pp. 389–425. [http://www.case.edu/orgs/jil/vol.37.2.3/Bassiouni.pdf].

——— (1981). Terrorism, law enforcement, and the mass media: Perspectives, problems, proposals. *Journal of Criminal Law and Criminology*, 72:1, pp. 1–51.

Beale, S.S. and Feldman, J.E. (2002). The consequence of enlisting federal grand juries in the war on terrorism: Assessing the USA Patriot Act's changes to grand jury secrecy. *Harvard Journal of Law and Public Policy*, 25:2 pp. 699–720.

Becker, J.S. (2003). A legal war on terrorism: Extending New York v. Quarles and the departure from enemy combatant designations. *DePaul Law Review*, 53:2, pp. 831–873.

Bell, J.T. (2010). Trying Al-Qaeda: Bringing terrorists to justice. *Perspectives on Terrorism*, 4:4, pp. 73–81. [http://www.terrorismanalysts.com/pt/index.php/pot/article/view/115].

Bellamy, A.J. (2006). No pain, no gain?: Torture and ethics in the war on terror. *International Affairs*, 82:1, pp. 121–148.

Bennett, G. (2005). Legislative responses to terrorism: A view from Britain. *Penn State Law Review*, 109:4, pp. 947–966.

Bennoune, K. (2010). Terror/Torture redux. *Tulane Journal of International and Comparative Law*, 19:1, pp. 173–185.

Ben-Yehuda, N. (1997). Political assassination events as a cross-cultural form of alternative justice. *International Journal of Comparative Sociology*, 38:1, pp. 25–47.

Bergen, P. (2001). The Bin Laden trial: What did we learn? *Studies in Conflict and Terrorism*, 24:6, pp. 429–434.

Betti, S. (2006). The duty to bring terrorists to justice and discretionary prosecution. *Journal of International Criminal Justice*, 4:5, pp. 1104–1116.

Bianchini, S. (1990). Purges and political trials in Jugoslavia, 1948–1954. *Rivista Di Storia Contemporanea*, 19:4, pp. 587–615.

Blaauw-Wolf, L. (2004). The Hamburg terror trials—American political poker and German legal procedure: An unlikely combination to fight international terrorism. *German Law Journal*, 5:7, pp. 791–828. [http://www.germanlawjournal.com/pdfs/Vol05No07/PDF_Vol_05_No_07_791-828_Public_Wolf.pdf].

Black, R. (2004). Lockerbie: A satisfactory process but a flawed result. *Case Western Reserve Journal of International Law*, 36:2–3, pp. 443–451.

Blakeley, R. (2011). Dirty hands, clean conscience? The CIA Inspector General's investigation of 'enhanced interrogation techniques' in the war on terror and the torture debate. *Journal of Human Rights*, 10:4, pp. 544–561.

Blank, L.R. (2010). Defining the battlefield in contemporary conflict and counterterrorism: Understanding the parameters of the zone of combat. *Georgia Journal of International and Comparative Law*, 39:1, pp. 1–38.

Boeving, J.N. (2007). The right to be present before military commissions and federal courts: Protecting national security in an age of classified information. *Harvard Journal of Law and Public Policy*, 30:2, pp. 463–577. [http://www.law.harvard.edu/students/orgs/jlpp/Vol30_No2_Boevingonline.pdf].

Bolgiano, D.G. and Banks, L.M. (2010). Military interrogation of terror suspects: Imaginative does not have to be mean unlawful. *Military Review*, 90:6, pp. 2–9.

Bonner, D. (1988). Combating terrorism: Supergrass trials in Northern Ireland. *Modern Law Review*, 51:1, pp. 23–53.

Bradley-Engen, M.S., Damphousse, K.R., and Smith, B.L. (2009). Punishing terrorists: A re-examination of U.S. federal sentencing in the postguidelines era. *International Criminal Justice Review*, 19:4, pp. 433–455.

Brill, S. (2010). The national security court we already have. *Yale Law and Policy Review*, 28:2, pp. 525–537. [http://yalelawandpolicy.org/sites/default/files/Brill_28.pdf].

Broxmeyer, E. (2004). The problems of security and freedom: Procedural due process and the designation of foreign terrorist organizations under the Anti-Terrorism and Effective Death Penalty Act. *Berkeley Journal of International Law*, 22:3, pp. 439–488.

Bryant, A.C. and Tobias, C. (2002). Youngstown revisited. *Hastings Constitutional Law Quarterly*, 29:3, pp. 373–438. [http://papers.ssrn.com/sol3/papers.cfm?abstract_id=1090205].

Callen, J. (2004). Unlawful combatants and the Geneva Conventions. *Virginia Journal of International Law*, 44:4, pp. 1025–1072.

Caro Coria, D.C. (2010). Prosecuting international crimes in Peru. *International Criminal Law Review*, 10:4, pp. 583–600.

Cassel, D. (2008). Pretrial and preventive detention of suspected terrorists: Options and constraints under international law. *Journal of Criminal Law and Criminology*, 98:3, pp. 811–852. [http://www.law.northwestern.edu/jclc/symposium/Cassel.pdf].

Chadha, S. (2006, Winter). Lynne Stewart, jihadi lawyer. *Middle East Quarterly*, 13:1, pp. 59–65. [http://www.meforum.org/887/lynne-stewart-jihadi-lawyer].

Chanbonpin, K.D. (2008). Ditching the disposal plan: Revisiting Miranda in an age of terror. *St. Thomas Law Review*, 20:2, pp. 155–182.

——— (2011). 'We don't want dollars, just change': Narrative counter-terrorism strategy, an inclusive model for social healing, and the truth about torture commission. *Northwestern University Journal of Law and Social Policy*, 6:1, pp. 1–46.

Chesney, R.M. (2007). Federal prosecution of terrorism-related offenses: Conviction and sentencing data in light of the 'soft-sentence' and 'data reliability' critiques. *Lewis and Clark Law Review*, 11:4, pp. 851–901.

——— (2005). The sleeper scenario: Terrorism-support laws and the demands of prevention. *Harvard Journal on Legislation*, 42:1, pp. 1–89. [http://papers.ssrn.com/sol3/papers.cfm?abstract_id=587442].

Choi, E.Y. (2007). Veritas, not vengeance: An examination of the evidentiary rules for military commissions in the war against terrorism. *Harvard Civil Rights-Civil Liberties Law Review*, 42:1, pp. 139–189. [http://www.law.harvard.edu/students/orgs/crcl/vol42_1/choi.pdf].

Claeys, G. (1983). The concept of political justice in Godwin political justice—A reconsideration. *Political Theory*, 11:4, pp. 565–584.

Clarke, A. (2003). Terrorism, extradition, and the death penalty. *William Mitchell Law Review*, 29:3, pp. 783–808.

Clark, K. (2005). Ethical issues raised by the OLC torture memorandum. *Journal of National Security Law and Policy*, 1:2, pp. 455–472.

Clover, J.S. (2004). 'Remember, we're the good guys': The classification and trial of the Guantanamo Bay detainees. *South Texas Law Review*, 45:2, pp. 351–393.

Cohen, S. (2009). Inside a terror trial. *City Journal*, 19:3. [http://www.city-journal.org/2009/19_3_al-kassar.html].

Colb, S. (2009). Why is torture 'different' and how 'different' is it? *Cardozo Law Review*, 30:4, pp. 1411–1473.

Cole, D. (2012). The taint of torture: The roles of law and policy in our descent to the dark side. *Houston Law Review*, 49:1, pp. 53–69.

——— (2012). Torture and just war. *Journal of Religious Ethics*, 40:1, pp. 26–51.

Collins, J.M. (2002). And the walls came tumbling down: Sharing grand jury information with the intelligence community under the USA Patriot Act. *American Criminal Law Review*, 39:3, pp. 1261–1286.

Condon, J.B. (2008). Extraterritorial interrogation: The porous border, torture and U.S. criminal trials. *Rutgers Law Review*, 60:3, pp. 647–704.

Connors, T.P. (2010). How not to process stateless enemies: A review of Andrew McCarthy's *Willful Blindness: A Memoir of the Jihad*. *Pace Law Review*, 30:2, pp. 832–839.

Corn, G.S. and Finegan, S. (2011). America's longest held prisoner of war: Lessons learned from the capture, prosecution, and extradition of General Manuel Noriega. *Louisiana Law Review*, 71:4, pp. 1–31. [http://papers.ssrn.com/sol3/papers.cfm?abstract_id=1762898].

Coughenour, J.C. (2003). Reflections on Russia's revival of trial by jury: History demands that we ask difficult questions regarding terror trials, procedures to combat terrorism, and our federal sentencing regime. *Seattle University Law Review*, 26:3, pp. 399–430.

Crenshaw, M. (1992). Current research on terrorism: The academic perspective. *Studies in Conflict and Terrorism*, 15:1, pp. 1–11.

Creegan, E. (2011). Cooperation in foreign terrorism prosecutions. *Georgetown Journal of International Law*, 42:2, pp. 491–529.

Cullinan, K. (2010, January). Tracking terrorist trials. *News Media and the Law*, 34:1, pp. 4–6.

Cunningham, K.V. and Srader, J.L. (2004). The post 9–11 war on terrorism ... What does it mean for the attorney-client privilege? *Wyoming Law Review*, 4:1, pp. 311–363.

Damphousse, K. and Shields, C. (2007). The morning after: Assessing the effect of major terrorism events on prosecution strategies and outcomes. *Journal of Contemporary Criminal Justice*, 23:2, pp. 174–194.

Danner, A.M. (2005). Beyond the Geneva Conventions: Lessons from the Tokyo tribunal in prosecuting war and terrorism. *Virginia Journal of International Law*, 46:1, pp. 83–130.

Davidson, S. (1997). Blood money: When media expose others to risk of bodily harm. *Hastings Communication and Entertainment Law Journal*, 19:2, pp. 225–307.

Davis, M. (2005). The moral justifiability of torture and other cruel, inhuman, or degrading treatment. *International Journal of Applied Philosophy*, 19:1, pp. 161–178.

Davis, M.D. (2009). Historical perspective on Guantanamo Bay: The arrival of the high value detainees. *Case Western Reserve Journal of International Law*, 42: 1–2, pp. 115–124.

Davis, S.W. (2006). Incitement to terrorism in media coverage: Solutions to Al-Jazeera after the Rwandan media trials. *George Washington International Law Review*, 38:4, pp. 749–778

Debowski, A. (2009). Old dogs, new tricks: Public interest lawyering in an age of terror. *Alternative Law Journal*, 34:1, pp. 15–20.

Della Porta, D. (1992). Institutional responses to terrorism: The Italian case. *Terrorism and Political Violence*, 4:4, pp. 151–170.

Dervan, L.E. (2010). The surprising lessons from plea bargaining in the shadow of terror. *Georgia State University Law Review*, 27:2, pp. 239–298.

Desai, A.R. (2003). How we should think about the constitutional status of the suspected terrorist detainees at Guantanamo Bay: Examining theories that interpret the constitution's scope. *Vanderbilt Journal of Transnational Law*, 36:5, pp. 1579–1618.

Deutsch, M.E. and Susler, J. (1991). Political prisoners in the United States: The hidden reality. *Social Justice*, 18:3, pp. 92–106.

Dickinson, L.A. (2002). Using legal process to fight terrorism: Detentions, military commissions, international tribunals, and the rule of law. *Southern California Law Review*, 75:6, pp. 1407–1492.

——— (2006). Torture and contract. *Case Western Reserve Journal of International Law*, 37:2–3, pp. 267–275.

Donohue, L.K. (2007). Terrorism and trial by jury: The vices and virtues of British and American criminal law. *Stanford Law Review*, 59:5, pp. 1321–1364. [http://cisac.stanford.edu/publications/terrorism_and_trial_by_jury_the_vices_and_virtues_of_british_and_american_criminal_law].

Dratel, J.L. (2003). Ethical issues in defending a terrorism case: How secrecy and security impair the defense of a terrorism case. *Cardozo Public Law, Policy and Ethics Journal*, 2:1, pp. 81–105.

Drumbl, M.A. (2002). Terrorist crime, Taliban guilt, Western victims, and international law. *Denver Journal of International Law and Policy*, 31:1, pp. 69–79.

Ducos, M. (1990). The concept of justice in the works of Tacitus. *Revue des Etudes Latines*, 68, pp. 99–111.

Dunlap, C.J. (2008). Lawfare today: A perspective. *Yale Journal of International Affairs*, 3:1, pp. 146–154.

——— and Letendre, L.A. (2008). Military lawyering and professional independence in the war on terror: A response to David Luban. *Stanford Law Review*, 61:2, pp. 417–442. [http://www.stanfordlawreview.org/print/article/military-lawyering-and-professional-independence-war-terror-response-david-luban].

Eckhardt, W.G. (2003). Lawyering for Uncle Sam when he draws his sword. *Chicago Journal of International Law*, 4:2, pp. 431–444.

Eijkman, Q. and Ginkel, B. van (2011). Compatible or incompatible? Intelligence and human rights in terrorist trials. *Amsterdam Law Forum*, 3:4, pp. 3–6. [http://www.clingendael.nl/publications/2011/20111100_cscp_artikel_ginkel.pdf].

Eldredge, J. (2004). Detainment of United States citizens as enemy combatants under a Fourth Amendment historical analysis. *Journal of Law and Social Challenges*, 6, pp. 19–43.

Eler, J. (2010). Rights trump torture: How Dworkin's system of rights should include a right not to be tortured and defeat ticking time-bomb scenario type arguments. *Macalester Journal of Philosophy*, 19:1, pp. 66–87.

Elias, S.B. (2009). Rethinking 'preventive detention' from a comparative perspective: Three frameworks for detaining terrorist suspects. *Columbia Human Rights Law Review*, 41:1, pp. 100–234.

Elsea, J.K. (2007). Lawfulness of interrogation techniques under the Geneva Conventions. *International Journal of Terrorism and Political Hot Spots*, 2:1–2, pp. 35–70.

——— (2008). Treatment of 'battlefield detainees' in the war on terrorism. *International Journal of Terrorism and Political Hot Spots*, 3:1–2, pp. 125–178.

Emerson, S. (2004). The Lockerbie terrorist attack and Libya: A retrospective analysis. *Case Western Reserve Journal of International Law*, 36:2–3, pp. 487–490.

Enders, W. and Jindapon, P. (2011). On the economics of interrogation: The big 4 versus the little fish game. *Journal of Peace Research*, 48:3, pp. 287–301.

Esposito, S.A. (1998). Source utilization in legal journalism: Network TV news coverage of the Timothy McVeigh Oklahoma City bombing trial. *Communications and the Law*, 20:2, pp. 15–34.

Evans, J.R. (et al.). (2010). Criminal versus HUMINT interrogations: The importance of psychological science to improving interrogative practice. *Journal of Psychiatry and Law*, 38:1–2, pp. 215–249.

Falvey, J.L. and Eck, B.D. (2010). Holding the high ground: The operational calculus of torture and coercive interrogation. *Campbell Law Review*, 32:4, pp. 561–593.

Farhang, M. (1994). Terrorism and military trials in Egypt: Presidential decree no. 375 and the consequences for judicial authority. *Harvard International Law Journal*, 35:1, pp. 225–237.

Ferrara, A. (2003). Two notions of humanity and the judgment argument for human rights. *Filosoficky Casopis*, 51:4, pp. 639–663.

Fichtelberg, A. (2005). Crimes beyond justice? Retributivism and war crimes. *Criminal Justice Ethics*, 24:1, pp. 31–46.

Findlay, W. (2002). Deciphering the 'humpty-dumpty' protocol: Political crime, political prisoners and 19th-century Ireland. *Cahiers Victoriens and Edouardiens*, 55, pp. 363–376.

Findlay, M. (2007). Terrorism and relative justice. *Crime, Law and Social Change*, 47:1, pp. 57–68.

Finnin, S.J. (2003). The proposed trials by the US military commissions. *Yearbook of International Humanitarian Law*, 6, pp. 409–423.

——— (2007). Update on United States military commissions. *Yearbook of International Humanitarian Law*, 10, pp. 198–231.

Fiss, O.M. (2006). The war against terrorism and the rule of law. *Oxford Journal of Legal Studies*, 26:2, pp. 235–256.

Fitzpatrick, J. (2003). Speaking law to power: The war against terrorism and human rights. *European Journal of International Law*, 14:2, pp. 241–264.

——— (2003). Rendition and transfer in the war against terrorism: Guantanamo and beyond. *Loyola of Los Angeles International and Comparative Law Review*, 25:3, pp. 457–492.

Flanagan-Hyde, K. (2006). The public's right to access to the military tribunals and trials of enemy combatants. *Arizona Law Review*, 48:3, pp. 585–613. [http://www.arizonalawreview.org/pdf/48-3/48arizlrev585.pdf].

Fokkens, J.W. (2004). Strafrecht en terrorisme. *Nederlands Juristenblad*, pp. 1347–1351.

Foley, B.J. (2007). Guantanamo and beyond: Dangers of rigging the rules. *Journal of Criminal Law and Criminology*, 97:4, pp. 1009–10069.

Frouville, O. de (2011). The influence of the European Court of Human Rights' case law on international criminal of torture and inhuman or degrading treatment. *Journal of International Criminal Justice*, 9:3, pp. 633–649.

Gallagher, K. (2008). Universal jurisdiction in practice: Efforts to hold Donald Rumsfeld and other high-level United States officials accountable for torture. *Journal of International Criminal Justice*, 7:5, pp. 1087–1116.

Garcia, M.J. (2009). Renditions: Constraints imposed by laws on torture. *International Journal of Terrorism and Political Hot Spots*, 4:3–4, pp. 297–326.

——— (2009). U.N. Convention Against Torture (CAT): Overview and application to interrogation techniques. *International Journal of Terrorism and Political Hot Spots*, 4:3–4, pp. 411–436.

——— (2009). Interrogation of detainees: Requirements of the Detainee Treatment Act. *International Journal of Terrorism and Political Hot Spots*, 4:3–4, pp. 437–453.

Gardella, T.M. (2006). Beyond terrorism: The potential chilling effect on the internet of broad law enforcement legislation. *St. John's Law Review*, 80:2, pp. 655–692.

Gardes, J. (1988). Terrorist on trial: The legal dilemmas. *Criminal Justice Journal*, 11:1, pp. 235–265

Garrison, A.H. (2003). Hamdi, Padilla and Rasul: The war on terrorism on the judicial front. *American Journal of Trial Advocacy*, 27:1, pp. 99–148.

——— (2004). The war on terrorism on the judicial front, part II: The courts strike back. *American Journal of Trial Advocacy*, 27:3, pp. 473–516.

Gauthier, A. (2002). Secret justice: Access to terrorism proceedings. *News Media and the Law*, 26:1.

Gershman, B.L. (2005). How juries get it wrong. Anatomy of the Detroit terror case. *Washburn Law Journal*, 44:2, pp. 327–354. [http://digitalcommons.pace.edu/cgi/viewcontent.cgi?article=1123andcontext=lawfaculty].

Ghetti, M.W. (2008). The terrorist is a star! Regulating media coverage of publicity-seeking crimes. *Federal Communications Law Journal*, 60:3, pp. 481–533.

Gibbons, J.J. (2011). Does 9/11 justify a war on the judicial branch. *Rutgers Law Review*, 63:4, pp. 1101–1116.

Gilbert, G. (1992). The Irish interpretation of the political offense exemption. *International and Comparative Law Quarterly*, 41:1, pp. 66–84.

Glazier, D.W. (2005, Fall). Precedent lost: The neglected history of the military commission. *Virginia Journal of International Law*, 46:1, pp. 5–82.

Goede, M. de and Graaf, B.A. de (2013). Sentencing risk. Temporality and precaution in terrorism trials. *International Political Sociology*, 7:3, pp. 313–331.

Goldstone, R. (2006). Combating terrorism: Zero tolerance for torture. *Case Western Reserve Journal of International Law*, 37:2–3, pp. 343–348.

Green, L.C. (1981). Terrorism and the courts. *Manitoba Law Journal*, 11:4, pp. 333–358.

Greer, C. and McLaughlin, E. (2011). Trial by media: Policing, the 24–7 news media sphere and the politics of outrage. *Theoretical Criminology*, 15:1, pp. 23–46. [http://tcr.sagepub.com/content/15/1/23.full.pdf+html].

Greer, E. (2004). 'We don't torture people in America': Coercive interrogation in the global village. *New Political Violence*, 26:3, pp. 371–387.

Gregory, E.J. (2010). Trying unlawful combatants at general courts-martial: Amending the UCMJ in light of the military commissions experience. *Military Law Review*, 203:1, pp. 150–188. [http://www.loc.gov/rr/frd/Military_Law/Military_Law_Review/pdf-files/203-spring-2010.pdf].

Gross, E. (2003). Trying terrorists–Justification for differing trial rules: The balance between security consideration and human rights. *Indiana International and Comparative Law Review*, 13:3, pp. 777–786.

Guiora, A.N. (2005). Legislative and policy responses to terrorism. A global perspective. *San Diego Journal of International Law*, 7:1, pp. 125–172.

——— (2007). Where are terrorists to be tried: A comparative analysis of rights granted to suspected terrorists. *Catholic University Law Review*, 56:2, pp. 805–836.

——— (2008). Creating a domestic terror court. *Washburn Law Journal*, 48:3, pp. 617–632.

——— (2008). Interrogation of detainees: Extending a hand or a boot? *University of Michigan Journal of Law Reform*, 41:2, pp. 375–420.

——— (2008). Military commissions and national security courts after Guantanamo. *Northwestern University Law Review*, 103, pp. 199–208.

——— (2010). The quest for individual adjudication and accountability: Are international tribunals the right response to terrorism? *Emory International Law Review*, 24:2, pp. 497–513.

——— (2012). Due process and counterterrorism. *Emory International Law Review*, 26:1, pp. 163–188. [http://www.law.emory.edu/fileadmin/journals/eilr/26/26.1/Guiora.pdf].

——— and Page, E.M. (2006). The unholy trinity: Intelligence, interrogation and torture. *Case Western Reserve Journal of International Law*, 37:2–3, pp. 427–446.

——— and Parry, J.T. (2008). Light at the end of the pipeline?: Choosing a forum for suspected terrorists. *University Pennsylvania Law Review*, 156, pp. 356–378.

Haines, S.M. (2004). Rounding up all the usual suspects: The rights of Arab detainees in a post-September 11 world. *Arkansas Law Review*, 57:1, pp. 105–142.

Hajjar, L. (2002). The making of a political trial: The Marwan Barghouti case. *Middle East Report*, 225, pp. 30–37.

Hannay, W.M. (1980). International terrorism and the political offense exception to extradition. *Columbia Journal of Transnational Law*, 18:3, pp. 381–412.

Harel, A. and Sharon, A. (2008). What is really wrong with torture? *Journal of International Criminal Justice*, 6:2, pp. 241–259.

Harper, J. (2009). Defining torture: Bridging the gap between rhetoric and reality. *Santa Clara Law Review*, 49:3, pp. 893–928.

Harris, G.C. (2003). Terrorism, war and justice: The concept of the unlawful enemy combatant. *Loyola of Los Angeles International and Comparative Law Journal*, 26:1, pp. 31–36.

Heilbrunn, J. (1991, Winter). The NY Times and the Moscow show trials. *World Affairs*, 15:3, pp. 87–101.

Hemming, S. (2010). The practical application of counter-terrorism legislation in England and Wales: A prosecutor's perspective, *International Affairs*, 86:4, pp. 955–969.

Herrmann, K.L. (2010). Reviewing Bush-Era counterterrorism policy after 9/11: Reconciling ethical and practical considerations. *Homeland Security Review*, 4:2, pp. 139–155.

Hert, P.J.A. de (2005). Balancing security and liberty within the European Human Rights framework: A critical reading of the court's case law in the light of surveillance and criminal law enforcement strategies after 9/11. *Utrecht Law Review*, 1:1, pp. 68–96.

Herzig, M. (2002). Is Korematsu good law in the face of terrorism? Procedural due process in the security versus liberty debate. *Georgetown Immigration Law Journal*, 16:3, pp. 685–703.

Hill, S. (2001). Extradition and international terrorism: Part II. *Crime and Justice International*, 17:52.

Hocking, J. (2003). Counter-terrorism and the criminalization of politics: Australia's new security powers of detention, proscription, and control. *Australian Journal of Politics and History*, 49:3, pp. 355–371.

Hodgkinson, S.L. (2010). Are ad hoc tribunals an effective tool for prosecuting international terrorism cases? *Emory International Law Review*, 24:2, pp. 515–525.

Holmes, S. (2009). In case of emergency: Misunderstanding tradeoffs in the war on terror. *California Law Review*, 97:2, pp. 301–355.

Hooks, G. and Mosher, C. (2005). Outrages against personal dignity: Rationalizing abuse and torture in the war on terror. *Social Forces*, 83:4, pp. 1627–1645.

Hufnagel, S.M. (2008). German perspectives on the right to life and human dignity in the 'war on terror.' *Criminal Law Journal*, 32:100, pp. 100–113.

Hughes, K. (2011). Anatomy of a terrorism prosecution: Dr. Rafil Dhafir and the help the needy Muslim charity case. *National Law Guild Review*, 68:4.

Huq, A.Z. (2012). Forum choice for terrorism suspects. *Duke Law Journal*, 61, pp. 1415–1509. [http://scholarship.law.duke.edu/cgi/viewcontent.cgi?article=1534andcontext=dlj].

Hutchinson, A.C. and Monahan, P.J. (1984). Law, politics and the critical legal scholars: The unfolding drama of American legal thought. *Stanford Law Review*, 36:1–2, pp. 199–245.

Ip, J. (2010). The Supreme Court and House of Lords in the war on terror: Inter arma silent leges? *Michigan State Journal of International Law*, 19:1, pp. 1–61.

——— (2009). Two narratives of torture. *Northwestern Journal of International Human Rights*, 7:1, pp. 35–77. [http://www.law.northwestern.edu/journals/jihr/v7/n1/2/Ip.pdf].

Iraola, R. (2003). Terrorism, grand juries, and the Federal Material Witness statute. *St. Mary's Law Journal*, 34, pp. 401–428.

Ivey, L.M. (2002–2003). Ready, aim, fire? The president's executive order authorizing detention, treatment and trial of certain non-citizens in the war on terrorism is a powerful weapon, but should it be upheld? *Cumberland Law Review*, 33, pp. 107–134.

Jackola, A.T. (2004). A second bite at the apple: How the government's use of the doctrine of enemy combatants in the case of Zacarias Moussaoui threatens to upset the future of the crime justice system. *Hamline Law Review*, 27, pp. 101–132.

Jackson, J. (2003–2004). Trial of the accused Taliban and al Qaeda operatives captured in Afghanistan and detained on a U.S. military base in Cuba. *Cumberland Law Review*, 34, pp. 195–229.

Jackson, J.D. and Doran, S. (1993). Conventional trials in unconventional times: The Diplock court experience. *Criminal Law Forum*, 4:3, pp. 503–520.

Jacobs, L.M. (2010). It's time to leave the Troubles behind: Northern Ireland must try paramilitary suspects by jury rather than Diplock-type courts. *Texas International Law Journal*, 45:3, pp. 655–665.

Jaehnig, W.B. (1978). Journalists and terrorism: Captives of the libertarian tradition. *Indiana Law Journal*, 53, pp. 717–744.

Jakobs, G. (2006). Terroristen als Personen im Recht? *Zeitschrift für die gesamte Strafrechtswissenschaft*, 117:4, pp. 839–851.

Janik, Jr., A.L. (2002). Prosecuting Al-Qaeda: America's human rights policy interest are best served by trying terrorists under international tribunals. *Denver Journal of International Law and Policy*, 30:4, pp. 498–531.

Jenks, C. (2009). Notice otherwise given: Will in absentia trials at the special tribunal for Lebanon violate human rights? *Fordham International Law Journal*, 33:1, pp. 57–100.

——— and Jensen, E.T. (2010). All human rights are equal, but some are more equal than others: The extraordinary rendition of a terror suspect in Italy, the NATO SOFA, and human rights. *Harvard National Security Journal*, 1, pp. 171–202.

——— and Jensen, E.T. (2011). Indefinite detention under the laws of war. *Stanford Law and Policy Review*, 22:1, pp. 41–92.

Johnson, B.D. (2012). Cross-classified multilevel models: An application to the criminal case processing of indicted terrorists. *Journal of Quantitative Criminology*, 28:1, pp. 163–189.

Jonakait, R.N. (2003–2004). A double due process denial: The crime of providing material support or resources to designated foreign terrorist organizations. *New York Law School Law Review*, 48, pp. 125–172.

Joyce, D. (2007). The Judith Miller case and the relationship between reporter and source: Competing visions of the media's roll and function. *Fordham Intellectual Property Media and Entertainment Law Journal*, 17:3, pp. 555–589.

Joyner, C.C. (2003). International extradition and global terrorism: Bringing international criminals to justice. *Loyola of Los Angeles International and Comparative Law Review*, 25, pp. 493–451.

Kacprowski, N.A. (2003). Stacking the deck against suspected terrorists: The dwindling procedural limits on the government's power to indefinitely detain United States citizens as enemy combatants. *Seattle University Law Review*, 26, pp. 651–697.

Kadidal, S. (2011). Confronting ethical issues in national security cases: The Guantanamo habeas litigation. *Seton Hall Law Review*, 41:4, pp. 1397–1426. [http://erepository.law.shu.edu/cgi/viewcontent.cgi?article=1407andcontext=shlr].

Kane, J. (1996). Justice, impartiality, and equality: Why the concept of justice presume equality. *Political Theory*, 23:3, pp. 375–393.

Kantor, E. (2008, April). New threats, old problems: Adhering to Brandenburg's imminence requirement in terrorism prosecutions. *George Washington Law Review*, 76:3, pp. 752–785. [http://groups.law.gwu.edu/LR/ArticlePDF/76-3-Kantor.pdf].

Keith, D. (2004). In the name of national security or insecurity? The potential indefinite detention of noncitizen certified terrorists in the United States and the United Kingdom in the aftermath of September 11. *Florida Journal of International Law*, 16, pp. 405–481.

Kelly, C.A. (2003). The Pen is mightier than the sword or why the media should exercise self-restraint in time of war. *Florida Bar Journal*, 77, pp. 22–29.

Kelly, M.J. (2003). Executive excess v. judicial process: American judicial response to the government's war on terror. *Indiana International and Comparative Law Review*, 13, pp. 787–823.

——— (2003). Cheating justice by cheating death: The doctrinal collision for prosecuting foreign terrorists—Passage of aut dedere aut judicare into customary law and refusal to extradite based on the death penalty. *Arizona Journal of International and Comparative Law*, 20, pp. 491–532.

Kendall, E.C. (2011, Winter). The alien terrorist removal court and other national security measures you may have never heard of: The need for comprehensive national security reform. *Texas Wesleyan Law Review*, 18:2, pp. 253–274. [http://www.texaswesleyanlawreview.org/index.php?option=com_articlemanagerandItemid=andtask=detailsandid=53].

Keyes, T.W. (1985). Does Marx have a concept of justice. *Philosophical Topics*, 13:2, pp. 277–286.

Kim, J. (2004). Making state sponsors of terrorism pay: A separation of powers discourse under the Foreign Sovereign Immunities Act. *Berkeley Journal of International Law*, 22, pp. 513–540.

Kinneally, J.J., III (1987). The political offence exception: Is the United States-United Kingdom supplementary extradition treaty the beginning of the end? *American University Journal of International Law and Policy*, 2:1, pp. 203–227.

Kirtley, J.E. (2006). Transparency and accountability in a time of terror: The Bush' Administration's on freedom of information. *Communication Law and Policy*, 11, pp. 479–509.

Knowles, J.B. (2004). The Lockerbie judgments: A short analysis. *Case Western Reserve Journal of International Law*, 36, pp. 473–486.

Koh, H.H. (2002, April). The case against military commissions. *American Journal of International Law*, 96:2, pp. 337–344. [http://digitalcommons.law.yale.edu/cgi/viewcontent.cgi?article=2842andcontext=fss_papers].

Kontorovich, E. (2010). A Guantanamo on the sea: The difficulties of prosecuting pirates and terrorists. *California Law Review, 98*, pp. 234–276.

Korn, A. (2003). From refugees to infiltrators: Constructing political crime in Israel in the 1950s. *International Journal of the Sociology of Law*, 31:1, pp. 1–22.

Koskenniemi, M. (2002). Between show trials and impunity. *Max Planck Yearbook of United Nations Law*, pp. 1–15.

Kreimer, S.F. (2005). 'Torture lite', 'full bodied' torture, and the insulation of legal conscience. *Journal of National Security Law and Policy*, 1:2, pp. 187–229.

Krejci, O. (1985). The conservative concept of justice. *Filosoficky Casopis*, 33:6, pp. 845–859.

Kuhn, W. (2012). The modern development of homegrown creative justice: The speedy trial rights of military detainees. *Syracuse Law Review*, 62:2, pp. 209–253.

Kumar, M.A. (2011). Secret witnesses, secret information and secret evidence: Australia's response to terrorism. *Mississippi Law Journal*, 80:4, pp. 1371–1394. [http://papers.ssrn.com/sol3/papers.cfm?abstract_id=1949575].

Lasson, K. (2007). Civil liberties in uncivil times: The perilous quest to preserve American freedoms. *London Law Review*, 2, pp. 2–130.

Lebowitz, M.J. (2011). 'Terrorist speech': Detained propagandists and the issue of extraterritorial application of the First Amendment. *First Amendment Law Review*, 9, pp. 573–601.

——— (2011). The value of claiming torture: An analysis of al-Qaeda's tactical lawfare strategy and efforts to fight back. *Case Western Reserve Journal of International Law*, 43:1–2, pp. 357–392.

Lee, P. (2006). Interrogational torture. *American Journal of Jurisprudence*, 51, pp. 131–147.

Legge, Jr., J.S. (2011). Prosecuting Nazi collaborators and terrorists: Eli Rosenbaum and managing the Office of Special Investigations. *Public Administration Review*, 71:2, pp. 247–284.

Lederer, F.I. (2004). The potential use of courtroom technology in major terrorism cases. *William and Mary Bill of Rights Journal*, 12:3, pp. 887–938. [http://scholarship.law.wm.edu/wmborj/vol12/iss3/16/].

Leiken, J. (2004). Leaving wonderland: Distinguishing terrorism from other types of crime. *Case Western Reserve Journal of International Law*, 36:2–3, pp. 501–505.

Lepri, T.J. (2003). Safeguarding the enemy within: The need for procedural protections for U.S. citizens detained as enemy combatants under *Ex Parte Quirin*. *Fordham Law Review*, 71, pp. 2565–2598.

Levin, B. (2007, May). Trials for terrorists: The shifting legal landscape of the post-9/11 era. *Journal of Contemporary Criminal Justice*, 23:2, pp. 198–218.

Levinson, S. (2003, Summer). The debate on torture: War against virtual states. *Dissent*, 30:3, pp. 79–90.

——— (2005). In quest of a 'common conscience': Reflections on the current debate about torture. *Journal of National Security Law and Policy*, 1:2, pp. 231–252.

Levitt, K.J. (2005). The CIA and the torture controversy: Interrogation, authorities and practices in the war on terror. *Journal of National Security Law and Policy*, 1:2, pp. 341–356.

Lieberman, D.M. (2006). Sorting the revolutionary from the terrorist: The delicate application of the 'political offense' exception in US extradition cases. *Stanford Law Review*, 59:1, pp. 181–212.

Lippman, M. (1989). Political offender exception in international extradition law: Terrorism versus human rights. *International Journal of Comparative and Applied Criminal Justice*, 13:2, pp. 45–59.

Lochner, T. (2008, April). Sound and fury: Pretextual prosecution and Department of Justice antiterrorism efforts. *Law and Policy*, 30:2, pp. 168–193.

Locy, T. (2004). The trials of al Qaeda: Federal court vs. military commission. *Case Western Reserve Journal of International Law*, 36:2–3, pp. 507–512.

Luban, D. (2008). Lawfare and the legal ethics in Guantanamo. *Stanford Law Review*, 60:6, pp. 1981–2026. [http://papers.ssrn.com/sol3/papers.cfm?abstract_id=1092451].

——— (2009). Human dignity, humiliation and torture. *Kennedy Institute of Ethics Journal*, 19:3, pp. 211–230.

Lynch, A. (2006). Legislating with urgency—The enactment of The Anti-Terrorism Act [No 1] 2005. *Melbourne University Law Review*, 31, pp. 747–781.

——— (2006). Maximising the drama: 'Jihad Jack', the court of appeal and the Australian media. *Adelaide Law Review*, 27, pp. 311–334. http://www.gtcentre.unsw.edu.au/sites/gtcentre.unsw.edu.au/files/mdocs/ALynch_ALR.pdf

——— (2012). The impact of post-enactment review on anti-terrorism laws: Four jurisdictions compared. *Journal of Legislative Studies*, 18:1, pp. 63–81.

———, McGarrity, N., and Williams, G. (2009). The proscription of terrorist organizations in Australia. *Federal Law Review*, 37, pp. 1–39. [http://www.gtcentre.unsw.edu.au/sites/gtcentre.unsw.edu.au/files/mdocs/Prosciption.pdf].

Madison, B. (2006). Trial by jury or by military tribunal for accused terrorist detainees facing the death penalty? An examination of principles that transcend the U.S. Constitution. *University of Florida Journal of Law and Public Policy*, 17, pp. 347–428. [http://regentuniversity.org/acad/schlaw/faculty_staff/docs/madison/trialbyjury.pdf].

Margulies, P. (2003). The virtues and vices of solidarity: Regulating the roles of lawyers for clients accused of terrorist activity. *Maryland Law Review*, 62, pp. 173–217.

——— (2004). Judging terror in the 'zone of twilight': Exigency, institutional equity, and procedure after September 11. *Boston University Law Review*, 84, pp. 383–443.

Martinez, L. (2002). Prosecuting terrorists at the International Criminal Court: Possibilities and problems. *Rutgers Law Journal*, 34, pp. 1–62.

May, L. (2005). Torturing detainees during interrogation. *International Journal of Applied Philosophy*, 19:2, pp. 193–208.

McCarthy, A. (2004). Terrorism on trial: The trials of al Qaeda. *Case Western Reserve Journal of International Law*, 36:2–3, pp. 513–522.

McComas, B.C. (2010, Spring). Article III by default: Constitutional requirements for the capital prosecution of unprivileged enemy belligerents. *University of San Francisco Law Review*, 44, pp. 979–1005.

McDonnell, M.H.M., Nordgren, L. and Loewenstein, G. (2011). Torture in the eyes of the beholder: The psychological difficulty of defining torture in law and policy. *Vanderbilt Journal of Transnational Law*, 44:1, pp. 87–122. [http://law.vanderbilt.edu/publications/journal-of-transnational-law/archives/volume-44-number-1/index.aspx].

McGarrity, N. (2010). 'Testing' our counter-terrorism laws: The prosecution of individuals for terrorism offences in Australia. *Criminal Law Journal*, 34, pp. 92–127. [http://www.law.utoronto.ca/documents/workshops/Constitutional-111019-McGarrity.pdf].

——— (2011). Fourth estate or government lapdog? The role of the Australian media in the counter-terrorism context. *Continuum: Journal of Media and Cultural Studies*, 25:2, pp. 273–283.

McGregor, A. (2010). 'The Chechen network' on trial: Terrorist prosecutions in Paris. *North Caucasus Analysis*, 7:18. [http://www.jamestown.org/single/?no_cache=1andtx_ttnews%5Btt_news%5D=3232].

McMahan, J. (2006). Torture, morality and law. *Case Western Reserve Journal of International Law*, 37:2–3, pp. 241–248. [http://www.case.edu/orgs/jil/vol.37.2.3/McMahan.pdf].

McNeal, G.S. (2008). Organizational theory and counterterrorism prosecutions: A Preliminary Inquiry. *Regent University of Law Review*, 21, pp. 307–329.

Mégret, F. (2003). Justice in times of violence. *European Journal of International Law*, 14:2, pp. 327–345.

Meijers, T. and Glasius, M. (2013). Expression of Justice or Political Trial? Discursive battles in the Karadžić case. *Human Rights Quarterly*, 35:3, pp. 720–752.

Meringolo, J.C. (2010). The media, the jury, and the high-profile defendant: A defense perspective on the media circus. *New York Law School Law Review*, 55, pp. 981–1012.

Minor, W. (1975). Political crime, political justice, and political prisoners. *Criminology*, 12:4, pp. 385–398.

Moeckli, D. (2006). The selective 'war on terror': Executive detention of foreign nationals and the principles of non-discrimination. *Brooklyn Journal of International Law*, 31:2, pp. 1–40.

Montano, M. (2009). Who may be tried under the Military Commissions Act of 2006? *Standard Law Review*, 61:5, pp. 1281–1332. [http://www.stanfordlawreview.org/print/article/who-may-be-tried-under-military-commissions-act-2006].

Moore, K. (2007). The role of federal criminal prosecutions in the war on terrorism. *Lewis and Clark Law Review*, 11:4, pp. 837–849.

Morgan, R. (2000). The utilitarian justification of torture: Denial, desert, and disinformation. *Punishment and Society*, 2:2, pp. 181–196.

Mullenix, P. (2007). Interrogation strategies for an unconventional extremist enemy. *Polygraph*, 36:3, pp. 121–132.

Murali, J. (2004). Extraditing terrorists hits a death penalty kibosh. *Wisconsin International Law Journal*, 22, pp. 163–185.

Murray, C.R.G. (2011). The ripple effect: Guantanamo Bay in the United Kingdom's courts. *Pace International Law Review*, 23, pp. 15–40.

Nagel, T. (2005). The problem of global justice. *Philosophy and Public Affairs*, 33:2, pp. 113-147.

Neuman, G.L. (2004). Counter-terrorist operations and the rule of law. *European Journal of International Law*, 15:5, pp. 1019–1029.

Newton, M.A. (2003). International criminal law aspects of the war against terrorism. *U.S. Naval War College International Law Studies*, 79, pp. 323–352.

——— (2006). War by proxy: Legal and moral duties of 'other actors' derived from government affiliation. *Case Western Reserve Journal of International Law*, 37:2–3, pp. 249–265.

Nichols, G. (2008). Repercussions and recourse for specially designated terrorist organizations acquitted of materially supporting terrorism. *Review of Litigation*, 28:1, pp. 263–293.

Nordgren, L.F., McDonnell, M.H. and Loewenstein, G. (2011). What constitutes torture?: Psychological impediments to an objective evaluation of interrogation tactics. *Psychological Science*, 22:5, pp. 689–694.

Nouwen, S. and Werner, W. (2010). Doing justice to the political: The ICC in Uganda and Sudan. *European Journal of International Law*, 11:4. pp. 1–25.

Nugent-Borakove, M.E. (2008). Precursor crimes to terrorism and the local prosecutor's role in disruption. *International Journal of Comparative and Applied Criminal Justice*, 32:1, pp. 9–21.

O'Connell, M.E. (2005). Affirming the ban on harsh interrogation. *Ohio State Law Journal, 66:6*, pp. 1231–1267.

——— (2008). Defining armed conflict. *Journal of Conflict Security Law*, 13, pp. 393–400.

Odeshoo, J.R. (2004). Truth or dare? Terrorism and 'truth serum' in the 9/11 world. *Stanford Law Review*, 57, pp. 209–255.

O'Donnell, M. (2008). Stories of Jack: Myth, media and the law. *Law Text Culture*, 12:1, pp. 188–213. [http://ro.uow.edu.au/cgi/viewcontent.cgi?article=1013andcontext=ltc].

Ohlin, J.D. (2008). The bounds of necessity. *Journal of International Criminal Justice*, 6:2, pp. 289–308.

Olson, L.M. (2010). Prosecuting suspected terrorists: The 'war on terror' demands reminders about war, terrorism, and international law. *Emory International Law Review*, 24:2, pp. 479–496.

Packer, H.L. (1964). Two models of the criminal process. *University of Pennsylvania Law Review*, 113:1, pp. 1–68.

Padmanabhan, V.M. (2009). Norm internalization through trials for violations of international law: Four conditions for success and their application to trials of detainees at Guantanamo Bay. *University of Pennsylvania Journal of International Law*, 31:2, pp. 427–492. [http://scholarship.law.upenn.edu/cgi/viewcontent.cgi?article=1121&context=jil].

Parry, J.T. (2005). 'Just for fun': Understanding torture and understanding Abu Ghraib. *Journal of National Security Law and Policy*, 1:2, pp. 253–284.

——— (2009). Torture nation, torture law. *Georgetown Law Journal*, 97, pp. 1001–1054.

——— and White, W.S. (2002). Interrogating suspected terrorists: Should torture be an option. *University of Pittsburgh Law Review*, 63, pp. 743–766.

Paust, J.J. (2003). Judicial power to determine the status and rights of persons detained without trial. *Harvard International Law Journal*, 44, pp. 503–532.

——— (2009). Serial war crimes in response to terrorism can pose threats to national security. *William Mitchell Law Review*, 35:5, pp. 5201–5221.

Peterson, A. (2008) Addressing tomorrow's terrorists. *Journal of National Security Law and Policy*, 2:2, pp. 297–354.

Petty, K.A. (2009). Are you there, Geneva? It's me, Guantanamo. *Case Western Reserve Journal of International Law*, 42:1–2, pp. 171–186. [http://papers.ssrn.com/sol3/papers.cfm?abstract_id=1528491].

Phillips, R.S. (1997). The political offence exception and terrorism: Its place in the current extradition scheme and proposals for its future. *Dickinson Journal of International Law*, 15:1, pp. 337–362.

Posner, E. and Vermeule, A. (2006). Should coercive interrogation be legal? *Michigan Law Review*, 104:4, pp. 671–707.

Post, J.M. (2000). Terrorist on trial: The context of political crime. *Journal of the American Academy of Psychiatry and the Law*, 28:2, pp. 171–178.

Punch, M. and Cramphorn, C. (2007). The murder of Theo van Gogh and the Islamic Jihad Division (*Divisie Islamitische Jihad*) in the Netherlands. *Journal of Policing, Intelligence and Counter Terrorism*, 2:1, pp. 34–53.

Radsan, A.J. (2006). A better model for interrogating high-level terrorists. *Temple Law Review*, 79:4, pp. 1227–1286.

Rassera, M. (2005). The Dutch response to Moluccan terrorism, 1970–1978. *Studies in Conflict and Terrorism*, 28:6, pp. 481–492.

Ratner, E. (2012). Anonymous accusers in the Holy Land: Subverting the right of confrontation in the United States' largest terrorism-financing trial. *Loyola Journal of Public Interest Law*, 13, pp. 575–621.

Raven-Hansen, P. (2006–2007). National security secrecy in the courts: A comparative perspective from Israel and Ireland. *Cardozo Public Law Policy and Ethics Journal*, 5, pp. 63–74.

Raviv, A. (2004). Torture and justification: Defending the indefensible. *George Mason Law Review*, 13:1, pp. 135–181.

Rejali, D. (2003). Modern torture as a civic marker: Solving a global anxiety with a new political technology. *Journal of Human Rights*, 2:2, pp. 153–171.

Reid, M. (2010). Secrets behind secrets: Disclosure of classified information before and during trial and why CIPA should be revamped. *Seton Hall Legislative Journal*, 32:2, pp. 272–300.

Resnik, J. (2010). Detention, the war on terror, and the federal courts. *Columbia Law Review*, 110:2, pp. 579–686.

Reyes, H. (2007). The worst scars are in the mind: Psychological torture. *International Review of the Red Cross*, 89:867, pp. 591–617. [http://www.ikrk.org/eng/assets/files/other/irrc-867-reyes.pdf].

Rice, P.R. and Saul, B.P. (2002, Summer). Is the war on terrorism a war on attorney-client privilege? *Criminal Justice*, 17:2. [http://www.americanbar.org/publications/criminal_justice_magazine_home/crimjust_cjmag_17_2_privilege.html].

Richardson, C.L. (2010, Summer). The creation of judicial compromise: Prosecuting detainees in a national security court system in Guantanamo Bay, Cuba. *Homeland Security Review*, 4:2, pp. 119–138.

Rishikof, H. (2003). Is it time for a federalist terrorist court? Terrorists and prosecutions: Problems, paradigms, and paradoxes. *Suffolk Journal of Trial and Appellate Advocacy*, 7, pp. 1–37.

Roach, K. (2008). The consequences of compelled self-incrimination in terrorism investigations: A comparison of American grand juries and Canadian investigative hearings. *Cardozo Law Review*, 30:3, pp. 1089–1115. [http://papers.ssrn.com/sol3/papers.cfm?abstract_id=1622260].

Roach, K. (2011). 'Constitution chicken': National security confidentiality and terrorism prosecutions after R. v. Ahmad. *Supreme Court Law Review*, 54, pp. 357–390. [http://papers.ssrn.com/sol3/papers.cfm?abstract_id=2123496].

——— (2012). Uneasy neighbors: Comparative American and Canadian counter-terrorism. *William Mitchell Law Review*, 38:4, pp. 1701–1803.

——— and Trotter, G. (2005). Miscarriages of justice in the war against terrorism. *Penn State Law Review*, 109:4. pp. 967–1041.

Robbins, C.W. (2012). Finding terrorists' intent: Aligning civil antiterrorism law with national security. *St. John's Law Review*, 83:4, pp. 1201–1273. [http://scholarship.law.stjohns.edu/cgi/viewcontent.cgi?article=1046andcontext=lawreview].

Rose, G. and Nestorovska, D. (2007). Australian counter-terrorism offences: Necessity and clarity in federal criminal law reforms. *Criminal Law Journal*, 31, pp. 20–55. [http://ro.uow.edu.au/cgi/viewcontent.cgi?article=1029andcontext=lawpapers].

Ross, J. (2007). Black letter abuse: The US response to torture since 9/11. *International Review of the Red Cross*, 89:867, pp. 561–590. [http://www.icrc.org/eng/assets/files/other/irrc-867-ross.pdf].

Rostow, N. (2011). The laws of war and the killing of suspected terrorists: False starts, rabbit holes, and dead ends. *Rutgers Law Review*, 63:1, pp. 1215–1233.

Sadat, L.N. (2006). Ghost prisoners and black sites: Extraordinary rendition under international law. *Case Western Reserve Journal of International Law*, 37:2–3, pp. 309–342.

——— (2007). Extraordinary rendition, torture, and other nightmares from the war on terror. *George Washington Law Review*, 75:5–6, pp. 1200–1248.

Said, W.E. (2010). The terrorism informant. *Washington Law Quarterly*, 85:4, pp. 687–738.

——— (2012). Ten years after 9/11: Rethinking counterterrorism: The message and means of the modern terrorism prosecution. *Transnational Law and Contemporary Problems*, 21, pp. 175–195.

Sallon, C. (2006, Spring). Taking liberties with justice—The legal landscape in Britain post September 11th. *Stetson Law Review*, 34, pp. 983–999.

Sands, P. (2008). Torture team: The responsibility of lawyers for abusive interrogation. *Melbourne Journal of International Law*, 9:2, pp. 365–380.

Saul, B. (2011). Legislating from a radical The Hague: The UN special tribunal for Lebanon invents an international crime of transnational terrorism. *Leiden Journal of International Law*, 24:3, pp. 677–700.

Schabas, W.A. (2006). The crime of torture and the international criminal tribunals. *Case Western Reserve Journal of International Law*, 37:2–3, pp. 349–364.

Scharf, M.P. (2000). Terrorism on trial: The Lockerbie criminal proceedings. *ILSA Journal of International and Comparative Law*, 6, pp. 355–361.

Scheppele, K.L. (2005). Hypothetical torture in the 'war on terrorism'. *Journal of National Security Law and Policy*, 1:2, pp. 285–340.

——— (2005). 'We forgot about the ditches': Russian constitutional impatience and the challenge of terrorism. *Drake Law Review*, 53, pp. 963–1027.

Schlink, B. (2007). Problem with 'torture lite'. *Cardozo Law Review*, 29:1, pp. 85–89.

Schmid, A.P. (2004). Terrorism: The definitional problem. *Case Western Reserve Journal of International Law*, 36:2–3, pp. 375–419.

Schmid, E. (2009). The right to a fair trial in times of terrorism: A method to identify the non-derogable aspects of article 14 of the international covenant on civil and political rights. *Goettingen Journal of International Law*, 1:1, pp. 29–44.

Schmidt, S.A. and Dreatel, J.L. (2003/2004). Turning the tables: Using the government's secrecy and security arsenal for the benefit of the client in terrorism prosecutions. *New York Law School Law Review*, 48, pp. 69–90.

Schulhofer, S.J. (2008, Fall). Prosecuting suspected terrorists: The role of the civilian courts. *Advance: The Journal of the ACS Issue Groups*, 2:2, pp. 64–71. [http://www.acslaw.org/files/Prosecuting-Suspected-Terrorists.pdf].

Shah, T.A. (2001). Islam, Muslims and terrorism: Secret evidence and guilt by association. *Michigan State University-Detroit College of Law Journal of International Law*, 10, pp. 589–602.

Shields, C.A., Damphousse, K.R., and Smith, B.L. (2006, August). Their day in court: Assessing guilty plea rates among terrorists. *Journal of Contemporary Criminal Justice*, 22:3, pp. 261–276.

Shue, H. (2006). Torture in dreamland: Disposing of the ticking bomb. *Case Western Reserve Journal of International Law*, 37:2–3, pp. 231–239.

Shulman, M.R. (2009). National security courts: Star Chamber or specialized justice? *ILSA Journal of International and Comparative Law*, 15:2, pp. 533–549. [http://papers.ssrn.com/sol3/papers.cfm?abstract_id=1328427].

Sievert, R.J. (2002). War on terrorism or global law enforcement operation? *Notre Dame Law Review*, 78:2, pp. 307–353.

Silliman, S.L. (2009). The appropriate venue for trying terrorist case: Prosecuting alleged terrorists by military commission: A prudent option. *Case Western Reserve Journal of International Law*, 41:1–2, pp. 289–297.

Silver, D. (2011). Media censorship and access to terrorism trials: A social architecture analysis. *Notre Dame Journal of Law, Ethics and Public Policy*, 25, pp. 143–186.

Simmons, J.A. (2004). In civilian dress and with hostile purpose: The labeling of United States citizens captured on American soil as enemy combatants: Due process vs. national security. *Indiana Law Review*, 37, pp. 579–603.

Smith, B.L., Damphousse, K.R., Yang, S., and Ginther, C. (2005). Prosecuting politically motivated offenders: The impact of terrorist label on criminal case outcomes. *International Journal of Contemporary Sociology*, 42:2, pp. 209–226.

———, Damphousse, K.R., Jackson, F., and Sellers, A. (2002). The prosecution and punishment of international terrorists in federal courts: 1980–1998. *Criminology and Public Policy*, 1:3, pp. 311–338.

Smolla, R.A. (2002). From 'Hit Man to Encyclopedia of Jihad': How to distinguish freedom of speech from terrorist training. *Loyola of Los Angeles Entertainment Law Review*, 22, pp. 479–490.

Stratton, S.N. (2004). Taking terrorists to court: A practical evaluation of civil suits against terrorists under the Anti-Terrorism Act. *Suffolk Journal of Trial and Appellate Advocacy*, 9, pp. 27–55.

Strassfeld, R.N. (2006). American innocence. *Case Western Reserve Journal of International Law*, 37:2–3, pp. 277–308.

Strauss, M. (2003). Torture. *New York Law School Law Review*, 48, pp. 201–274.

Sulmasy, G. (2009). The need for a national security court system. *St. John's Journal of Legal Commentary*, 23:4, pp. 1007–1016. [http://scholarship.law.stjohns.edu/cgi/viewcontent.cgi?article=1053andcontext=jcred].

Sussman, D. (2006). Defining torture. *Case Western Reserve Journal of International Law*, 37:2–3, pp. 225–230.

Tait, D. (2011, December). Deliberating about terrorism: Prejudice and jury verdicts in a mock terrorism trial. *Australian and New Zealand Journal of Criminology*, 44:3, pp. 387–403.

Tarin, D. (2004). Will an attack on America justify an attack on Americans?: Congressional and constitutional prohibitions on the executive's power to detain U.S. citizens as enemy combatants. *Virginia Journal of International Law*, 22, pp. 1145–1196.

Terry, J.P. (2010). Federal court or military commission: The legal dilemma posed by those charged with terrorist violence. *Naval Law Review*, 60, pp. 125–140. [http://www.jag.navy.mil/documents/navylawreview/NLRVolume60.pdf].

Thompson, D.K. (1983). The evolution of the political offence exception in an age of modern political violence. *Yale Journal of World Public Order*, 9:2, pp. 315–341.

Tilstra, S.E. (2003). Prosecuting international terrorists: The Abu Sayyaf attacks and the Bali bombing. *Pacific Rim Law and Policy Journal*, 12:3, pp. 835–869. [http://digital.law.washington.edu/dspace-law/bitstream/handle/1773.1/745/12PacRimLPolyJ835.pdf?sequence=1].

Tobias, C. (2004). Punishment and the war on terrorism. *University of Pennsylvania Journal of Constitutional Law*, 6, pp. 1116–1158.

Tortoroli, C. (2010, Winter). Gangs of New York are terrorists? The misapplication of the New York antiterrorism statute due to lack of comprehensive gang legislation. *St. John's Law Review*, 84:1, pp. 391–421.

Tracy, J. (2009). Detention and prosecution of alleged terrorists and combatants. *Human Rights Brief*, 16:3, pp. 15–18.

Trahan, J. (2002). Trying a Bin Laden and others: Evaluating the options for terrorist trials. *Houston Journal of International Law*, 24, pp. 475–508.

Tsai, R.L. (2010). John Brown's constitution. *Boston College Law Review*, 51:1, pp. 151–207.

Ulbrick, J.T. (2005). Tortured logic: The (il)legality of United States interrogation practices in the war on terror. *Northwestern University Journal of International Human Rights*, 5:1, pp. 210–237.

Valero-Garces, C. and Abkari, A. (2010). Learning from practice: Interpreting at the 11M terrorist attack trial. *The International Journal for Translation and Interpreting Research*, 2:2, pp. 44–56.

Vervaele, J.A. (2005). Terrorism and information sharing between the intelligence and law enforcement communities in the US and the Netherlands: Emergency criminal law? *Utrecht Law Review*, 1:1, pp. 1–27.

——— (2009). Special procedural measures and the protection of human rights, general report. *Utrecht Law Review*, 5:2, pp. 66–103.

Vidino, L. (2007). The Hofstad group: The new face of terrorist networks in Europe. *Studies in Conflict and Terrorism*, 30:7, pp. 579–592.

Vidmar, N. (2003). When all of us are victims: Juror prejudice and terrorist trials. *Chicago-Kent Law Review*, 78, pp. 1143–1178.

Villaverde, M.D. (2003). Structuring the prosecutor's duty to search the intelligence community for Brady material. *Cornell Law Review*, 88:5, pp. 1471–1548.

Vladeck, S.I. (2010). Terrorism trials and the Article III courts after Abu Ali. *Texas Law Review*, 88:7, pp. 1501–1532. [http://www.texaslrev.com/issues/vol/88/issue/7/vladeck].

——— (2010). The laws of war as a constitutional limit on military jurisdiction. *Journal of National Security and Policy*, 4:295, pp. 295–342.

Van der Vyver, J.D. (2010). Prosecuting terrorism in international tribunals. *Emory International Law Review*, 24:2, pp. 527–547.

Wahlquist, J. (2009). Enhancing interrogation: Advancing a new agenda. *Parameters*, pp. 38–49.

Waldron, J. (2005). Torture and positive law: Jurisprudence for the White House. *Columbia Law Review*, 105:6, pp. 1681–1750.

Walker, C. (2006). Intelligence and anti-terrorism legislation in the United Kingdom. *Crime, Law and Social Change*, 44, pp. 387–422.

——— (2009). Prosecuting terrorism: the Old Bailey versus Belmarsh. *Amicus Curiae*, 79, pp. 21–25. [http://sas-space.sas.ac.uk/2564/1/Amicus79_Walker.pdf].

Wallace, D.H. and Kreisel, B. (2003). Martial law as a counterterrorism response to terrorist attacks: Domestic and international dimensions. *International Criminal Justice Review*, 13:1, pp. 50–75.

Wallace, D.A. (2008). Torture v. the basic principles of the US military. *Journal of International Criminal Justice*, 6:2, pp. 309–322.

Wattellier, J.J. (2003). Comparative legal responses to terrorism: Lessons from Europe. *Hastings International and Comparative Law Review*, 27:2, pp. 397–420.

Weissbrodt, D. and Bergquist, A. (2006). Extraordinary rendition and the torture convention. *Virginia Journal of International Law*, 46, pp. 585–650.

Weisselberg, C.D. (2008). Terror in the courts: Beginning to assess the impact of terrorism-related prosecutions on domestic criminal law and procedure in the USA. *Crime, Law and Social Change*, 50:1–2, pp. 25–46.

Werner, W. (2010). The curious career of lawfare. *Case Western Reserve Journal of International Law*, 43:1–2, pp. 61–72.

——— (2010). The changing face of enmity: Carl Schmitt's international theory and the evolution of the legal concept of war. *International Theory*, 2:3, pp. 351–380.

Whealy, A. (2007). Impact of terrorism related laws on judges conducting criminal trials. *The Judicial Review*, 8:3, pp. 353–383.

Wheatley, J. (2006). The Hamburg 9/11 terrorism trials: Prospects for German legal reform and intelligence sharing. *Journal of International Law and Policy*, 3, pp. 1–25. [https://www.law.upenn.edu/journals/jil/jilp/articles/3-1_Wheatley_Joseph.pdf].

White, M.J. (2001, Spring). Prosecuting terrorism in New York. *Middle East Quarterly*, 8:2, pp. 11–18. [http://www.meforum.org/25/prosecuting-terrorism-in-new-york].

Wilke, C. (2005, December). War vs. justice: Terrorism cases, enemy combatants, and political justice in US courts. *Politics and Society*, 33:4, pp. 637–669.

Wilson, R.J. (2003, Fall). Can U.S. courts learn from failed terrorist trials by military commission in Turkey and Peru? *Human Rights Brief*, 11, pp. 12–14. [http://digitalcommons.wcl.american.edu/cgi/viewcontent.cgi?article=1338andcontext=hrbrief].

Winter, B.T. (1996). Invidious prosecution: The history of seditious conspiracy-Foreshadowing the recent convictions of Sheik Omar Abdel-Rahman and his immigrant followers. *Georgetown Immigration Law Journal*, 10, pp. 185.

Wolfendale, J. (2006). Training torturers: A critique of the 'ticking bomb' argument. *Social Theory and Practice*, 32:2, pp. 269–287.

——— (2009). The myth of 'torture lite'. *Ethics and International Affairs*, 23:1, pp. 47–61.

Wood, L. (2008). Overview and analysis of Senate amendment concerning interrogation of detainees. *International Journal of Terrorism and Political Hot Spots*, 3:1–2, pp. 1–6.

Woods, J.C. (2003). The third tower: The effect of the September 11th terrorist attacks on the American jury system. *Alabama Law Review*, 55, pp. 209–229.

Wright, J. (2011). Mirandizing terrorists? An empirical analysis of the public safety exception. *Columbia Law Review*, 111:6, pp. 1296–1331.

Yin, T. (2009). Boumediene and lawfare. *University of Richmond Law Review*, 48, pp. 865–892.

Zarrella, J. (2005). Why the traditional First Amendment right to a public trial cannot be applied to military tribunals. *CommLaw Conspectus*, 14, pp. 269–284. [http://commlaw.cua.edu/articles/v14/Zarrella.pdf].

Zelikow, P. (2012). Codes of conduct for a twilight war. *Houston Law Review*, 49:1, pp. 1–52. [http://www.houstonlawreview.org/wp-content/uploads/2012/05/1-Zelikow.pdf].

13.3. Non-conventional Sources

Abrams, N. (2012). *Terrorism prosecutions in federal court: Exceptions to constitutional evidence rules and development of a cabined exception for coerced confessions*. (Research Paper No. 11–14). UCLA School of Law. [http://papers.ssrn.com/sol3/papers.cfm?abstract_id=1846963].

American Bar Association Standing Committee on Law and National Security, National Strategy Forum, McCormick Foundation (2009, July). *Trying terrorists in Article III courts—A post-workshop report*. Washington, DC. [http://www.americanbar.org/content/dam/aba/migrated/natsecurity/trying_terrorists_artIII_report_final.authcheckdam.pdf].

Amnesty International (1998). *Fair Trials Manual.* London: Amnesty International Publications.

——— (2005, December, 14). USA: *The trial of Ahmed Abu Ali—Findings of Amnesty International's trial observation.* [http://web.archive.org/web/20070617045947/http://web.amnesty.org/library/index/engamr511922005].

Brown, M.A. (2011, March). *Freed: Ripples of the convicted and released terrorist in America.* Naval Postgraduate School.

Buchhandler-Raphel, M. (2011). *What's terrorism got to do with it? The perils of prosecutorial misuse of terrorism offenses.* [http://works.bepress.com/michal_buchhandler_raphael/15/].

The Center on Law and Security at NYU School of Law (2006, April). *Prosecuting Terrorism: The Legal Challenge.* The NYU Review of Law and Security. [http://www.lawandsecurity.org/Portals/0/Documents/n07_Prosecuting-Terrorism-the-Legal-Challenge.pdf].

——— (2011). *Terrorist trial report card: September 11, 2001—September 11, 2011.*

Center on Law and Security (2009). *Highlights from the Terrorist Trial Report Card, 2001–2009: Lessons Learned.* New York: CLS.

Council of Europe (1950, amendments 2010). *Convention for the Protection of Human Rights and Fundamental Freedoms.* [http://conventions.coe.int/treaty/en/treaties/html/005.htm].

Donohue, L.A. (2001). *In the name of national security: U.S. counterterrorist measures, 1960–2000.* Belfer Center for Science and International Affairs. [http://belfercenter.ksg.harvard.edu/files/in_the_name_of_national_security.pdf].

Elsea, J.F. (2012, May 9). *Comparison of rights in military commission trials and trials in federal criminal court.* (Rep. No. R40932). Congressional Research Service. [http://www.fas.org/sgp/crs/natsec/R40932.pdf].

Fischer-Lichte, E. (1999, 23 November). Notwendige Ergänzung des Tekst-Modells. *Frankfurter Rundschau.*

——— (2000). Theater als Modell für eine performative Kultur. Zum performative turn in der europäischen Kultur des 20. Jahrhunderts. *Universitätsreden,* 46. Saarbrücken: Pressestelle der Universität des Saarlandes.

Goldsmith, J. (2009, February 4). *Long-term terrorist detention and our national security court.* Counterterrorism and American Statutory Law Series No. 5. Brookings Institution, the Georgetown University Law Center, and the Hoover Institution. [http://www.brookings.edu/research/papers/2009/02/09-detention-goldsmith].

Grave de Peralta, R. (2010). *Ensuring the end game: Facilitating the use of classified evidence in the prosecution of terrorist subjects.* Monterey, CA: Naval Postgraduate School. [http://www.dtic.mil/cgi-bin/GetTRDoc?AD=ADA518654].

Hodgson, J. (2006, November). *The investigation and prosecution of terrorists in France.* An Independent Report Commissioned by the Home Office, United Kingdom. [http://www2.warwick.ac.uk/fac/soc/law/staff/academic/hodgson/publications/horeportfinal2006.pdf].

Litt, R.S. and Bennett, W.C. (2009, May 8). *Better rules for terrorism trials.* Counterterrorism and American Statutory Law Series No. 7. Brookings Institution, the Georgetown University Law Center, and the Hoover Institution. [http://www.brookings.edu/research/papers/2009/05/08-terrorism-litt-bennett].

Paulussen, C. (2012, April). *Impunity for international terrorists? Key legal questions and practical considerations.* International Centre for Counter-Terrorism. The Hague. [http://www.icct.nl/download/file/ICCT-Paulussen-Impunity-April-2012.pdf].

Reagan, R.T. (2011, November 14). *National security case studies: Special case-management challenges.* Federal Judicial Center.

Rishikof, H. (2007, November). *A federal terrorism court.* Progressive Policy Institute.

Scheffer, D. (2001, November). *Options for prosecuting international terrorists.* Washington, DC: United States Institute of Peace. [http://www.usip.org/publications/options-prosecuting-international-terrorists].

Shields, C., Damphousse, K.R., and Smith, B.L. (2009, September). *An assessment of defense and prosecutorial strategies in terrorism trials: Implications for state and federal prosecutors.* Terrorism Research Center, Fulbright University. [https://www.ncjrs.gov/pdffiles1/nij/grants/228276.pdf].

Silver, A. (2006, March 27). *Prosecuting terrorists after September 11.* CFR Backgrounder, Council on Foreign Relations. [http://www.cfr.org/terrorism-and-the-law/prosecuting-terrorists-after-september-11/p10246].

Smith, B.L. and Damphousse, K.R. (2001). *American terrorism study: Patterns of behavior, investigation and prosecution of American terrorists, final report.* [https://www.ncjrs.gov/pdffiles1/nij/grants/193420.pdf].

Turner, S. and Schulhofer, S.J. (2005). *The secrecy problem in terrorism trials.* Brennan Center for Justice at NYU School of Law. [http://brennan.3cdn.net/2941d4bea7c3c450d2_4sm6iy66c.pdf].

United Nations Office on Drugs and Crime (UNODC) (ca. 2003). *Unpublished report of the UNODC on the treatment of the political offence exception in international anti-terrorism legal instruments.*

——— (2009). *Handbook on criminal justice responses to terrorism.* New York: United Nations.

United Nations (2002). *Report of the ad hoc committee established by General Assembly resolution 51/210 of 17 December 1996. Sixth session* (28 January – 1 February 2002). General Assembly. Official Records. Supplement No. 37 (A/57/37).

——— (2003). *Digest of jurisprudence of the United Nations and regional organizations on the protection of human rights while countering terrorism*. New York: United Nations.

U.S. Department of Defense (2011). *Regulation for trial by military commission*. [http://www.mc.mil/Portals/0/Reg_for_Trial_by_mcm.pdf].

Vidmar, N. (2006). *Trial by jury involving persons accused of terrorism*. Duke Law School Faculty Scholarship Series. (Paper 54). [http://lsr.nellco.org/duke_fs/54].

Whealy, A. (2010, April). *Terrorism and the right to a fair trial: Can the law stop terrorism? A comparative analysis*. A Paper presented to the British Institute of International and Comparative Law, London, UK. [http://www.biicl.org/files/5038_terrorism_and_the_right_to_a_fair_trial__2_.pdf].

Zabel, R.B. and Benjamin, Jr., J.J. (2008). *In pursuit of justice: Prosecuting terrorism cases in the federal courts*. Washington, DC: Human Rights First. [http://www.humanrightsfirst.org/wp-content/uploads/pdf/080521-USLS-pursuit-justice.pdf].

13.3.1. *Interrogation and Torture Debate*

Ferrara, P. (et al.) (n.d.). *The interrogation memos: Shall we be clueless on terrorism*. Alexandria, VA: American Civil Rights Union. [http://theacru.org/pdfs/TheInterrogationMemos.pdf].

Human Rights Center (2008). *Guantanamo and its aftermath: US detention and interrogation practices*.

Human Rights Watch (2011, July). *Getting away with torture: The Bush Administration and mistreatment of detainees*. [http://www.hrw.org/sites/default/files/reports/us0711webwcover.pdf].

Intelligence Science Board (2006, December). *Educing information: Interrogation: Science and art*. Washington, DC: National Defense Intelligence College. [http://www.fas.org/irp/dni/educing.pdf].

Laufer, J. (2011). By any means necessary: The quandary the CIA now faces in light of employing enhanced interrogation methods to combat the war on terror. (Master's thesis, Duquesne University). [http://gradworks.umi.com/14/90/1490849.html].

13.3.2. *Prosecution and Trial News Coverage By Defendant/Plot*

Anti-Terrorism Law General

Anti-terror tactics 'weaken law' (2009, February 16). BBC *News*. [http://news.bbc.co.uk/2/hi/europe/7892387.stm].

General Terrorism and Trials

Chronology of major terrorism trials in Britain (2007, July 9). *Reuters*. [http://uk.reuters.com/article/2007/07/09/idUKL0929297720070709].

Eggen, D. and Tate, J. (2005, June 12). U.S. campaign produces few convictions on terrorism charges; statistics often count lesser crimes. *Washington Post*. [http://www.washingtonpost.com/wp-dyn/content/article/2005/06/11/AR2005061100381.html].

Fazlollah, M. and Nicholas, P. (2001, December 1). U.S. overstates arrests in terrorism. *Philadelphia Inquirer*. [http://articles.philly.com/2001-12-16/news/25307839_1_terrorism-fbi-computer-system-justice-department].

I was put on trial by al-Qaeda (2009, February 7). BBC *News*. [http://news.bbc.co.uk/2/hi/europe/7870597.stm].

Justice department chronology of terrorism-related convictions (2006, June 23). *Wall Street Journal*. [http://online.wsj.com/article/SB115108663859289059.html].

Montgomery, L. and Ryan, E. (2011, February 24). Terrorist plots uncovered in the US since 9/11. *Christian Science Monitor*. [http://www.csmonitor.com/USA/2009/0926/p02s08-usgn.html].

Perelman, M. (2006, January 19). How the French fight terror. *Foreign Policy*. [http://www.foreignpolicy.com/articles/2006/01/18/how_the_french_fight_terror].

Recent terrorism-related cases in Canada (2012, June 8). CBC *News*. [http://www.cbc.ca/news/canada/story/2011/01/21/f-terror-cases-quickfacts.html].

Liquid Bomb Plot

7/7 'inspired airline plotters' (2008, April 7). BBC *News Online*. [http://news.bbc.co.uk/2/hi/uk_news/7334453.stm].

Aircraft bomb plot trial to begin (2008, April 2). BBC *News Online*. [http://news.bbc.co.uk/2/hi/uk_news/7326981.stm].

Airlines bomb plot: The e-mails. (2009, September 7). BBC *News*. [http://news.bbc.co.uk/2/hi/uk_news/8193501.stm].

Bin Laden 'inspired bomb plotter' (2008, April 10). BBC *News Online*. [http://news.bbc.co.uk/2/hi/uk_news/7340606.stm].

Casciani, D. (2009, September 7). Liquid bomb plot: What happened. BBC *News*. [http://news.bbc.co.uk/2/hi/uk_news/8242479.stm].

Corera, G. (2008, September 9). Bomb plot—the al-Qaeda connection. BBC *News*. [http://news.bbc.co.uk/2/hi/uk_news/7606107.stm].

Jury hears 'suicide recordings' (2008, May 7). BBC *News Online*. [http://news.bbc.co.uk/2/hi/uk_news/7387933.stm].

Profiles: Airline plot accused (2009, September 7). BBC *News*. [http://news.bbc.co.uk/2/hi/uk_news/7604808.stm].

Profiles: Operation Overt (2008, September 8). BBC *News Online*. [http://www.bbc.co.uk/news/10455915].

Reaction to airline convictions (2009, September 7). BBC *News*. [http://news.bbc.co.uk/2/hi/uk_news/8242515.stm].

Stringer, D. (2008, April 3). Airliner bomb plot trial begins in UK. USA *Today*. [http://www.usatoday.com/news/world/2008-04-02-4073236149_x.htm].

'Suicide videos': What they said (2008, April 4). BBC *News Online*. [http://news.bbc.co.uk/2/hi/uk_news/7330367.stm].

Sullivan, A. (2008, April 5). British jury in terror case shown 'martyrdom tapes.' *Washington Post*. [http://www.washingtonpost.com/wp-dyn/content/article/2008/04/04/AR2008040403468.html].

Three guilty of airline bomb plot (2009, September 7). BBC *News*. [http://news.bbc.co.uk/2/hi/uk_news/8242238.stm].

UK terror suspect says bombs were stunt (2008, June 2). USA *Today*. [http://www.usatoday.com/news/world/2008-06-02-terrorist-uk_N.htm].

Anders Behring Breivik

Anda, L.G. (2012, April 10). Breivik's sanity: Norway psychiatrists at odds. BBC *News*. [http://www.bbc.co.uk/news/world-europe-17667261].

Anders Behring Breivik wants acquittal or death penalty (2012, April 18). BBC *News*. [http://www.bbc.co.uk/news/world-europe-17752189].

Anderson, C. (2012, May 11). Shoe thrown at defendant in Norway murder trial. *New York Times*. [http://www.nytimes.com/2012/05/12/world/europe/breivik-trial-in-norway-killings-is-disrupted.html].

Deshayes, P.H. (2012, May 23). Norway shooting massacre survivor calls bullet scars 'the price of democracy.' *National Post* (Canada). [http://news.nationalpost.com/2012/05/23/norway-shooting-massacre-survivor-calls-bullet-scars-the-price-for-democracy/].

Lewis, M. (2012, June 21). Prosecutors in Norway seek hospital for gunman. *New York Times*. [http://www.nytimes.com/2012/06/22/world/europe/anders-breivik-prosecutors-seek-psychiatric-confinement.html].

——— (2012, June 22). At trial's end, lawyers say Norway killer is not insane. *New York Times*.

——— and Cowell, A. (2012, April 16). Norwegian man claims self-defense in killings. *New York Times*. [http://www.nytimes.com/2012/04/17/world/europe/trial-of-anders-behring-breivik-opens-in-norway.html?pagewanted=alland_moc.semityn].

——— and Cowell, A. (2012, April 17). On witness stand, Norwegian says he would kill again. *New York Times*. [http://www.nytimes.com/2012/04/18/world/europe/anders-behring-breivik-trial-in-norway.html?pagewanted=all].

——— and Jolly, D. (2012, April 18). Prosecutors press Norwegian on extremist affiliations. *New York Times*. [http://www.nytimes.com/2012/04/19/world/europe/norway-anders-behring-breivik-trial-extremist-affiliations.html].

No appeal from Breivik as case formally ends (2012, September 7). *Seattle Times*. [http://seattletimes.com/html/nationworld/2019089020_apeunorwaymassacre.html].

Shane, S. (2011, July 24). Killings in Norway spotlight anti-Muslim thought in U.S. *New York Times*. [http://www.nytimes.com/2011/07/25/us/25debate.html?pagewanted=all].

Stephens, B. (2011, July 26). What is Anders Breivik? *Wall Street Journal*. [http://online.wsj.com/article/SB10001424053111903591104576467773477916948.html].

Nidal Hassan—Fort Hood Shooting

Brown, A.K. (2012, September 6). Nidal Hasan, Fort Hood shooting suspect, must shave beard. *Huffington Post*. [http://www.huffingtonpost.com/2012/09/06/nidal-hasan-shave-beard-fort-hood-shooting_n_1862241.html].

Fernandez, M. (2012, August 15). Fort Hood shooting trial delayed pending ruling on beard. *New York Times*. [http://www.nytimes.com/2012/08/16/us/fort-hood-shooting-trial-delayed-pending-ruling-on-beard.html].

Hennessy-Fiske, M. (2012, August 14). Judge fines Ft. Hood suspect for beard, denies trial delay. *Los Angeles Times*. [http://www.latimes.com/news/nation/nationnow/la-na-nn-fort-hood-shooter-20120814,0,5364782.story].

Rizzo, J. (2012, August 30). Accused Fort Hood shooter makes first statement in court. CNN *Security Clearance*. [http://security.blogs.cnn.com/2012/08/30/accused-fort-hood-shooter-makes-first-statement-in-court/].

El-Masri

Court rejects lawsuit related to C.I.A. kidnapping (2010, December 11). *New York Times*. [http://www.nytimes.com/2010/12/11/world/europe/11briefs-Germany.html].

Fleishman, J. and Goetz, J. (2007, January 31). Germany may indict U.S. agents in abduction. *Los Angeles Times*. [http://articles.latimes.com/2007/jan/31/world/fg-cia31].

Landler, M. (2007, February 1). German court challenges CIA over abduction. *New York Times*. [http://www.nytimes.com/2007/02/01/world/europe/01germany.html].

Whitlock, C. (2007, February 1). Germans charge 13 CIA operatives. *Washington*

Post. [http://www.washingtonpost.com/wp-dyn/content/article/2007/01/31/AR2007013100356.html].

Virginia Jihad

Lichtblau, E. (2003, June 28). Group of Muslims charged with plotting against India. *New York Times*. [http://www.nytimes.com/2003/06/28/us/group-of-muslims-charged-with-plotting-against-india.html].

——— (2007, November 21). Wiretap issues leads judge to warn of retrial in terror case. *New York Times*. [http://www.nytimes.com/2007/11/21/washington/21nsa.html].

Markon, J. (2004, March 10). Final 'Va. jihad' defendant acquitted. *Washington Post*. [http://www.washingtonpost.com/wp-dyn/articles/A44463-2004Mar9.html].

——— (2005, July 30). U.S. judge reduces 'Va. jihad' sentences. *Washington Post*. [http://www.washingtonpost.com/wp-dyn/content/article/2005/07/29/AR2005072901893.html].

——— (2006, April 26). Va. terror case sent back to lower court. *Washington Post*. [http://www.washingtonpost.com/wp-dyn/content/article/2006/04/25/AR2006042502004.html].

——— (2006, June 8). Va. jihad case hailed as key in war on terror. *Washington Post*. [http://www.washingtonpost.com/wp-dyn/content/article/2006/06/07/AR2006060702109.html].

——— (2007, November 21). Government secrecy may lead to new trial in Va. terrorism case. *Washington Post*. [http://www.washingtonpost.com/wp-dyn/content/article/2007/11/20/AR2007112001913.html].

O'Dell, L. (2006, May 26). Court hears appeal of jihad cases. *Richmond Times Dispatch*.

Sentences lengthy for Virginia jihad (2004, June 15). *USA Today*. [http://www.usatoday.com/news/nation/2004-06-15-virginia-jihad-sentence_x.htm].

Smith, B. (2007, October 29). Chandia challenges law on terror group. *Legal Times*.

9/11 Guantanamo

American female defense lawyer covers up in traditional Islamic dress at 9/11 Guantanamo trial 'out of respect' for her client's religious beliefs (2012, May 6). *Daily News* (UK). [http://www.dailymail.co.uk/news/article-2140393/9-11-Guantanamo-trial-American-female-defense-lawyer-covers-traditional-Islamic-dress.html].

Khalid Sheikh Mohammed Guantanamo hearing gets chaotic start (2012, May 6). BBC *News*. [http://www.bbc.co.uk/news/world-us-canada-17966362].

McGreal, C. (2012, May 5). 9/11 suspects refuse to answer judge's questions as Guantánamo trial opens. *The Guardian* (UK). [http://www.guardian.co.uk/world/2012/may/05/9-11-suspects-guantanamo-trial].

Pilkington, E. (2008, February 11). US seeks the death penalty as six detained in Guantánamo are charged over 9/11. *The Guardian*. [http://www.guardian.co.uk/world/2008/feb/12/guantanamo.september11?INTCMP=ILCNETTXT3487].

Schulz, D. (2012, April 18). Guantánamo trials should be open. *New York Times*.

Selsky, A.O. (2008, June 5). Accused 9/11 mastermind asks judge to be executed. (2008, June 5). *USA Today*. [http://www.usatoday.com/news/topstories/2008-06-04-146165448_x.htm].

The Guantanamo docket (n.d.). *New York Times*. [http://projects.nytimes.com/guantanamo/].

Tran, M. (2009, November 13). Guantánamo Bay detainees to face September 11 trial in New York. *The Guardian* (UK). [http://www.guardian.co.uk/world/2009/nov/13/guantanamo-bay-september-11-trial?INTCMP=ILCNETTXT3487].

Wittes, B. and Bennett, W. (2012, May 5–6). 9/11 arraignment. *Lawfare Blog*. (Note: there are 14 parts to this). [http://www.lawfareblog.com/category/event-coverage/page/3/].

Abd al-Rahim al-Nashiri—USS Cole

Savage, C. (2011, November 9). Abd al-Rahim al-Nashiri arraigned in U.S.S. Cole bombing. *New York Times*. [http://www.nytimes.com/2011/11/10/us/abd-al-rahim-al-nashiri-arraigned-in-uss-cole-bombing.html].

——— (2012, April 12). Ruling averts testimony by a detainee, for now. *New York Times*. [http://www.nytimes.com/2012/04/12/us/politics/judges-ruling-averts-detainees-testimony-for-now.html].

Fort Dix Six

Anastasia, G. (2007, May 13). A radical shift in reputation for 6 men. *Philadelphia Inquirer*. [http://articles.philly.com/2007-05-13/news/25229153_1_dritan-duka-agron-abdullahu-shain-duka].

Erminio, V. (2008, December 17). Terror trial defense's last word: It was all hot air. *Star Ledger* (New Jersey). [http://blog.nj.com/ledgerarchives/2008/12/terror_trial_defenses_last_wor.html].

Martin, J. (2008, June 6). Jury pool for Fort Dix trial starts big. *Star Ledger* (New Jersey). [http://blog.nj.com/ledgerarchives/2008/06/jury_pool_for_fort_dix_trial_s.html].

Mittica, C.J. (2011, April). A shadow in the suburbs. *South Jersey Magazine*. [http://www.southjersey.com/articles/?articleID=24040].

Aafia Siddiqui

Ambinder, M. (2010, February 11). A terrorist tried in federal court: The case of Aafia Siddiqui. *The Atlantic*. [http://www.theatlantic.com/politics/archive/2010/02/a-terrorist-tried-in-federal-court-the-case-of-aafia-siddiqui/35793/].

North Carolina—Daniel Body Cell

Convicted NC terror plotters get long prison terms (2012, August 24). *Washington Examiner*. [http://washingtonexaminer.com/convicted-nc-terror-plotters-get-long-prison-terms/article/feed/2027373].

Foot Hood Bomb Plot

Brown, A.K. (2012, May 25). Naser Jason Abdo guilty in Fort Hood bomb plot. *Huffington Post*. [http://www.huffingtonpost.com/2012/05/25/fort-hood-soldier-guilty_n_1545207.html].

Hennessy-Fiske, M. (2012, August 10). Jason Abdo, former AWOL soldier, sentenced in Ft. Hood bomb plot. *Los Angeles Times*. [http://www.latimes.com/news/nation/nationnow/la-na-nn-ft-hood-bomb-20120810,0,2708863.story].

Naser Jason Abdo sentencing delayed in Fort Hood bomb plot trial (2012, August 9). *Huffington Post*. [http://www.huffingtonpost.com/2012/08/09/naser-jason-abdo_n_1762276.html].

Lockerbie

Lockerbie evidence not disclosed (2008, August 28). *BBC News Online*. [http://news.bbc.co.uk/2/hi/uk_news/scotland/south_of_scotland/7573244.stm].

Trial of El Sayyid Nosair

Farber, M.A. (1991, December 9). Kahane trial sets off squabbles by lawyers. *New York Times*. [http://www.nytimes.com/1991/12/09/nyregion/reporter-s-notebook-kahane-trial-sets-off-squabbles-by-lawyers.html?pagewanted=allandsrc=pm].

McFadden, R.D. (1991, December 23). For jurors, evidence in Kahane case was riddled with gaps. *New York Times*. [http://www.nytimes.com/1991/12/23/nyregion/for-jurors-evidence-in-kahane-case-was-riddled-with-gaps.html?pagewanted=allandsrc=pm].

Hofstad Group

Vermaat, E. (2008, January 31). Wrong decision by Dutch appeals court in Hofstad group terror case. *PipeLineNews*. [http://www.investigativeproject.org/595/wrong-decision-by-dutch-appeals-court-in-hofstad-group].

——— (2010, November 1). Dutch Hofstad group member Jason Walters renounces terrorism, violence and salafism. *PipeLineNews*. [http://www.pipelinenews.org/2010/nov/01/Dutch-Hofstad-Group-Member-Jason-Walters-Renounces-Terrorism.html].

NGOs, *Charities and Corporations and Terrorism*

Apuzzo, M. (2007). Chiquita pleads guilty in terrorism probe. *Washington Post*. [http://www.washingtonpost.com/wp-dyn/content/article/2007/03/19/AR2007031900641_pf.html].

Kovach, G.C. (2008, November 24). Five convicted in terrorism financing trial. *New York Times*. [http://www.nytimes.com/2008/11/25/us/25charity.html].

Millennium Bomber: Ressam and Haouari

Coughenour, J.C. (2007, November 1). Op-Ed, How to Try a Terrorist. *N.Y. Times*. [http://www.nytimes.com/2007/11/01/opinion/01coughenour.html].

——— (2008, July 27). Op-Ed, The Right Place to Try Terrorism Cases. *Washington Post*. [http://www.washingtonpost.com/wp-dyn/content/article/2008/07/25/AR2008072502759.html].

Lovett, I. (2012, March 12). Appeals court overturns millennium bomb-plot sentence; calls it too light. *New York Times*. [http://www.nytimes.com/2012/03/13/us/appeals-court-overturns-millennium-bomb-plot-sentence.html].

Schwartz, J. (2010, February 3). Appeals court throws out sentence in bombing plot, calling it too light. *New York Times*. [http://www.nytimes.com/2010/02/03/us/03bomber.html?_r=1].

Sullivan, J. (2010, February 3). Court: Ressam sentence failed to protect public. *Seattle Times*. [http://seattletimes.com/html/localnews/2010963552_ressam03m.html].

Lodi Trials

Archibold, R.C. and Kearns, J. (2006, April 26). In California terror case, a mistrial for a father, but a son is guilty. *New York Times*. [http://www.nytimes.com/2006/04/26/us/26mistrial.html].

Marshall, C. (2006, May 6). Government will retry terror case. *New York Times*. [http://www.nytimes.com/2006/05/06/us/06lodi.html].

Bali Bombing Trial

Bali bombing suspect Umar Patek on trial in Indonesia (2012, February 13). *BBC News*. [http://www.bbc.co.uk/news/world-asia-17008398].

Hussain, Z. (2012, March 23). Osama bin Laden Funded Bali Bombing, Terror Trial Reveals. *Jakarta Globe*. [http://www.thejakartaglobe.com/home/osama-bin-laden-funded-bali-bombing-terror-trial-reveals/506694].

Madanir, R. and Whiteman, H. (2012, June 21). Indonesian court sentences Bali bomber to 20 years in jail. CNN. [http://www.cnn.com/2012/06/21/world/asia/patek-bali-bombing-verdict/index.html].

'Jihad' Jack Thomas

Allard, T. (2006, August 29). Jihad Jack wife's terror link. *Sydney Morning Herald*. [http://www.smh.com.au/news/national/jihad-jack-wifes-terror-link/2006/08/28/1156617275236.html?page=fullpage].

———, Munro, I. and Nguyen, K. (2006, August 29). Order puts rights of all at risk: Lawyer. *Sydney Morning Herald*. [http://www.smh.com.au/news/national/order-puts-rights-of-all-at-risk-lawyer/2006/08/28/1156617275327.html].

'Jihad Jack' guilty in Melbourne (2006, February 26). BBC *News*. [http://news.bbc.co.uk/2/hi/asia-pacific/4751958.stm].

'Jihad Jack' given five-year term (2006, March 31). BBC *News*. [http://news.bbc.co.uk/2/hi/asia-pacific/4863422.stm].

'Jihad Jack' conviction quashed (2006, August 18). BBC *News*. [http://news.bbc.co.uk/2/hi/asia-pacific/5262114.stm].

Leys, N. (2011, May 2). 'Jihad' Jack Thomas welcomes bin Laden death but warns of martyrdom. *Herald Sun*. [http://www.heraldsun.com.au/news/jihad-jack-welcomes-bin-laden-death/story-e6frf7jo-1226048407755].

Neighbour, S. (2008, October 24). Accused's trial by media. *The Australian*. [http://www.theaustralian.com.au/opinion/columnists/accuseds-trial-by-media/story-e6frg7ef-1111117839224].

Schuster, H. (2006, March 3). The story of Jihad Jack. CNN. [http://edition.cnn.com/2006/WORLD/asiapcf/03/03/schuster.column/index.html].

Squires, N. (2006, August 19). Bin Laden's friend Jihad Jack freed by Australian judges. *The Telegraph* (UK). [http://www.telegraph.co.uk/news/1526744/Bin-Ladens-friend-Jihad-Jack-freed-by-Australian-judges.html].

Jack Roche

The Jack Roche story (2004, May 28). *Sydney Morning Herald*. [http://www.smh.com.au/articles/2004/05/28/1085641707742.html].

Zeky Mallah—2003

McGarrity, N. (2008, September 17). Identifying clear and present danger. *Sydney Morning Herald.* [http://www.smh.com.au/news/opinion/identifying-clear-and-present-danger/2008/09/16/1221330832350.html].

Neighbour, S. (2007, July 19). Guilty until proven innocent. *The Australian.* [http://www.theaustralian.com.au/business/legal-affairs/guilty-until-proven-innocent/story-e6frg97x-1111113987106].

O'Brien, N. (2009, February 21). First charged with terrorism Zeky Mallah gains passport. *The Australian.* [http://www.theaustralian.com.au/news/first-terrorism-charged-gains-passport/story-e6frg606-1111118919770].

Faheem Khalid Lodhi—2006

Lamont, L. (2006, August 23). Lodhi gets 20-year terror term. *Sydney Morning Herald.* [http://www.smh.com.au/news/national/lodhi-gets-20year-terror-term/2006/08/23/1156012585950.html].

Wallace, N. (2006, June 19). Lodhi guilty of terror plot. *Sydney Morning Herald.* [http://www.smh.com.au/news/national/lodhi-guilty-of-terror-plot/2006/06/19/1150569264287.html].

'Terrorist Training Camps' Case

Bowcott, O. (2008, February 26). Preacher guilty of organising terror training camps. *The Guardian* (UK). [http://www.guardian.co.uk/uk/2008/feb/26/uksecurity].

Capaccio, T. (2011, June 21). Pentagon Crosses $1 Trillion Threshold In War On Terror Spending, *Bloomberg News.* [http://www.bloomberg.com/news/articles/2011-06-21/afghanistan-pushes-pentagon-over-1-trillion-mark-for-war-on-terror-costs].

Terror training camps trial marks another first for the Crown Prosecution Service (2008, February 26). *The Crown Prosecution Service.* [http://www.cps.gov.uk/news/latest_news/112_08/].

The evidence that convicted Hamid (2008, February 28). *The Guardian.* [http://www.guardian.co.uk/uk/video/2008/feb/26/mohammed.hamid.terror.training?INTCMP=ILCNETTXT3487].

Note

1 Assisted by Susanne Keesman, Hannah Joosse, Jorrit Steehouder, Mike Spaans, Alex P. Schmid and Daan Weggemans.

14. Notes on Contributors

Editors

PROFESSOR BEATRICE DE GRAAF is professor of History of International Relations & Global Governance at Utrecht University, within the Strategic Theme of Institutions. She was co-founder of the Centre for Terrorism and Counterterrorism at Leiden University, Campus The Hague, and, amongst other things, fellow of the Netherlands Institute for Advanced Study (NIAS) where she initiated the research theme group on 'Terrorists on Trial'. She publishes widely on matters of terrorism, conflict and security. Her book *Evaluating Counterterrorism Performance* (Routledge, 2011) was internationally ranked amongst the top 150 terrorism books. Her current research, financed by means of an ERC Consolidator Grant, investigates the origins and makings of a European Security Culture in the long 19th century. Furthermore, De Graaf often features in the media as a commentator on matters of international and national security.

PROFESSOR EM. ALEX P. SCHMID is a Research Fellow of the International Centre for Counter-Terrorism (ICCT) in The Hague. He is also Director of the Terrorism Research Initiative (TRI), an international network of 15 institutes and more than 100 individual scholars and professionals seeking to improve security through collaborative research. Dr. Schmid is Editor-in-Chief of the online journal 'Perspectives on Terrorism' and former co-editor of 'Terrorism and Political Violence'. Previous positions held included Officer-in-Charge of the United Nations Terrorism Prevention Branch (UNODC/TPB) in Vienna and Director of the Centre for the Study of Terrorism and Political Violence (CSTPV) at the University of St. Andrews, Scotland, where Schmid also held a chair in International Relations. He has more than 180 reports and publications to his name, including the acclaimed 'Routledge Handbook of Terrorism Research' (2011/13), a sequel to his award-winning handbook on Political Terrorism (1984/1988/2005).

Contributors

JOOST AUGUSTEIJN is senior lecturer in history at Leiden University. He has previously held posts at the University of Amsterdam, Trinity College Dublin and Queens' University Belfast, and has taught at the College of William and Mary. He is the author of *From Public Defiance to Guerrilla Warfare: The Experience of Ordinary Volunteers in the Irish War of Independence 1916–1921* (1996), and *Patrick Pearse: The Making of a Revolutionary* (2010), as well as the editor of several volumes on Irish history and beyond.

TORE BJØRGO is Professor of Police Science at the Norwegian Police University College and Adjunct Professor at the Norwegian Institute of International Affairs (NUPI). A social anthropologist by training (University of Oslo), he received his doctoral degree from the University of Leiden. His main fields of research have been political extremism and terrorism; racist and right-wing violence; delinquent youth gangs; disengagement from violent groups; political communication; crime prevention and policing. He has (co-)authored or (co-)edited several books, amongst others *Terror from the Extreme Right* (1995); *Root Causes of Terrorism* (2005) and *Strategies for Preventing Terrorism* (2013). He was the initiator of the 'Exit' project to promote disengagement from racist groups in Norway, a project that was later adopted in Sweden, Finland and Germany, and has attracted interest in several other European countries.

FRED L. BORCH is the Regimental Historian and Archivist for the US Army Judge Advocate General's Corps. He served for 25 years as a soldier before retiring from active service in 2005. A lawyer and historian by education and profession, he has a Bachelor's (History) from Davidson College (North Carolina), and a Juris Doctor (Law) from the University of North Carolina. He also has a Master's of Law (International and Comparative Law) from the University of Brussels (Vrije Universiteit Brussel) and a Master's of Law (Military Law) from The Judge Advocate General's School (Virginia). Finally, he has a Master's (National Security Studies) from the US Naval War College (Rhode Island) and a Master's (American History) from the University of Virginia. From August 2012 to January 2013, he was a Fulbright Scholar in the Netherlands and a Visiting Professor at the Centre for Terrorism and Counter-Terrorism, University of Leiden (Campus The Hague) and a Visiting Researcher at the Netherlands Institute for Military History (The Hague).

LIESBETH VAN DER HEIDE is a researcher and lecturer at the Centre for Terrorism and Counterterrorism (CTC), Leiden University, Campus the Hague. Her fields of interest are: rehabilitation and de-radicalisation of violent extremist offenders in prison; security in International Relations; lone wolf terrorism and effective counter-terrorism. She coordinates the International Centre for Counter-Terrorism (ICCT)'s activities on the rehabilitation and reintegration of violent extremist offenders.

PROFESSOR GEERTJAN KNOOPS is visiting professor of International Criminal Law at Shandong University (Jinan, China). From 2003 to 2013 he was professor of International Criminal Law at Utrecht University. He holds two PhD degrees, one in criminal law (duress) from the University of Leiden (The Netherlands) and one in international criminal law from the University of Ireland, at the Human Rights Centre in Galway. He practises as a lawyer at Knoops' attorneys in Amsterdam, the Netherlands, and has appeared as defence counsel before the ICTR, ICTY and SCSL. In his capacity as an international criminal law expert, Professor Knoops has appeared as an expert witness before the Dutch Parliamentary Commission on the ISAF mission (Uruzgan, Afghanistan), as well as before the Parliamentary Commission on Combatting Piracy.

CATO HEMMINGBY is a research fellow at the Norwegian Police University College, also holding a position as Senior Advisor at the Norwegian Government Security and Service Organisation. He is working on terrorism and security-related issues, currently writing a PhD on terrorist target selection processes. He is also an expert on Israel's security policy, the Israeli Defence Forces, Hezbollah and Palestinian militant groups, as well as the conflict in Northern Ireland. Mr Hemmingby has 20 years of experience of security work within the governmental sector. He holds a BA and MA in Middle East studies and Modern Hebrew from the University of Oslo, supplemented by relevant studies at the Hebrew University of Jerusalem and the University of St Andrews. In 2014 he was a guest researcher at John Jay College of Criminal Science in New York. Hemmingby comments regularly in national and international media.

JACCO PEKELDER is a historian specialising in modern German history and Dutch–German relations. Since late 2007 he has been senior lecturer at the History Department of Utrecht University, after having had positions as researcher at the Centre for Parliamentary History (CPG) at Nijmegen University (1999–2001) and as research coordinator at the Germany Institute (DIA) in Amsterdam (2002–2007). In 2015, Pekelder was appointed as honorary professor of contemporary history of Western Europe at Saarland University. Among other themes, Pekelder has published extensively about left-wing terrorism in 1970s West Germany, in Dutch, German, and English. In 2011 he co-edited the volume *Between Prague Spring and French May. Opposition and Revolt in Europe, 1960–1980* (New York: Berghahn Books). His latest book on Baader Meinhof appeared in 2012: *"Ich liebe Ulrike": Die R.A.F. in den Niederlanden 1970–1980* (Münster: Agenda Verlag).

JACLYN A. PETERSON is a freelance research analyst and editor, based in Wilmington, Delaware. She obtained her Juris Doctor in 2010 from Widener University School of Law, Delaware. She also holds dual Bachelor of Science degrees in biology and psychology from West Virginia University. Currently she is completing her Master's in Criminal Justice and Homeland Security. Peterson specialises in open source research and analysis.

CAROLIJN TERWINDT graduated with distinction in law (LL.M.) and cultural anthropology (M.Sc.) from Utrecht University. Subsequently, she wrote her doctoral thesis 'Ethnographies of Contentious Criminalization' at Columbia Law School, NYC, for which she conducted fieldwork in Chile, the United States and Spain. She was a lecturer and researcher at the Centre for Conflict Studies in Utrecht, the Graduate School for Social Sciences in Amsterdam and the Max Planck Institute for Foreign and International Criminal Law in Freiburg, and her work has been published in a variety of journals, including *Nationalism and Ethnic Politics*, *Development in Practice*, the *Oñati Social Legal Series*, and *Crime, Law, and Social Change*. She further co-authored the book *NGOs under Pressure in Partial Democracies* (Palgrave Macmillan). Currently, she works as a legal advisor at the European Centre for Constitutional and Human Rights.

DAAN WEGGEMANS is a PhD Student at the Centre for Terrorism and Counterterrorism (CTC), Leiden University, Campus the Hague. He conducted research in Oslo on the Anders Breivik trial. Earlier publications focused on radicalisation, new technologies and counterterrorism measures. In 2013 he received a research grant to study the reintegration of violent extremists. Weggemans is country coordinator for the Terrorism Research Initiative (TRI) and a member of the board of the Dutch-Flemish Network for Terrorism Researchers.

KLAUS WEINHAUER is Professor of Modern History at Bielefeld University, Centre for Inter-American Studies. He was awarded his PhD at Hamburg University. He was fellow of the Netherlands Institute for Advanced Study (NIAS) and of the Modern European History Research Centre (MEHRC), Oxford University. He is currently conducting research on violence in European, US and Latin American cities during the 20th century. Among his research interests are also the social and cultural history of terrorism, policing, juvenile delinquency, drugs, social movements and labour history. His most recent publications are: *Germany 1916–1923. A Revolution in Context*, forthcoming Columbia UP 2015 (edited with K. Heinsohn etc.); *Terrorism, Gender, and History* (Historical Social Research 2/2014, edited with S. Schraut); *Stadt, Raum und Gewalt seit dem 19. Jahrhundert* (*Informationen zur modernen Stadtgeschichte* 2/2013, edited with D. Ellerbrock); *Gewalt ohne Ausweg? Terrorismus als Kommunikationsprozess in Europa seit dem 19. Jahrhundert* (Campus, 2012).

15. Index

Compiled by Joost Augusteijn, Susanne Keesman, Jorrit Steehouder

1916 Rising, 173
2083—A European Declaration of Independence, 457, 459
9/11, 18
  See September 11, 2001
Abbasi, Feroz, 350, 354, 357
Abida, 402–403, 404
Abu Khaled, 374
  See Al-Issa, Redouan
Abu Sayyaf Group (ASG), 355
Academic Consensus Definition of Terrorism, 31–33
Accusation
  self, 117, 129
Achille Lauro Affair, 523
Act on Terrorism Crimes, 384
Acusación popular, 434, 436, 439, 446
Aer Lingus, 191
Afghanistan, 33, 38, 312, 315, 318, 328, 346, 351–356, 505
Ahmed A., 391
Akhnikh, Ismail, 374–375, 380, 387–392
Akoudad, Abdeladim, 374
Al Bahlul, Ali Hamza, 350, 352–353, 356, 360
Al Haramein International, 373
Al Qaeda, 9, 33, 375, 376, 383, 398, 424, 459, 505
Al Qosi, Ibrahim, 350, 353, 360–361
Al Zawahari, Ayman, 356, 396
Albrecht, Susanne, 255
Alegal, 433
Alexander II, Tsar, 51–54, 60, 77, 79, 82–83
Alexander III, Tsar, 76
Alexandrov, Peter A., 63–69, 73–75, 77, 79
Alfonso XII, King, 82
Algemene Inlichtingen- en Veiligheidsdienst (AIVD), 373–381, 384–386, 394, 395–397, 401, 403, 406
Allo, Awol Kassim, 11, 509
Amnesty, 76, 427, 429, 442
Amnesty International, 217, 440, 522
Amoore, Louise, 518
Andersonstown, 191
Andropov, Yuri, 144
Angela Davis Defence Committee, 215
Anti-Internment League, 215
Anti-terrorism legislation, 245–246, 262, 278, 372, 405
Apartheid, 506
Aradau, Claudia, 372, 405
Arc, Jeanne d', 75
Ard Fheis (Sinn Fein), 180
Arendt, Hannah, 520
Aristotle, 35, 36
Arles case, 371, 384–394, 395
Armed Islamic Group (GIA), 355
Armed organisation, 424, 426
Armenia, 462

Armstrong, William Joseph, 206, 209
Arntzen, Wenche E., 465, 467, 475, 476, 480
Arrowsmith, Pat, 215
Article 58 (of Penal Code of 1927), 101, 104, 111, 125, 130, 149
Asociación de Víctimas del Terrorismo, 434
Asociación Dignidad y Justicia, 434
Association of Legal Justice, 188, 217
Asylum, 28, 135
Attentat clause, 28
Audiencia Nacional, 419–447
Augustin, Ronald, 252
Aust, Stefan, 235–236, 241–243, 276, 278
Australia, 328, 353, 360
Austria, 462
Aut dedere aut judicare [extradite or bring to court], 38
Authorization for Use of Military Force Against Terrorists (AUMF), 312
Azzola, Axel, 265–267, 268, 289
Azzouz, Samir, 374–376, 388, 389, 394–396, 398–407
Baader-Meinhof Gruppe, 231
See Red Army Faction
Baader, Andreas, 517
Bakayev, Ivan F., 103, 106–107, 109, 115–118, 127
Bakker Schut, Pieter Herman, 236, 252, 278, 279
Balmoral Furniture Company, 220
Balticum, 462
Barr, William 'Bill', 358
Barroso, José Manuel Durao, 375
Barry, Tom, 189
Basayev, Shamil, 33
Basque left-nationalist movement, 425, 427, 434
Bayat, 325, 352
BBC, 214
Becker, Marieluise, 259, 289
Bedny, Demian, 132
Begg, Moazzam, 350, 354, 357, 358
Bejer Engh, Inga, 466–469, 471, 482, 483
Belfast
Ten, 174, 175, 222
Belgium, 252, 374
Ben-Yehuda, Nachman, 34
Bender, Traugott, 275
Benelux, 462
Benson, Constable, 204
Bergen-Belsen, 217
Beria, Lavrentiy, 142, 144–146
Berlin, 119, 210, 247–248, 250–251, 255, 281, 283, 374
Berman-Yurin, 110, 119, 129–131
Berroth, Ulrich, 288
Biesenbach, Klaus, 281
Bin Laden, Osama, 9, 23, 33–34, 38, 311–312, 320, 325, 328–329, 331, 390, 396, 506
Bin Oqlaa' al Sjou'abi, Hamoud, 380
Birkenmaier, Werner, 291
Black Panthers, 231
Black sites, 313
Bloody Sunday, 216
Bogoliubov, Arkhip Petrovich, 51–84
Böhler, Britta, 391, 393
Bolshevik Party, 96–98, 101, 109, 141
Bombings
1879 Moscow, 82
1972 Germany, 232, 240, 261
1972 Northern Ireland, 174

1973 London, 174, 199
1998 Kenya, 10, 321, 352
1998 Tanzania, 10, 321, 352
2003 Casablanca, 376
2004 Madrid, 376
2005 London, 393, 396, 398
2011 Oslo, 458
Borch, Frederic 'Fred', 349–361
Border Campaign (IRA), 173
Borisov, M.D., 100
Bouyeri, Mohammed, 515
Brackman, Roman, 107
Bradford, Roy, 190
Brady v. Maryland, 327
Brady, Martin, 206, 211
Brandt, Willy, 239, 266, 291
Braunmühl, Gerold von, 279–280
Breivik trial, 18
court strategy, 465, 467–469, 471, 474, 482–483, 489, 490
defence strategy, 483–485, 489, 490, 520
performance in court, 420, 432
Breivik, Anders Behring, 18
manifesto, 457–465, 466, 469, 476, 484
Breloer, Heinrich, 281
Brezhnev, Leonid, 144
Bridewell police station, 185
Brinkema, Leonie, 323–331
Brixton Prison, 217
Bruecker, Kurt, 288
Brundtland, Gro Harlem, 459, 467
Buback, Siegfried, 239, 262–264, 270, 276, 280, 289, 290
Buckingham Palace, 211
Bukharin, Nikolai, 94, 98, 120–121, 137, 140–144, 146–147
Bundeskriminalamt (BKA, the Federal Criminal Police Office), 232, 248
Bundesrat (Federal Council), 247
Bundestag (Federal Diet), 247
Burns, Bernard, 176
Busche, Jürgen, 291
Bush, George W., 33, 314, 323, 345–350, 351, 355, 359–360
Administration, 43, 323–324, 357, 504
Bystanders, 215, 284
Canada, 328, 354, 361
captivity, 232
See Prison
Card, Francis, 174–180, 181–182, 188, 201, 219, 220
Carr, John, 361
Cassese, Antonio, 523
Catechism of a Revolutionary, 57
Censorship, 51, 55, 80
Challenge (on grounds of bias), 258, 264, 276
Charing Cross, 215
Chechnya, 328, 374, 376
Cheka, 97, 109, 127
Chekist, 100, 141
Cheney, Dick, 9, 504
China, 463
Civil war
Irish, 173, 183
Russian, 97–98, 101, 109, 117, 120, 143
Spanish, 146
Clausewitz, Carl von, 11, 12
Closure, 14, 17, 18, 140, 420, 481, 486, 488, 513, 514
Code of Criminal Procedure, 250, 256–260, 269, 272, 327
Colby, William, 266

Cold War
  end, 23, 282, 283
Collard, Dudley, 111
Collectivisation, 98, 140
Colombia, 38
Comintern, 95, 99, 109, 119, 121, 128, 132, 142
Commission
  military, 23
    See Military Commission (US)
Committee for Prevention of Torture (CPT), 403
Communication
  terrorism (as process of), 234, 235, 237, 509
  victim-based, 280–283
  victim-focused, 281
  victim-led, 280
Communicative process (law as a), 280, 507
Communist Party, 112
  Armenian, 109
  German, 109, 110
Confessions
  by torture, 104, 105, 428
  in show trials, 94, 104
  under police pressure, 39
Congress of Berlin, 51
Conservative Party (British), 182, 214
Conspiracy
  theory, 315, 326, 355, 394
  trial, 38, 103, 315, 320, 325, 329, 380, 506, 519
Copenhagen, 119
Coping mechanisms, 458, 481, 486–489, 490–491
Corday, Charlotte, 75
Cork, 191, 193
Corrigan, Aidan, 186
Cossaks, 79
Council for Civil Liberties, 215
Council of Europe, 27
Counter-terrorism, 33, 327, 331, 373, 377, 424, 505, 506, 510, 523
Counter-terrorist policy, 232, 237, 238
Court of Military Commission Review, 360
Court
  authority of the, 13, 316
  civilian, 9, 351, 503–506
  Constitutional, 245, 246, 257, 260
  Diplock, 175
    See Diplock courts
  European Human Rights, 37, 217
  High, 215, 219, 241, 257, 276, 473
  Higher Regional (Oberlandes-gericht), 238, 241, 242, 256, 267
  kangaroo, 35, 517
  military, 36, 78, 347, 351, 423, 439, 504, 505, 523
  Military Collegium of the Supreme, 94, 138, 144
  of Appeals (Amsterdam), 393
  of Appeals (Russian), 63, 74
  of Appeals (The Hague), 392, 403, 404, 515
  of Appeals (US), 328, 360
  of Cassation, 78, 392
  of Military Commission Review, 360
    See Court of Military Commission Review
  refusal to recognise, 212
  Special (Sondergerichte), 242
  Special Criminal, 181, 184, 219

Supreme (Netherlands), 392, 397, 404, 516
Supreme (USA), 314, 316, 323, 327, 359, 360
Supreme (USSR), 94, 131, 139
Crime
non-political, 25, 61, 240, 333
political, 18, 54, 61, 79, 205, 239, 513
quasi-political, 25, 53
war, 24, 27, 31, 265, 266, 345, 347, 348, 351, 355–357, 360, 505, 520
Criminal
association, 240–241, 248, 250, 284
behaviour, 243, 263
code, 111, 122, 130, 239–240, 245, 261, 284, 384, 392
justice, 13, 17, 18, 23, 42, 43, 52, 138, 177, 326, 329, 332, 351, 373, 394, 422–424, 425, 429, 437, 485–487, 506, 508, 511, 516
liability, 315, 345, 354–356, 432, 442
organisation, 261–262, 263, 380, 393, 515
Croissant, Klaus, 248, 250–254, 290
Cronin, Sean, 189
Crown witness, 284
See Witness
Cubar, Vlas, 144
Cyprus, 463
Czech Republic, 485
Dahrendorf, Ralf, 285
Dáil Eireann, 180–181, 186, 187, 192, 193–194, 197
Dam, Alexander van, 386, 388, 395, 400
David, Fritz (aka I. Kruglansky), 110, 119, 129–130, 131
Davis, Joseph, 134
Death penalty, 9, 26, 27, 38, 66, 101, 103–106, 130, 132, 134, 137–140, 142, 201, 219, 324–325, 327–331, 345, 354, 357, 477, 479
Débray, Régis, 253
Deich, Lev, 81
Democratic values, 486–487, 490
Democratisation, 53, 282
Denmark, 119, 462, 485
Derry (London-), 186, 187, 189, 192, 193, 216
Detention
administrative, 58, 78
House of preliminary, 53–55, 60–66, 67, 74
indefinite, 504, 524
military, 504
non-criminal, 331
pre-trial, 425, 430, 431, 440
preventive, 36, 428, 469, 473, 480, 487
temporary, 71, 375
without charge, 43
youth, 402
Deutscher Herbst, 236
See German Autumn
Dewey Commission, 135–136
Dewey, John, 135
Diplock courts, 36, 38, 175, 219–220, 221
Disciplinary
measures, 270
procedure, 276
punishment, 272
Disclosure obligations, 327, 331
Dostoyevsky, F., 64, 69
Dramaturgy, 15, 16, 267, 268, 284, 505, 510, 511, 519
Dreitzer, E.A., 103, 106, 114, 141
Drenkmann, Günter von, 247, 251
Drenteln, Alexander, 82

Dublin, 173–223
Dunlap, Charles, 12
Dzerzhinski, Felix, 97
Eckhardt, William, 12
Edelman, Joseph, 111
Eggler, Ernst, 290
Egyptian Islamic Jihad (EIJ), 355
Ehmke, Horst, 239
Ehrenburg, Ilya, 146
Eiche, Roberts, 144
Eijkman, Quirine, 385
El Fatmi, Nouriddin, 375, 377, 380–381, 386–388, 392, 394, 396, 398–399
El Tawheed Mosque, 373–377
Ellis, Lee, 25
Eminent Jurists Panel, 505
Emmet, Robert, 173
Ensslin, Gudrun, 231–291, 517
ETA
  commandos, 425, 430, 434
  environment (*entorno de* ETA), 425
  prisoners collective, 424, 427, 430, 440, 443, 445
  trial, 18
Etxerat, 430
European Commission of Human Rights, 28, 423
European Convention on Human Rights, 258, 277, 392, 480, 508
European Convention on the Suppression of Terrorism, 27
European Court of Human Rights, 37, 217
European Soccer Championship (2004), 375
Euskal Herria, 426, 427, 444
Euskara, 438
Evdokimov, G.E., 102, 106, 118, 126
Eviction, 244
  See Trials, eviction from
Exile, 53, 58, 67, 76, 98, 100, 109, 110, 116, 119, 124, 130, 136, 140
Extradition, 23, 26–28, 188, 190, 330
Faerber, Renate, 291
Fahmi Boughaba, Mohamed, 374, 375
Fair trial, 13, 18, 27, 36–37, 38, 42, 94, 194, 242, 258, 311, 323, 324, 327, 331–333, 345, 348, 351, 358, 360, 361, 385, 391, 394, 405, 428, 440, 481, 483, 485–487, 490, 491, 504, 508, 512, 516, 521
  prevention, 481, 485–487, 490
  re-establishing stability, 13, 481, 486
  rehabilitation, 481, 490
  restoring Democratic Rule of Law, 481, 483, 485, 487
  truth-finding, 481, 483, 486, 490
Fakir case, 381–384
Famine, 98, 107
Fascism, 127, 128, 132, 136, 137, 148, 253, 265
Fast, 195
  See Hunger strike
Faulkner, Brian, 192
Fedorov, G.F., 74, 102
Feeney, Hugh, 200, 206–213
Female Warriors of Allah, 397
Fenian rebellion, 173
Fianna Fáil, 181, 186, 192, 193
Figner, Vera, 52
Five-Year Plan, 98, 101, 134
Fjordman, 485
  See Nøstvold Jensen, Peder Are
Flogging, 55, 59, 61, 65, 67, 68, 77
Foth, Eberhard, 273–276, 288
Foucault, Michel, 518

France, 27, 76, 252, 254, 316, 317, 421, 426, 427, 430, 462
Franz Ferdinand, Archduke, 52
Free State (Irish), 183, 185
Freedom fighter, 29, 33, 266
Freuer, Hans-Jürgen, 288
Gaelic Athletic Association (GAA), 191
Garda, 197
Garzón, Baltasar, 425, 430, 433, 440, 443
Geiking, Baron F.E., 82
Geneva Conventions, 264–267, 314, 323, 359
Gerhard, Rudolf, 291
German Autumn, 233–234, 236, 276, 277–278, 281–282
German U-boat saboteurs
    trial of, 348
Gestapo, 109, 113, 117–119, 125, 132, 134
Ghailani, Ahmed Khalfan, 10, 321, 332, 504, 505, 509
Ginkel, Bibi van, 385
Goebbels, Joseph, 99
Goede, Marieke de, 13, 372
Gogarty, Frank, 179
Gogh, Theo van, 515
Goldsmith, Jack, 504
Goldsmith, Peter, 358
Good Friday Agreement, 174
Gorchakov, Prince, 64, 71, 75
Goulding, Cathal, 195, 196
Graaf, Janny de, 234, 237
Great Britain, 27, 76, 488
Great Purges, 95, 100, 133, 140, 143, 146, 149
Great Terror, 101, 143, 145, 149
Greaves, Desmond, 186
Greece, 374, 462
Greenfield, Jeff, 9
Griffin, Frank, 184, 188
Grigat, Peter, 290
Groenewold, Kurt, 248, 250, 254, 290
Gromyko, Andrei, 144
Grosser, Alfred, 282
Grusin, Richard, 372
Guantánamo Bay (Cuba), 9, 18, 311–314, 315, 323, 331–332, 402, 504, 518, 523
Guerrilla
    movement, 186, 231, 249, 261
    tactics, 252
    warfare, 32, 173, 253, 284
Guevara, Ernesto 'Che', 253
Gulag, 105, 147, 149
Gunn, William 'Will', 349, 357
Haag, Siegfried, 248
Habeas corpus, 36, 215, 359, 392, 513
Haersma Buma, Sybrand van, 402
Hakimiyyat Allah (The sovereignty of God), 515
Hamdan v. Rumsfeld, 314, 316, 323, 359, 360
Hamdan, Salim, 311, 350, 352, 359, 360
Hannover, Heinrich, 254
Hardy, Deborah, 84
Hartigh, Bart den, 395
Haynes, William J. 'Jim' II, 349, 358
Heath, Edward, 182
Heintz, Aryeh Leib, 403
Heldmann, Hans-Heinz, 257, 263, 265, 271, 273, 276, 289
Herold, Horst, 232
Heydrich, Reinhard, 99
Hicks, David M., 350, 353–355, 360
High Court, 215
    See Court
Himmler, Heinrich, 99, 117, 125

Hirsi Ali, Ayaan, 379–381, 394, 402
Hitler, Adolf, 95, 99, 146
Hoecke, Mark van, 507
Hoff, Dierk, 261, 262, 290
Hofstad Group, 18, 512, 515
    trials, 381–404, 515
Holden, Svein, 467–469, 471
Holder, Eric, 9, 322, 323
Holland, Klaus, 264, 289
Hollander, Leo, 404
Holmes, Paul Joseph, 203, 212
House of Lords, 197
Human rights
    instrument, 37
    law, 392
    violations, 25, 37
Hume, John, 190
Hungary, 462
Hunger strike, 15, 26, 32, 175, 180–199, 211–219, 223, 233, 247, 249–252, 254, 259–262, 276, 429, 520
Hyde Park, 215
Ignatieff, Michael, 505
Imprisonment, 105
    See Prison
Incarceration, 278
    See Prison
Incorporated Law Society, 186
Indictment, 65, 102, 104, 106, 107, 111, 117, 239, 267, 284, 320, 325, 356, 426, 430, 433, 464, 471
Indonesia, 514, 523
Injustice frame, 199, 510
Intelligence evidence, 385, 396
Intelligentsia, 51, 52, 58, 136
International Committee for the Defence of Political Prisoners, 251
International Covenant on Civil and Political Rights, 37, 508
International law, 18, 27, 29, 32, 242, 265, 266, 359, 508
International Red Cross, 30, 217
International Socialist, 215
Inverse investigation, 385, 406
Irish Political Hostages Campaign, 218
Irish Republican Army (IRA)
    Army Council, 213
    campaigns, 173
    Green Book, 35
    leaders, 173, 174, 176, 180, 189, 195, 198, 210
    Official IRA, 182, 195, 197
    policy, 182, 188, 207, 220
    prisoners, 26, 216, 218, 223
    Provisional IRA, 26, 173, 175, 179, 180, 212, 213
    trials, 18
Islamisation
    of Europe, 460, 461, 477
    of Germany, 476
    of Norway, 475
Israel, 29, 34, 131, 328, 379
Al-Issa, Redouan, 373–378, 380
Italy, 207, 210, 252, 374, 462, 520
ITGWU (Irish Trade Union), 189
Jail, 326
    See Prison
Jemaah Islamiyah, 355
Jenkins, Brian M., 509
Jneid, Fawaz, 399, 403
Judicial
    catharsis, 522–525
    consequences, 77–79, 136–139
    goals, 458, 481, 485–487, 490

independence, 36
power, 41
reforms, 52, 53, 57
system, 13, 37, 38, 52, 93, 179, 222, 240, 244, 245, 254, 255, 262, 264, 276, 312, 326, 329, 332, 349, 373, 394, 401, 422, 423, 431, 437, 447, 457, 464, 478, 485, 504, 506, 511, 515, 516
Judicialisation of the repression, 443, 445
Jünschke, Klaus, 272
Kabat, Alexander, 60
Kaczynski, Theodore, 471
Kaganovich, Lazar, 104, 107–108, 112, 116, 120, 129–131, 132, 138, 140, 144
Kaiserreich, 240
Kaplan, Lewis, 332
Kelly, Gerard, 200, 209, 212
Kennedy, David, 12
Kennedy, Joseph, 192
Kennedy, Robert, 192
Kenya, 10, 321, 352
Kenyatta, Jomo, 186
Kessel, Konstantin, 63–67, 73, 77–78
Khadr, Omar Ahmed, 315, 332, 354, 361
Khalid Sheikh Mohammed (KSM), 9, 311, 313, 318, 319, 324, 331
Khalturin, Stephan, 82
Khrushchev, Nikita, 100, 104, 113, 132, 133, 139, 140
Kibalchich, N.I., 81
Kinkel, Klaus, 283
Kirchheimer, Otto, 25, 39, 40, 95, 269, 508
Knight, Amy, 148
Knights Templar, 459–462, 466–470, 473, 474, 476
Kolchak, Admiral, 109, 117
Kolenkina, Masha (Maria), 58, 59
Komsomol, 138
Koni, Anatoli Fedorovich, 61–64, 70, 72–78, 79
König, Dieter, 290
Koning, Karina M.E. de, 399
Koppe, Victor, 391, 393, 398, 402
Kosior, Stanislav, 104, 112, 116, 130, 144
Kravchinskii, Sergei (aka 'Stepniak'), 81
Kremlin, 105, 107, 116, 131, 132, 144, 145
Kringlen, Einar, 469
Kropotkin, Dimitri, 82
Kruglansky, I., 129
See David, Fritz
Krumm, Karl-Heinz, 291
Krupskaya, Nadezhda, 132
Kühnert, Hanno, 291
Künzel, Manfred, 271, 290
Kurneev, Fedor, Major, 65–67
L'Estrange, Gerald, 181
Labour camp, 55, 101, 102, 131, 138
Labour Party
British, 135
Irish, 190
See Social Democratic and Labour Party of Northern Ireland
Norwegian, 458, 459, 464, 479
Landshut airplane, 517
Lang, Scott, 349
Lashkar-e-Tayyiba, 353, 355
Lawfare, 11–17, 41, 326, 328, 420, 503, 507, 510, 512–514
Lawfare Project, The, 12
Laws of war, 12, 29, 315, 356
Lawyer
commissioned, 247, 257, 258
of choice, 247, 248, 256–259, 263, 270, 271, 275–277, 289, 290

substitute, 247, 257, 258, 268, 271, 273, 275, 276, 290
Lazarus, Robert, 111
Leaderless Jihad, 375
Lebanon, 462
Left-wing
lawyers, 244, 245, 248, 517
organisation, 215, 216, 218, 231, 237
terrorism, 231, 236–238, 247, 255, 281–283
Lenin, Vladimir I., 94, 97, 98, 106, 109, 110, 121–123, 129, 132, 133, 142, 143
Leningrad, 98
See St. Petersburg
Liberal democracy, 27, 28, 36, 43, 243, 428
Liberia, 462, 468
Linke, Karl-Heinz, 290
Linksanwälte, 244, 245, 517
Lippestad, Geir, 461–464, 469–480
London, 251, 317, 318, 321, 358, 393, 396, 398, 461, 462, 468
London Metropolitan Police, 178
Lone wolf, 383, 487, 489
Long War strategy (IRA's), 174
Lopukhin, Alexander, 62, 74
Lord Dunleath, 197
Lorenz, Peter, 255
Loris-Melikov, General Count, 82
Lover boys, 393, 397
Loyalist, 179, 191, 205, 211
Lubbe, Marinus van der, 94
Lubianka (NKVD headquarter and prison), 130, 145
Lurye, Moissei, 106, 113, 125, 130
Lurye, Nathan, 106, 113, 125, 130
Lynch, Jack, 182, 185, 190, 192, 194, 195
MacManus, Fr Sean, 195
MacStiofáin, Mary, 190
MacStiofáin, Sean, 174, 213
Madame Tussaud's, 211
Maguire, Maura, 213, 215
Mahler, Horst, 231, 233
Maier, Hubert, 288
Maihofer, Werner, 275
Main stakeholders, 14, 17
Malaysia, 318
Malika, 387
Malraux, André, 135
Malta, 463
Mandela, Nelson, 506
Mansfield, Michael, 204, 205
Martin, Ludwig, 289
Martine van den O., 381
Martyr, 38, 77, 81, 192, 198, 250, 320, 328–330, 353, 375, 379, 383, 468, 477, 517
Marxism, 80, 116
cultural, 460, 462, 470, 476
Masood Azhar, Maulana, 375
Mater Hospital (Dublin), 189–193
Mathiesen, Thomas, 485
Mauz, Gerhard, 264, 278, 291
Mayer, Albrecht, 272, 273, 276
McAirt, Pronnsias, 176
See Card, Francis
McCann, Eamonn, 204, 215
McKee, William, 174–180, 182, 188, 201, 219, 220
McLarnon, William Patrick, 200, 204, 210, 212
McNearney, Roisin, 199–218
McQuaid, Dr. John Charles, 193
Media show, 371, 420, 438, 441, 445, 446, 514, 520
Medical doctor, 259, 260

Medved, Philip, 100
Meinhof, Ulrike, 517
Meinhold, Werner, 288
Meins, Holger, 247, 251, 255, 258, 261–262, 271
Mercader, Ramon, 146
Meshchersky, Prince Vladimir P., 75
Mexico, 98, 135, 139, 145, 463
Mezentsev, General, 81, 82
Mikhailov, Alexander, 59
Mikoyan, Anastas, 99, 100
Military campaigns in Iraq and Afghanistan, 505
Military Commission (US), 313, 314
  Act of 2006, 314, 316, 323, 359
  Act of 2009, 316, 323
  Instruction No. 2, Crimes and Elements, 356
  manual, 360
  proceedings, 311, 312, 323, 331, 350
  trials, 311, 314, 315, 322, 331, 332
  U-Boat, 348
Military Order (November 13, 2001), 314, 321, 346–350, 355, 359
Military tribunal, 36
  See Court, military
Miliutin, Dimitri A., 60, 64, 76
Mimesis, poiesis, kinesis, 15
Ministry of Justice, 63, 78, 137
Miscarriages of justice, 39, 71–74, 79, 93, 139, 219, 244, 285
  typology, 39
Mogadishu, 233, 517
Mohamed Atta, 318
Mohamed El M., 375
Mohammed B., 376
  See Bouyeri, Mohammed
Mohammed C., 400, 403
Mohammed el B., 390
Mohammed H., 400, 404
Mohnhaupt, Brigitte, 262
Molotov, Vyacheslav, 106, 107, 138, 141, 142, 144, 146
Monaghan, 193
Montesquieu, Charles de, 40
Morocco, 316, 317, 376
Mosque
  Brixton, 317
  El Tawheed, 373
    See El Tawheed Mosque
  Finsbury, 317
Moussaoui, Zacarias, 18
Mrachkovsky, Sergei V., 102–107, 109, 114–115, 118, 126, 135
Müller, Gerhard, 261–263, 290
Munster, Rens van, 372, 405
Musolff, Andreas, 256
My Lai cases, 12
Nadir A., 389
Naoufel, 374
  See (Akoudad, Abdeladim)
Narodnaya Rasprava, 57
  See People's Revenge
Narodnaya Volya, 52
  See People's Will
Narodniki, 54
  See Populists
Narrative
  counter-, 221, 483, 490
  master, 283, 286
  meta-, 523
  of (in)justice, 11, 16, 175, 235, 419, 421, 431, 436, 438, 445–447, 481, 509, 521, 523, 524

of injustice, 179, 183, 184, 186, 213, 406, 445, 509, 510, 524
of justice, 248
pre-existing, 447
prosecutorial, 428, 433, 443
victim, 522
Naryshkin-Kurakin, Elizabeth, 71
National Graves Association, 191
National Police Services Agencies (KLPD), 375
National Socialism, 508
Nazi, 95, 241, 242, 266, 277, 313, 400, 402
neo-, 463, 488
Nechaev, Sergei, 56, 57, 60, 64, 66, 78
Nerlich, Heinz, 288
Nesser, Petter, 379
Netherlands, 18, 23, 235, 252, 371–407, 505, 511, 514
Nève, Marc, 403
New York, 9, 10, 313, 321, 332, 346, 355, 383
Nickels, Christa, 281
Nigeria, 463
Nihilism, 56, 60, 66, 524
Nikolayev, Leonid, 94, 100–102, 112, 115, 140, 142
Nixon, Richard, 266, 291
Nooitgedagt, Bart, 403, 404
Norgaard Principles, 28
Northern Alliance, 353
Northern Ireland, 38
Northern Ireland Civil Rights Association, 179
Norway, 98, 110, 119, 135, 145
Nøstvold Jensen, Peder Are (aka Fjordman), 476, 485
O Bradaigh, Ruari, 190, 194
O Connaill, Daithi, 190, 197
O'Kelly, Kevin, 181–183, 198
O'Malley, Desmond, 181–186
Obama, Barack, 314, 504
Administration, 43, 313, 322, 323, 360
Okhrana, 145
Olberg, Valentine, 103, 110, 113, 118, 130, 131
Old Bailey, 199, 202–206, 210
Old Bolsheviks, 94, 99, 101, 104–110, 117, 120, 128, 130, 137, 139, 146, 147
Olmo, Juan del, 433
Operation *Geronimo*, 9
Ordzhonikidze, Grigory, 104, 120, 130
Organisation of Islamic Cooperation (OIC), 29
Orlov, Alexander, 105–106, 109–131, 137
Orlov, Vladimir, 57
Osinsky, Valerian, 82
Oslo, 18, 457–491
Oxford Union, 189
Özdemir, Yasser, 400
Pahlen, Count Konstantin K., 55, 58, 61–65, 77–78
Pakistan, 23, 38, 312, 313, 321, 352, 353, 375
Palestine, 328
Paranoid schizophrenia, 318, 329, 469–474
Paris, 217, 252, 461
Parker, Thomas, 521
Pasternak, Boris, 146
Pauker, Karl, 131
Pearse, Patrick, 186, 212
People's Revenge (Narodnaya Rasprava), 57
People's Will (Narodnaya Volya), 52, 80, 82–84, 125

Perception
of justice, 35
of social norms, 507
of truth, 506
Performance
of justice, 419, 420, 432, 436, 441, 444, 446, 490–491, 509, 514, 520–522
Performative
acts, 11, 14–17, 503, 512, 521
perspective, 9, 11, 235, 284, 324, 382, 404, 489, 503
power, 11, 93, 149, 173, 175, 180, 192, 218, 220, 222, 223, 243
strategies, 13, 18, 41, 175, 312, 324–331, 371, 419–421, 429, 431, 436–438, 445–446, 458, 467, 484, 485, 489, 506, 509–511, 512, 520, 522
theories, 15
Performativity, 14, 17, 19, 507, 510
Peter and Paul Fortress, 58
Peters, Butz, 282
Peters, Ruud, 379, 387, 389
Peterson, Jeremy, 94
Philosophy of the Bomb, 83
Pickel, Richard V., 110, 116, 127, 141
Pirandello play, 522
Piranha case, 371, 381, 384–386, 512
Plasman, Peter, 382, 387, 393
Plechanov, Georgi V., 53, 80
Plooy, Koos, 386, 397, 398
Plottnitz, Rupert von, 260, 264, 289
Politburo, 97, 99, 102–104, 105–109, 111, 130, 133, 134, 137–143, 144, 145
Political
defence, 244, 245, 254, 517
justice, 23–43
offence exception, 24–29
prisoners, 55–56, 67–69, 149, 212, 216, 219, 250–252, 255, 259, 424, 427–430, 435, 440, 441, 444
trials, 11, 13, 16, 23, 29, 39–42, 43, 212, 214, 236, 239–241, 284, 508, 509, 552
violence, 11, 29, 31, 32, 43, 84, 232, 234, 251
Otto Kirchheimer's definition of, 25, 39, 95, 269, 508
Politicisation
of justice, 420, 514
of trials, 13, 41
Populists, 54, 59, 80, 83, 176
Narodniki, 54, 58
Portugal, 375
Postyshev, Pavel, 104, 112, 116, 130, 144
Power, Michael, 373, 405
Pre-emption, 405, 519
Premediation, 372, 384, 396, 400, 405, 519, 523
Preston, Rob, 361
Presumption of innocence, 43, 242, 258, 323
Preventive detention, 36, 428, 469, 473, 480, 487
Price, Dolours, 200, 202–210, 212, 217
Price, Marian, 200, 212
Prinzing, Theodor, 241–243, 247–248, 256–260, 264, 269–271, 271–277, 285, 288
Prison
sentence, 58, 67, 94, 101, 102, 105, 117, 126, 130, 140, 173, 178–180, 183, 188, 190, 193, 195, 198, 200, 213, 233, 246, 248, 249, 263, 277, 311, 325, 328, 330, 332, 348, 360, 377, 385, 392, 394, 397,

401–403, 431, 439, 471, 473, 474, 480, 482, 487, 490, 515
struggle, 233, 249–251, 429, 439, 441
Prisoner
Action Committee, 215
collective, 424
See ETA, prisoners collective
ghost, 10, 504
military, 504
of war, 42, 256, 268, 358, 505
political, 67
See Political
support, 174, 213, 215, 218, 250, 251, 271, 446, 485, 489, 520
Pritt, Denis Noel, 111, 135
Propaganda, 54, 80, 99, 109, 148, 176, 250, 252, 253, 259, 264, 286, 439, 470, 474, 477, 484, 485
by the deed, 30, 52
counter, 255
illegal, 59
phase, 457, 470
support, 132
Prosecution
anticipatory, 372, 373
deal, 262
strategy, 11, 41, 202, 261, 311, 312, 321–324, 345, 354, 386, 394, 397, 405, 490
Provocation-repression theory, 510
Prussia, 11, 99, 240
Psychiatry
role of, 465, 469, 470–474
Public Affairs Office, 351
Public opinion, 10, 12, 39, 41, 51, 63, 65, 76, 80, 81, 133, 232, 244, 254, 259, 350, 439, 480, 481, 506, 517, 518, 520, 521
Pyatakov, Levid, 94, 98, 120, 132–133, 135, 142
Rachid B., 378, 389, 390
Radek, Karl, 94, 120–121, 132–133, 135, 136, 142
radicalisation, 278, 317–318, 372, 377, 384, 395, 402, 403, 468, 510
research on, 14
Radzinsky, Edvard, 73
Rakovsky, Khristian, 132
Raspe, Jan-Carl, 233, 238, 257, 262, 263, 268–272, 275–277, 288, 517
Rawlinson, Sir Peter, 201, 202, 209, 210
Rebellion of 1803 (Ireland), 173
Rebmann, Kurt, 289
Red Army, 97, 117, 143, 144
Red Army Faction (RAF), 18
accusation, 240, 245, 249
accused, 267–271
Armed Struggle, 232, 253, 255
art exhibition, 281, 283
Red Terror, 83, 98
Regime of truth, 445
Reid, Richard, 319
Reingold, Isak, 110, 116, 120, 126, 127
Repentance, 101, 443
Republican Clubs, 191
Revenge, 24, 33–36, 42, 43, 55, 59, 61, 66, 82, 97, 107, 147, 213, 243, 247, 251, 351, 485–487, 515
Revolution, 28, 32, 56, 58, 121, 231, 253, 485, 514, 517, 519
Bolshevik, 96, 137, 145
counter-, 103, 112, 123, 127, 246
French, 33
Russian, 52, 74, 83
Riedel, Helmut, 289

Right-wing
extremism, 470, 472, 478, 488
radicals, 465, 468, 469, 471, 484
terrorism, 487
Right
of resistance, 267
of self-defence, 266, 267
Risk management, 373, 384–386, 400, 405, 407, 432, 513, 518, 519, 523
secondary, 373, 405
Robespierre, Maximilien, 33
Rogovin, Vadim, 146
Röhm, Ernst, 99
Rolland, Romain, 135
Romano, Unai, 437
Roosevelt, Franklin D., 347, 348
Rote Armee Fraktion (RAF), 231
See Red Army Faction
Rote Hilfe (Red Assistance), 244
Roth, Christopher, 282
Royal Ulster Constabulary (RUC), 188
Rudzutak, Janis, 144
Rule of law, 10–13, 15, 36, 38, 179, 194, 221, 246, 253, 254, 260, 278, 322, 332, 371, 388, 389, 394, 398, 400, 404–407, 419, 440, 481, 485–487, 506, 512–516, 520, 523
Rumsfeld, Donald, 349, 358, 359
Rupture, 14, 17, 18, 326–328, 512–514, 516
Russia, 17, 125, 133, 136, 148, 149, 328, 374, 462
Russian government, 51
Russian Penal Code, 71
Ryan, Dr. Dermot, 193
Rykov, Alexei, 94, 97, 120, 132, 140, 143
Safonova, A.N., 113, 114, 117
Sageman, Marc, 375
Saif al-Adel, 33
Saif al-Din (Sword of religion), 379
Saifu Deen al-Muwahhied, 379
Salafism, 373, 376, 377, 382, 384, 394, 399
Sands, Bobby, 175, 219–221, 520
Sanity assessment, 465, 472, 482, 490
Sartre, Jean-Paul, 251
Saudi Arabia, 346
Saul, Ben, 43
Schiller, Margrit, 263
Schily, Otto, 245, 246, 254, 258, 263, 265, 266, 272, 273, 275, 276, 289
Schlägel, Stefan, 290
Schleyer, Hanns Martin, 233, 277–281
Schmid, Alex, 234
Schmidt, Helmut, 258, 266
Schnabel, Dieter, 290
Schueler, Hans, 291
Schwarz, Eberhard, 290
Schwurgericht, 251, 263
Scotland Yard, 179, 199–202, 213, 214
Secondary risk management, 373, 405
Security
internal (Innere Sicherheit), 237
national, 12, 42, 258, 373–376, 487, 489, 505, 508, 513
Sedov, Lev, 113, 119, 130, 135, 146
Sedov, Sergei, 146
Semantics, 286
of communication, 238
September 11, 2001
attacks, 34, 278, 311, 312, 318, 320, 322, 323, 346–356, 372, 380, 505
legacy, 312–316
prosecuting suspects, 312–313, 313–314, 321
Serebryakov, Leonid, 120, 142

Serfdom, 51, 52
Sharia, 35, 38, 371, 390, 402
Shaw, Bernard, 135
Shaw, Sebag, 203–213
Sheinin, Lev, 108, 143
Sherwin, Sean, 193, 197
Shkiryatov, Matvei, 103
Show trial, 9, 18, 214, 242, 258, 322, 387, 393, 439, 489, 504, 507–510, 513, 517–519, 522, 524
  political, 284
Shura Council, 355
Siberia, 53, 101, 109
Sidoratskii, Grigorii, 75
Sinn Fein, 177, 179, 180, 185, 186, 189–192, 194, 196, 214, 216
Smirnov, Ivan N., 97, 103, 106, 109, 113–124, 128–131, 140
Smolny Institute, 100, 102
Sochi, 103, 104, 108, 140
Social Democratic and Labour Party of Northern Ireland (SDLP), 190
Social-Democratic Party, 53, 80
Social drama, 16, 514, 525
Socialist-Revolutionary Party, 80
Socialist Workers Movement, 191
Sokolnikov, Mikhail, 120, 142
Solidarity
  campaign, 213, 215, 233, 250, 259, 271, 424
  movement, 248, 249
Soloviev, A.K., 82
Solsky, Dmitri M., 64
Soumaya S., 381, 387, 392, 394–404, 406, 516
South Africa, 506
Southern Rebels, 58, 59
Sovereignty
  national, 23, 461
  of God, 515
    See Hakimiyyat Allah
Spain, 18, 82, 254, 373–376, 462
Special Branch (Irish), 191, 200, 205
Special Forces
  GSG-9, 233
  Netherlands, 380
  US, 315, 354
Special Powers Act, 210
Special tribunal
  for Lebanon, 23
  NKVD, 149
St. Joseph's College (Belfast), 217
St. Mary's College (Belfast), 217
Stammheim, 231, 241
  courthouse, 241, 242
  legacy, 277–283
  prison, 233, 241, 249, 251, 259, 277, 283
  trial, 18, 39, 513, 517, 523
State Council, 57, 64, 78
State of exception, 506
State repression, 31, 179, 277, 427, 436, 437, 443
Steinfeld, Thomas, 282
Straelen, Frits van, 381
Strasbourg, 212
Ströbele, Hans-Christian, 248, 261, 290
Stroganoff, Count, 64
Stuberger, Ulf G., 236, 242, 243, 263–264, 267–269, 273–275, 276, 290, 291
Students, 54, 57, 67, 79, 217, 218, 374, 484
  demonstration, 53, 79
  organisation, 215
  rebellion, 244
Submission, 378

Sudan, 312, 353
Suicide, 62, 72, 99, 100, 120, 140, 145, 233, 252, 264, 269–271, 277, 517
  attack, 30, 352, 396
  by cop, 380, 383
  political, 32
Sweden, 462, 467
Switzerland, 57, 76, 78
Sympathisers, 10, 18, 83, 178, 201, 218, 232, 233, 250, 251, 262, 271, 279, 291, 383, 406, 421, 433, 439–441, 446, 459, 470, 472, 476, 480, 489, 513, 514, 516, 520, 523
Syria, 374, 377
Syrian Muslim Brotherhood, 374
Taliban, 33, 38, 312, 346, 355
Tanzania, 321, 352
Taranto, James, 504
Target audience, 13–17, 175, 371, 382, 404, 429, 436–438, 438–441, 446, 510, 523
Tawheed, 377
  confessor of (*al-Muwahhid*), 379
Taybi, Zakaria, 375, 391
Tell, William, 75
Temming, Gerd, 268
Tenfelde, Christopher R., 236, 240, 246, 260, 272, 273
Ter-Vaganyan, Vargarshak A., 109
Ter-Vaganyan, Vargarshak A., 103, 106, 107, 115, 129
Terrorism
  definition, 29–33
  is theatre, 509
Testimony
  bought, 261–267
  false, 54, 110
  pre-trial, 113
Teuns, Sjef, 259, 260
Thatcher, Margaret, 26
The Sheikh, 374
  See Al-Issa, Redouan
Theatre
  of lawfare, 328, 420, 513, 514
  terrorism trials as form of, 10, 372, 457, 519, 522
Theatrics, 256
  See Theatre
Tolmein, Oliver, 279
Tomsky, Mikhail, 97, 120, 140
Tone, Wolfe, 173
Torture, 27, 32, 37, 68, 104, 108, 142, 144, 145, 149, 215, 217, 245, 249, 250, 255, 259, 314, 316, 323, 332, 361, 424, 428, 437, 438, 444, 446, 463, 479, 480, 489
  Isolationsfolter, 249
Tory/Tories, 214
  See Conservative Party (British)
Traube, Klaus, 275
Trials
  Abu Bakar Ba'asyir, 523
  Breivik, 18
    See Breivik Trial
  Eichmann, 520
  ETA, 18
    See ETA, trial
  eviction from, 244–248, 256–260, 290
  fair, 392
  fair, 13
    See Fair Trial
  for conspiracy, 38
    See Conspiracy
  ghost, 255–277
  in absentia, 246
  Lockerbie, 23

macro-, 420–427, 432–435, 437, 440, 445
Moluccan (1970s), 514, 516
Nuremberg, 509
O.J. Simpson, 16
political, 11
See Political, trials
show, 9
See Show Trial
Stammheim, 39
See Stammheim trial
status-quo, 512
status-quo, 514
Trial of the 193, 54, 59–64, 66, 74, 78, 104
virtual, 371
See Virtual trial
Trotzkyists, 93–149
German, 118
Trotzkyite-Zinovievite Terrorist Centre, 18
Troubles, the, 174, 199, 219, 221
Tucker, Robert, 108, 133, 136, 147, 148
Tukhachevsky, Mikhail, 144
Tumyr, Arne, 475
Tupamaros, 231
Turkey, 51
Tvedt, Tore, 475
Twomey, Maurice, 189
Typology
of crime, 24–27, 72
of miscarriages of justice, 39
of terrorism trials, 11, 14, 19, 420, 503, 512–522
Tyrannicide, 32–33
Uglanov, Nikolai, 120
Ukraine, 107, 132
Ulrich, Vasily, 110, 129, 130
Ulster Defence Association (UDA), 210
Ulster Volunteer Force (UVF), 211
Umberto I, King, 82
Unionists, 180, 181–190, 192, 221
United Kingdom, 328, 358, 462, 488
United Nations, 31
Ad Hoc Committee on Terrorism, 29, 31
Comprehensive Convention on International Terrorism, 29
Convention against Torture, 480
draft definition of terrorism, 30
General Assembly, 29
Human Rights Committee, 423
Special Rapporteur, 440
United States of America, 9, 23, 27, 38, 42, 231, 264, 283, 345–361, 379, 505
Air Force, 346, 349, 361
anti-terrorism legislation, 312
Army, 12, 232, 241, 266, 269, 315, 346, 349
Article III, 350
CIA, 266, 269, 313, 332
Commission of Inquiry, 135
Congress, 313, 314, 323, 359, 361
Constitution, 324, 359
Department of Defense, 351
Intelligence, 319, 327
Navy, 349
Patriot Act, 312
Pentagon, 312, 358
Special Forces, 315, 354
Supreme Court, 314
See Court, Supreme (USA)
Unlawful combatant, 314, 356
Uruguay, 231

USS Cole, 352, 356
Utøya, 18, 457–459, 463, 466–467, 479, 482
Valbert, Gustave, 75
Veiel, Andreas, 281
Verdict, 75
 See: Conviction
Victim
 narratives, 522
 organisation, 422, 425, 434, 436, 439, 440, 445
Vietcong, 265
Vietnam, 265, 269
 war, 256, 264, 266
Virtual trial, 371, 372, 386, 407, 420, 431, 441, 445, 513, 519, 521
Vogel, Hans-Jochen, 263
Vollmer, Antje, 281
Voroshilov, Kliment Y., 104, 105, 112, 116, 128–131, 138, 144
Vötsch, Otto, 288
Waldmann, Peter, 509
Walker, Clive, 39
Wallace, Donald Mackenzie, 72
Walsh, Anthony, 25
Walsh, Robert, 200, 205
Walters, Jason, 374–375, 380–381, 387–392, 406, 515, 516
Walters, Jermaine, 381
War crime, 24
 See Crime
War on terror, 33, 42, 43, 312–313, 361, 394
Weimar Republic, 240
Weiss, Franz, 125
Werner, Wouter, 12
Werth, Nikolaus, 149
Wesel, Uwe, 278
West Germany, 231, 232, 236, 246, 247, 260, 278, 280, 282, 283
White Guards, 97, 100–103, 109, 117, 134
Widera, Werner, 289
Wilders, Geert, 402
William I, Kaiser, 82
Wilson, Detective Chief Inspector Robert, 178
Wilson, Harold, 187
Winchester, 174, 199–201, 213–214
 Winchester 9, 209
  See Belfast Ten
Winkel, Detlef zum, 279
Witness
 character, 403
 crown, 100, 256, 284, 290, 401
 hearing, 37, 38, 58, 65–67, 75, 113, 134, 177, 178, 243, 261, 263, 266, 272, 275, 276, 319, 328, 376, 384, 386, 387, 391, 399, 424, 436, 437, 446, 457, 465, 473, 475, 479, 481, 510, 518
Wolfowitz, Paul, 349, 351, 357–359, 361
World Trade Center, 312, 318, 346, 353
Wormwood Scrubs, 217
Wunder, Heinrich, 263–267, 289
Yagoda, Genrikh G., 94, 100, 107, 108, 129, 130, 137, 143
Yagoda, Ghenrikh G., 102–104, 140–141
Yenukidze, Arel, 143
Yezhov, Nikolai I., 94, 102–108, 111, 120, 126, 130, 132, 137–146, 146
Zalm, Gerrit, 383
Zasulich, Feoktista, 56
Zasulich, Ivan, 56
Zasulich, Vera, 18
Zeis, Peter, 264, 275, 289

Zemlia I Volia (Land and Freedom), 59, 80
Zhdanov, Andrei, 103, 104, 112, 130, 138, 141, 144
Zhelekhovskii, Vladislav, 54, 60
Zinovievites, 102, 103, 112, 114, 120, 142
Zschäpe, Beate, 470, 476